Why Do You Need This New Edition?

If you're wondering why you should buy this new edition of *One Hundred Great Essays,* here are four good reasons:

❶ Twenty new selections include essays by authors not included in the previous edition of this anthology, as well as new selections by previously anthologized authors.

❷ New essays by contemporary writers include selections by David Sedaris, Alice Walker, David Foster Wallace, and others.

❸ New essays from widely admired essayists include contributions from Annie Dillard, Nancy Mairs, and Anne Fadiman.

❹ A diverse range of voices includes new selections from Kwame Anthony Appiah, Jamaica Kincaid, Zora Neale Hurston, Judy Ruiz, and Linda Hogan.

PEARSON

 **ROBERT DIYANNI** is Director of International Services for The College Board. Dr. DiYanni, who holds a B.A. from Rutgers University and a Ph.D. from the City University of New York, has taught English and Humanities at a variety of institutions, including NYU, CUNY, and Harvard. An Adjunct Professor of English and Humanities at New York University, he has written and edited more than thirty-five books, mostly for college students of writing, literature, and humanities.

PENGUIN ACADEMICS

ONE HUNDRED
GREAT ESSAYS

FOURTH EDITION

Edited by

Robert DiYanni
New York University

Longman

Boston   Columbus   Indianapolis   New York   San Francisco   Upper Saddle River
Amsterdam   Cape Town   Dubai   London   Madrid   Milan   Munich   Paris   Montreal   Toronto
Delhi   Mexico City   Sao Paulo   Sydney   Hong Kong   Seoul   Singapore   Taipei   Tokyo

Senior Sponsoring Editor: Virginia L. Blanford
Senior Marketing Manager: Sandra McGuire
Production Manager: Frances Russello
Project Coordination, Text Design, and Electronic Page Makeup: Suganya
  Karuppasamy, GGS Higher Education Resources PMG.
Creative Art Director: Jayne Conti
Cover Designer: Karen Salzbach
Cover Illustration/Photo: James Merrell/Dorling Kindersley
Printer and Binder: Courier Companies, Inc.

For more information about the Penguin Academic series, please contact us
by mail at Pearson Education, attn. Marketing Department, 51 Madison
Avenue, 29th floor, New York, New York 10010 or by e-mail at
English.Service@Pearson.com.

For permission to use copyrighted material, grateful acknowledgment is
made to the copyright holders on pp. 715–719, which are hereby made part of
this copyright page.

Library of Congress Cataloging-in-Publication Data

One hundred great essays / edited by Robert DiYanni.—4th ed.
    p. cm.
    Includes bibliographical references and index.
    ISBN-13: 978-0-205-70680-8
    ISBN-10: 0-205-70680-0
  1. College readers. 2. English language—Rhetoric—Problems,
exercises, etc. 3. Report writing—Problems, exercises, etc. 4. Essays.
I. DiYanni, Robert. II. Title: 100 great essays.
    PE1417.O56 2011
    808'.0427—dc22
                                                        2009041327

Longman
is an imprint of

PEARSON
www.pearsonhighered.com

3 4 5 6 7 8 9 10 — V013 — 13 12 11

ISBN-13: 978-0-205-70680-8
ISBN-10:   0-205-70680-0

For Pat C. Hoy
Cherished Colleague and Friend

contents

One Hundred Great Essays is one volume of a three-book series designed to provide college students and teachers with an outstanding collection of essays for use in university writing courses. The other volumes are *Fifty Great Essays* and *Twenty-Five Great Essays*. All three volumes are based upon the conviction that reading and writing are reciprocal acts that should be married rather than divorced. Because reading and writing stimulate and reinforce one another, it is best that they be allied rather than separated. In learning to read and respond critically both to their own writing and to the writing of others, students mature as writers themselves.

One Hundred Great Essays offers a compendium of the best essays written during the past seven hundred years. Readers will find here essays by the great early practitioners of the genre, Montaigne and Bacon, as well as numerous examples from the centuries that follow, both classic and contemporary. Taken together, the essayists whose work is anthologized here offer an abundance of nonfiction that takes the form of autobiographical and polemical essays, observations and speculations, reminiscences and sketches, meditations and expostulations, celebrations and attacks. Overall, the selections balance and blend the flamboyant and innovative with the restrained and classically lucid.

Each of the essays in *One Hundred Great Essays* can be considered "great," but is not necessarily great in the same way. Montaigne's greatness as an essayist is not Franklin's, nor is Hazlitt's essay writing matched equivalently by Swift's. And Orwell's greatness, inspired by a political animus, differs dramatically from that of E. B. White, whose inspiration and emphasis derive less from grand social issues than from personal observation and experience. Yet however much these essayists and essays differ, two aspects of greatness they share are readability and teachability. Whether classic, modern, or contemporary, and whatever their styles, subjects, and rhetorical strategies, these one hundred essays are worth reading and teaching. They have served students and teachers of reading and writing well for many years.

The fourth edition of *One Hundred Great Essays* deviates only slightly from the first three editions. The introduction to reading and writing essays and the format for the collection of great essays remain the same. The changes occur in the anthology of essays, with twenty essays from the third edition replaced by twenty new selections. The new essays are provided with the same apparatus—author biography, essay headnote, and questions—just as the selections carried over from the third edition.

This collection should be of great value to university instructors who are teaching writing courses both introductory and advanced. They will find here an abundance of outstanding writing to serve as models for their students—models of style and structure, models of thought and feeling expressed in, with, and through carefully wrought language.

Students will find in this valuable collection a source of ideas and models for their own writing. They will also discover here writers who will serve as inspiration and influence as they develop their own styles and voices. In studying these essays as models of good writing, students will profit from analyzing not so much what these writers say as how they say what they do.

Writers, too, can benefit from reading the essays collected here and studying the craftsmanship they embody. Montaigne's ease and elegance, and his quirky individuality, while not easily imitated, provide an example of how the familiar material of everyday life can be artfully blended with the exploration of ideas. Bacon's pithy prose exemplifies ideas expressed with aphoristic acuteness. And while these early stars of the constellation of essayists may shine more brightly than others, writers who read with care the contemporary pieces collected here will learn new tricks of the trade and discover unexpected surprises and pleasures.

The heart and soul of *One Hundred Great Essays* are one hundred outstanding essays that span seven centuries. The essays provide a rich sampling of styles and voices across a wide spectrum of topics. They range in length and complexity—some more accessible, others more challenging—all worth reading. These one hundred essays provide excellent opportunities for readers to meet new writers and to become reacquainted with writers and essays they already know. General readers—both those who have completed their formal education and those still in college—will find in these excellent essays promises and provocations, ideas to respond to and wrestle with, and sometimes argue against.

The Introduction to *One Hundred Great Essays* provides an historical overview of the essay from antiquity to the present. It traces developments in the ways writers used essays to entertain readers as well as to inform and persuade them, and it describes the wide range of interests that writers of essays have pursued over the centuries. The Introduction also includes discussion of various types of essays and the pleasures that readers find in them.

Guidelines for reading essays are identified and exemplified with a close reading of a contemporary essay—Annie Dillard's "Living Like Weasels." Readers are provided with a series of guiding questions, commentary about the essay's style and voice, as well as its structure and ideas. The guidelines for reading essays are supplemented by guidelines for writing them. A discussion of the qualities of good writing is supplemented by an approach to the writing process, which includes consideration of three major phases or stages—planning, drafting, and revising.

In addition to a set of general essay writing guidelines, the Introduction provides an approach to writing about reading, with sample text from Susan Sontag's essay "A Woman's Beauty: Put-Down or Power Source?" The approach to writing about Sontag's essay takes the form of strategies for blending critical reading and writing, including annotating, freewriting, using a double-column notebook, and writing a summary. A further set of guidelines linking reading with writing focuses on observing details, making connections, drawing inferences, generating questions and formulating an interpretation. Throughout the discussion of writing and the sample demonstration, the emphasis is on analysis, reflection, and deliberation—on considering what the essayist is saying, what the reader thinks of it, and why.

Students should be interested in the Introduction's advice about how to read essays critically and thoughtfully. Other readers may be interested in the historical overview of the essay's development. And all readers can practice their reading skills by reading Susan Sontag's essay "A Woman's Beauty: Put-Down or Power Source?" along with the commentary that explains and explores the writer's ideas.

Each essay in *One Hundred Great Essays* is preceded by a headnote, which includes a biographical sketch along with an overview of the essay's key ideas. The biographical information provides context, while the commentary provides a starting point for consideration of the writer's ideas and values. A brief set of questions for thinking and writing follows each essay. All in all, *One Hundred Great Essays* should provide readers with many hours of reading pleasure and numerous ideas and models for writing.

Patient and persistent work with *One Hundred Great Essays* in the classroom and out will help users understand the qualities of good writing and discover ways to emulate it. With the guided practice in critical reading and essay writing that *One Hundred Great Essays* provides, students will increase both their competence and their confidence as perceptive readers and as cogent and able writers. Through repeated acts of attention to their own writing and to the writing of others, students can be expected to acquire a sense of the original meaning of "essay": a foray into thought, an attempt to discover an idea, work out its implications, and express it with distinctiveness. Readers and users of *One Hundred Great Essays* should come to see the essay as a way of enriching their experience and their thinking while discovering effective ways to share them with others.

Robert DiYanni
New York University

Introduction: Reading and Writing Essays

History and Context

The essay has a long and distinguished history. Its roots go back to Greco-Roman antiquity. Forerunners of the essay include the Greek writer Plutarch (46–120), whose *Parallel Lives* of noble Greeks and Romans influenced the art of biography, and who also wrote essays in his *Moralia*. The early Roman writer Seneca, a philosopher, dramatist, and orator, also wrote essays in the grand manner of classical oratory, on topics that include "Asthma" and "Noise." These two early western writers of essays are complemented by a pair of Japanese writers: Sei Shonagon, a court lady who lived and wrote in the tenth century, and Yoshida Kenko (1283–1350), a poet and Buddhist monk, whose brief, fragmentary essays echo the quick brushstrokes of Zen painting.

In one sense, the modern essay begins with Michel de Montaigne in France and with Francis Bacon in England. Both writers published books of essays at the end of the sixteenth century. Montaigne's first two books of essays came out together in 1580 and Bacon's first collection in 1597. Each followed with additional volumes, Montaigne in 1588, Bacon in 1612 and 1625. With each later volume, both writers revised and expanded essays previously published in the earlier volumes as well as added new ones. Both writers also wrote longer and more elaborate essays from one collection to the next.

Generally recognized as the father of the essay, Michel de Montaigne called his works "essais," French for attempts. In his essays, Montaigne explored his thinking on a wide variety of subjects, including virtue and vice, customs and behavior, children and cannibals. Although Montaigne's first essays began as reflections about his reading and made liberal use of quoted passages, his later essays relied much less on external sources for impetus and inspiration.

The power of Montaigne's essays derives largely from their personal tone, their improvisatory nature, and their display of an energetic and inquiring mind. In his essays, Montaigne talks about himself and the world as he experienced it. He repeatedly tests his opinions and presents an encyclopedia of information that sets him thinking. Amidst an essay's varied details, Montaigne reveals himself, telling us what he likes, thinks, and believes. The openness and flexibility of his essay form make its direction unpredictable, its argument arranged less as a logical structure than as a meandering exploration of its subject. But what is most revealing about Montaigne's essays is that they reveal his mind in the act of thinking. The self-revelatory circling around his subject constitutes the essential subject of the essays. Ironically, in reading him we learn not only about Montaigne but about ourselves.

Another Renaissance writer credited with an influential role in the development of the essay is Francis Bacon—statesman, philosopher, scientist, and essayist. Unlike Montaigne, who retired from active political life early to read, reflect, and write in his private library tower, Bacon remained politically active and intellectually prominent until the last few years of his life. His life and work exhibit a curious interplay between ancient and modern forms of thought. Coupled with a modernity that valued experiment and individual experience was a respect for the authority of tradition. Bacon's scientific and literary writings both display this uneasy alliance of tradition and innovation.

Bacon's essays differ from Montaigne's in striking ways. First, most of Bacon's essays are short. Second, his essays are much less personal than Montaigne's. And third, many of Bacon's essays offer advice on how to live. Their admonitory intent differs from Montaigne's more exploratory temper.

Eighteenth-century America included a profusion of essayists writing in a variety of nonfictional forms. Thomas Paine wrote essays of political persuasion in the periodical *The Crisis*. J. Hector St. John de Crèvecoeur wrote his essayistic *Letters from an American Farmer*. And Benjamin Franklin compiled his *Autobiography* and his *Poor Richard's Almanack*, which is a loosely stitched collection of aphorisms, including "haste makes waste," "a stitch in time saves nine," and "Fish and visitors stink after three days."

During the eighteenth century, more and more writers produced essays, along with their work in other genres. Among them are Samuel Johnson (1709–1784), whose philosophical and moral periodical essays appeared regularly in his own *Rambler*, *Idler*, and *Adventurer*. The gravity and sobriety of Johnson's essays were complemented by the more lighthearted and satirical vein mined by Joseph Addison (1672–1719), and Richard Steele (1672–1729), whose essays in their *Tatler* and *Spectator* periodicals, which they jointly wrote and published, were avidly awaited when they appeared, as often as three times a week. Jonathan Swift (1667–1745), best known for his satire, *Gulliver's Travels*, also wrote a number of essays, including what is perhaps the most famous satirical essay ever written (and the essay with one of the longest titles): "A Modest Proposal for Preventing the Children of the Poor People in Ireland from being a Burden to their Parents or Country; and for making them beneficial to their Publick."

The nineteenth century saw the rise of the essay less as moralistic and satirical than as entertaining and even a bit eccentric. Among the most notable practitioners were Charles Lamb (1775–1834), whose *Essays of Elia* and *More Essays of Elia* are constructed to read less like random assortments than as books centered on characters, and whose stories form a loose plot. Among these essays is his "A Bachelor's Complaint," in which Lamb, himself a lifelong bachelor, takes up a list of grievances he holds against his married friends and acquaintances. Complementing the playful essays of Charles Lamb during this time are the passionate and highly opinionated essays of William Hazlitt (1778–1830), a friend of the English Romantic poets William Wordsworth and Samuel Taylor Coleridge. Hazlitt's "On the Pleasure of Hating" is written with his customary "gusto," a characteristic he brought to his writing from his life and one in synch with the Romantic poets' emphasis on the importance of feeling.

Nineteenth-century American essayists include the powerful twosome of Ralph Waldo Emerson and Henry David Thoreau. Emerson's essays grew out of his public lectures. He was at home in the form and wrote a large number of essays in a highly aphoristic style that contained nuggets of wisdom served up in striking images and memorably pithy expressions. A few quotable examples include "hitch your wagon to a star," "trust thyself," and "give all to love." Much of Emerson's writing focused on nature, which he envisioned as a divine moral guide to life.

Thoreau, a friend and protégé of Emerson, was another New Englander who limned the natural world in prose. Like Emerson, Thoreau wrote essays on a variety of topics, but mostly about nature. Thoreau's most famous essay, however, is political—his "On the Duty of Civil Disobedience," in which he argues that each individual human being has not only the right but the obligation to break the law when the law is unjust or immoral. Thoreau's "Civil Disobedience," a much cited essay, has also been an influential one, affecting the stances of peaceful nonviolent political resistance taken up by both Mahatma Gandhi and Martin Luther King, Jr. But it is Thoreau's *Walden* that contains his most beautifully crafted essays in his most artfully composed book. Who can forget the matchless prose of sentences such as "If a man cannot keep pace with his companions, perhaps he hears the sound of a different drummer. Let him step to the music which he hears, however measured or far away."

If in one sense the Renaissance can be considered the beginnings of the modern essay, in another, the modern essay is synonymous with the twentieth-century essay, a period in which the essay developed into a literary genre that began to rival fiction and poetry in importance. George Orwell (1903–1950), best known for his satirical *Animal Farm* and *1984*, is equally eminent for the four thick volumes of essays and letters he produced. Orwell's "A Hanging" and "Shooting an Elephant" are modern classics of the genre, as is his "Politics and the English Language," perhaps the best-known essay on language in English. Another English writer better known for her work as a novelist, Virginia Woolf (1882–1941), like Orwell, left a splendid set of essay volumes, including her "Common Reader" series, in which she presents her views on a wide range of authors and works of literature in a relaxed, casual style. "The Death of a Moth" is deservedly among her most highly regarded essays.

On the twentieth-century American scene, E. B. White (1899–1985) stands out as a modern master of the genre. White, too, is best known for his fiction, in his case the books he wrote for children, all gems with the diamond among them the ever-popular *Charlotte's Web*. White published many of his essays in the *New Yorker* and a number of others in *Harper's* magazine. "Once More to the Lake," his best known and oft reprinted essay, is also among his most beautifully written, and some would argue, among his most enduring contributions to literature.

Along with White, who rarely wrote about social issues per se, there is James Baldwin (1924–1987), who wrote almost exclusively about race, particularly about race relations in America and about his place in society as a black man and a writer. In fact, Baldwin's consistent theme is identity, his identity as a black writer, who became an expatriate, living in Paris, in part to discover what it meant for him to be an American. A third modern American essayist is James Thurber, a humorist who published satirical cartoons, humorous stories, and parables, as well as journalism. His "The Secret Life of Walter Mitty" and "The Catbird Seat" are two comic story masterpieces. His *My Life and Hard Times* is a classic of American autobiography, and his *Is Sex Necessary?* a spoof on pop psychology.

At the beginning of the twenty-first century, the essay is continuing to thrive. Essayists of all stripes and persuasions continue to publish in magazines and anthologies and in books of collected essays. The annual series, *The Best American Essays*, has recently celebrated its twentieth anniversary. Other annual series of essays have joined it, notably *The Anchor Essay Annual*. These essay volumes are joined by others that are not part of any annual series, but which, nevertheless, come out with great frequency and regularity. The essay, in short, is alive and well in the new millennium.

Pleasures of the Essay

But why has the essay been so well regarded for such a long time? What attracts readers to essays? And what attracts writers to the form? Why has the essay endured?

One answer lies in the wide variety the genre affords. There are essays for everybody, essay voices and visions and styles to suit every taste, to satisfy every kind of intellectual craving. There is variety of subject—of topic—from matters of immediate and practical concern to those of apparently purely theoretical interest; from essays of somber gravity to those in a lighter more playful vein; from easy essays on familiar topics to complex and challenging ones on subjects outside the bounds of most readers' knowledge and experience.

An essay can be about anything. And essayists have written about every topic under the sun, from their own lives and experience to what they have read and observed in the world, to their speculations and imaginings. All of these are available, for example, in Montaigne's little essay, "Of Smells." In fact, to list just a handful of the more than one hundred essays Montaigne alone wrote is to convey a sense of the essay's bewildering variety. In addition to "Of Smells," Montaigne wrote "Of Friendship," "Of Sadness," "Of Idleness," "Of Liars," "Of Constancy," "Of Solitude," "Of Sleep," "Of Fear," "Of Age," "Of Prayers," "Of Conscience," "How We Cry and Laugh for the Same Thing," "Of Moderation," "Of Thumbs," "Of Cannibals," "Of Names," "Of Virtue," "Of Anger," "Of Vanity," "Of Cruelty," "Of Cripples," "Of Glory," "Of Presumption," "Of Books," "How Our Mind Hinders Itself," "That Our Desire Is Increased By Difficulty," "Of the Inconsistency of Our Actions," "Of the Love of Fathers for Their Children," and "That to Philosophize Is to Learn to Die." A similarly wide-ranging list of topics could be culled from Bacon's essays, expressing an equally strong interest in the human condition.

For all his essayistic variety, Montaigne did not write much about nature. Many others, however, have written about the natural world, including Ralph Waldo Emerson in "Nature," N. Scott Momaday in "The Way to Rainy Mountain," Annie Dillard in "Living Like Weasels," Mark Twain in "Reading the River," and Virginia Woolf in "The Death of the Moth." In each of these essays the writer describes an encounter with nature and explores his or her relationship to it.

When not writing about themselves or about nature, and when not speculating on one or another aspect of the human condition, essayists often write about the social world. Joan Didion's "Marrying Absurd" is about Las Vegas weddings; James Thurber's "University Days," about college; and Pico Iyer's "Nowhere Man," about living in multiple places and being a member of no single social group.

Identity, in fact, is a frequent topic among contemporary essayists, with writers exploring their roots and their relationships in essays that touch on race and gender, and on broad social and cultural values. James Baldwin explores what it means to be a black man in a white world. Frederick Douglass writes about his struggle for literacy as a black slave; Judith Ortiz Cofer writes about her dual cultural and linguistic identity; Martin Luther King, Jr., writes about racial prejudice and injustice, and what must be done to establish and ensure racial equality, and why; and Jamaica Kincaid writes about finding and valuing her Caribbean Antiguan identity under the seductive influence of British colonial culture.

Issues of gender are equally important for essayists. Gretel Ehrlich writes about what it means to be a cowboy who cares for animals as an integral part of his life, and of how cowboys, if they are to be good at what they do, need as much maternalism as machismo, if not a good deal more. Maxine Hong Kingston writes about the power and place of gender in traditional China by telling the story of a man, Tang Ao, who visits the land of women, is captured, and is transformed into a woman. Another strong woman who appears in an essay is N. Scott Momaday's Kiowa Indian grandmother, who reflects the cultural values of her tribe and its Native American tradition.

Besides a wide variety of topic and a broad spectrum of human concerns, including gender, race, culture, and identity, essays appeal, too, because of their style, the craftsmanship and beauty with which they are written. And just as there are many essay subjects, so also are there many styles. There are as many styles, in fact, as essayists, for each essayist of distinction develops his or her own style, finding a voice and tone appropriate to the topic, audience, and situation that occasioned the writing of each essay.

E. B. White's "Once More to the Lake" is written in a style at once easy and elegant, familiar and formal, in a splendid blend of language that is as easy on the ear as it is on the eye. For the sheer beauty of language, it begs to be read aloud. George Orwell's "Shooting an Elephant" is less lyrical but no less memorable, written in a style that seems to be no style at all—as clear as a windowpane. Amy Tan's "Mother Tongue" is written in a mixture of styles, an indication that she speaks more than one brand of English, as she describes the worlds of English both she and her Chinese mother inhabit. Langston Hughes uses a simple and direct style in his "Salvation," which tells the story of his religious "anti-conversion." Martin Luther King, Jr., writes in a style that appeals to thinking people, as he develops his own arguments and rebuts the arguments of others about the right of African Americans to protest against racial injustice.

Types of Essays

The word "essay" comes from the French "essai" (essay), which derives from the French verb "essayer"—to try or attempt. The word "essay" suggests less a formal and systematic approach to a topic than a casual, even random one. In this sense, an essay differs from other prose forms such as the magazine article, whose purpose is usually to inform or persuade, and the review, which evaluates a book or performance.

Essays, to be sure, may also evaluate, and they often inform as well as persuade. But their manner of going about offering information, making a case, and providing an evaluation differs from those less variable genres.

The essay can be compared with the short story in that some essays, like short stories, include narrative. But the short story is fiction, the essay fact. And fiction works largely by implication, the essay mostly by expository discursiveness. Essays explain what stories imply. This is not to say that essayists don't make use of fictional techniques and strategies. They do so often, particularly in personal or familiar essays, which include narration and description.

The essay can also be linked with poetry, particularly with the more discursive poems that explain as well as image ideas that tell straightforwardly rather than hint or suggest in a more oblique manner. Essayists, on the other hand, typically say what's on their mind fairly directly. They explain what they are thinking. Poets more often write about one thing in terms of another (they write about love, for example, in terms of war). And they prefer implication to explication, which is more characteristic of the essay writer.

Kinds of essays include, broadly, personal essays and formal essays. Personal essays are those in which the writer is amply evident—front and center. Employing the personal pronoun "I," personal essays include opinions and perspectives explicitly presented as the writer's own in a personal, even idiosyncratic, manner. Formal essays, by contrast, typically avoid the pronoun "I," and they omit personal details. Formal essays include expository essays, analytical essays, and argumentative, or persuasive, essays. Expository essays explain ideas and scenarios, using standard patterns of organization, including comparison and contrast, classification, and cause and effect. Analytical essays offer an analysis and interpretation of a text or performance, typically breaking that text or performance into parts or aspects, and presenting both an evaluative judgment and the evidence on which it is based. Argumentative, or persuasive, essays advance a thesis or claim and present evidence that is organized as part of a logical demonstration, utilizing the modes of deductive and inductive reasoning, and including support for the argumentative claim in the form of reasons, examples, and data as evidence.

Most essays, even the most personal ones, are composites and blends. They may tell personal stories rich in descriptive detail to provide evidence to support an idea or claim to persuasion. They may use traditional patterns of expository organization such as comparison and contrast in the cause of developing a logical argument. And they may include information and explanation along with personal experience and argumentation. More often than not, the most interesting and memorable of essays mix and match what are typically thought of as distinct essay types and the conventions associated with them. Contemporary essayists, in particular, cross borders and mix modes, as they write essays that break the rules in a quest to be engaging, persuasive, and interesting.

Reading Essays

Reading essays is a lot like reading other forms of literature. It requires careful attention to language—to the words on the page and to what's "written between the lines." Reading essays involves essentially five interrelated mental acts: observing, connecting, inferring, questioning, and concluding. Good readers attend to the details of language and structure of the essays they read. They note not only the information that writers of essays provide, but also how that information is presented, how any stories are told, how arguments are made, and evidence presented. Good readers of essays look for connections among the details they observe—details of image and structure, argument and evidence. And good readers draw inferences based on those connected observations, inferences that prepare them to make an interpretive conclusion from their inferences.

Good readers are also engaged by what they read. They respond with questions that echo in their minds as they read. They make their reading an active engagement with the essay text, an involvement that continues after their actual reading of the words on the page has been completed.

Reading in this manner—observing, connecting, inferring, questioning, and concluding—alerts readers to nuances, to things rendered but not explained or elaborated by the writer. Active, deliberative reading of this sort involves both intellectual comprehension and emotional apprehension, a consideration of the feelings essays generate as well as the thinking they stimulate. This reading process requires that readers make sense of gaps in texts; that they recognize linguistic, literary, and cultural conventions; that they generalize on the basis of textual details; that they bring their values to bear on the essays they read; and that they do all these things concurrently and simultaneously.

Reading Annie Dillard's "Living Like Weasels"

We can illustrate this kind of active, engaged reading by looking at the opening paragraphs of Annie Dillard's "Living Like Weasels," an essay printed in full on pages 164–168.

> A weasel is wild. Who knows what he thinks? He sleeps in his underground den, his tail draped over his nose. Sometimes he lives in his den for two days without leaving. Outside, he stalks rabbits, mice, muskrats, and birds, killing more bodies than he can eat warm, and often dragging the carcasses home. Obedient to instinct, he bites his prey at the neck, either splitting the jugular vein at the throat or crunching the brain at the base of the skull, and he does not let go. One naturalist refused to kill a weasel who was socketed into his hand deeply as a rattlesnake. The man could in no way pry the tiny weasel off, and he had to walk half a mile to water, the weasel dangling from his palm, and soak him off like a stubborn label.

First, a few questions. What strikes us most about this passage? What do we notice on first reading it? What observations would we most like to make about it? What questions do we have? What feelings does the text inspire? What expectations do we have about where the essayist is taking us?

Next, some observations. The first sentence is abrupt. It announces forcefully the key point that a weasel is wild. But what does it imply? What do we understand by the word "wild"? How wild? In what way is the weasel wild? The second sentence is a question, one that invites us to consider what a weasel thinks about. (Or perhaps it suggests that we shouldn't bother because we simply cannot know.) "Who knows what he thinks?" How we take this sentence depends on how we hear it, which in turn, affects how we say it. Here's one way: Who knows what he *thinks?* Here's another: Who knows *what* he thinks? And still another: Who *knows* what he thinks? Whichever way we prefer, we recognize the possibility of alternative emphases and thus, alternative ways of understanding what the writer is saying and suggesting about weasels.

Dillard's next two sentences provide information—that weasels sleep in dens where they can remain for up to two days at a time. There's nothing really surprising here. But what about that other little bit of information—*how* the weasel sleeps: with his tail draped over his nose. Whether factual or fanciful, that draped tail is a lovely surprise, a gratuitous image offered to engage and entertain as well as inform.

The fifth and sixth sentences of the opening paragraph reveal the weasel as hunter—stalking prey, killing it, dragging it to his den, where he eats it and then, presumably, sleeps. When we are told that the weasel is obedient to instinct and are shown exactly how he kills—by splitting the jugular vein or by crunching his victim's brain—we remember the opening sentence: "A weasel is wild." And we begin to understand in a new way just what this means. Although we "understood" before, on first encountering the sentence, that vague and general knowledge is now particularized. We have since acquired specific information that we can understand intellectually and respond to emotionally. Now, we know more fully what it means to say that a weasel is "wild."

It is here, in the middle of the paragraph, that we perhaps register our strongest emotional response. How do we respond to Dillard's details about the weasel's method of killing its victims? Are we amazed? Engaged? Appalled? Or what? That question about response is directed at our experience of the essay. We can also ask a technical question: Does Dillard need that degree of detail? Suppose she had diluted it or perhaps even omitted such concrete details entirely. Or conversely, suppose that she had provided an even fuller rendition of the killing. How would such alternatives have affected our response?

Dillard's opening paragraph concludes with an anecdote about a naturalist bitten by the tenacious weasel. The anecdote makes a point, to be sure. But it does more. The image impresses itself on our minds in language worth noting: the verb "socketed"; the comparison with the rattlesnake; the image of the stubborn label. To make sense of Dillard's opening paragraph, even a preliminary kind of sense, is to make such observations and to wonder about their significance. And it is to wonder, too, where the essay is heading, where the writer is taking us. What *do* we expect at this point? Why?

Once we read the second paragraph of Dillard's essay, we can consider how it affects our understanding of and response to the first. How does it follow from the opening paragraph? What does it do rhetorically? That is, what effect does it have on us, and how does it advance Dillard's point about the wildness of the weasel?

Here is Dillard's next paragraph:

> And once, says Ernest Thompson Seton—once, a man shot an eagle
> out of the sky. He examined the eagle and found the dry skull of a
> weasel fixed by the jaws to his throat. The supposition is that the eagle
> had pounced on the weasel and the weasel swiveled and bit as instinct

*taught him, tooth to neck, and nearly won. I would like to have seen
that eagle from the air a few weeks or months before he was shot: was
the whole weasel still attached to his feathered throat, a fur pendant?
Or did the eagle eat what he could reach, gutting the living weasel with
his talons before his breast, bending his beak, cleaning the beautiful
airborne bones?*

Our questions at the beginning of this second paragraph of Dillard's
essay necessarily invite our responses, both intellectual and emotional.
In asking what strikes us about the details or the language of this paragraph, we move from subjective responses to objective considerations.
On the basis of the details we notice and relate, we form inferences.
We move backward, in a way, from our initial response to a set of observations about the essay's rhetoric. We might observe, for example, that
the second paragraph begins with an image very much like the one at
the end of the opening paragraph. The tenacious weasel holds on
fiercely, in one instance to a man's hand, and in another, to an eagle's
throat. And we might register the justness of this pair of images, the
more striking image of the eagle following and intensifying the first
image of the weasel socketed to a man's hand. We might also observe
that the second paragraph begins with statements—with declarative
sentences—and ends with questions. We might notice, further, that it
includes a reference to another written text (did we notice that this
occurs in the opening paragraph as well?). And, finally, that the writer
speaks personally, using the personal pronoun "I," revealing her desire
to have seen the amazing thing she had only read about.

In addition, we should note Dillard's profusion of precise, vivid,
strong verbs, which contribute to the power of her prose. We should
note, too, the image of the eagle gutting the living weasel, bending his
beak and cleaning the weasel's bones of its flesh—an image brought
forward and elaborated from the previous sentence, where it exists as a
pair of adjectives and corresponding nouns: "his feathered throat, a fur
pendant." Dillard actually brings the dormant image to life in that
string of participles: *gutting, living, bending, cleaning.*

The repeated words in this second paragraph create a litany of eagle
and weasel, their rhyming sound echoed again in "*eat*," "*reach*," "*beak*,"
and "*cleaning*." We should notice, as well, the alliterative b's of the final
sentence: "his talons before his breast, bending his beak, cleaning the
beautiful airborne bones." And further, we might see how the paragraph's
monosyllabic diction is counterpointed against both the polysyllabic

name of the naturalist, Ernest Thompson Seton, and the continual yoking and re-yoking of the animals, eagle and weasel always coming together. To hear the remarkable sound play of Dillard's prose, including its subtle yet muscular rhythms, we must read it aloud.

We can make some observations about the overall structure of Dillard's complete essay. We have described how the first two paragraphs present facts about weasels, especially about their wildness and their tenaciousness. This introductory section of the essay is followed by a section, paragraphs 3–7, that depicts Dillard's encounter with a weasel and their exchange of glances. The middle paragraphs of that section—4 through 6—set the scene, while paragraphs 3 and 7 frame this section, with an emphasis on Dillard's and the weasel's repeated locked glances. Paragraph 5 is of particular interest in its mix of details that contrast wilderness and civilization. They exist, surprisingly, side by side, one within the other: beer cans coexist with muskrat holes; turtle eggs sit in motorcycle tracks; a highway runs alongside a duck pond.

Dillard's next large section of the essay, paragraphs 8–13, provides a crescendo and a climax. Dillard describes the weasel in detail, emphasizing the shock of their locked looks and the shattering of the spell. She also laments her unsuccessful attempt to re-forge the link with the weasel after the spell had been broken. The section ends with Dillard and her readers pondering the mysterious encounter she experienced.

In her concluding section, paragraphs 14–17, Dillard speculates about the meaning of her encounter with the weasel. She contemplates living like a weasel—what it means, why it appeals to her. She explores the implications of what a weasel's life is like, and how its life relates to the life of human beings like her own. She concludes with an image from the opening: an eagle carrying something that is clinging fiercely to it, not letting go, holding on into and beyond death. The image brings the essay full circle—but with the important difference that we, Dillard's readers, have taken the weasel's place.

We are now poised to consider the ideas, the meaning, of "Living Like Weasels," though, clearly, it is necessary to read the essay in its entirety at least once for the following remarks to be completely comprehensible.

What begins as an expository essay that outlines facts about the wildness and tenacity of weasels turns into a meditation on the value of wildness and the necessity of tenacity in human life. By the end of the essay, Dillard has made the weasel a symbol and a model of how human beings might, even should, live. And her tone changes from the factual declaration of the essay's introductory section to speculative wonder, and finally to admonition. Dillard encourages her readers to identify their one necessity, and then, like the weasel, to latch on to it and never let it go.

Dillard also suggests that there is between human and animal the possibility of communication, of understanding. She opts for a mystical communion between woman and weasel, by necessity a brief communion, one beyond the power of words to describe. The experience for Dillard stuns her into stillness and momentarily stops time. In linking her mind even briefly with the weasel, Dillard undergoes an extraordinary transforming experience. But it's an experience that, as much as she wishes it to continue, she cannot prolong because her own consciousness, the distinctive human quality of her thinking mind, which enables her to appreciate the experience in the first place, prevents her, finally, from staying at one with an animal.

There seems to be, thus, in Dillard's essay, a pull in two directions. On one hand, there is the suggestion that human beings can link themselves with the animal world, and like the weasel, live in necessity instinctively. On the other hand sits an opposing idea: that human beings cannot stay linked with the weasel or any animal, primarily because our minds prohibit it. We are creatures for whom remembering is necessary, vital. The mindlessness of the weasel, thus, can never be ours, for we are mindful creatures, not mindless ones. Our living as we should is necessarily different from the weasel's living as it should. And although we can certainly learn from the weasel's tenacity and purity of living, we can follow it only so far on the way to wildness.

Writing Essays

Reading actively and with critical judgment is a necessary adjunct to writing well. In reading carefully and critically, we learn about suggestiveness, about allusion, about economy, about richness. We learn about rhetorical and stylistic possibilities for our own essay writing.

The Qualities of Good Writing

But what constitutes good writing, the kind of writing expected of students in college courses, the kind expected of professional employees on the job? Writing, essentially, that is characterized by the following qualities: (1) clarity; (2) coherence; (3) logical organization; (4) accuracy and correctness; (5) sufficiency; and (6) style.

Good writing is *clear* writing. Readers can follow and understand it easily. This is harder to accomplish than it sounds because what is clear to the writer may not be clear to the reader. Writers need to remember that the entire context of their thinking is not readily apparent to their readers. Readers can determine what a writer is saying only from the words on the page.

Good writing is *coherent* writing. Coherence refers to how a writer's sentences "hang together," how those sentences relate to one another sensibly and logically. We can think of coherence, first, though not exclusively, as a quality of paragraphs. Good writing allows readers to determine the focus and point of every paragraph, and to determine, further, the relation of one paragraph to another. This aspect of coherence reveals a writer's inescapable concern with essay organization overall.

Good writing is carefully *organized* writing. A well-written essay has a discernible beginning, middle, and ending (a clearly identifiable introduction, body, and conclusion). Each of these three main parts of an essay need not be baldly announced, but each should be readily discernible by a careful reader. But the organization of an essay requires more than including these three broad aspects. Of particular importance is how the essay unfolds, how its information and evidence are deployed, how each aspect of the writer's idea leads into the next, how the paragraphs that make up the middle, or body, of an essay exhibit a logical structure.

Good writing is also *accurate* and *correct* both in terms of information included and in terms of its language. Grammatical accuracy is essential. So are accurate spelling and punctuation. These elements of good writing can be assisted through the use of grammar and spell-check features of word processing programs, through the use of a college dictionary, and through keeping a reliable handbook, such as *The Scribner Handbook for Writers*, nearby.

Good writing is also *sufficient* to the scope of its subject and the limits of its topic. Short essays may be adequate to discussing highly focused aspects of a topic, while broader and more inclusive topics require longer, more detailed writing. Sufficiency, of course, is a relative concept. But it is important for a writer to include enough evidence to support an idea persuasively, enough examples to illustrate a concept clearly, a sufficient number of reasons to support a claim in developing an argument.

Good writing, finally, has a sense of *style*. Every writer needs to develop his or her own way with words. Paradoxically, one of the best ways to do this is to observe and imitate the style of other writers.

Good writers attend to how other successful writers structure their essays, shape their sentences, and select their words. One of the reasons to develop skillful habits of reading is to glean, from that attentiveness, strategies and techniques for good writing.

An Overview of the Writing Process

These six qualities of good writing require patience, persistence, and practice. Good writing can't be rushed. It requires planning, drafting, and revising.

Planning

In the planning stage of the writing process, it is important to take notes and to make notes. Taking notes involves mostly marking or copying passages, which you might use in your essay. It also involves summarizing and paraphrasing what you read—putting it into your own words. Making notes refers to the act of thinking about what you have marked, copied, summarized, or paraphrased. Writing out notes about what you think about your reading, beginning to formulate your own thinking about it, is an active and reflective process that provides an important step toward drafting your essay.

Planning your essay requires making notes to yourself in other ways as well. You can make lists of observations from your reading or lists of aspects or elements of your topic to consider in your essay draft. You can jot down questions, and you can do some freewriting to jumpstart your thinking. These and other preliminary planning strategies are necessary for all but the most informal of writing projects. Time spent on them pays off later during the drafting stage.

Drafting

A draft is a first take, one that provides an overview of your essay, including some kind of beginning and ending, and much of the body or middle, with its examples and evidence to support and develop your ideas. First drafts of essays are often called "rough" drafts, and for good reason. The preliminary draft is not meant to be worried into final form. The first draft is not intended to be a finished product, fit for public display. It is, rather, an attempt the writer makes to see where the topic is going, and whether there are sufficient examples and evidence to support the idea. The idea too, may very well require adjustment and revision, more often than not.

In drafting an essay, it is important to consider your purpose. Are you writing to provide information? To convey an experience? To amuse and entertain? To present an idea for your readers' consideration? To persuade your readers to see something your way? Being clear about your purpose will help with decisions about other aspects of writing your essay, including how to begin and end, as well as choices of language and tone.

Your draft should also make a good start toward providing the supporting evidence necessary for making your ideas persuasive. In marshalling evidence for your ideas from your reading of primary sources, such as works of literature (including the essays in this book), and from secondary sources written about the primary sources, keep the following guidelines in mind:

1. Be fair-minded. Be careful not to oversimplify or distort either a primary or secondary source.
2. Be cautious. Qualify your claims. Limit your assertions to what you can comfortably demonstrate.
3. Be logical. See that the various elements of your argument fit together and that you don't contradict yourself.
4. Be accurate. Present facts, details, and quotations with care.
5. Be confident. Believe in your ideas and present them with conviction.

After writing a draft of an essay, put it aside for a while—ideally for at least a day or two. When you return to it, assess whether what you are saying still makes sense, whether you have provided enough examples to clarify your ideas and presented sufficient evidence to make them persuasive. Read the draft critically, asking yourself what is convincing and what is not, what makes sense and what doesn't. Consider whether the draft centers on a single idea and stays on track.

If the first draft accomplishes these things, you can begin thinking about how to tighten its organization and refine its style. If, on the other hand, the draft contains frequent changes of direction, confusions of thought, multiple unrelated ideas, incoherent paragraphs, and more, you will need to decide what to salvage and what to discard. You will need to return to the planning stage—though now with a clearer sense of your essay's possibilities, and begin the process of drafting your essay again—a second attempt in a second draft. This scenario, by the way, is not uncommon. It simply represents the way first efforts often begin: in some degree of confusion that is eventually dispelled. This common scenario, moreover, argues for leaving enough time to do a second (and, if necessary, a third) draft.

Revising

Revision is not something that occurs only once, at the end of the writing process. Redrafting your essay to consider the ordering of paragraphs and the use of examples is itself a significant act of revision. So, too, is doing additional reading and even rereading some materials to reconsider your original idea. Revision occurs throughout the entire arc of the writing process. It requires you to reconsider your writing and your thinking not once, but several times. This reconsideration is made on three levels: conceptual, organizational, and stylistic.

Conceptual revision involves reconsidering your ideas. As you write your first and subsequent drafts, your understanding of the topic may change. While accumulating evidence in support of your idea, you may find evidence that subverts or challenges it. And you might decide, if not to change your idea dramatically, at least to qualify it to account for this contradictory or complicating evidence. On the other hand, as you write your various drafts, you might find yourself thinking of additional ways to develop and strengthen your idea, to support it with additional evidence, examples, and reasons.

Organizational or structural revision involves asking yourself whether your essay's arrangement best presents your line of thinking. You might ask yourself questions such as these: Is the organizational framework readily discernible? Does it make sense? Have you written an introduction that identifies your topic and clarifies your intent? Have you organized your supporting details in a sensible and logical manner? Does your conclusion follow from your discussion, and does it bring your essay to a satisfying close? However you choose to end your essay, your conclusion should answer the question "So what?" for the reader. Even though you may have presented details, reasons, and examples to support your idea, your readers will still expect you to explain their significance, and in ways that they themselves will want to see as interesting and valuable.

Stylistic revision concerns smaller-scale details, such as matters of syntax or word order, of diction or word choice, of tone, imagery, and rhythm. Even though you may think about some of these things a bit in early drafts, it is better to defer critical attention to them until your final draft, largely because such microscopic stylistic considerations may undergo significant alteration as you rethink and reorganize your essay. You might find, for example, that a paragraph you worked on carefully for style in a first draft is no longer important or relevant, and thus disappears from the final draft.

Focus on aspects of style that may require revision with the following questions:

1. Are your sentences concise and clear?
2. Can you eliminate words that are not doing their job?
3. Is your tone consistent? (For example, you need to avoid shifts from a formal to an informal or colloquial tone.)
4. Is your level of language appropriate for the subject of your essay?
5. Are there any grammatical errors? Any mistakes in spelling or punctuation? And, finally, before letting an essay go public, be sure to proofread it to check for typos and other unintended mistakes.

Writing from Reading—An Example

In order to write essays about what you read, it is always useful to work through some preliminary, informal writing en route to preparing a more formal piece, whether a short summary or a longer, full-fledged essay.

Earlier, some types of preliminary writing were mentioned. Here they will be illustrated with a short excerpt from Susan Sontag's essay, "A Woman's Beauty" (pp. 588–591).

We begin with annotation.

Annotations are brief notes you write about a text while reading it. You can underline and circle words and phrases that strike you as important. You can highlight passages. You can make marginal comments that reflect your understanding of and attitude toward the text. Your annotations might also include arrows that link related points, question marks that indicate possible confusion, and exclamation marks to express surprise or agreement.

Annotations can be single words or brief phrases; they can be written as statements or as questions. And depending on how extensively you annotate a text, your annotations may form a secondary text that reminds you of the one you are reading and analyzing. Annotations used this way serve as an abbreviated guide to what the text says and what you think about it.

As you read the following passage, notice the various types of annotations, and, if you like, add additional annotations of your own.

Here, first, for convenience, is an excerpt from Sontag's essay.

Excerpt from Susan Sontag's

A Woman's Beauty: Put-Down or Power Source?

Is beauty really essential? Seems exaggerated. Society defines names of beauty. Women are pushed into over concern with their appearance Contrast: men do well; women look good.

To be called beautiful is thought to name something essential to women's character and concerns. (In contrast to men—whose essence is to be strong, or effective, or competent.) It does not take someone in the throes of advanced feminist awareness to perceive that the way women are taught to be involved with beauty encourages narcissism, reinforces dependence and immaturity. Everybody (women and men) knows that. For it is "everybody," a whole society, that has identified being feminine with caring about how one looks. (In contrast to being masculine—which is identified with caring about what one is and does and only secondarily, if at all, about how one looks.) [. . .]

Contrast: desire for beauty versus obligation to be beautiful strong palletizes the issue—beauty as means of oppression. Women + beauty = body parts.

It is not, of course, the desire to be beautiful that is wrong but the obligation to be—or to try. What is accepted by most women as a flattering idealization of their sex is a way of making women feel inferior to what they actually are—or normally grow to be. For the ideal of beauty is administered as a form of self-oppression. Women are taught to see their bodies in parts, and to evaluate each part separately. Breasts, feet, hips, waistline, neck, eyes, nose, complexion, hair, and so on—each in turn is submitted to an anxious, fretful, often despairing scrutiny. Even if some pass muster, some will always be found wanting. [. . .]

In <u>men, good looks is a whole</u>, something taken in at a glance. It does not need to be confirmed by giving measurements of different regions of the body; nobody encourages a man to dissect his appearance, feature by feature. As for <u>perfection</u>, that is considered trivial—almost unmanly.

Doesn't author exaggerate here about perfection?
Nice distinction here on beauty and the sexes.

Freewriting

Your initial impressions of a text, which you can record with annotations, will often lead you to further thoughts about it. You can begin developing these thoughts with freewriting. As with annotating, in freewriting you record ideas, reactions, or feelings about a text without arranging them in any special order. Freewriting is free-form writing. You simply write down what you think about the passage, without worrying about logical organization. The point is to get your ideas down on paper and not to censor or judge them prematurely. Freewriting, in fact, provides a way to pursue an idea and develop your thinking to see where it may lead.

Both annotation and freewriting precede the more intricate and deliberative work of analysis, interpretation, and evaluation. Annotation and freewriting also provide a convenient way to prepare for writing essays and reports. These two informal techniques work well together; the brief, quickly noted annotations complement the more leisurely paced, longer elaborations of freewriting.

Here is an example of freewriting about the Susan Sontag essay excerpt annotated earlier. Notice how the freewriting includes questions that stimulate reflection on the passage.

Example of Freewriting

Interesting questions. Women do seem to think more about their looks than men do. But since it's men women wish to please by looking good, men may be responsible (some? much?) for women's obsession with appearance. How far have women bought into the beauty myth? How much are they responsible for obsessing about beauty? How about money and profit? And at whose expense?

Why don't men *need* to be beautiful? To please parents—employers? To attract a mate? To be considered "normal"? Sontag says beauty is irrelevant for men—men judged by different standards—strength, competence, effectiveness. She doesn't mention power, money, status—leaves out intelligence and moral qualities—kindness, decency, generosity? How important?

Distinction between *desiring* to be beautiful (perhaps to be desired or admired) and *needing* to be. Nothing wrong with women wanting to be attractive, to look good. Problem is when desire becomes *obligation*—a waste of women's talents—minimizes them, keeps them subservient.

Parts and whole—are women concerned with *parts* of their bodies—certain parts? Their overall appearance? Their sense of self? Silicone breast implants? Face lifts? (But men have nose jobs, pec implants.) Men are concerned with *some parts* of their bodies more than others—like women? Or not?

What about the words for good-looking women—and men? Beautiful women, but handsome men. Foxy lady—gorgeous woman (guy?) attractive girl. And what of men? Handsome, good-looking. Pretty boy? Hunk—derogatory for men. A real "he-man."

Double-Column Notebook

Still another way to develop your thinking about what you read is to make entries in a double-column notebook. To create a double-column notebook, simply divide a page in half. One half is for summarizing and interpreting what you read. Use this side to record your understanding of the text. Use the other side to respond to what you read, to think about implications, and to relate it to knowledge gleaned elsewhere.

The advantage of a double-column notebook is that it encourages you to be an active reader, to think about your reading, and to make connections with your other reading and with your experience. You can use the double-column notebook to think further about your earlier reactions and thoughts recorded in your annotations and freewriting.

Here are, first, a generic look at how a double-column notebook page appears, and then an example based on the Sontag essay excerpt.

Double-Column Notebook Page

Summary	Comments
Summarize the text.	Respond to your summary.
Interpret the author's ideas.	Reflect on the author's ideas.
Explain the ideas succinctly.	Consider your agreement or disagreement.
Identify important details.	Raise questions about those details.
Relate details to central idea.	Relate main idea to reading & experience.

The following sample page details how a double-column notebook page might look based on Sontag's essay excerpt. But it's not an attempt to comment on every aspect of her essay.

Double-Column Notebook

for Sontag Essay Excerpt

Summary	Comments
Sontag argues that women's beauty is more dangerous than beneficial. Their beauty and their concern with it hurt women by distracting them from more important things, such as intellectual pursuits and political opportunities.	Sontag's agenda here seems genuine. She values women as intelligent people with a contribution to make to society. She seems genuinely angry by their being forced to be overly concerned with their appearance.
Sontag claims that women are seen as superficial and frivolous because they occupy much of their time with attempting to improve their appearance.	Sontag implies that women are damned if they do and damned if they don't. Women have to look their best in a world that expects nothing less of them. If women neglect

Summary

She criticizes a society that relegates women to a form of second-class citizenship in which beauty counts less than brains, and in which obsessing about appearance instead of devoting time and energy to power and status allow women to be dismissed as superficial and decorative.

She sets the standards and ideals for women's beauty over and against those for men, and she finds the standards for men's appearance more sensible, reasonable, and meaningful.

Comments

their looks they are criticized for it; if they labor to be beautiful, they are equally criticized. It's a no-win situation for them.

In blaming society for women's beauty dilemma, is she really blaming men? Isn't it men who continue to rule the world and set the standards and expectations? Or is she blaming the consumerism and commercialism that dominate contemporary culture?

Writing a Summary

A summary is a compressed version of a text in which you explain the author's meaning in your own words. You summarize a text when you need to give your readers the gist of what it says. A summary should present the author's text accurately and represent his or her views fairly. You build your summary on the observations, connections, and inferences you make while reading. Although there is no rule for how long or short a summary should be, a summary of a text is always shorter than the text itself.

Writing a summary requires careful reading, in part to ensure that you thoroughly understand what you are reading. Writing a summary helps you respond to what you read by requiring careful analysis and consideration of its details.

Writing a summary requires essentially two kinds of skills: identifying the idea of the text you are summarizing and recognizing the evidence that supports that idea. One strategy for writing a summary is to find the key points that support the main idea. You can do this by looking for clusters of sentences or groups of paragraphs that convey the writer's meaning. Because paragraphs work together, you cannot simply summarize each paragraph independently. You may need to summarize a cluster of paragraphs to convey the idea of a text effectively. It all depends on the length and complexity of the text you are summarizing and on how it is organized.

Here is an example of the process applied to the essay excerpt by Sontag.

Sample Notes toward Summary

General idea of passage: Women are seen as superficial and trivial, concerned with surface beauty rather than with deeper qualities of character. Women are viewed as beautiful objects, valued for how they look rather than for who they are and what they have achieved.

Key supporting points:

- Women's preoccupation with their beauty is a sign of their self-absorption.
- Women's concern for beauty is a form of enslavement to appearances.
- Men are less concerned with appearances, especially with perfecting their appearance.
- Women are objectified in connection with parts of their bodies.
- Women are deemed inconsequential and frivolous.

To create a smooth summary from these key-supporting points, it is necessary to expand and elaborate on them a bit. It is also necessary to put them in a logical order, and to create introductory and concluding sentences for the summary paragraph. Transitions also need to be provided.

Here is an example of such a summary. This one avoids direct quotation from Sontag's text, though quoting her essay is certainly permissible in a summary. Opinions and judgmental words and phrases are avoided, and the writer and text are identified in the opening sentence.

Sample Summary
Sontag Essay Excerpt

In her essay "A Woman's Beauty: Put-Down or Power Source?" Susan Sontag explains how women's need to appear beautiful trivializes them, making them sound superficial and identifying them as creatures preoccupied with how they look rather than with who they are and what they have achieved. Sontag suggests that women's preoccupation with physical beauty is a sign of their self-absorption and triviality. Through being taught to see themselves as mere body parts, women become both objectified and ridden with anxiety that their parts may not measure up. Unlike women, men are viewed as a whole rather than for their parts. Their looks are considered as part of an overall package, one that includes not only the appearance they present, but their knowledge, intelligence, and status. Unlike women, who lack power, men are perceived as more serious, more confident, and more powerful than the women who anxiously labor to be beautiful in order to please them.

Going Further

Once you have gotten far enough to be comfortable with the writer's idea so that you can summarize it accurately, you are ready to return to the text to look for additional evidence to develop and expand your summary into a full-fledged essay. Earlier a process for accomplishing this revisionary reading was described. Now we will add some notes which, coupled with the summary, can prepare for the writing of a more elaborate essay about Sontag's perspective on women's beauty. The notes can help you expand your summary.

There are four basic steps in this process: observing details of the text, connecting or relating them, making inferences based on those connections, and drawing a conclusion, or interpretation, about the text's meaning and significance. This four-stage process allows for the accumulation of the evidence needed to support a textual interpretation that could be formulated in an essay about it.

Observing Details

The kinds of observations you make about text depend on the kind of text you are reading. Here are some observations about Sontag's essay excerpt:

- Sontag focuses throughout on surface beauty—on appearance.
- She distinguishes between beauty in women and in men.
- She sees women's obsession with beauty as dangerous.
- She describes men as strong and competent.

- She italicizes certain key words.
- She places certain sentences in parentheses.
- She puts some words in quotation marks.
- She punctuates heavily with dashes.

Look back at the passage. Make your own observations about the ideas in Sontag's comments; select one sentence in each paragraph that crystallizes her thought. Make a few observations about Sontag's sentences: their type, length, and form. Notice how she begins and ends her paragraphs. Observe what evidence she provides to support her views.

Connecting Details

It is not enough, however, simply to observe details about a text. You must also connect them; relate them to one another. To make a connection is to see one thing in relation to another. You may notice that some details reinforce others, or that the writer repeats certain words or ideas. Perhaps she sets up a contrast, as Sontag does between men's and women's attitudes toward beauty.

While you are noticing aspects of a text, you can also begin making connections among its details. Your goal is to see how the connected details help you make sense of the text as a whole. One way to do this is to group information in lists or in outline form. This involves setting up categories or headings for related kinds of details. In the Sontag passage, for example, you could create heads for details about men and about women. Or you could group observations about style under one head and observations about ideas under another. Notice, for example, how the list of observations made earlier can be divided exactly in this manner, with the first four items concerning Sontag's ideas and the last four her style.

Making observations about a text and establishing connections among them form the basis of analysis. From that basis you begin to consider the significance of what you observe and proceed to develop an interpretation of the text overall. Breaking the interpretive process down in this manner enables you to understand what it involves and should prepare you to practice it on other occasions.

Making Inferences

An inference is a statement based on what has been observed. You infer a writer's idea or point of view, for instance, from the examples and evidence he or she provides. Inferences drive the interpretive process. They push readers beyond making observations and toward explaining their significance. Without inferences there can be no interpretation based on textual evidence.

There is nothing mysterious about the process of making inferences. We do it all the time in our everyday lives, from inferring what someone feels when they complain about something we have done (or failed to do) to inferring the significance of a situation based upon visual observation, as when we see someone with a large ring of keys opening rooms in an academic building early in the morning.

The same is true of making inferences about a text. The inferences we make in reading represent our way of "reading between the lines" by discovering what is implied rather than explicitly stated. The freewriting sample about the Sontag essay excerpt contains inferences. Here are a few additional inferences a reader could draw from the Sontag passage:

- Sontag thinks that the double standard by which women are judged for their beauty and men for other qualities is wrong (paragraph 1).
- She implies that few women can meet the high standards for beauty that society imposes (paragraph 2).
- She seems to approve of the way masculine beauty is considered as a sum of each feature of a man's overall appearance (paragraph 3).
- She implies that women would be better off regarded as whole beings as well.

Sontag does not say any of these things outright. But readers can infer them based on what she does say explicitly. Remember that an inference can be right or wrong, and thus different readers might debate the reliability of these or other inferences we might make about Sontag's essay excerpt. The important thing is not to be afraid to make inferences because of uncertainty about their accuracy. Critical reading and writing involve thinking, and thinking involves making inferences. It is this kind of inferential thinking, moreover, that is essential to good reading and good writing.

Arriving at an Interpretation

The step from making inferences to arriving at an interpretation is not an overly large one. An interpretation is a way of explaining the meaning of a text; it represents your way of understanding the text expressed as an idea. In formulating an interpretation of the Sontag essay, you might write something like the following:

> *Sontag examines the meaning of beauty in the lives of women, seeing women's beauty, to echo her title, as more of a "put-down" than a source of power. Although she recognizes that beautiful women can use their attractive appearance to their advantage, she argues that the very beauty that gives beautiful women a social advantage, simultaneously detracts from the overall estimation and regard which others have of them.*

This interpretation can be debated, and it can be, indeed needs to be, further elaborated and explained. But the interpretation is based on the inferences made while reading the text, and upon the observations and connections among them that provided the foundation for those inferences. In arriving at this or any interpretation, it is necessary to look back at the text's details to reconsider your initial observations, as well as to review the connections and inferences based upon them. Your inferences must be defensible, that is supportable, either by textual evidence or by logical reasoning.

In looking back at the Sontag passage, you might notice something you overlooked earlier. You might notice, for example, that Sontag mentions society's responsibility for foisting certain ideals of beauty upon women. In thinking about the implications of that observation, you might make other inferences, which may lead you to an interpretive emphasis that differs from your previous understanding of her text. You might decide that the central issue for Sontag is society's role and responsibility in forcing such an ideal of beauty upon women. In that case, you would probably select your evidence from the essay differently to support this new focus of your interpretation.

In writing a full-fledged interpretive essay based on Sontag's piece, or in writing your own essay on the subject of beauty—whether or not you restrict it to "women's beauty"—you would go through the same process described here. The only difference is that the essay you develop would be long enough to provide a full explanation of your ideas and sufficient evidence to make your ideas worthy of a reader's consideration, and that it be long and detailed enough either to fulfill the demands of an assignment to which it might be a response, or to satisfy you as its writer that you have said what you wanted to with enough evidence to make it convincing to others.

Gloria Anzaldúa *(1942–2004) grew up in the Rio Grande Valley of south Texas, a rural area near the Mexican border that was home to many Chicanos. She graduated from Pan American University in Austin, taught high school, and later found her way to San Francisco, where she became an outspoken member of the feminist movement. A lesbian and a woman of mixed cultural heritage, she has described herself as the "new mestiza," straddling many personal and cultural influences. In addition to several children's stories, Anzaldúa has published two highly influential books in the field of cultural studies:* Borderlands/La Frontera: The New Mestiza *(1987), which mixes prose and poetry, narrative and polemic, and* Making Face, Making Soul/Haciendo Caras: Creative and Critical Perspectives by Women of Color, *co-edited with Cherie Moraga.*

How to Tame a Wild Tongue

In "How to Tame a Wild Tongue," from her book *Borderlands/La Frontera,* Gloria Anzaldúa addresses intertwined issues of language, culture, identity, and power. Her essay is radical in idea, organization, and style. Anzaldúa's idea includes suggestions about the need for a broader view of what constitutes both "English" and "Spanish." She argues for the usefulness of a Chicano Spanish, which deviates in many ways from the Spanish brought from Europe to Mexico and to Central and South America. She also argues for the value of a border-crossing Tex-Mex blend of Spanish and English in a kind of "Spanglish."

The structure of Anzaldúa's essay follows less the logical and systematic development of a single idea than a network of related ideas, each developed within a chunked unit of her essay, and each with its own topical heading. Anzaldúa's style is noteworthy for the border-crossing fusion of the forms of language she describes, as she argues that language is bound up inextricably with ethnic personal identity.

"We're going to have to control your tongue," the dentist says, pulling out all the metal from my mouth. Silver bits plop and tinkle into the basin. My mouth is a motherlode.

The dentist is cleaning out my roots. I get a whiff of the stench when I gasp. "I can't cap that tooth yet, you're still draining," he says.

"We're going to have to do something about your tongue," I hear the anger rising in his voice. My tongue keeps pushing out the wads of cotton, pushing back the drills, the long thin needles. "I've never seen anything as strong or as stubborn," he says. And I think, how do you tame a wild tongue, train it to be quiet, how do you bridle and saddle it? How do you make it lie down?

Who is to say that robbing a people of its language is less violent than war?

—Ray Gwyn Smith[1]

[1]Ray Gwyn Smith, *Moorland Is Cold Country,* unpublished book.

I remember being caught speaking Spanish at recess—that was good for three licks on the knuckles with a sharp ruler. I remember being sent to the corner of the classroom for "talking back" to the Anglo teacher when all I was trying to do was tell her how to pronounce my name. "If you want to be American, speak 'American.' If you don't like it, go back to Mexico where you belong."

"I want you to speak English. *Pa'hallar buen trabajo tienes que saber hablar el inglés bien. Qué vale toda tu educación si todavía hablas inglés con un 'accent',*" my mother would say, mortified that I spoke English like a Mexican. At Pan American University, I and all Chicano students were required to take two speech classes. Their purpose: to get rid of our accents.

Attacks on one's form of expression with the intent to censor are a violation of the First Amendment. *El Anglo con cara de inocente nos arrancó la lengua.* Wild tongues can't be tamed, they can only be cut out.

Overcoming the Tradition of Silence

> Ahogadas, escupimos el oscuro.
> Peleando con nuestra propia sombra
> el silencio nos sepulta.

En boca cerrada no entran moscas. "Flies don't enter a closed mouth" is a saying I kept hearing when I was a child. *Ser habladora* was to be a gossip and a liar, to talk too much. *Muchachitas bien criadas,* well-bred girls don't answer back. *Es una falta de respeto* to talk back to one's mother or father. I remember one of the sins I'd recite to the priest in the confession box the few times I went to confession: talking back to my mother, *hablar pa' 'tras, repelar. Hocicona, repelona, chismosa,* having a big mouth, questioning, carrying tales are all signs of being *mal criada.* In my culture they are all words that are derogatory if applied to women—I've never heard them applied to men.

The first time I heard two women, a Puerto Rican and a Cuban, say the word "*nosotras,*" I was shocked. I had not known the word existed. Chicanas use *nosotros* whether we're male or female. We are robbed of our female being by the masculine plural. Language is a male discourse.

> And our tongues have become
> dry   the wilderness has

dried out our tongues   and
we have forgotten speech.

—IRENA KLEPFISZ[2]

Even our own people, other Spanish speakers *nos quieren poner canda-
dos en la boca.* They would hold us back with their bag of *reglas de academia.*

Oyé como ladra:
el lenguaje de la frontera

Quien tiene boca se equivoca.

—MEXICAN SAYING

"*Pocho,* cultural traitor, you're speaking the oppressor's language by
speaking English, you're ruining the Spanish language," I have been
accused by various Latinos and Latinas. Chicano Spanish is considered
by the purist and by most Latinos deficient, a mutilation of Spanish.

But Chicano Spanish is a border tongue which developed naturally.
Change, *evolución, enriquecimiento de palabras nuevas por invención o
adopción* have created variants of Chicano Spanish, *un nuevo lenguaje.
Un lenguaje que corresponde a un modo de vivir.* Chicano Spanish is not
incorrect, it is a living language.

For a people who are neither Spanish nor live in a country in which
Spanish is the first language; for a people who live in a country in which
English is the reigning tongue but who are not Anglo; for a people who
cannot entirely identify with either standard (formal, Castilian) Spanish
nor standard English, what recourse is left to them but to create their
own language? A language which they can connect their identity to, one
capable of communicating the realities and values true to themselves—
a language with terms that are neither *español ni inglés,* but both. We
speak a patois, a forked tongue, a variation of two languages.

Chicano Spanish sprang out of the Chicanos' need to identify
ourselves as a distinct people. We needed a language with which we
could communicate with ourselves, a secret language. For some of us,
language is a homeland closer than the Southwest—for many Chicanos
today live in the Midwest and the East. And because we are a complex,
heterogeneous people, we speak many languages. Some of the
languages we speak are

1. Standard English
2. Working class and slang English

GLORIA ANZALDÚA

32

[2]Irena Klepfisz, "*Di rayze aheym*/The Journey Home," in *The Tribe of Dina: A Jewish Women's Anthology,*
Melanie Kaye/Kantrowitz and Irena Klepfisz, eds. (Montpelier, VT: Sinister Wisdom Books, 1986), 49.

3. Standard Spanish
4. Standard Mexican Spanish
5. North Mexican Spanish dialect
6. Chicano Spanish (Texas, New Mexico, Arizona, and California have regional variations)
7. Tex-Mex
8. *Pachuco* (called *caló*)

My "home" tongues are the languages I speak with my sister and brothers, with my friends. They are the last five listed, with 6 and 7 being closest to my heart. From school, the media, and job situations, I've picked up standard and working class English. From Mamagrande Locha and from reading Spanish and Mexican literature, I've picked up Standard Spanish and Standard Mexican Spanish. From *los recién llegados*, Mexican immigrants, and *braceros*, I learned the North Mexican dialect. With Mexicans I'll try to speak either Standard Mexican Spanish or the North Mexican dialect. From my parents and Chicanos living in the Valley, I picked up Chicano Texas Spanish, and I speak it with my mom, younger brother (who married a Mexican and who rarely mixes Spanish with English), aunts, and older relatives.

With Chicanas from *Nuevo México* or *Arizona* I will speak Chicano Spanish a little, but often they don't understand what I'm saying. With most California Chicanas I speak entirely in English (unless I forget). When I first moved to San Francisco, I'd rattle off something in Spanish, unintentionally embarrassing them. Often it is only with another Chicana *tejano* that I can talk freely.

Words distorted by English are known as anglicisms or *pochismos*. The *pocho* is an anglicized Mexican or American of Mexican origin who speaks Spanish with an accent characteristic of North Americans and who distorts and reconstructs the language according to the influence of English.[3] Tex-Mex, or Spanglish, comes most naturally to me. I may switch back and forth from English to Spanish in the same sentence or in the same word. With my sister and my brother Nune and with Chicano *tejano* contemporaries I speak in Tex-Mex.

From kids and people my own age I picked up *Pachuco. Pachuco* (the language of the zoot suiters) is a language of rebellion, both against Standard Spanish and Standard English. It is a secret language. Adults of the culture and outsiders cannot understand it. It is made up of

[3]R. C. Ortega, *Dialectología Del Barrio*, trans. Hortencia S. Alwan (Los Angeles, CA: R. C. Ortega Publisher & Bookseller, 1977), 132.

slang words from both English and Spanish. *Ruca* means girl or woman, *vato* means guy or dude, *chale* means no, *simón* means yes, *churro* is sure, talk is *periquiar*, *pigionear* means petting, *que gacho* means how nerdy, *ponte águila* means watch out, death is called *la pelona*. Through lack of practice and not having others who can speak it, I've lost most of the *Pachuco* tongue.

Chicano Spanish

Chicanos, after 250 years of Spanish/Anglo colonization, have developed significant differences in the Spanish we speak. We collapse two adjacent vowels into a single syllable and sometimes shift the stress in certain words such as *maíz/maiz, cohete/cuete*. We leave out certain consonants when they appear between vowels: *lado/lao, mojado/mojao*. Chicanos from South Texas pronounce *f* as *j* as in *jue (fue)*. Chicanos use "archaisms," words that are no longer in the Spanish language, words that have been evolved out. We say *semos, truje, haiga, ansina*, and *naiden*. We retain the "archaic" *j*, as in *jalar*, that derives from an earlier *h* (the French *halar* or the Germanic *halon*, which was lost to standard Spanish in the sixteenth century), but which is still found in several regional dialects such as the one spoken in South Texas. (Due to geography, Chicanos from the Valley of South Texas were cut off linguistically from other Spanish speakers. We tend to use words that the Spaniards brought over from Medieval Spain. The majority of the Spanish colonizers in Mexico and the Southwest came from Extremadura—Hernán Cortés was one of them—and Andalucía. Andalucians pronounce *ll* like a *y*, and their *d*'s tend to be absorbed by adjacent vowels: *tirado* becomes *tirao*. They brought *el lenguaje popular, dialectos y regionalismos*.[4])

Chicanos and other Spanish speakers also shift *ll* to *y* and *z* to *s*.[5] We leave out initial syllables, saying *tar* for *estar*, *toy* for *estoy*, *hora* for *ahora* (*cubanos* and *puertorriqueños* also leave out initial letters of some words). We also leave out the final syllable such as *pa* for *para*. The intervocalic *y*, the *ll* as in *tortilla, ella, botella*, gets replaced by *tortia* or *tortiya, ea, botea*. We add an additional syllable at the beginning of certain words: *atocar* for *tocar*, *agastar* for *gastar*. Sometimes we'll say

[4]Eduardo Hernandéz-Chávez, Andrew D. Cohen, and Anthony F. Beltramo, El Lenguaje de los Chicanos: *Regional and Social Characteristics of Language Used By Mexican Americans* (Arlington, VA: Center for Applied Linguistics, 1975), 39.
[5]Hernandéz-Chávez, xvii.

lavaste las vacijas, other times *lavates* (substituting the *ates* verb endings for the *aste*).

We used anglicisms, words borrowed from English: *bola* from ball, *carpeta* from carpet, *máchina de lavar* (instead of *lavadora*) from washing machine. Tex-Mex argot, created by adding a Spanish sound at the beginning or end of an English word, such as *cookiar* for cook, *watchar* for watch, *parkiar* for park, and *rapiar* for rape, is the result of the pressures on Spanish speakers to adapt to English.

We don't use the word *vosotros/as* or its accompanying verb form. We don't say *claro* (to mean *yes*), *imaginate*, or *me emociona*, unless we picked up Spanish from Latinas, out of a book, or in a classroom. Other Spanish-speaking groups are going through the same, or similar, development in their Spanish.

Linguistic Terrorism

> *Deslenguadas. Somos los del español deficiente. We are your linguistic nightmare, your linguistic aberration, your linguistic mestisaje, the subject of your burla. Because we speak with tongues of fire we are culturally crucified. Racially, culturally, and linguistically somos huérfanos—we speak an orphan tongue.*

Chicanas who grew up speaking Chicano Spanish have internalized the belief that we speak poor Spanish. It is illegitimate, a bastard language. And because we internalize how our language has been used against us by the dominant culture, we use our language differences against each other.

Chicana feminists often skirt around each other with suspicion and hesitation. For the longest time I couldn't figure it out. Then it dawned on me. To be close to another Chicana is like looking into the mirror. We are afraid of what we'll see there. *Pena*. Shame. Low estimation of self. In childhood we are told that our language is wrong. Repeated attacks on our native tongue diminish our sense of self. The attacks continue throughout our lives.

Chicanas feel uncomfortable talking in Spanish to Latinas, afraid of their censure. Their language was not outlawed in their countries. They had a whole lifetime of being immersed in their native tongue; generations, centuries in which Spanish was a first language, taught in school, heard on radio and TV, and read in the newspaper.

If a person, Chicana or Latina, has a low estimation of my native tongue, she also has a low estimation of me. Often with *mexicanas y latinas* we'll speak English as a neutral language. Even among Chicanas we tend to speak English at parties or conferences. Yet, at the same time, we're afraid the other will think we're *agringadas* because we don't speak Chicano Spanish. We oppress each other trying to out-Chicano each other, vying to be the "real" Chicanas, to speak like Chicanos. There is no one Chicano language just as there is no one Chicano experience. A monolingual Chicana whose first language is English or Spanish is just as much a Chicana as one who speaks several variants of Spanish. A Chicana from Michigan or Chicago or Detroit is just as much a Chicana as one from the Southwest. Chicano Spanish is as diverse linguistically as it is regionally.

By the end of this century, Spanish speakers will comprise the biggest minority group in the United States, a country where students in high schools and colleges are encouraged to take French classes because French is considered more "cultured." But for a language to remain alive it must be used.[6] By the end of this century English, and not Spanish, will be the mother tongue of most Chicanos and Latinos.

So, if you want to really hurt me, talk badly about my language. Ethnic identity is twin skin to linguistic identity—I am my language. Until I can take pride in my language, I cannot take pride in myself. Until I can accept as legitimate Chicano Texas Spanish, Tex-Mex, and all the other languages I speak, I cannot accept the legitimacy of myself. Until I am free to write bilingually and to switch codes without having always to translate, while I still have to speak English or Spanish when I would rather speak Spanglish, and as long as I have to accommodate the English speakers rather than having them accommodate me, my tongue will be illegitimate.

I will no longer be made to feel ashamed of existing. I will have my voice: Indian, Spanish, white. I will have my serpent's tongue—my woman's voice, my sexual voice, my poet's voice. I will overcome the tradition of silence.

> My fingers
> move sly against your palm
> Like women everywhere, we speak in code.
>
> —MELANIE KAYE/KANTROWITZ[7]

"Vistas," corridos, y comida:

[6]Irena Klepfisz, "Secular Jewish Identity: Yidishkayt in America," in *The Tribe of Dina*, Kaye/Kantrowitz and Klepfisz, eds., 43.
[7]Melanie Kaye/Kantrowitz, "Sign," in *We Speak In Code: Poems and Other Writings* (Pittsburgh, PA: Motheroot Publications, Inc., 1980), 85.

My Native Tongue

In the 1960s, I read my first Chicano novel. It was *City of Night* by John Rechy, a gay Texan, son of a Scottish father and a Mexican mother. For days I walked around in stunned amazement that a Chicano could write and could get published. When I read *I Am Joaquín*[8] I was surprised to see a bilingual book by a Chicano in print. When I saw poetry written in Tex-Mex for the first time, a feeling of pure joy flashed through me. I felt like we really existed as a people. In 1971, when I started teaching High School English to Chicano students, I tried to supplement the required texts with works by Chicanos, only to be reprimanded and forbidden to do so by the principal. He claimed that I was supposed to teach "American" and English literature. At the risk of being fired, I swore my students to secrecy and slipped in Chicano short stories, poems, a play. In graduate school, while working toward a Ph.D., I had to "argue" with one adviser after the other, semester after semester, before I was allowed to make Chicano literature an area of focus.

Even before I read books by Chicanos or Mexicans, it was the Mexican movies I saw at the drive-in—the Thursday night special of $1.00 a carload—that gave me a sense of belonging. "*Vámonos a las vistas*," my mother would call out and we'd all—grandmother, brothers, sister, and cousins—squeeze into the car. We'd wolf down cheese and bologna white bread sandwiches while watching Pedro Infante in melodramatic tearjerkers like *Nosotros los pobres*, the first "real" Mexican movie (that was not an imitation of European movies). I remember seeing *Cuando los hijos se van* and surmising that all Mexican movies played up the love a mother has for her children and what ungrateful sons and daughters suffer when they are not devoted to their mothers. I remember the singing-type "westerns" of Jorge Negrete and Miquel Aceves Mejía. When watching Mexican movies, I felt a sense of homecoming as well as alienation. People who were to amount to something didn't go to Mexican movies, or *bailes*, or tune their radios to *bolero, rancherita*, and *corrido* music.

The whole time I was growing up, there was *norteño* music sometimes called North Mexican border music, or Tex-Mex music, or Chicano music, or *cantina* (bar) music. I grew up listening to *conjuntos*, three- or four-piece bands made up of folk musicians playing guitar, *bajo sexto*, drums, and button accordion, which Chicanos had borrowed from the German immigrants who had come to Central Texas and

---

[8]Rodolfo Gonzales, *I Am Joaquín/Yo Soy Joaquín* (New York, NY: Bantam Books, 1972). It was first published in 1967.

Mexico to farm and build breweries. In the Rio Grande Valley, Steve Jordan and Little Joe Hernández were popular, and Flaco Jiménez was the accordion king. The rhythms of Tex-Mex music are those of the polka, also adapted from the Germans, who in turn had borrowed the polka from the Czechs and Bohemians.

I remember the hot, sultry evenings when *corridos*—songs of love and death on the Texas-Mexican borderlands—reverberated out of cheap amplifiers from the local *cantinas* and wafted in through my bedroom window.

Corridos first became widely used along the South Texas/Mexican border during the early conflict between Chicanos and Anglos. The *corridos* are usually about Mexican heroes who do valiant deeds against the Anglo oppressors. Pancho Villa's song, "*La cucaracha,*" is the most famous one. *Corridos* of John F. Kennedy and his death are still very popular in the Valley. Older Chicanos remember Lydia Mendoza, one of the great border *corrido* singers who was called *la Gloria de Tejas.* Her "*El tango negro,*" sung during the Great Depression, made her a singer of the people. The ever-present *corridos* narrated one hundred years of border history, bringing news of events as well as entertaining. These folk musicians and folk songs are our chief cultural mythmakers, and they made our hard lives seem bearable.

I grew up feeling ambivalent about our music. Country-western and rock-and-roll had more status. In the fifties and sixties, for the slightly educated and *agringado* Chicanos, there existed a sense of shame at being caught listening to our music. Yet I couldn't stop my feet from thumping to the music, could not stop humming the words, nor hide from myself the exhilaration I felt when I heard it.

There are more subtle ways that we internalize identification, especially in the forms of images and emotions. For me food and certain smells are tied to my identity, to my homeland. Woodsmoke curling up to an immense blue sky; woodsmoke perfuming my grandmother's clothes, her skin. The stench of cow manure and the yellow patches on the ground; the crack of a .22 rifle and the reek of cordite. Homemade white cheese sizzling in a pan, melting inside a folded *tortilla.* My sister Hilda's hot, spicy *menudo, chile colorado* making it deep red, pieces of *panza* and hominy floating on top. My brother Carito barbequing *fajitas* in the backyard. Even now and 3,000 miles away, I can see my mother spicing the ground beef, pork, and venison with *chile.* My mouth salivates at the thought of the hot steaming *tamales* I would be eating if I were home.

Si le preguntas a mi mamá, "¿Qué eres?"

> Identity is the essential core of who
> we are as individuals, the conscious
> experience of the self inside.
> —GERSHEN KAUFMAN[9]

Nosotros los Chicanos straddle the borderlands. On one side of us, we are constantly exposed to the Spanish of the Mexicans, on the other side we hear the Anglos' incessant clamoring so that we forget our language. Among ourselves we don't say *nosotros los americanos, o nosotros los españoles, o nosotros los hispanos.* We say *nosotros los mexicanos* (by *mexicanos* we do not mean citizens of Mexico; we do not mean a national identity, but a racial one). We distinguish between *mexicanos del otro lado* and *mexicanos de este lado.* Deep in our hearts we believe that being Mexican has nothing to do with which country one lives in. Being Mexican is a state of soul—not one of mind, not one of citizenship. Neither eagle nor serpent, but both. And like the ocean, neither animal respects borders.

> *Dime con quien and as y te diré quien eres.*
> (Tell me who your friends are and I'll tell you who you are.)
> —MEXICAN SAYING

Si le preguntas a mi mamá, "¿Qué eres?" te dirá, *"Soy mexicana."* My brothers and sister say the same. I sometimes will answer *"soy mexicana"* and at others will say *"soy Chicana" o "soy tejana."* But I identified as *"Raza"* before I ever identified as *"mexicana"* or *"Chicana."*

As a culture, we call ourselves Spanish when referring to ourselves as a linguistic group and when copping out. It is then that we forget our predominant Indian genes. We are 70–80 percent Indian.[10] We call ourselves Hispanic[11] or Spanish-American or Latin American or Latin when linking ourselves to other Spanish-speaking peoples of the Western hemisphere and when copping out. We call ourselves Mexican-American[12] to signify we are neither Mexican nor American, but more the noun "American" than the adjective "Mexican" (and when copping out).

---

[9]Kaufman, 68.
[10]Chávez, 88–90.
[11]"Hispanic" is derived from *Hispanis* (*España*, a name given to the Iberian Peninsula in ancient times when it was part of the Roman Empire) and is a term designated by the U.S. government to make it easier to handle us on paper.
[12]The Treaty of Guadalupe Hidalgo created the Mexican-American in 1848.

Chicanos and other people of color suffer economically for not acculturating. This voluntary (yet forced) alienation makes for psychological conflict, a kind of dual identity—we don't identify with the Anglo-American cultural values and we don't totally identify with the Mexican cultural values. We are a synergy of two cultures with various degrees of Mexicanness or Angloness. I have so internalized the borderland conflict that sometimes I feel like one cancels out the other and we are zero, nothing, no one. *A veces no soy nada ni nadie. Pero hasta cuando no lo soy, lo soy.*

When not copping out, when we know we are more than nothing, we call ourselves Mexican, referring to race and ancestry; *mestizo* when affirming both our Indian and Spanish (but we hardly ever own our Black) ancestry; Chicano when referring to a politically aware people born and/or raised in the United States; *Raza* when referring to Chicanos; *tejanos* when we are Chicanos from Texas.

Chicanos did not know we were a people until 1965 when Cesar Chavez and the farmworkers united and *I Am Joaquín* was published and *la Raza Unida* party was formed in Texas. With that recognition, we became a distinct people. Something momentous happened to the Chicano soul—we became aware of our reality and acquired a name and a language (Chicano Spanish) that reflected that reality. Now that we had a name, some of the fragmented pieces began to fall together— who we were, what we were, how we had evolved. We began to get glimpses of what we might eventually become.

Yet the struggle of identities continues, the struggle of borders is our reality still. One day the inner struggle will cease and a true integration take place. In the meantime, *tenémos que hacer la lucha. ¿Quién está protegiendo los ranchos de mi gente? ¿Quién está tratando de cerrar la fisura entre la india y el blanco en nuestra sangre? El Chicano, si, el Chicano que anda como un landrón en su propia casa.*

Los Chicanos, how patient we seem, how very patient. There is the quiet of the Indian about us.[13] We know how to survive. When other races have given up their tongue we've kept ours. We know what it is to live under the hammer blow of the dominant *norteamericano* culture. But more than we count the blows, we count the days the weeks the years the centuries the aeons until the white laws and commerce and

[13]Anglos, in order to alleviate their guilt for dispossessing the Chicano, stressed the Spanish part of us and perpetrated the myth of the Spanish Southwest. We have accepted the fiction that we are Hispanic, that is Spanish, in order to accommodate ourselves to the dominant culture and its abhorrence of Indians. Chávez, 88–91.

customs will rot in the deserts they've created, lie bleached. *Humildes* yet proud, *quietos* yet wild, *nosotros los mexicanos-Chicanos* will walk by the crumbling ashes as we go about our business. Stubborn, persevering, impenetrable as stone, yet possessing a malleability that renders us unbreakable, we, the *mestizas* and *mestizos,* will remain.

POSSIBILITIES FOR WRITING

1. Anzaldúa focuses here not only on language but on other aspects of culture as well, including music and movies. How do these various examples contribute to her overall argument?
2. After the introductory paragraphs, the essay is divided into four separately headed sections. What points does Anzaldúa make in each section? What links can you find among the sections? For you, does she succeed in making a coherent argument?
3. Think about your own use of language—at home, at school, at work, among friends, with strangers, in formal and informal situations. When do you feel most comfortable and when least comfortable? How do you account for your feelings? Are they in any way related to the point Anzaldúa is making?

KWAME ANTHONY APPIAH

Facts on the Ground

In "Facts on the Ground," Kwame Anthony Appiah describes the belief system of his Ghanian family on his father's side. He takes pains to explain how their beliefs in spirits and witchcraft, along with behaviors associated with them, make sense to his family—how they cohere in a reasonable way. He explains how his family's theory guides their interpretation of facts and details, and how this is the way belief systems in general always operate.

The essay is divided into three parts: an introductory section, "Living with Spirits"; a middle part, "Arguing with Akosua"; and a concluding section, "Duhem's Discovery." In the first part, Appiah lays out the belief system of his ancestors, explaining how they see things. In the second, he explains why belief systems are so difficult to change and how physical events, such as diseases and injuries, can be explained coherently in different ways by different systems of belief. In the last section, Appiah invokes the French physicist Pierre Duhem to show how any theory is not determined by the available evidence. Appiah argues, further, that "there will always be more than one possible, reasonable account of the facts."

Living with Spirits

Late one evening, at home in Ghana many years ago, I was watching television with my father. As the broadcast day came to a close, the Ghana Broadcasting Corporation played the national anthem. My father loved hymns, and so he sang along. "God bless our homeland, Ghana . . ." As the singing ended and the screen faded to the test card, he remarked that he was glad that the government had modified the words of the independence national anthem, which I had learned in primary school. That one began, "Lift high the flag of Ghana." I was a newly minted philosophy graduate at the time, who had recently read

John Rawls's modern liberal classic, *A Theory of Justice*, and my response was to say that the old anthem had the advantage that you could sing along with it happily without believing in God. My father laughed. "Nobody in Ghana is silly enough not to believe in God," he said.

That's not how I would have put it; but it's true that Ghana's atheists could hold their meetings in a phone booth. Almost everybody in Ghana believes not just in a powerful divine creator but in a whole range of other spirits. One reflection of this belief is that at funerals, naming ceremonies, marriages, confirmations, birthday parties—indeed, at almost any social gathering—people of all religions will pour libations to their ancestors. When they open a bottle of whisky or gin or schnapps, they will pour some on the ground and ask various dead ancestors, by name, to accept the offering and to keep watch over the interests of the *abusua*, the matriclan. This is not just a symbolic gesture. While they don't think the ancestors literally need liquor, they do think they, and other largely invisible spirits, can hear and respond by helping their living relatives in everyday life. My father—a member of one of the London Inns of Court; an elder in the Methodist church of Ghana; a man whose favorite bedside reading, apart from the Bible, was Cicero—certainly believed this. And he wasn't embarrassed by the fact. His autobiography is full of episodes in which he sought and received the assistance of spirits. When he opened a bottle of whisky at home, after pouring off a little onto the floor of the sitting room, he would speak some words to Akroma-Ampim, an eighteenth-century Asante general who laid the foundations of the family fortune, and Yao Antony, my great-great-uncle (both of whose names, as it happens, I bear), as well as to my great-great-aunt, Yao Antony's sister.

If this were all symbolic, we could suppose that these acts expressed family values or something of the sort. The trouble is the fundamental belief wasn't remotely symbolic. If you don't think your late great-uncle could hear you and help you in your doings, you disagree with my father about the facts.

Here's another thing about which you are likely to disagree with my Ghanaian kin. Most of them believe in witchcraft. They think that there are certain evil people—women and men—who have the power to harm others they dislike without using ordinary everyday means. When my father died, one of my sisters was convinced that an aunt of ours might be practicing witchcraft against us. She wouldn't eat any of the food that our aunt sent us during the period of mourning, and she wouldn't let the rest of the family eat it either. But she thought it was fine for other people in the household to eat it. It wasn't poisoned. Witchcraft medicines know the difference between the people they're aimed at and the ones they're not: the food would harm only us. Since my aunt was supposed to be a powerful witch, this wasn't the only danger we faced. So it was fortunate that there are also practitioners of good witchcraft—many of them Muslim *malaams*, actually—who could counteract bad witchcraft. My sister made sure we bought a white ram to be sacrificed to protect us.

Asante beliefs about spirits and beliefs about witchcraft are extensive, complex, and interconnected. And, as you'd expect, not everybody believes exactly the same things about them. Some evangelical Christians identify the traditional spirits—whose shrines and priests you will find scattered through the country—with devils or with what the New Testament, in the King James translation, calls "principalities and powers." Not so my father, who took his appeals to spirits to be consistent with his Methodism. You could say that most people in Asante believe in a sort of theory, in which the world contains many spirits and invisible forces that work, like witchcraft, to affect human life. And, since some of the theory is about invisible personal beings—to whom you can pray for help—you might also say that it was part of Asante religion.

Of course, the place where I grew up is, in this way, like most places in the world. Even where the great world religions—Christianity, Islam, Hinduism, Buddhism—have come in, they overlie a set of traditions that include all kinds of invisible spirits who can be invoked both to do good and to do harm.

Now, the Positivist is likely to contrast these beliefs with modern scientific views. "These traditional religions are not just false, they are irrational: anyone who exposed them to the rigorous examination that scientists practice would be forced to give them up." This is, in fact, very far from evident. In the last chapter, I argued that values aren't as flighty as the Positivist supposes. Here I want to suggest that facts aren't quite so solid. Not because I'm a skeptic about truth. (I once wrote a book called *For Truth in Semantics*.) But because finding the truth isn't just a matter of having open eyes and a level head.

Arguing with Akosua

Take the simple-seeming question of whether you can be harmed by witchcraft. How would you go about persuading one of my Asante kinfolk that it could not be? People do get sick for unaccountable reasons all the time, do they not? Many of them have reason to think that there are people who dislike them. So that once you have the idea of witch-craft, there will be plenty of occasions when the general theory will seem to be confirmed. To rule out the theory of witchcraft, you would first have to understand it better, and then you would have to persuade my relatives both that the theory gets it wrong over and over again and that you have a better story. That could take a very long time. In a real cross-cultural encounter of this sort, you would be invited to explain all sorts of facts you were unaware of, whose explanations you did not know. Akosua, your Asante interlocutor, has an aunt who fell ill last year, and everyone knows that it was caused by witchcraft by her daughter-in-law. The family went to a *malaam* and slaughtered a sheep. She got better. Akosua wants to know why her aunt got better, if the sheep had nothing to do with it; why she got ill, if there's no witch-craft. And, of course, while you think that these questions have an-swers, you don't know for sure what they are.

On the other hand, you have to persuade Akosua of the existence of tiny, invisible atoms, strung together to make viruses, particles so small that you cannot see them with the most powerful magnifying lens, yet so potent that they can kill a healthy adult. Consider how long it took to persuade European scientists that this was so, how complex the chain of inferences that led first to the germ theory of disease and then to the identification of viruses. Why should anyone believe this story, just because you said so? And could you—and I mean you, not some biology professor—provide her with convincing evidence? Akosua might well be willing to do one of the experiments you propose. You might, for example, try to show that there's no correlation between whether someone who is thought to be a witch hates you and whether you fall sick. But what if there *were* such a correlation? If Akosua's view made the right prediction—that people who are hated by witches get sicker more often than people who aren't—you wouldn't come to be-lieve in witchcraft. You'd have an alternative explanation. (People who think they are hated by powerful witches might well be more likely to fall ill, mightn't they? Something to do with stress, perhaps?) So it shouldn't surprise you that when your predictions are borne out, she has her explanations, too.

There's an oft-told anecdote about a medical missionary in a re-mote place, who watches, in horror, as people give untreated well water to their babies. The children regularly get diarrhea, and many of them die. The missionary explains that, even though the water looks clear, there are tiny, invisible creatures in it that make the children sick. Fortunately, she says, if they boil the water, it will kill these bacteria. A month later she's back, and they're still giving the babies the dirty water. After all, if a stranger came into your community and told you that your children got influenza because of witchcraft, would you respond by going out and slaughtering a sheep? Then the missionary has another idea. Look, she says, let me show you something. She takes some water and boils it. See, she says, there are spirits in the water, and when you put it on the fire they flee: those bubbles you see are the spirits escaping, the spirits that are making your children sick. Now boiling water makes sense. Now the babies stop dying. In belief, as in everything else, each of us must start from where we are.

When people get sick for unaccountable reasons in Manhattan, there is much talk of viruses and bacteria. Since doctors do not claim to be able to do much about most viruses, they do not put much effort into identifying them. Nor will the course of a viral infection be much changed by a visit to the doctor. In short, most appeals in everyday life to viruses are like most everyday appeals to witchcraft. They are supported only by a general conviction that sickness can be explained, and the conviction that viruses can make you sick.

If you ask most people in Manhattan why they believe in viruses, they will say two kinds of things: First, they will appeal to authority. "Science has shown," they will say, though if you ask them how science showed it, you will pretty quickly reach an impasse (even with scientists, by the way, unless they happen to be virologists unusually curious about the history of medicine). Second, they will point to phenomena—the spread of HIV or the common cold, the death of their great-aunt last winter, a picture of a virus they once saw in a magazine—where the viral theory explains what happened.

Similarly, in Kumasi, people who are asked why they believe in witchcraft will appeal to authority, too. "Our ancestors taught us about it." And they will then go on to tell you of cases of witch-craft they have seen or heard of, filling in for you all the things that it explains. Sir Edward Evans-Pritchard, one of the greatest anthropologists of the twentieth century, wrote a wonderful book called *Witchcraft, Oracles and Magic among the Azande*, about a people of that name who live in the Sudan. Having explained their ideas about witchcraft in great detail, he observes at one point that sometimes, in the evenings, when he saw a flash of flame in the bush around the Azande settlement where he was living, he found himself thinking, "Look, a witch." Of course, he didn't believe it, really. He knew it was probably someone from the village going off to relieve himself, carrying a flaming torch to guide him on his way. But what he was teaching us is that what you see depends on what you believe. What it's reasonable for you to think, faced with a particular experience, depends on what ideas you already have.

Duhem's Discovery

That's as true of Western science as of traditional religion. In the early twentieth century, the French physicist Pierre Duhem noticed an interesting fact about the way scientists behave. When they do experiments or collect data to support their theories, other scientists, often those attached to different theories, deny that the evidence shows any such thing. The objections can be of many different kinds. They might say, for example, that the experiment really hasn't been done properly. (Your test tubes were contaminated.) They might say that the so-called data are simply incorrect. (We did the same experiment, and that's not what happened.) Or they could point out that their own theory explained the data just as well. (The theory that life on Earth arrived in the form of basic organisms on a meteorite explains the fossil data just as well as the theory that life evolved by the creation of its basic elements as a result of electrochemical processes in the primeval oceans.) Starting with this observation, he went on to propose a general claim that philosophers know as the Duhem thesis. However much data you have, Duhem said, there will be many theories that explain it equally well. Theories, to use the jargon, are underdetermined by the evidence.

For Positivism, the underdetermination of theory by evidence is a problem. If science is rational, then we want the process of scientific theorizing to give us reasons to believe the theories. And presumably we want to get the best theory we can, given the evidence. But if two people can always reasonably respond with different theories to the same evidence, then something other than reason or evidence must account for their choices. Furthermore, if this is true however much evidence we have, *there will always be more than one possible reasonable account of the facts.* And that will mean that no amount of scientific exploration will allow us to settle on a single picture of the way things are. If Positivism understates the place of reason in the justification of desires, and thus of values, it overstates the power of reason in the justification of belief, and thus of facts.

Underdetermination is worrying enough. But a later student of scientific thinking, the philosopher N. R. Hanson, noticed something equally troubling for the Positivist view about scientific thinking. The way the Positivists thought about getting evidence for our theories was this. First you collect the data; then you see what theories it supports. Observation and experiment, the collection of the basic facts, was supposed to be used as an independent support for theories. What Hanson noticed was that the data never came free of theoretical commitments. When Galileo said that he saw through the telescope that the moon had mountains, he was assuming—as some of his opponents at the time pointed out—that telescopes work just as well in space as on Earth. That happens to be right. But how did he know? No one, at that point, had ever taken a telescope up into space to check. He just theorized that it was so. And, in fact, it turns out to be enormously difficult—Hanson thought it was literally impossible—to present data in language that isn't infused with theoretical ideas.

It doesn't matter for our purposes whether Hanson was right about the impossibility of separating theory and data, because what's certain is that we don't. When scientists looked at the tracks of charged particles in photographs of cloud chambers—this was the scientific example that Hanson knew best—they said things like, "Like, there's the path of an electron." That's what was reasonable for them to believe. Yet for the rest of us, who don't know the relevant physics or understand how the cloud chamber works, it all looks just like a fuzzy line in a photograph. Hanson's insight was that what it's reasonable for you to believe, as you look out on the world, depends both on what you believe already and on what ideas you have been introduced to. If you don't know about electricity—if you don't have the idea of it—you'll have no reason to wonder, as Benjamin Franklin wondered, whether that is what lightning is made of.

If what it's reasonable to believe depends on what you believe already, however, then you can't check the reasonableness of all your beliefs. You respond to new evidence in the light of what you already believe, and that gives you need beliefs. Were the original beliefs reasonable? Well, you can test them, but only by taking yet other beliefs for granted. You can't get into the game of belief by starting from nothing. And, of course, we all grow up in a family and society that start us out with a great raft of beliefs that we could not have developed on our own. Concepts and ideas develop in our upbringing. Some concepts and ideas are based in our biological natures—like color concepts, or the idea that there are physical objects in the world. But some ideas we wouldn't be using if we hadn't been given them—like electron, gene, democracy, contract, superego, witchcraft.

There is nothing unreasonable, then, about my kinsmen's belief in witchcraft. They think only what most people would think, given the concepts and beliefs they inherited; if you grew up with their beliefs and had their experiences, that is what you would believe, too. (Nor is belief in the agency of supernatural beings at all alien to the industrialized West: more than half of Americans believe in angels; roughly 40 percent think it's likely that Jesus will return to earth to render judgment sometime in the next half century.)

Those of us who were given scientific educations have a significant advantage. It's not that we are individually more reasonable; it's that we have been given better materials with which to think about the world. The institutions of science mean that the theories and ideas that scientists have developed are far superior to the ones that we human beings had before the growth of modern science. If we borrow their concepts, we are plugging ourselves into reality in ways that will make it easier for us to understand and to master the world. The best traditional predictors of the weather in Asante—and that is something that matters for a farming civilization—are simply not as good as the ones that the National Meteorological Office now provides, using modern scientific models. Who knows where we would be with the HIV/AIDS pandemic in Africa if we did not have modern scientific tools: tests for the virus, drugs for treatment, the understanding that predicts that condoms will prevent transmission of the disease? The advance of reason in the industrialized world is not the product of greater individual powers of reasoning. It is the result of the fact that we have developed institutions that can allow ordinary human beings to develop, test, and refine their ideas. What's wrong with the theory of witchcraft is not that it doesn't make sense but that it isn't true. And to find that out—in the way scientists gradually developed our modern understanding of disease—requires enormous, organized institutions or research, reflection, and analysis.

There is only one reality, and theories about witchcraft, like the germ theory of disease, are attempts to understand that one reality. Current medical theories of disease don't get everything right: otherwise, when you went to the doctor you could be guaranteed a diagnosis, a prognosis, perhaps even a cure. When an American gets a fever and assumes he has an infection, he's just doing what people have always done everywhere: he's applying the concepts that his culture has given him for thinking about disease. If, as I believe, this is a better story than a story about witchcraft, it's not because he's a better person. It's because he has the good fortune to live in a society that has spent enormous amounts of human resources to get that better story.

Scientific stories are not the only words we live by, I began with the ways our language of values helps guide us to a shared approach to the decisions that face us all. And one thing that is right in the Positivist picture is this: the methods of the natural sciences have not led to the kind of progress in our understanding of values that they have led to in our grasp of the facts. So we may be able to learn about values from societies where science is less deeply implanted than in ours: if scientific method has not advanced our understanding of values, then its superiority offers no reason to suppose that our understanding of values is superior. In fact, we have every reason to think that we can learn from other peoples, in ways both positive and negative. And if the Positivist asks *us* what guarantee we have that there is always going to be a way of persuading everyone of the value of everything valuable, we can ask *him* what guarantee he has that we can always persuade everyone of the facts. For the question presupposes that facts are in better shape than values here. And, even within the Positivist picture, as Duhem saw, there is no good reason to accept that claim.

That there are many ways of arguing for values of many kinds should be a good deal less puzzling when we recall that there are many kinds of facts for which we must offer different kinds of support, too. Mathematical beliefs can be justified by proofs. Beliefs about the colors of things get support from how they look in ordinary lighting. Psychological beliefs about the people get support from what they do and say. Beliefs about our own mental lives gain evidence, sometimes, from introspection. In the end, though, with facts as with values, nothing guarantees that we will be able to persuade everyone else of our view: this is a constraint that cosmopolitans, like everyone else, must accept. The Positivist holds that with facts, when we disagree, one of us has the truth, one of us is underwritten by the way things are, whereas with values, there is nothing to underwrite our claims. But even if we granted this picture, what would entitle us to think that the universe's being determinately one way or another guarantees that we can reach agreement as to which way it is? We enter every conversation—whether with neighbors or with strangers—without a promise of final agreement.

POSSIBILITIES FOR WRITING

1. Discuss the extent to which you find Appiah's explanation of his ancestors' and family's belief system convincing. Illustrate with an example from your own experience.

2. Provide an example to support, qualify, or challenge Appiah's statement that "what you see depends upon what you believe." Consider his related comment that "What is reasonable for you to think . . . depends on ideas you already have." Consider the kinds of evidence Appiah provides to support this claim.

3. What distinction does Appiah make between facts and values? Why does he make that distinction, and what conclusion does he draw from it? What implications might you draw from Appiah's final sentence? Discuss.

Francis Bacon (1561–1626) was born in London to parents who were members of the court of Queen Elizabeth I. He attended Trinity College, entered the practice of law in his late teens, and became a member of the House of Commons at the age of 23. His career flourished under King James I, but later scandals ended his life as a politician. A philosopher/scientist by nature and one of the most admired thinkers of his day, Bacon was a founder of the modern empirical tradition based on closely observing the physical world, conducting controlled experiments, and interpreting results rationally to discover the workings of the universe. Of his many published works, he is best remembered today for his Essays (collected from 1597 until after his death), brief meditations noted for their wit and insight.

Of Studies

In his classic essay, "Of Studies," Francis Bacon explains how and why study—knowledge—is important. Along with Michel de Montaigne, who published his first essays less than twenty years before Francis Bacon published his first collection in 1597, Bacon is considered the father of the English essay (with Montaigne the father of the French essay). Bacon's essays differ from Montaigne's in being more compact and more formal. Where Montaigne conceived of the essay as an opportunity to explore a subject through mental association and a casual ramble of the mind, Bacon envisioned the essay as an opportunity to offer advice. The title of his essay collection: "Essays or Counsels: Civil and Moral," suggests that didactic intent.

In "Of Studies," Bacon lays out the value of knowledge in practical terms. Bacon considers to what use studies might be put. He is less interested in their theoretical promise than in their practical utility—a proclivity more English, perhaps, than French. Bacon's writing in "Of Studies" is direct and pointed. It avoids the meandering find-your-way free form of Montaigne's essays. From his opening sentence Bacon gets directly to the point: "Studies serve for delight, for ornament, and for ability." He then elaborates on how studies are useful in these three ways. And he wastes no words in detailing the uses of "studies" for a Renaissance gentleman.

One of the attractions of Bacon's essay is his skillful use of parallel sentence structure, as exemplified in the opening sentence and throughout "Of Studies." This stylistic technique lends clarity and order to the writing, as in "crafty men contemn studies, simple men admire them, and wise men use them," which in its straightforward assertiveness exhibits confidence and elegance in addition to clarity and emphasis.

Studies serve for delight, for ornament, and for ability. Their chief use for delight is in privateness and retiring; for ornament, is in discourse;

and for ability, is in the judgment and disposition of business. For expert men can execute, and perhaps judge of particulars, one by one; but the general counsels, and the plots and marshaling of affairs, come best from those that are learned. To spend too much time in studies is sloth; to use them too much for ornament is affectation; to make judgment wholly by their rules is the humor of a scholar. They perfect nature, and are perfected by experience; for natural abilities are like natural plants, that need pruning by study; and studies themselves do give forth directions too much at large, except they be bounded in by experience. Crafty men contemn studies, simple men admire them, and wise men use them, for they teach not their own use; but that is a wisdom without them, and above them, won by observation. Read not to contradict and confute, nor to believe and take for granted, nor to find talk and discourse, but to weigh and consider. Some books are to be tasted, others to be swallowed, and some few to be chewed and digested; that is, some books are to be read only in parts; others to be read, but not curiously and some few to be read wholly, and with diligence and attention. Some books also may be read by deputy and extracts made of them by others, but that would be only in the less important arguments and the meaner sort of books; else distilled books are like common distilled waters, flashy things. Reading maketh a full man, conference a ready man, and writing an exact man. And therefore, if a man write little, he had need have a great memory; if he confer little, he had need have a present wit and if he read little, he had need have much cunning, to seem to know that he doth not. Histories make men wise; poets, witty, the mathematics, subtle; natural philosophy, deep; moral, grave; logic and rhetoric, able to contend. *Abeunt studia in mores,* Nay, there is no stond or impediment in the wit but may be wrought out by fit studies, like as diseases of the body may have appropriate exercises. Bowling is good for the stone and reins, shooting for the lungs and breast, gentle walking for the stomach, riding for the head, and the like. So if a man's wit be wandering, let him study the mathematics; for in demonstrations, if his wit be called away never so little, he must begin again. If his wit be not apt to distinguish or find differences, let him study the schoolmen, for they are *cumini sectores*. If he be not apt to beat over matters and to call up one thing to prove and illustrate another, let him study the lawyer's cases. So every defect of the mind may have a special receipt.

POSSIBILITIES FOR WRITING

1. Bacon's essay was composed some four hundred years ago in a society that was in many ways very different from ours today. Write an analysis of "Of Studies" in which you summarize the main points Bacon makes and then go on to explore the extent to which his remarks continue to seem relevant. As you reread "Of Studies" and make preliminary notes, you will need to find ways to "translate" much of his vocabulary into its modern equivalent.

2. Bacon's brief essay contains many aphorisms, concise statements of a general principle or truth—for example, "Read not to contradict and confute, nor to believe and take for granted, nor to find talk and discourse, but to weigh and consider." Take one of these, put it into your own words, and use it as the starting point for an essay of your own. Elaborate on the statement with examples and further details that come from your own experience or imagination.

3. Changing Bacon's focus a bit, write an essay for modern audiences titled "On Reading." In it consider different types of reading, purposes for reading, benefits of reading, difficulties involved in reading, and so forth. Your essay may be quite personal, focusing on your own experiences as a reader, or, like Bacon's, more formal.

Russell Baker (b. 1925) was born in rural Virginia and grew up in Baltimore, Maryland, where he graduated from Johns Hopkins University with a degree in English. He began his career in journalism at the Baltimore Sun, then moved on to the New York Times, where he worked for over thirty years. His op-ed column, "Observer," was particularly popular, and Baker was awarded the Pulitzer Prize for commentary in 1979; these columns have been collected in such volumes as So This Is Depravity (1983) and The Good Times (1989). Baker also won a Pulitzer for his memoir Growing Up (1982), about his Depression-era childhood. For a number of years, he was the host of Masterpiece Theatre on PBS.

RUSSELL BAKER

Growing Up

In this excerpt from his autobiographical volume, *Growing Up*, Russell Baker describes his mother after she had lapsed into senility. In this first chapter from that book Baker describes visiting her in a Baltimore hospital when she is unable to identify him and when she confuses present reality with past memories, some from Russell Baker's childhood and some from her own.

Baker brings his mother vividly to life with carefully articulated descriptive detail and crisp, revelatory dialogue. He reveals her character in all its tough mindedness, in its no-nonsense, formidable determination. Baker's mother tells people exactly what's on her mind, including the young doctor whose lack of knowledge about the Guy Fawkes Gunpowder plot rouses her criticism of his ignorance of history.

Midway through this excerpt Baker shifts from characterizing and memorializing his mother to speculating on the bonds and relations between parents and children. His autobiographical stance takes a meditative turn, as he reflects on the importance of memory and the value of the past, and how he, as both a parent and a writer, has a responsibility to preserve that past and demonstrate its relation to the present.

Throughout this excerpt from his memoir, Baker writes about common matters with grace and humor. Two of the pleasures of this piece are the precision of its style and its leavening of seriousness with humor. The tolerance and affection with which Baker writes about his mother and the honesty with which he characterizes himself are additional bonuses. So too is the image of "a braided cord of humanity" that he uses to convey the intimate and intricate relations of parents and children across generations.

At the age of eighty my mother had her last bad fall, and after that her mind wandered free through time. Some days she went to weddings and funerals that had taken place half a century earlier. On others she presided over family dinners cooked on Sunday afternoons for children who were now gray with age. Through all this she lay in bed but moved across time, traveling among the dead decades with a speed and ease beyond the gift of physical science.

"Where's Russell?" she asked one day when I came to visit at the nursing home.

"I'm Russell," I said.

She gazed at this improbably overgrown figure out of an inconceivable future and promptly dismissed it.

"Russell's only this big," she said, holding her hand, palm down, two feet from the floor. That day she was a young country wife with chickens in the backyard and a view of hazy blue Virginia mountains behind the apple orchard, and I was a stranger old enough to be her father.

Early one morning she phoned me in New York. "Are you coming to my funeral today?" she asked.

It was an awkward question with which to be awakened. "What are you talking about, for God's sake?" was the best reply I could manage.

"I'm being buried today," she declared briskly, as though announcing an important social event.

"I'll phone you back," I said and hung up, and when I did phone back she was all right, although she wasn't all right, of course, and we all knew she wasn't.

She had always been a small woman—short, light-boned, delicately structured—but now, under the white hospital sheet, she was becoming tiny. I thought of a doll with huge, fierce eyes. There had always been a fierceness in her. It showed in that angry, challenging thrust of the chin when she issued an opinion, and a great one she had been for issuing opinions.

"I tell people exactly what's on my mind," she had been fond of boasting. "I tell them what I think, whether they like it or not." Often they had not liked it. She could be sarcastic to people in whom she detected evidence of the ignoramus or the fool.

"It's not always good policy to tell people exactly what's on your mind," I used to caution her.

"If they don't like it, that's too bad," was her customary reply, "because that's the way I am."

And so she was. A formidable woman. Determined to speak her mind, determined to have her way, determined to bend those who opposed her. In that time when I had known her best, my mother had hurled herself at life with chin thrust forward, eyes blazing, and an energy that made her seem always on the run.

She ran after squawking chickens, an axe in her hand, determined on a beheading that would put dinner in the pot. She ran when she made beds, ran when she set the table. One Thanksgiving she burned herself badly when, running up from the cellar oven with the ceremonial turkey, she tripped on the stairs and tumbled back down, ending at the bottom in the debris of giblets, hot gravy, and battered turkey. Life was combat, and victory was not to the lazy, the timid, the slugabed, the drugstore cowboy, the libertine, the mushmouth afraid to tell people exactly what was on his mind whether people liked it or not. She ran.

But now the running was over. For a time I could not accept the inevitable. As I sat by her bed, my impulse was to argue her back to reality. On my first visit to the hospital in Baltimore, she asked who I was.

"Russell," I said.

"Russell's way out west," she advised me.

"No, I'm right here."

"Guess where I came from today?" was her response.

"Where?"

"All the way from New Jersey."

"When?"

"Tonight."

"No. You've been in the hospital for three days," I insisted.

"I suggest the thing to do is calm down a little bit," she replied. "Go over to the house and shut the door."

Now she was years deep into the past, living in the neighborhood where she had settled forty years earlier, and she had just been talking with Mrs. Hoffman, a neighbor across the street.

"It's like Mrs. Hoffman said today: The children always wander back to where they come from," she remarked.

"Mrs. Hoffman has been dead for fifteen years."

"Russ got married today," she replied.

"I got married in 1950," I said, which was the fact.

"The house is unlocked," she said.

So it went until a doctor came by to give one of those oral quizzes that medical men apply in such cases. She failed catastrophically, giving wrong answers or none at all to "What day is this?" "Do you know where you are?" "How old are you?" and so on. Then, a surprise.

"When is your birthday?" he asked.

"November 5, 1897," she said. Correct. Absolutely correct.

"How do you remember that?" the doctor asked.

"Because I was born on Guy Fawkes Day," she said.

"Guy Fawkes?" asked the doctor. "Who is Guy Fawkes?"

She replied with a rhyme I had heard her recite time and again over the years when the subject of her birth date arose:

> "Please to remember the Fifth of November,
> Gunpowder treason and plot.
> I see no reason why gunpowder treason
> Should ever be forgot."

Then she glared at this young doctor so ill informed about Guy Fawkes' failed scheme to blow King James off his throne with barrels of gunpowder in 1605. She had been a schoolteacher, after all, and knew how to glare at a dolt. "You may know a lot about medicine, but you obviously don't know any history," she said. Having told him exactly what was on her mind, she left us again.

The doctors diagnosed a hopeless senility. Not unusual, they said. "Hardening of the arteries" was the explanation for laymen. I thought it was more complicated than that. For ten years or more the ferocity with which she had once attacked life had been turning to a rage against the weakness, the boredom, and the absence of love that too much age had brought her. Now, after the last bad fall, she seemed to have broken chains that imprisoned her in a life she had come to hate and to return to a time inhabited by people who loved her, a time in which she was needed. Gradually I understood. It was the first time in years I had seen her happy.

She had written a letter three years earlier which explained more than "hardening of the arteries." I had gone down from New York to Baltimore, where she lived, for one of my infrequent visits and, afterwards, had written her with some banal advice to look for the silver lining, to count her blessings instead of burdening others with her miseries. I suppose what it really amounted to was a threat that if she was not more cheerful during my visits I would not come to see her very often. Sons are capable of such letters. This one was written out of a childish faith in the eternal strength of parents, a naive belief that age and wear could be overcome by an effort of will, that all she needed was a good pep talk to recharge a flagging spirit. It was such a foolish, innocent idea, but one thinks of parents differently from other people. Other people can become frail and break, but not parents.

She wrote back in an unusually cheery vein intended to demonstrate, I suppose, that she was mending her ways. She was never a woman to apologize, but for one moment with the pen in her hand she came very close. Referring to my visit, she wrote: "If I seemed unhappy to you at times—" Here she drew back, reconsidered, and said something quite different:

"If I seemed unhappy to you at times, I am, but there's really nothing anyone can do about it, because I'm just so very tired and lonely that I'll just go to sleep and forget it." She was then seventy-eight.

Now, three years later, after the last bad fall, she had managed to forget the fatigue and loneliness and, in these free-wheeling excursions back through time, to recapture happiness. I soon stopped trying to wrest her back to what I considered the real world and tried to travel along with her on those fantastic swoops into the past. One day when I arrived at her bedside she was radiant.

"Feeling good today," I said.

"Why shouldn't I feel good?" she asked. "Papa's going to take me up to Baltimore on the boat today."

At that moment she was a young girl standing on a wharf at Merry Point, Virginia, waiting for the Chesapeake Bay steamer with her father, who had been dead sixty-one years. William Howard Taft was in the White House, Europe still drowsed in the dusk of the great century of peace, America was a young country, and the future stretched before it in beams of crystal sunlight. "The greatest country on God's green earth," her father might have said, if I had been able to step into my mother's time machine and join him on the wharf with the satchels packed for Baltimore.

I could imagine her there quite clearly. She was wearing a blue dress with big puffy sleeves and long black stockings. There was a ribbon in her hair and a big bow tied on the side of her head. There had been a childhood photograph in her bedroom which showed all this, although the colors of course had been added years later by a restorer who tinted the picture.

About her father, my grandfather, I could only guess, and indeed, about the girl on the wharf with the bow in her hair, I was merely sentimentalizing. Of my mother's childhood and her people, of their time and place, I knew very little. A world had lived and died, and though it was part of my blood and bone I knew little more about it than I knew of the world of the pharaohs. It was useless now to ask for help from my mother. The orbits of her mind rarely touched present interrogators for more than a moment.

Sitting at her bedside, forever out of touch with her, I wondered about my own children, and their children, and children in general, and about the disconnections between children and parents that prevent them from knowing each other. Children rarely want to know who their parents were before they were parents, and when age finally stirs their curiosity there is no parent left to tell them. If a parent does lift the curtain a bit, it is often only to stun the young with some exemplary tale of how much harder life was in the old days.

I had been guilty of this when my children were small in the early 1960s and living the affluent life. It galled me that their childhoods should be, as I thought, so easy when my own had been, as I thought, so hard. I had developed the habit, when they complained about the steak being overcooked or the television being cut off, of lecturing them on the harshness of life in my day.

"In my day all we got for dinner was macaroni and cheese, and we were glad to get it."

"In my day we didn't have any television."

"In my day . . ."

"In my day . . ."

At dinner one evening a son had offended me with an inadequate report card, and as I leaned back and cleared my throat to lecture, he gazed at me with an expression of unutterable resignation and said, "Tell me how it was in your days, Dad."

I was angry with him for that, but angrier with myself for having become one of those ancient bores whose highly selective memories of the past become transparently dishonest even to small children. I tried to break the habit, but must have failed. A few years later my son was referring to me when I was out of earshot as "the old-timer." Between us there was a dispute about time. He looked upon the time that had been my future in a disturbing way. My future was his past, and being young, he was indifferent to the past.

As I hovered over my mother's bed listening for muffled signals from her childhood, I realized that this same dispute had existed between her and me. When she was young, with life ahead of her, I had been her future and resented it. Instinctively, I wanted to break free, cease being a creature defined by her time, consign her future to the past, and create my own. Well, I had finally done that, and then with my own children, I had seen my exciting future become their boring past.

These hopeless end-of-the-line visits with my mother made me wish I had not thrown off my own past so carelessly. We all come from the past, and children ought to know what it was that went into their making, to know that life is a braided cord of humanity stretching up from time long gone, and that it cannot be defined by the span of a single journey from diaper to shroud.

I thought that someday my own children would understand that. I thought that, when I am beyond explaining, they would want to know what the world was like when my mother was young and I was younger, and we two relics passed together through strange times. I thought I should try to tell them how it was to be young in the time before jet planes, superhighways, H-bombs, and the global village of television. I realized I would have to start with my mother and her passion for improving the male of the species, which in my case took the form of forcing me to "make something of myself."

Lord, how I hated those words. . . .

POSSIBILITIES FOR WRITING

1. In this memoir Baker provides a portrait of his mother that reveals her honestly, warts and all. Analyze the essay carefully to explore how he balances her positive and negative traits.
2. Baker makes several generalizations about children and their relationship to their parents—and vice versa. How do you respond to these generalizations? To what extent do they tend to reflect your own experience?
3. Write an essay about your relationship to a parent or adult guardian. As Baker does, present your subject honestly and without sentimentality.

James Baldwin (1924–1987) is widely considered one of the premiere stylists of modern American letters and among its most impassioned chroniclers of the African-American experience. Born in Harlem, Baldwin became interested in literature as a child, and he began publishing essays and reviews in his early twenties. He used the proceeds of a 1948 fellowship to relocate to Paris, where he lived for much of the rest of his life. There he worked on the novel Go Tell It on the Mountain, *which was published in 1953 to great praise. This was followed by* Giovanni's Room *(1956) and* Another Country *(1962), both of which dealt openly with issues of homosexuality as well as race. A major figure in the civil rights movement, Baldwin also published a number of acclaimed essay collections, mostly based on the experiences of blacks grappling with prejudice and social injustice.*

JAMES BALDWIN

Notes of a Native Son

In "Notes of a Native Son," James Baldwin takes up the major theme of his work, the relations between the black and white races in America. As in many of his essays, Baldwin here defines himself as an American, a writer, and a black man, which for him, were inextricably and inexorably intertwined. In coming to terms with these interrelated aspects of his complex identity, Baldwin produced some of the most powerful and the most passionate prose ever written about race relations in the United States.

Baldwin describes his family, especially his father, and his own thorny relationship with him. Setting his relationship with his father and family in the context of racial tensions in urban America, Baldwin looks into his heart and finds there a hatred so deep that it frightens him into an important personal realization: that this hatred of the other destroys not only other people, but also himself.

As an essayist, Baldwin writes out of a tradition of black pulpit oratory. Baldwin's father was a preacher, and he himself had pursued that vocation for a short time before deciding that his true calling was writing. His prose bears the hallmarks of spoken language, not the everyday idioms of street talk but rather the long rolling sentences of an elevated discourse, full of repetitions of word and phrase, of exalted diction, and of carefully balanced grammatical structures. In "Notes of a Native Son," we encounter a prose whose style persuades as much by its beauty as by its logic.

I

On the 29th of July, in 1943, my father died. On the same day, a few hours later, his last child was born. Over a month before this, while all our energies were concentrated in waiting for these events, there had been, in Detroit, one of the bloodiest race riots of the century. A few hours after my father's funeral, while he lay in state in the undertaker's chapel, a race riot broke out in Harlem. On the morning of the 3rd of August, we drove my father to the graveyard through a wilderness of smashed plate glass.

The day of my father's funeral had also been my nineteenth birthday. As we drove him to the graveyard, the spoils of injustice, anarchy, discontent, and hatred were all around us. It seemed to me that God himself had devised, to mark my father's end, the most sustained and brutally dissonant of codas. And it seemed to me, too, that the violence which rose all about us as my father left the world had been devised as a corrective for the pride of his eldest son. I had declined to believe in that apocalypse which had been central to my father's vision; very well, life seemed to be saying, here is something that will certainly pass for an apocalypse until the real thing comes along. I had inclined to be contemptuous of my father for the conditions of his life, for the conditions of our lives. When his life had ended I began to wonder about that life and also, in a new way, to be apprehensive about my own.

I had not known my father very well. We had got on badly, partly because we shared, in our different fashions, the vice of stubborn pride. When he was dead I realized that I had hardly ever spoken to him. When he had been dead a long time I began to wish I had. It seems to be typical of life in America, where opportunities, real and fancied, are thicker than anywhere else on the globe, that the second generation has no time to talk to the first. No one, including my father, seems to have known exactly how old he was, but his mother had been born during slavery. He was of the first generation of free men. He, along with thousands of other Negroes, came North after 1919 and I was part of that generation which had never seen the landscape of what Negroes sometimes call the Old Country.

He had been born in New Orleans and had been a quiet young man there during the time that Louis Armstrong, a boy, was running errands for the dives and honky-tonks of what was always presented to me as one of the most wicked of cities—to this day, whenever I think of New Orleans, I also helplessly think of Sodom and Gomorrah. My father never mentioned Louis Armstrong, except to forbid us to play his records; but there was a picture of him on our wall for a long time. One of my father's strong-willed female relatives had placed it there and forbade my father to take it down. He never did, but he eventually maneuvered her out of the house and when, some years later, she was in trouble and near death, he refused to do anything to help her.

He was, I think, very handsome. I gather this from photographs and from my own memories of him, dressed in his Sunday best and on his way to preach a sermon somewhere, when I was little. Handsome, proud, and ingrown, "like a toe-nail," somebody said. But he looked to me, as I grew older, like pictures I had seen of African tribal chieftains: he really should have been naked, with war-paint on and barbaric mementos, standing among spears. He could be chilling in the pulpit and indescribably cruel in his personal life and he was certainly the most bitter man I have ever met; yet it must be said that there was something else in him, buried in him, which lent him his tremendous power and, even, a rather crushing charm. It had something to do with his blackness, I think—he was very black—with his blackness and his beauty, and with the fact that he knew that he was black but did not know that he was beautiful. He claimed to be proud of his blackness but it had also been the cause of much humiliation and it had fixed bleak boundaries to his life. He was not a young man when we were growing up and he had already suffered many kinds of ruin; in his outrageously demanding and protective way he loved his children, who were black like him and menaced, like him; and all these things sometimes showed in his face when he tried, never to my knowledge with any success, to establish contact with any of us. When he took one of his children on his knee to play, the child always became fretful and began to cry; when he tried to help one of us with our homework the absolutely unabating tension which emanated from him caused our minds and our tongues to become paralyzed, so that he, scarcely knowing why, flew into a rage and the child, not knowing why, was punished. If it ever entered his head to bring a surprise home for his children, it was, almost unfailingly, the wrong surprise and even the big watermelons he often brought home on his back in the summertime led to the most appalling scenes. I do not remember, in all those years, that one of his children was ever glad to see him come home. From what I was able to gather of his early life, it seemed that this inability to establish contact with other people had always marked him and had been one of the things which had driven him out of New Orleans. There was something in him, therefore, groping and tentative, which was never expressed and which was buried with him. One saw it most clearly when he was facing new people and hoping to impress them. But he never did, not for long. We went from church to smaller and more improbable church, he found himself in less and less demand as a minister, and by the time he died none of his friends had come to see him for a long time. He had lived and died in an intolerable bitterness of spirit and it frightened me, as we drove him to the graveyard through those unquiet, ruined streets, to see how powerful and overflowing this bitterness could be and to realize that this bitterness now was mine.

When he died I had been away from home for a little over a year. In that year I had had time to become aware of the meaning of all my father's bitter warnings, had discovered the secret of his proudly pursed lips and rigid carriage: I had discovered the weight of white people in the world. I saw that this had been for my ancestors and now would be for me an awful thing to live with and that the bitterness which had helped to kill my father could also kill me.

He had been ill a long time—in the mind, as we now realized, reliving instances of his fantastic intransigence in the new light of his affliction and endeavoring to feel a sorrow for him which never, quite, came true. We had not known that he was being eaten up by paranoia, and the discovery that his cruelty, to our bodies and our minds, had been one of the symptoms of his illness was not, then, enough to enable us to forgive him. The younger children felt, quite simply, relief that he would not be coming home anymore. My mother's observation that it was he, after all, who had kept them alive all these years meant nothing because the problems of keeping children alive are not real for children. The older children felt, with my father gone, that they could invite their friends to the house without fear that their friends would be insulted or, as had sometimes happened with me, being told that their friends were in league with the devil and intended to rob our family of everything we owned. (I didn't fail to wonder, and it made me hate him, what on earth we owned that anybody else would want.)

His illness was beyond all hope of healing before anyone realized that he was ill. He had always been so strange and had lived, like a prophet, in such unimaginably close communion with the Lord that his long silences which were punctuated by moans and hallelujahs and snatches of old songs while he sat at the living-room window never seemed odd to us. It was not until he refused to eat because, he said, his family was trying to poison him that my mother was forced to accept as a fact what had, until then, been only an unwilling suspicion. When he was committed, it was discovered that he had tuberculosis and, as it turned out, the disease of his mind allowed the disease of his body to destroy him. For the doctors could not force him to eat, either, and, though he was fed intravenously, it was clear from the beginning that there was no hope for him.

In my mind's eye I could see him, sitting at the window, locked up in his terrors; hating and fearing every living soul including his children who had betrayed him, too, by reaching toward the world which had despised him. There were nine of us. I began to wonder what it could have felt like for such a man to have had nine children whom he could barely feed. He used to make little jokes about our poverty, which never, of course, seemed very funny to us; they could not have seemed very funny to him, either, or else our all too feeble response to them would never have caused such rages. He spent great energy and achieved, to our chagrin, no small amount of success in keeping us away from the people who surrounded us, people who had all-night rent parties to which we listened when we should have been sleeping, people who cursed and drank and flashed razor blades on Lenox Avenue. He could not understand why, if they had so much energy to spare, they could not use it to make their lives better. He treated almost everybody on our block with a most uncharitable asperity and neither they, nor, of course, their children were slow to reciprocate.

The only white people who came to our house were welfare workers and bill collectors. It was almost always my mother who dealt with them, for my father's temper, which was at the mercy of his pride, was never to be trusted. It was clear that he felt their very presence in his home to be a violation: this was conveyed by his carriage, almost ludicrously stiff, and by his voice, harsh and vindictively polite. When I was around nine or ten I wrote a play which was directed by a young, white schoolteacher, a woman, who then took an interest in me, and gave me books to read and, in order to corroborate my theatrical bent, decided to take me to see what she somewhat tactlessly referred to as "real" plays. Theatergoing was forbidden in our house, but, with the really cruel intuitiveness of a child, I suspected that the color of this woman's skin would carry the day for me. When, at school, she suggested taking me to the theater, I did not, as I might have done if she had been a Negro, find a way of discouraging her, but agreed that she should pick me up at my house one evening. I then, very cleverly, left all the rest to my mother, who suggested to my father, as I knew she would, that it would not be very nice to let such a kind woman make the trip for nothing. Also, since it was a schoolteacher, I imagine that my mother countered the idea of sin with the idea of "education," which word, even with my father, carried a kind of bitter weight.

Before the teacher came my father took me aside to ask *why* she was coming, what *interest* she could possibly have in our house, in a boy like me. I said I didn't know but I, too, suggested that it had something to do with education. And I understood that my father was waiting for me to say something—I didn't quite know what; perhaps that I wanted his protection against this teacher and her "education." I said none of these things and the teacher came and we went out. It was clear, during the brief interview in our living room, that my father was agreeing very much against his will and that he would have refused permission if he had dared. The fact that he did not dare caused me to despise him: I had no way of knowing that he was facing in that living room a wholly unprecedented and frightening situation.

Later, when my father had been laid off from his job, this woman became very important to us. She was really a very sweet and generous woman and went to a great deal of trouble to be of help to us, particularly during one awful winter. My mother called her by the highest name she knew. She said she was a "christian." My father could scarcely disagree but during the four or five years of our relatively close association he never trusted her and was always trying to surprise in her open, Midwestern face the genuine, cunningly hidden, and hideous motivation. In later years, particularly when it began to be clear that this "education" of mine was going to lead me to perdition, he became more explicit and warned me that my white friends in high school were not really my friends and that I would see, when I was older, how white people would do anything to keep a Negro down. Some of them could be nice, he admitted, but none of them were to be trusted and most of them were not even nice. The best thing was to have as little to do with them as possible. I did not feel this way and I was certain, in my innocence, that I never would.

But the year which preceded my father's death had made a great change in my life. I had been living in New Jersey, working in defense plants, working and living among southerners, white and black. I knew about the south, of course, and about how southerners treated Negroes and how they expected them to behave, but it had never entered my mind that anyone would look at me and expect *me* to behave that way. I learned in New Jersey that to be a Negro meant, precisely, that one was never looked at but was simply at the mercy of the reflexes the color of one's skin caused in other people. I acted in New Jersey as I had always acted, that is as though I thought a great deal of myself—I had to *act* that way—with results that were, simply, unbelievable. I had scarcely arrived before I had earned the enmity, which was extraordinarily ingenious, of all my superiors and nearly all my coworkers. In the beginning, to make matters worse, I simply did not know what was happening. I did not know what I had done, and I shortly began to wonder what *anyone* could possibly do, to bring about such unanimous, active, and unbearably vocal hostility. I knew about jim-crow but I had never experienced it. I went to the same self-service restaurant three times and stood with all the Princeton boys before the counter, waiting for a hamburger and coffee; it was always an extraordinarily long time before anything was set before me; but it was not until the fourth visit that I learned that, in fact, nothing had ever been set before me: I had simply picked something up. Negroes were not served there, I was told, and they had been waiting for me to realize that I was always the only Negro present. Once I was told this, I determined to go there all the time. But now they were ready for me and, though some dreadful scenes were subsequently enacted in that restaurant, I never ate there again.

It was the same story all over New Jersey, in bars, bowling alleys, diners, places to live. I was always being forced to leave, silently, or with mutual imprecations. I very shortly became notorious and children giggled behind me when I passed and their elders whispered or shouted—they really believed that I was mad. And it did begin to work on my mind, of course; I began to be afraid to go anywhere and to compensate for this I went places to which I really should not have gone and where, God knows, I had no desire to be. My reputation in town naturally enhanced my reputation at work and my working day became one long series of acrobatics designed to keep me out of trouble. I cannot say that these acrobatics succeeded. It began to seem that the machinery of the organization I worked for was turning over, day and night, with but one aim: to eject me. I was fired once, and contrived, with the aid of a friend from New York, to get back on the payroll; was fired again, and bounced back again. It took a while to fire me for the third time, but the third time took. There were no loopholes anywhere. There was not even any way of getting back inside the gates.

That year in New Jersey lives in my mind as though it were the year during which, having an unsuspected predilection for it, I first contracted some dread, chronic disease, the unfailing symptom of which is a kind of blind fever, a pounding in the skull and fire in the bowels. Once this disease is contracted, one can never be really carefree again, for the fever, without an instant's warning, can recur at any moment. It can wreck more important things than race relations. There is not a Negro alive who does not have this rage in his blood—one has the choice, merely, of living with it consciously or surrendering to it. As for me, this fever has recurred in me, and does, and will until the day I die.

My last night in New Jersey, a white friend from New York took me to the nearest big town, Trenton, to go to the movies and have a few drinks. As it turned out, he also saved me from, at the very least, a violent whipping. Almost every detail of that night stands out very clearly in my memory. I even remember the name of the movie we saw because its title impressed me as being so patly ironical. It was a movie about the German occupation of France, starring Maureen O'Hara and Charles Laughton and called *This Land Is Mine.* I remember the name of the diner we walked into when the movie ended: it was the "American Diner." When we walked in the counterman asked what we wanted and I remember answering with the casual sharpness which had become my habit: "We want a hamburger and a cup of coffee, what do you think we want?" I do not know why, after a year of such rebuffs, I so completely failed to anticipate his answer, which was, of course, "We don't serve Negroes here." This reply failed to discompose me, at least for the moment. I made some sardonic comment about the name of the diner and we walked out into the streets.

This was the time of what was called the "brown-out," when the lights in all American cities were very dim. When we reentered the streets something happened to me which had the force of an optical illusion, or a nightmare. The streets were very crowded and I was facing north. People were moving in every direction but it seemed to me, in that instant, that all of the people I could see, and many more than that, were moving toward me, against me, and that everyone was white. I remember how their faces gleamed. And I felt, like a physical sensation, a *click* at the nape of my neck as though some interior string connecting my head to my body had been cut. I began to walk. I heard my friend call after me, but I ignored him. Heaven only knows what was going on in his mind, but he had the good sense not to touch me— I don't know what would have happened if he had—and to keep me in sight. I don't know what was going on in my mind, either; I certainly had no conscious plan. I wanted to do something to crush these white faces, which were crushing me. I walked for perhaps a block or two until I came to an enormous, glittering, and fashionable restaurant in which I knew not even the intercession of the Virgin would cause me to be served. I pushed through the doors and took the first vacant seat I saw, at a table for two, and waited.

I do not know how long I waited and I rather wonder, until today, what I could possibly have looked like. Whatever I looked like, I frightened the waitress who shortly appeared, and the moment she appeared all of my fury flowed towards her. I hated her for her white face, and for her great, astounded, frightened eyes. I felt that if she found a black man so frightening I would make her fright worthwhile.

She did not ask me what I wanted, but repeated, as though she had learned it somewhere, "We don't serve Negroes here." She did not say it with the blunt, derisive hostility to which I had grown so accustomed, but, rather, with a note of apology in her voice, and fear. This made me colder and more murderous than ever. I felt I had to do something with my hands. I wanted her to come close enough for me to get her neck between my hands.

So I pretended not to have understood her, hoping to draw her closer. And she did step a very short step closer, with her pencil poised incongruously over her pad, and repeated the formula: ". . . don't serve Negroes here."

Somehow, with the repetition of that phrase, which was already ringing in my head like a thousand bells of a nightmare, I realized that she would never come any closer and that I would have to strike from a distance. There was nothing on the table but an ordinary water-mug half full of water, and I picked this up and hurled it with all my strength at her. She ducked and it missed her and shattered against the mirror behind the bar. And, with that sound, my frozen blood abruptly thawed, I returned from wherever I had been, I *saw*, for the first time, the restaurant, the people with their mouths open, already, as it seemed to me, rising as one man, and I realized what I had done, and where I was, and I was frightened. I rose and began running for the door. A round, pot-bellied man grabbed me by the nape of the neck just as I reached the doors and began to beat me about the face. I kicked him and got loose and ran into the streets. My friend whispered, *"Run!"* and I ran.

My friend stayed outside the restaurant long enough to misdirect my pursuers and the police, who arrived, he told me, at once. I do not know what I said to him when he came to my room that night. I could not have said much. I felt, in the oddest, most awful way, that I had somehow betrayed him. I lived it over and over and over again, the way one relives an automobile accident after it has happened and one finds oneself alone and safe. I could not get over two facts, both equally difficult for the imagination to grasp, and one was that I could have been murdered. But the other was that I had been ready to commit murder. I saw nothing very clearly but I did see this: that my life, my *real* life, was in danger, and not from anything other people might do but from the hatred I carried in my own heart.

II

I had returned home around the second week in June—in great haste because it seemed that my father's death and my mother's confinement were both but a matter of hours. In the case of my mother, it soon became clear that she had simply made a miscalculation. This had always been her tendency and I don't believe that a single one of us arrived in the world, or has since arrived anywhere else, on time. But none of us dawdled so intolerably about the business of being born as did my baby sister. We sometimes amused ourselves, during those endless, stifling weeks, by picturing the baby sitting within in the safe, warm dark, bitterly regretting the necessity of becoming a part of our chaos and stubbornly putting it off as long as possible. I understood her perfectly and congratulated her on showing such good sense so soon. Death, however, sat as purposefully at my father's bedside as life stirred within my mother's womb and it was harder to understand why he so lingered in that long shadow. It seemed that he had bent, and for a long time, too, all of his energies towards dying. Now death was ready for him but my father held back.

All of Harlem, indeed, seemed to be infected by waiting. I had never before known it to be so violently still. Racial tensions throughout this country were exacerbated during the early years of the war, partly because the labor market brought together hundreds of thousands of ill-prepared people and partly because Negro soldiers, regardless of where they were born, received their military training in the south. What happened in defense plants and army camps had repercussions, naturally, in every Negro ghetto. The situation in Harlem had grown bad enough for clergymen, policemen, educators, politicians, and social workers to assert in one breath that there was no "crime wave" and to offer, in the very next breath, suggestions as to how to combat it. These suggestions always seemed to involve playgrounds, despite the fact that racial skirmishes were occurring in the playgrounds, too. Playground or not, crime wave or not, the Harlem police force had been augmented in March, and the unrest grew—perhaps, in fact, partly as a result of the ghetto's instinctive hatred of policemen. Perhaps the most revealing news item, out of the steady parade of reports of muggings, stabbings, shootings, assaults, gang wars, and accusations of police brutality is the item concerning six Negro girls who set upon a white girl in the subway because, as they all too accurately put it, she was stepping on their toes. Indeed she was, all over the nation.

I had never before been so aware of policemen, on foot, on horse-back, on corners, everywhere, always two by two. Nor had I ever been so aware of small knots of people. They were on stoops and on corners and in doorways, and what was striking about them, I think, was that they did not seem to be talking. Never, when I passed these groups, did the usual sound of a curse or a laugh ring out and neither did there seem to be any hum of gossip. There was certainly, on the other hand, occurring between them communication extraordinarily intense. An-other thing that was striking was the unexpected diversity of the peo-ple who made up these groups. Usually, for example, one would see a group of sharpies standing on the street corner, jiving the passing chicks; or a group of older men, usually, for some reason, in the vicin-ity of a barber shop, discussing baseball scores, or the numbers or making rather chilling observations about women they had known. Women, in a general way, tended to be seen less often together—unless they were church women, or very young girls, or prostitutes met together for an unprofessional instant. But that summer I saw the strangest combina-tions: large, respectable, churchly matrons standing on the stoops or the corners with their hair tied up, together with a girl in sleazy satin whose face bore the marks of gin and the razor, or heavy-set, abrupt, no-nonsense older men, in company with the most disreputable and fanatical "race" men, or these same "race" men with the sharpies, or these sharpies with the churchly women. Seventh Day Adventists and Methodists and Spiritualists seemed to be hobnobbing with Holy-rollers and they were all, alike, entangled with the most flagrant disbe-lievers; something heavy in their stance seemed to indicate that they had all, incredibly, seen a common vision, and on each face there seemed to be the same strange, bitter shadow.

The churchly women and the matter-of-fact, no-nonsense men had children in the Army. The sleazy girls they talked to had lovers there, the sharpies and the "race" men had friends and brothers there. It would have demanded an unquestioning patriotism, happily as un-common in this country as it is undesirable, for these people not to have been disturbed by the bitter letters they received, by the newspa-per stories they read, not to have been enraged by the posters, then to be found all over New York, which described the Japanese as "yellow-bellied Japs." It was only the "race" men, to be sure, who spoke ceaselessly of being revenged—how this vengeance was to be exacted was not clear—for the indignities and dangers suffered by Negro boys in uniform; but everybody felt a directionless, hopeless bitterness, as well as that panic which can scarcely be suppressed when one knows that a human being one loves is beyond one's reach, and in danger. This helplessness and this gnawing uneasiness does something, at length, to even the toughest mind. Perhaps the best way to sum all this up is to say that the people I knew felt, mainly, a peculiar kind of relief when they knew that their boys were being shipped out of the south, to do battle overseas. It was, perhaps, like feeling that the most dangerous part of a dangerous journey had been passed and that now, even if death should come, it would come with honor and without the complicity of their countrymen. Such a death would be, in short, a fact with which one could hope to live.

It was on the 28th of July, which I believe was a Wednesday, that I visited my father for the first time during his illness and for the last time in his life. The moment I saw him I knew why I had put off this visit so long. I had told my mother that I did not want to see him because I hated him. But this was not true. It was only that I *had* hated him and I wanted to hold on to this hatred. I did not want to look on him as a ruin: it was not a ruin I had hated. I imagine that one of the reasons people cling to their hates so stubbornly is because they sense, once hate is gone, that they will be forced to deal with pain.

We traveled out to him, his older sister and myself, to what seemed to be the very end of a very Long Island. It was hot and dusty and we wrangled, my aunt and I, all the way out, over the fact that I had recently begun to smoke and, as she said, to give myself airs. But I knew that she wrangled with me because she could not bear to face the fact of her brother's dying. Neither could I endure the reality of her despair, her unstated bafflement as to what had happened to her brother's life, and her own. So we wrangled and I smoked and from time to time she fell into a heavy reverie. Covertly, I watched her face, which was the face of an old woman; it had fallen in, the eyes were sunken and lightless; soon she would be dying, too.

In my childhood—it had not been so long ago—I had thought her beautiful. She had been quick-witted and quick-moving and very generous with all the children and each of her visits had been an event. At one time one of my brothers and myself had thought of running away to live with her. Now she could no longer produce out of her handbag some unexpected and yet familiar delight. She made me feel pity and revulsion and fear. It was awful to realize that she no longer caused me to feel affection. The closer we came to the hospital the more querulous she became and at the same time, naturally, grew more dependent on me. Between pity and guilt and fear I began to feel that there was another me trapped in my skull like a jack-in-the-box who might escape my control at any moment and fill the air with screaming.

She began to cry the moment we entered the room and she saw him lying there, all shriveled and still, like a little black monkey. The great, gleaming apparatus which fed him and would have compelled him to be still even if he had been able to move brought to mind, not beneficence, but torture; the tubes entering his arm made me think of pictures I had seen when a child, of Gulliver, tied down by the pygmies on that island. My aunt wept and wept, there was a whistling sound in my father's throat; nothing was said; he could not speak. I wanted to take his hand, to say something. But I do not know what I could have said, even if he could have heard me. He was not really in that room with us, he had at last really embarked on his journey; and though my aunt told me that he said he was going to meet Jesus, I did not hear anything except that whistling in his throat. The doctor came back and we left, into that unbearable train again, and home. In the morning came the telegram saying that he was dead. Then the house was suddenly full of relatives, friends, hysteria, and confusion and I quickly left my mother and the children to the care of those impressive women, who, in Negro communities at least, automatically appear at times of bereavement armed with lotions, proverbs, and patience, and an ability to cook. I went downtown. By the time I returned, later the same day, my mother had been carried to the hospital and the baby had been born.

III

For my father's funeral I had nothing black to wear and this posed a nagging problem all day long. It was one of those problems, simple, or impossible of solution, to which the mind insanely clings in order to avoid the mind's real trouble. I spent most of that day at the downtown apartment of a girl I knew, celebrating my birthday with whiskey and wondering what to wear that night. When planning a birthday celebration one naturally does not expect that it will be up against competition from a funeral and this girl had anticipated taking me out that night, for a big dinner and a night club afterwards. Sometime during the course of that long day we decided that we would go out anyway, when my father's funeral service was over. I imagine I decided it, since, as the funeral hour approached, it became clearer and clearer to me that I would not know what to do with myself when it was over. The girl, stifling her very lively concern as to the possible effects of the whiskey on one of my father's chief mourners, concentrated on being conciliatory and practically helpful. She found a black shirt for me somewhere and ironed it and, dressed in the darkest pants and jacket I owned, and slightly drunk, I made my way to my father's funeral.

The chapel was full, but not packed, and very quiet. There were, mainly, my father's relatives, and his children, and here and there I saw faces I had not seen since childhood, the faces of my father's one-time friends. They were very dark and solemn now, seeming somehow to suggest that they had known all along that something like this would happen. Chief among the mourners was my aunt, who had quarreled with my father all his life; by which I do not mean to suggest that her mourning was insincere or that she had not loved him. I suppose that she was one of the few people in the world who had, and their incessant quarreling proved precisely the strength of the tie that bound them. The only other person in the world, as far as I knew, whose relationship to my father rivaled my aunt's in depth was my mother, who was not there.

It seemed to me, of course, that it was a very long funeral. But it was, if anything, a rather shorter funeral than most, nor, since there were no overwhelming, uncontrollable expressions of grief, could it becalled—if I dare to use the word—successful. The minister who preached my father's funeral sermon was one of the few my father had still been seeing as he neared his end. He presented to us in his sermon a man whom none of us had ever seen—a man thoughtful, patient, and forbearing, a Christian inspiration to all who knew him, and a model for his children. And no doubt the children, in their disturbed and guilty state, were almost ready to believe this; he had been remote enough to be anything and, anyway, the shock of the incontrovertible, that it was really our father lying up there in that casket, prepared the mind for anything. His sister moaned and this grief-stricken moaning was taken as corroboration. The other faces held a dark, non-committal thoughtfulness. This was not the man they had known, but they had scarcely expected to be confronted with *him*; this was, in a sense deeper than questions of fact, the man they had not known, and the man they had not known may have been the real one. The real man, whoever he had been, had suffered and now he was dead: this was all that was sure and all that mattered now. Every man in the chapel hoped that when his hour came he, too, would be eulogized, which is to say forgiven, and that all of his lapses, greeds, errors, and strayings from the truth would be invested with coherence and looked upon with charity. This was perhaps the last thing human beings could give each other and it was what they demanded, after all, of the Lord. Only the Lord saw the midnight tears, only He was present when one of His children, moaning and wringing hands, paced up and down the room. When one slapped one's child in anger the recoil in the heart reverberated through heaven and became part of the pain of the universe. And when the children were hungry and sullen and distrustful and one watched them, daily, growing wilder, and further away, and running headlong into danger, it was the Lord who knew what the charged heart endured as the strap was laid to the backside; the Lord alone who knew what one *would* have said if one had had, like the Lord, the gift of the living word. It was the Lord who knew of the impossibility every parent in that room faced: how to prepare the child for the day when the child would be despised and how to *create* in the child—by what means?—a stronger antidote to this poison than one had found for oneself. The avenues, side streets, bars, billiard halls, hospitals, police stations, and even the playgrounds of Harlem—not to mention the houses of correction, the jails, and the morgue—testified to the potency of the poison while remaining silent as to the efficacy of whatever antidote, irresistibly raising the question of whether or not such an antidote existed; raising, which was worse, the question of whether or not an antidote was desirable; perhaps poison should be fought with poison. With these several schisms in the mind and with more terrors in the heart than could be named, it was better not to judge the man who had gone down under an impossible burden. It was better to remember. *Thou knowest this man's fall; but thou knowest not his wrassling.*

While the preacher talked and I watched the children—years of changing their diapers, scrubbing them, slapping them, taking them to school, and scolding them had had the perhaps inevitable result of making me love them, though I am not sure I knew this then—my mind was busily breaking out with a rash of disconnected impressions. Snatches of popular songs, indecent jokes, bits of books I had read, movie sequences, faces, voices, political issues—I thought I was going mad; all these impressions suspended, as it were, in the solution of the faint nausea produced in me by the heat and liquor. For a moment I had the impression that my alcoholic breath, inefficiently disguised with chewing gum, filled the entire chapel. Then someone began singing one of my father's favorite songs and, abruptly, I was with him, sitting on his knee, in the hot, enormous, crowded church which was the first church we attended. It was the Abyssinia Baptist Church on 138th Street. We had not gone there long. With this image, a host of others came. I had forgotten, in the rage of my growing up, how proud my father had been of me when I was little. Apparently, I had had a voice and my father had liked to show me off before the members of the church. I had forgotten what he had looked like when he was pleased but now I remembered that he had always been grinning with pleasure when my solos ended. I even remembered certain expressions on his face when he teased my mother—had he loved her? I would never know. And when had it all begun to change? For now it seemed that he had not always been cruel. I remembered being taken for a haircut and scraping my knee on the footrest of the barber's chair and I remembered my father's face as he soothed my crying and applied the stinging iodine. Then I remembered our fights, fights which had been of the worst possible kind because my technique had been silence.

I remembered the one time in all our life together when we had really spoken to each other.

It was on a Sunday and it must have been shortly before I left home. We were walking, just the two of us, in our usual silence, to or from church. I was in high school and had been doing a lot of writing and I was, at about this time, the editor of the high school magazine. But I had also been a Young Minister and had been preaching from the pulpit. Lately, I had been taking fewer engagements and preached as rarely as possible. It was said in the church, quite truthfully, that I was "cooling off."

My father asked me abruptly, "You'd rather write than preach, wouldn't you?"

I was astonished at his question—because it was a real question. I answered, "Yes."

That was all we said. It was awful to remember that that was all we had *ever* said.

The casket now was opened and mourners were being led up the aisle to look for the last time on the deceased. The assumption was that the family was too overcome with grief to be allowed to make this journey alone and I watched while my aunt was led to the casket and, muffled in black, and shaking, led back to her seat. I disapproved of forcing the children to look on their dead father, considering that the shock of his death, or, more truthfully, the shock of death as a reality, was already a little more than a child could bear, but my judgment in this matter had been overruled and there they were, bewildered and frightened and very small, being led, one by one, to the casket. But there is also something very gallant about children at such moments. It has something to do with their silence and gravity and with the fact that one cannot help them. Their legs, somehow, seem *exposed,* so that it is at once incredible and terribly clear that their legs are all they have to hold them up.

I had not wanted to go to the casket myself and I certainly had not wished to be led there, but there was no way of avoiding either of these forms. One of the deacons led me up and I looked on my father's face. I cannot say that it looked like him at all. His blackness had been equivocated by powder and there was no suggestion in that casket of what his power had or could have been. He was simply an old man dead, and it was hard to believe that he had ever given anyone either joy or pain. Yet, his life filled that room. Further up the avenue his wife was holding his newborn child. Life and death so close together, and love and hatred, and right and wrong, said something to me which I did not want to hear concerning man, concerning the life of man.

After the funeral, while I was downtown desperately celebrating my birthday, a Negro soldier, in the lobby of the Hotel Braddock, got into a fight with a white policeman over a Negro girl. Negro girls, white policemen, in or out of uniform, and Negro males—in or out of uniform—were part of the furniture of the lobby of the Hotel Braddock and this was certainly not the first time such an incident had occurred. It was destined, however, to receive an unprecedented publicity, for the fight between the policeman and the soldier ended with the shooting of the soldier. Rumor, flowing immediately to the streets outside, stated that the soldier had been shot in the back, an instantaneous and revealing invention, and that the soldier had died protecting a Negro woman. The facts were somewhat different—for example, the soldier had not been shot in the back, and was not dead, and the girl seems to have been as dubious a symbol of womanhood as her white counterpart in Georgia usually is, but no one was interested in the facts. They preferred the invention because this invention expressed and corroborated their hates and fears so perfectly. It is just as well to remember that people are always doing this. Perhaps many of those legends, including Christianity, to which the world clings began their conquest of the world with just some such concerted surrender to distortion. The effect, in Harlem, of this particular legend was like the effect of a lit match in a tin of gasoline. The mob gathered before the doors of the Hotel Braddock simply began to swell and to spread in every direction, and Harlem exploded.

The mob did not cross the ghetto lines. It would have been easy, for example, to have gone over Morningside Park on the west side or to have crossed the Grand Central railroad tracks at 125th Street on the east side, to wreak havoc in white neighborhoods. The mob seems to have been mainly interested in something more potent and real than the white face, that is, in white power, and the principal damage done during the riot of the summer of 1943 was to white business establishments in Harlem. It might have been a far bloodier story, of course, if, at the hour the riot began, these establishments had still been open. From the Hotel Braddock the mob fanned out, east and west along 125th Street, and for the entire length of Lenox, Seventh, and Eighth avenues. Along each of these avenues, and along each major side street—116th, 125th, 135th, and so on—bars, stores, pawnshops, restaurants, even little luncheonettes had been smashed open and entered and looted—looted, it might be added, with more haste than efficiency. The shelves really looked as though a bomb had struck them. Cans of beans and soup and dog food, along with toilet paper, corn flakes, sardines and milk tumbled every which way, and abandoned cash registers and cases of beer leaned crazily out of the splintered windows and were strewn along the avenues. Sheets, blankets, and clothing of every description formed a kind of path, as though people had dropped them while running. I truly had not realized that Harlem *had* so many stores until I saw them all smashed open; the first time the word *wealth* ever entered my mind in relation to Harlem was when I saw it scattered in the streets. But one's first, incongruous impression of plenty was countered immediately by an impression of waste. None of this was doing anybody any good. It would have been better to have left the plate glass as it had been and the goods lying in the stores.

It would have been better, but it would also have been intolerable, for Harlem had needed something to smash. To smash something is the ghetto's chronic need. Most of the time it is the members of the ghetto who smash each other, and themselves. But as long as the ghetto walls are standing there will always come a moment when these outlets do not work. That summer, for example, it was not enough to get into a fight on Lenox Avenue, or curse out one's cronies in the barber shops. If ever, indeed, the violence which fills Harlem's churches, pool halls, and bars erupts outward in a more direct fashion, Harlem and its citizens are likely to vanish in an apocalyptic flood. That this is not likely to happen is due to a great many reasons, most hidden and powerful among them the Negro's real relation to the white American. This relation prohibits, simply, anything as uncomplicated and satisfactory as pure hatred. In order really to hate white people, one has to blot so much out of the mind—and the heart—that this hatred itself becomes an exhausting and self-destructive pose. But this does not mean, on the other hand, that love comes easily: the white world is too powerful, too complacent, too ready with gratuitous humiliation, and, above all, too ignorant and too innocent for that. One is absolutely forced to make perpetual qualifications and one's own reactions are always canceling each other out. It is this, really, which has driven so many people mad, both white and black. One is always in the position of having to decide between amputation and gangrene. Amputation is swift but time may prove that the amputation was not necessary—or one may delay the amputation too long. Gangrene is slow, but it is impossible to be sure that one is reading one's symptoms right. The idea of going through life as a cripple is more than one can bear, and equally unbearable is the risk of swelling up slowly, in agony, with poison. And the trouble, finally, is that the risks are real even if the choices do not exist.

"But as for me and my house," my father had said, "we will serve the Lord." I wondered, as we drove him to his resting place, what this line had meant for him. I had heard him preach it many times. I had preached it once myself, proudly giving it an interpretation different from my father's. Now the whole thing came back to me, as though my father and I were on our way to Sunday school and I were memorizing the golden text: *And if it seem evil unto you to serve the Lord, choose you this day whom you will serve; whether the gods which your fathers served that were on the other side of the flood, or the gods of the Amorites, in whose land ye dwell: but as for me and my house, we will serve the Lord.* I suspected in these familiar lines a meaning which had never been there for me before. All of my father's texts and songs, which I had decided were meaningless, were arranged before me at his death like empty bottles, waiting to hold the meaning which life would give them for me. This was his legacy: nothing is ever escaped. That bleakly memorable morning I hated the unbelievable streets and the Negroes and whites who had, equally, made them that way. But I knew that it was folly, as my father would have said, this bitterness was folly. It was necessary to hold on to the things that mattered. The dead man mattered, the new life mattered; blackness and whiteness did not matter; to believe that they did was to acquiesce in one's own destruction. Hatred, which could destroy so much, never failed to destroy the man who hated and this was an immutable law.

It began to seem that one would have to hold in the mind forever two ideas which seemed to be in opposition. The first idea was acceptance, the acceptance, totally without rancor, of life as it is, and men as they are: in the light of this idea, it goes without saying that injustice is a commonplace. But this did not mean that one could be complacent, for the second idea was of equal power: that one must never, in one's own life, accept these injustices as commonplace but must fight them with all one's strength. This fight begins, however, in the heart and it now had been laid to my charge to keep my own heart free of hatred and despair. This intimation made my heart heavy and, now that my father was irrecoverable, I wished that he had been beside me so that I could have searched his face for the answers which only the future would give me now.

POSSIBILITIES FOR WRITING

1. Analyze Baldwin's essay as a *narrative*, one with several strands that move backward and forward in time. To do so, you will first need to read and annotate carefully, picking out the main narrative line involving his father's death and funeral and the ride to the cemetery. You will need to look as well at the various incidents Baldwin narrates from earlier in his life and his report of the conflict that led to the rioting. How does he weave these together? How do the subsidiary stories contribute to the central narrative? Finally, explore how these narrative strands serve to embody Baldwin's central idea.

2. Much of "Notes of a Native Son" is a portrait of Baldwin's father and of the son's relationship to his father. In an essay focus specifically on this aspect of the piece. How do you interpret this complex, difficult man? In writing about him some ten years later (the essay was published in 1955), to what extent does Baldwin seem to have a different view of his father than he had at the time of his death?

3. "Hatred, which could destroy so much," Baldwin writes, "never failed to destroy the man who hated and this was an immutable law." Using this idea, along with the "two ideas which seemed to be in opposition" that Baldwin describes in his final paragraph, write an essay that explores your own ideas about how best to deal with bigotry and injustice.

Dave Barry (b. 1947), *a native of Armonk, New York, graduated from Haverford College. After ten years of working as a newspaper reporter and later as a business writing consultant, he began turning out a freelance humor column in 1980. He is now on the staff of the* Miami Herald, *and his popular column is syndicated in more than one hundred fifty papers around the country. Barry has published many collections of these columns, which often find irony and humor in the everyday circumstances of middle-class Americans; among his collections is* Dave Barry Is Not Taking This Sitting Down *(2000). Barry was awarded a Pulitzer Prize for commentary in 1988.*

DAVE BARRY

Road Warrior

In "Road Warrior," the humor columnist Dave Barry writes about the recently diagnosed quality of "road rage" that is said to afflict America's motorists. "Road rage" refers to the pent-up and explosively released anger and hostility that drivers feel and express in an era of increasing automobile traffic congestion and ever-increasing delays. Social analysts attribute driver "road rage" not only to all the additional cars and drivers clogging the roads, but also to a decline in civility that seems to many to afflict American society today.

Barry pokes fun at the drivers who flout the rules of the road, and in criticizing their misbehavior, he works himself up into a kind of rage, indicated by his use of CAPITAL LETTERS. In venting a bit over road rage, Barry segues into describing what he calls "Parking Lot Rage" and "Shopping Cart Rage," two forms of anger that push Barry's discussion of road rage into comic territory.

Barry has some fun as he describes the frustration that drivers feel when, looking for a parking space, they see someone sitting in a car, apparently ready to pull out, without finally doing so. They just sit there, leading, as Barry suggests, to "Parking Lot Rage." He also describes the congestion of shopping carts in supermarket aisles, which leads to still another kind of rage that Barry describes while offering up criticism of both the proliferation of product choices confronting supermarket patrons, and the automated telephone service—which leads to yet another kind of "rage." Barry's humor both describes these various reasons for anger and simultaneously defuses that anger.

If you do much driving on our nation's highways, you've probably noticed that, more and more often, bullets are coming through your windshield. This is a common sign of Road Rage, which the opinionmakers in the news media have decided is a serious problem, currently ranking just behind global warming and several points ahead of Asia.

How widespread is Road Rage? To answer that question, researchers for the National Institute of Traffic Safety recently did a study in which they drove on the interstate highway system in a specially equipped observation van. By the third day, they were deliberately running other motorists off the road.

"These people are MORONS!" was their official report.

That is the main cause of Road Rage: the realization that many of your fellow motorists have the same brain structure as a cashew. The most common example, of course, is the motorists who feel a need to drive in the left-hand, or "passing," lane, even though they are going slower than everybody else. Nobody knows why these motorists do this. Maybe they belong to some kind of religious cult that believes the right lane is sacred and must never come in direct contact with tires. Maybe one time, years ago, these motorists happened to be driving in the left lane when their favorite song came on the radio, so they've driven over there ever since, in hopes that the radio will play that song again.

But whatever makes these people drive this way, there's nothing you can do about it. You can honk at them, but it will have no effect. People have been honking at them for years: It's a normal part of their environment. They've decided that, for some mysterious reason, wherever they drive, there is honking. They choose not to ponder this mystery any further, lest they overburden their cashews.

I am very familiar with this problem, because I live and drive in Miami, which proudly bills itself as The Inappropriate-Lane-Driving Capital Of The World, a place where the left lane is thought of not so much as a thoroughfare as a public recreational area, where motorists feel free to stop, hold family reunions, barbecue pigs, play volleyball, etc. Compounding this problem is another common type of Miami motorist, the aggressive young male whose car has a sound system so powerful that the driver must go faster than the speed of sound at all times, because otherwise the nuclear bass notes emanating from his rear speakers will catch up to him and cause his head to explode.

So the tiny minority of us Miami drivers who actually qualify as normal find ourselves constantly being trapped behind people drifting along on the interstate at the speed of diseased livestock, while at the same time we are being tailgated and occasionally bumped from behind by testosterone-deranged youths who got their driver training from watching the space-fighter battle scenes in *Star Wars*. And of course nobody EVER signals or yields, and people are CONSTANTLY cutting us off, and AFTER A WHILE WE START TO FEEL SOME RAGE, OK? YOU GOT A PROBLEM WITH THAT, MISTER NEWS MEDIA OPINION-MAKER??

In addition to Road Rage, I frequently experience Parking Lot Rage, which occurs when I pull into a crowded supermarket parking lot, and I see people get into their car, clearly ready to leave, so I stop my car and wait for them to vacate the spot, and . . . nothing happens! They just stay there! WHAT THE HELL ARE THEY DOING IN THERE??!! COOKING DINNER???

When I finally get into the supermarket, I often experience Shopping Cart Rage. This is caused by the people—and you just KNOW these are the same people who always drive in the left-hand lane—who routinely manage, by careful placement, to block the entire aisle with a single shopping cart. If we really want to keep illegal immigrants from entering the United States, we should employ Miami residents armed with shopping carts; we'd only need about two dozen to block the entire Mexican border.

What makes the supermarket congestion even worse is that shoppers are taking longer and longer to decide what to buy, because every product in America now comes in an insane number of styles and sizes. For example, I recently went to the supermarket to get orange juice. For just *one brand* of orange juice, Tropicana, I had to decide whether I wanted Original, HomeStyle, Pulp Plus, Double Vitamin C, Grovestand, Calcium, or Old-Fashioned; I also had to decide whether I wanted the 16-ounce, 32-ounce, 64-ounce, 96-ounce, or six-pack size. This is WAY too many product choices. It caused me to experience Way Too Many Product Choices Rage. I would have called Tropicana and complained, but I probably would have wound up experiencing Automated Phone Answering System Rage. (". . . For questions about Pulp Plus in the 32-ounce size, press 23. For questions about Pulp Plus in the 64-ounce size, press 24. For questions about . . . .")

My point is that there are many causes for rage in our modern world, and if we're going to avoid unnecessary violence, we all need to "keep our cool." So let's try to be more considerate, OK? Otherwise I will kill you.

POSSIBILITIES FOR WRITING

1. Barry's point, he writes, is that "there are many causes for rage in our modern world, and if we're going to avoid unnecessary violence, we all need to 'keep our cool'." Use this idea as the basis for a more serious essay on the topic of controlling conflict and violence.

2. Write a comic essay about other sorts of behavior that can spark irritation or "rage." Don't be afraid to use exaggeration, as Barry does, but do so in ways that readers will find amusing rather than offensive.

3. Scan some newspapers or magazines for another recent social trend, being reported in the media. Examine this trend from your own perspective and using your own examples—either comically, as Barry does, or more seriously.

ROLAND BARTHES

Toys

In "Toys," Barthes meditates on the cultural significance of French toys, seeing them as a "microcosm" of the adult world. Barthes analyzes the social implications of French toys, arguing that it is no accident that toys reflect the "myths and techniques" of modern life. Toys, according to Barthes, epitomize what is socially important and culturally validated by the country in which they are produced and purchased.

A second area Barthes investigates concerns the forms and materials from which French toys are made. He considers the extent to which certain kinds of toys are imitative of actual life—girl's dolls that take in and eliminate water being one example. He contrasts such imitative toys with simple toys such as wooden blocks, which allow children to be more creative in their play.

French toys: one could not find a better illustration of the fact that the adult Frenchman sees the child as another self. All the toys one commonly sees are essentially a microcosm of the adult world; they are all reduced copies of human objects, as if in the eyes of the public the child was, all told, nothing but a smaller man, a homunculus to whom must be supplied objects of his own size.

Invented forms are very rare: a few sets of blocks, which appeal to the spirit of do-it-yourself, are the only ones which offer dynamic forms. As for the others, French toys *always mean something*, and this something is always entirely socialized, constituted by the myths or the techniques of modern adult life: the Army, Broadcasting, the Post Office, Medicine (miniature instrument-cases, operating theatres for dolls), School, Hair-Styling (driers for permanent-waving), the Air Force (Parachutists), Transport (trains, Citroëns, Vedettes, Vespas, petrol-stations), Science (Martian toys).

The fact that French toys *literally* prefigure the world of adult functions obviously cannot but prepare the child to accept them all, by constituting for him, even before he can think about it, the alibi of a Nature which has at all times created soldiers, postmen, and Vespas. Toys here reveal the list of all the things the adult does not find unusual: war, bureaucracy, ugliness, Martians, etc. It is not so much, in fact, the imitation which is the sign of an abdication, as its literalness: French toys are like a Jivaro head, in which one recognizes, shrunken to the size of an apple, the wrinkles and hair of an adult. There exist, for instance, dolls which urinate; they have an oesophagus, one gives them a bottle, they wet their nappies; soon, no doubt, milk will turn to water in their stomachs. This is meant to prepare the little girl for the causality of house-keeping, to "condition" her to her future role as mother. However, faced with this world of faithful and complicated objects, the child can only identify himself as owner, as user, never as creator; he does not invent the world, he uses it: there are, prepared for him, actions without adventure, without wonder, without joy. He is turned into a little stay-at-home householder who does not even have to invent the mainsprings of adult causality; they are supplied to him ready-made: he has only to help himself, he is never allowed to discover anything from start to finish. The merest set of blocks, provided it is not too refined, implies a very different learning of the world: then, the child does not in any way create meaningful objects, it matters little to him whether they have an adult name; the actions he performs are not those of a user but those of a demiurge. He creates forms which walk, which roll, he creates life, not property: objects now act by themselves, they are no longer an inert and complicated material in the palm of his hand. But such toys are rather rare: French toys are usually based on imitation, they are meant to produce children who are users, not creators.

The bourgeois status of toys can be recognized not only in their forms, which are all functional, but also in their substances. Current toys are made of a graceless material, the product of chemistry, not of nature. Many are now molded from complicated mixtures; the plastic material of which they are made has an appearance at once gross and hygienic, it destroys all the pleasure, the sweetness, the humanity of touch. A sign which fills one with consternation is the gradual disappearance of wood, in spite of its being an ideal material because of its firmness and its softness, and the natural warmth of its touch. Wood removes, from all the forms which it supports, the wounding quality of angles which are too sharp, the chemical coldness of metal. When the child handles it and knocks it, it neither vibrates nor grates, it has a sound at once muffled and sharp. It is a familiar and poetic substance, which does not sever the child from close contact with the tree, the table, the floor. Wood does not wound or break down; it does not shatter, it wears out, it can last a long time, live with the child, alter little by little the relations between the object and the hand. If it dies, it is in dwindling, not in swelling out like those mechanical toys which disappear behind the hernia of a broken spring. Wood makes essential objects, objects for all time. Yet there hardly remain any of these wooden toys from the Vosges, these fretwork farms with their animals, which were only possible, it is true, in the days of the craftsman. Henceforth, toys are chemical in substance and color; their very material introduces one to a coenaesthesis of use, not pleasure. These toys die in fact very quickly, and once dead, they have no posthumous life for the child.

POSSIBILITIES FOR WRITING

1. Barthes suggests that French toys "always mean something." Consider the examples he provides and identify just how and what they signify about French society and culture at the time the essay was written.
2. To what extent do you agree with Barthes that toys can stifle as well as stimulate creativity? What sorts of toys limit the imagination of children, and what kinds of toys help them develop their imaginative capacity? Why?
3. Write an essay in which you explore and analyze contemporary American toys and the extent to which they convey implications about American cultural and social life today. Or write an essay in which you analyze another aspect of American popular culture, such as fast food, wrestling, casino gambling, or video games, to explain how and what they reveal about American social and cultural life.

Sven Birkerts (b. 1951) is a literary critic and writing teacher. Birkerts has taught at Emerson and Bennington Colleges, at Mount Holyoke, Amherst, and Harvard. His essays and reviews have appeared in many journals, including the New York Times Book Review, Harper's, the Atlantic, the New Republic, and the New York Review of Books. He has published collections of essays on twentieth-century literature, a book of essays, Readings (1999), a memoir, My Sky Blue Trades (2002), and college textbooks on writing and studying literature. Currently editor of the journal Agni, Birkerts is best known for his 1994 book, The Gutenberg Elegies: The Fate of Reading in an Electronic Age.

SVEN BIRKERTS

Into the Electronic Millennium

In "Into the Electronic Millennium," Sven Birkerts takes aim at what were then, in 1994, recent developments in electronic culture. As Birkerts notes, the move toward electronic forms of information was well under way at that time and no longer even then the imaginings of an avant-garde. It's clear from the anecdotes he includes that Birkerts is both concerned with and upset about the developments and consequences of a rapidly rising electronic culture.

Birkerts compares the changes that occurred in the later twentieth century, when print began to be supplanted by electronic forms of communication, with the way written words came to dominate oral culture in ancient Greece, and then how print became the central and essential mode of communication with the advent of movable type and the invention of the printing press in the fifteenth century. He invites readers to imagine how the world was different fifty or a hundred years ago in an effort to convey just how significant a change has begun to occur with the development of electronic technologies, a change, he notes, that is resulting in a "reweaving" of society and culture.

Some years ago, a friend and I comanaged a used and rare book shop in Ann Arbor, Michigan. We were often asked to appraise and purchase libraries—by retiring academics, widows, and disgruntled graduate students. One day we took a call from a professor of English at one of the community colleges outside Detroit. When he answered the buzzer I did a double take—he looked to be only a year or two older than we were. "I'm selling everything," he said, leading the way through a large apartment. As he opened the door of his study I felt a nudge from my partner. The room was wall-to-wall books and as neat as a chapel.

The professor had a remarkable collection. It reflected not only the needs of his vocation—he taught nineteenth- and twentieth-century literature—but a book lover's sensibility as well. The shelves were strictly arranged, and the books themselves were in superb condition. When he left the room we set to work inspecting, counting, and estimating. This is always a delicate procedure, for the buyer is at once anxious to avoid insult to the seller and eager to get the goods for the best price. We adopted our usual strategy, working out a lower offer and a more generous fallback price. But there was no need to worry. The professor took our first offer without batting an eye.

As we boxed up the books, we chatted. My partner asked the man if he was moving. "No," he said, "but I am getting out." We both looked up. "Out of the teaching business, I mean. Out of books." He then said that he wanted to show us something. And indeed, as soon as the books were packed and loaded, he led us back through the apartment and down a set of stairs. When we reached the basement, he flicked on the light. There, on a long table, displayed like an exhibit in the Space Museum, was a computer. I didn't know what kind it was then, nor could I tell you now, fifteen years later. But the professor was keen to explain and demonstrate.

While he and my partner hunched over the terminal, I roamed to and fro, inspecting the shelves. It was purely a reflex gesture, for they held nothing but thick binders and paperbound manuals. "I'm changing my life," the ex-professor was saying. "This is definitely where it's all going to happen." He told us that he already had several good job offers. And the books? I asked. Why was he selling them all? He paused for a few beats. "The whole profession represents a lot of pain to me," he said. "I don't want to see any of these books again."

The scene has stuck with me. It is now a kind of marker in my mental life. That afternoon I got my first serious inkling that all was not well in the world of print and letters. All sorts of corroborations followed. Our professor was by no means an isolated case. Over a period of two years we met with several others like him. New men and new women who had glimpsed the future and had decided to get out while the getting was good. The selling off of books was sometimes done for financial reasons, but the need to burn bridges was usually there as well. It was as if heading to the future also required the destruction of tokens from the past.

A change is upon us—nothing could be clearer. The printed word is part of a vestigial order that we are moving away from—by choice and by societal compulsion. I'm not just talking about disaffected academics, either. This shift is happening throughout our culture, away from the patterns and habits of the printed page and toward a new world distinguished by its reliance on electronic communications.

This is not, of course, the first such shift in our long history. In Greece, in the time of Socrates, several centuries after Homer, the dominant oral culture was overtaken by the writing technology. And in Europe another epochal transition was effected in the late fifteenth century after Gutenberg invented movable type. In both cases the long-term societal effects were overwhelming, as they will be for us in the years to come.

The evidence of the change is all around us, though possibly in the manner of the forest that we cannot see for the trees. The electronic media, while conspicuous in gadgetry, are very nearly invisible in their functioning. They have slipped deeply and irrevocably into our midst, creating sluices and circulating through them. I'm not referring to any one product or function in isolation, such as television or fax machines or the networks that make them possible. I mean the interdependent totality that has arisen from the conjoining of parts—the disk drives hooked to modems, transmissions linked to technologies of reception, recording, duplication, and storage. Numbers and codes and frequencies. Buttons and signals. And this is no longer "the future," except for the poor or the self-consciously atavistic—it is now. . . .

To get a sense of the enormity of the change, you must force yourself to imagine—deeply and in nontelevisual terms—what the world was like a hundred, even fifty, years ago. If the feat is too difficult, spend some time with a novel from the period. Read between the lines and reconstruct. Move through the sequence of a character's day and then juxtapose the images and sensations you find with those in the life of the average urban or suburban dweller today.

Inevitably, one of the first realizations is that a communications net, a soft and pliable mesh woven from invisible threads, has fallen over everything. The so-called natural world, the place we used to live, which served us so long as the yardstick for all measurements, can now only be perceived through a scrim. Nature was then; this is now. Trees and rocks have receded. And the great geographical Other, the faraway rest of the world, has been transformed by the pure possibility of access. The numbers of distance and time no longer mean what they used to. Every place, once unique, itself, is strangely shot through with radiations from every other place. "There" was then; "here" is now. . . .

To underscore my point, I have been making it sound as if we were all abruptly walking out of one room and into another, leaving our books to the moths while we settle ourselves in front of our state-of-the-art terminals. The truth is that we are living through a period of overlap; one way of being is pushed athwart another. Antonio Gramsci's often-cited sentence comes inevitably to mind: "The crisis consists precisely in the fact that the old is dying and the new cannot be born; in this interregnum a great variety of morbid symptoms appears." The old surely is dying, but I'm not so sure that the new is having any great difficulty being born. As for the morbid symptoms, these we have in abundance.

The overlap in communications modes, and the ways of living that they are associated with, invites comparison with the transitional epoch in ancient Greek society, certainly in terms of the relative degree of disturbance. Historian Eric Havelock designated that period as one of "protoliteracy," of which his fellow scholar Oswyn Murray has written:

> To him [Havelock] the basic shift from oral to literate culture was a slow process; for centuries, despite the existence of writing, Greece remained essentially an oral culture. This culture was one which depended heavily on the encoding of information in poetic texts, to be learned by rote and to provide a cultural encyclopedia of conduct. It was not until the age of Plato in the fourth century that the dominance of poetry in an oral culture was challenged in the final triumph of literacy.

That challenge came in the form of philosophy, among other things, and poetry has never recovered its cultural primacy. What oral poetry was for the Greeks, printed books in general are for us. But our historical moment, which we might call "proto-electronic," will not require a transition period of two centuries. The very essence of electronic transmissions is to surmount impedances and to hasten transitions. Fifty years, I'm sure, will suffice. As for what the conversion will bring—and *mean*—to us, we might glean a few clues by looking to some of the "morbid symptoms" of the change. But to understand what these portend, we need to remark a few of the more obvious ways in which our various technologies condition our senses and sensibilities.

I won't tire my reader with an extended rehash of the differences between the print orientation and that of electronic systems. Media theorists from Marshall McLuhan to Walter Ong to Neil Postman have discoursed upon these at length. What's more, they are reasonably commonsensical. I therefore will abbreviate.

The order of print is linear, and is bound to logic by the imperatives of syntax. Syntax is the substructure of discourse, a mapping of the ways that the mind makes sense through language. Print communication requires the active engagement of the reader's attention, for reading is fundamentally an act of translation. Symbols are turned into their verbal referents and these are in turn interpreted. The print engagement is essentially private. While it does represent an act of communication, the contents pass from the privacy of the sender to the privacy of the receiver. Print also posits a time axis; the turning of pages, not to mention the vertical descent down the page, is a forward-moving succession, with earlier contents at every point serving as a ground for what follows. Moreover, the printed material is static—it is the reader, not the book, that moves forward. The physical arrangements of print are in accord with our traditional sense of history. Materials are layered; they lend themselves to rereading and to sustained attention. The pace of reading is variable, with progress determined by the reader's focus and comprehension.

The electronic order is in most ways opposite. Information and contents do not simply move from one private space to another, but they travel along a network. Engagement is intrinsically public, taking place within a circuit of larger connectedness. The vast resources of the network are always there, potential, even if they do not impinge on the immediate communication. Electronic communication can be passive, as with television watching, or interactive, as with computers. Contents, unless they are printed out (at which point they become part of the static order of print) are felt to be evanescent. They can be changed or deleted with the stroke of a key. With visual media (television, projected graphs, highlighted "bullets"), impression and image take precedence over logic and concept, and detail and linear sequentiality are sacrificed. The pace is rapid, driven by jump-cut increments, and the basic movement is laterally associative rather than vertically cumulative. The presentation structures the reception and, in time, the expectation about how information is organized.

Further, the visual and nonvisual technology in every way encourages in the user a heightened and ever-changing awareness of the present. It works against historical perception, which must depend on the inimical notions of logic and sequential succession. If the print medium exalts the word, fixing it into permanence, the electronic counterpart reduces it to a signal, a means to an end.

Transitions like the one from print to electronic media do not take place without rippling or, more likely, *reweaving* the entire social and cultural web. The tendencies outlined above are already at work. We don't need to look far to find their effects. We can begin with the newspaper headlines and the millennial lamentations sounded in the op-ed pages: that our educational systems are in decline; that our students are less and less able to read and comprehend their required texts, and that their aptitude scores have leveled off well below those of previous generations. Tag-line communication, called "bite-speak" by some, is destroying the last remnants of political discourse; spin doctors and media consultants are our new shamans. As communications empires fight for control of all information outlets, including publishers, the latter have succumbed to the tyranny of the bottom line; they are less and less willing to publish work, however worthy, that will not make a tidy profit. And, on every front, funding for the arts is being cut while the arts themselves appear to be suffering a deep crisis of relevance. And so on.

Every one of these developments is, of course, overdetermined, but there can be no doubt that they are connected, perhaps profoundly, to the transition that is underway.

Certain other trends bear watching. One could argue, for instance, that the entire movement of postmodernism in the arts is a consequence of this same macroscopic shift. For what is postmodernism at root but an aesthetic that rebukes the idea of an historical time line, as well as previously uncontested assumptions of cultural hierarchy. The postmodern artifact manipulates its stylistic signatures like Lego blocks and makes free with combinations from the formerly sequestered spheres of high and popular art. Its combinatory momentum and relentless referencing of the surrounding culture mirror perfectly the associative dynamics of electronic media.

One might argue likewise, that the virulent debate within academia over the canon and multiculturalism may not be a simple struggle between the entrenched ideologies of white male elites and the forces of formerly disenfranchised gender, racial, and cultural groups. Many of those who would revise the canon (or end it altogether) are trying to outflank the assumption of historical tradition itself. The underlying question, avoided by many, may be not only whether the tradition is relevant, but whether it might not be too taxing a system for students to comprehend. Both the traditionalists and the progressives have valid arguments, and we must certainly have sympathy for those who would try to expose and eradicate the hidden assumptions of bias in the Western tradition. But it also seems clear that this debate could only have taken the form it has in a society that has begun to come loose from its textual moorings. To challenge repression is salutary. To challenge history itself, proclaiming it to be simply an archive of repressions and justifications, is idiotic.*...

A collective change of sensibility may already be upon us. We need to take seriously the possibility that the young truly "know no other way," that they are not made of the same stuff that their elders are. In her *Harper's* magazine debate with Neil Postman, Camille Paglia observed:

> *Some people have more developed sensoriums than others. I've found that most people born before World War II are turned off by the modern media. They can't understand how we who were born after the war can read and watch TV at the same time. But we can. When I wrote my book, I had earphones on, blasting rock music or Puccini and Brahms. The soap operas—with the sound turned down—flickered on my TV. I'd be talking on the phone at the same time. Baby boomers have a multilayered, multitrack ability to deal with the world.*

I don't know whether to be impressed or depressed by Paglia's ability to disperse her focus in so many directions. Nor can I say, not having read her book, in what ways her multitrack sensibility has informed her prose. But I'm baffled by what she means when she talks about an ability to "deal with the world." From the context, "dealing" sounds more like a matter of incessantly repositioning the self within a barrage of on-rushing stimuli....

My final exhibit—I don't know if it qualifies as a morbid symptom as such—is drawn from a *Washington Post Magazine* essay on the future of the Library of Congress, our national shrine to the printed word. One of the individuals interviewed in the piece is Robert Zich, so-called "special projects czar" of the institution. Zich, too, has seen the future, and he is surprisingly candid with his interlocutor. Before long, Zich maintains, people will be able to get what information they want directly off their terminals. The function of the Library of Congress

---

*The outcry against the modification of the canon can be seen as a plea for old reflexes and routines. And the cry for multicultural representation may be a last-ditch bid for connection to the fading legacy of print. The logic is simple. When a resource is threatened—made scarce—people fight over it. In this case the struggle is over textual power in an increasingly nontextual age. The future of books and reading is what is at stake, and a dim intuition of this drives the contending factions.

As Katha Pollitt argued so shrewdly in her much-cited article in *The Nation*: If we were a nation of readers, there would be no issue. No one would be arguing about whether to put Toni Morrison on the syllabus because her work would be a staple of the reader's regular diet anyway. These lists are suddenly so important because they represent, very often, the only serious works that the student is ever likely to be exposed to. Whoever controls the lists comes out ahead in the struggle for the hearts and minds of the young.

(and perhaps libraries in general) will change. He envisions his library becoming more like a museum: "Just as you go to the National Gallery to see its Leonardo or go to the Smithsonian to see the Spirit of St. Louis and so on, you will want to go to libraries to see the Gutenberg or the original printing of Shakespeare's plays or to see Lincoln's hand-written version of the Gettysburg Address."

Zich is outspoken, voicing what other administrators must be thinking privately. The big research libraries, he says, "and the great national libraries and their buildings will go the way of the railroad stations and the movie palaces of an earlier era which were really vital institutions in their time.... Somehow folks moved away from that when the technology changed."

And books? Zich expresses excitement about Sony's hand-held electronic book, and a miniature encyclopedia coming from Franklin Electronic Publishers. "Slip it in your pocket," he says. "Little keyboard, punch in your words and it will do the full text searching and all the rest of it. Its limitation, of course, is that it's devoted just to that one book." Zich is likewise interested in the possibility of memory cards. What he likes about the Sony product is the portability: one machine, a screen that will display the contents of whatever electronic card you feed it.

I cite Zich's views at some length here because he is not some Silicon Valley research and development visionary, but a highly placed executive at what might be called, in a very literal sense, our most conservative public institution. When men like Zich embrace the electronic future, we can be sure it's well on its way.

Others might argue that the technologies cited by Zich merely represent a modification in the "form" of reading, and that reading itself will be unaffected, as there is little difference between following words on a pocket screen or a printed page. Here I have to hold my line. The context cannot but condition the process. Screen and book may exhibit the same string of words, but the assumptions that underlie their significance are entirely different depending on whether we are staring at a book or a circuit-generated text. As the nature of looking—at the natural world, at paintings—changed with the arrival of photography and mechanical reproduction, so will the collective relation to language alter as new modes of dissemination prevail.

Whether all of this sounds dire or merely "different" will depend upon the reader's own values and priorities. I find these portents of change depressing, but also exhilarating—at least to speculate about. On the one hand, I have a great feeling of loss and a fear about what habitations will exist for self and soul in the future. But there is also a quickening, a sense that important things are on the line. As Heraclitus once observed, "The mixture that is not shaken soon stagnates." Well, the mixture is being shaken, no doubt about it. And here are some of the kinds of developments we might watch for as our "proto-electronic" era yields to an all-electronic future:

1. *Language erosion.* There is no question but that the transition from the culture of the book to the culture of electronic communication will radically alter the ways in which we use language on every societal level. The complexity and distinctiveness of spoken and written expression, which are deeply bound to traditions of print literacy, will gradually be replaced by a more telegraphic sort of "plainspeak." Syntactic masonry is already a dying art. Neil Postman and others have already suggested what losses have been incurred by the advent of telegraphy and television—how the complex discourse patterns of the nineteenth century were flattened by the requirements of communication over distances. That tendency runs riot as the layers of mediation thicken. Simple linguistic prefab is now the norm, while ambiguity, paradox, irony, subtlety, and wit are fast disappearing. In their place, the simple "vision thing" and myriad other "things." Verbal intelligence, which has long been viewed as suspect as the act of reading, will come to seem positively conspiratorial. The greater part of any articulate person's energy will be deployed in dumbing-down her discourse.

Language will grow increasingly impoverished through a series of vicious cycles. For, of course, the usages of literature and scholarship are connected in fundamental ways to the general speech of the tribe. We can expect that curricula will be further streamlined, and difficult texts in the humanities will be pruned and glossed. One need only compare a college textbook from twenty years ago to its contemporary version. A poem by Milton, a play by Shakespeare—one can hardly find the text among the explanatory notes nowadays. Fewer and fewer people will be able to contend with the so-called masterworks of literature or ideas. Joyce, Woolf, Soyinka, not to mention the masters who preceded them, will go unread, and the civilizing energies of their prose will circulate aimlessly between closed covers.

2. *Flattening of historical perspectives.* As the circuit supplants the printed page, and as more and more of our communications involve us in network processes—which of their nature plant us in a perpetual present—our perception of history will inevitably alter. Changes in information storage and access are bound to impinge on our historical

memory. The depth of field that is our sense of the past is not only a linguistic construct, but is in some essential way represented by the book and the physical accumulation of books in library spaces. In the contemplation of the single volume, or mass of volumes, we form a picture of time past as a growing deposit of sediment; we capture a sense of its depth and dimensionality. Moreover, we meet the past as much in the presentation of words in books of specific vintage as we do in any isolated fact or statistic. The database, useful as it is, expunges this context, this sense of chronology, and admits us to a weightless order in which all information is equally accessible....

3. *The waning of the private self.* We may even now be in the first stages of a process of social collectivization that will over time all but vanquish the ideal of the isolated individual. For some decades now we have been edging away from the perception of private life as something opaque, closed off to the world; we increasingly accept the transparency of a life lived within a set of systems, electronic or otherwise. Our technologies are not bound by season or light—it's always the same time in the circuit. And so long as time is money and money matters, those circuits will keep humming. The doors and walls of our habitations matter less and less—the world sweeps through the wires as it needs to, or as we need it to. The monitor light is always blinking; we are always potentially on-line.

I am not suggesting that we are all about to become mindless, soulless robots, or that personality will disappear altogether into an oceanic homogeneity. But certainly the idea of what it means to be a person living a life will be much changed. The figure-ground model, which has always featured a solitary self before a background that is the society of other selves, is romantic in the extreme. It is ever less tenable in the world as it is becoming. There are no more wildernesses, no more lonely homesteads, and, outside of cinema, no more emblems of the exalted individual.

The self must change as the nature of subjective space changes. And one of the many incremental transformations of our age has been the slow but steady destruction of subjective space. The physical and psychological distance between individuals has been shrinking for at least a century. In the process, the figure-ground image has begun to blur its boundary distinctions. One day we will conduct our public and private lives within networks so dense, among so many channels of instantaneous information, that it will make almost no sense to speak of the differentiations of subjective individualism.

We are already captive in our webs. Our slight solitudes are transected by codes, wires, and pulsations. We punch a number to check in with the answering machine, another to tape a show that we are too busy to watch. The strands of the web grow finer and finer—this is obvious. What is no less obvious is the fact that they will continue to proliferate, gaining in sophistication, merging functions so that one can bank by phone, shop via television, and so on. The natural tendency is toward streamlining: The smart dollar keeps finding ways to shorten the path, double-up the function. We might think in terms of a circuit-board model, picturing ourselves as the contact points. The expansion of electronic options is always at the cost of contractions in the private sphere. We will soon be navigating with ease among cataracts of organized pulsations, putting out and taking in signals. We will bring our terminals, our modems, and menus further and further into our former privacies; we will implicate ourselves by degrees in the unitary life, and there may come a day when we no longer remember that there was any other life....

Trafficking with tendencies—extrapolating and projecting as I have been doing—must finally remain a kind of gambling. One bets high on the validity of a notion and low on the human capacity for resistance and for unpredictable initiatives. No one can really predict how we will adapt to the transformations taking place all around us. We may discover, too, that language is a hardier thing than I have allowed. It may flourish among the beep and the click and the monitor as readily as it ever did on the printed page. I hope so, for language is the soul's ozone layer and we thin it at our peril.

POSSIBILITIES FOR WRITING

1. Identify the anecdotes that Birkerts includes as part of his essay, and explain his purpose in using each. Consider the extent to which they are useful to Birkerts in making his point about the development of electronic culture.

2. Summarize the three main consequences that Birkerts foresees as outcomes of the rise of an electronic culture and its dominance of print. Consider the extent to which you agree with his assessment.

3. Reflect on your own use of computer technology and your reliance on print culture. Write an essay in which you explore Birkerts's ideas in light of your personal experience, your observation of others, and your reading.

Judy Brady (b. 1937) *was born in San Francisco and attended the University of Iowa, graduating with a B.A. in 1962. A feminist and political activist, she edited* Women and Cancer (1990) *and* 1 in 3: Women with Cancer Confront an Epidemic *(1991). Her essays and articles have appeared in Greenpeace magazine and in the* Women's Review of Books. *Her best known essay is "I Want a Wife."*

JUDY BRADY

I Want a Wife

"I Want a Wife" first appeared in the feminist magazine *Ms.*, in its preview issue in 1972, under the name Judy Syfers, Brady's married name. The essay was twice reprinted in the magazine, in 1979 and in 1990. And it has been a popular and frequently anthologized piece for three decades.

A large part of the essay's appeal and power derives from its wit and irony. Part derives from its humor and part from its style, particularly its use of repetition. But its biggest draw for many readers is the truths it tells in characterizing the endless work of a wife as she provides every imaginable service for her husband and children.

I belong to that classification of people known as wives. I am a Wife. And, not altogether incidentally, I am a mother.

Not too long ago a male friend of mine appeared on the scene fresh from a recent divorce. He had one child, who is, of course, with his ex-wife. He is obviously looking for another wife. As I thought about him while I was ironing one evening, it suddenly occurred to me that I, too, would like to have a wife. Why do I want a wife?

I would like to go back to school so that I can become economically independent, support myself, and, if need be, support those dependent upon me. I want a wife who will work and send me to school. And while I am going to school I want a wife to take care of my children. I want a wife to keep track of the children's doctor and dentist appointments. And to keep track of mine, too. I want a wife to make sure my children eat properly and are kept clean. I want a wife who will wash the children's clothes and keep them mended. I want a wife who is a good nurturant attendant to my children, who arranges for their schooling, makes sure that they have an adequate social life with their peers, takes them to the park, the zoo, etc. I want a wife who takes care of the children when they are sick, a wife who arranges to be around when the children need special care, because, of course, I cannot miss classes at school. My wife must arrange to lose time at work and not lose the job. It may mean a small cut in my wife's income from time to time, but I guess I can tolerate that. Needless to say, my wife will arrange and pay for the care of the children while my wife is working.

I want a wife who will take care of *my* physical needs. I want a wife who will keep my house clean. A wife who will pick up after me. I want a wife who will keep my clothes clean, ironed, mended, replaced when need be, and who will see to it that my personal things are kept in their proper place so that I can find what I need the minute I need it. I want a wife who cooks the meals, a wife who is a *good* cook. I want a wife who will plan the menus, do the necessary grocery shopping, prepare the meals, serve them pleasantly, and then do the cleaning up while I do my studying. I want a wife who will care for me when I am sick and sympathize with my pain and loss of time from school. I want a wife to go along when our family takes a vacation so that someone can continue to care for me and my children when I need a rest and change of scene.

I want a wife who will not bother me with rambling complaints about a wife's duties. But I want a wife who will listen to me when I feel the need to explain a rather difficult point I have come across in my course of studies. And I want a wife who will type my papers for me when I have written them.

I want a wife who will take care of the details of my social life. When my wife and I are invited out by my friends, I want a wife who will take care of the babysitting arrangements. When I meet people at school that I like and want to entertain, I want a wife who will have the house clean, will prepare a special meal, serve it to me and my friends, and not interrupt when I talk about the things that interest me and my friends. I want a wife who will have arranged that the children are fed and ready for bed before my guests arrive so that the children do not bother us. I want a wife who takes care of the needs of my guests so that they feel comfortable, who makes sure that they have an ashtray, that they are passed the hors d'oeuvres, that they are offered a second helping of the food, that their wine glasses are replenished when necessary, that their coffee is served to them as they like it. And I want a wife who knows that sometimes I need a night out by myself.

I want a wife who is sensitive to my sexual needs, a wife who makes love passionately and eagerly when I feel like it, a wife who makes sure that I am satisfied. And, of course, I want a wife who will not demand sexual attention when I am not in the mood for it. I want a wife who assumes the complete responsibility for birth control, because I do not want more children. I want a wife who will remain sexually faithful to me so that I do not have to clutter up my intellectual life with jealousies. And I want a wife who understands that *my* sexual needs may entail more than strict adherence to monogamy. I must, after all, be able to relate to people as fully as possible.

If, by chance, I find another person more suitable as a wife than the wife I already have, I want the liberty to replace my present wife with another one. Naturally, I will expect a fresh, new life; my wife will take the children and be solely responsible for them so that I am left free.

When I am through with school and have a job, I want my wife to quit working and remain at home so that my wife can more fully and completely take care of a wife's duties.

My God, who *wouldn't* want a wife?

POSSIBILITIES FOR WRITING

1. How does Brady define what it means to be a "wife"? How does she organize the many services a wife provides her husband and family? What do you think of Brady's characterization of a wife and her responsibilities? How do you think she wants her readers to respond to this characterization? Why?

2. Write a letter to Brady responding to "I Want a Wife." Let her know what you admire or don't admire about the essay and the extent to which you consider it effective and/or persuasive.

3. Write your own piece entitled "I Want a/an X." You can use Brady's essay as a model, and in the process, imitate some of her stylistic techniques. Or, alternatively, write an essay about the role of a "wife" in the early twenty-first century, explaining how a wife's responsibilities complement and are complemented by those of a spouse.

Jane Brox (b. 1956) *grew up on a farm near the small town of Dracut, Massachusetts. Brox is noted primarily for her poetry and essays, and her work has appeared in* Georgia Review, Salamander, *and* Hudson Review, *as well as* The Best American Essays of 1996. *She has also published* Here and Nowhere Else: Late Seasons of a Farm and Its Family (1995) *and* Five Thousand Days Like This One (1999).

JANE BROX

Influenza 1918

In her essay "Influenza 1918," originally published in the *Georgia Review*, Jane Brox describes the epidemic of influenza, or flu, that took the lives of hundreds of thousands of people around the world. To convey a sense of just what this epidemic was like, Brox focuses on the small farming community of Lawrence, Massachusetts, where she grew up. Brox takes us close to the people whose lives were at first disrupted and then devastated by the outbreak of the disease. She makes us care about these local people by putting them before us through carefully controlled descriptive detail.

By zeroing in closely on the commonplace lives of ordinary people in an unexceptional place, Brox is able to suggest the immensity of the human tragedy the influenza epidemic wrought. She brings us into the streets of the town where the flu was raging. She takes us behind the closed doors of houses, where entire families were suffering, many to die while tended by each other, and still others to succumb to the inevitable onslaught of the disease in the makeshift hospital tent the town constructed on Tower Hill. Making the past present, Brox writes a kind of "you are there" history with immediacy and power.

In ordinary times, the bankers, lawyers, and mill owners who lived on Tower Hill opened their doors to a quiet broken only by the jostle of a laden milk wagon, the first stirrings of a wind in the elms, or the quavering notes of a sparrow. It was the height of country; the air, sweet and clear. Looking east from their porches they could survey miles of red-brick textile mills that banked the canals and the sluggish Merrimack, as well as the broad central plain mazed with tenements. To their west was a patchwork of small dairy holdings giving over to the blue distance. But for the thirty-one mornings of October 1918 those men adjusted gauze masks over their mouths and noses as they set out for work in the cold-tinged dawn, and they kept their eyes to the ground so as not to see what they couldn't help but hear: the clatter of motorcars and horse-drawn wagons over the paving stones, as day and night without ceasing the ambulances ran up the hill bringing sufferers from the heart of the city and the hearses carried them away.

It had started as a seemingly common thing—what the line-storm season always brings, born on its wind and on our breath, something that would run its course in the comfort of camphor and bed rest. At first there had been no more than six or eight or ten cases a day reported in the city, and such news hardly took up a side column in the papers, which were full of soldiers' obituaries and reports of a weakening Germany. As September wore on, however, the death notices of victims of the flu began to outnumber the casualties of war. Finally it laid low so many the Lawrence Board of Health set aside its usual work of granting permits to keep roosters, charting the milk supply, and inspecting tenements. The flu took up all its talk—how it was to be treated, how contained, how to stay ahead of the dead. The sufferers needed fresh air and isolation, and their care had to be consolidated to make the most of the scarce nurses and orderlies. So the board took a page from other stricken cities and voted to construct a makeshift tent hospital on their highest, most open land that offered the best air, which was the leeward side of Tower Hill where a farm still spread across the slope.

Lawrence, Massachusetts, in 1918 was largely a city of immigrants who had come for work in the textile mills. Most had been in the city for only a short time and still spoke Polish, Arabic, French, Italian, German—forty-five different languages and dialects within the few square miles of the central district. They made worsteds and woolens; they were dyers, cutters, and weavers. They fixed the looms, rigged the warps, and felt along the yardage for slubs, working more than fifty hours a week, breathing in air white with cloth dust. At home they breathed in the smells of rubbish and night soil that drifted up from the alleyways between tenements. Where they lived was low-lying, so such smells, together with smoke and ash, hung in the air. Their heat was sparse. They were crowded into their rooms. The flu cut right through, spreading ahead of its own rumors, passing on a handshake and on the wind and with the lightest kiss. No spitting. No sharing food. Keep your hands clean. Avoid crowds. Walk everywhere. Sleep with your windows open.

They slept to the sound of rain—rain pouring from their gutterless roofs turning the alleyways into thick mud, rain on the wandering hens pecking at stones in the streets, rain on the silenced pigeons puffed and caged in their coops. At times it was hard, driven from the north like mare's hooves on their roofs, drowning the parsley and oregano set in enamel basins on the window ledges. Other times it fell soft and fine out of a pale gray sky, making circles fragile as wrists on the surfaces of the canals before being lost to the brown, frothy water there. And sometimes it was no more than a mist that settled in the low places, obscuring the bottoms of the stairwells and the barrels and the piles of sawdust, only to shift and reveal the same world as always. Then the rain would gather its strength again, seeming to rake their lives all that much harder. Scrap coal couldn't keep away its chill.

A doctor may as well have gone house to house down Common, Haverhill, and Jackson streets, so numerous were the cases. Often his knock would go unanswered, since it wasn't the family who had sought him out. More likely the sickness had been reported by their landlord or neighbor—afraid that the influenza would spread—so the doctor heard a sudden silence within and a face at the window disappearing into shadow. What kept the families from responding wasn't a lack of a common language so much as the fear that the doctor would tack a card to the door warning of the infection within, and the greater fear that their sick children would be ordered to the tent hospital. Once there, they wouldn't be seen again until they were dead or cured.

When the doctor finally gained entrance—at times with the help of the police—he could find whole families had been laid low, with the sick tending those who were sicker. They had sacks of camphor around their necks, or mustard spread on their chests, a cup of chamomile by the cot. Whiskey, Garlic and onions weighed in the air. Some sufferers lay in windowless rooms where the damp had kept in the smoke from a low coal fire, and what light there was wavered from a kerosene lamp. Almost always the disease had gone beyond a cough and aches and a runny nose. There was blood mixed in with their phlegm, and they couldn't move from their beds. In the worst cases their skin was tinted blue.

One doctor could see hundreds of cases a day, and in his haste to complete his records, he sometimes left out the ages of the victims and often the names. They come down now in the *Influenza Journal* distinguished only by their address or their nationality: *four Cases, 384 Common Street (downstairs)*. Or: *Mother and Child. Baby Rossano. Father and Son. A Syrian fellow. Polish man.* When the rain finally let up and days of mist lifted to bring on clear dry air, the number of influenza cases still didn't slow. Every woman who gave birth, it seems, died. The elderly, schoolchildren, and infants, yes—but strangest of all was how it took the young and healthy who had never been sick in their lives. Just yesterday they had worked a full day.

The entrance to the tent hospital on Tower Hill was clotted with ambulances arriving with patients and standing ambulances awaiting their dispatch orders. Many were still horse drawn, and the mares stood uneasy in the confusion. The motorized cars idled and choked the air with gasoline, the tang of which overlay the warm, familiar smells of hay and animal sweat. Everyone wore gauze masks, and there was no talk but orders. *Don't back up. Bring that one over here.* Nurses checked the pulse and color of patients and listened to their lungs. *We need more masks. Find me a doctor. Help me with this one.* The gate was patrolled by a military guard to assure that only the sufferers and those who tended them went beyond. Waiting black hacks stood three deep.

Every day at 5 A.M. a soldier blew reveille. The quick, bright notes parted the confusion at the entrance and gleamed above the hospital grounds—a far call from a country those patients no longer came from. The general din at the gate may as well have been the sound of a market day in a port city, and they, drowsing on a ship that had pulled away. They didn't stir. It was no concern of theirs, each in his or her own tent, the tent flap open to the back of a neighboring tent. Tents were arranged in rows, in wards, and in precincts, making a grid of the old hayfield. Its crickets were silent. Its summer birds had flown. Electrical wires hung on make-shift poles, and you could hear them swaying in the storms. The soaked canvas flanks of the tents ballooned in a wind and settled back on their frames. Boardwalks had been laid down between the tents, and footfalls, softened by the drenched wood, came near and receded. The nuns' habits swished. What country was this? A cough. A groan. The stricken tossed in their fevers. Their muscles ached. One moment they had the sweats; the next, chills. In forty-five different languages and dialects they called for water and warmth.

Many were cared for in words they couldn't understand. The student nurses and sisters of Saint Jeanne d'Arc spoke both English and French, but to the Germans and Italians and Syrians their voices may just as well have been more soft rain. A face half covered with gauze leaned near their own. They were given water to drink. Cool cloths were placed on their brows. They were wrapped in blankets and wheeled outside for more air. Someone listened to their hearts and then to their bogged-down lungs. A spoonful of thick serum was lifted to their lips. Their toes and fingertips turned blue from a lack of oxygen. In many pneumonia set in.

It was the same suffering in each tent, in each ward, in each precinct of the hospital. And the same in the surrounding country, in all cities, in all the known nations of the world. It struck those already stricken with war in the military camps, the troop ships, the trenches, in the besieged villages along the Meuse, in the devastated plain called the Somme, in the Argonne woods. It struck those who knew nothing of the war—all the Eskimos in a remote outpost, villagers in China. Some died without having given it a name. Others called it "the grippe," the flu—influenza—meaning "under the influence of the stars," under Orion and the Southern Cross, under the Bear, the Pole Star, and the Pleiades.

When care failed in the Tower Hill hospital, the sisters of Saint Jeanne d'Arc closed the eyes of the dead, blessed the body in the language that they knew, blessed themselves, and closed the tent flap. The sisters on the next shift said a last prayer in front of each closed tent and turned to the living.

In the central city those who were spared became captive to a strange, altered music. All the sounds of their streets—voices and songs, teams hauling loads over paving stones, elm whips cracking the air and animals, bottles nudging one another in the back of a truck, the deliberate tread of the iceman on their stairs—all these were no longer heard. Or they weren't heard as usual. Survivors strained at the absence, as if they were listening for flowing water after a cold snap, water now trapped and nearly silenced by clear ice. Schools and movie houses had been ordered closed and bolted shut; public gatherings were curtailed. Workers, their numbers halved, walked down Essex Street to the mills in a slackened ribbon. Their tamped-down gossip touched only on who had been stricken, who had died in the night. They traded preventions and cures, some wearing masks, others with garlic hung around their necks. More pronounced than the usual smells of the fouled canals or lanolin or grease were the head-clearing scents of camphor and carbolic soap.

The flow of supply wagons slowed as well. There was no commerce in bolts of velvet, silk puffs, worsted suits, or pianos. Bakers who used to shape one hundred granary loaves a day—split and seeded and washed with a glaze of milk—took to preparing fifty or sixty unadorned loaves. In the corner groceries, scab spread on the early apple crop, grapes softened then soured, and pears turned overripe in their crates.

The absence filled with uncommon sounds. Children with nowhere to go played in the streets and in the parks as if it were another kind of summer. They sang their jump-rope songs and called out sides in the letups between rains. The pharmacies swarmed with customers looking for Vaporub, germicide, and ice. And all the carpenters—whether they had formerly spent their days roughing out tenements or carving details into table legs—had turned to making pine boxes. Their sawing and the sound of bright nails driving into soft wood could be heard long into the night. Even so, coffins remained scarce and expensive.

The streets running up to Tower Hill rushed with ambulances, police cars, and fire engines. The alleyways and side streets were clogged with passing funerals. Meager corteges were everywhere—there, out of the corner of an eye, or coming straight on. In hopes of slowing the spread of the epidemic, the board of health had limited the size of the funerals to one carriage. They prohibited church services for the dead, and forbade anyone other than the immediate family to accompany the coffin. So, a black hack or a utility wagon with a loose knot of mourners following on foot behind was all. Some of the grieving were sick themselves, some barely recovered, and they had trouble keeping up if the hack driver was proceeding faster than he should—there were so many, had been so many, and someone else was waiting for his services. The processions appeared to be blown by a directionless wind down home streets past the millworks and across the bridge to the burial grounds on the outskirts of the city.

The mourners entered a place starred with freshly closed graves and open graves with piles of earth next to them—clay, sea-worn gravel, sodden sandy loam. The gravediggers kept on shoveling—they had long stopped looking up from their work. Even so, they couldn't stay ahead, and most of the coffins had to be escorted to the yard and left near the entrance along with others to await a later burial. Few of the processions were accompanied by ministers or priests. The parents or children or sisters of the deceased bowed their heads and said their own prayers. Perhaps they threw a handful of earth on the set-aside box. Maybe they lay a clutch of asters on the top. So plain and unsacred, it may just as well have been a death in the wilderness. Small. A winter spider crawling across an old white wall.

"We knew it was serious, but we didn't know how serious," my father says. The farm is less than five miles to the west of Lawrence, but by the time news reached here, it was muted and slowed—no more than a rumor on the sea winds biting in from Cape Ann. Their eastward view was open then, and they could see the leeward slope of Tower Hill, though it was far enough away to appear plainly blue. On the first of October 1918 they woke to see the flanks of those white canvas tents set in columns and rows across the hill. And that night the horizon was so crowded with lights that it must have seemed as if the heart of the city had grown closer.

As in the city, whole families on some farms were stricken, others spared. His family was spared—all he knew of the flu then was white chips of camphor in an old sock around his neck, and his mother whispering to his father in the evenings: "You'll bring it here. . . . " His aunt and uncle, who had a nearby farm, and his cousins all came down with it in turn. It had begun when his uncle, for all his old strength, just couldn't get up. His aunt cared for him, until the whole household was confined to their beds. No doctor came. My grandfather, after he had tended his own herd, saw to theirs—to their water and grain, as well as the milking. He drew water for the house and brought them bread. He'd light the fires and bring in a day's supply of wood. Even so, with the windows open the rooms felt as cold as quarried granite.

The last to contract it, the youngest boy, died. The parents, still weak, were slow to perform the offices of the strong. They washed the body and had to rest. It seemed to take most of a day to make a respectable, small pine coffin. They cleaned the front room, set the coffin in the bay window, and took their turns sitting beside it. Not even small things were the same. Not the rust-colored chrysanthemums blooming against the kitchen door. Not the lingering fragrance of thyme and mint in the yard.

And the large things to be done—the work that had waited all through their sickness—waited still and weighed heavier. It was late enough in the year so that the weeding didn't matter anymore. But carrots, potatoes, and cabbages had to be harvested and stored. Wood to be gotten in. The late apple tree was laden with fruit—Ben Davis apples would cling to the branches all winter if you let them. Enough work to fill their days for as long as they could foresee.

There are two small, walled-in graveyards in the middle of our farm. They seem odd and adrift now among our fields and woods, though in the early part of this century there had been a Protestant church adjoining them. It was pulled down for salvage sométime in the forties, and its granite steps are now my parents' doorstone. My father sits on one of the pews when he pulls off his work boots. He will be buried among those graves, just up the hill behind a white birch. But in those years only the names of the settlers—Richardson, Coburn, Clough—had been chiseled into the stones. It wasn't a place for recent immigrants to be buried, so his uncle's family walked behind the coffin to

Lawrence and set their child beside all the recent victims in the city. The mounds of earth beside the open graves were composed of heavier and stonier soils than any they had cultivated in the arid land they had been born to. Impossible to return to that country now, though they said their words in Arabic before turning west out of the gate.

For another week after the funeral they could still see the tents, white in the new days, just like yesterday. Then at the end of October the epidemic broke, the fires were banked. The tent hospital was taken down in a driving rain, and the stricken were moved to winter quarters at the General Hospital. At night Tower Hill once again appeared darker than the night sky. Predictable quiet returned to the neighborhood of mill owners, bankers, lawyers. The schools opened again, then the theaters. The policemen and firemen took off their gauze masks. On the twelfth of November, even the Red Cross workers marched in the Victory Day parade. When the city looked up, they counted more dead of the flu than of the war.

The winter of 1918 was so cold that the water over the Lawrence dam froze and had to be dynamited. The following spring, the field where the tent hospital had stood was seeded in hay. It was mown three times that summer and winds swept the timothy and redtop. Here, after the child had become bone, a liturgy was said for him. A child whose life is no longer given a name or a length, so short it is remembered by the one fact of his death.

It is a summer evening, and my father sits on his porch, looking at our own horizon. The long simple line of the hill is gone. Pine and maple have grown up and buildings square off against the sky. Out of nowhere he mentions the lights of the tent hospital, as if he could still see them, strange and clear.

AUTHOR'S NOTE

I am indebted to the Immigrant City Archives Historical Society of Lawrence, Massachusetts, where I was able to consult the *Records of the Board of Health, January 1918–April 1931*, and the *Board of Health Influenza Journal, 1918–1920*. In addition, the Archives house recordings of oral histories. Listening to these voices was invaluable to my understanding of the atmosphere of the time. The recordings made of the recollections of Daniel Murphy and Sister Jeanne d'Arc were particularly helpful. I am also indebted to Alfred Crosby's *America's Forgotten Pandemic: The Influenza of 1918*

(Cambridge: Cambridge University Press, 1989) and to two local newspapers, the *Lawrence Telegram* and the *Lawrence Sun American* (September–November 1918).

POSSIBILITIES FOR WRITING

1. Brox's essay is marked by careful attention to descriptive detail—to sights, sounds, smells, and tactile images. Analyze the essay to comment on this use of descriptive detail.
2. Consider the structure of Brox's essay. How does the way she paces the narrative contribute to its overall effect?
3. Write about an experience you have had with a life-threatening illness or injury—either your own or that of someone close to you. Use strong descriptive detail to enhance your depiction of the experience.

Angela Carter (1940–1992) *was born in South London, England, and attended the University of Bristol. Her novels, including* Shadowdance *(1966),* Heroes and Villains *(1969),* Nights at the Circus *(1985), and* Wise Children *(1991), are often marked by Gothic eroticism and extravagant prose. Her work was also influenced by myths and fairy tales, most notably* The Old Wives' Fairy Tale Book *(1990), which reworked traditional stories with a decidedly contemporary slant. In addition to fiction, Carter published the highly influential* The Sadeian Woman and the Ideology of Pornography *(1979), as well as the collection* Nothing Sacred: Selected Journalism *(1982).*

ANGELA CARTER

The Wound in the Face

The wound that Angela Carter refers to in the title of her essay, "The Wound in the Face," is the red oval of lips colored with lipstick. She describes the red lipsticked mouth as "a bloody gash, a visible wound" that "bleeds over everything, cups, ice-cream, table napkins, towels." Carter is interested in this "wound" as a symbol of other deeper wounds in the culture of women's beauty and self-perception. Her essay delves beneath the surface or the face of beauty to investigate what lies beneath.

Carter's essay ranges across history, as she considers how "the hard, bland face with which women brazened their way through the tough 1930s, the tough 1940s" disappears for a while only to resurface in the 1970s. She describes the 1960s look as one of "Rousseauesque naturalism" with its face including a "bee-stung underlip, enormous eyes and a lot of disordered hair." It was, she notes, "a wild, sweet, gypsyish, vulnerable face." And she mentions Queen Elizabeth I, who colored her lips red in the late 1500s.

I spent a hallucinatory weekend, staring at faces I'd cut out of women's magazines, either from the beauty page or from the ads—all this season's faces. I stuck twenty or thirty faces on the wall and tried to work out from the evidence before me (a) what women's faces are supposed to be looking like, now; and (b) why. It was something of an exercise in pure form, because the magazine models' faces aren't exactly the face in the street—not low-style, do-it-yourself assemblages, but more a platonic, ideal face. Further, they reflect, as well as the mood of the moment, what the manufacturers are trying to push this year. Nevertheless, the *zeitgeist* works through the manufacturers, too. They do not understand their own imagery, any more than the consumer who demonstrates it does. I am still working on the nature of the imagery of cosmetics. I think it scares me.

Construing the imagery was an unnerving experience because all the models appeared to be staring straight at me with such a heavy, static quality of *being there* that it was difficult to escape the feeling they were accusing me of something. (How rarely women look one another in the eye.) Only two of the faces wear anything like smiles, and only one is showing a hint of her teeth. This season's is not an extravert face. Because there is not much to smile about this season? Surely. It is a bland, hard, bright face; it is also curiously familiar, though I have never seen it before.

The face of the seventies matches the fashions in clothes that have dictated some of its features, and is directly related to the social environment which produces it. Like fashions in clothes, fashions in faces have been stuck in pastiche for the past four or five years. This bankruptcy is disguised by ever more ingenious pastiche—of the thirties, the forties, the fifties, the Middle East, Xanadu, Wessex (those smocks). Compared with the short skirts and flat shoes of ten years ago, style in women's clothes has regressed. Designers are trying to make us cripple our feet again with high-heeled shoes and make us trail long skirts in dogshit. The re-introduction of rouge is part of this regression; rouge, coyly re-introduced under the nineteenth-century euphemism of 'blusher.'

The rather older face—the *Vogue* face, as opposed to the *Honey* face—is strongly under the 1930s influence, the iconographic, androgynous face of Dietrich and Garbo, with heavily emphasised bone structures, hollow cheeks and hooded eyelids. Warhol's transvestite superstars, too, and his magazine, *Interview*—with its passion for the tacky, the kitschy, for fake glamour, for rhinestones, sequins, Joan Crawford, Ann-Margaret—have exercised a profound influence. As a result, fashionable women now tend to look like women imitating men imitating women, an interesting reversal. The face currently perpetuated by the glossies aspires to the condition of that of Warhol's Candy Darling.

The main message is that the hard, bland face with which women brazened their way through the tough 1930s, the tough 1940s and the decreasingly tough 1950s (at the end of the 1950s, when things got less tough, they abandoned it) is back to sustain us through the tough 1970s. It recapitulates the glazed, self-contained look typical of times of austerity.

But what is one to make of the transvestite influence? Is it that the physical image of women took such a battering in the sixties that when femininity did, for want of anything better, return, the only people we could go to to find out what it had looked like were the dedicated male impersonators who had kept the concept alive in the sequined gowns, their spike-heeled shoes and their peony lipsticks? Probably. 'The feminine character, and the idea of femininity on which it is modelled, are products of masculine society,' says Theodore Adorno. Clearly a female impersonator knows more about his idea of the character he is mimicking than I do, because it is his very own invention, and has nothing to do with me.

Yet what about the Rousseauesque naturalism of the dominant image of women in the mid-1960s? Adorno can account for that, sociologically, too. 'The image of undistorted nature arises only in distortion, as its opposite.' The sixties face was described early in the decade by *Queen* (as it was then) as a 'look of luminous vacancy.'

The sixties face had a bee-stung underlip, enormous eyes and a lot of disordered hair. It saw itself as a wild, sweet, gipsyish, vulnerable face. Its very lack of artifice suggested sexual licence in a period that had learned to equate cosmetics, not with profligacy as in the nineteenth century, but with conformity to the standard social and sexual female norm. Nice girls wore lipstick, in the fifties.

When the sixties face used cosmetics at all, it explored imports such as kohl and henna from Indian shops. These had the twin advantages of being extremely exotic and very, very cheap. For purposes of pure decoration, for fun, it sometimes stuck sequins to itself, or those little gold and silver 'good conduct' stars. It bought sticks of stage make-up, and did extraordinary things around its eyes with them, at about the time of Flower Power. It was, basically, a low-style or do-it-yourself face. Ever in search of the new, the magazines eventually caught up with it, and high-style faces caught on to flowered cheeks and stars on the eyelids at about the time the manufacturers did. So women had to pay considerably more for their pleasures.

The sixties look gloried in its open pores and, if your eye wasn't into the particular look, you probably thought it didn't wash itself much. But it was just that, after all those years of pancake makeup, people had forgotten what the real colour of female skin was. This face cost very little in upkeep. Indeed, it was basically a most economical and serviceable model and it was quite a shock to realise, as the years passed, that all the beauty experts were wrong and, unless exposed to the most violent weather, it did not erode if it was left ungreased. A face is not a bicycle. Nevertheless, since this face had adopted naturalism as an ingenious form of artifice, it *was* a mask, like the grease masks of cosmetics, though frequently refreshingly eccentric.

At the end of that decade, in a brief period of delirium, there was a startling vogue of black lipstick and red eyeshadow. For a little while we were painting ourselves up just as arbitrarily as Larionov did before the Revolution. Dada in the boudoir! What a witty parody of the whole theory of cosmetics!

The basic theory of cosmetics is that they make a woman beautiful. Or, as the advertisers say, more beautiful. You blot out your noxious wens and warts and blemishes, shade your nose to make it bigger or smaller, draw attention to your good features by bright colours, and distract it from your bad features by more reticent tones. But those manic and desperate styles—leapt on and exploited instantly by desperate manufacturers—seemed to be about to break the ground for a whole new aesthetic of appearance, which would have nothing to do with the conformist ideology of 'beauty' at all. Might—ah, might—it be possible to use cosmetics to free women from the burden of having to look beautiful altogether?

Because black lipstick and red eyeshadow never 'beautified' anybody. They were the cosmetic equivalent of Duchamp's moustache on the Mona Lisa. They were cosmetics used as satire on cosmetics, on the arbitrary convention that puts blue on eyelids and pink on lips. Why not the other way round? The best part of the joke was that the look itself was utterly monstrous. It instantly converted the most beautiful women into outrageous grotesques; every face a work of anti-art. I enjoyed it very, very much.

However, it takes a helluva lot of guts to maintain oneself in a perpetual state of visual offensiveness. Most women could not resist keeping open a treacherous little corner on sex appeal. Besides, the joke went a little too near the bone. To do up your eyes so that they look like self-inflicted wounds is to wear on your face the evidence of the violence your environment inflicts on you.

Black paint around the eyes is such a familiar convention it seems natural; so does red paint on the mouth. We are so used to the bright red mouth we no longer see it as the wound it mimics, except in the treacherous lucidity of paranoia. But the shock of the red-painted eye recalls, directly, the blinding of Gloucester in *Lear*; or, worse and more aptly, the symbolic blinding of Oedipus. Women are allowed—indeed, encouraged—to exhibit the sign of their symbolic castration, but only in the socially sanctioned place. To transpose it upwards is to allow its significance to become apparent. We went too far, that time. Scrub it all off and start again.

And once we started again, red lipstick came back. Elizabeth I seems to have got a fine, bright carmine with which to touch up her far from generous lips. The Victorian beauty's 'rosebud mouth'—the mouth so tiny it was a wonder how it managed to contain her teeth—was a restrained pink. Flappers' lips spread out and went red again, and the 'generous mouth' became one of the great glamour conventions of the entire twentieth century and has remained so, even if its colour is modified.

White-based lipsticks, colourless glosses, or no lipstick at all, were used in the 1960s. Now the mouth is back as a bloody gash, a visible wound. This mouth bleeds over everything, cups, ice-cream, table napkins, towels. Mary Quant has a shade called (of course) 'Bloody Mary,' to ram the point home. We will leave our bloody spoor behind us, to show we have been there.

In the thirties, that spoor was the trademark of the sophisticate, the type of Baudelairean female dandy Dietrich impersonated so well. Dietrich always transcended self-pity and self-destruction, wore the wound like a badge of triumph, and came out on top. But Iris Storm in Michael Arlen's *The Green Hat*, the heroines of Maurice Dekobra, the wicked film star in Chandler's *The Little Sister* who always dressed in black to offset her fire-engine of a mouth—*they* all dripped blood over everything as they stalked sophisticatedly to their dooms. In their wake, lipstick traces on a cigarette stub; the perfect imprint, like half a heart, of a scarlet lower lip on a drained Martini glass; the tell-tale scarlet letter. *A* for adultery, on a shirt collar . . . the kitsch poetry of it all!

Elizabeth Taylor scrawls 'Not for sale' on her bedroom mirror in her red, red lipstick in *Butterfield 8*. The generosity the mouth has given so freely will be spurned with brutal ingratitude. The open wound will never heal. Perhaps, sometimes, she will lament the loss of the tight rosebud; but it has gone forever.

The revival of red lipstick indicates, above all, I suppose, that women's sense of security was transient.

POSSIBILITIES FOR WRITING

1. What is Carter's purpose in this essay? Focus particularly on her imagery of the wound.

2. Carter refers to "the burden of having to look beautiful." Do women today continue to suffer this burden? Do men? What is your own take on what society considers beautiful? You may wish to consider Susan Sontag's essay, "A Woman's Beauty," on pp. 588–591.

3. Re-create Carter's study, as described in her first paragraph, using images from contemporary women's magazines. What are women's faces today "supposed to be looking like"? Why?

Philip Dormer Stanhope (1694–1773), the Fourth Earl of Chesterfield, was an English statesman and author. He was renowned as a clever and witty man who was an eloquent public speaker, traits that served him well in the diplomatic and state work of his long public career. He was an ambassador to the Hague in the Netherlands, held a seat in Parliament, and had a successful tenure as Lord Lieutenant of Ireland. Chesterfield, however, is perhaps best known for his literary writing, especially for his letters to his son, designed to offer advice about how to educate himself in the ways of the world.

Letter to His Son

In "Letter to his Son," Lord Chesterfield provides advice about how to live—what to do and what not to do in order to avoid making mistakes in life. Chesterfield focuses his letter on pleasure, advising his son to be careful about letting others decide what pleasures he ought to seek, encouraging him to avoid the mistakes that he, his father, has made in the pursuit of pleasure. In the process, Lord Chesterfield encourages his son to distinguish between false, or ephemeral, pleasures and real, or lasting and more valuable, ones.

London, March 27, O.S. 1747.

Dear Boy,

Pleasure is the rock which most people split upon; they launch out with crowded sails in quest of it, but without a compass to direct their course, or reason sufficient to steer the vessel; for want of which, pain and shame, instead of Pleasure, are the returns of their voyage. Do not think that I mean to snarl at Pleasure, like a Stoic, or to preach against it, like a parson; no, I mean to point it out, and recommend it to you, like an Epicurean: I wish you a great deal; and my only view is to hinder you from mistaking it.

The character which most young men first aim at is, that of a Man of Pleasure; but they generally take it upon trust; and, instead of consulting their own taste and inclinations, they blindly adopt whatever those, with whom they chiefly converse, are pleased to call by the name of Pleasure; and a *Man of Pleasure*, in the vulgar acceptation of that phrase, means only a beastly drunkard, an abandoned . . ., and a profligate swearer and curser. As it may be of use to you, I am not unwilling, though at the same time ashamed, to own, that the vices of my youth proceeded much more from my silly resolution of being what I heard called a Man of Pleasure, than from my own inclinations. I always naturally hated drinking; and yet I have often drunk, with disgust at the time, attended by great sickness the next day, only because I then considered drinking as a necessary qualification for a fine gentleman, and a Man of Pleasure.

The same as to gaming. I did not want money, and consequently had no occasion to play for it; but I thought Play another necessary ingredient in the composition of a Man of Pleasure, and accordingly I plunged into it without desire, at first; sacrificed a thousand real pleasures to it; and made myself solidly uneasy by it, for thirty of the best years of my life.

I was even absurd enough, for a little while, to swear, by way of adorning and completing the shining character which I affected; but this folly I soon laid aside, upon finding both the guilt and the indecency of it.

Thus seduced by fashion, and blindly adopting nominal pleasures, I lost real ones; and my fortune impaired, and my constitution shattered, are, I must confess, the just punishment of my errors.

Take warning then by them; choose your pleasures for yourself, and do not let them be imposed upon you. Follow nature, and not fashion: weigh the present enjoyment of your pleasures against the necessary consequences of them, and then let your own common sense determine your choice.

POSSIBILITIES FOR WRITING

1. Summarize the gist of what Lord Chesterfield says to his son about the pursuit of pleasure. To what extent do you agree with his advice?
2. Compare Lord Chesterfield's letter of advice to his son Philip with that of Nicola Sacco to his son Dante (see pp. 525–528). What kind of relationship does each father have with his son, based on the details of their respective letters?
3. Write a letter to someone important in your life—a parent or child, a sibling, a grandparent or other relative, or a friend. Convey in your letter to this person some advice about what is important to you and how you might like him or her to live in the future.

Christopher Clausen (b. 1942) is a professor of English at Pennsylvania State University. Dr. Clausen has a Bachelor of Arts from Earlham College, a Master of Arts from the University of Chicago, and a doctorate from Queen's University in Canada. His books include The Place of Poetry: Two Centuries of an Art in Crisis *(1981),* The Moral Imagination: Essays on Literature and Ethics *(1986),* My Life with President Kennedy *(1994), and* Faded Mosaic: The Emergence of Post-Cultural America *(2000).*

CHRISTOPHER CLAUSEN

Against Work

In "Against Work," which originally appeared in the journal, the *American Scholar*, Christopher Clausen makes a case for not working, for becoming one of the leisured class. Clausen identifies and analyzes the reasons people work, and he decides that many would be better off simply not working.

Clausen both locates and enlarges his discussion of not working by contrasting American attitudes toward work with those of French and German workers. In the process, he addresses fundamental questions about the nature of work and about our reasons for spending so much of our lives engaged in it.

A history of my suburban early ambitions would sound utterly conventional. At the age of six I wanted to be a cowboy. At twelve I decided instead to become a professional football player, which, for someone who would never weigh more than a hundred and thirty pounds, was even more hopeless. In high school I made up my mind to be a writer. As in most such cases, it wasn't the work of writing that appealed to me. It was that, secretly, I never wanted to do any work at all. But teenagers are rarely of one mind, and their inconsistent wishes seldom come true in a recognizable way.

"What is the use of having money if you have to work for it?" Violet Malone disdainfully asks her father-in-law, a self-made Irish-American billionaire, in George Bernard Shaw's play *Man and Superman*. A century ago, when Shaw was writing, the different valuation that Americans and Europeans set on work as an abstract ideal was already evident to anyone who had a chance to compare them. By that time the "gospel of work" preached by Thomas Carlyle, who repeated endlessly that "work is alone noble," was a mid-Victorian relic.

To her perfectly reasonable question, the Englishwoman Violet receives no answer. She would be just as baffled a hundred years later. If humans are the only animal that doesn't think the purpose of life is to enjoy it, Americans are an especially hard case. Today those of us with full-time employment typically put in several hundred more hours per year than western Europeans—the equivalent of seven additional weeks, according to some surveys. Even the proverbially hard-working Germans spend only about three-quarters as many hours on the job and retire younger. Our disposable income is correspondingly higher, though when asked whether we would prefer more leisure to greater wealth, most of us opt for leisure. Statistics on voluntary overtime, however, suggest that we may not be telling the truth. A long American tradition leads people to define themselves not just by their occupations but also by the amount of labor they put in.

Captain John Smith's declaration that those who do not work shall not eat is the real national motto, ratified by subsequent authorities from Benjamin Franklin to Donald Trump. Rockefellers and Kennedys, whose international counterparts would spend all their time collecting works of art, instead work conspicuously hard at finance or politics. The American way is to prove one's worth by long hours, almost regardless of what one actually accomplishes. The fact that many people appear to work hard while actually coasting through the week merely confirms the gap between what they think they should be doing and their actual preferences.

Consider the fate of the word *workaholism,* coined by W.E. Oates in 1968 to identify a disturbing psychological obsession—an "addiction," a "compulsion"—that Oates had noticed around him. Others took up the new term enthusiastically. "The workaholic, as an addict is called, neglects his family, withdraws from social life, and loses interest in sex," the *Sydney Bulletin* explained ominously in 1973. But within a decade the term lost all connotation of pathology and became a compliment. "Unlike their workaholic American cousins," *Time* reported in 1981, "Europeans tend to see lengthy vacations as somehow part of the natural order of things." Today the word is most often heard in the proud boast. "I'm a workaholic," recited ad nauseam by type A personalities in corporations, politics, and the professions. Carlyle lives, if only in America.

Why on earth do we do it? Do most of us really prefer to work—to spend our lives in labor as an end rather than as an unavoidable means to our own or others' happiness? Of course not. Most jobs are boring at best, with few psychic rewards. Nobody works on an assembly line or at Wal-Mart, or recites the weather on Channel 9, simply for lack of a pleasanter way to spend two thousand hours every year. It's true that the most energetic and gregarious of us, the kind who have been claiming since high school that they "want to work with people," often find even jobs like these a relief from loneliness. One suspects, though, that if they suddenly didn't need the money or respect, they would quickly turn to playing games instead, or traveling the world, or finding innovative new ways to cope. The upper-middle-class professions are supposed to be a different story. Doctors, lawyers, and college professors usually think of themselves as "committed," with the implication that there is nothing they would rather be doing.

Speaking from experience, I can attest that being a senior academic is one of the more privileged assignments in life, although anyone who thinks universities are relaxed, humane centers for the free play of intellect hasn't spent much time in one lately. Plenty of hard work goes into getting a Ph.D., achieving tenure, and practicing a profession that despite its flattering self-image involves as much stress, conformity, and tedium as other occupations. In response to charges made a few years ago that professors are slackers, the Department of Education released a survey concluding that the average full-time university faculty member puts in between forty-five and fifty-five hours a week. Some of what I do for a living is fun—though I discovered early that writing anything meant to be read by others involves a good deal of labor—and the rest is pleasanter than what many people have to do. But still. Most of your waking hours for forty years?

There is something deeply conflicted about the devotion to work, vocation, career as an ideal in any society, but especially in one that has zealously cast off so many of its other repressions. Americans at the beginning of the twenty-first century pursue pleasure with the same avid desperations as upscale high school students pursue getting into the right college—that is, with a hell of a lot of work. We have all been so oversocialized that unnatural devotion to toil leaves its mark on every area of life. It could even be argued that the most highly prized pleasures have themselves become a form of work, complete with their own uniforms, disciplines, and special lingo.

My own conflicted attitude probably owes something to the fact that during the summer between high school and college, I worked as an information clerk for the National Heart Institute in a suburb of the capital. As a temporary, I spent my days keeping track of off-prints from medical journals, answering requests for the Heart Institute's own publications, and cleaning out the primitive photocopier. Much of the time there was not enough work to keep me busy, and like other low-level civil servants, I soon discovered that the Washington summer in a building with no air conditioning called for a relaxed approach to the public's business.

Most mornings I stayed in my office filling orders from school-teachers for our most popular publication, a garish poster titled "The Living Pump." Having answered the mail as best I could, I generally re-treated in the heat of the afternoon to the comfortable underground vault where our own materials and hundreds of articles on heart dis-ease were stored. This fastness lay beneath a building that had been constructed with nuclear attack in mind. In addition to a normal base-ment, it had four subbasements reached by a freight elevator that no one else seemed to use. Once I got to the bottom, I made my way through nearly half a mile of corridors filled with abandoned office furniture. I never encountered another human being down there, just thousands of desks and chairs and filing cabinets that nobody wanted anymore. After several hours in this environment, it was easy to believe the world had ended, and all that was left of the United States govern-ment was one GS-2 surrounded by acres of junk five levels below ground zero. It seemed odd to me that reams of Living Pumps would survive Armageddon while the doctors who ran the National Institutes of Health turned into dust, but eighteen-year-olds have a high toler-ance for irrationality. That's one reason they make good soldiers. I cat-alogued the contents of my bunker, restocked as necessary, composed juvenile light verse, and read a lot of novels in the cool silence. Some July afternoons I thought seriously about canceling my college plans and staying underground in the government forever.

The Department of Health, Education, and Welfare, as it was then called, had its headquarters on Independence Avenue in downtown Washington. Olive, a Southern widow who must have been in her fifties, presided over the Heart Institute's offices there. She had worked in similar offices since the New Deal and had seen bosses come and go. A slim woman of vast charm and presence, she liked young men who would spend Friday afternoons in her office drinking coffee and conversing. I retain only the general impression of an elegant lady from a different world where manners and human contact counted for nearly everything and bureaucratic procedures for nothing. Without ever saying so, she conveyed through her demeanor that the government was too absurd to worry about. My guess, although I really have no idea, is that Olive did her job very well, if in an unconven-tional fashion. Whoever was nominally her superior must have had a difficult time until he tacitly agreed that everything she did would be done her way.

As I look back, it's hard for me to believe what her way meant to my weekly routine. Every Thursday I would receive a slip entitling me to take a pickup truck out of the motor pool on Friday and drive it downtown to HEW. On alternate Friday mornings I would load the truck with publications from the bunker. Then I would have lunch, drive to Olive's office, unload the truck, and spend the afternoon listening, like a young man out of a Faulkner novel. The next Friday I would drive an empty truck to HEW, load it up with the same publications I had delivered the previous week, and return them to Bethesda. It sounds worse than it seemed at the time. Perhaps I'm forgetting some deliveries that served a real purpose beyond bringing me into Olive's presence. The possibility that my cheerful, un-ambitious colleagues would object to these excursions did not occur to me, and nobody ever did.

Everyone has met people who boast (sometimes repetitively) of loving their work so much that they rarely take vacations and can't bear the thought of retirement. Star athletes, successful artists, and research scientists are sometimes credible when they make these assertions. Occasionally an obstetrician goes on delivering babies into his nineties, and the local newspaper praises his enthusiasm for life. But who believes middle managers when they claim to spend the weekend looking forward to Monday? Who takes teachers seriously in June when they say they can't wait for September? If hypocrisy is the tribute vice pays to virtue, the oddity here is that so many people believe work as such, work divorced from any particular achievement, is especially virtuous. Working to earn one's bread is something few people can escape. Working out of moral vanity is sheer self-deception.

Of course Americans didn't invent the idea. As with so many things, we merely perfected it. To get people to do their best over a long period of time, it has always been necessary to make what they do seem both a duty and a pleasure, something like rearing children. Seneca assured affluent Roman parents, "Nothing is so certain as that the evils of idleness can be shaken off by hard work." In a similar vein, Voltaire wrote, "Work keeps us from three great evils, boredom, vice, and need." These are the homilies of the fortunate. Those who have been forced to work hard are often more realistic about what is at stake. "I don't like work—no man does," Joseph Conrad's alter ego Marlow announces in *Heart of Darkness*, and then adds, "—but I like what is in work—the chance to find yourself. Your own reality—for yourself, not for others—what no other man can ever know." The self-respect that comes from being financially self-supporting, as well as capable of some useful accomplishment for oneself or others, is a worthy goal for anyone. Fetishizing the labor itself is merely a form of bondage, workaholism in the true, perverse sense.

Because it serves so many different practical and psychic purposes, it's no wonder that, in the celebrated words of C. Northcote Parkinson, "work expands so as to fill the time available for its completion." Still, much can be said not just for the strenuous, cultivated leisure that hardworking professionals sometimes allow themselves to imagine as an alternative to virtuous toil, but for bone-idleness. There is in fact no indication that those who work are happier than those who choose not to. After surveying a mass of research on what it takes to make people happy, the psychologist David Watson declares, "With the notable exception of involuntary unemployment, we see little evidence that occupational and employment status have a major impact on well-being. Generally speaking, people in seemingly uninteresting, low-status jobs report levels of happiness and life satisfaction that are quite comparable to those of individuals in high-status occupations. Moreover, the employed and voluntarily unemployed report extremely similar levels of affect and well-being." He concludes, "One particularly interesting implication of this literature is that people apparently devote much of their lives to striving after things—education, marriage, money, and so on—that ultimately have little effect on their happiness." Although having some goals in life seems to work better than having none, "happiness is primarily a subjective phenomenon . . . not highly constrained by objective circumstances."

If your work won't make you or anyone else happier, why do more of it than you have to? Believers in the gospel of work typically consider happiness irrelevant. Deep down, they think we have a duty to be miserable. As usual, the bullying Carlyle put it most brutally: "'Happy,' my brother? First of all, what difference is it whether thou art happy or not! . . . The only happiness a brave man ever troubled himself with asking much about was, happiness enough to get his work done. Not 'I can't eat!' but 'I can't work!' that was the burden of all wise complaining among men." Men must work, and women must weep, as Carlyle's friend Charles Kingsley decreed. Work itself, work as a sacred abstraction, had become a substitute for the God that Carlyle and many of his readers no longer believed in.

In America this grim pseudo-religion continues to draw worshippers on a scale no longer seen elsewhere in the Western world.

The only major change is that women are now expected to work like men. We speak in reverent tones of the "work ethic"; politicians praise "working families" and, even in times of relatively low unemployment, make job creation an issue in every campaign. A few years ago, cutting the work week was a central promise in a French election, and the government actually passed laws on the subject. In the United States, by contrast, legislation has been introduced to make overtime easier for companies to afford. We abolished mandatory retirement in the 1980s. Despite the growth in productivity and affluence over the past decades, all the social pressures are for working longer hours and later in life rather than cashing in on the promise of greater leisure—partly to take some of the pressure off Social Security and Medicare, but mostly because work is such an ingrained American value.

I don't know about the civil service, but not many Olives are left in major universities. Sometimes I dream of my vault full of Living Pumps. A colleague and I recently passed the time by talking speculatively of retirement. "You wouldn't actually retire at sixty-five, would you?" this proud workaholic asked with incredulity.

"Of course," I gulped, suddenly and unexpectedly defensive about my secret plan to quit at sixty-two. "Why not?"

He shrugged disdainfully and went back to writing his next book on Chaucer. Truly, we are the last Puritans.

POSSIBILITIES FOR WRITING

1. Summarize the reasons Clausen presents for why people work. Explain what he thinks of each of those reasons. And explain what you think of them, as well.
2. Identify the conflicts between the different pleasures of work and leisure that Clausen discusses. Describe your own attitudes toward work and leisure. What, for you, is the ideal balance between work and leisure? Explain why this is so.
3. Write an essay about a job you have had. Describe what it was like to do the work you did, why you did it, how you felt about it. You might wish to compare two jobs in your essay.

Judith Ortiz Cofer (b. 1952) spent her childhood in the small Puerto Rican town where she was born and in Paterson, New Jersey, where her family lived for most of each year, from the time she was three. She attended Catholic schools in Paterson and she holds degrees from the University of Georgia and Florida Atlantic University. She has published several volumes of poetry, including Reaching for the Mainland *(1996), and her 1989 novel* The Line of the Sun *was nominated for a Pulitzer Prize. Cofer has also published two autobiographical works:* Silent Dancing: A Partial Remembrance of a Puerto Rican Childhood *(1990) and* The Latin Deli: Prose and Poetry *(1993). Some recent books are* Woman in Front of the Sun: On Becoming a Writer *(2000),* The Meaning of Consuelo *(2003), and* Call Me Maria *(2004). She currently teaches creative writing at the University of Georgia.*

JUDITH ORTIZ COFER

Casa: A Partial Remembrance of a Puerto Rican Childhood

In "Casa: A Partial Remembrance of a Puerto Rican Childhood," Judith Ortiz Cofer describes the bonds that obtain among a community of women—three generations of a family headed by the matriarch, Mamá, the author's grandmother. In celebrating the intertwined lives of these women of her family, Cofer simultaneously celebrates the power of storytelling. Weaving these two strands of her essay together—family and stories—Cofer conveys some important ideas about women and their relations with men, along with important ideas about culture and its significance for identity.

Cofer's "Casa" is about living in and moving between two worlds—the warm world of her Puerto Rican tropical home and the cold new world of New York and Paterson, New Jersey. Cofer alludes to this dual existence early on and explains its significance later in her essay, referring to herself as an outsider who spoke English with a Spanish accent and Spanish with an English accent. And although this dual linguistic identity made her stand out in both groups, Cofer benefits from her double linguistic and cultural heritage. It allows her to shift back and forth readily between two very different worlds, with their different sets of cultural values.

At three or four o'clock in the afternoon, the hour of *café con leche*, the women of my family gathered in Mamá's living room to speak of important things and retell familiar stories meant to be overheard by us young girls, their daughters. In Mamá's house (everyone called my grandmother Mamá) was a large parlor built by my grandfather to his wife's exact specifications so that it was always cool, facing away from the sun. The doorway was on the side of the house so no one could walk directly into her living room. First they had to take a little stroll through and around her beautiful garden where prize-winning orchids grew in the trunk of an ancient tree she had hollowed out for that purpose. This room was furnished with several mahogany rocking chairs, acquired at the births of her children, and one intricately carved rocker that had passed down to Mamá at the death of her own mother.

It was on these rockers that my mother, her sisters, and my grandmother sat on these afternoons of my childhood to tell their stories, teaching each other, and my cousin and me, what it was like to be a woman, more specifically, a Puerto Rican woman. They talked about life on the island, and life in *Los Nueva Yores*, their way of referring to the United States from New York City to California: the other place, not home, all the same. They told real-life stories though, as I later learned, always embellishing them with a little or a lot of dramatic detail. And they told *cuentos*, the morality and cautionary tales told by the women in our family for generations: stories that became a part of my subconscious as I grew up in two worlds, the tropical island and the cold city, and that would later surface in my dreams and in my poetry.

One of these tales was about the woman who was left at the altar. Mamá liked to tell that one with histrionic intensity. I remember the rise and fall of her voice, the sighs, and her constantly gesturing hands, like two birds swooping through her words. This particular story usually would come up in a conversation as a result of someone mentioning a forthcoming engagement or wedding. The first time I remember hearing it, I was sitting on the floor at Mamá's feet, pretending to read a comic book. I may have been eleven or twelve years old, at that difficult age when a girl was no longer a child who could be ordered to leave the room if the women wanted freedom to take their talk into forbidden zones, nor really old enough to be considered a part of their conclave. I could only sit quietly, pretending to be in another world, while absorbing it all in a sort of unspoken agreement of my status as silent auditor. On this day, Mamá had taken my long, tangled mane of hair into her ever-busy hands. Without looking down at me and with no interruption of her flow of words, she began braiding my hair, working at it with the quickness and determination that characterized all her actions. My mother was watching us impassively from her rocker across the room. On her lips played a little ironic smile. I would never sit still for *her* ministrations, but even then, I instinctively knew that she did not possess Mamá's matriarchal power to command and keep everyone's attention. This was never more evident than in the spell she cast when telling a story.

"It is not like it used to be when I was a girl," Mamá announced. "Then, a man could leave a girl standing at the church altar with a bouquet of fresh flowers in her hands and disappear off the face of the earth. No way to track him down if he was from another town. He could be a married man, with maybe even two or three families all over the island. There was no way to know. And there were men who did this. Hombres with the devil in their flesh who would come to a pueblo, like this one, take a job at one of the haciendas, never meaning to stay, only to have a good time and to seduce the women."

The whole time she was speaking, Mamá would be weaving my hair into a flat plait that required pulling apart the two sections of hair with little jerks that made my eyes water; but knowing how grandmother detested whining and *boba* (sissy) tears, as she called them, I just sat up as straight and stiff as I did at La Escuela San José, where the nuns enforced good posture with a flexible plastic ruler they bounced off of slumped shoulders and heads. As Mamá's story progressed, I noticed how my young Aunt Laura lowered her eyes, refusing to meet Mamá's meaningful gaze. Laura was seventeen, in her last year of high school, and already engaged to a boy from another town who had staked his claim with a tiny diamond ring, then left for Los Nueva Yores to make his fortune. They were planning to get married in a year. Mamá had expressed serious doubts that the wedding would ever take place. In Mamá's eyes, a man set free without a legal contract was a man lost. She believed that marriage was not something men desired, but simply the price they had to pay for the privilege of children and, of course, for what no decent (synonymous with "smart") woman would give away for free.

"María La Loca was only seventeen when *it* happened to her." I listened closely at the mention of this name. María was a town character, a fat middle-aged woman who lived with her old mother on the outskirts of town. She was to be seen around the pueblo delivering the meat pies the two women made for a living. The most peculiar thing about María, in my eyes, was that she walked and moved like a little girl though she had the thick body and wrinkled face of an old woman. She would swing her hips in an exaggerated, clownish way, and sometimes even hop and skip up to someone's house. She spoke to no one. Even if you asked her a question, she would just look at you and smile, showing her yellow teeth. But I had heard that if you got close enough, you could hear her humming a tune without words. The kids yelled out nasty things at her calling her *La Loca*, and the men who hang out at the bodega playing dominoes sometimes whistled mockingly as she passed by with her funny, outlandish walk. But María seemed impervious to it all, carrying her basket of *pasteles* like a grotesque Little Red Riding Hood through the forest.

María La Loca interested me, as did all the eccentrics and crazies of our pueblo. Their weirdness was a measuring stick I used in my serious quest for a definition of normal. As a Navy brat shuttling between New Jersey and the pueblo, I was constantly made to feel like an oddball by my peers, who made fun of my two-way accent: a Spanish accent when I spoke English, and when I spoke Spanish I was told that I sounded like a *Gringa*. Being the outsider had already turned my brother and me into cultural chameleons. We developed early on the ability to blend into a crowd, to sit and read quietly in a fifth story apartment building for days and days when it was too bitterly cold to play outside, or, set free, to run wild in Mamá's realm, where she took charge of our lives, releasing Mother for a while from the intense fear for our safety that our father's absences instilled in her. In order to keep us from harm when Father was away, Mother kept us under strict surveillance. She even walked us to and from Public School No. 11, which we attended during the months we lived in Paterson, New Jersey, our home base in the states. Mamá freed all three of us like pigeons from a cage. I saw her as my liberator and my model. Her stories were parables from which to glean the *Truth*.

"María La Loca was once a beautiful girl. Everyone thought she would marry the Méndez boy." As everyone knew, Rogelio Méndez was the richest man in town. "But," Mamá continued, knitting my hair with the same intensity she was putting into her story, "this *macho* made a fool out of her and ruined her life." She paused for the effect of her use of the word "Macho," which at that time had not yet become a popular epithet for an unliberated man. This word had for us the crude and comical connotation of "male of the species," stud; a *macho* was what you put in a pen to increase your stock.

I peeked over my comic book at my mother. She too was under Mamá's spell, smiling conspiratorially at this little swipe at men. She was safe from Mamá's contempt in this area. Married at an early age, an unspotted lamb, she had been accepted by a good family of strict Spaniards whose name was old and respected, though their fortune had been lost long before my birth. In a rocker Papá had painted sky blue sat Mamá's oldest child, Aunt Nena. Mother of three children, stepmother of two more, she was a quiet woman who liked books but had married an ignorant and abusive widower whose main interest in life was accumulating wealth. He too was in the mainland working on his dream of returning home rich and triumphant to buy the *finca* of his dreams. She was waiting for him to send for her. She would leave her children with Mamá for several years while the two of them slaved away in factories. He would one day be a rich man, and she a sadder woman. Even now her life-light was dimming. She spoke little, an aberration in Mamá's house, and she read avidly, as if storing up spiritual food for the long winters that awaited her in Los Nueva Yores without her family. But even Aunt Nena came alive to Mamá's words, rocking gently, her hands over a thick book in her lap.

Her daughter, my cousin Sara, played jacks by herself on the tile porch outside the room where we sat. She was a year older than I. We shared a bed and all our family's secrets. Collaborators in search of answers, Sara and I discussed everything we heard the women say, trying to fit it all together like a puzzle that, once assembled, would reveal life's mysteries to us. Though she and I still enjoyed taking part in boys' games—chase, volleyball, and even *vaqueros*, the island version of cowboys and Indians involving cap-gun battles and violent shoot-outs under the mango tree in Mamá's backyard—we loved best the quiet hours in the afternoon when the men were still at work, and the boys had gone to play serious baseball at the park. Then Mamá's house belonged only to us women. The aroma of coffee perking in the kitchen, the mesmerizing creaks and groans of the rockers, and the women telling their lives in *cuentos* are forever woven into the fabric of my imagination, braided like my hair that day I felt my grandmother's hands teaching me about strength, her voice convincing me of the power of storytelling.

That day Mamá told how the beautiful María had fallen prey to a man whose name was never the same in subsequent versions of the story; it was Juan one time, José, Rafael, Diego, another. We understood that neither the name nor any of the *facts* were important, only that a woman had allowed love to defeat her. Mamá put each of us in María's place by describing her wedding dress in loving detail: how she looked like a princess in her lace as she waited at the altar. Then, as Mamá approached the tragic denouement of her story, I was distracted by the sound of my aunt Laura's violent rocking. She seemed on the verge of tears. She knew the fable was intended for her. That week she was going to have her wedding gown fitted, though no firm date had been set for the marriage. Mamá ignored Laura's obvious discomfort, digging out a ribbon from the sewing basket she kept by her rocker while describing María's long illness, "a fever that would not break for days." She spoke of a mother's despair: "that woman climbed the church steps on her knees every morning, wore only black as a *promesa* to the Holy Virgin in exchange for her daughter's health." By the time María returned from her honeymoon with death, she was ravished, no longer young or sane. "As you can see, she is almost as old as her mother already," Mamá lamented while tying the ribbon to the ends of my hair, pulling it back with such force that I just knew I would never be able to close my eyes completely again.

"That María's getting crazier every day." Mamá's voice would take a lighter tone now, expressing satisfaction, either for the perfection of my braid, or for a story well told—it was hard to tell. "You know that tune María is always humming?" Carried away by her enthusiasm, I tried to nod, but Mamá still had me pinned between her knees.

"Well, that's the wedding march." Surprising us all, Mamá sang out, "Da, da, dara . . . da, da, dara." Then lifting me off the floor by my skinny shoulders, she would lead me around the room in an im-promptu waltz—another session ending with the laughter of women, all of us caught up in the infectious joke of our lives.

POSSIBILITIES FOR WRITING

1. The longest and most elaborate example Cofer uses is that of María La Loca. Explain the significance of this example, and identify and explain the significance of another example that Cofer includes.

2. Cofer uses a number of Spanish words and phrases in "Casa," some of which she translates and others of which she leaves untranslated. What is the effect of these Spanish words and phrases? What would be gained or lost if they were omitted?

3. Use the following quotation as a springboard to write about identity as a theme in "Casa": "It was on these rockers that my mother, her sisters, and my grandmother sat on these afternoons of my childhood to tell their stories, teaching each other, and my cousin and me, what it was like to be a woman, more specifically, a Puerto Rican woman."

K. C. Cole (b. 1946), *a science writer for the* Los Angeles Times, *was born in Detroit, Michigan, and was educated at Columbia University, from which she received her B.A. She has taught science at the University of California and the University of Wisconsin. Cole began doing science writing in the 1970s and has written for publications that include* Smithsonian, Omni, *and* Discover *magazines. Her books include* Visions *(1978),* Sympathetic Vibrations *(1984),* The Universe and the Teacup: The Mathematics of Truth and Beauty *(1998), and* The Hole in the Universe *(2001).*

K. C. COLE

Calculated Risks

In "Calculated Risks," from her book *The Universe and the Teacup: The Mathematics of Truth and Beauty* (1998), K. C. Cole explains why people take some risks and not others, and how their risk assessment analysis typically lacks a sound mathematical or scientific basis. Using a clear, direct style of writing, and providing numerous examples from everyday experience, Cole is able to explain complex ideas lucidly and engagingly.

Throughout "Calculated Risks," Cole shows how irrational people's behavior choices often are and how little real analysis typically precedes them. She explains how personal risks differ from societal ones and why certain kinds of risks are more widely publicized than others.

Newsweek magazine plunged American women into a state of near panic some years ago when it announced that the chance of a college-educated thirty-five-year-old woman finding a husband was less than her chance of being killed by a terrorist. Although Susan Faludi made mincemeat of this so-called statistic in her book *Backlash*, the notion that we can precisely quantify risk has a strong hold on the Western psyche. Scientists, statisticians, and policy makers attach numbers to the risk of getting breast cancer or AIDS, to flying and food additives, to getting hit by lightning or falling in the bathtub.

Yet despite (or perhaps because of) all the numbers floating around, most people are quite properly confused about risk. I know people who live happily on the San Andreas Fault and yet are afraid to ride the New York subways (and vice versa). I've known smokers who can't stand to be in the same room with a fatty steak, and women afraid of the side effects of birth control pills who have unprotected sex with strangers. Risk assessment is rarely based on purely rational considerations—even if people could agree on what those considerations were. We worry about negligible quantities of Alar in apples, yet shrug off the much higher probability of dying from smoking. We worry about flying, but not driving. We worry about getting brain cancer from cellular phones, although the link is quite tenuous. In fact, it's easy to make a statistical argument—albeit a fallacious one—that cellular phones prevent cancer, because the proportion of people with brain tumors is smaller among cell phone users than among the general population.[1]

Even simple pleasures such as eating and breathing have become suspect. Love has always been risky, and AIDS has made intimacy more perilous than ever. On the other hand, not having relationships may be riskier still. According to at least one study, the average male faces three times the threat of early death associated with not being married as he does from cancer.

Of course, risk isn't all bad. Without knowingly taking risks, no one would ever walk out the door, much less go to school, drive a car, have a baby, submit a proposal for a research grant, fall in love, or swim in the ocean. It's hard to have any fun, accomplish anything productive, or experience life without taking on risks—sometimes substantial ones. Life, after all, is a fatal disease, and the mortality rate for humans, at the end of the day, is 100 percent.

Yet, people are notoriously bad at risk assessment. I couldn't get over this feeling watching the aftermath of the crash of TWA Flight 800 and the horror it spread about flying, with the long lines at airports, the increased security measures, the stories about grieving families day after day in the newspaper, the ongoing attempt to figure out why and who and what could be done to prevent such a tragedy from happening again.

Meanwhile, tens of thousands of children die every day around the world from common causes such as malnutrition and disease. That's roughly the same as a hundred exploding jumbo jets full of children every single day. People who care more about the victims of Flight 800 aren't callous or ignorant. It's just the way our minds work. Certain kinds of tragedies make an impact; others don't. Our perceptual apparatus is geared toward threats that are exotic, personal, erratic, and dramatic. This doesn't mean we're ignorant; just human.

This skewed perception of risk has serious social consequences, however. We aim our resources at phantoms, while real hazards are ignored. Parents, for example, tend to rate drug abuse and abduction by strangers as the greatest threats to their children. Yet hundreds of

---

[1]John Allen Paulos was the first person I know of to make this calculation; it is probably related to the fact that people who use cellular phones are on average richer, and therefore healthier, than people who don't.

times more children die each year from choking, burns, falls, drowning, and other accidents that public safety efforts generally ignore.

We spend millions to fight international terrorism and wear combat fatigues for a morning walk to protect against Lyme disease. At the same time, "we see several very major problems that have received relatively little attention," write Bernard Cohen and I-Sing Lee in *Health Physics*. The physicists suggest—not entirely tongue in cheek—that resources might be far more efficiently spent on programs such as government-organized computer dating services. "Favorable publicity on the advantages of marriage might be encouraged."

It's as if we incarcerated every petty criminal with zeal, while inviting mass murderers into our bedrooms. If we wanted to put the money on the real killers, we'd go after suicide, not asbestos.

Even in terms of simple dollars, our policies don't make any sense. It's well known, for example, that prenatal care for pregnant women saves enormous amounts of money—in terms of care infants need in the first year of life—and costs a pittance. Yet millions of low-income women don't get it.

Numbers are clearly not enough to make sense of risk assessment. Context counts, too. Take cancer statistics. It's always frightening to hear that cancer is on the rise. However, at least one reason for the increase is simply that people are living longer—long enough to get the disease.

Certain conclusions we draw from statistics are downright silly. Physicist Hal Lewis writes in *Technological Risk* that per mile traveled a person is more likely to be killed by a car as a pedestrian than as a driver or passenger. Should we conclude that driving is safer than walking and therefore that all pedestrians should be forced into cars?

Charles Dickens made a point about the absurdity of misunderstanding numbers associated with risk by refusing to ride the train. One day late in December, the story goes, Dickens announced that he couldn't travel by train any more that year, "on the grounds that the average annual quota of railroad accidents in Britain had not been filled and therefore further disasters were obviously imminent."

Purely numerical comparisons also may be socially unacceptable. When the state of Oregon decided to rank its medical services according to benefit-cost ratios, some results had to be thrown out—despite their statistical validity. Treatment for thumb sucking, crooked teeth, and headaches, for example, came out on the priorities list ahead of therapy for cystic fibrosis and AIDS.

What you consider risky, after all, depends somewhat on the circumstances of your life and lifestyle. People who don't have enough to eat don't worry about apples contaminated with Alar. People who face daily violence at their front door don't worry about hijackings on flights to the Bahamas. Attitudes toward risk evolve in cultural contexts and are influenced by everything from psychology to ethics to beliefs about personal responsibility.

In addition to context, another factor needed to see through the maze of conflicting messages about risk is human psychology. For example, imminent risks strike much more fear in our hearts than distant ones; it's much harder to get a teenager than an older person to take long-term dangers like smoking seriously.

Smoking is also a habit people believe they can control, which makes the risk far more acceptable. (People seem to get more upset about the effects of passive smoking than smoking itself—at least in part because smokers get to choose, and breathers don't.)

As a general principle, people tend to grossly exaggerate the risk of any danger perceived to be beyond their control, while shrugging off risks they think they can manage. Thus, we go skiing and skydiving, but fear asbestos. We resent and fear the idea that anonymous chemical companies are putting additives into our food; yet the additives we load onto our own food—salt, sugar, butter—are millions of times more dangerous.

This is one reason that airline accidents seem so unacceptable—because strapped into our seats in the cabin, what happens is completely beyond our control. In a poll taken soon after the TWA Flight 800 crash, an overwhelming majority of people said they'd be willing to pay up to fifty dollars more for a round-trip ticket if it increased airline safety. Yet the same people resist moves to improve automobile safety, for example, especially if it costs money.

The idea that we can control what happens also influences who we blame when things go wrong. Most people don't like to pay the costs for treating people injured by cigarettes or riding motorcycles because we think they brought these things on themselves. Some people also hold these attitudes toward victims of AIDS, or mental illness, because they think the illness results from lack of character or personal morals.

In another curious perceptual twist, risks associated with losing something and gaining something appear to be calculated in our minds according to quite different scales. In a now-classic series of studies, Stanford psychologist Amos Tversky and colleague Daniel Kahneman concluded that most people will bend over backward to avoid small risks, even if that means sacrificing great potential rewards. "The threat of a loss has a greater impact on a decision than the possibility of an equivalent gain," they concluded.

In one of their tests, Tversky and Kahneman asked physicians to choose between two strategies for combating a rare disease, expected to kill 600 people. Strategy A promised to save 200 people (the rest would die), while Strategy B offered a one-third probability that everyone would be saved, and a two-thirds probability that no one would be saved. Betting on a sure thing, the physicians choose A. But presented with the identical choice, stated differently, they choose B. The difference in language was simply this: Instead of stating that Strategy A would guarantee 200 out of 600 saved lives, it stated that Strategy A would mean 400 sure deaths.

People will risk a lot to prevent a loss, in other words, but risk very little for possible gain. Running into a burning house to save a pet or fighting back when a mugger asks for your wallet are both high-risk gambles that people take repeatedly in order to hang on to something they care about. The same people might not risk the hassle of, say, fastening a seat belt in a car even though the potential gain might be much higher.

The bird in the hand always seems more attractive than the two in the bush. Even if holding on to the one in your hand comes at a higher risk and the two in the bush are gold-plated.

The reverse situation comes into play when we judge risks of commission versus risks of omission. A risk that you assume by actually doing something seems far more risky than a risk you take by not doing something, even though the risk of doing nothing may be greater.

Deaths from natural causes, like cancer, are more readily acceptable than deaths from accidents or murder. That's probably one reason it's so much easier to accept thousands of starving children than the death of one in a drive-by shooting. The former is an act of omission—a failure to step in and help, send food or medicine. The latter is the commission of a crime—somebody pulled the trigger.

In the same way, the Food and Drug Administration is far more likely to withhold a drug that might help a great number of people if it threatens to harm a few; better to hurt a lot of people by failing to do something than act with the deliberate knowledge that some people will be hurt. Or as the doctors' credo puts it: First do no harm.

For obvious reasons, dramatic or exotic risks seem far more dangerous than more familiar ones. Plane crashes and AIDS are risks associated with ambulances and flashing lights, sex and drugs. While red dye #2 strikes terror in our hearts, that great glob of butter melting into our baked potato is accepted as an old friend. "A woman drives down the street with her child romping around in the front seat," says John Allen Paulos. "Then they arrive at the shopping mall, and she grabs the child's hand so hard it hurts, because she's afraid he'll be kidnapped."

Children who are kidnapped are far more likely to be whisked away by relatives than strangers, just as most people are murdered by people they know.

Familiar risks creep up on us like age and are often difficult to see until it's too late to take action. Mathematician Sam C. Saunders of Washington State University reminds us that a frog placed in hot water will struggle to escape, but the same frog placed in cool water that's slowly warmed up will sit peacefully until it's cooked. "One cannot anticipate what one does not perceive," he says, which is why gradual accumulations of risk due to lifestyle choices (like smoking or eating) are so often ignored. We're in hot water, but it's gotten hot so slowly that no one notices.

To bring home his point, Saunders asks us to imagine that cigarettes are not harmful—with the exception of an occasional one that has been packed with explosives instead of tobacco. These dynamite-stuffed cigarettes look just like normal ones. There's only one hidden away in every 18,250 packs—not a grave risk, you might say. The only catch is, if you smoke one of those explosive cigarettes, it might blow your head off.

The mathematician speculates, I think correctly, that given such a situation, cigarettes would surely be banned outright. After all, if 30 million packs of cigarettes are sold each day, an average of 1,600 people a day would die in gruesome explosions. Yet the number of deaths is the same to be expected from normal smoking. "The total expected loss of life or health to smokers using dynamite-loaded (but otherwise harmless) cigarettes over forty years would not be as great as with ordinary filtered cigarettes," says Saunders.

We can accept getting cooked like a frog, in other words, but not getting blown up like a firecracker.

It won't come as a great surprise to anyone that ego also plays a role in the way we assess risks. Psychological self-protection leads us to draw consistently wrong conclusions. In general, we overestimate the risks of bad things happening to others, while vastly underrating the possibility that they will happen to ourselves. Indeed, the lengths people go to minimize their own perceived risks can be downright "ingenious," according to Rutgers psychologist Neil Weinstein. For example, people asked about the risk of finding radon in their houses always rate their risk as "low" or "average," never "high." "If you ask them why," says Weinstein, "they take anything and twist it around in a way that reassures them. Some say their risk is low because the house is new; others, because the house is old. Some will say their risk is low because their house is at the top of a hill; others, because it's at the bottom of a hill."

Whatever the evidence to the contrary, we think: "It won't happen to me." Weinstein and others speculate that this has something to do with preservation of self-esteem. We don't like to see ourselves as vulnerable. We like to think we've got some magical edge over the others. Ego gets involved especially in cases where being vulnerable to risk implies personal failure—for example, the risk of depression, suicide, alcoholism, drug addiction. "If you admit you're at risk," says Weinstein, "you're admitting that you can't handle stress. You're not as strong as the next person."

Average people, studies have shown, believe that they will enjoy longer lives, healthier lives, and longer marriages than the "average" person. Despite the obvious fact that they themselves are, well, average people, too. According to a recent poll, 3 out of 4 baby boomers (those born between 1946 and 1964) think they look younger than their peers, and 4 out of 5 say they have fewer wrinkles than other people their age—a statistical impossibility.

Kahneman and Tversky studied this phenomenon as well and found that people think they'll beat the odds because they're special. This is no doubt a necessary psychological defense mechanism, or no one would ever get married again without thinking seriously about the potential for divorce. A clear view of personal vulnerability, however, could go a long way toward preventing activities like drunken driving. But then again, most people think they are better than average drivers— even when intoxicated.

We also seem to believe it won't happen to us if it hasn't happened yet. That is, we extrapolate from the past to the future. "I've been taking that highway at eighty miles per hour for ten years and I haven't crashed yet," we tell ourselves. This is rather like reasoning that flipping a coin ten times that comes up heads guarantees that heads will continue to come up indefinitely.

Curiously, one advertising campaign against drunken driving that was quite successful featured the faces of children killed by drunken drivers. These children looked real to us. We could identify with them. In the same way as we could identify with the people on TWA Flight 800. It's much easier to empathize with someone who has a name and a face than a statistic.

That explains in part why we go to great expense to rescue children who fall down mine shafts, but not children dying from preventable diseases. Economists call this the "rule of rescue." If you know that someone is in danger and you know that you can help, you have a moral obligation to do so. If you don't know about it, however, you have no obligation. Columnist Roger Simon speculates that's one reason the National Rifle Association lobbied successfully to eliminate the program at the Centers for Disease Control that keeps track of gun deaths. If we don't have to face what's happening, we won't feel obligated to do anything about it.

Even without the complication of all these psychological factors, however, calculating risks can be tricky because not everything is known about every situation. "We have to concede that a single neglected or unrecognized risk can invalidate all the reliability calculations, which are based on known risk," writes Ivar Ekeland. There is always a risk, in other words, that the risk assessment itself is wrong.

Genetic screening, like tests for HIV infection, has a certain probability of being wrong. If your results come back positive, how much should you worry? If they come back negative, how safe should you feel?

The more factors involved, the more complicated the risk assessment becomes. When you get to truly complex systems like nationwide telephone networks and power grids, worldwide computer networks and hugely complex machines like space shuttles, the risk of disaster becomes infinitely harder to pin down. No one knows when a minor glitch will set off a chain reaction of events that will culminate in disaster. Potential risks in complex systems, in other words, are subject to the same kinds of exponential amplification discussed in the previous chapter.

Needless to say, the way a society assesses risk is very different from the way an individual views the same choices. Whether or not you wish to ride a motorcycle is your own business. Whether society pays the bills for the thousands of people maimed by cycle accidents, however, is everybody's business. Any one of us might view our own survival on a transatlantic flight as more important than the needs of the nation's children. Governments, one presumes, ought to have a somewhat different agenda.

But how far does society want to go in strictly numerical accounting? It certainly hasn't helped much in the all-important issue of health care, where an ounce of prevention has been proven again and again to be worth many pounds of cures. Most experts agree that we should be spending much more money preventing common diseases and accidents, especially in children. But no one wants to take health dollars away from precarious newborns or the elderly—where most of it goes. These are decisions that ultimately will not be made by numbers alone. Calculating risk only helps us to see more clearly what exactly is going on.

According to anthropologist Melvin Konner, author of *Why the Reckless Survive*, our poor judgment about potential risks may well be the legacy of evolution. Early peoples lived at constant risk from predators, disease, accidents. They died young. And in evolutionary terms, "winning" means not longevity, but merely sticking around long enough to pass on your genes to the next generation. Taking risk was therefore a "winning" strategy, especially if it meant a chance to mate before dying. Besides, decisions had to be made quickly. If going for a meal of ripe berries meant risking an attack from a saber-toothed tiger, you dove for the berries. For a half-starved cave dweller, this was a relatively simple choice. Perhaps our brains are simply not wired, speculates Konner, for the careful calculations presented by the risks of modern life.

Indeed, some of our optimistic biases toward personal risk may still serve important psychological purposes. In times of stress and danger, they help us to put one foot in front of the other; they help us to get on with our lives, and out the door.

In the end, Konner, the cautious professor, ruminates somewhat wistfully about his risk-taking friends—who smoke, and ride motorcycles, and drive with their seat belts fastened behind them. Beside them, he feels "safe and virtuous," yet somehow uneasy. "I sometimes think," he muses, "that the more reckless among us may have something to teach the careful about the sort of immortality that comes from living fully every day."

POSSIBILITIES FOR WRITING

1. Select any three of K. C. Cole's examples and explain why you do or do not agree with what she says about people's behavior (your own included) with respect to each.

2. Identify two analogies or uses of exaggeration (or two instances where she uses analogy and exaggeration together) and discuss the point of the analogy/exaggeration and the extent to which you think it is effective.

3. Write a personal essay explaining your own attitudes toward taking risks. Illustrate your essay with examples from your own experience in deciding to engage in or to avoid particular kinds of behaviors. You may use examples from Cole's essay or provide others.

Charles Darwin (1809–1882) was born in Shrewsbury, England, and studied both medicine and religion before turning his attention full time to his first love, natural history. From 1831 to 1836, he served as official naturalist on an ocean voyage exploring the coast of South America, and his studies there, along with the many specimens he shipped back to England, led him to develop the theory of organic evolution based on natural selection that still predominates in scientific thinking today. His seminal Origin of Species *(1859) outlined his theory with abundant supporting detail and was followed by subsequent works in which he refined and elaborated on the theory, including* The Descent of Man *(1871). He is considered one of the most original thinkers in history.*

CHARLES DARWIN

Natural Selection

In the following excerpt from "Natural Selection," a chapter from *The Origin of Species*, Charles Darwin explains the concept of natural selection and provides scientific evidence for its existence and its ramifications. According to Darwin, natural selection is the process by which the evolution of species occurs. He lays out his theory of evolution by natural selection in great detail, postulating a world governed not by the providential design of an almighty creator, but by the irrevocable laws of species' adaptation to their environment.

Darwin's emphasis on the mechanism of natural selection undermined conventional theological and philosophical assumptions about the special place of human beings in the divine order of creation. According to this view, human beings are simply a species of animal that has adapted successfully to changing conditions, thus ensuring its capacity for survival.

How will the struggle for existence, discussed too briefly in the last chapter, act in regard to variation? Can the principle of selection, which we have seen is so potent in the hands of man, apply in nature? I think we shall see that it can act most effectually. Let it be borne in mind in what an endless number of strange peculiarities our domestic productions, and, in a lesser degree, those under nature, vary; and how strong the hereditary tendency is. Under domestication, it may be truly said that the whole organisation becomes in some degree plastic. Let it be borne in mind how infinitely complex and close-fitting are the mutual relations of all organic beings to each other and to their physical conditions of life. Can it, then, be thought improbable, seeing that variations useful to man have undoubtedly occurred, that other variations useful in some way to each being in the great and complex battle of life, should sometimes occur in the course of thousands of generations? If such do occur, can we doubt (remembering that many more individuals are born than can possibly survive) that individuals having any advantage, however slight, over others, would have the best chance of surviving and of procreating their kind? On the other hand, we may feel sure that any variation in the least degree injurious would be rigidly destroyed. This preservation of favourable variations and the rejection of injurious variations, I call Natural Selection. Variations neither useful nor injurious would not be affected by natural selection, and would be left a fluctuating element, as perhaps we see in the species called polymorphic.

We shall best understand the probable course of natural selection by taking the case of a country undergoing some physical change, for instance, of climate. The proportional numbers of its inhabitants would almost immediately undergo a change, and some species might become extinct. We may conclude, from what we have seen of the intimate and complex manner in which the inhabitants of each country are bound together, that any change in the numerical proportions of some of the inhabitants, independently of the change of climate itself, would most seriously affect many of the others. If the country were open on its borders, new forms would certainly immigrate, and this also would seriously disturb the relations of some of the former inhabitants. Let it be remembered how powerful the influence of a single introduced tree or mammal has been shown to be. But in the case of an island, or of a country partly surrounded by barriers, into which new and better adapted forms could not freely enter, we should then have places in the economy of nature which would assuredly be better filled up, if some of the original inhabitants were in some manner modified; for, had the area been open to immigration, these same places would have been seized on by intruders. In such case, every slight modification, which in the course of ages chanced to arise, and which in any way favoured the individuals of any of the species, by better adapting them to their altered conditions, would tend to be preserved; and natural selection would thus have free scope for the work of improvement.

We have reason to believe, as stated in the first chapter, that a change in the conditions of life, by specially acting on the reproductive system, causes or increases variability; and in the foregoing case the conditions of life are supposed to have undergone a change, and this would manifestly be favourable to natural selection, by giving a better chance of profitable variations occurring; and unless profitable variations do occur, natural selection can do nothing. Not that, as I believe, any extreme amount of variability is necessary; as man can certainly produce great results by adding up in any given direction mere individual differences, so could Nature, but far more easily, from having incomparably longer time at her disposal. Nor do I believe that any great physical change, as of climate, or any unusual degree of isolation to check immigration, is actually necessary to produce new and unoccupied places for natural selection to fill up by modifying and improving some of the varying inhabitants. For as all the inhabitants of each country are struggling together with nicely balanced forces, extremely slight modifications in the structure or habits of one inhabitant would often give it an advantage over others; and still further modifications of the same kind would often still further increase the advantage. No country can be named in which all the native inhabitants are now so perfectly adapted to each other and to the physical conditions under which they live, that none of them could anyhow be improved; for in all countries, the natives have been so far conquered by naturalised productions, that they have allowed foreigners to take firm possession of the land. And as foreigners have thus everywhere beaten some of the natives, we may safely conclude that the natives might have been modified with advantage, so as to have better resisted such intruders.

As man can produce and certainly has produced a great result by his methodical and unconscious means of selection, what may not nature effect? Man can act only on external and visible characters: nature cares nothing for appearances, except in so far as they may be useful to any being. She can act on every internal organ, on every shade of constitutional difference, on the whole machinery of life. Man selects only for his own good; Nature only for that of the being which she tends. Every selected character is fully exercised by her; and the being is placed under well-suited conditions of life. Man keeps the natives of many climates in the same country; he seldom exercises each selected character in some peculiar and fitting manner; he feeds a long and a short beaked pigeon on the same food; he does not exercise a long-backed or long-legged quadruped in any peculiar manner; he exposes sheep with long and short wool to the same climate. He does not allow the most vigorous males to struggle for the females. He does not rigidly destroy all inferior animals, but protects during each varying season, as far as lies in his power, all his productions. He often begins his selection by some half-monstrous form; or at least by some modification prominent enough to catch his eye, or to be plainly useful to him. Under nature, the slightest difference of structure or constitution may well turn the nicely-balanced scale in the struggle for life, and to be preserved. How fleeting are the wishes and efforts of man! How short his time! and consequently how poor will his products be, compared with those accumulated by nature during whole geological periods. Can we wonder, then, that nature's productions should be far 'truer' in character than man's productions; that they should be infinitely better adapted to the most complex conditions of life, and should plainly bear the stamp of far higher workmanship?

It may be said that natural selection is daily and hourly scrutinising, throughout the world, every variation, even the slightest; rejecting that which is bad, preserving and adding up all that is good; silently and insensibly working, whenever and wherever opportunity offers, at the improvement of each organic being in relation to its organic and inorganic conditions of life. We see nothing of these slow changes in progress, until the hand of time has marked the long lapses of ages, and then so imperfect is our view into long past geological ages, that we only see that the forms of life are now different from what they formerly were.

Although natural selection can act only through and for the good of each being, yet characters and structures, which we are apt to consider as of very trifling importance, may thus be acted on. When we see leaf-eating insects green, and bark-feeders mottled-grey; the alpine ptarmigan white in winter, the red-grouse the colour of heather, and the black-grouse that of peaty earth, we must believe that these tints are of service to these birds and insects in preserving them from danger. Grouse, if not destroyed at some period of their lives, would increase in countless numbers; they are known to suffer largely from birds of prey; and hawks are guided by eyesight to their prey,—so much so, that on parts of the Continent persons are warned not to keep white pigeons, as being the most liable to destruction. Hence I can see no reason to doubt that natural selection might be most effective in giving the proper colour to each kind of grouse, and in keeping that colour, when once acquired, true and constant. Nor ought we to think that the occasional destruction of an animal of any particular colour would produce little effect: we should remember how essential it is in a flock of white sheep to destroy every lamb with the faintest trace of black. In plants the down on the fruit and the colour of the flesh are considered by botanists as characters of the most trifling importance: yet we hear from an excellent horticulturist, Downing, that in the United States smooth-skinned fruits suffer far more from a beetle, a curculio, than those with down; that purple plums suffer far more from a certain disease than yellow plums; whereas another disease attacks yellow-fleshed peaches far more than those with other coloured flesh. If, with all the aids of art, these slight differences make a great difference in cultivating the several varieties, assuredly, in a state of nature, where the trees would have to struggle with other trees and with a host of enemies, such differences would effectually settle which variety, whether a smooth or downy, a yellow or purple fleshed fruit, should succeed.

In looking at many small points of difference between species, which, as far as our ignorance permits us to judge, seem to be quite unimportant, we must not forget that climate, food, probably produce some slight and direct effect. It is, however far more necessary to bear in mind that there are many unknown laws of correlation of growth, which, when one part of the organisation is modified through variation, and the modifications are accumulated by natural selection for the good of the being, will cause other modifications, often of the most unexpected nature.

As we see that those variations which under domestication appear at any particular period of life, tend to reappear in the offspring at the same period; —for instance, in the seeds of the many varieties of our culinary and agricultural plants; in the caterpillar and cocoon stages of the varieties of the silkworm; in the eggs of poultry, and in the colour of the down of their chickens; in the horns of our sheep and cattle when nearly adult; —so in a state of nature, natural selection will be enabled to act on and modify organic beings at any age, by the accumulation of profitable variations at that age, and by their inheritance at a corresponding age. If it profit a plant to have its seeds more and more widely disseminated by the wind, I can see no greater difficulty in this being effected through natural selection, than in the cotton-planter increasing and improving by selection the down in the pods on his cotton-trees. Natural selection may modify and adapt the larva of an insect to a score of contingencies, wholly different from those which concern the mature insect. These modifications will no doubt affect, through the laws of correlation, the structure of the adult; and probably in the case of those insects which live only for a few hours, and which never feed, a large part of their structure is merely the correlated result of successive changes in the structure of their larvae. So, conversely, modifications in the adult will probably often affect the structure of the larva; but in all cases natural selection will ensure that modifications consequent on other modifications at a different period of life, shall not be in the least degree injurious: for if they became so, they would cause the extinction of the species.

Natural selection will modify the structure of the young in relation to the parent, and of the parent in relation to the young. In social animals it will adapt the structure of each individual for the benefit of the community; if each in consequence profits by the selected change. What natural selection cannot do, is to modify the structure of one species, without giving it any advantage, for the good of another species; and though statements to this effect may be found in works of natural history, I cannot find one case which will bear investigation. A structure used only once in an animal's whole life, if of high importance to it, might be modified to any extent by natural selection; for instance, the great jaws possessed by certain insects, and used exclusively for opening the cocoon—or the hard tip to the beak of nestling birds, used for breaking the egg. It has been asserted, that of the best short-beaked tumbler-pigeons more perish in the egg than are able to get out of it; so that fanciers assist in the act of hatching. Now, if nature had to make the beak of a full-grown pigeon very short for the bird's own advantage, the process of modification would be very slow, and there would be simultaneously the most rigorous selection of the young birds within the egg, which had the most powerful and hardest beaks, for all with weak beaks would inevitably perish: or, more delicate and more easily broken shells might be selected, the thickness of the shell being known to vary like every other structure. . . .

Illustrations of the Action of Natural Selection

In order to make it clear how, as I believe, natural selection acts, I must beg permission to give one or two imaginary illustrations. Let us take the case of a wolf, which preys on various animals, securing some by craft, some by strength, and some by fleetness; and let us suppose that the fleetest prey, a deer for instance, had from any change in the country increased in numbers, or that other prey had decreased in numbers, during that season of the year when the wolf is hardest pressed for food. I can under such circumstances see no reason to doubt that the swiftest and slimmest wolves would have the best chance of surviving, and so be preserved or selected—provided always that they retained strength to master their prey at this or at some other period of the year, when they might be compelled to prey on other animals. I can see no more reason to doubt this, than that man can improve the fleetness of his greyhounds by careful and methodical selection, or by that unconscious selection which results from each man trying to keep the best dogs without any thought of modifying the breed.

Even without any change in the proportional numbers of the animals on which our wolf preyed, a cub might be born with an innate tendency to pursue certain kinds of prey. Nor can this be thought very improbable; for we often observe great differences in the natural tendencies of our domestic animals; one cat, for instance, taking to catch rats, another mice; one cat according to Mr. St. John, bringing home winged game, another hares or rabbits, and another hunting on marshy ground and almost nightly catching woodcocks or snipes. The tendency to catch rats rather than mice is known to be inherited. Now, if any slight innate change of habit or of structure benefited an individual wolf, it would have the best chance of surviving and of leaving offspring. Some of its young would probably inherit the same habits or structure, and by the repetition of this process, a new variety might be formed which would either supplant or coexist with the parent-form of wolf. Or, again, the wolves inhabiting a mountainous district, and those frequenting the lowlands, would naturally be forced to hunt different prey; and from the continued preservation of the individuals best fitted for the two sites, two varieties might slowly be formed. These varieties would cross and blend where they met; but to this subject of intercrossing we shall soon have to return. I may add, that, according to Mr. Pierce, there are two varieties of the wolf inhabiting the Catskill Mountains in the United States, one with a light greyhound-like form, which pursues deer, and the other more bulky, with shorter legs, which more frequently attacks the shepherd's flocks.

Let us now take a more complex case. Certain plants excrete a sweet juice, apparently for the sake of eliminating something injurious from their sap: this is effected by glands at the base of the stipules in some Leguminosae, and at the back of the leaf of the common laurel. This juice, though small in quantity, is greedily sought by insects. Let us now suppose a little sweet juice or nectar to be excreted by the inner bases of the petals of a flower. In this case insects in seeking the nectar would get dusted with pollen, and would certainly often transport the pollen from one flower to the stigma of another flower. The flowers of two distinct individuals of the same species would thus get crossed; and the act of crossing, we have good reason to believe (as will hereafter be more fully alluded to), would produce very vigorous seedlings, which consequently would have the best chance of flourishing and surviving. Some of these seedlings would probably inherit the nectar-excreting power. Those individual flowers which had the largest glands or nectaries, and which excreted most nectar, would be oftenest visited by insects and would be oftenest crossed; and so in the long-run would gain the upper hand. Those flowers, also, which had their stamens and pistils placed, in relation to the size and habits of the particular insects which visited them, so as to favour in any degree the transportal of their pollen from flower to flower, would likewise be favoured or selected. We might have taken the case of insects visiting flowers for the sake of collecting pollen instead of nectar; and as pollen is formed for the sole object of fertilisation, its destruction appears a simple loss to the plant; yet if a little pollen were carried, at first occasionally and then habitually, by the pollen-devouring insects from flower to flower, and a cross thus effected, although nine-tenths of the pollen were destroyed, it might still be a great gain to the plant; and those individuals which produced more and more pollen, and had larger and larger anthers, would be selected.

When our plant, by this process of the continued preservation or natural selection of more and more attractive flowers, had been rendered highly attractive to insects, they would, unintentionally on their part, regularly carry pollen from flower to flower; and that they can most effectually do this, I could easily show by many striking instances. I will give only one—not as a very striking case, but as likewise illustrating one step in the separation of the sexes of plants, presently to be alluded to. Some holly-trees bear only male flowers, which have four stamens producing rather a small quantity of pollen, and a rudimentary pistil; other holly-trees bear only female flowers; these have a full-sized pistil, and four stamens with shrivelled anthers, in which not a grain of pollen can be detected. Having found a female tree exactly sixty yards from a male tree, I put the stigmas of twenty flowers, taken from different branches, under the microscope, and on all, without exception, there were pollen-grains, and on some a profusion of pollen. As the wind had set for several days from the female to the male tree, the pollen could not thus have been carried. The weather had been cold and boisterous, and therefore not favourable to bees, nevertheless every female flower which I examined had been effectually fertilised by the bees, accidentally dusted with pollen, having flown from tree to tree in search of nectar. But to return to our imaginary case: as soon as the plant had been rendered so highly attractive to insects that pollen was regularly carried from flower to flower, another process might commence. No naturalist doubts the advantage of what has been called the physiological division of labour; hence we may believe that it would be advantageous to a plant to produce stamens alone in one flower or on one whole plant, and pistils alone in another flower or on another plant. In plants under culture and placed under new conditions of life, sometimes the male organs and sometimes the female organs become more or less impotent; now if we suppose this to occur in ever so slight a degree under nature, then as pollen is already carried regularly from flower to flower, and as a more complete separation of the sexes of our plant would be advantageous on the principle of the division of labour, individuals with this tendency more and more increased, would be continually favoured or selected, until at last a complete separation of the sexes would be effected.

Let us now turn to the nectar-feeding insects in our imaginary case: we may suppose the plant of which we have been slowly increasing the nectar by continued selection, to be a common plant; and that certain insects depended in main part on its nectar for food. I could give many facts, showing how anxious bees are to save time; for instance, their habit of cutting holes and sucking the nectar at the bases of certain flowers, which they can, with a very little more trouble, enter by the mouth. Bearing such facts in mind, I can see no reason to doubt that an accidental deviation in the size and form of the body, or in the curvature and length of the proboscis, far too slight to be appreciated by us, might profit a bee or other insect, so that an individual so characterised would be able to obtain its food more quickly, and so have a better chance of living and leaving descendants. Its descendants would probably inherit a tendency to a similar slight deviation of structure. The tubes of the corollas of the common red and incarnate clovers (Trifolium pratense and incarnatum) do not on a hasty glance appear to differ in length; yet the hive-bee can easily suck the nectar out of the incarnate clover, but not out of the common red clover, which is visited by humble-bees alone; so that whole fields of the red clover offer in vain an abundant supply of precious nectar to the hive-bee. Thus it might be a great advantage to the hive-bee to have a slightly longer or differently constructed proboscis. On the other hand, I have found by experiment that the fertility of clover greatly depends on bees visiting and moving parts of the corolla, so as to push the pollen on to the stigmatic surface. Hence, again, if humble-bees were to become rare in any country, it might be a great advantage to the red clover to have a shorter or more deeply divided tube to its corolla, so that the hive-bee could visit its flowers. Thus I can understand how a flower and a bee might slowly become, either simultaneously or one after the other, modified and adapted in the most perfect manner to each other, by the continued preservation of individuals presenting mutual and slightly favourable deviations of structure.

I am well aware that this doctrine of natural selection, exemplified in the above imaginary instances, is open to the same objections which were at first urged against Sir Charles Lyell's noble views on 'the modern changes of the earth, as illustrative of geology;' but we now very seldom hear the action, for instance, of the coast-waves, called a trifling and insignificant cause, when applied to the excavation of gigantic valleys or to the formation of the longest lines of inland cliffs. Natural selection can act only by the preservation and accumulation of infinitesimally small inherited modifications, each profitable to the preserved being; and as modern geology has almost banished such views as the excavation of a great valley by a single diluvial wave, so will natural selection, if it be a true principle, banish the belief of the continued creation of new organic beings, or of any great and sudden modification in their structure.

Summary of Chapter

If during the long course of ages and under varying conditions of life, organic beings vary at all in the several parts of their organisation, and I think this cannot be disputed; if there be, owing to the high geometrical powers of increase of each species, at some age, season, or year, a severe struggle for life, and this certainly cannot be disputed; then, considering the infinite complexity of the relations of all organic beings to each other and to their conditions of existence, causing an infinite diversity in structure, constitution, and habits, to be advantageous to them, I think it would be a most extraordinary fact if no variation ever had occurred useful to each being's own welfare, in the same way as so many variations have occurred useful to man. But if variations useful to any organic being do occur, assuredly individuals thus characterised will have the best chance of being preserved in the struggle for life; and from the strong principle of inheritance they will tend to produce offspring similarly characterised. This principle of preservation, I have called, for the sake of brevity, Natural Selection. Natural selection, on the principle of qualities being inherited at corresponding ages, can modify the egg, seed, or young, as easily as the adult. Amongst many animals, sexual selection will give its aid to ordinary selection, by assuring to the most vigorous and best adapted males the greatest number of offspring. Sexual selection will also give characters useful to the males alone, in their struggles with other males.

Whether natural selection has really thus acted in nature, in modifying and adapting the various forms of life to their several conditions and stations, must be judged of by the general tenour and balance of evidence given in the following chapters. But we already see how it entails extinction; and how largely extinction has acted in the world's history, geology plainly declares. Natural selection, also, leads to divergence of character; for more living beings can be supported on the same area the more they diverge in structure, habits, and constitution, of which we see proof by looking at the inhabitants of any small spot or at naturalised productions. Therefore during the modification of the descendants of any one species, and during the incessant struggle of all species to increase in numbers, the more diversified these descendants become, the better will be their chance of succeeding in the battle of life. Thus the small differences distinguishing varieties of the same species, will steadily tend to increase till they come to equal the greater differences between species of the same genus, or even of distinct genera.

We have seen that it is the common, the widely-diffused, and widely-ranging species, belonging to the larger genera, which vary most; and these will tend to transmit to their modified offspring that superiority which now makes them dominant in their own countries. Natural selection, as has just been remarked, leads to divergence of character and to much extinction of the less improved and intermediate forms of life. On these principles, I believe, the nature of the affinities of all organic beings may be explained. It is a truly wonderful fact—the wonder of which we are apt to overlook from familiarity—that all animals and all plants throughout all time and space should be related to each other in group subordinate to group, in the manner which we everywhere behold—namely, varieties of the same species most closely related together, species of the same genus less closely and unequally related together, forming sections and sub-genera, species of distinct genera much less closely related, and genera related in different degrees, forming subfamilies, families, orders, sub-classes, and classes. The several subordinate groups in any class cannot be ranked in a single file, but seem rather to be clustered round points, and these round other points, and so on in almost endless cycles. On the view that each species has been independently created, I can see no explanation of this great fact in the classification of all organic beings; but, to the best of my judgment, it is explained through inheritance and the complex action of natural selection, entailing extinction and divergence of character, as we have seen illustrated in the diagram.

The affinities of all the beings of the same class have sometimes been represented by a great tree. I believe this simile largely speaks the truth. The green and budding twigs may represent existing species; and those produced during each former year may represent the long succession of extinct species. At each period of growth all the growing twigs have tried to branch out on all sides, and to overtop and kill the surrounding twigs and branches, in the same manner as species and groups of species have tried to overmaster other species in the great battle for life. The limbs divided into great branches, and these into lesser and lesser branches, were themselves once, when the tree was small, budding twigs; and this connexion of the former and present buds by ramifying branches may well represent the classification of all extinct and living species in groups subordinate to groups. Of the many twigs which flourished when the tree was a mere bush, only two or three, now grown into great branches, yet survive and bear all the other branches; so with the species which lived during long-past geological periods, very few now have living and modified descendants. From the first growth of the tree, many a limb and branch has decayed and dropped off; and these lost branches of various sizes may represent those whole orders, families, and genera which have now no living representatives, and which are known to us only from having been found in a fossil state. As we here and there see a thin straggling branch springing from a fork low down in a tree, and which by some chance has been favoured and is still alive on its summit, so we occasionally see an animal like the Ornithorhynchus or Lepidosiren, which in some small degree connects by its affinities two large branches of life, and which has apparently been saved from fatal competition by having inhabited a protected station. As buds give rise by growth to fresh buds, and these, if vigorous, branch out and overtop on all sides many a feebler branch, so by generation I believe it has been with the great Tree of Life, which fills with its dead and broken branches the crust of the earth, and covers the surface with its ever branching and beautiful ramifications.

POSSIBILITIES FOR WRITING

1. Based on Darwin's explanations here, define "natural selection." You may quote from the text, but cast your definition primarily in your own words.
2. Focusing on the "Summary of Chapter" at the conclusion of the essay, analyze Darwin's logic. How does Darwin lay out his case and distill his primary ideas?
3. Do some research to write an essay focusing on current controversies surrounding teaching evolution in public schools. Why do Darwin's discoveries continue to trouble some, and where does the scientific community stand on the question of evolution?

Joan Didion (b. 1934) grew up in central California, where her family had lived for many generations. After graduating from the University of California at Berkeley in 1956, she joined the staff of Vogue *magazine, where she worked until the publication of her first novel,* Run River, *in 1963. Other novels followed—including* Play It As It Lays *(1970),* A Book of Common Prayer *(1977), and* The Last Thing He Wanted *(1996)—but it is her essays, particularly those collected in* Slouching Towards Bethlehem *(1968) and* The White Album *(1979), that established Didion as one of the most admired voices of her generation. A meticulous stylist who combines sharply observed detail with wry—even bracing—irony, she has examined subjects that range from life in Southern California to the Washington political scene to the war in El Salvador to marriage Las Vegas–style. Among her recent books is* The Year of Magical Thinking *(2005).*

JOAN DIDION

Marrying Absurd

In "Marrying Absurd," Joan Didion takes a critical look at the Las Vegas wedding industry. In keeping with the portraits of people and places throughout her work, Didion uses carefully selected details to convey her impression of Las Vegas and to render her judgment of its values. She uses a number of ironic techniques to establish and sustain her satiric tone, most significantly, perhaps, including details that mean one thing to the Las Vegas wedding people and something quite different to the reader. Examples include the signs advertising weddings posted throughout the city, as well as comments made by participants, in which they condemn themselves, unwittingly. Some of the most damning examples of this ironic use of dialogue occur in the essay's concluding paragraph.

"Marrying Absurd," however, conveys more than Joan Didion's acerbic criticism of Las Vegas marriages. It also suggests something of Didion's attitude toward the larger national problem of what she describes as "venality" and a "devotion to immediate gratification."

To be married in Las Vegas, Clark County, Nevada, a bride must swear that she is eighteen or has parental permission and a bridegroom that he is twenty-one or has parental permission. Someone must put up five dollars for the license. (On Sundays and holidays, fifteen dollars. The Clark County Courthouse issues marriage licenses at any time of the day or night except between noon and one in the afternoon, between eight and nine in the evening, and between four and five in the morning.) Nothing else is required. The State of Nevada, alone among these United States, demands neither a premarital blood test nor a waiting period before or after the issuance of a marriage license. Driving in across the Mojave from Los Angeles, one sees the signs way out on the desert, looming up from that moonscape of rattlesnakes and mesquite, even before the Las Vegas lights appear like a mirage on the horizon: "GET-TING MARRIED? Free License Information First Strip Exit." Perhaps the Las Vegas wedding industry achieved its peak operational efficiency between 9:00 p.m. and midnight of August 26, 1965, an otherwise unremarkable Thursday which happened to be, by Presidential order, the last day on which anyone could improve his draft status merely by getting married. One hundred and seventy-one couples were pronounced man and wife in the name of Clark County and the State of Nevada that night, sixty-seven of them by a single justice of the peace, Mr. James A. Brennan. Mr. Brennan did one wedding at the Dunes and the other sixty-six in his office, and charged each couple eight dollars. One bride lent her veil to six others. "I got it down from five to three minutes," Mr. Brennan said later of his feat. "I could've married them *en masse*, but they're people, not cattle. People expect more when they get married."

What people who get married in Las Vegas actually do expect—what, in the largest sense, their "expectations" are—strikes one as a curious and self-contradictory business. Las Vegas is the most extreme and allegorical of American settlements, bizarre and beautiful in its venality and in its devotion to immediate gratification, a place the tone of which is set by mobsters and call girls and ladies' room attendants with amyl nitrite poppers in their uniform pockets. Almost everyone notes that there is no "time" in Las Vegas, no night and no day and no past and no future (no Las Vegas casino, however, has taken the obliteration of the ordinary time sense quite so far as Harold's Club in Reno, which for a while issued, at odd intervals in the day and night, mimeographed "bulletins" carrying news from the world outside); neither is there any logical sense of where one is. One is standing on a highway in the middle of a vast hostile desert looking at an eighty-foot sign which blinks "Stardust" or "Caesar's Palace." Yes, but what does that explain? This geographical implausibility reinforces the sense that what happens there has no connection with "real" life; Nevada cities like Reno and Carson are ranch towns, Western towns, places behind which there is some historical imperative. But Las Vegas seems to exist only in the eye of the beholder. All of which makes it an extraordinarily stimulating and interesting place, but an odd one in which to want to wear a candlelight satin Priscilla of Boston wedding dress with Chantilly lace insets, tapered sleeves and a detachable modified train.

And yet the Las Vegas wedding business seems to appeal to precisely that impulse. "Sincere and Dignified Since 1954," one wedding chapel advertises. There are nineteen such wedding chapels in Las

Vegas, intensely competitive, each offering better, faster, and, by implication, more sincere services than the next: Our Photos Best Anywhere, Your Wedding on A Phonograph Record, Candlelight with Your Ceremony, Honeymoon Accommodations, Free Transportation from Your Motel to Courthouse to Chapel and Return to Motel, Religious or Civil Ceremonies, Dressing Rooms, Flowers, Rings, Announcements, Witnesses Available, and Ample Parking. All of these services, like most others in Las Vegas (sauna baths, payroll-check cashing, chinchilla coats for sale or rent), are offered twenty-four hours a day, seven days a week, presumably on the premise that marriage, like craps, is a game to be played when the table seems hot.

But what strikes one most about the Strip chapels, with their wishing wells and stained-glass paper windows and their artificial bouvardia, is that so much of their business is by no means a matter of simple convenience, of late-night liaisons between show girls and baby Crosbys. Of course there is some of that. (One night about eleven o'clock in Las Vegas I watched a bride in an orange minidress and masses of flame-colored hair stumble from a Strip chapel on the arm of her bridegroom, who looked the part of the expendable nephew in movies like *Miami Syndicate*. "I gotta get the kids," the bride whimpered. "I gotta pick up the sitter, I gotta get to the midnight show." "What you gotta get," the bridegroom said, opening the door of a Cadillac Coupe de Ville and watching her crumple on the seat, "is sober.") But Las Vegas seems to offer something other than "convenience"; it is merchandising "niceness," the facsimile of proper ritual, to children who do not know how else to find it, how to make the arrangements, how to do it "right." All day and evening long on the Strip, one sees actual wedding parties, waiting under the harsh lights at a crosswalk, standing uneasily in the parking lot of the Frontier while the photographer hired by The Little Church of the West ("Wedding Place of the Stars") certifies the occasion, takes the picture: the bride in a veil and white satin pumps, the bridegroom usually in a white dinner jacket, and even an attendant or two, a sister or a best friend in hot-pink *peau de soie,* a flirtation veil, a carnation nosegay. "When I Fall in Love It Will Be Forever," the organist plays, and then a few bars of Lohengrin. The mother cries; the stepfather, awkward in his role, invites the chapel hostess to join them for a drink at the Sands. The hostess declines with a professional smile; she has already transferred her interest to the group waiting outside. One bride out, another in, and again the sign goes up on the chapel door: "One Moment please—Wedding."

I sat next to one such wedding party in a Strip restaurant the last time I was in Las Vegas. The marriage had just taken place; the bride still wore her dress, the mother her corsage. A bored waiter poured out a few swallows of pink champagne ("on the house") for everyone but the bride, who was too young to be served. "You'll need something with more kick than that," the bride's father said with heavy jocularity to his new son-in-law; the ritual jokes about the wedding night had a certain Pangiossian character, since the bride was clearly several months pregnant. Another round of pink champagne, this time not on the house, and the bride began to cry. "It was just as nice," she sobbed, "as I hoped and dreamed it would be."

POSSIBILITIES FOR WRITING

1. Didion inevitably conveys an air of superiority in this essay—her purpose, after all, is to point out what she sees as the absurdity of the marriage business in Las Vegas. In an essay, analyze how you respond to this tone and this attitude toward her subjects. Use specific quotations to elaborate on the reasons for your response.

2. One of Didion's main points is that many of those who marry in Las Vegas chapels do so in order to have "the facsimile of proper ritual"; they are "children who do not know how else to find it, how to make the arrangements, how to do it 'right.' " Didion was writing in 1967. What is most people's notion of "proper ritual" today? In considering this question, think not only of weddings but of anything that is traditionally considered a "solemn occasion": graduations, church services, funerals, and the like. What do you think is the proper level of formality for such occasions?

3. Pick a setting where you think people engage in "absurd" behavior. Either spend some time observing what happens there, or re-create these activities in detail from memory. Then write an essay, as Didion does, in which you describe this setting and these activities in an ironic light. Be as specific as possible.

On Self-Respect

The title of Didion's essay promises an exploration of the meaning of self-respect, and, not surprisingly, it delivers on that promise. Along the way it also says what self-respect is not: a technique of "negative definition" writers often use when explaining an abstract concept. Besides using negative definition, Didion provides examples to clarify what she means by self-respect.

Didion's essay is loosely structured. Its form, like its title, owes something to Montaigne, who envisioned the essay as an exploration of a topic, without a strictly logical structure and a clearly defined thesis. Didion asserts the importance of self-respect, and she identifies a number of key qualities it comprises, including honesty, integrity, and discipline.

Once, in a dry season, I wrote in large letters across two pages of a notebook that innocence ends when one is stripped of the delusion that one likes oneself. Although now, some years later, I marvel that a mind on the outs with itself should have nonetheless made painstaking record of its every tremor, I recall with embarrassing clarity the flavor of those particular ashes. It was a matter of misplaced self-respect.

I had not been elected to Phi Beta Kappa. This failure could scarcely have been more predictable or less ambiguous (I simply did not have the grades), but I was unnerved by it; I had somehow thought myself a kind of academic Raskolnikov, curiously exempt from the cause-effect relationships which hampered others. Although even the humorless nineteen-year-old that I was must have recognized that the situation lacked real tragic stature, the day that I did not make Phi Beta Kappa nonetheless marked the end of something, and innocence may well be the word for it. I lost the conviction that lights would always turn green for me, the pleasant certainty that those rather passive virtues which had won me approval as a child automatically guaranteed me not only Phi Beta Kappa keys but happiness, honor, and the love of a good man; lost a certain touching faith in the totem power of good manners, clean hair, and proven competence on the Stanford-Binet scale. To such doubtful amulets had my self-respect been pinned, and I faced myself that day with the nonplused apprehension of someone who has come across a vampire and has no crucifix at hand.

Although to be driven back upon oneself is an uneasy affair at best, rather like trying to cross a border with borrowed credentials, it seems to me now the one condition necessary to the beginnings of real self-respect. Most of our platitudes notwithstanding, self-deception remains the most difficult deception. The tricks that work on others count for nothing in that very well-lit back alley where one keeps assignations with oneself: no winning smiles will do here, no prettily drawn lists of good intentions. One shuffles flashily but in vain through one's marked cards—the kindness done for the wrong reason, the apparent triumph which involved no real effort, the seemingly heroic act into which one had been shamed. The dismal fact is that self-respect has nothing to do with the approval of others—who are, after all, deceived easily enough; has nothing to do with reputation, which, as Rhett Butler told Scarlett O'Hara, is something people with courage can do without.

To do without self-respect, on the other hand, is to be an unwilling audience of one to an interminable documentary that details one's failings, both real and imagined, with fresh footage spliced in for every screening. *There's the glass you broke in anger, there's the hurt on X's face; watch now, this next scene, the night Y came back from Houston, see how you muff this one.* To live without self-respect is to lie awake some night, beyond the reach of warm milk, phenobarbital, and the sleeping hand on the coverlet, counting up the sins of commission and omission, the trusts betrayed, the promises subtly broken, the gifts irrevocably wasted through sloth or cowardice or carelessness. However long we postpone it, we eventually lie down alone in that notoriously uncomfortable bed, the one we make ourselves. Whether or not we sleep in it depends, of course, on whether or not we respect ourselves.

To protest that some fairly improbable people, some people who *could not possibly respect themselves* seem to sleep easily enough is to miss the point entirely, as surely as those people miss it who think that self-respect has necessarily to do with not having safety pins in one's underwear. There is a common superstition that "self-respect" is a kind of charm against snakes, something that keeps those who have it locked in some unblighted Eden, out of strange beds, ambivalent conversations, and trouble in general. It does not at all. It has nothing to do with the face of things, but concerns instead a separate peace, a private reconciliation. Although the careless, suicidal Julian English in *Appointment in Samarra* and the careless, incurably dishonest Jordan Baker in *The Great Gatsby* seem equally improbable candidates for self-respect, Jordan Baker had it, Julian English did not. With that genius for accommodation more often seen in women than in men, Jordan took her own measure, made her own peace, avoided threats to that peace: "I hate careless people." she told Nick Carraway. "It takes two to make an accident."

Like Jordan Baker, people with self-respect have the courage of their mistakes. They know the price of things. If they choose to commit adultery, they do not then go running, in an access of bad conscience, to receive absolution from the wronged parties; nor do they complain unduly of the unfairness, the undeserved embarrassment, of being named co-respondent. In brief, people with self-respect exhibit a certain toughness, a kind of moral nerve; they display what was once called *character*, a quality which, although approved in the abstract, sometimes loses ground to other, more instantly negotiable virtues. The measure of its slipping prestige is that one tends to think of it only in connection with homely children and United States senators who have been defeated, preferably in the primary, for reelection. Nonetheless, character— the willingness to accept responsibility for one's own life—is the source from which self-respect springs.

Self-respect is something that our grandparents, whether or not they had it, knew all about. They had instilled in them, young, a certain discipline, the sense that one lives by doing things one does not particularly want to do, by putting fears and doubts to one side, by weighing immediate comforts against the possibility of larger, even intangible, comforts. It seemed to the nineteenth century admirable, but not remarkable, that Chinese Gordon put on a clean white suit and held Khartoum against the Mahdi; it did not seem unjust that the way to free land in California involved death and difficulty and dirt. In a diary kept during the winter of 1846, an emigrating twelve-year-old named Narcissa Cornwall noted coolly: "Father was busy reading and did not notice that the house was being filled with strange Indians until Mother spoke about it." Even lacking any clue as to what Mother said, one can scarcely fail to be impressed by the entire incident: the father reading, the Indians filing in, the mother choosing the words that would not alarm, the child duly recording the event and noting further that those particular Indians were not, "fortunately for us," hostile. Indians were simply part of the *donnée*.

In one guise or another, Indians always are. Again, it is a question of recognizing that anything worth having has its price. People who respect themselves are willing to accept the risk that the Indians will be hostile, that the venture will go bankrupt, that the liaison may not turn out to be one in which *every day is a holiday because you're married to me*. They are willing to invest something of themselves; they may not play at all, but when they do play, they know the odds.

That kind of self-respect is a discipline, a habit of mind that can never be faked but can be developed, trained, coaxed forth. It was once suggested to me that, as an antidote to crying, I put my head in a paper bag. As it happens, there is a sound physiological reason, something to do with oxygen, for doing exactly that, but the psychological effect alone is incalculable: it is difficult in the extreme to continue fancying oneself Cathy in *Wuthering Heights* with one's head in a Food Fair bag. There is a similar case for all the small disciplines, unimportant in themselves; imagine maintaining any kind of swoon, commiserative or carnal, in a cold shower.

But those small disciplines are valuable only insofar as they represent larger ones. To say that Waterloo was won on the playing fields of Eton is not to say that Napoleon might have been saved by a crash program in cricket; to give formal dinners in the rain forest would be pointless did not the candlelight flickering on the liana call forth deeper, stronger disciplines, values instilled long before. It is a kind of ritual, helping us to remember who and what we are. In order to remember it, one must have known it.

To have that sense of one's intrinsic worth which constitutes self-respect is potentially to have everything: the ability to discriminate, to love and to remain indifferent. To lack it is to be locked within oneself, paradoxically incapable of either love or indifference. If we do not respect ourselves, we are on the one hand forced to despise those who have so few resources as to consort with us, so little perception as to remain blind to our fatal weaknesses. On the other, we are peculiarly in thrall to everyone we see, curiously determined to live out—since our self-image is untenable—their false notions of us. We flatter ourselves by thinking this compulsion to please others an attractive trait: a gist for imaginative empathy, evidence of our willingness to give. *Of course* I will play Francesca to your Paolo, Helen Keller to anyone's Annie Sullivan: no expectation is too misplaced, no role too ludicrous. At the mercy of those we cannot but hold in contempt, we play roles doomed to failure before they are begun, each defeat generating fresh despair at the urgency of divining and meeting the next demand made upon us.

It is the phenomenon sometimes called "alienation from self." In its advanced stages, we no longer answer the telephone, because someone might want something; that we could say *no* without drowning in self-reproach is an idea alien to this game. Every encounter demands too much, tears the nerves, drains the will, and the specter of something as small as an unanswered letter arouses such disproportionate guilt that answering it becomes out of the question. To assign unanswered letters their proper weight, to free us from the expectations of others, to give us back to ourselves—there lies the great, the singular power of self-respect. Without it, one eventually discovers the final turn of the screw: one runs away to find oneself, and finds no one at home.

POSSIBILITIES FOR WRITING

1. Didion's definition of "self-respect" is based primarily on examples. Analyze her use of these, making sure to look up any references or allusions with which you are unfamiliar.
2. Didion uses a variety of closely related words in defining "self-respect," among them "character," "courage," "discipline," and "private reconciliation." Using these and others you find in the essay, consider how the nuances of these terms help contribute to the overall definition.
3. Define "self-respect" from your own perspective, offering examples to suggest people you believe do and do not possess it.

Annie Dillard (b. 1945) *developed an interest in nature at the age of ten, after discovering* The Field Book of Ponds and Streams *in a branch of the Pittsburgh library system. While studying creative writing and theology at Hollins College in rural Virginia, she began a journal of observations of natural phenomena that would eventually become the Pulitzer Prize–winning* Pilgrim at Tinker Creek *(1974), her first published work of nonfiction. This was followed by* Holy the Firm *(1977), a mystical meditation on the natural world, and* Teaching a Stone to Talk *(1982), a collection of philosophical essays. A professor at Wesleyan College, Dillard has also published several volumes of poetry, a novel, and a memoir of her youth,* An American Childhood *(1987). Her most recent book is a novel,* The Maytrees *(2007).*

ANNIE DILLARD

Living Like Weasels

In "Living Like Weasels," Annie Dillard describes an encounter with a weasel she had one day while resting on a log in a patch of woods near a housing development in Virginia. Dillard begins in the expository mode, detailing facts about weasels, especially their tenacity and wildness. But she shifts, before long, into a meditation on the value and necessity of instinct and tenacity in human life. Dillard's tone changes from the factual declaration of the opening into speculative wonder at the weasel's virtues and, finally, into urgent admonition. By the end of the essay Dillard has made the weasel a symbol of how human beings might live.

As a "nature writer," Dillard is compelling. She digs deep beneath the surface of her subjects, always looking for connections between the natural and human worlds. In "Living Like Weasels," these connections take the form of speculating about the connections and disjunctions between the wildness and ferocity of a little brown-bodied, furry creature, and the human need to find our necessity, lock onto it, and never let go. Dillard privileges wildness over civilization, mystical communion over separateness, instinct over intellect. She clearly values the weasel's tenacity.

I

A weasel is wild. Who knows what he thinks? He sleeps in his underground den, his tail draped over his nose. Sometimes he lives in his den for two days without leaving. Outside, he stalks rabbits, mice, muskrats, and birds, killing more bodies than he can eat warm, and often dragging the carcasses home. Obedient to instinct, he bites his prey at the neck, either splitting the jugular vein at the throat or crunching the brain at the base of the skull, and he does not let go. One naturalist refused to kill a weasel who was socketed into his hand deeply as a rattlesnake. The man could in no way pry the tiny weasel off, and he had to walk half a mile to water, the weasel dangling from his palm, and soak him off like a stubborn label.

And once, says Ernest Thompson Seton—once, a man shot an eagle out of the sky. He examined the eagle and found the dry skull of a weasel fixed by the jaws to his throat. The supposition is that the eagle had pounced on the weasel and the weasel swiveled and bit as instinct taught him, tooth to neck, and nearly won. I would like to have seen that eagle from the air a few weeks or months before he was shot: was the whole weasel still attached to his feathered throat, a fur pendant? Or did the eagle eat what he could reach, gutting the living weasel with his talons before his breast, bending his beak, cleaning the beautiful airborne bones?

II

I have been reading about weasels because I saw one last week. I startled a weasel who startled me, and we exchanged a long glance.

Twenty minutes from my house, through the woods by the quarry and across the highway, is Hollins Pond, a remarkable piece of shallowness, where I like to go at sunset and sit on a tree trunk. Hollins Pond is also called Murray's Pond; it covers two acres of bottomland near Tinker Creek with six inches of water and six thousand lily pads. In winter, brown-and-white steers stand in the middle of it, merely dampening their hooves; from the distant shore they look like miracle itself, complete with miracle's nonchalance. Now, in summer, the steers are gone. The water lilies have blossomed and spread to a green horizontal plane that is terra firma to plodding blackbirds, and tremulous ceiling to black leeches, cray fish, and carp.

This is, mind you, suburbia. It is a five-minute walk in three directions to rows of houses, though none is visible here. There's a 55 mph highway at one end of the pond, and a nesting pair of wood ducks at the other. Under every bush is a muskrat hole or a beer can. The far end is an alternating series of fields and woods, fields and woods, threaded everywhere with motorcycle tracks—in whose bare clay wild turtles lay eggs.

So, I had crossed the highway, stepped over two low barbed-wire fences, and traced the motorcycle path in all gratitude through the wild rose and poison ivy of the pond's shoreline up into high grassy fields. Then I cut down through the woods to the mossy fallen tree where I sit. This tree is excellent. It makes a dry, upholstered bench at the upper, marshy end of the pond, a plush jetty raised from the thorn shore between a shallow blue body of water and a deep blue body of sky.

The sun had just set. I was relaxed on the tree trunk, ensconced in the lap of lichen, watching the lily pads at my feet tremble and part dreamily over the thrusting path of a carp. A yellow bird appeared to my right and flew behind me. It caught my eye; I swiveled around—and the next instant, inexplicably, I was looking down at a weasel, who was looking up at me.

III

Weasel! I'd never seen one wild before. He was ten inches long, thin as a curve, a muscled ribbon, brown as fruitwood, soft-furred, alert. His face was fierce, small and pointed as a lizard's; he would have made a good arrowhead. There was just a dot of chin, maybe two brown hairs' worth, and then the pure white fur began that spread down his underside. He had two black eyes I didn't see, any more than you see a window.

The weasel was stunned into stillness as he was emerging from beneath an enormous shaggy wild rose bush four feet away. I was stunned into stillness twisted backward on the tree trunk. Our eyes locked, and someone threw away the key.

Our look was as if two lovers, or deadly enemies, met unexpectedly on an overgrown path when each had been thinking of something else: a clearing blow to the gut. It was also a bright blow to the brain, or a sudden beating of brains with all the charge and intimate grate of rubbed balloons. It emptied our lungs. It felled the forest, moved the fields, and drained the pond; the world dismantled and tumbled into that black hole of eyes. If you and I looked at each other that way, our skulls would split and drop to our shoulders. But we don't. We keep our skulls. So.

He disappeared. This was only last week, and already I don't remember what shattered the enchantment. I think I blinked, I think I retrieved my brain from the weasel's brain, and tried to memorize what I was seeing, and the weasel felt the yank of separation, the careening splashdown into real life and the urgent current of instinct. He vanished under the wild rose. I waited motionless, my mind suddenly full of data and my spirit with pleadings, but he didn't return.

Please do not tell me about "approach-avoidance conflicts." I tell you I've been in that weasel's brain for sixty seconds, and he was in mine. Brains are private places, muttering through unique and secret tapes—but the weasel and I both plugged into another tape simultaneously, for a sweet and shocking time. Can I help it if it was a blank?

What goes on in his brain the rest of the time? What does a weasel think about? He won't say. His journal is tracks in clay, a spray of feathers, mouse blood and bone: uncollected, unconnected, loose-leaf, and blown.

IV

I would like to learn, or remember, how to live. I come to Hollins Pond not so much to learn how to live as, frankly, to forget about it. That is, I don't think I can learn from a wild animal how to live in particular—shall I suck warm blood, hold my tail high, walk with my footprints precisely over the prints of my hands?—but I might learn something of mindlessness, something of the purity of living in the physical senses and the dignity of living without bias or motive. The weasel lives in necessity and we live in choice, hating necessity and dying at the last ignobly in its talons. I would like to live as I should, as the weasel lives as he should. And I suspect that for me the way is like the weasel's: open to time and death painlessly, noticing everything, remembering nothing, choosing the given with a fierce and pointed will.

V

I missed my chance. I should have gone for the throat. I should have lunged for that streak of white under the weasel's chin and held on, held on through mud and into the wild rose, held on for a dearer life. We could live under the wild rose wild as weasels, mute and uncomprehending. I could very calmly go wild. I could live two days in the den, curled, leaning on mouse fur, sniffing bird bones, blinking, licking, breathing musk, my hair tangled in the roots of grasses. Down is a good place to go, where the mind is single. Down is out, out of your ever-loving mind and back to your careless senses. I remember muteness as a prolonged and giddy fast, where every moment is a feast of utterance received. Time and events are merely poured, unremarked, and ingested directly, like blood pulsed into my gut through a jugular vein. Could two live that way? Could two live under the wild rose, and explore by the pond, so that the smooth mind of each is as everywhere present to the other, and as received and as unchallenged, as falling snow?

We could, you know. We can live any way we want. People take vows of poverty, chastity, and obedience—even of silence—by choice. The thing is to stalk your calling in a certain skilled and supple way, to locate the most tender and live spot and plug into that pulse. This is yielding, not fighting. A weasel doesn't 'attack' anything; a weasel lives as he's meant to, yielding at every moment to the perfect freedom of single necessity.

VI

I think it would be well, and proper, and obedient, and pure, to grasp your one necessity and not let it go, to dangle from it limp wherever it takes you. Then even death, where you're going no matter how you live, cannot you part. Seize it and let it seize you up aloft even, till your eyes burn out and drop; let your musky flesh fall off in shreds, and let your very bones unhinge and scatter, loosened over fields, over fields and woods, lightly, thoughtless, from any height at all, from as high as eagles.

POSSIBILITIES FOR WRITING

1. Central to Dillard's point here are the concepts of "mindlessness" and "necessity" as opposed to consciousness and choice. In an essay, explore what Dillard means by these terms and what value she apparently finds in giving oneself over to mindlessness and necessity.

2. Dillard's essay is divided into six parts, all linked by repeated images and words. Analyze the essay to note as many of these linkages as you can. Then explore how several of these threads function meaningfully in the essay.

3. Dillard's encounter with the weasel provides her with a profound insight about humans and the natural world. Recall a time when an encounter or experience led you to see some aspect of life in a new light. In an essay explore the circumstances of this sudden insight.

ANNIE DILLARD

Heaven and Earth in Jest

In "Heaven and Earth in Jest," an excerpt from her 1974 book, *Pilgrim at Tinker Creek*, Annie Dillard presents three scenes. The first is a shocking scene, one that leaves her "dumbstruck": a giant waterbug sucks the life out of an unsuspecting frog, who is victimized by the poison that dissolves its bones and internal organs, reducing them to a juice that the predator ingests.

Balancing this horrifying scene is another: a moment of grace and joy in which Dillard describes a mockingbird diving nearly to its destruction from a rooftop until it unfurls its wings at the last moment to float gracefully onto the grass. Dillard's third and final descriptive sketch describes a group of sharks swimming together in a roil of foaming water. The image is one of beauty and terror, which combines the shocking horror of the waterbug vignette with the beauty of the mockingbird scene. In describing all tree scenes. Dillard wonders about their meaning, probing with philosophical questions that lack easy answers, or indeed any satisfying answers at all.

A couple of summers ago I was walking along the edge of the island to see what I could see in the water, and mainly to scare frogs. Frogs have an inelegant way of taking off from invisible positions on the bank just ahead of your feet, in dire panic, emitting a froggy "Yike!" and splashing into the water. Incredibly, this amused me, and, incredibly, it amuses me still. As I walked along the grassy edge of the island, I got better and better at seeing frogs both in and out of the water. I learned to recognize, slowing down, the difference in texture of the light reflected from mudbank, water, grass, or frog. Frogs were flying all around me. At the end of the island I noticed a small green frog. He was exactly half in and half out of the water, looking like a schematic diagram of an amphibian, and he didn't jump.

He didn't jump; I crept closer. At last I knelt on the island's winterkilled grass, lost, dumbstruck, staring at the frog in the creek just four feet away. He was a very small frog with wide, dull eyes. And just as I looked at him, he slowly crumpled and began to sag. The spirit vanished from his eyes as if snuffed. His skin emptied and drooped; his very skull seemed to collapse and settle like a kicked tent. He was shrinking before my eyes like a deflating football. I watched the taut, glistening skin on his shoulders rack, and rumple, and fall. Soon, part of his skin, formless as a pricked balloon, lay in floating folds like bright scum on top of the water: it was a monstrous and terrifying thing. I gaped bewildered, appalled. An oval shadow hung in the water behind the drained frog; then the shadow glided away. The frog skin bag started to sink.

I had read about the giant water bug, but never seen one. "Giant water bug" is really the name of the creature, which is an enormous, heavy-bodied brown beetle. It eats insects, tadpoles, fish, and frogs. Its grasping forelegs are mighty and hooked inward. It seizes a victim with these legs, hugs it tight, and paralyzes it with enzymes injected during a vicious bite. That one bite is the only bite it ever takes. Through the puncture shoot the poisons that dissolve the victim's muscles and bones and organs—all but the skin—and through it the giant water bug sucks out the victim's body, reduced to a juice. This event is quite common in warm fresh water. The frog I saw was being sucked by a giant water bag. I had been kneeling on the island grass; when the unrecognizable flap of frog skin settled on the creek bottom, swaying, I stood up and brushed the knees of my pants. I couldn't catch my breath.

Of course, many carnivorous animals devour their prey alive. The usual method seems to be to subdue the victim by downing or grasping it so it can't flee, then eating it whole or in a series of bloody bites. Frogs eat everything whole, stuffing prey into their mouths with their thumbs. People have seen frogs with their wide jaws so full of live dragonflies they couldn't close them. Ants don't even have to catch their prey: in the spring they swarm over newly hatched, featherless birds in the nest and eat them tiny bite by bite.

That it's rough out there and chancy is no surprise. Every live thing is a survivor on a kind of extended emergency bivouac. But at the same time we are also created. In the Koran, Allah asks, "The heaven and the earth and all in between, thinkest thou I made them *in jest?*" It's a good question. What do we think of the created universe, spanning an unthinkable void with an unthinkable profusion of forms? Or what do we think of nothingness, those sickening reaches of time in either direction? If the giant water bug was not made in jest, was it then made in earnest? Pascal uses a nice term to describe the notion of the creator's, once having called forth the universe, turning his back to it: *Deus Absconditus.* Is this what we think happened? Was the sense of it there, and God absconded with it, ate it, like a wolf who disappears round the edge of the house with the Thanksgiving turkey? "God is subtle," Einstein said, "but not malicious." Again, Einstein said that "nature conceals her mystery by means of her essential grandeur, not by her cunning." It could be that God has not absconded but spread, as our vision and understanding of the universe have spread, to a fabric of spirit and sense so grand and subtle, so powerful in a new way, that we can only feel blindly of its hem. In making the thick darkness a swaddling band for the sea, God "set bars and doors" and said, "Hitherto shalt thou come, but no further." But have we come even that far? Have we rowed out to the thick darkness, or are we all playing pinochle in the bottom of the boat?

Cruelty is a mystery, and the waste of pain. But if we describe a world to compass these things, a world that is a long, brute game, then we bump against another mystery: the inrush of power and light, the canary that sings on the skull. Unless all ages and races of men have been deluded by the same mass hypnotist (who?), there seems to be such a thing as beauty, a grace wholly gratuitous. About five years ago I saw a mockingbird make a straight vertical descent from the roof gutter of a four-story building. It was an act as careless and spontaneous as the curl of a stem or the kindling of a star.

The mockingbird took a single step into the air and dropped. His wings were still folded against his sides as though he were singing from a limb and not falling, accelerating thirty-two feet per second, through empty air. Just a breath before he would have been dashed to the ground, he unfurled his wings with exact, deliberate care, revealing the broad bars of white, spread his elegant, white-banded tail, and so floated onto the grass. I had just rounded a corner when his insouciant step caught my eye; there was no one else in sight. The fact of his free fall was like the old philosophical conundrum about the tree that falls in the forest. The answer must be, I think, that beauty and grace are performed whether or not we will or sense them. The least we can do is try to be there.

Another time I saw another wonder: sharks off the Atlantic coast of Florida. There is a way a wave rises about the ocean horizon, a triangular wedge against the sky. If you stand where the ocean breaks on a shallow beach, you see the raised water in a wave is translucent, shot with lights. One late afternoon at low tide a hundred big sharks passed the beach near the mouth of a tidal river in a feeding frenzy. As each green wave rose from the churning water, it illuminated within itself the six- or eight-foot-long bodies of twisting sharks. The sharks disappeared as each wave rolled toward me; then a new wave would swell above the horizon, containing in it, like scorpions in amber, sharks that roiled and heaved. The sight held awesome wonders: power and beauty, grace tangled in a rapture with violence.

We don't know what's going on here. If these tremendous events are random combinations of matter run amok, the yield of millions of monkeys at millions of typewriters, then what is it in us, hammered out of those same typewriters, that they ignite? We don't know. Our life is a faint tracing on the surface of mystery, like the idle, curved tunnels of leaf miners on the face of a leaf. We must somehow take a wider view, look at the whole landscape, really see it, and describe what's going on here. Then we can at least wail the right question into the swaddling band of darkness, or, if it comes to that, choir the proper praise.

At the time of Lewis and Clark, setting the prairies on fire was well-known signal that meant, "Come down to the water." It was an extravagant gesture, but we can't do less. If the landscape reveals one certainty, it is that the extravagant gesture is the very stuff of creation. After the one extravagant gesture of creation in the first place, the universe has continued to deal exclusively in extravagances, flinging intricacies and colossi down aeons of emptiness, heaping profusions on profligacies with ever-fresh vigor. The whole show has been on fire from the word go. I come down to the water to cool my eyes. But everywhere I look I see fire; that which isn't flint is tinder, and the whole world sparks and flames.

POSSIBILITIES FOR WRITING

1. Dillard organizes "Heaven and Earth in Jest" by presenting three scenes: the waterbug and frog, the mockingbird, and the sharks. Explain what Dillard conveys in each scene and why each scene is important for the overall meaning about nature that she conveys in this piece.

2. Two rhetorical devices important for Dillard in this essay are the imagery of light and darkness, and the use of quotation and allusion. Identify Dillard's uses of either her imagery or her external references, and explain their function in "Heaven and Earth in Jest."

3. Write your own essay based on close observation of a scene in nature or in a public place. After making a list of the things you notice, select three or four details or elements that can be linked together, details or elements that stand out, and which can form the basis of an essay in which you speculate on their significance.

John Donne (1572–1631) *was born in London and attended Cambridge University before studying law. For some years a member of the British government, he also established a reputation as a poet of great wit and verbal dexterity. His later poems, especially those written after the death of his wife, take on a more somber tone, and Donne increasingly turned to overtly religious themes. Ordained as a minister in 1615, he later became a royal chaplain and dean of St. Paul's Cathedral. There, he composed highly original sermons that brought him considerable renown as a preacher. Although his reputation dimmed after his death, he was rediscovered in the early twentieth century as one of the greatest of English writers.*

JOHN DONNE

No Man Is an Island

John Donne's oft-quoted statement—"No man is an island"—occurs in a book of meditations he wrote when he lay sick and presumably dying. Donne collected his meditations in a volume and published it as *Devotions Upon Emergent Occasions.* Meditation XVII from that volume is excerpted here.

Donne's images are both conventional and distinctive. He writes from within a tradition that sees human life as fulfilled in an afterlife, and that regards sickness and suffering in this life as a valuable reminder of eternity and of the salvation that is the religious person's final goal. What remains most memorable about this piece today, however, for believers and non-believers alike, is the splendid way that Donne explains how all human lives are intertwined, and how human pain and sorrow and death, wherever they occur, concern us all. And that is why the bell, which ostensibly tolls for another, also tolls for each of us.

Perchance he for whom this bell tolls may be so ill, as that he knows not it tolls for him; and perchance I may think myself so much better than I am, as that they who are about me, and see my state, may have caused it to toll for me, and I know not that. The church is Catholic, universal, so are all her actions; all that she does belongs to all. When she baptizes a child, that action concerns me; for that child is thereby connected to that body which is my head too, and ingrafted into that body whereof I am a member. And when she buries a man, that action concerns me: all mankind is of one author, and is one volume; when one man dies, one chapter is not torn out of the book, but translated into a better language; and every chapter must be so translated; God employs several translators; some pieces are translated by age, some by sickness, some by war, some by justice; but God's hand is in every translation, and his hand shall bind up all our scattered leaves again for that library where every book shall lie open to one another.

As therefore the bell that rings to a sermon calls not upon the preacher only, but upon the congregation to come, so this bell calls us all; but how much more me, who am brought so near the door by this sickness. Here was a contention as far as a suit (in which both piety and dignity, religion and estimation, were mingled), which of the religious orders should ring to prayers first in the morning; and it was determined, that they should ring first that rose earliest. If we understand aright the dignity of this bell that tolls for our evening prayer, we would be glad to make it ours by rising early, in that application, that it might be ours as well as his, whose indeed it is. The bell doth toll for him that thinks it doth; and though it intermit again, yet from that minute that that occasion wrought upon him, he is united to God.

Who casts not up his eye to the sun when it rises? but who takes off his eye from a comet when that breaks out? Who bends not his ear to any bell which upon any occasion rings? but who can remove it from that bell which is passing a piece of himself out of this world?

No man is an island, entire of itself; every man is a piece of the continent, a part of the main. If a clod be washed away by the sea, Europe is the less, as well as if a promontory were, as well as if a manor of thy friend's or of thine own were: any man's death diminishes me, because I am involved in mankind, and therefore never send to know for whom the bell tolls; it tolls for thee.

Neither can we call this a begging of misery, or a borrowing of misery, as though we were not miserable enough of ourselves, but must fetch in more from the next house, in taking upon us the misery of our neighbors. Truly it were an excusable covetousness if we did, for affliction is a treasure, and scarce any man hath enough of it.

No man hath affliction enough that is not matured and ripened by it, and made fit for God by that affliction. If a man carry treasure in bullion, or in a wedge of gold, and have none coined into current money, his treasure will not defray him as he travels. Tribulation is treasure in the nature of it, but it is not current money in the use of it, except we get nearer and nearer our home, heaven, by it. Another man may be sick too, and sick to death, and this affliction may lie in his bowels, as gold in a mine, and be of no use to him; but this bell, that tells me of his affliction, digs out and applies that gold to me: if by this consideration of another's danger I take mine own into contemplation, and so secure myself, by making my recourse to my God, who is our only security.

POSSIBILITIES FOR WRITING

1. Analyze Donne's use of metaphor and other imagery. How does his poetic language contribute to the meditation's effect?
2. Paragraph by paragraph, closely analyze your own response to Donne's prose. What does the meditation communicate to you?
3. Apply Donne's message to the contemporary world. Use examples to suggest the extent to which people follow Donne's words and the extent to which they do not.

Frederick Douglass (1817–1895) was born a slave in rural Maryland and as a boy worked as a house servant in Baltimore, where his mistress taught him the rudiments of reading until her husband objected. Continuing his education surreptitiously on his own, Douglass escaped to New York when he was twenty. Within three years, he had become an ardent campaigner against slavery and for the rights of free blacks. In 1846 his freedom was officially purchased by British supporters, and in 1847 he began publishing a weekly newspaper, North Star. *During the Civil War, he promoted the use of black troops to fight the Confederacy, and following the war he held several government posts, including U. S. Minister to Haiti. Today he is best known for his autobiographical works, most notably his first publication,* Narrative of the Life of Frederick Douglass *(1845).*

FREDERICK DOUGLASS

Learning to Read and Write

In this excerpt from his autobiography, Frederick Douglass, an American slave, describes how he learned to read and write, and the consequences that his literacy brought him. Douglass entwines the story of his entry into literacy with that of his enslavement. He makes clear how, by keeping black slaves ignorant through denying them literacy, white slaveowners kept them under control. In telling this part of his life story, Douglass conveys a sense of the power of literacy. Learning to read and write transformed Douglass from a passive person to an active one, from an obedient slave who accepted his lot to a thoughtful critic of the institution of slavery and a spirited rebel against it.

Douglass links the stories of how he learned to read and to write with a bridge anecdote about his resolve to run away from his master. In this section, Douglass reveals his mistrust of white people, some of whom were actually eager to help him, and he reveals as well his gradual understanding of the abolitionist movement, in which he himself would later become a prominent figure. Douglass exercised the same ingenuity and determination in learning to write as he did in learning to read. Ingenuity and determination, in fact, are central themes of Douglass's story.

I lived in Master Hugh's family about seven years. During this time, I succeeded in learning to read and write. In accomplishing this, I was compelled to resort to various stratagems. I had no regular teacher. My mistress, who had kindly commenced to instruct me, had, in compliance with the advice and direction of her husband, not only ceased to instruct, but had set her face against my being instructed by any one else. It is due, however, to my mistress to say of her, that she did not adopt this course of treatment immediately. She at first lacked the depravity indispensable to shutting me up in mental darkness. It was at least necessary for her to have some training in the exercise of irre-sponsible power, to make her equal to the task of treating me as though I were a brute.

My mistress was, as I have said, a kind and tender-hearted woman; and in the simplicity of her soul she commenced, when I first went to live with her, to treat me as she supposed one human being ought to treat another. In entering upon the duties of a slaveholder, she did not seem to perceive that I sustained to her the relation of a mere chattel, and that for her to treat me as a human being was not only wrong, but dangerously so. Slavery proved as injurious to her as it did to me. When I went there, she was a pious, warm, and tender-hearted woman. There was no sorrow or suffering for which she had not a tear. She had bread for the hungry, clothes for the naked, and comfort for every mourner that came within her reach. Slavery soon proved its ability to divest her of these heavenly qualities. Under its influence, the tender heart be-came stone, and the lamb-like disposition gave way to one of tiger-like fierceness. The first step in her downward course was in her ceasing to instruct me. She now commenced to practise her husband's precepts. She finally became even more violent in her opposition than her hus-band himself. She was not satisfied with simply doing as well as he had commanded; she seemed anxious to do better. Nothing seemed to make her more angry than to see me with a newspaper. She seemed to think that here lay the danger. I have had her rush at me with a face made all up of fury, and snatch from me a newspaper, in a manner that fully revealed her apprehension. She was an apt woman; and a little ex-perience soon demonstrated, to her satisfaction, that education and slavery were incompatible with each other.

From this time I was most narrowly watched. If I was in a separate room any considerable length of time, I was sure to be suspected of having a book, and was at once called to give an account of myself. All this, however, was too late. The first step had been taken. Mistress, in teaching me the alphabet, had given me the *inch*, and no precaution could prevent me from taking the *ell*.

The plan which I adopted, and the one by which I was most suc-cessful, was that of making friends of all the little white boys whom I met in the street. As many of these as I could, I converted into teach-ers. With their kindly aid, obtained at different times and in different places, I finally succeeded in learning to read. When I was sent of er-rands, I always took my book with me, and by going one part of my er-rand quickly, I found time to get a lesson before my return. I used also to carry bread with me, enough of which was always in the house, and to which I was always welcome; for I was much better off in this regard than many of the poor white children in our neighborhood. This bread I used to bestow upon the hungry little urchins, who, in return, would give me that more valuable bread of knowledge. I am strongly tempted to give the names of two or three of those little boys, as a testimonial of the gratitude and affection I bear them; but prudence forbids:—not that it would injure me, but it might embarrass them; for it is almost an unpardonable offence to teach slaves to read in this Christian country. It is enough to say of the dear little fellows, that they lived on Philpot Street, very near Durgin and Bailey's ship-yard. I used to talk this matter of slavery over with them. I would sometimes say to them, I wished I could be as free as they would be when they got to be men. "You will be free as soon as you are twenty-one, *but I am a slave for life!* Have not I as good a right to be free as you have?" These words used to trouble them; they would express for me the liveliest sympathy, and console me with the hope that something would occur by which I might be free.

I was now about twelve years old, and the thought of being *a slave for life* began to bear heavily upon my heart. Just about this time, I got hold of a book entitled "The Columbian Orator." Every opportunity I got, I used to read this book. Among much of other interesting matter, I found in it a dialogue between a master and his slave. The slave was represented as having run away from his master three times. The dialogue represented the conversation which took place between them, when the slave was retaken the third time. In this dialogue, the whole argument in behalf of slavery was brought forward by the master, all of which was disposed of by the slave. The slave was made to say some very smart as well as impressive things in reply to his master—things which had the desired though unexpected effect; for the conversation resulted in the voluntary emancipation of the slave on the part of the master.

In the same book, I met with one of Sheridan's mighty speeches on and in behalf of Catholic emancipation. These were choice documents to me. I read them over and over again with unabated interest. They gave tongue to interesting thoughts of my own soul, which had frequently flashed through my mind, and died away for want of utterance. The moral which I gained from the dialogue was the power of truth over the conscience of even a slaveholder. What I got from Sheridan was a bold denunciation of slavery, and a powerful vindication of human rights. The reading of these documents enabled me to utter my thoughts, and to meet the arguments brought forward to sustain slavery; but while they relieved me of one difficulty, they brought on another even more painful than the one of which I was relieved. The more I read, the more I was led to abhor and detest my enslavers. I could regard them in no other light than a band of successful robbers, who had left their homes, and gone to Africa, and stolen us from our homes, and in a strange land reduced us to slavery. I loathed them as being the meanest as well as the most wicked of men. As I read and contemplated the subject, behold! that very discontentment which Master Hugh had predicted would follow my learning to read had already come, to torment and sting my soul to unutterable anguish. As I writhed under it, I would at times feel that learning to read had been a curse rather than a blessing. It had given me a view of my wretched condition, without the remedy. It opened my eyes to the horrible pit, but to no ladder upon which to get out. In moments of agony, I envied my fellow-slaves for their stupidity. I have often wished myself a beast. I preferred the condition of the meanest reptile to my own. Any thing, no matter what, to get rid of thinking! It was this everlasting thinking of my condition that tormented me. There was no getting rid of it. It was pressed upon me by every object within sight or hearing, animate or inanimate. The silver trump of freedom had roused my soul to eternal wakefulness. Freedom now appeared, to disappear no more forever. It was heard in every sound, and seen in every thing. It was ever present to torment me with a sense of my wretched condition. I saw nothing without seeing it, I heard nothing without hearing it, and felt nothing without feeling it. It looked from every star, it smiled in every calm, breathed in every wind, and moved in every storm.

I often found myself regretting my own existence, and wishing myself dead; and but for the hope of being free, I have no doubt but that I should have killed myself, or done something for which I should have been killed. While in this state of mind, I was eager to hear anyone speak of slavery. I was a ready listener. Every little while, I could hear something about the abolitionists. It was some time before I found what the word meant. It was always used in such connections as to make it an interesting word to me. If a slave ran away and succeeded in getting clear, or if a slave killed his master, set fire to a barn, or did any thing very wrong in the mind of a slaveholder, it was spoken of as the fruit of *abolition*. Hearing the word in this connection very often, I set about learning what it meant. The dictionary afforded me little or no help. I found it was "the act of abolishing;" but then I did not know what was to be abolished. Here I was perplexed. I did not dare to ask any one about its meaning, for I was satisfied that it was something they wanted me to know very little about. After a patient waiting, I got one of our city papers, containing an account of the number of petitions from the north, praying for the abolition of slavery in the District of Columbia, and of the slave trade between the States. From this time I understood the words *abolition* and *abolitionist,* and always drew near when that word was spoken, expecting to hear something of importance to myself and fellow-slaves. The light broke in upon me by degrees. I went one day down on the wharf of Mr. Waters; and seeing two Irishmen unloading a scow of stone, I went, unasked, and helped them. When we had finished, one of them came to me and asked me if I were a slave. I told him I was. He asked, "Are ye a slave for life?" I told him that I was. The good Irishman seemed to be deeply affected by the statement. He said to the other that it was a pity so fine a little fellow as myself should be a slave for life. He said it was a shame to hold me. They both advised me to run away to the north; that I should find friends there, and that I should be free. I pretended not to be interested in what they said, and treated them as if I did not understand them; for I feared they might be treacherous. White men have been known to encourage slaves to escape, and then, to get the reward, catch them and return them to their masters. I was afraid that these seemingly good men might use me so; but I nevertheless remembered their advice, and from that time I resolved to run away. I looked forward to a time at which it would be safe for me to escape. I was too young to think of doing so immediately; besides, I wished to learn how to write, as I might have occasion to write my own pass. I consoled myself with the hope that I should one day find a good chance. Meanwhile, I would learn to write.

The idea as to how I might learn to write was suggested to me by being in Durgin and Bailey's ship-yard, and frequently seeing the ship carpenters, after hewing, and getting a piece of timber ready for use, write on the timber the name of that part of the ship for which it was intended. When a piece of timber was intended for the larboard side, it would be marked thus—"L." When a piece was for the starboard side, it would be marked thus—"S." A piece for the larboard side forward, would be marked thus—"L. F." When a piece was for starboard side forward, it would be marked thus—"S. F." For larboard aft, it would be marked thus—"L. A." For starboard aft, it would be marked thus—"S. A."

I soon learned the names of these letters, and for what they were intended when placed upon a piece of timber in the shipyard. I immediately commenced copying them, and in a short time was able to make the four letters named. After that, when I met with any boy who I knew could write, I would tell him I could write as well as he. The next word would be, "I don't believe you. Let me see you try it." I would then make the letters which I had been so fortunate as to learn, and ask him to beat that. In this way I got a good many lessons in writing, which it is quite possible I should never have gotten in any other way. During this time, my copy-book was the board fence, brick wall, and pavement; my pen and ink was a lump of chalk. With these, I learned mainly how to write. I then commenced and continued copying the Italics in Webster's Spelling Book, until I could make them all without looking on the book. By this time, my little Master Thomas had gone to school, and learned how to write, and had written over a number of copy-books. These had been brought home, and shown to some of our near neighbors, and then laid aside. My mistress used to go to class meeting at the Wilk Street meetinghouse every Monday afternoon, and leave me to take care of the house. When left thus, I used to spend the time in writing in the spaces left in Master Thomas's copy-book, copying what he had written. I continued to do this until I could write a hand very similar to that of Master Thomas. Thus, after a long, tedious effort for years, I finally succeeded in learning how to write.

POSSIBILITIES FOR WRITING

1. In various ways throughout this essay, Douglass makes the point that education—learning to read and write—and slavery are "incompatible with each other," for both slaves and those who own them. Using evidence from the text, as well as your own conclusions, explore why this would be so.
2. Douglass's autobiography was written before slavery was fully abolished in the United States. In what ways can his narrative be read as an argument against slavery? Consider this issue from the perspective of readers who might be slaveholders, those who were already abolitionists, and those who did not own slaves but were undecided on the question.
3. How do you respond to Douglass's situation and to the portrait he presents of himself as you read it today, more than a hundred and fifty years after it was written? Do you find that you can apply any of what he says to the world you live in today? Explain why you feel as you do.

Brian Doyle *(b. 1956) is the editor of* Portland *magazine at the University of Portland, Oregon. His essays have appeared in the* American Scholar, *the* Atlantic Monthly, Harper's, Orion, Commonweal, *and the* Georgia Review. *A number of his essays have been selected to appear in the annual* Best American Essays *series. Among his books are an edited collection of spiritual writing,* God Is Love, *and two of his own five collections of essays,* Leaping: Revelations & Epiphanies *(2004), and* The Wet Engine *(2005), in which "Joyas Voladoras" appears.*

BRIAN DOYLE

Joyas Voladoras

In "Joyas Voladoras," Brian Doyle's characteristic wit, grace, and writerly elegance are in evidence as he explores one of life's mysteries—the beautiful jewel-like hummingbird. The essay blends scientific information with spiritual appreciation of this miniature marvel of creation. Doyle celebrates the wonders of the hummingbird, cataloging its myriad species and highlighting the intensity of its life force.

Beyond describing and celebrating the life of the hummingbird, Doyle branches out to mention other marvels of creation, especially the largest of all creatures, the blue whale. It is the heart of this great beast that interests Doyle, as well as the heart of the hummingbird, and then beyond these hearts great and small, the heart of that other marvel of creation—the human species.

Consider the hummingbird for a long moment. A hummingbird's heart beats ten times a second. A hummingbird's heart is the size of a pencil eraser. A hummingbird's heart is a lot of the hummingbird. *Joyas voladoras,* flying jewels, the first white explorers in the Americas called them, and the white men had never seen such creatures, for hummingbirds came into the world only in the Americas, nowhere else in the universe, more than three hundred species of them whirring and zooming and nectaring in hummer time zones nine times removed from ours, their hearts hammering faster than we could clearly hear if we pressed our elephantine ears to their infinitesimal chests.

Each one visits a thousand flowers a day. They can dive at sixty miles an hour. They can fly backward. They can fly more than five hundred miles without pausing to rest. But when they rest they come close to death: on frigid nights, or when they are starving, they retreat into torpor, their metabolic rate slowing to a fifteenth of their normal sleep rate, their hearts sludging nearly to a halt, barely beating, and if they are not soon warmed, if they do not soon find that which is sweet, their hearts grow cold, and they cease to be. Consider for a moment those hummingbirds who did not open their eyes again today, this very day, in the Americas: bearded helmetcrests and booted racket-tails, violet-tailed sylphs and violet-capped woodnymphs, crimson topazes and purple-crowned fairies, red-tailed comets and amethyst woodstars, rainbow-bearded thornbills and glittering-bellied emeralds, velvet-purple coronets and golden-bellied star-frontlets, fiery-tailed awlbills and Andean hillstars, spatuletails and pufflegs, each the most amazing thing you have never seen, each thunderous wild heart the size of an infant's fingernail, each mad heart silent, a brilliant music stilled.

Hummingbirds, like all flying birds but more so, have incredible enormous immense ferocious metabolisms. To drive those metabolisms they have racecar hearts that eat oxygen at an eye-popping rate. Their hearts are built of thinner, leaner fibers than ours. Their arteries are stiffer and more taut. They have more mitochondria in their heart muscles—anything to gulp more oxygen. Their hearts are stripped to the skin for the war against gravity and inertia, the mad search for food, the insane idea of flight. The price of their ambition is a life closer to death; they suffer more heart attacks and aneurysms and ruptures than any other living creature. It's expensive to fly. You burn out. You fry the machine. You melt the engine. Every creature on earth has approximately two billion heartbeats to spend in a lifetime. You can spend them slowly, like a tortoise, and live to be two hundred years old, or you can spend them fast, like a hummingbird, and live to be two years old.

The biggest heart in the world is inside the blue whale. It weighs more than seven tons. It's as big as a room. It *is* a room, with four chambers. A child could walk around in it, head high, bending only to step through the valves. The valves are as big as the swinging doors in a saloon. This house of a heart drives a creature a hundred feet long. When this creature is born it is twenty feet long and weighs four tons. It is waaaaay bigger than your car. It drinks a hundred gallons of milk from its mama every day and gains two hundred pounds a day, and when it is seven or eight years old it endures an unimaginable puberty and then it essentially disappears from human ken, for next to nothing is known of the mating habits, travel patterns, diet, social life, language, social structure, diseases, spirituality, wars, stories, despairs, and arts of the blue whale. There are perhaps ten thousand blue whales in the world, living in every ocean on earth, and of the largest mammal who ever lived we know nearly nothing. But we know this: the animals with the largest hearts in the world generally travel in pairs, and their penetrating moaning cries, their piercing yearning tongue, can be heard underwater for miles and miles.

Mammals and birds have hearts with four chambers. Reptiles and turtles have hearts with three chambers. Fish have hearts with two chambers. Insects and mollusks have hearts with one chamber. Worms have hearts with one chamber, although they may have as many as eleven single-chambered hearts. Unicellular bacteria have no hearts at all; but even they have fluid eternally in motion, washing from one side of the cell to the other, swirling and whirling. No living being is without interior liquid motion. We all churn inside.

So much held in a heart in a lifetime. So much held in a heart in a day, an hour, a moment. We are utterly open with no one, in the end— not mother and father, not wife or husband, not lover, not child, not friend. We open windows to each but we live alone in the house of the heart. Perhaps we must. Perhaps we could not bear to be so naked, for fear of a constantly harrowed heart. When young we think there will come one person who will savor and sustain us always; when we are older we know this is the dream of a child, that all hearts finally are bruised and scarred, scored and torn, repaired by time and will, patched by force of character, yet fragile and rickety forevermore, no matter how ferocious the defense and how many bricks you bring to the wall. You can brick up your heart as stout and tight and hard and cold and impregnable as you possibly can and down it comes in an instant, felled by a woman's second glance, a child's apple breath, the shatter of glass in the road, the words "I have something to tell you," a cat with a broken spine dragging itself into the forest to die, the brush of your mother's papery ancient hand in the thicket of your hair, the memory of your father's voice early in the morning echoing from the kitchen where he is making pancakes for his children.

POSSIBILITIES FOR WRITING

1. Why do you think Doyle wrote this little essay? What is his main idea? How does his discussion of the hummingbird contribute to the development of this idea? What is the purpose of his including the description of the heart of the blue whale?

2. Take an inventory of Doyle's essay, identifying the places where his writing anchors itself in scientific detail and description, where it verges

on spiritual celebration rather than the factual, and where it seems to blend or shift rapidly between the two modes of writing.

3. Write an essay in which you celebrate one of the marvels of creation. You may wish to choose something very large or very small to write about—and you may wish, like Doyle, to work in a contrast to whatever you choose to describe. You should do some research so you can present a number of factual details; and you should do some reflecting so you can provide a perspective that transcends the factual information you include.

W(illiam) E(dward) B(urghardt) DuBois (1868–1963) was born in Great Barrington, Massachusetts, and received his B.A., M.A., and Ph.D from Harvard University, an unusual achievement for a black man of his day. A tireless advocate of full civil rights for African Americans, he was a founder of the organization that would later become the National Association for the Advancement of Colored People (NAACP) and for several years edited its official magazine, Crisis. *He organized a number of international conferences on the condition of Black people worldwide, and he also advised U.S. government representatives on policy issues with regard to civil rights. His writings include* The Souls of Black Folk *(1903),* The Negro *(1915), and* Color and Democracy *(1945).*

W.E.B. DUBOIS

Of Our Spiritual Striving

In this excerpt from *The Souls of Black Folk,* W. E. B. DuBois describes the American Negro's desire to be able "to husband and use his best powers and his latent genius," after having been freed from slavery in the 1860s and given the right to vote in 1870, by the fifteenth amendment to the Constitution. DuBois makes clear his belief in the dignity of Black people, who possess two cultures—their adopted American culture and their African ancestral culture. DuBois sees the value of not so much mingling these two cultures as of preserving each of them intact.

DuBois describes the problem of the "veil" that separates American Blacks from their African past and from their American present. He sees that to a large extent American Blacks in 1900 had yet to be integrated and accepted on their own terms into American society and culture. DuBois's ideas were revolutionary when advocated a century ago, as he urged African Americans not to deny their African heritage and roots and become culturally indistinguishable from white society. Instead, he encouraged them to preserve their distinctiveness while claiming political and social equality.

> O water, voice of my heart, crying in the sand,
>   All night long crying with a mournful cry,
> As I lie and listen, and cannot understand
>   The voice of my heart in my side or the voice of the sea,
>   O water, crying for rest, is it I, is it I?
>   All night long the water is crying to me.
> Unresting water, there shall never be rest
>   Till the last moon droop and the last tide fail,
> And the fire of the end begin to burn in the west;
>   And the heart shall be weary and wonder and cry like the sea,
>   All life long crying without avail,
>   As the water all night long is crying to me.

> —ARTHUR SYMONS

Between me and the other world there is ever an unasked question: unasked by some through feelings of delicacy; by others through the difficulty of rightly framing it. All, nevertheless, flutter round it. They approach me in a half-hesitant sort of way, eye me curiously or compassionately, and then, instead of saying directly, How does it feel to be a problem? they say, I know an excellent colored man in my town; or, I fought at Mechanicsville; or, Do not these Southern outrages make your blood boil? At these I smile, or am interested, or reduce the boiling to a simmer, as the occasion may require. To the real question, How does it feel to be a problem? I answer seldom a word.

And yet, being a problem is a strange experience,—peculiar even for one who has never been anything else, save perhaps in babyhood and in Europe. It is the early days of rollicking boyhood that the revelation first bursts upon one, all in a day, as it were. I remember well when the shadow swept across me. I was a little thing, away up in the hills of New England, where the dark Housatonic winds between Hoosac and Taghkanic to the sea. In a wee wooden schoolhouse, something put it into the boys' and girls' heads to buy gorgeous visiting-cards—ten cents a package—and exchange. The exchange was merry, till one girl, a tall newcomer, refused my card,—refused it peremptorily, with a glance. Then it dawned upon me with a certain suddenness that I was different from the others; or like, mayhap, in heart and life and longing, but shut out from their world by a vast veil. I had thereafter no desire to tear down that veil, to creep through; I held all beyond it in common contempt, and lived above it in a region of blue sky and great wandering shadows. That sky was bluest when I could beat my mates at examination-time, or beat them at a foot-race, or even beat their stringy heads. Alas, with the years all this fine contempt began to fade; for the worlds I longed for, and all their dazzling opportunities, were theirs, not mine. But they should not keep these prizes, I said; some, all, I would wrest from them. Just how I would do it I could never decide: by reading law, by healing the sick, by telling the wonderful tales that swam in my head,—some way. With other black boys the strife was not so fiercely sunny: their youth shrunk into tasteless sycophancy, or into silent hatred of the pale world about them and mocking distrust of everything white; or wasted itself in a bitter cry, Why did God make me an outcast and a stranger in mine own house? The shades of the prison-house closed round about us all: walls strait and stubborn to the whitest, but relentlessly narrow, tall, and unscalable to sons of night who must plod darkly on in resignation, or beat unavailing palms against the stone, or steadily, half hopelessly, watch the streak of blue above.

After the Egyptian and Indian, the Greek and Roman, the Teuton and Mongolian, the Negro is a sort of seventh son, born with a veil, and gifted with second-sight in this American world,—a world which yields him no true self-consciousness, but only lets him see himself through the revelation of the other world. It is a peculiar sensation, this double-consciousness, this sense of always looking at one's self through the eyes of others, of measuring one's soul by the tape of a world that looks on in amused contempt and pity. One ever feels his two-ness,—an American, a Negro; two souls, two thoughts, two unreconciled strivings; two warring ideals in one dark body, whose dogged strength alone keeps it from being torn asunder.

The history of the American Negro is the history of this strife,— this longing to attain self-conscious manhood, to merge his double self into a better and truer self. In this merging he wishes neither of the older selves to be lost. He would not Africanize America, for America has too much to teach the world and Africa. He would not bleach his Negro soul in a flood of white Americanism, for he knows that Negro blood has a message for the world. He simply wishes to make it possible for a man to be both a Negro and an American, without being cursed and spit upon by his fellows, without having the doors of Opportunity closed roughly in his face.

This, then, is the end of his striving: to be a co-worker in the kingdom of culture, to escape both death and isolation, to husband and use his best powers and his latent genius. These powers of body and mind have in the past been strangely wasted, dispersed, or forgotten. The shadow of a mighty Negro past flits through the tale of Ethiopia the Shadowy and of Egypt the Sphinx. Throughout history, the powers of single black men flash here and there like falling stars, and die sometimes before the world has rightly gauged their brightness. Here in America, in the few days since Emancipation, the black man's turning hither and thither in hesitant and doubtful striving has often made his very strength to lose effectiveness, to seem like absence of power, like weakness. And yet it is not weakness,—it is the contradiction of double aims. The double-aimed struggle of the black artisan—on the one hand to escape white contempt for a nation of mere hewers of wood and drawers of water, and on the other hand to plough and nail and dig for a poverty-stricken horde—could only result in making him a poor craftsman, for he had but half a heart in either cause. By the poverty and ignorance of his people, the Negro minister or doctor was tempted toward quackery and demagogy; and by the criticism of the other world, toward ideals that made him ashamed of his lowly tasks. The would-be black *savant* was confronted by the paradox that the knowledge his people needed was a twice-told tale to his white neighbors, while the knowledge which would teach the white world was Greek to his own flesh and blood. The innate love of harmony and beauty that set the rude souls of his people a-dancing and a-singing raised but confusion and doubt in the soul of the black artist; for the beauty revealed to him was the soul-beauty of a race which his larger audience despised, and he could not articulate the message of another people. This waste of double aims, this seeking to satisfy two unreconciled ideals, has wrought sad havoc with the courage and faith and deeds of ten thou-sand thousand people,—has sent them often wooing false gods and invoking false means of salvation, and at times has even seemed about to make them ashamed of themselves.

Away back in the days of bondage they thought to see in one divine event the end of all doubt and disappointment; few men ever worshipped Freedom with half such unquestioning faith as did the American Negro for two centuries. To him, so far as he thought and dreamed, slavery was indeed the sum of all villainies, the cause of all sorrow, the root of all prejudice; Emancipation was the key to a promised land of sweeter beauty than ever stretched before the eyes of wearied Israelites. In song and exhortation swelled one refrain—Liberty; in his tears and curses the God he implored had Freedom in his right hand. At last it came,—suddenly, fearfully, like a dream. With one wild carnival of blood and passion came the message in his own plaintive cadences:—

> "Shout, O children!
> Shout, you're free!
> For God has bought your liberty!"

Years have passed away since then,—ten, twenty, forty; forty years of national life, forty years of renewal and development, and yet the swarthy spectre sits in its accustomed seat at the Nation's feast. In vain do we cry to this our vastest social problem:—

> "Take any shape but that, and my firm nerves
> Shall never tremble!"

The Nation has not yet found peace from its sins; the freedman has not yet found in freedom his promised land. Whatever of good may have come in these years of change, the shadow of a deep disappointment rests upon the Negro people,—a disappointment all the more bitter because the unattained ideal was unbounded save by the simple ignorance of a lowly people.

The first decade was merely a prolongation of the vain search for freedom, the boon that seemed ever barely to elude their grasp,—like a tantalizing will-o'-the-wisp, maddening and misleading the headless host. The holocaust of war, the terrors of the Ku-Klux Klan, the lies of carpet-baggers, the disorganization of industry, and the contradictory advice of friends and foes, left the bewildered serf with no new watchword beyond the old cry for freedom. As the time flew, however, he began to grasp a new idea. The ideal of liberty demanded for its attainment powerful means, and these the Fifteenth Amendment gave him. The ballot, which before he had looked upon as a visible sign of freedom, he now regarded as the chief means of gaining and perfecting the liberty with which war had partially endowed him. And why not? Had not votes made war and emancipated millions? Had not votes enfranchised the freedmen? Was anything impossible to a power that had done all this? A million black men started with renewed zeal to vote themselves into the kingdom. So the decade flew away, the revolution of 1876 came, and left the half-free serf weary, wondering, but still inspired. Slowly but steadily, in the following years, a new vision began gradually to replace the dream of political power,—a powerful movement, the rise of another ideal to guide the unguided, another pillar of fire by night after a clouded day. It was the ideal of "book-learning"; the curiosity, born of compulsory ignorance, to know and test the power of the cabalistic letters of the white man, the longing to know. Here at last seemed to have been discovered the mountain path to Canaan; longer than the highway of Emancipation and law, steep and rugged, but straight, leading to heights high enough to overlook life.

Up the new path the advance guard toiled, slowly, heavily, doggedly; only those who have watched and guided the faltering feet, the misty minds, the dull understandings, of the dark pupils of these schools know how faithfully, how piteously, this people strove to learn. It was weary work. The cold statistician wrote down the inches of progress here and there, noted also where here and there a foot had slipped or some one had fallen. To the tired climbers, the horizon was ever dark, the mists were often cold, the Canaan was always dim and far away. If, however, the vistas disclosed as yet no goal, no resting-place, little but flattery and criticism, the journey at least gave leisure for reflection and self-examination; it changed the child of Emancipation to the youth with dawning self-consciousness, self-realization, self-respect. In those sombre forests of his striving his own soul rose before him, and he saw himself,—darkly as through a veil; and yet he saw in himself some faint revelation of his power, of his mission. He began to have a dim feeling that, to attain his place in the world, he must be himself, and not another. For the first time he sought to analyze the burden he bore upon his back, that dead-weight of social degradation partially masked behind a half-named Negro problem. He felt his poverty; without a cent, without a home, without land, tools, or savings, he had entered into competition with rich, landed, skilled neighbors. To be a poor man is hard, but to be a poor race in a land of dollars is the very bottom of hardships. He felt the weight of his ignorance,—not simply of letters, but of life, of business, of the humanities; the accumulated sloth and shirking and awkwardness of decades and centuries shackled his hands and feet. Nor was his burden all poverty and ignorance. The red stain of bastardy, which two centuries of systematic legal defilement of Negro women had stamped upon his race, meant not only the loss of ancient African chastity, but also the hereditary weight of a mass of corruption from white adulterers, threatening almost the obliteration of the Negro home.

A people thus handicapped ought not to be asked to race with the world, but rather allowed to give all its time and thought to its own social problems. But alas! While sociologists gleefully count his bastards and his prostitutes, the very soul of the toiling, sweating black man is darkened by the shadow of a vast despair. Men call the shadow prejudice, and learnedly explain it as the natural defence of culture against barbarism, learning against ignorance, purity against crime, the "higher" against the "lower" races. To which the Negro cries Amen! and swears that to so much of this strange prejudice as is founded on just homage to civilization, culture, righteousness, and progress, he humbly bows and meekly does obeisance. But before that nameless prejudice that leaps beyond all this he stands helpless, dismayed, and well-nigh speechless; before that personal disrespect and mockery, the ridicule and systematic humiliation, the distortion of fact and wanton license of fancy, the cynical ignoring of the better and the boisterous welcoming of the worse, the all-pervading desire to inculcate disdain for everything black, from Toussaint to the devil,—before this there rises a sickening despair that would disarm and discourage any nation save that black host to whom "discouragement" is an unwritten word.

But the facing of so vast a prejudice could not but bring the inevitable self-questioning, self-disparagement, and lowering of ideals which ever accompany repression and breed in an atmosphere of contempt and hate. Whisperings and portents came borne upon the four winds: Lo! we are diseased and dying, cried the dark hosts; we cannot write, our voting is vain; what need of education, since we must always cook and serve? And the Nation echoed and enforced this self-criticism, saying: Be content to be servants, and nothing more; what need of higher culture for half-men? Away with the black man's ballot, by force or fraud,—and behold the suicide of a race! Nevertheless, out of the evil came something of good,—the more careful adjustment of education to real life, the clearer perception of the Negroes' social responsibilities, and the sobering realization of the meaning of progress.

So dawned the time of *Sturm und Drang*: storm and stress to-day rocks our little boat on the mad waters of the world-sea; there is within and without the sound of conflict, the burning of body and rending of soul; inspiration strives with doubt, and faith with vain questionings. The bright ideals of the past,—physical freedom, political power, the training of brains and the training of hands,—all these in turn have waxed and waned, until even the last grows dim and overcast. Are they all wrong,—all false? No, not that, but each alone was over-simple and incomplete,—the dreams of a credulous race-childhood, or the fond imaginings of the other world which does not know and does not want to know our power. To be really true, all these ideals must be melted and welded into one. The training of the schools we need to-day more than ever,—the training of deft hands, quick eyes and ears, and above all the broader, deeper, higher culture of gifted minds and pure hearts. The power of the ballot we need in sheer self-defence,—else what shall save us from a second slavery? Freedom, too, the long-sought, we still seek,—the freedom of life and limb, the freedom to work and think, the freedom to love and aspire. Work, culture, liberty,—all these we need, not singly but together, not successively but together, each growing and aiding each, and all striving toward that vaster ideal that swims before the Negro people, the ideal of human brotherhood, gained through the unifying ideal of Race; the ideal of fostering and developing the traits and talents of the Negro, not in opposition to or contempt for other races, but rather in large conformity to the greater ideals of the American Republic, in order that some day on American soil two world-races may give each to each those characteristics both so sadly lack. We the darker ones come even now not altogether empty-handed: there are to-day no truer exponents of the pure human spirit of the Declaration of Independence than the American Negroes; there is no true American music but the wild sweet melodies of the Negro slave; the American fairy tales and folklore are Indian and African; and, all in all, we black men seem the sole oasis of simple faith and reverence in a dusty desert of dollars and smartness. Will America be poorer if she replace her brutal dyspeptic blundering with light-hearted but determined Negro humility? or her coarse and cruel wit with loving jovial good-humor? or her vulgar music with the soul of the Sorrow Songs?

Merely a concrete test of the underlying principles of the great republic is the Negro Problem, and the spiritual striving of the freed-men's sons is the travail of souls whose burden is almost beyond the measure of their strength, but who bear it in the name of an historic race, in the name of this the land of their fathers' fathers, and in the name of human opportunity.

And now what I have briefly sketched in large outline let me on coming pages tell again in many ways, with loving emphasis and deeper detail, that men may listen to the striving in the souls of black folk.

POSSIBILITIES FOR WRITING

1. What are DuBois's main themes here, and how does he relate them to the past, to his present day, and to a possible future?
2. DuBois's later paragraphs focus on "the shadow prejudice." What does he see as the causes and results of prejudice? How, in his view, can prejudice be overcome?
3. DuBois was one of the first defenders of full social and civil equality for African Americans. How are the ideas he puts forth here reflected in contemporary cultural reality and societal attitudes?

Andre Dubus (1936–1999) *was born in Lake Charles, Louisiana, attended McNeese State College, and received an M.F.A. from the University of Iowa. He taught writing at Bradford College from 1966 to 1984 and then was a popular visting lecturer. Winner of a prestigious MacArthur Foundation award, Dubus published many short stories, collected in* Separate Flights (1975) *and* Dancing After Hours (1992), *among others, as well as novels and essay collections, including* Broken Vessels (1991) *and* Meditations From a Moveable Chair (1998). *After he was disabled in an auto accident in 1986, he often wrote about his confined condition. His work is noted for its examination of the loneliness and isolation of contemporary culture.*

ANDRE DUBUS

Lights of the Long Night

In "Lights of the Long Night," Andre Dubus describes what he remembers of the night he was struck by a car as he stopped to assist an injured motorist. Dubus was struck by a car that swerved into him as he tried to protect a woman whose husband was killed that night. Dubus himself suffered an injury that took him to the hospital and left him, in his words, "a cripple," his left leg amputated below the knee.

The essay is an act of remembrance and an attempt to reconstruct what happened from fragments of his own memory, from the memories of the doctor who saved his life, and from those of the woman whose life Dubus himself saved. It is also a vivid description of the final moments leading up to the accident, a description that begins vividly with the words "I remember the headlights." The essay's title, "Lights of the Long Night," images both the lights of the oncoming car's headlights and the hospital operating room lights where Dubus lost his leg. It was indeed a "long night," the longest of Dubus's life.

But the essay is also a memorial for the young man who lost his life that night, twenty-three-year-old Luis Santiago, who had come from Puerto Rico, and who that night had been in an accident with his sister Luz. Dubus records the young man's last words: "Por favor, señor, please help, no hablo Ingles." By presenting these words without comment and by describing the action simply and directly, Dubus achieves a powerful emotional effect. And, finally, writing the essay is a form of therapy for Dubus. Through his reconstruction of the scene and the incident, and through his memorializing of the young man and his sister, Dubus comes to terms with his own sacrifice, with the fact that his life was forever altered by the lights of that long night.

I remember the headlights, but I do not remember the car hitting Luis Santiago and me, and I do not remember the sounds our bodies made. Luis died, either in the ambulance, or later that night in the hospital. He was twenty-three years old. I do not remember leaving the ground my two legs stood on for the last instant in my life, then moving through the air, over the car's hood and windshield and roof, and falling on its trunk. I remember lying on my back on that trunk and asking someone: *What happened?*

I did not lose consciousness. The car did not injure my head or my neck or my spine. It broke my right hand and scraped both arms near my wrists, so my wife believes I covered my face with my arms as I fell. I lay for a while on the trunk, talking to a young man, then to a woman who is a state trooper, then I was in an ambulance, stopped on the highway talking to a state trooper, a man, while he cut my trousers and my right western boot. That morning my wife saw the left boot on the side of the highway, while she was driving home from the hospital in Boston. The car had knocked it off my foot. The state troopers got the boot for my wife, but I did not leave the hospital with a left foot or, below the middle of my knee, a left leg.

While the state trooper was cutting and we were talking, I saw Luis Santiago on a stretcher. People were putting him into an ambulance. Looking in the ambulance and watching Luis I knew something terrible had happened and I said to the trooper: *Did that guy die?* I do not remember what the trooper said, but I knew then that Luis was either dead or soon would be. Then I went by ambulance to a clinic in Wilmington where Dr. Wayne Sharaf saved my life, and my wife Peggy and my son Jeb were there, then an ambulance took me to Massachusetts General Hospital in Boston, where they operated on me for twelve hours.

Luis Santiago said what were probably his last words on earth to me: *Por favor, señor, please help, no hablo Ingles.* This was around one o'clock in the morning of 23 July 1986. I was driving north on route 93, going from Boston to my home in Haverhill, Massachusetts. The highway has four lanes and I was driving in the third. That stretch of road is straight and the visibility on 23 July was very good, so when I saw the Santiagos' car I did not have to apply the brakes or make any other sudden motions. It was ahead of me, stopped in the third lane, its tail lights darkened. I slowed my car. To the right of the Santiagos' car, in the breakdown lane, a car was parked and, behind it, a woman stood talking into the emergency call box. Her back was to me. I was driving a standard shift Subaru, and I shifted down to third, then second, and drove to the left, into the speed lane, so I could pass the left side of the Santiagos' car and look into it for a driver, and see whether or not the driver was hurt. There were no cars behind me. Luz Santiago stood beside the car, at the door to the driver's side, and her forehead was bleeding and she was crying. I drove to the left side of the road and parked near the guard rail and turned on my emergency blinker lights. Because of the guard rail, part of my car was still in the speed lane. I left the car and walked back to Luz Santiago. She was still crying and bleeding and she asked me to help her. She said: *There's a motorcycle under my car.*

I looked down. Dark liquid flowed from under her engine and formed a pool on the highway, and I imagined a motorcycle under there and a man dead and crushed between the motorcycle and the engine and I knew I would have to look at him. Then, for the first time, I saw Luis Santiago. He came from the passenger's side, circling the rear of the car, and walked up to me and Luz, standing beside the driver's door and the pool of what I believed was blood on the pavement. Later I learned that it was oil from the crankcase and the abandoned motorcycle Luz had run over was no longer under her car. Luis was Luz's brother and he was young and I believe his chest and shoulders were broad. He stopped short of Luz, so that she stood between us. That is when he spoke to me, mostly in his native tongue, learned in Puerto Rico.

I do not remember what I said to him, or to Luz. But I know what I was feeling, thinking: first I had to get Luz off the highway and lie her down and raise her legs and cover her with my jacket, for I believed she was in danger of shock. Then I would leave Luis with Luz and return to her car and look under its engine at the crushed man. We left her car and walked across the speed lane to the left side of the highway. We did not have to hurry. No cars were coming. We walked in column: I was in front, Luz was behind me, and Luis was in the rear. At the side of the road we stopped. I saw headlights coming north, toward us. We were not in danger then. If we had known the car was going to swerve toward us, we could have stepped over the guard rail. I waved at the headlights, the driver, my raised arms crossing in front of my face. I wanted the driver to stop and help us. I wanted the driver to be with me when I looked under Luz's car. We were standing abreast, looking at the car. I was on the right, near the guard rail: Luz was in the middle, and Luis stood on her left. I was still waving at the car when it came too fast to Luz's car and the driver swerved left, into the speed lane, toward my Subaru's blinking emergency lights, and toward us. Then I was lying on the car's trunk and asking someone: *What happened?*

Only Luis Santiago knows. While I was in Massachusetts General Hospital my wife told me that Luz Santiago told our lawyer I had pushed her away from the car. I knew it was true. Maybe because my left thigh was the only part of my two legs that did not break, and because the car broke my right hip. When the car hit us, Luis was facing its passenger side, Luz was between its headlights, and I was facing the driver. In the hospital I assumed that I had grabbed Luz with my left hand and jerked and threw her behind me and to my right, onto the side of the highway. That motion would have turned my body enough to the left to protect my left thigh, and expose my right hip to the car. But I do not think the patterns of my wounds told me I had pushed Luz. I knew, from the first moments in the stationary ambulance, that a car struck me because I was standing where I should have been; and, some time later, in the hospital, I knew I had chosen to stand there, rather than leap toward the guard rail.

On 17 September 1986 I left the hospital and came home. In December, Dr. Wayne Sharaf talked to me on the phone. He is young, and he told me I was the first person whose life he had saved, when he worked on me at the clinic in Wilmington. Then he said that, after working on me, he worked on Luz Santiago, and she told him I had pushed her away from the car. I thanked him for saving my life and telling me what Luz had told him. I said: *Now I can never be angry at myself for stopping that night.* He said: *Don't ever be. You saved that woman's life.* Perhaps not. She may have survived, as I have. I am forever a cripple, but I am alive, and I am a father and a husband, and in 1987 I am sitting in the sunlight of June and writing this.

POSSIBILITIES FOR WRITING

1. Many powerful emotions underlie the seemingly low-key surface of Dubus's essay. Explore what you can of the writer's inner drama. Why do you think he keeps his emotions so contained?

2. The essay is based on an almost circular repetition of key moments and narrative details. Carefully analyze these repetitions. How would you describe their effect?

3. Write an essay of your own about a traffic accident or another brush with danger. Include details so that readers will share what happened to you as well as what you felt both physically and emotionally.

Gretel Ehrlich (b. 1946), a native Californian, attended Bennington College and later the film school at New York University. Her work as a documentary filmmaker took her to Wyoming in 1979, and she found herself drawn to the state's sweeping open countryside and to the people who inhabit it. During her seventeen years working as a rancher there, she produced several books of reflections on her experiences, including The Solace of Open Spaces *(1985) and* A Match to the Heart *(1994), as well a novel and other works. Currently dividing her time between California and Wyoming, she has most recently published* Questions from Heaven *(1997), an account of her pilgrimage as a Buddhist to shrines in China, and* John Muir: Nature's Visionary *(2000), a biography of the great American naturalist and conservationist.*

GRETEL EHRLICH

About Men

Ehrlich's brief essay, "About Men," originally appeared in *Time* magazine, and was included in her first essay collection, *The Solace of Open Spaces.* Ehrlich's primary purpose in the essay is to reconsider some basic stereotypes about men—particularly western men, including, of course, "cowboys." Through a series of carefully chosen examples graced by vivid description, revealing dialogue, and sharply etched details, Ehrlich reveals the complex nature of the American cowboy. She suggests that cowboys, usually thought of as rugged and tough, are kind and tender hearted. In debunking stereotypes about cowboys, Ehrlich encourages readers to consider how manliness is a quality which, for cowboys, also requires a balancing of more conventionally typical feminine qualities, such as caring and compassion. The cowboys Ehrlich knows and describes are, as she writes, "androgynous at the core."

While describing what cowboys are really like, Ehrlich also conveys a powerful impression of the natural world, which so dramatically and inescapably affects their lives. She describes the sheer beauty of nature, while not ignoring the darker dangers it poses for beasts and men alike. But it's clear from her tone of respectful admiration, she wouldn't trade her western world and the western men she describes for anything, regardless of the challenges both nature and cowboys present.

When I'm in New York but feeling lonely for Wyoming I look for the Marlboro ads in the subway. What I'm aching to see is horseflesh, the glint of a spur, a line of distant mountains, brimming creeks, and a reminder of the ranchers and cowboys I've ridden with for the last eight years. But the men I see in those posters with their stern, humorless looks remind me of no one I know here. In our hellbent earnestness to romanticize the cowboy we've ironically disesteemed his true character. If he's "strong and silent" it's because there's probably no one to talk to. If he "rides away into the sunset" it's because he's been on horseback since four in the morning moving cattle and he's trying, fifteen hours later, to get home to his family. If he's "a rugged individualist" he's also part of a team: ranch work is teamwork and even the glorified open-range cowboys of the 1880s rode up and down the Chisholm Trail in the company of twenty or thirty other riders. Instead of the macho, trigger-happy man our culture has perversely wanted him to be, the cowboy is more apt to be convivial, quirky, and softhearted. To be "tough" on a ranch has nothing to do with conquests and displays of power. More often than not, circumstances—like the colt he's riding or an unexpected blizzard—are overpowering him. It's not toughness but "toughing it out" that counts. In other words, this macho, cultural artifact the cowboy has become is simply a man who possesses resilience, patience, and an instinct for survival. "Cowboys are just like a pile of rocks—everything happens to them. They get climbed on, kicked, rained and snowed on, scuffed up by wind. Their job is 'just to take it,'" one old-timer told me.

A cowboy is someone who loves his work. Since the hours are long—ten to fifteen hours a day—and the pay is $30 he has to. What's required of him is an odd mixture of physical vigor and maternalism. His part of the beef-raising industry is to birth and nurture calves and take care of their mothers. For the most part his work is done on horseback and in a lifetime he sees and comes to know more animals than people. The iconic myth surrounding him is built on American notions of heroism: the index of a man's value as measured in physical courage. Such ideas have perverted manliness into a self-absorbed race for cheap thrills. In a rancher's world, courage has less to do with facing danger than with acting spontaneously—usually on behalf of an animal or another rider. If a cow is stuck in a boghole he throws a loop around her neck, takes his dally (a half hitch around the saddle horn), and pulls her out with horsepower. If a calf is born sick, he may take her home, warm her in front of the kitchen fire, and massage her legs until dawn. One friend, whose favorite horse was trying to swim a lake with hobbles on, dove under water and cut her legs loose with a knife, then swam her to shore, his arm around her neck lifeguard-style, and saved her from drowning. Because these incidents are usually linked to someone or something outside himself, the westerner's courage is selfless, a form of compassion.

The physical punishment that goes with cowboying is greatly underplayed. Once fear is dispensed with, the threshold of pain rises to meet the demands of the job. When Jane Fonda asked Robert Redford (in the film *The Electric Horseman*) if he was sick as he struggled to his feet one morning, he replied, "No, just bent." For once the movies had it right. The cowboys I was sitting with laughed in agreement. Cowboys are rarely complainers; they show their stoicism by laughing at themselves.

If a rancher or cowboy has been thought of as a "man's man"—laconic, hard-drinking, inscrutable—there's almost no place in which the balancing act between male and female, manliness and femininity, can be more natural. If he's gruff, handsome, and physically fit on the outside, he's androgynous at the core. Ranchers are midwives, hunters, nurturers, providers, and conservationists all at once. What we've interpreted as toughness—weathered skin, calloused hands, a squint in the eye and a growl in the voice—only masks the tenderness inside. "Now don't go telling me these lambs are cute," one rancher warned me the first day I walked into the football-field-sized lambing sheds. The next thing I knew he was holding a black lamb. "Ain't this little rat good-lookin'?"

So many of the men who came to the West were southerners—men looking for work and a new life after the Civil War—that chivalrousness and strict codes of honor were soon thought of as western traits. There were very few women in Wyoming during territorial days, so when they did arrive (some as mail-order brides from places like Philadelphia) there was a stand-offishness between the sexes and a formality that persists now. Ranchers still tip their hats and say, "Howdy, ma'am" instead of shaking hands with me.

Even young cowboys are often evasive with women. It's not that they're Jekyll and Hyde creatures—gentle with animals and rough on women—but rather, that they don't know how to bring their tenderness into the house and lack the vocabulary to express the complexity of what they feel. Dancing wildly all night becomes a metaphor for the explosive emotions pent up inside, and when these are, on occasion, released, they're so battery-charged and potent that one caress of the face or one "I love you" will peal for a long while.

The geographical vastness and the social isolation here make emotional evolution seem impossible. Those contradictions of the heart between respectability, logic, and convention on the one hand, and impulse, passion, and intuition on the other, played out wordlessly against the paradisical beauty of the West, give cowboys a wide-eyed but drawn look. Their lips pucker up, not with kisses but with immutability. They may want to break out, staying up all night with a lover just to talk, but they don't know how and can't imagine what the consequences will be. Those rare occasions when they do bare themselves result in confusion. "I feel as if I'd sprained my heart," one friend told me a month after such a meeting.

My friend Ted Hoagland wrote, "No one is as fragile as a woman but no one is as fragile as a man." For all the women here who use "fragileness" to avoid work or as a sexual ploy, there are men who try to hide theirs, all the while clinging to an adolescent dependency on women to cook their meals, wash their clothes, and keep the ranch house warm in winter. But there is true vulnerability in evidence here. Because these men work with animals, not machines or numbers, because they live outside in landscapes of torrential beauty, because they are confined to a place and a routine embellished with awesome variables, because calves die in the arms that pulled others into life, because they go to the mountains as if on a pilgrimage to find out what makes a herd of elk tick, their strength is also a softness, their toughness, a rare delicacy.

POSSIBILITIES FOR WRITING

1. What does Ehrlich find so admirable and so sympathetic about the cowboys and ranchers she encounters in Wyoming? What does this suggest about her view of male roles more generally in our culture? Using specific examples from her essay, explore her central themes.

2. Cowboys, as Ehrlich describes them, seem to have trouble communicating with and relating to women, yet cling to an "adolescent dependency" on women to take care of them. How does Ehrlich square this with her positive image of cowboys? Do you think she does so effectively, or does this point diminish her image of cowboys in your eyes?

3. The media depict many different stereotypes in terms of gender, ethnicity, and so on. Choose a particular stereotype you have encountered, describe it and how it is exemplified in the media, then, as Ehrlich does, question the stereotype based on your own experiences.

Elizabeth I (1533–1603) *reigned as Queen of England from 1558 until her death, a period noted for its flowering of intellectual, artistic, and political achievement. A woman of great intellect, stamina, and cunning, Elizabeth was able to survive many intrigues against the crown and establish England as a preeminent world power. Although she had many suitors—and several lovers—she never married, devoting herself instead to her country and its people. The subject of innumerable biographies and dramatizations, Elizabeth has been embodied on screen in the films* Elizabeth, Shakespeare in Love, *and* The Queen.

QUEEN ELIZABETH I

Speech to the Troops at Tilbury

In the following speech Queen Elizabeth I of England addresses her land forces on horseback as they are assembled at Tilbury in Essex to repel the anticipated invasion of the Spanish Armada. This fleet of warships sent against England by the Spanish King, Philip II, was defeated at sea, never to reach the shores of England.

Elizabeth's speech is a little jewel of persuasion and inspiration, one of a number of excellent speeches she made during her long reign. She begins and ends by using a familiar and winning term of address, "my loving people" and "my people," for she indeed believed and often referred to her subjects as "loyal" and "loving," and portrayed herself as their able and devoted political and military leader. The rhetorical effectiveness of Elizabeth's speech is due in part to her repeated assurances of her love for her people and her willingness to put her life in jeopardy. Its stylistic effectiveness resides in its carefully crafted parallel sentences, with balanced phrases and clauses used to highlight Elizabeth's inspiring message.

My loving people: We have been persuaded by some that are careful of our safety, to take heed how we commit ourselves to armed multitudes, for fear of treachery. But I assure you I do not desire to live to distrust my faithful and loving people. Let tyrants fear! I have always so behaved myself that, under God, I have placed my chief strength and safeguard in the loyal hearts and goodwill of my subjects; and therefore I am come amongst you, as you see, at this time, not for my recreation and disport, but being resolved, in the midst of the heat of the battle, to live or die amongst you all; to lay down for my God, and for my kingdom, and for my people, my honor and my blood, even in the dust. I know I have the body but of a weak and feeble woman; but I have the heart and stomach of a king, and of a king of England too, and think foul scorn that Parma or Spain, or any prince of Europe, should dare to invade the borders of my realm; to which, rather than any dishonor should grow by me, I myself will take up arms, I myself will be your general, judge, and rewarder of every one of your virtues in the field. I know already, for your forwardness you have deserved rewards and crowns; and we do assure you on the word of a prince, they shall be duly paid you. In the meantime, my lieutenant-general shall be in my stead, than whom never prince commanded a more noble or worthy subject; not doubting but by your obedience to my general, by your concord in the camp, and your valor in the field, we shall shortly have a famous victory over those enemies of my God, of my kingdoms, and of my people.

POSSIBILITIES FOR WRITING

1. Elizabeth's is a political speech rallying her citizens to war. Compare it with the transcript of a twentieth-century example, such as that by George Bush, Sr., in announcing the attacks on Iraq at the time of the Persian Gulf War, or of George W. Bush in his speech announcing the war against terrorism.
2. Do some research on the reign of Elizabeth I using a good encyclopedia entry or another detailed source. Compare the historical image of the woman with the way she presents herself here.
3. Write your own "speech to the troops," rallying others to participate in a cause you believe in.

Ralph Ellison (1914–1994) was born in Oklahoma City, the grandson of slaves. Named for Ralph Waldo Emerson, Ellison was a voracious reader from an early age, a strong student, and well trained in music. He attended the Tuskegee Institute on a music scholarship but moved to Harlem in 1936, a year shy of graduating. There he began to write reviews and short stories under the tutelage of Richard Wright. His major work is Invisible Man *(1952), a novel that has continued to receive wide critical acclaim. A professor at New York University for many years, Ellison also published several highly regarded collections of essays, including* Shadow and Act *(1964) and* Going to the Territory *(1986). His second, unfinished novel,* Juneteenth, *was published posthumously in 1999 in a controversial edited version.*

Living with Music

In "Living with Music," Ellison describes himself as a young man living between two musical worlds—the world of classical music and the world of jazz. As a young writer struggling to find his voice and hone his art, Ellison lived amidst the sounds of musicians practicing and performing music in these diverse styles and forms. As a lover of music, Ellison was, by turns, distracted and inspired by what he heard from these musicians, who themselves were perfecting their own art through intense practice and inspired performance.

Ellison's essay mixes humor with reverence as he tells stories about musicians and about his own experiences as a budding trumpeter. Ellison explains the power of music to soothe and ennoble humanity, and he highlights the inspiration we can take from musicians who struggle daily with their art, much as Ellison himself does with his writing. Nor does Ellison ignore the cultural context of the music he describes or its historical significance, claiming no less than that music helps us understand ourselves, gives order and meaning to our lives, and contributes, as well, to our social and cultural identity.

In those days it was either live with music or die with noise, and we chose rather desperately to live. In the process our apartment—what with its booby-trappings of audio equipment, wires, discs and tapes—came to resemble the Collier mansion, but that was later. First there was the neighborhood, assorted drunks and a singer.

We were living at the time in a tiny ground-floor-rear apartment in which I was also trying to write. I say "trying" advisedly. To our right, separated by a thin wall, was a small restaurant with a juke box the size of the Roxy. To our left, a night-employed swing enthusiast who took his lullaby music so loud that every morning promptly at nine Basie's brasses started blasting my typewriter off its stand. Our living room looked out across a small back yard to a rough stone wall to an apartment building which, towering above, caught every passing thoroughfare sound and rifled it straight down to me. There were also howling cats and barking dogs, none capable of music worth living with, so we'll pass them by.

But the court behind the wall, which on the far side came knee-high to a short Iroquois, was a forum for various singing and/or preaching drunks who wandered back from the corner bar. From these you sometimes heard a fair barbershop style "Bill Bailey," free-wheeling versions of "The Bastard King of England," the saga of Uncle Bud, or a deeply felt rendition of Leroy Carr's "How Long Blues." The preaching drunks took on any topic that came to mind: current events, the fate of the long-sunk *Titanic* or the relative merits of the Giants and the Dodgers. Naturally there was great argument and occasional fighting—none of it fatal but all of it loud.

I shouldn't complain, however, for these were rather entertaining drunks, who like the birds appeared in the spring and left with the first fall cold. A more dedicated fellow was there all the time, day and night, come rain, come shine. Up on the corner lived a drunk of legend, a true phenomenon, who could surely have qualified as the king of all the world's winos—not excluding the French. He was neither poetic like the others nor ambitious like the singer (to whom we'll presently come) but his drinking bouts were truly awe-inspiring and he was not without his sensitivity. In the throes of his passion he would shout to the whole wide world one concise command, "Shut up!" Which was disconcerting enough to all who heard (except, perhaps, the singer), but such were the labyrinthine acoustics of courtyards and areaways that he seemed to direct his command at me. The writer's block which this produced is indescribable. On one heroic occasion he yelled his obsessive command without one interruption longer than necessary to take another drink (and with no appreciable loss of volume, penetration or authority) for three long summer days and nights, and shortly afterwards he died. Just how many lines of agitated prose he cost me I'll never know, but in all that chaos of sound I sympathized with his obsession, for I, too, hungered and thirsted for quiet. Nor did he inspire me to a painful identification, and for that I was thankful. Identification, after all, involves feelings of guilt and responsibility, and since I could hardly hear my own typewriter keys I felt in no way accountable for his condition. We were simply fellow victims of the madding crowd. May he rest in peace.

No, these more involved feelings were aroused by a more intimate source of noise, one that got beneath the skin and worked into the very structure of one's consciousness—like the "fate" motif in Beethoven's Fifth or the knocking-at-the-gates scene in *Macbeth*. For at the top of our pyramid of noise there was a singer who lived directly above us, you might say we had a singer on our ceiling.

Now, I had learned from the jazz musicians I had known as a boy in Oklahoma City something of the discipline and devotion to his art required of the artist. Hence I knew something of what the singer faced. These jazzmen, many of them now world-famous, lived for and with music intensely. Their driving motivation was neither money nor fame, but the will to achieve the most eloquent expression of idea-emotions through the technical mastery of their instruments (which, incidentally, some of them wore as a priest wears the cross) and the give and take, the subtle rhythmical shaping and blending of idea, tone and imagination demanded of group improvisation. The delicate balance struck between strong individual personality and the group during those early jam sessions was a marvel of social organization. I had learned too that the end of all this discipline and technical mastery was the desire to express an affirmative way of life through its musical tradition and that this tradition insisted that each artist achieve his creativity within its frame. He must learn the best of the past, and add to it his personal vision. Life could be harsh, loud and wrong if it wished, but they lived it fully, and when they expressed their attitude toward the world it was with a fluid style that reduced the chaos of living to form.

The objectives of these jazzmen were not at all those of the singer on our ceiling, but though a purist committed to the mastery of the *bel canto* style, German *lieder*, modern French art songs and a few American slave songs sung as if *bel canto*, she was intensely devoted to her art. From morning to night she vocalized, regardless of the condition of her voice, the weather or my screaming nerves. There were times when her notes, sifting through her floor and my ceiling, bouncing down the walls and ricocheting off the building in the rear, whistled like ten-penny nails, buzzed like a saw, wheezed like the asthma of a Hercules, trumpeted like an enraged African elephant—and the squeaky pedal of her piano rested plumb center above my typing chair. After a year of non-co-operation from the neighbor on my left I became desperate enough to cool down the hot blast of his phongraph by calling the cops, but the singer presented a serious ethical problem: Could I, an aspiring artist, complain against the hard work and devotion to craft of another aspiring artist?

Then there was my sense of guilt. Each time I prepared to shatter the ceiling in protest I was restrained by the knowledge that I, too, during my boyhood, had tried to master a musical instrument and to the great distress of my neighbors—perhaps even greater than that which I now suffered. For while our singer was concerned basically with a single tradition and style, I had been caught actively between two: that of the Negro folk music, both sacred and profane, slave song and jazz, and that of Western classical music. It was most confusing; the folk tradition demanded that I play what I heard and felt around me, while those who were seeking to teach the classical tradition in the schools insisted that I play strictly according to the book and express that which I was *supposed* to feel. This sometimes led to heated clashes of wills. Once during a third-grade music appreciation class a friend of mine insisted that it was a large green snake he saw swimming down a quiet brook instead of the snowy bird the teacher felt that Saint-Saëns' *Carnival of the Animals* should evoke. The rest of us sat there and lied like little black, brown and yellow Trojans about that swan, but our stalwart classmate held firm to his snake. In the end he got himself spanked and reduced the teacher to tears, but truth, reality and our environment were redeemed. For we were all familiar with snakes, while a swan was simply something the Ugly Duckling of the story grew up to be. Fortunately some of us grew up with a genuine appreciation of classical music *despite* such teaching methods. But as an inspiring trumpeter I was to wallow in sin for years before being awakened to guilt by our singer.

Caught mid-range between my two traditions, where one attitude often clashed with the other and one technique of playing was by the other opposed, I caused whole blocks of people to suffer.

Indeed, I terrorized a good part of an entire city section. During summer vacation I blew sustained tones out of the window for hours, usually starting—especially on Sunday mornings—before breakfast. I sputtered whole days through M. Arban's (he's the great authority on the instrument) double- and triple-tonguing exercises—with an effect like that of a jackass hiccupping off a big meal of briars. During school-term mornings I practiced a truly exhibitionist "Reveille" before leaving for school, and in the evening I generously gave the ever-listening world a long, slow version of "Taps," ineptly played but throbbing with what I in my adolescent vagueness felt was a romantic sadness. For it was farewell to day and a love song to life and a peace-be-with-you to all the dead and dying.

On hot summer afternoons I tormented the ears of all not blessedly deaf with imitations of the latest hot solos of Hot Lips Paige (then a local hero), the leaping right hand of Earl "Fatha" Hines, or the rowdy poetic flights of Louis Armstrong. Naturally I rehearsed also such school-band standbys as the *Light Cavalry* Overture, Sousa's "Stars and Stripes Forever," the *William Tell* Overture, and "Tiger Rag." (Not even an after-school job as office boy to a dentist could stop my efforts. Frequently, by way of encouraging my development in the proper cultural direction, the dentist asked me proudly to render Schubert's *Serenade* for some poor devil with his jaw propped open in the dental chair. When the drill got going, or the forceps bit deep, I blew real strong.)

Sometimes, inspired by the even then considerable virtuosity of the late Charlie Christian (who during our school days played marvelous riffs on a cigar box banjo), I'd give whole summer afternoons and the evening hours after heavy suppers of black-eyed peas and turnip greens, cracklin' bread and buttermilk, lemonade and sweet potato cobbler, to practicing hard-driving blues. Such food oversupplied me with bursting energy, and from listening to Ma Rainey, Ida Cox and Clara Smith, who made regular appearances in our town, I knew exactly how I wanted my horn to sound. But in the effort to make it do so (I was no embryo Joe Smith or Tricky Sam Nanton) I sustained the curses of both Christian and infidel—along with the encouragement of those more sympathetic citizens who understood the profound satisfaction to be found in expressing oneself in the blues.

Despite those who complained and cried to heaven for Gabriel to blow a chorus so heavenly sweet and so hellishly hot that I'd forever put down my horn, there were more tolerant ones who were willing to pay in present pain for future pride.

For who knew what skinny kid with his chops wrapped around a trumpet mouthpiece and a faraway look in his eyes might become the next Armstrong? Yes, and send you, at some big dance a few years hence, into an ecstasy of rhythm and memory and brassy affirmation of the goodness of being alive and part of the community? Someone had to; for it was part of the group tradition—though that was not how they said it.

"Let that boy blow," they'd say to the protesting ones. "He's got to talk baby talk on that thing before he can preach on it. Next thing you know he's liable to be up there with Duke Ellington. Sure, plenty

Oklahoma boys are up there with the big bands. Son, let's hear you try those 'Trouble in Mind Blues.' Now try and make it sound like ole Ida Cox sings it."

And I'd draw in my breath and do Miss Cox great violence.

Thus the crimes and aspirations of my youth. It had been years since I had played the trumpet or irritated a single ear with other than the spoken or written word, but as far as my singing neighbor was concerned I had to hold my peace. I was forced to listen, and in listening I soon became involved to the point of identification. If she sang badly I'd hear my own futility in the windy sound; if well, I'd stare at my typewriter and despair that I should ever make my prose so sing. She left me neither night nor day, this singer on our ceiling, and as my writing languished I became more and more upset. Thus one desperate morning I decided that since I seemed doomed to live within a shrieking chaos I might as well contribute my share; perhaps if I fought noise with noise I'd attain some small peace. Then a miracle: I turned on my radio (an old Philco AM set connected to a small Pilot FM tuner) and I heard the words

> Art thou troubled?
> Music will calm thee ...

I stopped as though struck by the voice of an angel. It was Kathleen Ferrier, that loveliest of singers, giving voice to the aria from Handel's *Rodelinda*. The voice was so completely expressive of words and music that I accepted it without question—what lover of the vocal art could resist her?

Yet it was ironic, for after giving up my trumpet for the typewriter I had avoided too close a contact with the very art which she recommended as balm. For I had started music early and lived with it daily, and when I broke I tried to break clean. Now in this magical moment all the old love, the old fascination with music superbly rendered, flooded back. When she finished I realized that with such music in my own apartment, the chaotic sounds from without and above had sunk, if not into silence, then well below the level where they mattered. Here was a way out. If I was to live and write in that apartment, it would be only through the grace of music. I had tuned in a Ferrier recital, and when it ended I rushed out for several of her records, certain that now deliverance was mine.

But not yet. Between the hi-fi record and the ear, I learned, there was a new electronic world. In that realization our apartment was well on its way toward becoming an audio booby trap. It was 1949 and I rushed to the Audio Fair. I have, I confess, as much gadget-resistance as the next American of my age, weight and slight income; but little did I dream of the test to which it would be put. I had hardly entered the fair before I heard David Sarser's and Mel Sprinkle's Musician's Amplifier, took a look at its schematic and, recalling a boyhood acquaintance with such matters, decided that I could build one. I did, several times before it measured within specifications. And still our system was lacking. Fortunately my wife shared my passion for music, so we went on to buy, piece by piece, a fine speaker system, a first-rate AM-FM tuner, a transcription turntable and a speaker cabinet. I built half a dozen or more preamplifiers and record compensators before finding a commercial one that satisfied my ear, and, finally, we acquired an arm, a magnetic cartridge and—glory of the house—a tape recorder. All this plunge into electronics, mind you, had as its simple end the enjoyment of recorded music as it was intended to be heard. I was obsessed with the idea of reproducing sound with such fidelity that even when using music as a defense behind which I could write, it would reach the unconscious levels of the mind with the least distortion. And it didn't come easily. There were wires and pieces of equipment all over the tiny apartment (I became a compulsive experimenter) and it was worth your life to move about without first taking careful bearings. Once we were almost crushed in our sleep by the tape machine, for which there was space only on a shelf at the head of our bed. But it was worth it.

For now when we played a recording on our system even the drunks on the wall could recognize its quality. I'm ashamed to admit, however, that I did not always restrict its use to the demands of pleasure or defense. Indeed, with such marvels of science at my control I lost my humility. My ethical consideration for the singer up above shriveled like a plant in too much sunlight. For instead of soothing, music seemed to release the beast in me. Now when jarred from my writer's reveries by some especially enthusiastic flourish of our singer, I'd rush to my music system with blood in my eyes and burst a few decibels in her direction. If she defied me with a few more pounds of pressure against her diaphragm, then a war of decibels was declared.

If, let us say, she were singing *"Depuis le Jour"* from *Louise,* I'd put on a tape of Bidu Sayâo performing the same aria, and let the rafters ring. If it was some song by Mahler, I'd match her spitefully with Marian Anderson or Kathleen Ferrier; if she offended with something from *Der Rosenkavalier,* I'd attack her flank with Lotte Lehmann. If she brought me up from my desk with art songs by Ravel or Rachmaninoff, I'd defend myself with Maggie Teyte or Jennie Tourel. If she polished a spiritual to a meaningless artiness I'd play Bessie Smith to remind her of the earth out of which we came. Once in a while I'd forget completely that I was supposed to be a gentleman and blast her with Strauss' *Zarathustra*, Bartók's *Concerto for Orchestra*, Ellington's "Flaming Sword," the famous crescendo from *The Pines of Rome*, or Satchmo scatting, "I'll be Glad When You're Dead" (you rascal you!). Oh, I was living with music with a sweet vengeance.

One might think that all this would have made me her most hated enemy, but not at all. When I met her on the stoop a few weeks after my rebellion, expecting her fully to slap my face, she astonished me by complimenting our music system. She even questioned me concerning the artists I had used against her. After that, on days when the acoustics were right, she'd stop singing until the piece was finished and then applaud—not always, I guessed, without a justifiable touch of sarcasm. And although I was now getting on with my writing, the unfairness of this business bore in upon me. Aware that I could not have withstood a similar comparison with literary artists of like caliber, I grew remorseful. I also came to admire the singer's courage and control, for she was neither intimidated into silence nor goaded into undisciplined screaming; she persevered, she marked the phrasing of the great singers I sent her way, she improved her style.

Better still, she vocalized more softly, and I, in turn, used music less and less as a weapon and more for its magic with mood and memory. After a while a simple twirl of the volume control up a few decibels and down again would bring a live-and-let-live reduction of her volume. We have long since moved from that apartment and that most interesting neighborhood and now the floors and walls of our present apartment are adequately thick and there is even a closet large enough to house the audio system; the only wire visible is that leading from the closet to the corner speaker system. Still we are indebted to the singer and the old environment for forcing us to discover one of the most deeply satisfying aspects of our living. Perhaps the enjoyment of music is always suffused with past experience; for me, at least, this is true.

It seems a long way and a long time from the glorious days of Oklahoma jazz dances, the jam sessions at Halley Richardson's place on Deep Second, from the phonographs shouting the blues in the back alleys I knew as a delivery boy and from the days when watermelon men with voices like mellow bugles shouted their wares in time with the rhythm of their horses' hoofs and farther still from the washerwomen singing slave songs as they stirred sooty tubs in sunny yards, and a long time, too, from those intense, conflicting days when the school music program of Oklahoma City was tuning our earthy young ears to classical accents—with music appreciation classes and free musical instruments and basic instruction for any child who cared to learn and uniforms for all who made the band. There was a mistaken notion on the part of some of the teachers that classical music had nothing to do with the rhythms, relaxed or hectic, of daily living, and that one should crook the little finger when listening to such refined strains. And the blues and the spirituals—jazz—? they would have destroyed them and scattered the pieces. Nevertheless, we learned some of it all, for in the United States when traditions are juxtaposed they tend, regardless of what we do to prevent it, irresistibly to merge. Thus musically at least each child in our town was an heir of all the ages. One learns by moving from the familiar to the unfamiliar, and while it might sound incongruous at first, the step from the spirituality of the spirituals to that of the Beethoven of the symphonies or the Bach of the chorales is not as vast as it seems. Nor is the romanticism of a Brahms or Chopin completely unrelated to that of Louis Armstrong. Those who know their native culture and love it unchauvinistically are never lost when encountering the unfamiliar.

Living with music today we find Mozart and Ellington, Kirsten Flagstad and Chippie Hill, William L. Dawson and Carl Orff all forming part of our regular fare. For all exalt life in rhythm and melody; all add to its significance. Perhaps in the swift change of American society in which the meanings of one's origin are so quickly lost, one of the chief values of living with music lies in its power to give us an orientation in time. In doing so, it gives significance to all those indefinable aspects of experience which nevertheless help to make us what we are. In the swift whirl of time music is a constant, reminding us of what we were and of that toward which we aspired. Art thou troubled? Music will not only calm, it will ennoble thee.

POSSIBILITIES FOR WRITING

1. Ellison suggests that music has meant many things to him over the course of his life, from the days of his childhood to the years in the apartment he describes here to the time when he was writing this essay. Focusing on each of these stages in his life, analyze his various feelings about music.

2. Ellison's tone in this essay ranges from serious to light, from outraged to self-deprecating, from "classical" to "jazzy." Analyze these various elements of his voice and how they work together to help make his larger point.

3. Write an essay of your own about "living with music," focusing on the music you grew up with, were taught in school, learned to play yourself, listen to now, and so forth. Try to draw some larger conclusions, as Ellison does, about your relationship with music.

Anne Fadiman (b. 1953) won the National Book Critics Circle Award for The Spirit Catches You and You Fall Down, *her 1997 report on the medical and cultural struggles of an immigrant Hmong family living in California with an epileptic child. A graduate of Harvard University, Fadiman was a founding editor of the Library of Congress magazine* Civilization *and, in 1997, became the editor of the Phi Beta Kappa quarterly the* American Scholar. *In 2005, she became the first Paul E. Francis Writer in Residence at Yale University. She is the author of* Ex Libris: Confessions of a Common Reader *(1998) and the editor of* Re-readings *(2003), a collection of essays in which the writers discuss their rereading of classic books.*

ANNE FADIMAN

Birth

In "Birth," the first chapter of *The Spirit Catches You and You Fall Down*, Anne Fadiman describes the birth of the children of a Hmong woman, Foua Yang, in the north of Laos. Fadiman describes the normal birthing procedure for Laotian women, such as Foua had for the first twelve of her children. After birthing her thirteenth child in a refugee camp, Foua gave birth to her fourteenth, Lia, in an American hospital in a process Fadiman describes, contrasting it, without comment, with the traditional birth process.

Throughout the essay, Fadiman presents fact after fact about Hmong beliefs, customs, and cultural values—all without comment or judgment. The essay reads, thus, largely like an anthropologist's report about a family transplanted from a very different world, who, nevertheless, accommodated themselves to the customs of their new country.

If Lia Lee had been born in the highlands of northwest Laos, where her parents and twelve of her brothers and sisters were born, her mother would have squatted on the floor of the house that her father had built from ax-hewn planks thatched with bamboo and grass. The floor was dirt, but it was clean. Her mother, Foua, sprinkled it regularly with water to keep the dust down and swept it every morning and evening with a broom she had made of grass and bark. She used a bamboo dustpan, which she had also made herself, to collect the feces of the children who were too young to defecate outside, and emptied its contents in the forest. Even if Foua had been a less fastidious housekeeper, her newborn babies wouldn't have gotten dirty, since she never let them actually touch the floor. She remains proud to this day that she delivered each of them into her own hands, reaching between her legs to ease out the head and then letting the rest of the body slip out onto her bent forearms. No birth attendant was present, though if her throat became dry during labor, her husband, Nao Kao, was permitted to bring her a cup of hot water, as long as he averted his eyes from her body. Because Foua believed that moaning or screaming would thwart the birth, she labored in silence, with the exception of an occasional prayer to her ancestors. She was so quiet that although most of her babies were born at night, her older children slept undisturbed on a communal bamboo pallet a few feet away, and woke only when they heard the cry of their new brother or sister. After each birth, Nao Kao cut the umbilical cord with heated scissors and tied it with string. Then Foua washed the baby with water she had carried from the stream, usually in the early phases of labor, in a wooden and bamboo pack-barrel strapped to her back.

Foua conceived, carried, and bore all her children with ease, but had there been any problems, she would have had recourse to a variety of remedies that were commonly used by the Hmong, the hilltribe to which her family belonged. If a Hmong couple failed to produce children, they could call in a *txiv neeb*, a shaman who was believed to have the ability to enter a trance, summon a posse of helpful familiars, ride a winged horse over the twelve mountains between the earth and the sky, cross an ocean inhabited by dragons, and (starting with bribes of food and money and, if necessary, working up to a necromantic sword) negotiate for his patients' health with the spirits who lived in the realm of the unseen. A *txiv neeb* might be able to cure infertility by asking the couple to sacrifice a dog, a cat, a chicken, or a sheep. After the animal's throat was cut, the *txiv neeb* would string a rope bridge from the doorpost to the marriage bed, over which the soul of the couple's future baby, which had been detained by a malevolent spirit called a *dab*, could now freely travel to earth. One could also take certain precautions to avoid becoming infertile in the first place. For example, no Hmong woman of childbearing age would ever think of setting foot inside a cave, because a particularly unpleasant king of *dab* sometimes lived there who liked to eat flesh and drink blood and could make his victim sterile by having sexual intercourse with her.

Once a Hmong woman became pregnant, she could ensure the health of her child by paying close attention to her food cravings. If she craved ginger and failed to eat it, her child would be born with an extra finger or toe. If she craved chicken flesh and did not eat it, her child would have a blemish near its ear. If she craved eggs and did not eat them, her child would have a lumpy head. When a Hmong woman felt the first pangs of labor, she would hurry home from the rice or opium fields, where she had continued to work throughout her pregnancy. It was important to reach her own house, or at least the house of one of her husband's cousins, because if she gave birth anywhere else a *dab* might injure her. A long or arduous labor could be eased by drinking the water in which a key had been boiled, in order to unlock the birth canal; by having her family array bowls of sacred water around the room and chant prayers over them; or, if the difficulty stemmed from having treated an elder member of the family with insufficient respect, by washing the offended relative's fingertips and apologizing like crazy until the relative finally said, "I forgive you."

Soon after the birth, while the mother and baby were still lying together next to the fire pit, the father dug a hole at least two feet deep in the dirt floor and buried the placenta. If it was a girl, her placenta was buried under her parents' bed; if it was a boy, his placenta was buried in a place of greater honor, near the base of the house's central wooden pillar, in which a male spirit, a domestic guardian who held up the roof of the house and watched over its residents, made his home. The placenta was always buried with the smooth side, the side that had faced the fetus inside the womb, turned upward, since if it was upside down, the baby might vomit after nursing. If the baby's face erupted in spots, that meant the placenta was being attacked by ants underground, and boiling water was poured into the burial hole as an insecticide. In the Hmong language, the word for placenta means "jacket." It is considered one's first and finest garment. When a Hmong dies, his or her soul must travel back from place to place, retracing the path of its life geography, until it reaches the burial place of its placental jacket, and puts it on. Only after the soul is properly dressed in the clothing in which it was born can it continue its dangerous journey, past murderous *dabs* and giant poisonous caterpillars, around man-eating rocks and impassable oceans, to the place beyond the sky where it is reunited with its ancestors and from which it will someday be sent to be reborn as the soul of a new baby. If the soul cannot find its jacket, it is condemned to an eternity of wandering, naked and alone.

Because the Lees are among the 150,000 Hmong who have fled Laos since their country fell to communist forces in 1975, they do not know if their house is still standing, or if the five male and seven female placentas that Nao Kao buried under the dirt floor are still there. They believe that half of the placentas have already been put to their final use, since four of their sons and two of their daughters died of various causes before the Lees came to the United States. The Lees believe that someday the souls of most of the rest of their family will have a long way to travel, since they will have to retrace their steps from Merced, California, where the family has spent fifteen of its seventeen years in this country; to Portland, Oregon, where they lived before Merced; to Honolulu, Hawaii, where their airplane from Thailand first landed; to two Thai refugee camps; and finally back to their home village in Laos.

The Lee's thirteenth child, Mai, was born in a refugee camp in Thailand. Her placenta was buried under their hut. Their fourteenth child, Lia, was born in the Merced Community Medical Center, a modern public hospital that serves an agricultural county in California's Central Valley, where many Hmong refugees have resettled. Lia's placenta was incinerated. Some Hmong women have asked the doctors at MCMC, as the hospital is commonly called, if they could take their babies' placentas home. Several of the doctors have acquiesced, packing the placentas in plastic bags or take-out containers from the hospital cafeteria; most have refused, in some cases because they have assumed that the women planned to eat the placentas, and have found that idea disgusting, and in some cases because they have feared the possible spread of hepatitis B, which is carried by at least fifteen percent of the Hmong refugees in the United States. Foua never thought to ask, since she speaks no English, and when she delivered Lia, no one present spoke Hmong. In any case, the Lee's apartment had a wooden floor covered with wall-to-wall carpeting, so burying the placenta would have been a difficult proposition.

When Lia was born, at 7:09 p.m. on July 19, 1982, Foua was lying on her back on a steel table, her body covered with sterile drapes, her genital area painted with a brown Betadine solution, with a high-wattage lamp trained on her perineum. There were no family members in the room. Gary Thueson, a family practice resident who did the delivery, noted in the chart that in order to speed the labor, he had artificially ruptured Foua's amniotic sac by poking it with a foot-long plastic "amni-hook"; that no anesthesia was used; that no episiotomy, an incision to enlarge the vaginal opening, was necessary; and that after the birth, Foua received a standard intravenous dose of Pitocin to constrict her uterus. Dr. Thueson also noted that Lia was a "healthy infant" whose weight, 8 pounds 7 ounces, and condition were "appropriate for gestational age" (an estimate he based on observation alone, since Foua had received no prenatal care, was not certain how long she had been pregnant, and could not have told Dr. Thueson even if she had known). Foua thinks that Lia was her largest baby, although she isn't sure, since none of her thirteen elder children were weighted at birth. Lia's Apgar scores, an assessment of a newborn infant's heart rate, respiration, muscle tone, color, and reflexes, were good: one minute after her birth she scored 7 on a scale of 10, and four minutes later she scored 9. When she was six minutes old, her color was described as "pink" and her activity as "crying." Lia was shown briefly to her mother. Then she was placed in a steel and Plexiglas warmer, where a nurse fastened a plastic identification band around her wrist and recorded her footprints by inking the soles of her feet with a stamp pad and pressing them against a Newborn Identification form. After that, Lia was removed to the central nursery, where she received an injection of Vitamin K in one of her thighs to prevent hemorrhagic disease; was treated with two drops of silver nitrate solution in each eye, to prevent an infection from gonococcal bacteria; and was bathed with Safeguard soap.

Foua's own date of birth was recorded on Lia's Delivery Room Record as October 6, 1944. In fact, she has no idea when she was born, and on various other occasions during the next several years she would inform MCMC personnel, through English-speaking relatives such as the nephew's wife who had helped her check into the hospital for Lia's delivery, that her date of birth was October 6, 1942, or, more frequently, October 6, 1926. Not a single admitting clerk ever appears to have questioned the latter date, though it would imply that Foua gave birth to Lia at the age of 55. Foua is quite sure, however, that October is correct, since she was told by her parents that she was born during the season in which the opium fields are weeded for the second time and the harvested rice stalks are stacked. She invented the precise day of the month, like the year, in order to satisfy the many Americans who have evinced an abhorrence of unfilled blanks on the innumerable forms the Lees have encountered since their admission to the United States in 1980. Most Hmong refugees are familiar with this American trait and have accommodated it in the same way. Nao Kao Lee has a first cousin who told the immigration officials that all nine of his children were born on July 15, in nine consecutive years, and this information was duly recorded on their resident alien documents.

When Lia Lee was released from MCMC, at the age of three days, her mother was asked to sign a piece of paper that read:

> I CERTIFY that during the discharge procedure I received my baby, examined it and determined that it was mine. I checked the Ident-A-Band® parts sealed on the baby and on me and found that they were identically numbered 5043 and contained correct identifying information.

Since Foua cannot read and has never learned to recognize Arabic numerals, it is unlikely that she followed these instructions. However, she had been asked for her signature so often in the United States that she had mastered the capital forms of the seven different letters contained in her name, Foua Yang. (The Yangs and the Lees are among the largest of the Hmong clans; the other major ones are the Chas, the Chengs, the Hangs, the Hers, the Kues, the Los, the Mouas, the Thaos, the Vues, the Xiongs, and the Vangs. In Laos, the clan name came first, but most Hmong refugees in the United States use it as a surname. Children belong to their father's clan; women traditionally retain their clan name after marriage. Marrying a member of one's own clan is strictly taboo.) Foua's signature is no less legible than the signatures of most of MCMC's resident physicians-in-training, which, particularly if they are written toward the end of a twenty-four-hour shift, tend to re-semble EEGs. However, it has the unique distinction of looking differ-ent each time it appears on a hospital document. On this occasion, FOUAYANG was written as a single word. One A is canted to the left and one to the right, the Y looks like an X, and the legs of the N undulate gracefully, like a child's drawing of a wave.

It is a credit to Foua's general equanimity, as well as her character-istic desire not to think ill of anyone, that although she found Lia's birth a peculiar experience, she has few criticisms of the way the hospi-tal handled it. Her doubts about MCMC in particular, and American medicine in general, would not begin to gather force until Lia had vis-ited the hospital many times. On this occasion, she thought the doctor was gentle and kind, she was impressed that so many people were there to help her, and although she felt that the nurses who bathed Lia with Safeguard did not get her quite as clean as she had gotten her newborns with Laotian stream water, her only major complaint con-cerned the hospital food. She was surprised to be offered ice water af-ter the birth, since many Hmong believe that cold foods during the postpartum period make the blood congeal in the womb instead of cleansing it by flowing freely, and that a woman who does not observe the taboo against them will develop itchy skin or diarrhea in her old age. Foua did accept several cups of what she remembers as hot black water. This was probably either tea or beef broth; Foua is sure it wasn't coffee, which she had seen before and would have recognized. The black water was the only MCMC-provided food that passed her lips during her stay in the maternity ward. Each day, Nao Kao cooked and brought her the diet that is strictly prescribed for Hmong women dur-ing the thirty days following childbirth: steamed rice, and chicken boiled in water with five special postpartum herbs (which the Lees had grown for this purpose on the edge of the parking lot behind their apartment building). This diet was familiar to the doctors on the Labor and Delivery floor at MCMC, whose assessments of it were fairly accurate gauges of their general opinion of the Hmong. One obstetrician, Raquel Arias, recalled, "The Hmong men carried these nice little silver cans to the hospital that always has some kind of chicken soup in them and always smelled great." Another obstetrician, Robert Small, said, "They always brought some horrible stinking concoction that smelled like the chicken had been dead for a week." Foua never shared her meals with anyone, because there is a postpartum taboo against spilling grains of rice accidentally into the chicken pot. If that occurs, the newborn is likely to break out across the nose and cheeks with little white pimples whose name in the Hmong language is the same as the word for "rice."

Some Hmong parents in Merced have given their children American names. In addition to many standard ones, these have included Kennedy, Nixon, Pajama, Guitar, Main (after Merced's Main Street), and, until a nurse counseled otherwise, Baby Boy, which one mother, seeing it written on her son's hospital paper, assumed was the name the doctor had already chosen for him. The lees chose to give their daughter a Hmong name, Lia. Her name was officially conferred in a ceremony called a *bu plig*, or soul-calling, which in Laos always took place on the third day after birth. Until this ceremony was performed, a baby was not considered to be fully a member of the human race, and if it died during its first three days it was not accorded the customary funerary rites. (This may have been a cultural adaptation to the fifty-percent infant mortality rate, a way of steeling Hmong mothers against the frequent loss of their babies during or shortly after childbirth by encouraging them to postpone their attachment.) In the United States, the naming is usually celebrated at a latter time, since on its third day a baby may still be hospitalized, especially if the birth was complicated. It took the lee family about a month to save enough money from their welfare checks, and from gifts from their relatives' welfare checks, to finance a soul-calling party for Lia.

Although the Hmong believe that illness can be caused by a variety of sources—including eating the wrong food, drinking contaminated water, being affected by a change in the weather, failing to ejaculate completely during sexual intercourse, neglecting to make offerings to one's ancestors, being punished for one's ancestors' transgressions, being cursed, being hit by a whirlwind, having a stone implanted in one's body by an evil spirit master, having one's blood sucked by a *dab*, bumping into a *dab* who lives in a tree or a stream, digging a well in a *dab's* living place, catching sight of a dwarf female *dab* who eats earthworms, having a *dab* sit on one's chest while one is sleeping, doing one's laundry in a lake inhabited by a dragon, pointing one's finger at the full moon, touching a newborn mouse, killing a large snake, urinating on a rock that looks like a tiger, urinating on or kicking a benevolent house spirit, or having bird droppings fall on one's head—by far the most common cause of illness is soul loss. Although the Hmong do not agree on just how many souls people have (estimates range from one to thirty-two; the Lees believe there is only one), there is a general consensus that whatever that number, it is the life-soul, whose presence is necessary for health and happiness, that tends to get lost. A life-soul can become separated from its body through anger, grief, fear, curiosity, or wanderlust. The life-souls of newborn babies are especially prone to disappearance, since they are so small, so vulnerable, and so precariously poised between the realm of the unseen, from which they have just traveled, and the realm of the living. Babies' souls may wander away, drawn by bright colors, sweet sounds, or fragrant smells; they may leave if a baby is sad, lonely, or insufficiently loved by its parents; they may be frightened away by a sudden loud noise; or they may be stolen by a *dab*. Some Hmong are careful never to say aloud that a baby is pretty, lest a *dab* be listening. Hmong babies are often dressed in intricately embroidered hats (Foua made several for Lia) which, when seen from a heavenly perspective, might fool a predatory *dab* into thinking the child was a flower. They spend much of their time swaddled against their mothers' backs in cloth carriers called *nyias* (Foua made Lia several of these too) that have been embroidered with soul-retaining motifs, such as the pigpen, which symbolizes enclosure. They may wear silver necklaces fastened with soul-shackling locks. When babies or small children go on an outing, their parents may call loudly to their souls before the family returns home, to make sure that none remain behind. Hmong families in Merced can sometimes be heard doing this when they leave local parks after a picnic. None of these ploys can work, however, unless the soul-calling ritual has already been properly observed.

Lia's *bu plig* took place in the living room of her family's apartment. There were so many guests, all of them Hmong and most of them members of the Lee and Yang clans, that it was nearly impossible to turn around. Foua and Nao Kao were proud that so many people had come to celebrate their good fortune in being favored with such a healthy and beautiful daughter. That morning Nao Kao had sacrificed a pig in order to invite the soul of one of Lia's ancestors, which was probably hungry and would appreciate an offering of food, to be reborn in her body. After the guests arrived, an elder of the Yang clan stood at the apartment's open front door, facing East 12th Street, with two live chickens in a bag on the floor next to him, and chanted a greeting to Lia's soul. The two chickens were then killed, plucked, eviscerated, partially boiled, retrieved from the cooking pot, and examined to see if their skulls were translucent and their tongues curled upward, both signs that Lia's new soul was pleased to take up residence in her body and that her name was a good one. (If the signs had been inauspicious, the soul-caller would have recommended that another name be chosen.) After the reading of the auguries, the chickens were put back in the cooking pot. The guests would later eat them and the pig for dinner. Before the meal, the soul-caller brushed Lia's hands with a bundle of short white strings and said, "I am sweeping away the ways of sickness." Then Lia's parents and all of the elders present in the room each tied a string around one of Lia's wrists in order to bind her soul securely to her body. Foua and Nao Kao promised to love her; the elders blessed her and prayed that she would have a long life and that she would never become sick.

POSSIBILITIES FOR WRITING

1. Fadiman writes largely as a reporter in "Birth." She describes without explaining, analyzing, or judging. Yet there are places in the text, where a reader can make inferences about the Hmong. Identify one such place where you formed an impression of Foua Yang. Explain your impression of her.

2. Summarize in a paragraph what you consider the main idea(s) conveyed in "Birth." Why do you think Fadiman began a book about the Hmong people with this chapter?

3. Write an essay in which you convey an impression of an individual or a group of people strictly through describing them. Include a description of an action or event as part of your essay. Avoid any overt or explicit comment, explanation, or judgment. Let the details convey your idea and impression through implication.

Richard Feynman (1918–1988) grew up in Far Rockaway, New York, where he attended school and became interested in science at an early age. He received a Doctor of Philosophy in Physics from Princeton University in 1942. During the Second World War Feynman played an important role in the development of the atomic bomb, an experience he discusses a number of times in his works. After the war, Feynman taught at Cornell University and the California Institute of Technology. In 1965, he was awarded the Nobel Prize in Physics for his research in quantum electrodynamics. And after the explosion of the Challenger *in 1986, Feynman was consulted to identify the cause of the disaster. In addition to his work as a physicist, Feynman was an artist, bongo player, raconteur, and safecracker. He was an engaging and entertaining lecturer on physics, with many of his lectures having been published. Among his best known books are* Six Easy Pieces; Six Not So Easy Pieces; Surely, You Are Joking, Mr. Feynman; *and* The Pleasure of Finding Things Out, *from which "The Value of Science" has been taken.*

RICHARD FEYNMAN

The Value of Science

In "The Value of Science," a lecture for fellow scientists, Richard Feynman considers why science is important and why scientists should focus the great bulk of their energy and attention on scientific questions, rather than on social problems. He argues that scientific knowledge is morally neutral, that although people can use scientific knowledge either for good or for ill, science is not something that can be ignored or stopped.

Among the values Feynman assigns to scientific investigations are its practical results, including technological advances and applications that flow from scientific discoveries. Besides the many practical benefits of science, such as medical applications, for example, Feynman argues for the value of science in stimulating the imagination, in providing intellectual enjoyment, which he calls simply, "the pleasure of finding things out." But the most important value of science, in Feynman's view, resides in its capacity to doubt, to use doubt and uncertainty to investigate all manner of unanswered and partly answered questions.

From time to time, people suggest to me that scientists ought to give more consideration to social problems—especially that they should be more responsible in considering the impact of science upon society. This same suggestion must be made to many other scientists, and it seems to be generally believed that if the scientists would only look at these very difficult social problems and not spend so much time fooling with the less vital scientific ones, great success would come of it.

It seems to me that we do think about these problems from time to time, but we don't put full-time effort into them—the reason being that we know we don't have any magic formula for solving problems, that social problems are very much harder than scientific ones, and that we usually don't get anywhere when we do think about them.

I believe that a scientist looking at nonscientific problems is just as dumb as the next guy—and when he talks about a nonscientific matter, he will sound as naive as anyone untrained in the matter. Since the question of the value of science is not a scientific subject, this discussion is dedicated to proving my point—by example.

The first way in which science is of value is familiar to everyone. It is that scientific knowledge enables us to do all kinds of things and to make all kinds of things. Of course if we make good things, it is not only to the credit of science; it is also to the credit of the moral choice which led us to good work. Scientific knowledge is an enabling power to do either good or bad—but it does not carry instructions on how to use it. Such power has evident value—even though the power may be negated by what one does.

I learned a way of expressing this common human problem on a trip to Honolulu. In a Buddhist temple there, the man in charge explained a little bit about the Buddhist religion for tourists, and then ended his talk by telling them he had something to say to them that they would *never* forget—and I have never forgotten it. It was a proverb of the Buddhist religion:

"To every man is given the key to the gates of heaven; the same key opens the gates of hell."

What, then, is the value of the key to heaven? It is true that if we lack clear instructions that determine which is the gate to heaven and which the gate to hell, the key may be a dangerous object to use, but it obviously has value. How can we enter heaven without it?

The instructions, also, would be of no value without the key. So it is evident that, in spite of the fact that science could produce enormous horror in the world, it is of value because it *can* produce *something.*

Another value of science is the fun called intellectual enjoyment which some people get from reading and learning and thinking about it, and which others get from working in it. This is a very real and important point and one which is not considered enough by those who tell us it is our social responsibility to reflect on the impact of science on society.

Is this mere personal enjoyment of value to society as a whole? No! But it is also a responsibility to consider the value of society itself. Is it, in the last analysis, to arrange things so that people can enjoy things? If so, the enjoyment of science is as important as anything else.

But I would like *not* to underestimate the value of the worldview which is the result of scientific effort. We have been led to imagine all sorts of things infinitely more marvelous than the imaginings of poets and dreamers of the past. It shows that the imagination of nature is far, far greater than the imagination of man. For instance, how much more remarkable it is for us all to be stuck—half of us upside down—by a mysterious attraction, to a spinning ball that has been swinging in space for billions of years, than to be carried on the back of an elephant supported on a tortoise swimming in a bottomless sea.

I have thought about these things so many times alone that I hope you will excuse me if I remind you of some thoughts that I am sure you have all had—or this type of thought—which no one could ever have had in the past, because people then didn't have the information we have about the world today.

For instance, I stand at the seashore, alone, and start to think. There are the rushing waves ... mountains of molecules, each stupidly minding its own business ... trillions apart ... yet forming white surf in unison.

Ages on ages ... before any eyes could see ... year after year ... thunderously pounding the shore as now. For whom, for what? ... on a dead planet, with no life to entertain.

Never at rest ... tortured by energy ... wasted prodigiously by the sun ... poured into space. A mite makes the sea roar.

Deep in the sea, all molecules repeat the patterns of one another till complex new ones are formed. They make others like themselves ... and a new dance starts.

Growing in size and complexity ... living things, masses of atoms, DNA, protein ... dancing a pattern ever more intricate.

Out of the cradle onto the dry land ... here it is standing ... atoms with consciousness ... matter with curiosity.

Stands at the sea ... wonders at wondering ... I ... a universe of atoms ... an atom in the universe.

The Grand Adventure

The same thrill, the same awe and mystery, come again and again when we look at any problem deeply enough. With more knowledge comes deeper, more wonderful mystery, luring one on to penetrate deeper still. Never concerned that the answer may prove disappointing, but with pleasure and confidence we turn over each new stone to find unimagined strangeness leading on to more wonderful questions and mysteries—certainly a grand adventure!

It is true that few unscientific people have this particular type of religious experience. Our poets do not write about it; our artists do not try to portray this remarkable thing. I don't know why. Is nobody inspired by our present picture of the universe? The value of science remains unsung by singers, so you are reduced to hearing—not a song or a poem, but an evening lecture about it. This is not yet a scientific age.

Perhaps one of the reasons is that you have to know how to read the music. For instance, the scientific article says, perhaps, something like this: "The radioactive phosphorus content of the cerebrum of the rat decreases to one-half in a period of two weeks." Now, what does that mean?

It means that phosphorus that is in the brain of a rat (and also in mine, and yours) is not the same phosphorus as it was two weeks ago, but that all of the atoms that are in the brain are being replaced, and the ones that were there before have gone away.

So what is this mind, what are these atoms with consciousness? Last week's potatoes! That is what now can *remember* what was going on in my mind a year ago—a mind which has long ago been replaced.

That is what it means when one discovers how long it takes for the atoms of the brain to be replaced by other atoms, to note that the thing which I call my individuality is only a pattern or dance. The atoms come into my brain, dance a dance, then go out; always new atoms but always doing the same dance, remembering what the dance was yesterday.

The Remarkable Idea

When we read about this in the newspaper, it says, "The scientist says that this discovery may have importance in the cure of cancer." The paper is only interested in the use of the idea, not the idea itself. Hardly anyone can understand the importance of an idea, it is so remarkable. Except that, possibly, some children catch on. And when a child catches on to an idea like that, we have a scientist. These ideas do filter down (in spite of all the conversation about TV replacing thinking), and lots of kids get the spirit—and when they have the spirit you have a scientist. It's too late for them to get the spirit when they are in our universities, so we must attempt to explain these ideas to children.

I would now like to turn to a third value that science has. It is a little more indirect, but not much. The scientist has a lot of experience with ignorance and doubt and uncertainty, and this experience is of very great importance, I think. When a scientist doesn't know the answer to a problem, he is ignorant. When he has a hunch as to what the result is, he is uncertain. And when he is pretty darn sure of what the result is going to be, he is in some doubt. We have found it of paramount importance that in order to progress we must recognize the ignorance and leave room for doubt. Scientific knowledge is a body of statements of varying degrees of certainty—some most unsure, some nearly sure, none *absolutely* certain.

Now, we scientists are used to this, and we take it for granted that it is perfectly consistent to be unsure—that it is possible to live and *not* know. But I don't know whether everyone realizes that this is true. Our freedom to doubt was born of a struggle against authority in the early days of science. It was a very deep and strong struggle. Permit us to question—to doubt, that's all—not to be sure. And I think it is important that we do not forget the importance of this struggle and thus perhaps lose what we have gained. Here lies a responsibility to society.

We are all sad when we think of the wondrous potentialities human beings seem to have, as contrasted with their small accomplishments. Again and again people have thought that we could do much better. They of the past saw in the nightmare of their times a dream for the future. We, of their future, see that their dreams, in certain ways surpassed, have in many ways remained dreams. The hopes for the future today are, in good share, those of yesterday.

Education, for Good and Evil

Once some thought that the possibilities people had were not developed because most of those people were ignorant. With education universal, could all men be Voltaires? Bad can be taught at least as efficiently as good. Education is a strong force, but for either good or evil.

Communications between nations must promote understanding: So went another dream. But the machines of communication can be channeled or choked. What is communicated can be truth or lie. Communication is a strong force also, but for either good or bad.

The applied sciences should free men of material problems at least. Medicine controls diseases. And the record here seems all to the good. Yet there are men patiently working to create great plagues and poisons. They are to be used in warfare tomorrow.

Nearly everybody dislikes war. Our dream today is peace. In peace, man can develop best the enormous possibilities he seems to have.

But maybe future men will find that peace, too, can be good and bad. Perhaps peaceful men will drink out of boredom. Then perhaps drink will become the great problem which seems to keep man from getting all he thinks he should out of his abilities.

Clearly, peace is a great force, as is sobriety, as are material power, communication, education, honesty, and the ideals of many dreamers.

We have more of these forces to control than did the ancients. And maybe we are doing a little better than most of them could do. But what we ought to be able to do seems gigantic compared with our confused accomplishments.

Why is this? Why can't we conquer ourselves?

Because we find that even great forces and abilities do not seem to carry with them clear instructions on how to use them. As an example, the great accumulation of understanding as to how the physical world behaves only convinces one that this behavior seems to have a kind of meaninglessness. The sciences do not directly teach good and bad.

Through all ages men have tried to fathom the meaning of life. They have realized that if some direction or meaning could be given to our actions, great human forces would be unleashed. So, very many answers must have been given to the question of the meaning of it all. But they have been of all different sorts, and the proponents of one answer have looked with horror at the actions of the believers in another. Horror, because from a disagreeing point of view all the great potentialities of the race were being channeled into a false and confining blind alley. In fact, it is from the history of the enormous monstrosities created by false belief that philosophers have realized the apparently infinite and wondrous capacities of human beings. The dream is to find the open channel.

What, then, is the meaning of it all? What can we say to dispel the mystery of existence?

If we take everything into account, not only what the ancients knew, but all of what we know today that they didn't know, then I think that we must frankly admit that *we do not know*.

But, in admitting this, we have probably found the open channel.

This is not a new idea; this is the idea of the age of reason. This is the philosophy that guided the men who made the democracy that we live under. The idea that no one really knew how to run a government led to the idea that we should arrange a system by which new ideas could be developed, tried out, tossed out, more new ideas brought in; a trial and error system. This method was a result of the fact that science was already showing itself to be a successful venture at the end of the 18th century. Even then it was clear to socially minded people that the openness of the possibilities was an opportunity, and that doubt and discussion were essential to progress into the unknown. If we want to solve a problem that we have never solved before, we must leave the door to the unknown ajar.

Our Responsibility as Scientists

We are at the very beginning of time for the human race. It is not unreasonable that we grapple with problems. There are tens of thousands of years in the future. Our responsibility is to do what we can, learn what we can, improve the solutions and pass them on. It is our responsibility to leave the men of the future a free hand. In the impetuous youth of humanity, we can make grave errors that can stunt our growth for a long time. This we will do if we say we have the answers now, so young and ignorant; if we suppress all discussion, all criticism, saying, "This is it, boys, man is saved!" and thus doom man for a long time to the chains of authority, confined to the limits of our present imagination. It has been done so many times before.

It is our responsibility as scientists, knowing the great progress and great value of a satisfactory philosophy of ignorance, the great progress that is the fruit of freedom of thought, to proclaim the value of this freedom, to teach how doubt is not to be feared but welcomed and discussed, and to demand this freedom as our duty to all coming generations.

POSSIBILITIES FOR WRITING

1. Summarize the key points Feynman makes about the value of science. Identify the values of science and provide a brief explanation of each.
2. To what extent do you agree with the values Feynman sees in science? Are there any you would dispute or modify? Are there any you would add? Explain.
3. Write an essay in which you consider the benefits and the dangers of scientific knowledge. You might wish to focus on a particular area of scientific investigation, such as stem cell research and its relation to cloning.

Benjamin Franklin (1706–1790), *one of the most versatile and widely admired figures in American history, was born in Boston and apprenticed at an early age to a printer and newspaper publisher. As a young man, he moved to Philadelphia to make his fortune, eventually acquiring his own printing and newspaper house where he produced the popular* Poor Richard's Almanack *from 1732 to 1757. Essentially self-taught, Franklin helped to establish what became the American Philosophical Society and the University of Pennsylvania, and his experiments with electricity were noted worldwide. A leading figure in the American Revolution and the establishment of the United States as a democracy, Franklin has been referred to as the "wisest American." His autobiography of his early years is considered a classic of American literature.*

BENJAMIN FRANKLIN

Arriving at Perfection

In "Arriving at Perfection," an excerpt from his *Autobiography,* Benjamin Franklin lays out a plan for his own self-improvement. Franklin was a conscious and a conscientious perfectionist. His little essay on self-improvement reflects the enlightenment ideals of his time with their emphasis on reason and progress. But it also reflects an older tendency in American culture: the tendency toward self-examination and self-correction, a meditative cast of mind Franklin inherited from his Puritan ancestors. Franklin weds these two tendencies toward self-examination and toward self-improvement, toward the moral and the practical.

Franklin's goal for what he calls this "bold and arduous Project" is to live each day without committing any faults. As a rationalist, he sees no reason why he shouldn't be able to live according to a standard of moral propriety. He comes to realize, however, that there are many ways he can lapse from his high standard—through habit, carelessness, inclination, and bad example.

It was about this time that I conceiv'd the bold and arduous Project of arriving at moral Perfection. I wish'd to live without committing any Fault at any time; I would conquer all that either Natural Inclination, Custom, or Company might lead me into. As I knew, or thought I knew, what was right and wrong, I did not see why I might not *always* do the one and avoid the other. But I soon found I had undertaken a Task of more Difficulty than I had imagined: While my Care was employ'd in guarding against one Fault, I was often surpriz'd by another. Habit took the Advantage of Inattention. Inclination was sometimes too strong for Reason. I concluded at length, that the mere speculative Conviction that it was our Interest to be compleatly virtuous, was not sufficient to prevent our Slipping, and that the contrary Habits must be broken and good Ones acquired and established, before we can have any Dependance on a steady uniform Rectitude of Conduct. For this purpose I therefore contriv'd the following Method.

In the various Enumerations of the moral Virtues I had met with in my Reading, I found the Catalogue more or less numerous, as different Writers included more or fewer Ideas under the same Name. Temperance, for Example, was by some confin'd to Eating and Drinking, while by others it was extended to mean the moderating every other Pleasure, Appetite, Inclination or Passion, bodily or mental, even to our Avarice and Ambition. I propos'd to myself, for the sake of Clearness, to use rather more Names with fewer Ideas annex'd to each, than a few Names with more Ideas; and I included after Thirteen Names of Virtues all that at that time occurr'd to me as necessary or desirable, and annex'd to each a short Precept, which fully express'd the Extent I gave to its Meaning.

These Names of Virtues with their Precepts were

1. **Temperance.** Eat not to Dulness. Drink not to Elevation.
2. **Silence.** Speak not but what may benefit others or your self. Avoid trifling conversation.
3. **Order.** Let all your Things have their Places. Let each Part of your Business have its Time.
4. **Resolution.** Resolve to perform what you ought. Perform without fail what you resolve.
5. **Frugality.** Make no Expence but to do good to others or yourself: i.e. Waste nothing.
6. **Industry.** Lose no Time. Be always employ'd in something useful. Cut off all unnecessary Actions.
7. **Sincerity.** Use no hurtful Deceit. Think innocently and justly; and, if you speak; speak accordingly.
8. **Justice.** Wrong none, by doing Injuries or omitting the Benefits that are your Duty.
9. **Moderation.** Avoid Extreams. Forbear resenting Injuries so much as you think they deserve.
10. **Cleanliness.** Tolerate no Uncleanness in Body, Cloaths or Habitation.
11. **Tranquility.** Be not disturbed at Trifles, or at Accidents common or unavoidable.
12. **Chastity.** Rarely use Venery but for Health or Offspring; Never to Dulness, Weakness, or the Injury of your own or another's Peace or Reputation.
13. **Humility.** Imitate Jesus and Socrates.

My intention being to acquire the *Habitude* of all these Virtues, I judg'd it would be well not to distract my Attention by attempting the whole at once, but to fix it on one of them at a time, and when I should be Master of that, then to proceed to another, and so on till I should have gone thro' the thirteen. And as the previous Acquisition of some might facilitate the Acquisition of certain others, I arrang'd them with that View as they stand above. *Temperance* first, as it tends to procure that Coolness and Clearness of Head, which is so necessary where constant Vigilance was to be kept up, and Guard maintained, against the unremitting Attraction of ancient Habits, and the Force of perpetual Temptations. This being acquir'd and establish'd, *Silence* would be more easy, and my Desire being to gain Knowledge at the same time that I improv'd in Virtue, and considering that in Conversation it was obtain'd rather by the Use of the Ears than of the Tongue, and therefore wishing to break a Habit I was getting into of Prattling, Punning and Joking, which only made me acceptable to trifling Company, I gave *Silence* the second Place. This, and the next, *Order*, I expected would allow me more Time for attending to my Project and my Studies; RESOLUTION once become habitual, would keep me firm in my Endeavors to obtain all the subsequent Virtues; *Frugality* and *Industry*, by freeing me from my remaining Debt, and producing Affluence and Independance would make more easy the Practice of *Sincerity* and *Justice*, etc. etc. Conceiving then that agreable to the Advice of Pythagoras in his Golden Verses, daily examination would be necessary, I contriv'd the following Method for conducting that Examination.

I made a little Book in which I allotted a Page for each of the Virtues. I rul'd each Page with red Ink so as to have seven Columns, one for each Day of the Week, marking each Column with a Letter for the Day. I cross'd these Columns with thirteen red Lines, marking the Beginning of each Line with the first Letter of one of the Virtues, on which Line and in its proper Column I might mark by a little black Spot every Fault I found upon Examination, to have been committed respecting that Virtue upon that Day.

I determined to give a Week's strict Attention to each of the Virtues successively. Thus in the first Week my great Guard was to avoid every the least Offence against Temperance, leaving the other Virtues to their ordinary Chance, only marking every Evening the faults of the Day. Thus if in the first Week I could keep my first Line marked T clear of Spots, I suppos'd the Habit of that Virtue so much strengthen'd and its opposite weaken'd, that I might venture extending my Attention to include the next, and for the following Week keep both Lines clear of Spots. Proceeding thus to the last, I could go thro' a Course compleat in Thirteen Weeks, and four Courses in a Year. And like him who having a Garden to weed, does not attempt to eradicate all the bad Herbs at

TEMPERANCE						
Eat not to Dulness. Drink not to Elevation.						
	S	M	T	W	T	F	S

	S	M	T	W	T	F	S
T							
S	••	•		•		•	
O	•	•	•		•	•	•
R			•			•	
F		•			•		
I			•				
S							
J							
M							
Cl.							
T							
Ch.							
H							

once, which would exceed his Reach and his Strength, but works on one of the Beds at a time, and having accomplish'd the first proceeds to a second; so I should have, (I hoped) the encouraging Pleasure of seeing on my Pages the Progress I made in Virtue, by clearing successively my Lines of their Spots, till in the End by a Number of Courses.

I should be happy in viewing a clean Book after a thirteen Weeks daily Examination. . . .

POSSIBILITIES FOR WRITING

1. Revise, reorder, and supplement Franklin's list of practical virtues as a guide for contemporary college students. Why do you make any changes that you do?
2. Compare Franklin's program for self-improvement with contemporary self-improvement books found in the advice section of a bookstore. To what extent are the values expressed similar and different?
3. Franklin's goal here is not just moral behavior but moral "perfection." Why do you think so few people today believe in such perfection?

Sigmund Freud (1856–1939), the father of psychoanalysis, spent most of his life in Vienna, Austria, where he received his medical degree and developed a practice that initially involved the use of hypnosis in treating mental disorders. Based on the idea that most such disorders stemmed from the repression of traumatic childhood experiences, Freud's methodology later came to involve free association to encourage his patients to recover these unconscious memories. Freud's important works in the field of psychoanalysis include The Interpretation of Dreams *(1900),* Three Essays on the Theory of Sexuality *(1905), and* The Ego and the Id *(1923). Although many of Freud's specific emphases are questioned today, his overall theory of the unconscious continues to be highly influential in the methodologies of psychotherapy.*

SIGMUND FREUD

The Interpretation of Dreams

In the following essay, an excerpt from his *Interpretation of Dreams,* Sigmund Freud explains his theory of dreams as the fulfillment of wishes that people harbor in their waking lives, but which lie hidden only to surface during sleep. Freud argues against the notion that dreams are meaningless random events. He contends, instead, that dreams are filled with meaning, but that to understand our dreams we need to understand their origin along with the psychological mechanism that triggers them.

Freud illustrates his ideas with numerous examples of dreams, including his own. His first and simplest example is of a dream in which being thirsty as he sleeps, Freud dreams of drinking water to quench that thirst. In such "dreams of convenience," as Freud designates them, the dreamer conveniently continues sleeping while the need is satisfied or the wish fulfilled.

When, after passing through a narrow defile, we suddenly emerge upon a piece of high ground, where the path divides and the finest prospects open up on every side, we may pause for a moment and consider in which direction we shall first turn our steps. Such is the case with us, now that we have surmounted the first interpretation of a dream. We find ourselves in the full daylight of a sudden discovery. Dreams are not to be likened to the unregulated sounds that rise from a musical instrument struck by the blow of some external force instead of by a player's hand; they are not meaningless, they are not absurd; they do not imply that one portion of our store of ideas is asleep while another portion is beginning to wake. On the contrary, they are psychical phenomena of complete validity—fulfillments of wishes; they can be inserted into the chain of intelligible waking mental acts; they are contracted by a highly complicated activity of the mind.

But no sooner have we begun to rejoice at this discovery than we are assailed by a flood of questions. If, as we are told by dream-interpretation, a dream represents a fulfilled wish, what is the origin of the remarkable and puzzling form in which the wish-fulfillment is expressed? What alteration have the dream-thoughts undergone before being changed into the manifest dream which we remember when we wake up? How does that alteration take place? What is the source of the material that has been modified into the dream? What is the source of the many peculiarities that are to be observed in the dream-thoughts—such, for instance, as the fact that they may be mutually contradictory? Can a dream tell us anything new about our internal psychical processes? Can its content correct opinions we have held during the day?

I propose that for the moment we should leave all these questions on one side and pursue our way further along one particular path. We have learnt that a dream can represent a wish as fulfilled. Our first concern must be to enquire whether this is a universal characteristic of dreams or whether it merely happened to be the content of the particular dream (the dream of Irma's injection) which was the first that we analyzed. For even if we are prepared to find that every dream has a meaning and a psychical value, the possibility must remain open of this meaning not being the same in every dream. Our first dream was the fulfillment of a wish; a second one might turn out to be a fulfilled fear; the content of a third might be a reflection; while a fourth might merely reproduce a memory. Shall we find other wishful dreams besides this one? Or are there perhaps no dreams but wishful ones?

It is easy to prove that dreams often reveal themselves without any disguise as fulfillments of wishes; so that it may seem surprising that the language of dreams was not understood long ago. For instance, there is a dream that I can produce in myself as often as I like—experimentally, as it were. If I eat anchovies or olives or any other highly salted food in the evening, I develop thirst during the night which wakes me up. But my waking is preceded by a dream, and this always has the same content, namely, that I am drinking. I dream I am swallowing down water in great gulps, and it has the delicious taste that nothing can equal but a cool drink when one is parched with thirst. Then I wake up and have to have a real drink. This simple dream is occasioned by the thirst which I become aware of when I wake. The thirst gives rise to a wish to drink, and the dream shows me that wish fulfilled. In doing so it is performing a function—which it was easy to divine. I am a good sleeper and not accustomed to be woken by any physical need. If I can succeed in appeasing my thirst by *dreaming* that I am drinking, then I need not wake up in order to quench it. This, then, is a dream of convenience. Dreaming has taken the place of action, as it often does elsewhere in life. Unluckily my need for water to quench my thirst cannot be satisfied by a dream in the same way as my thirst for revenge against my friend Otto and Dr. M.; but the good intention is there in both cases. Not long ago this same dream of mine showed some modification. I had felt thirsty even before I fell asleep, and I had emptied a glass of water that stood on the table beside my bed. A few hours later during the night I had a fresh attack of thirst, and this had inconvenient results. In order to provide myself with some water I should have had to get up and fetch the glass standing on the table by my wife's bed. I therefore had an appropriate dream that my wife was giving me a drink out of a vase; this vase was an Etruscan cinerary urn which I had brought back from a journey to Italy and had since given away. But the water in it tasted so salty (evidently because of the ashes in the urn) that I woke up. It will be noticed how conveniently everything was arranged in this dream. Since its only purpose was to fulfil a wish, it could be completely egotistical. A love of comfort and convenience is not really compatible with consideration for other people. The introduction of the cinerary urn was probably yet another wish-fulfillment. I was sorry that the vase was no longer in my possession—just as the glass of water on my wife's table was out of my reach. The urn with its ashes fitted in, too, with the salty taste in my mouth which had now grown stronger and which I knew was bound to wake me.

Dreams of convenience like these were very frequent in my youth. Having made it a practice as far back as I can remember to work late into the night, I always found it difficult to wake early. I used then to have a dream of being out of bed and standing by the washing stand; after a while I was no longer able to disguise from myself the fact that I was really still in bed, but in the meantime I had had a little more sleep. A slothful dream of this kind, which was expressed in a particularly amusing and elegant form, has been reported to me by a young medical colleague who seems to share my liking for sleep. The landlady of his lodgings in the neighborhood of the hospital had strict instructions to wake him in time every morning but found it no easy job to carry them out. One morning sleep seemed peculiarly sweet. The landlady called through the door: "Wake up, Herr Pepi! It's time to go to the hospital!" In response to this he had a dream that he was lying in bed in a room in the hospital, and that there was a card over the bed on which was written: "Pepi H., medical student, age 22." While he was dreaming, he said to himself "As I'm already *in* the hospital, there's no need for me to go there"—and turned over and went on sleeping. In this way he openly confessed the motive for his dream.

Here is another dream in which once again the stimulus produced its effect during actual sleep. One of my women patients, who had been obliged to undergo an operation on her jaw which had taken an unfavorable course, was ordered by her doctors to wear a cooling apparatus on the side of her face day and night. But as soon as she fell asleep she used to throw it off. One day, after she had once more thrown the apparatus on the floor, I was asked to speak to her seriously about it. "This time I really couldn't help it," she answered. "It was because of a dream I had in the night. I dreamed I was in a box at the opera and very much enjoying the performance. But Herr Karl Meyer was in the nursing home and complaining bitterly of pains in his jaw. So I told myself that as I hadn't any pain I didn't need the apparatus; and I threw it away." The dream of this poor sufferer seems almost like a concrete representation of a phrase that sometimes forces its way on to people's lips in unpleasant situations: "I must say I could think of something more agreeable than this." The dream gives a picture of this more agreeable thing. The Herr Karl Meyer on to whom the dreamer transplanted her pains was the most indifferent young man of her acquaintance that she could call to mind.

The wish-fulfillment can be detected equally easily in some other dreams which I have collected from normal people. A friend of mine, who knows my theory of dreams and has told his wife of it, said to me one day: "My wife has asked me to tell you that she had a dream yesterday that she was having her period. You can guess what that means." I could indeed guess it. The fact that this young married woman dreamed that she was having her period meant that she had missed her period. I could well believe that she would have been glad to go on enjoying her freedom a little longer before shouldering the burden of motherhood. It was a neat way of announcing her first pregnancy. Another friend of mine wrote and told me that, not long before, his wife had dreamed that she had noticed some milk stains on the front of her vest. This too was an announcement of pregnancy, but not of a first one. The young mother was wishing that she might have more nourishment to give her second child than she had had for her first.

A young woman had been cut off from society for weeks on end while she nursed her child through an infectious illness. After the child's recovery, she had a dream of being at a party at which, among others, she met Alphonse Daudet, Paul Bourget, and Marcel Prévost; they were all most affable to her and highly amusing. All of the authors resembled their portraits, except Marcel Prévost, of whom she had never seen a picture; and he looked like . . . the disinfection officer who had fumigated the sick room the day before and who had been her first visitor for so long. Thus it seems possible to give a complete translation of the dream: "It's about time for something more amusing than this perpetual sick-nursing."

These examples will perhaps be enough to show that dreams which can only be understood as fulfillments of wishes and which bear their meaning upon their faces without disguise are to be found under the most frequent and various conditions. They are mostly short and simple dreams, which afford a pleasant contrast to the confused and exuberant compositions that have in the main attracted the attention of the authorities. Nevertheless, it will repay us to pause for a moment over these simple dreams. We may expect to find the very simplest forms of dreams in *children,* since there can be no doubt that their psychical productions are less complicated than those of adults. Child psychology, in my opinion, is destined to perform the same useful services for adult psychology that the investigation of the structure or development of the lower animals has performed for research into the structure of the higher classes of animals. Few deliberate efforts have hitherto been made to make use of child psychology for this purpose.

The dreams of young children are frequently pure wish-fulfillments and are in that case quite uninteresting compared with the dreams of adults. They raise no problems for solution; but on the other hand they are of inestimable importance in proving that, in their essential nature, dreams represent fulfillments of wishes. I have been able to collect a few instances of such dreams from material provided by my own children.

I have to thank an excursion which we made from Aussee to the lovely village of Hallstatt in the summer of 1896 for two dreams: One of these was dreamed by my daughter, who was then eight and a half, and the other by her brother of five and a quarter. I must explain by way of preamble that we had been spending the summer on a hillside near Aussee, from which, in fine weather, we enjoyed a splendid view of the Dachstein. The Simony Hütte could be clearly distinguished through a telescope. The children made repeated attempts at seeing it through the telescope—I cannot say with what success. Before our excursion, I had told the children that Hallstatt lay at the foot of the Dachstein. They very much looked forward to the day. From Hallstatt we walked up the Echerntal, which delighted the children with its succession of changing landscapes. One of them, however, the five-year-old boy, gradually became fretful. Each time a new mountain came into view he asked if that was the Dachstein and I had to say, "No, only one of the foothills." After he had asked the question several times, he fell completely silent; and he refused point blank to come with us up the steep path to the waterfall. I thought he was tired. But next morning he came to me with a radiant face and said: "Last night I dreamed we were at the Simony Hütte." I understood him then. When I had spoken about the Dachstein, he had expected to climb the mountain in the course of our excursion to Hallstatt and to find himself at close quarters with the hut which there had been so much talk about in connection with the telescope. But when he found that he was being fobbed off with foothills and a waterfall, he felt disappointed and out of spirits. The dream was a compensation. I tried to discover its details, but they were scanty: "You have to climb up steps for six hours"—which was what he had been told.

The same excursion stirred up wishes in the eight-and-a-half-year-old girl as well—wishes which had to be satisfied in a dream. We had taken our neighbor's twelve-year-old son with us to Hallstatt. He was already a full-blown gallant, and there were signs that he had engaged the young lady's affections. Next morning she told me the following dream: "Just fancy! I had a dream that Emil was one of the family and called you 'Father' and 'Mother' and slept with us in the big room like the boys. Then Mother came in and threw a handful of big bars of chocolate, wrapped up in blue and green paper, under our beds." Her brothers, who have evidently not inherited a faculty for understanding dreams, followed the lead of the authorities and declared that the dream was nonsense. The girl herself defended one part of the dream at least; and it throws light on the theory of neuroses to learn which part. "Of course it's nonsense Emil being one of the family; but the part about the bars of chocolate isn't." It had been precisely on that point that I had been in the dark, but the girl's mother now gave me the explanation. On their way home from the station the children had stopped in front of a slot machine from which they were accustomed to obtain bars of chocolate of that very kind, wrapped in shiny metallic paper. They had wanted to get some; but their mother rightly decided that the day had already fulfilled enough wishes and left this one over to be fulfilled by the dream. I myself had not observed the incident. But the part of the dream which had been proscribed by my daughter was immediately clear to me. I myself had heard our well-behaved guest telling the children on the walk to wait till Father and Mother caught up with them. The little girl's dream turned this temporary kinship into permanent adoption. Her affection was not yet able to picture any other forms of companionship than those which were represented in the dream and which were based on her relation to her brothers. It was of course impossible to discover without questioning her why the bars of chocolate were thrown under the beds.

A friend of mine has reported a dream to me which was very much like my son's. The dreamer was an eight-year-old girl. Her father had started off with several children on a walk to Dornbach, with the idea of visiting the Rohrer Hütte. As it was getting late, however, he had turned back, promising the children to make up for the disappointment another time. On their way home they had passed the sign post that marks the path up to the Hameau. The children had then asked to be taken up to the Hameau; but once again for the same reason they had to be consoled with the promise of another day. Next morning the eight-year-old girl came to her father and said in satisfied tones: "Daddy, I dreamed last night that you went with us to the Rohrer Hütte and the Hameau." In her impatience she had anticipated the fulfillment of her father's promises.

Here is an equally straightforward dream, provoked by the beauty of the scenery at Aussee in another of my daughters, who was at that time three and a quarter. She had crossed the lake for the first time, and the crossing had been too short for her: When we reached the landing-stage she had not wanted to leave the boat and had wept bitterly. Next morning she said: "Last night I went on the lake." Let us hope that her dream-crossing had been of a more satisfying length.

My eldest boy, then eight years old, already had dreams of his fantasies coming true: He dreamed that he was driving in a chariot with Achilles and that Diomede was the charioteer. As may be guessed, he had been excited the day before by a book on the legends of Greece which had been given to his elder sister.

If I may include words spoken by children in their sleep under the heading of dreams, I can at this point quote one of the most youthful dreams in my whole collection. My youngest daughter, then nineteen months old, had had an attack of vomiting one morning and had consequently been kept without food all day. During the night after this day of starvation she was heard calling out excitedly in her sleep: "Anna Fweud, stwawbewwies, wild stwawbewwies, omblet, pudden!" At that time she was in the habit of using her own name to express the idea of taking possession of something. The menu included pretty well everything that must have seemed to her to make up a desirable meal. The fact that strawberries appeared in it two varieties was a demonstration against the domestic health regulations. It was based upon the circumstance, which she had no doubt observed, that her nurse had attributed her indisposition to a surfeit of strawberries. She was thus retaliating in her dream against this unwelcome verdict.

Though we think highly of the happiness of childhood because it is still innocent of sexual desires, we should not forget what a fruitful source of disappointment and renunciation, and consequently what a stimulus to dreaming, may be provided by the other of the two great vital instincts. Here is another instance of this. My nephew, aged 22 months, had been entrusted with the duty of congratulating me on my birthday and of presenting me with a basket of cherries, which are still scarcely in season at that time of year. He seems to have found the task a hard one, for he kept on repeating "Chewwies in it" but could not be induced to hand the present over. However, he found a means of compensation. He had been in the habit every morning of telling his mother that he had a dream of the "white soldier"—a Guards officer in his white cloak whom he had once gazed at admiringly in the street. On the day after his birthday sacrifice he awoke with a cheerful piece of news, which could only have originated from a dream: "Hermann eaten all the chewwies!"

I do not myself know what animals dream of. But a proverb, to which my attention was drawn by one of my students, does claim to know. "What," asks the proverb, "do geese dream of?" And it replies: "Of maize." The whole theory that dreams are wish-fulfillments is contained in these two phrases.

It will be seen that we might have arrived at our theory of the hidden meaning of dreams most rapidly merely by following linguistic usage. It is true that common language sometimes speaks of dreams with contempt. (The phrase "*Träume sind Schäume* [Dreams are froth]" seems intended to support the scientific estimate of dreams.) But, on the whole, ordinary usage treats dreams above all as the blessed fulfillers of wishes. If ever we find our expectation surpassed by the event, we exclaim in our delight: "I should never have imagined such a thing even in my wildest dreams."

POSSIBILITIES FOR WRITING

1. Part of Freud's purpose here is to convince readers to take more sophisticated dream analysis seriously. How does he go about doing so? Do his persuasive strategies work for you? Why or why not?
2. Freud refers to "dreams of convenience." What does he mean? Offer examples of your own to supplement those Freud suggests.
3. What is your attitude toward dreams? Do you think dreams can be related to "internal psychical processes"? Why do you think some dreams can have so potent an effect?

Henry Louis Gates, Jr. (b. 1950) grew up in the small West Virginia town of Keyser and received degrees from Yale and Cambridge universities. Currently chair of the Department of Afro-American Studies at Harvard, Gates has written and edited a number of scholarly works, such as Loose Canons: Notes on the Culture Wars *(1992). In addition, he has published many books and magazine articles aimed at a popular audience, including* Colored People *(1994), a memoir; and* Thirteen Ways of Looking at a Black Man *(1997).* Wonders of the African World *(1999) was the basis for a PBS documentary series he hosted about life in Africa. He is also general editor of the* Norton Anthology of African American Literature *(1997) and co-editor of* Africana: The Encyclopedia of the African and African-American Experience *(1999).*

HENRY LOUIS GATES, JR.

In the Kitchen

In his autobiographical essay, "In the Kitchen," Henry Louis Gates, Jr. memorializes his mother by writing about hair—his own hair, his mother's hair, and the hair of the women his mother straightens in her kitchen. It was in the kitchen that Gates's mother made her friends' kinky hair wavy with her "hot comb." Gates captures the joy of the experience for his mother and for her friends. In this nostalgic backward look, Gates celebrates the memory of his mother with zest and humor.

Through his discussion of hair, however, Gates also suggests something about standards of beauty. According to the way beauty is evaluated, hair can be either "good" or "bad." Wavy hair is "good" and kinky hair "bad". This standard is cultural as well as aesthetic. It suggests that the standard of beauty of one group—white people with wavy hair—is the ideal to which others aspire (black women with kinky hair, for example). Gates describes the effort, energy, time, and money that African Americans once invested to get the kink out of their hair.

We always had a gas stove in the kitchen, in our house in Piedmont, West Virginia, where I grew up. Never electric, though using electric became fashionable in Piedmont in the sixties, like using Crest toothpaste rather than Colgate, or watching Huntley and Brinkley rather than Walter Cronkite. But not us: gas, Colgate, and good ole Walter Cronkite, come what may. We used gas partly out of loyalty to Big Mom, Mama's Mama, because she was mostly blind and still loved to cook, and could feel her way more easily with gas than with electric. But the most important thing about our gas-equipped kitchen was that Mama used to do hair there. The "hot comb" was a fine-toothed iron instrument with a long wooden handle and a pair of iron curlers that opened and closed like scissors. Mama would put it in the gas fire until it glowed. You could smell those prongs heating up.

I liked that smell. Not the smell so much, I guess, as what the smell meant for the shape of my day. There was an intimate warmth in the women's tones as they talked with my Mama, doing their hair. I knew what the women had been through to get their hair ready to be "done," because I would watch Mama do it to herself. How that kink could be transformed through grease and fire into that magnificent head of wavy hair was a miracle to me, and still is.

Mama would wash her hair over the sink, a towel wrapped around her shoulders, wearing just her slip and her white bra. (We had no shower—just a galvanized tub that we stored in the kitchen—until we moved down Rat Toil Road into Doc Wolverton's house, in 1954). After she dried it, she would grease her scalp thoroughly with blue Bergamot hair grease, which came in a short, fat jar with a picture of a beautiful colored lady on it. It's important to grease your scalp real good, my Mama would explain, to keep from burning yourself. Of course, her hair would return to its natural kink almost as soon as the hot water and shampoo hit it. To me, it was another miracle how hair so "straight" would so quickly become kinky again the second it even approached some water.

My Mama had only a few "clients" whose heads she "did"—did, I think, because she enjoyed it, rather than for the few pennies it brought in. They would sit on one of our red plastic kitchen chairs, the kind with the shiny metal legs, and brace themselves for the process. Mama would stroke that red-hot iron—which by this time had been in the gas fire for half an hour or more—slowly but firmly through their hair, from scalp to strand's end. It made a scorching, crinkly sound, the hot iron did, as it burned its way through kink, leaving in its wake straight strands of hair, standing long and tall but drooping over at the ends, their shape like the top of a heavy willow tree. Slowly, steadily, Mama's hands would transform a round mound of Odetta kink into a darkened swamp of everglades. The Bergamot made the hair shiny; the heat of the hot iron gave it a brownish-red cast. Once all the hair was as straight as God allows kink to get, Mama would take the well-heated curling iron and twirl the straightened strands into more or less loosely wrapped curls. She claimed that she owed her skill as a hair-dresser to the strength in her wrists, and as she worked her little finger would poke out, the way it did when she sipped tea. Mama was a south-paw, and wrote upside down and backward to produce the cleanest, roundest letters you've ever seen.

The "kitchen" she would all but remove from sight with a handheld pair of shears, bought just for this purpose. Now, the kitchen was the room in which we were sitting—the room where Mama did hair and washed clothes, and where we all took a bath in that galvanized tub. But the word has another meaning, and the kitchen that I'm speaking of is the very kinky bit of hair at the back of your head, where your neck meets your shirt collar. If there was ever a part of our African past that resisted assimilation, it was the kitchen. No matter how hot the iron, no matter how powerful the chemical, no matter how stringent the mashed-potatoes-and-lye formula of a man's "process," neither God nor woman nor Sammy Davis, Jr., could straighten the kitchen. The kitchen was permanent, irredeemable, irresistible kink. Unassimilably African. No matter what you did, no matter how hard you tried, you couldn't de-kink a person's kitchen. So you trimmed it off as best you could.

When hair had begun to "turn," as they'd say—to return to its natural kinky glory—it was the kitchen that turned first (the kitchen around the back, and nappy edges at the temples). When the kitchen started creeping up the back of the neck, it was time to get your hair done again.

Sometimes, after dark, a man would come to have his hair done. It was Mr. Charlie Carroll. He was very light-completed and had a ruddy nose—it made me think of Edmund Gwenn, who played Kris Kringle in "Miracle on 34th Street." At first, Mama did him after my brother, Rocky, and I had gone to sleep. It was only later that we found out that he had come to our house so Mama could iron his hair—not with a hot comb or a curling iron but with our very own Proctor-Silex steam iron. For some reason I never understood, Mr. Charlie would conceal . . . is Frederick Douglass-like mane under a big white Stetson hat. I never saw him take it off except when he came to our house, at night, to have his hair pressed. (Later, Daddy would tell us about Mr. Charlie's most prized piece of knowledge, something that the man would only confide after his hair had been pressed, as a token of intimacy. "Not many people know this," he'd say, in a tone of circumspection, "but George Washington was Abraham Lincoln's daddy." Nodding solemnly, he'd add the clincher: "A white man told me." Though he was in dead earnest, this became a humorous refrain around our house—"a white man told me"—which we used to punctuate especially preposterous assertions.)

My mother examined my daughters' kitchens whenever we went home to visit, in the early eighties. It became a game between us. I had told her not to do it, because I didn't like the politics it suggested—the notion of "good" and "bad" hair. "Good" hair was "straight," "bad" hair kinky. Even in the late sixties, at the height of Black Power, almost nobody could bring themselves to say "bad" for good and "good" for bad. People still said that hair like white people's hair was "good," even if they encapsulated it in a disclaimer, like "what we used to call 'good.'"

Maggie would be seated in her high chair, throwing food this way and that, and Mama would be cooing about how cute it all was, how I used to do just like Maggie was doing, and wondering whether her flinging her food with her left hand meant thàt she was going to be left-handed like Mama. When my daughter was just about covered with Chef Boyardee Spaghetti-O's, Mama would seize the opportunity: wiping her clean, she would tilt Maggie's head to one side and reach down the back of her neck. Sometimes Mama would even rub a curl between her fingers, just to make sure that her bifocals had not deceived her. Then she'd sigh with satisfaction and relief: No Kink . . . yet. Mama! I'd shout, pretending to be angry. Every once in a while, if no one was looking. I'd peek, too.

I say "yet" because most black babies are born with soft, silken hair. But after a few months it begins to turn, as inevitably as do the seasons or the leaves on a tree. People once thought baby oil would stop it. They were wrong.

Everybody I knew as a child wanted to have good hair. You could be as ugly as homemade sin dipped in misery and still be thought attractive if you had good hair. "Jesus moss," the girls at Camp Lee, Virginia, had called Daddy's naturally "good" hair during the war. I know that he played that thick head of hair for all it was worth, too.

My own hair was "not a bad grade," as barbers would tell me when they cut it for the first time. It was like a doctor reporting the results of the first full physical he has given you. Like "You're in good shape" or "Blood pressure's kind of high—better eat down on salt."

I spent most of my childhood and adolescence messing with my hair. I definitely wanted straight hair. Like Pop's. When I was about three, I tried to stick a wad of Bazooka bubble gum to that straight hair of his. I suppose what fixed that memory for me is the spanking I got for doing so: he turned me upside down, holding me by my feet, the better to paddle my behind. Little *nigger*, he had shouted, walloping away. I started to laugh about it two days later, when my behind stopped hurting.

When black people say "straight," of course, they don't usually mean literally straight—they're not describing hair like, say, Peggy Lipton's (she was the white girl on "The Mod Squad"), or like Mary's of Peter, Paul & Mary fame; black people call that "stringy" hair. No, "straight" just means not kinky, no matter what contours the curl may take. I would have done *anything* to have straight hair—and I used to try everything, short of getting a process.

Of the wide variety of techniques and methods I came to master in the challenging prestidigitation of the follicle, almost all had two things in common: a heavy grease and the application of pressure. It's not an accident that some of the biggest black-owned companies in the fifties and sixties made hair products. And I tried them all, in search of that certain silken touch, the one that would leave neither the hand nor the pillow sallied by grease.

I always wondered what Frederick Douglass put on *his* hair, or what Phillis Wheatley put on hers. Or why Wheatley has that rag on her head in the little engraving in the frontispiece of her book. One thing is for sure: you can bet that when Phillis Wheatley went to England and saw the Countess of Huntingdon she did not stop by the Queen's coiffeur on her way there. So many black people still get their hair straightened that it's a wonder we don't have a national holiday for Madame C.J. Walker, the woman who invented the process of straightening kinky hair. Call it Jheri-Kurled or call it "relaxed," it's still fried hair.

I used all the greases, from sea-blue Bergamot and creamy vanilla Duke (in its clear jar with the orange-white-and-green label) to the godfather of grease, the formidable Murray's. Now, Murray's was some *serious* grease. Whereas Bergamot was like oily jello, and Duke was viscous and sickly sweet, Murray's was light brown and *hard*. Hard as lard and twice as greasy, Daddy used to say. Murray's came in an orange can with a press-on top. It was so hard that some people would put a match to the can, just to soften the stuff and make it more manageable. Then, in the late sixties, when Afros came into style, I used Afro Sheen. From Murray's to Duke to Afro Sheen: that was my progression in black consciousness.

We used to put hot towels or washrags over our Murray-coated heads, in order to melt the wax into the scalp and the follicles.

Unfortunately, the wax also had the habit of running down your neck, ears, and forehead. Not to mention your pillowcase. Another problem was that if you put two palmfuls of Murray's on your head your hair turned white. (Duke did the same thing.) The challenge was to get rid of that white color. Because if you got rid of the white stuff you had a magnificent head of wavy hair. That was the beauty of it: Murray's was so hard that it froze your hair into the wavy style you brushed it into. It looked really good if you wore a part. A lot of guys had parts *cut* into their hair by a barber, either with the clippers or with a straight-edge razor. Especially if you had kinky hair—then you'd generally wear a short razor cut, or what we called a Quo Vadis.

We tried to be as innovative as possible. Everyone knew about using a stocking cap, because your father or your uncle wore one whenever something really big was about to happen, whether sacred or secular: a funeral or a dance, a wedding or a trip in which you confronted official white people. Any time you were trying to look really sharp, you wore a stocking cap in preparation. And if the event was really a big one, you made a new cap. You asked your mother for a pair of her hose, and cut it with scissors about six inches or so from the open end—the end with the elastic that goes up to the top of the thigh. Then you knotted the cut end, and it became a beehive-shaped hat, with an elastic band that you pulled down low on your forehead and down around your neck in the back. To work well, the cap had to fit tightly and snugly, like a press. And it had to fit that tightly because it was a press: it pressed your hair with the force of the hose's elastic. If you greased your hair down real good, and left the stocking cap on long enough, voilà: you got a head of pressed-against-the-scalp waves. (You also got a ring around your forehead when you woke up, but it went away.) And then you could enjoy your concrete do. Swore we were bad, too, with all that grease and those flat heads. My brother and I would brush it out a bit in the mornings, so that it looked—well, "natural." Grown men still wear stocking caps—especially older men, who generally keep their stocking caps in their top drawers, along with their cufflinks and their see-through silk socks, their "Maverick" ties, their silk handkerchiefs, and whatever else they prize the most.

A Murrayed-down stocking cap was the respectable version of the process, which, by contrast, was most definitely not a cool thing to have unless you were an entertainer by trade. Zeke and Keith and Poochie and a few other stars of the high-school basketball team all used to get a process once or twice a year. It was expensive, and you had to go somewhere like Pittsburgh or D.C. or Uniontown—somewhere where there were enough colored people to support a trade. The guys would disappear, then reappear a day or two later, strutting like peacocks, their hair burned slightly red from the lye base. They'd also wear "rags"— cloths or handkerchiefs—around their heads when they slept or played basketball. Do-rags, they were called. But the result was straight hair, with just a hint of wave. No curl. Do-it-yourselfers took their chances at home with a concoction of mashed potatoes and lye.

The most famous process of all, however, outside of the process Malcolm X describes in his "Autobiography," and maybe the process of Sammy Davis. Jr., was Nat King Cole's process. Nat King Cole had patent-leather hair. That man's got the finest process money can buy, or so Daddy said the night we saw Cole's TV show on NBC. It was November 5, 1956. I remember the date because everyone came to our house to watch it and to celebrate one of Daddy's buddies' birthdays. Yeah, Uncle Joe chimed in, they can do shit to his hair that the average Negro can't even *think* about—secret shit.

Nat King Cole was *clean.* I've had an ongoing argument with a Nigerian friend about Nat King Cole for twenty years now. Not about whether he could sing—any fool knows that he could—but about whether or not he was a handkerchief head for wearing that patent-leather process.

Sammy Davis, Jr.'s process was the one I detested. It didn't look good on him. Worse still, he liked to have a fried strand dangling down the middle of his forehead, so he could shake it out from the crown when he sang. But Nat King Cole's hair was a thing unto itself, a beautifully sculpted work of art that he and he alone had the right to wear. The only difference between a process and a stocking cap, really, was taste; but Nat King Cole, unlike, say, Michael Jackson, looked *good* in his. His head looked like Valentino's head in the twenties, and some say it was Valentino the process was imitating. But Nat King Cole wore a process because it suited his face, his demeanor, his name, his style. He was as clean as he wanted to be.

I had forgotten all about that patent-leather look until one day in 1971, when I was sitting in an Arab restaurant on the island of Zanzibar surrounded by men in fezzes and white caftans, trying to learn how to eat curried goat and rice with the fingers of my right hand and feeling two million miles from home. All of a sudden, an old transistor radio sitting on top of a china cupboard stopped blaring out its Swahili music and started playing "Fly Me to the Moon," by Nat King Cole. The restaurant's din was not affected at all, but in my mind's eye I saw it: the King's magnificent sleek black tiara. I managed, barely, to blink back the tears.

POSSIBILITIES FOR WRITING

1. Gates is writing not only personally here, but also as a cultural historian. How does his focus on hair help you to understand African Americans at a particular time and place?
2. Gates's style ranges from fairly formal to highly colloquial. Provide examples of these various levels of diction, and show how they work together to create a particular effect.
3. In what ways is hair style a marker among your peer group, and how does it distinguish people of other peer groups? Why is hair linked so closely to style?

Matthew Goulish, a graduate of Kalamazoo College, is a performer and writer. He has collaborated on the creation of performances with the group Goat Island. A founding member of that group, Goulish also teaches at the School of the Art Institute of Chicago. His book 39 Microlectures: In Proximity of Performance (2000) is a compendium of small stories, parables, essays, musings, and explorations of thinking about reading and writing, performance and collaboration, life and death—and more.

MATTHEW GOULISH

Criticism

In "Criticism," Matthew Goulish reflects on the implications of the critical act through three metaphors: glass, windows, and rain. Goulish explores the ways in which these three metaphors enable us to extend our capacity to feel, see, and hear art works and performances through tactile, visual, and auditory images.

Goulish identifies and explores the purpose of critical thought, which he sees as valuable in so far as it "causes a change" and as it helps us "understand how to understand." He pursues these ideas by asking what kinds of change an act of critical engagement with a work of art or performance might effect—and in whom. Throughout the essay, Goulish pushes his readers to think both critically and creatively along with him.

Criticism

The example of glass
The example of windows
The example of rain

The Example of Glass

Each time we experience a work of performance, we start over almost from nothing. Despite recognizable trends, we face infinite differences— individual or cultural details, opposing traditions, idiosyncratic forms and settings, all kinds of aesthetic extremes.

Where do we begin, how do we begin, to engage a critical mind?

This question does not limit itself to performance. It relates to all art forms. In fact, it applies to all human endeavors and perceptions, from the humanities to the sciences to the practice of everyday life. Irreducible complexity seems to characterize the late twentieth century itself.

As a result, each field structures itself by propagating its own specialized vocabulary so that its practitioners might share some basic concepts. Yet each field necessarily interfaces and intersects any number of other fields, sometimes even spawning hybrid fields. Even the purist, in order to reach any depth of understanding on any given subject, must confront conflicting discourses. A serious student of performance thus might encounter the terminology of theatre, literature, music, psychology, architecture, anthropology, and biology, among other disciplines.

One might say that we face a landscape of vistas opening only onto more vistas. On the threshold of this landscape we might pause to recall the writer Isaac Babel who described his grandmother's sobering admonition when, as a child, he told her he wanted to grow up to be writer, and she replied, "To be a writer, you must know everything."

Faced with the impossibility of the task of knowing everything, we sometimes feel the desire to reject intellectuality altogether in favor of passionate expression. Such expression may take the form of the urgently political, the assertion of a solidified identity, or the following of individual inspiration wherever it may lead. And yet even these roads, if sincerely followed lead back to the discourse of complexity.

We have no choice but to accept this terrain, with the hope of discovering its exhilarating creative possibilities. Such acceptance requires a softening of the dividing lines between traditional differences: artist and critic, passion and intellect, accessible and hermetic, success and failure.

The softening of dividing lines does not however imply the disintegration of difference. Take for example the problem of glass. What is glass? Until recently, glass was considered a mostly transparent solid. It behaved like a solid; if struck, it shattered. But then, in the ancient cathedrals of Europe, it was observed that the tops of windows let in more light than the bottoms. A simple measurement proved that a window of once uniform thickness had grown thicker at the bottom and thinner at the top. Only one explanation exists for this phenomenon. Glass flows in the direction of the pull of gravity, exhibiting the behavior of a liquid. Thus one cannot conclusively define glass without the inclusion of time. At any given moment, glass is a solid, but over a period of one thousand years, it is a liquid. The problem of glass forces us to accept the inaccuracy of the traditional distinctions of solid or liquid. While the qualities of solidity and liquidity retain their difference, glass in fact is both, depending on the duration of observation, thus proving that these two states inextricably coexist.

We must ask not only how to engage the critical mind, but also why. Any act of critical thought finds its value through fulfilling one or both two interrelated purposes:

1. to cause a change;
2. to understand how to understand.

As creative and critical thinkers, we may find it rewarding to attempt works of criticism, which, over time, reveal themselves as works of art, thus following the example of glass.

The Example of Windows

Most critics would not contest the idea that criticism exists to cause a change. But to cause a change in what?

Rarely has a work of critical thought successfully caused a change in the artwork it addresses. If a critic sees a film one day, and writes a review the next excoriating the weakness of the lead actor's performance, that same critic could return to the theater on the third day, and, despite the conviction of his argument, encounter the actor's performance unchanged. The same holds true for countless examples: condemned paintings, ridiculed concertos, buildings of reviled design, all survive, oblivious. Yet critics continue to offer their views. What are they trying to change?

Perhaps they attempt to change the future by effecting audience perceptions. If they can convince enough people, they believe they will achieve critical mass, causing an elimination of the despised, and an encouragement of the admired. But is this an accurate assessment of events? A critique may influence the thoughts of many audience members, but in the end they will make up their own minds. And those few powerful individuals who function in a producing capacity have the option of following the will of the majority, the minority, whatever sells the most tickets, or the advice of the critic. In this equation, the critic's power seems slight. If a critic believes in his or her own power to cause a change in audience thinking, that critic lives in delusion. Any changes of this kind are peripheral effects of a more central event.

Criticism only consistently changes the critic—whether further narrowing the views of the art policeman, or incrementally expanding the horizons of the open-minded thinker. If we accept this severe limitation—that in fact the first function of criticism is to cause a change in the critic—then we may begin to act accordingly.

We may agree on the premise that each work of art is at least in part perfect, while each critic is at least in part imperfect. We may then look to each work of art not for its faults and shortcomings, but for its moments of exhilaration, in an effort to bring our own imperfections into sympathetic vibration with these moments, and thus effect a creative change in ourselves. These moments will of course be somewhat subjective, and if we don't see one immediately, we will out of respect look again, because each work contains at least one, even if it occurs by accident. We may look at the totality of the work in the light of this moment—whether it be a moment of humor or sadness, an overarching structural element, a mood, a personal association, a distraction, an honest error, anything at all that speaks to us. In this way we will treat the work of art, in the words of South African composer Kevin Volans, not as an object in this world but as a window into another world. If we can articulate one window's particular exhilaration, we may open a way to inspire a change in ourselves, so that we may value and work from these recognitions.

What I advocate is not so unusual, because if we have been trained at all, we have probably been trained to spot the negatives, and to try to improve the work by eliminating them. Given, as we have established, that criticism always changes the critic, this approach means trouble. Whatever we fix our attention on seems to multiply before our eyes. If we look for problems, we will find them everywhere. Out of concern for ourselves and our psychic well-being, let us look instead for the aspects of wonder.

If others choose to change their own thinking as an inspired result of our critical articulations, or if they decide to dismiss us as idealists, that is their business, and we will leave it to them.

But can we recognize windows to other worlds without some formal, historical, or theoretical understanding of what we are looking at? If we deepen our understanding, might we increase our chances of locating these moments? How do we deepen our understanding?

We may think of critical thought itself as a process through which we deepen our understanding. This brings us to the second proposed function of criticism, to understand how to understand.

The Example of Rain

How do we understand something? We understand something by approaching it. How do we approach something? We approach it from any direction. We approach it using our eyes, our ears, our noses, our intellects, our imaginations. We approach it with silence. We approach it with childhood. We use pain or embarrassment. We use history. We take a safe route or a dangerous one. We discover our approach and we follow it.

In his 1968 essay "Rain and the Rhinoceros," the American Trappist monk Thomas Merton attempted to understand Eugene Ionesco's play *Rhinoceros* by comparing it to the rain. Trappist monks take vows of silence. They almost never speak. In keeping with their silent life, they live in a silent place. The sound of the rain on the tin roof of his isolated monastic cabin in the Kentucky woods must have given Merton the only inspiration he needed to approach Ionesco's rhinoceros. And when the rain stopped, he heard the sound of the military airplane overhead, leaving the nearby base, on its way to Vietnam. When the airplane passed, he heard the hiss of his lantern burning. The rain provided the window to the rhinoceros, and the rhinoceros the window to the rain. The essay's analysis balances the work of art, with the work of nature, with the work of war. Merton understood critical thought as an act of contemplation, not an act of production. At the same time, he understood it to be, like all human activity, absurd. And thus he liberated his critical mind to follow whatever might cross its path. As the zen saying goes, no matter where we go, we are never far from enlightenment.

How then can we understand the rain? We can understand it as a scientist might, by studying climatic conditions and learning the Latin names for clouds. Or we may understand the rain by looking at it and how it falls—straight down, or at an angle, or lashed by the wind. Is it a light drizzly rain, or is it only a mist and hardly rain at all? Is it the kind that falls when the sun is shining just down the street? We could understand rain by examining its effects—on plants, on people, on cities. Or we may catalogue the sounds it makes on glass, on water, on stone, on metal. We could even study the moods it evokes before it has started and after it has stopped. We could not look at it directly, but rather at what it reminds us of—childhood, violence, love, tears. Who could tell us that any of these approaches to rain is not valid? And yet we would be the first to admit their absurdity.

The modernists believed that each work of art somehow outstretches interpretation, that each criticism reduces the infinite possibilities of the work, that no critique is exhaustive. I agree to the extent that the opposite is also true—each artwork reduces its critique. Only when criticism can step a little away from the artwork that fostered it will it achieve a life of its own as a way of understanding. The way a critique discovers and explores becomes as personal, intellectual, and creative as any artwork; not to offer a comprehensive analysis of the rain, but instead one singular approach to it. Thus it might return us to our first purpose, that of causing a change. If our critique of rain allows us a different rain experience, then it has caused a change, if not in the rain, at least in the critic. And as our approaches to the rain increase, so too increases our understanding of the fleeting and fragile qualities of human life. And as our ways of understanding the rain multiply, so too will we begin to see the presence of rain in even the driest of subjects. We will realize at last that our objective all along was to understand that it is always raining.

POSSIBILITIES FOR WRITING

1. Define the concept of "glass" in your own words and then expand your definition to include Goulish's suggestions about the nature of glass. Do the same for the concept of "window" and of "rain."

2. Goulish's "Criticism" is an exploration of a few ideas, essential ideas, about the process of coming to terms with works of art and performance. It is also a demonstration of a critical mind at work. Describe the nature and the quality of mind and thinking at work and play in Goulish's essay. What kinds of mental acts do you have to perform in order to follow his thinking?

3. Use Goulish's approach to think critically and creatively about a poem, play, story, painting, sculpture, or other work of art or performance you have encountered and experienced. Write an essay applying Goulish's questions and concepts.

Ellen Goodman (b. 1941) is a native of Newton, Massachusetts, and a graduate of Radcliffe College. After working as a reporter for several news organizations, she joined the Boston Globe in 1967 and has been on the staff there ever since. She writes an editorial column titled "At Large" that mixes the personal with the political in a way that has achieved broad appeal among readers; it is currently syndicated in more than 250 newspapers nationwide. These columns have been collected in several volumes, including Paper Trail: Common Sense in Uncommon Times *(2004), Goodman won the Pulitzer Prize for commentary in 1980.*

ELLEN GOODMAN

The Company Man

In "The Company Man," Ellen Goodman presents a sketch of a character who sacrifices everything for his work. He gives up all pretension to a social life and becomes disconnected from his wife and family, while keeping his focus entirely on his job as a corporate vice president.

Goodman tells the story of "Phil," the company man, the phrase itself conveying the extent of his commitment to his career. She keeps her language general, making Phil a symbol of company men (and now women too) everywhere. Describing him as a "type A" workaholic who lives for his work on the job, Goodman simplifies the man and the choices he makes. What she loses in presenting Phil as a complete and complex human being, she gains in making a point about what matters, or should matter, most in our lives.

He worked himself to death, finally and precisely, at 3:00 A.M. Sunday morning.

The obituary didn't say that, of course. It said that he died of a coronary thrombosis—I think that was it—but everyone among his friends and acquaintances knew it instantly. He was a perfect Type A, a workaholic, a classic, they said to each other and shook their heads—and thought for five or ten minutes about the way they lived.

This man who worked himself to death finally and precisely at 3:00 A.M. Sunday morning—on his day off—was fifty-one years old and a vice-president. He was, however, one of six vice-presidents, and one of three who might conceivably—if the president died or retired soon enough—have moved to the top spot. Phil knew that.

He worked six days a week, five of them until eight or nine at night, during a time when his own company had begun the four-day week for everyone but the executives. He worked like the Important People. He had no outside "extracurricular interests," unless, of course, you think about a monthly golf game that way. To Phil, it was work. He always ate egg salad sandwiches at his desk. He was, of course, overweight, by 20 or 25 pounds. He thought it was okay, though, because he didn't smoke.

On Saturdays, Phil wore a sports jacket to the office instead of a suit, because it was the weekend.

He had a lot of people working for him, maybe sixty, and most of them liked him most of the time. Three of them will be seriously considered for his job. The obituary didn't mention that.

But it did list his "survivors" quite accurately. He is survived by his wife, Helen, forty-eight years old, a good woman of no particular marketable skills, who worked in an office before marrying and mothering. She had, according to her daughter, given up trying to compete with his work years ago, when the children were small. A company friend said, "I know how much you will miss him." And she answered, "I already have."

"Missing him all these years," she must have given up part of herself which had cared too much for the man. She would be "well taken care of."

His "dearly beloved" eldest of the "dearly beloved" children is a hardworking executive in a manufacturing firm down South. In the day and a half before the funeral, he went around the neighborhood researching his father, asking the neighbors what he was like. They were embarrassed.

His second child is a girl, who is twenty-four and newly married. She lives near her mother and they are close, but whenever she was alone with her father, in a car driving somewhere, they had nothing to say to each other.

The youngest is twenty, a boy, a high-school graduate who has spent the last couple of years, like a lot of his friends, doing enough odd jobs to stay in grass and food. He was the one who tried to grab at his father, and tried to mean enough to him to keep the man at home. He was his father's favorite. Over the last two years, Phil stayed up nights worrying about the boy.

The boy once said, "My father and I only board here."

At the funeral, the sixty-year-old company president told the forty-eight-year-old widow that the fifty-one-year-old deceased had meant much to the company and would be missed and would be hard to replace. The widow didn't look him in the eye. She was afraid he would read her bitterness and, after all, she would need him to straighten out the finances—the stock options and all that.

Phil was overweight and nervous and worked too hard. If he wasn't at the office, he was worried about it. Phil was a Type A, a heart-attack natural. You could have picked him out in a minute from a lineup.

So when he finally worked himself to death, at precisely 3:00 A.M. Sunday morning, no one was really surprised.

By 5:00 P.M. the afternoon of the funeral, the company president had begun, discreetly of course, with care and taste, to make inquiries about his replacement. One of three men. He asked around: "Who's been working the hardest?"

POSSIBILITIES FOR WRITING

1. Goodman's essay is marked by irony throughout. Analyze the use of irony here—in language, in juxtapositions of images, and within scenes. Do you find the level of irony appropriate, or does it ever strike you as heavy-handed?
2. Goodman wrote this essay in the early 1970s. What values and social constructs does it suggest were common at the time? Using evidence from your own experience, would you say that things today are different or pretty much the same?
3. Using Goodman as a model, write an ironic portrait of a personality type you know well. You may base your portrait on a real person or on a composite of different people. If appropriate to your subject, you may wish to focus more on humorous aspects of this personality type.

Mary Gordon (b. 1949) grew up in a working-class Catholic neighborhood in Far Rockaway, New York. She shocked her family by insisting on attending Barnard College rather than a school closer to home, and she later received a master's degree from Syracuse University. Her first novel, Final Payments (1978), was an immediate critical and popular success, and she followed this with the equally well received The Company of Women *(1981) and* The Other Side *(1989), as well as several collections of short stories. Much of her fiction focuses on tightly knit ethnic families like her own. Gordon has also published several essay collections, including* Good Boys and Dead Girls *(1992) and* Seeing through Places: Reflections on Geography and Identity *(2000), as well as two a memoirs. She currently teaches at Barnard.*

MARY GORDON

More than Just a Shrine— Ellis Island

In "More than Just a Shrine—Ellis Island," Mary Gordon describes a visit she made to Ellis Island, the gateway to America for immigrants throughout the last century. Ellis Island, the place, however, does not interest Gordon as much as the people who passed through it. Gordon imagines their dreams and their hopes as they pursued their destinies in a new and foreign land.

For Gordon, Ellis Island is an emblem, a shrine to the people who arrived in America with little more than their hopes of finding and making better lives than the ones they left behind in their native countries. Gordon does not sentimentalize either the people or the place. Rather, she tries to understand both as she celebrates their courage and their humanity.

I once sat in a hotel in Bloomsbury trying to have breakfast alone. A Russian with a habit of compulsively licking his lips asked if he could join me. I was afraid to say no; I thought it might be bad for détente. He explained to me that he was a linguist and that he always liked to talk to Americans to see if he could make any connection between their speech and their ethnic background. When I told him about my mixed ancestry—my mother is Irish and Italian, my father was a Lithuanian Jew—he began jumping up and down in his seat, rubbing his hands together and licking his lips even more frantically.

"Ah," he said, "so you are really somebody who comes from what is called the boiling pot of America." Yes, I told him; yes, I was; but I quickly rose to leave. I thought it would be too hard to explain to him the relation of the boiling potters to the main course, and I wanted to get to the British Museum. I told him that the only thing I could think of that united people whose backgrounds, histories, and points of view were utterly diverse was that their people had landed at a place called Ellis Island.

I didn't tell him that Ellis Island was the only American landmark I'd ever visited. How could I describe to him the estrangement I'd always felt from the kind of traveler who visits shrines to America's past greatness, those rebuilt forts with muskets behind glass and sabers mounted on the walls and gift shops selling maple sugar candy in the shape of Indian headdresses, those reconstructed villages with tables set for fifty and the Paul Revere silver gleaming? All that Americana— Plymouth Rock, Gettysburg, Mount Vernon, Valley Forge—it all inhabits for me a zone of blurred abstraction with far less hold on my imagination than the Bastille or Hampton Court. I suppose I've always known that my uninterest in it contains a large component of the willed: I am American, and those places purport to be my history. But they are not mine.

Ellis Island is, though; it's the one place I can be sure my people are connected to. And so I made a journey there to find my history, like any Rotarian traveling in his Winnebago to Antietam to find his. I had become part of that humbling democracy of people looking in some site for a past that has grown unreal. The monument I traveled to was not, however, a tribute to some old glory. The minute I set foot upon the island I could feel all that it stood for: insecurity, obedience, anxiety, dehumanization, the terrified and careful deference of the displaced. I hadn't traveled to the Battery and boarded a ferry across from the Statue of Liberty to raise flags or breathe a richer, more triumphant air. I wanted to do homage to the ghosts.

I felt them everywhere, from the moment I disembarked and saw the building with its high-minded brick, its hopeful little lawn, its ornamental cornices. The place was derelict when I arrived; it had not functioned for more than thirty years—almost as long as the time it had operated at full capacity as a major immigration center. I was surprised to learn what a small part of history Ellis Island had occupied. The main building was constructed in 1892, then rebuilt between 1898 and 1900 after a fire. Most of the immigrants who arrived during the latter half of the nineteenth century, mainly northern and western Europeans, landed not at Ellis Island but on the western tip of the Battery, at Castle Garden, which had opened as a receiving center for immigrants in 1855.

By the 1880s, the facilities at Castle Garden had grown scandalously inadequate. Officials looked for an island on which to build a new immigration center, because they thought that on an island immigrants could be more easily protected from swindlers and quickly transported to railroad terminals in New Jersey. Bedloe's Island was considered, but New Yorkers were aghast at the idea of a "Babel" ruining their beautiful new treasure, "Liberty Enlightening the World." The statue's sculptor, Frédéric-Auguste Bartholdi, reacted to the prospect of immigrants landing near his masterpiece in horror; he called it a "monstrous plan." So much for Emma Lazarus.

Ellis Island was finally chosen because the citizens of New Jersey petitioned the federal government to remove from the island an old naval powder magazine that they thought dangerously close to the Jersey shore. The explosives were removed; no one wanted the island for anything. It was the perfect place to build an immigration center.

I thought about the island's history as I walked into the building and made my way to the room that was the center in my imagination of the Ellis Island experience: the Great Hall. It had been made real for me in the stark, accusing photographs of Lewis Hine and others, who took those pictures to make a point. It was in the Great Hall that everyone had waited—waiting, always, the great vocation of the dispossessed. The room was empty, except for me and a handful of other visitors and the park ranger who showed us around. I felt myself grow insignificant in that room, with its huge semicircular windows, its air, even in dereliction, of solid and official probity.

I walked in the deathlike expansiveness of the room's disuse and tried to think of what it might have been like, filled and swarming. More than sixteen million immigrants came through that room; approximately 250,000 were rejected. Not really a large proportion, but the implications for the rejected were dreadful. For some, there was nothing to go back to, or there was certain death; for others, who left as adventurers, to return would be to adopt in local memory the fool's role, and the failure's. No wonder that the island's history includes reports of three thousand suicides.

Sometimes immigrants could pass through Ellis Island in mere hours, though for some the process took days. The particulars of the experience in the Great Hall were often influenced by the political events and attitudes on the mainland. In the 1890s and the first years of the new century, when cheap labor was needed, the newly built receiving center took in its immigrants with comparatively little question. But as the century progressed, the economy worsened, eugenics became both scientifically respectable and popular, and World War I made American xenophobia seem rooted in fact.

Immigration acts were passed; newcomers had to prove, besides moral correctness and financial solvency, their ability to read. Quota laws came into effect, limiting the number of immigrants from southern and eastern Europe to less than 14 percent of the total quota. Intelligence tests were biased against all non-English-speaking persons, and medical examinations became increasingly strict, until the machinery of immigration nearly collapsed under its own weight. The Second Quota Law of 1924 provided that all immigrants be inspected and issued visas at American consular offices in Europe, rendering the center almost obsolete.

On the day of my visit, my mind fastened upon the medical inspections, which had always seemed to me most emblematic of the ignominy and terror the immigrants endured. The medical inspectors, sometimes dressed in uniforms like soldiers, were particularly obsessed with a disease of the eyes called trachoma, which they checked for by flipping back the immigrants' top eyelids with a hook used for buttoning gloves—a method that sometimes resulted in the transmission of the disease to healthy people. Mothers feared that if their children cried too much, their red eyes would be mistaken for a symptom of the disease and the whole family would be sent home. Those immigrants suspected of some physical disability had initials chalked on their coats. I remembered the photographs I'd seen of people standing, dumbstruck and innocent as cattle, with their manifest numbers hung around their necks and initials marked in chalk upon their coats: "E" for eye trouble, "K" for hernia, "L" for lameness, "X" for mental defects, "H" for heart disease.

I thought of my grandparents as I stood in the room: my seventeen-year-old grandmother, coming alone from Ireland in 1896, vouched for by a stranger who had found her a place as a domestic servant to some Irish who had done well. I tried to imagine the assault it all must have been for her; I've been to her hometown, a collection of farms with a main street—smaller than the athletic field of my local public school. She must have watched the New York skyline as the first- and second-class passengers were whisked off the gangplank with the most cursory of inspections while she was made to board a ferry to the new immigration center.

What could she have made of it—this buff-painted wooden structure with its towers and its blue slate roof, a place *Harper's Weekly* described as "a latter-day watering place hotel"? It would have been the first time she had heard people speaking something other than English. She would have mingled with people carrying baskets on their heads and eating foods unlike any she had ever seen—dark-eyed people, like the Sicilian she would marry ten years later, who came over with his family at thirteen, the man of the family, responsible even then for his mother and sister. I don't know what they thought, my grandparents, for they were not expansive people, nor romantic; they didn't like to think of what they called "the hard times," and their trip across the ocean was the single adventurous act of lives devoted after landing to security, respectability, and fitting in.

What is the potency of Ellis Island for someone like me—an American, obviously, but one who has always felt that the country really belonged to the early settlers, that, as J. F. Powers wrote in *Morte D'Urban*, it had been "handed down to them by the Pilgrims, George Washington and others, and that they were taking a risk in letting you live in it." I have never been the victim of overt discrimination; nothing I have wanted has been denied me because of the accidents of blood. But I suppose it is part of being an American to be engaged in a somewhat tiresome but always self-absorbing process of national definition. And in this process, I have found in traveling to Ellis Island an important piece of evidence that could remind me I was right to feel my differentness. Something had happened to my people on that island, a result of the eternal wrongheadedness of American protectionism and the predictabilities of simple greed. I came to the island, too, so I could tell the ghosts that I was one of them, and that I honored them—their stoicism, and their innocence, the fear that turned them inward, and their pride. I wanted to tell them that I liked them better than I did the Americans who made them pass through the Great Hall and stole their names and chalked their weaknesses in public on their clothing. And to tell the ghosts what I have always thought: that American history was a very classy party that was not much fun until they arrived, brought the good food, turned up the music, and taught everyone to dance.

POSSIBILITIES FOR WRITING

1. Gordon's visit to Ellis Island evokes in her a variety of negative impressions, yet the overall experience does not seem to be a negative one for her. Analyze the essay to explore this apparent contradiction. What does she gain from the experience?

2. In this essay Gordon mixes personal narration, description, reporting of historical detail and images from her imagination, along with personal analysis and reflection. Look carefully at how she develops these strands of the essay, provides transitions, and moves from point to point. In an essay analyze and evaluate her technique.

3. Reflect on own sense of your heritage as an American. Are there any "shrines"—whether public or private—that have special meaning to you? Do you feel more an insider or an outsider? (If you are not a citizen, you may wish to reflect on what your experience has led you to believe it means to be an American.)

On the Pleasure of Hating

In "On the Pleasure of Hating," William Hazlitt catalogues the many ways human beings express and act out their anger and antipathy toward other creatures and toward one another. Hazlitt explores the reasons why hatred and its associated feelings fascinate and excite us. In the process Hazlitt shows people to be nasty, mean-spirited, and vengeful, enjoying the suffering of others as idle amusement.

Hazlitt's long paragraphs are replete with instances of humanity's splenetic nature and habits. He piles on example upon example, from our fear of and disgust with insects and spiders to our fascination with disasters such as fires, our cruelty toward those different from ourselves, and our eagerness to maintain old animosities and hostilities whose original causes are long buried in history. According to Hazlitt, we even enjoy hating our old friends, amusing ourselves with their weaknesses and eccentricities. He writes, "We grow tired of every thing but turning others into ridicule, and congratulating ourselves on their defects."

There is a spider crawling along the matted floor of the room where I sit (not the one which has been so well allegorised in the admirable *Lines to a Spider,* but another of the same edifying breed); he runs with heedless, hurried haste, he hobbles awkwardly towards me, he stops— he sees the giant shadow before him, and, at a loss whether to retreat or proceed, meditates his huge foe—but as I do not start up and seize upon the straggling caitiff, as he would upon a hapless fly within his toils, he takes heart, and ventures on with mingled cunning, impudence, and fear. As he passes me, I lift up the matting to assist his escape, am glad to get rid of the unwelcome intruder, and shudder at the recollection after he is gone. A child, a woman, a clown, or a moralist a century ago, would have crushed the little reptile to death—my philosophy has got beyond that—I bear the creature no ill-will, but still I hate the very sight of it. The spirit of malevolence survives the practical exertion of it. We learn to curb our will and keep our overt actions within the bounds of humanity, long before we can subdue our sentiments and imaginations to the same mild tone. We give up the external demonstration, the *brute* violence, but cannot part with the essence or principle of hostility. We do not tread upon the poor little animal in question (that seems barbarous and pitiful!) but we regard it with a sort of mystic horror and superstitious loathing. It will ask another hundred years of fine writing and hard thinking to cure us of the prejudice, and make us feel towards this ill-omened tribe with something of "the milk of human kindness," instead of their own shyness and venom.

Nature seems (the more we look into it) made up of antipathies: without something to hate, we should lose the very spring of thought and action. Life would turn to a stagnant pool, were it not ruffled by the jarring interests, the unruly passions, of men. The white streak in our own fortunes is brightened (or just rendered visible) by making all around it as dark as possible; so the rainbow paints its form upon the cloud. Is it pride? Is it envy? Is it the force of contrast? Is it weakness or malice? But so it is, that there is a secret affinity [with], a *hankering* after, evil in the human mind, and that it takes a perverse, but a fortunate delight in mischief, since it is a never-failing source of satisfaction. Pure good soon grows insipid, wants variety and spirit. Pain is a bittersweet, which never surfeits. Love turns, with a little indulgence, to indifference or disgust: hatred alone is immortal. Do we not see this principle at work everywhere? Animals torment and worry one another without mercy: children kill flies for sport: every one reads the accidents and offences in a newspaper as the cream of the jest: a whole town runs to be present at a fire, and the spectator by no means exults to see it extinguished. It is better to have it so, but it diminishes the interest; and our feelings take part with our passions rather than with our understandings. Men assemble in crowds, with eager enthusiasm, to witness a tragedy: but if there were an execution going forward in the next street, as Mr. Burke observes, the theatre would be left empty. A strange cur in a village, an idiot, a crazy woman, are set upon and baited by the whole community. Public nuisances are in the nature of public benefits. How long did the Pope, the Bourbons, and the Inquisition keep the people of England in breath, and supply them with nicknames to vent their spleen upon! Had they done us any harm of late? No: but we have always a quantity of superfluous bile upon the stomach, and we wanted an object to let it out upon. How loth were we to give up our pious belief in ghosts and witches, because we liked to persecute the one, and frighten ourselves to death with the other! It is not the quality so much as the quantity of excitement that we are anxious about: we cannot bear a state of indifference and *ennui:* the mind seems to abhor a *vacuum* as much as ever nature was supposed to do. Even when the spirit of the age (that is, the progress of intellectual refinement, warring with our natural infirmities) no longer allows us to carry our vindictive and headstrong humours into effect, we try to revive them in description, and keep up the old bugbears, the phantoms of our terror and our hate, in imagination. We burn Guy Fawx in effigy, and the hooting and buffeting and maltreating that poor tattered figure of rags and straw makes a festival in every village in England once a year. Protestants and Papists do not now burn one another at the stake: but we subscribe to new editions of Fox's *Book of Martyrs;* and the secret of the success of the *Scotch Novels* is much the same—they carry us back to the feuds, the heart-burnings, the havoc, the dismay, the wrongs, and the revenge of a barbarous age and people—to the rooted prejudices and deadly animosities of sects and parties in politics and religion, and of contending chiefs and clans in war and intrigue. We feel the full force of the spirit of hatred with all of them in turn. As we read, we throw aside the trammels of civilization, the flimsy veil of humanity. "Off, you lendings!" The wild beast resumes its sway within us, we feel like hunting-animals, and as the hound starts in his sleep and rushes on the chase in fancy, the heart rouses itself in its native lair, and utters a wild cry of joy, at being restored once more to freedom and lawless, unrestrained impulses. Every one has his full swing, or goes to the Devil his own way. Here are no Jeremy Bentham Panopticons, none of Mr. Owen's impassable Parallelograms (Rob Roy would have spurned and poured a thousand curses on them), no long calculations of self-interest—the will takes its instant way to its object, as the mountain-torrent flings itself over the precipice: the greatest possible good of each individual consists in doing all the mischief he can to his neighbour: that is charming, and finds a sure and sympathetic chord in every breast! So Mr. Irving, the celebrated preacher, has rekindled the old, original, almost exploded hell-fire in the aisles of the Caledonian Chapel, as they introduce the real water of the New River at Sadler's Wells, to the delight and astonishment of his fair audience. *'Tis pretty, though a plague,* to sit and peep into the pit of Tophet, to play at *snapdragon* with flames and brimstone (it gives a smart electrical shock, a lively filip to delicate constitutions), and to see Mr. Irving, like a huge Titan, looking as grim and swarthy as if he had to forge tortures for all the damned! What a strange being man is! Not content with doing all he can to vex and hurt his fellows here, "upon this bank and shoal of time," where one would think there were heartaches, pain, disappointment, anguish, tears, sighs, and groans enough, the bigoted maniac takes him to the top of the high peak of school divinity to hurl him down the yawning gulf of penal fire; his speculative malice asks eternity to wreak its infinite spite in, and calls on the Almighty to execute its relentless doom! The cannibals burn their enemies and eat them in good-fellowship with one another: meek Christian divines cast those who differ from them but a hair's-breadth, body and soul into hell-fire for the glory of God and the good of His creatures! It is well that the power of such persons is not co-ordinate with their wills: indeed, it is from the sense of their weakness and inability to control the opinions of others, that they thus "outdo termagant," and endeavour to frighten them into conformity by big words and monstrous denunciations.

The pleasure of hating, like a poisonous mineral, eats into the heart of religion, and turns it to rankling spleen and bigotry; it makes patriotism an excuse for carrying fire, pestilence, and famine into other lands: it leaves to virtue nothing but the spirit of censoriousness, and a narrow, jealous, inquisitorial watchfulness over the actions and motives of others. What have the different sects, creeds, doctrines in religion been but so many pretexts set up for men to wrangle, to quarrel, to tear one another in pieces about, like a target as a mark to shoot at? Does any one suppose that the love of country in an Englishman implies any friendly feeling or disposition to serve another bearing the same name? No, it means only hatred to the French or the inhabitants of any other country that we happen to be at war with for the time. Does the love of virtue denote any wish to discover or amend our own faults? No, but it atones for an obstinate adherence to our own vices by the most virulent intolerance to human frailties. This principle is of a most universal application. It extends to good as well as evil: if it makes us hate folly, it makes us no less dissatisfied with distinguished merit. If it inclines us to resent the wrongs of others, it impels us to be as impatient of their prosperity. We revenge injuries: we repay benefits with ingratitude. Even our strongest partialities and likings soon take this turn. "That which was luscious as locusts, anon becomes bitter as coloquintida;" and love and friendship melt in their own fires. We hate old friends: we hate old books: we hate old opinions; and at last we come to hate ourselves.

I have observed that few of those whom I have formerly known most intimate, continue on the same friendly footing, or combine the steadiness with the warmth of attachment. I have been acquainted with two or three knots of inseparable companions, who saw each other "six days in the week," that have broken up and dispersed. I have quarrelled with almost all my old friends, (they might say this is owing to my bad temper, but) they have also quarrelled with one another. What is become of "that set of whist-players," celebrated by ELIA in his notable *Epistle to Robert Southey, Esq.* (and now I think of it—that I myself have celebrated in this very volume) "that for so many years called Admiral Burney friend? They are scattered, like last year's snow. Some of them are dead, or gone to live at a distance, or pass one another in the street like strangers, or if they stop to speak, do it as coolly and try to *cut* one another as soon as possible." Some of us have grown rich, others poor. Some have got places under Government, others a *niche* in the *Quarterly Review.* Some of us have dearly earned a name in the world; whilst others remain in their original privacy. We despise the one, and envy and are glad to mortify the other. Times are changed; we cannot revive our old feelings; and we avoid the sight, and are uneasy in the presence of, those who remind us of our infirmity, and put us upon an effort at seeming cordiality which embarrasses ourselves, and does not impose upon our *quondam* associates. Old friendships are like meats served up repeatedly, cold, comfortless, and distasteful, the stomach turns against them. Either constant intercourse and familiarity breed weariness and contempt; or, if we meet again after an interval of absence, we appear no longer the same. One is too wise, another too foolish, for us; and we wonder we did not find this out before. We are disconcerted and kept in a state of continual alarm by the wit of one, or tired to death of the dullness of another. The *good things* of the first (besides leaving stings behind them) by repetition grow stale, and lose their startling effect; and the insipidity of the last becomes intolerable. The most amusing or instructive companion is at best like a favourite volume, that we wish after a time to *lay upon the shelf;* but as our friends are not willing to be laid there, this produces a misunderstanding and ill-blood between us. Or if the zeal and integrity of friendship is not abated, [n]or its career interrupted by any obstacle arising out of its own nature, we look out for other subjects of complaint and sources of dissatisfaction. We begin to criticize each other's dress, looks, and general character. "Such a one is a pleasant fellow, but it is a pity he sits so late!" Another fails to keep his appointments, and that is a sore that never heals. We get acquainted with some fashionable young men or with a mistress, and wish to introduce our friend; but he is awkward and a sloven, the interview does not answer, and this throws cold water on our intercourse. Or he makes himself obnoxious to opinion; and we shrink from our own convictions on the subject as an excuse for not defending him. All or any of these causes mount up in time to a ground of coolness or irritation; and at last they break out into open violence as the only amends we can make ourselves for suppressing them so long, or the readiest means of banishing recollections of former kindness so little compatible with our present feelings. We may try to tamper with the wounds or patch up the carcase of departed friendship; but the one will hardly bear the handling, and the other is not worth the trouble of embalming! The only way to be reconciled to old friends is to part with them for good: at a distance we may chance to be thrown back (in a waking dream) upon old times and old feelings: or at any rate we should not think of renewing our intimacy, till we have fairly *spit our spite,* or said, thought, and felt all the ill we can of each other. Or if we can pick a quarrel with some one else, and make him the scape-goat, this is an excellent contrivance to heal a broken bone. I think I must be friends with Lamb again, since he has written that magnanimous Letter to Southey, and told him a piece of his mind! I don't know what it is that attaches me to H——— so much, except that he and I, whenever we meet, sit in judgment on another set of old friends, and "carve them as a dish fit for the Gods." There was L[eigh] [Hunt], John Scott, Mrs. [Montagu], whose dark raven locks make a picturesque background to our discourse, B———, who is grown fat, and is, they say, married, R[ickman]; these had all separated long ago, and their foibles are the common link that holds us together. We do not affect to condole or whine over their follies; we enjoy, we laugh at them, till we are ready to burst our sides, "*sans* intermission, for hours by the dial." We serve up a course of anecdotes, *traits,* masterstrokes of character, and cut and hack at them till we are weary. Perhaps some of them are even with us. For my own part, as I once said, I like a friend the better for having faults that one can talk about. "Then," said Mrs. [Montagu], "you will never cease to be a philanthropist!" Those in question were some of the choice-spirits of the age, not "fellows of no mark or likelihood"; and we so far did them justice: but it is well they did not hear what we sometimes said of them. I care little what any one says of me, particularly behind my back, and in the way of critical and analytical discussion: it is looks of dislike and scorn that I answer with the worst venom of my pen. The expression of the face wounds me more than the expressions of the tongue. If I have in one instance mistaken this expression, or resorted to this remedy where I ought not, I am sorry for it. But the face was too fine over which it mantled, and I am too old to have misunderstood it! . . . I sometimes go up to ———'s; and as often as I do, resolve never to go again. I do not find the old homely welcome. The ghost of friendship meets me at the door, and sits with me all dinner-time. They have got a set of fine notions and new acquaintance. Allusions to past occurrences are thought trivial, nor is it always safe to touch upon more general subjects. M. does not begin as he formerly did every five minutes, "Fawcett used to say." That topic is something worn. The girls are grown up, and have a thousand accomplishments. I perceive there is a jealousy on both sides. They think I give myself airs, and I fancy the same of them. Every time I am asked, "If I do not think Mr. Washington Irving a very fine writer?" I shall not go again till I receive an invitation for Christmas Day in company with Mr. Liston. The only intimacy I never found to flinch or fade was a purely intellectual one. There was none of the cant of candour in it, none of the whine of mawkish sensibility. Our mutual acquaintance were considered merely as subjects of conversation and knowledge, not at all of affection. We regarded them no more in our experiments than "mice in an air-pump:" or like malefactors, they were regularly cut down and given over to the dissecting-knife. We spared neither friend nor foe. We sacrificed human infirmities at the shrine of truth. The skeletons of character might be seen, after the juice was extracted, dangling in the air like flies in cobwebs: or they were kept for future inspection in some refined acid. The demonstration was as beautiful as it was new. There is no surfeiting on gall: nothing keeps so well as a decoction of spleen. We grow tired of every thing but turning others into ridicule, and congratulating ourselves on their defects.

We take a dislike to our favourite books, after a time, for the same reason. We cannot read the same works for ever. Our honey-moon, even though we wed the Muse, must come to an end; and is followed by indifference, if not by disgust. There are some works, those indeed that produce the most striking effect at first by novelty and boldness of outline, that will not bear reading twice: others of a less extravagant character, and that excite and repay attention by a greater nicety of details, have hardly interest enough to keep alive our continued enthusiasm. The popularity of the most successful writers operates to wean us from them, by the cant and fuss that is made about them, by hearing their names everlastingly repeated, and by the number of ignorant and indiscriminate admirers they draw after them:—we as little like to have to drag others from their unmerited obscurity, lest we should be exposed to the charge of affectation and singularity of taste. There is nothing to be said respecting an author that all the world have made up their minds about: it is a thankless as well as hopeless task to recommend one that nobody has ever heard of. To cry up Shakespeare as the god of our idolatry, seems like a vulgar national prejudice: to take down a volume of Chaucer, or Spenser, or Beaumont and Fletcher, or Ford, or Marlowe, has very much the look of pedantry and egotism. I confess it makes me hate the very name of Fame and Genius, when works like these are "gone into the wastes of time," while each successive generation of fools is busily employed in reading the trash of the day, and women of fashion gravely join with their waiting-maids in discussing the preference between the *Paradise Lost* and Mr. Moore's *Loves of the Angels*. I was pleased the other day on going into a shop to ask, "If they had any of the *Scotch Novels?*" to be told—"That they had just sent out the last, *Sir Andrew Wylie!*"—Mr. Galt will also be pleased with this answer! The reputation of some books is raw and *unaired:* that of others is worm-eaten and mouldy. Why fix our affections on that which we cannot bring ourselves to have faith in, or which others have long ceased to trouble themselves about? I am half afraid to look into *Tom Jones,* lest it should not answer my expectations at this time of day; and if it did not, I should certainly be disposed to fling it into the fire, and never look into another novel while I lived. But surely, it may be said, there are some works that, like nature, can never grow old; and that must always touch the imagination and passions alike! Or there are passages that seem as if we might brood over them all our lives, and not exhaust the sentiments of love and admiration they excite: they become favourites, and we are fond of them to a sort of dotage. Here is one:

—"Sitting in my window

> Printing my thoughts in lawn, I saw a god,
> I thought (but it was you), enter our gates;
> My blood flew out and back again, as fast
> As I had puffed it forth and sucked it in
> Like breath; then was I called away in haste
> To entertain you: never was a man
> Thrust from a sheepcote to a sceptre, raised
> So high in thoughts as I; you left a kiss
> Upon these lips then, which I mean to keep
> From you for ever. I did hear you talk
> Far above singing!"

A passage like this, indeed, leaves a taste on the palate like nectar, and we seem in reading it to sit with the Gods at their golden tables: but if we repeat it often in ordinary moods, it loses its flavour, becomes vapid, "the wine of *poetry* is drank, and but the lees remain." Or, on the other hand, if we call in the aid of extraordinary circumstances to set it off to advantage, as the reciting it to a friend, or after having our feelings excited by a long walk in some romantic situation, or while we

> —"play with Amaryllis in the shade,
> Or with the tangles of Neaera's hair"—

we afterwards miss the accompanying circumstances, and instead of transferring the recollection of them to the favourable side, regret what we have lost, and strive in vain to bring back "the irrevocable hour"—wondering in some instances how we survive it, and at the melancholy blank that is left behind! The pleasure rises to its height in some moment of calm solitude or intoxicating sympathy, declines ever after, and from the comparison and a conscious falling-off, leaves rather a sense of satiety and irksomeness behind it. . . . "Is it the same in pictures?" I confess it is, with all but those from Titian's hand. I don't know why, but an air breathes from his landscapes, pure, refreshing, as if it came from other years; there is a look in his faces that never passes away. I saw one the other day. Amidst the heartless desolation and glittering finery of Fonthill, there is a portfolio of the Dresden Gallery. It opens, and a young female head looks from it; a child, yet woman grown; with an air of rustic innocence and the graces of a princess, her eyes like those of doves, the lips about to open, a smile of pleasure dimpling the whole face, the jewels sparkling in her crisped hair, her youthful shape compressed in a rich antique dress, as the bursting leaves contain the April buds! Why do I not call up this image of gentle sweetness, and place it as a perpetual barrier between mischance and me?—It is because pleasure asks a greater effort of the mind to support it than pain; and we turn after a little idle dalliance from what we love to what we hate!

As to my old opinions, I am heartily sick of them. I have reason, for they have deceived me sadly. I was taught to think, and I was willing to believe, that genius was not a bawd, that virtue was not a mask, that liberty was not a name, that love had its seat in the human heart. Now I would care little if these words were struck out of the dictionary, or if I had never heard them. They are become to my ears a mockery and a dream. Instead of patriots and friends of freedom, I see nothing but the tyrant and the slave, the people linked with kings to rivet on the chains of despotism and superstition. I see folly join with knavery, and together make up public spirit and public opinions. I see the insolent Tory, the blind Reformer, the coward Whig! If mankind had wished for what is right, they might have had it long ago. The theory is plain enough; but they are prone to mischief, "to every good work reprobate." I have seen all that had been done by the mighty yearnings of the spirit and intellect of men, "of whom the world was not worthy," and that promised a proud opening to truth and good through the vista of future years, undone by one man, with just glimmering of understanding enough to feel that he was a king, but not to comprehend how he could be king of a free people! I have seen this triumph celebrated by poets, the friends of my youth and the friends of man, but who were carried away by the infuriate tide that, setting in from a throne, bore down every distinction of right reason before it; and I have seen all those who did not join in applauding this insult and outrage on humanity proscribed, hunted down (they and their friends made a byword of), so that it has become an understood thing that no one can live by his talents or knowledge who is not ready to prostitute those talents and that knowledge to betray his species, and prey upon his fellowman. "This was some time a mystery: but the time gives evidence of it." The echoes of liberty had awakened once more in Spain, and the morning of human hope dawned again: but that dawn has been overcast by the foul breath of bigotry, and those reviving sounds stifled by fresh cries from the time-rent towers of the Inquisition— man yielding (as it is fit he should) first to brute force, but more to the innate perversity and dastard spirit of his own nature which leaves no room for farther hope or disappointment. And England, that arch-reformer, that heroic deliverer, that mouther about liberty, and tool of power, stands gaping by, not feeling the blight and mildew coming over it, nor its very bones crack and turn to a paste under the grasp and circling folds of this new monster, Legitimacy! In private life do we not see hypocrisy, servility, selfishness, folly, and impudence succeed, while modesty shrinks from the encounter, and merit is trodden under foot? How often is "the rose plucked from the forehead of a virtuous love to plant a blister there!" What chance is there of the success of real passion? What certainty of its continuance? Seeing all this as I do, and unravelling the web of human life into its various threads of meanness, spite, cowardice, want of feeling, and want of understanding, of indifference towards others, and ignorance of ourselves—seeing custom prevail over all excellence, itself giving way to infamy—mistaken as I have been in my public and private hopes, calculating others from myself, and calculating wrong; always disappointed where I placed most reliance; the dupe of friendship, and the fool of love;—have I not reason to hate and to despise myself? Indeed I do; and chiefly for not having hated and despised the world enough.

POSSIBILITIES FOR WRITING

1. As expressed here, are Hazlitt's views those of a pessimist, a realist, or something in between? How do you respond to the writer's views of hating?
2. "Hating" takes on a variety of meanings here, some more intense than others. Explore these various meanings, using examples from the text to explain your reasoning.
3. Pick a passage or two from Hazlitt's essay that you find relevant to contemporary life and write an essay exploring its implications for the world today.

Linda Hogan (b. 1947) was born in Colorado of Native American lineage, as her father was a member of the Chickasaw nation. While working with children as a young adult, Hogan discovered the expressive power of language, both reading and writing. She became a teacher and writer, as a result. Her novels, plays, poems, and essays display a holistic view of the environment grounded in the belief that all of life is connected. The following essay is taken from her book Dwellings: A Spiritual History of the Living World (1995).

LINDA HOGAN

Dwellings

In "Dwellings," Linda Hogan describes a variety of residences of different creatures, mostly small ones, such as bees, spiders, and mice, but also including her own human domiciles. Mostly, she tells stories of how she found the various dwellings she describes, and she lets her mind wander from the description of the insect and other animal dwellings to larger questions about her and our human relationship with these creatures. She invites us to go along with her on her ruminative excursion of thought about the kinds of shelter we and they inhabit.

Hogan writes with poetic flair, and with an easy grace. Her essay is more exploration than argument, more an invitation to think about what matters to her than an attempt at persuasion. She engages us with some surprising stories and some riveting details, but she leaves to us what to make of these astonishments.

Not far from where I live is a hill that was cut into by the moving water of a creek. Eroded this way, all that's left of it is a broken wall of earth that contains old roots and pebbles woven together and exposed. Seen from a distance, it is only a rise of raw earth. But up close it is something wonderful, a small cliff dwelling that looks almost as intricate and well made as those the Anasazi left behind when they vanished mysteriously centuries ago. This hill is a place that could be the starry skies at night turned inward into the thousand round holes where solitary bees have lived and died. It is a hill of tunneling rooms. At the mouths of some of the excavations, half-circles of clay beetle out like awnings shading a doorway. It is earth that was turned to clay in the mouths of the bees and spit out as they mined deeper into their dwelling places.

This place is where the bees reside at an angle safe from rain. It faces the southern sun. It is a warm and intelligent architecture of memory, learned by whatever memory lives in the blood. Many of the holes still contain gold husks of dead bees, their faces dry and gone, their flat eyes gazing out from death's land toward the other uninhabited half of the hill that is across the creek from the catacombs.

The first time I found the residence of the bees, it was dusty summer. The sun was hot, and land was the dry color of rust. Now and then a car tumbled along; the dirt road and dust rose up behind it before settling back down on older dust. In the silence, the bees made a soft droning hum. They were alive then, and working the hill, going out and returning with pollen, in and out through the holes, back and forth between daylight and the cooler, darker regions of the inner earth. They were flying an invisible map through air, a map charted by landmarks, the slant of light, and a circling story they told one another about the direction of food held inside the center of yellow flowers.

Sitting in the hot sun, watching the small bees fly in and out around the hill, hearing the summer birds, the light breeze. I felt right in the world. I belonged there. I thought of my own dwelling places, those real and those imagined. Once I lived in a town called Manitou, which means "Great Spirit," and where hot mineral springwater gurgled beneath the streets and rose into open wells. I felt safe there. With the underground movement of water and heat a constant reminder of other life, of what lives beneath us, it seemed to be the center of the world.

A few years after that, I wanted silence. My daydreams were full of places I longed to be, shelters and solitudes. I wanted a room apart from others, a hidden cabin to rest in. I wanted to be in a redwood forest with trees so tall the owls called out in the daytime. I daydreamed of living in a vapor cave a few hours away from here. Underground, warm, and moist, I thought it would be the perfect world for staying out of cold winter, for escaping the noise of living.

And how often I've wanted to escape to a wilderness where a human hand has not been in everything. But those were only dreams of peace, of comfort, of a nest inside stone or woods, a sanctuary where a dream or life wouldn't be invaded.

Years ago, in the next canyon west of here, there was a man who followed one of those dreams and moved into a cave that could only be reached by climbing down a rope. For years he lived there in comfort, like a troglodite. The inner weather was stable, never too hot, too cold, too wet, or too dry. But then he felt lonely. His utopia needed a woman. He went to town until he found a wife. For a while after the marriage, his wife climbed down the rope along with him, but before long she didn't want the mice scurrying about in the cave, or the untidy bats that wanted to hang from the stones of the ceiling. So they built a door. Because of the closed entryway, the temperature changed. They had to put in heat. Then the inner moisture of earth warped the door, so they had to have air conditioning, and after that the earth wanted to go about life in its own way and it didn't give in to the people.

In other days and places, people paid more attention to the strong-headed will of earth. Once homes were built of wood that had been felled from a single region in a forest. That way, it was thought, the house would hold together more harmoniously, and the family of walls would not fall or lend themselves to the unhappiness or arguments of the inhabitants.

An Italian immigrant to Chicago, Aldo Piacenzi, built birdhouses that were dwellings of harmony and peace. They were the incredible spired shapes of cathedrals in Italy. They housed not only the birds, but also his memories, his own past. He painted them the watery blue of his Mediterranean, the wild rose of flowers in a summer field. Inside them was straw and the droppings of lives that layed eggs, fledglings who grew there. What places to inhabit, the bright and sunny bird-houses in dreary alleyways of the city.

One beautiful afternoon, cool and moist, with the kind of yellow light that falls on earth in these arid regions, I waited for barn swallows to return from their daily work of food gathering. Inside the tunnel where they live, hundreds of swallows had mixed their saliva with mud and clay, much like the solitary bees, and formed nests that were perfect as a potter's bowl. At five in the evening, they returned all at once, a dark, flying shadow. Despite their enormous numbers and the crowding together of nests, they didn't pause for even a moment before entering the nests, nor did they crowd one another. Instantly they vanished into the nests. The tunnel went silent. It held no outward signs of life.

But I knew they were there, filled with the fire of living. And what a marriage of elements was in those nests. Not only mud's earth and water, the fire of sun and dry air, but even the elements contained one another. The bodies of prophets and crazy men were broken down in that soil.

I've noticed often how when a house is abandoned, it begins to sag. Without a tenant, it has no need to go on. If it were a person, we'd say it is depressed or lonely. The roof settles in, the paint cracks, the walls and floorboards warp and slope downward in their own natural ways, telling us that life must stay in everything as the world whirls and tilts and moves through boundless space.

One summer day, cleaning up after long-eared owls where I work at a rehabilitation facility for birds of prey, I was raking the gravel floor of a flight cage. Down on the ground, something looked like it was moving. I bent over to look into the pile of bones and pellets I'd just raked together. There, close to the ground, were two fetal mice. They were new to the planet, pink and hairless. They were so tenderly young. Their faces had swollen blue-veined eyes. They were nestled in a mound of feathers, soft as velvet, each one curled up smaller than an infant's ear, listening to the first sounds of earth. But the ants were biting them. They turned in agony, unable to pull away, not yet having the arms or legs to move, but feeling, twisting away from, the pain of the bites. I was horrified to see them bitten out of life that way. I dipped them in water, as if to take away the sting, and let the ants fall in the bucket. Then I held the tiny mice in the palm of my hand. Some of the ants were drowning in the water. I was trading one life for another, exchanging the lives of the ants for those of mice, but I hated their suffering, and hated even more that they had not yet grown to a life, and already they inhabited the miserable world of pain. Death and life feed each other. I know that.

Inside these rooms where birds are healed, there are other lives besides those of mice. There are fine gray globes the wasps have woven together, the white cocoons of spiders in a corner, the downward tunneling anthills. All these dwellings are inside one small walled space, but I think most about the mice. Sometimes the downy nests fall out of the walls where their mothers have placed them out of the way of their enemies. When one of the nests falls, they are so well made and soft, woven mostly from the chest feathers of birds. Sometimes the leg of a small quail holds the nest together like a slender cornerstone with dry, bent claws. The mice have adapted to life in the presence of their enemies, adapted to living in the thin wall between beak and beak, claw and claw. They move their nests often, as if a new rafter or wall will protect them from the inevitable fate of all our returns home to the deeper, wider nests of earth that houses us all.

One August at Zia Pueblo during the corn dance I noticed tourists picking up shards of all the old pottery that had been made and broken there. The residents of Zia know not to take the bowls and pots left behind by the older ones. They know that the fragments of those earlier lives need to be smoothed back to earth, but younger nations, travelers from continents across the world who have come to inhabit this land, have little of their own to grow on. The pieces of earth that were formed into bowls, even on their way home to dust, provide the new people a lifeline to an unknown land, help them remember that they live in the old nest of earth.

It was in early February, during the mating season of the great horned owl. It was dusk, and I hiked up the back of a mountain to where I'd heard the owls a year before. I wanted to hear them again, the voices so tender, so deep, like a memory of comfort. I was halfway up the trail when I found a soft, round nest. It had fallen from one of the bare-branched trees. It was a delicate nest, woven together of feathers, sage, and strands of wild grass. Holding it in my hand in the rosy twilight. I noticed that a blue thread was entwined with the other gatherings there. I pulled at the thread a little, and then I recognized it. It was a thread from one of my skirts. It was blue cotton. It was the unmistakable color and shape of a pattern I knew, I liked it, that a thread of my life was in an abandoned nest, one that had held eggs and new life. I took the nest home. At home, I held it to the light and looked more closely. There, to my surprise, nestled into the gray-green sage, was a gnarl of black hair. It was also unmistakable. It was my daughter's hair, cleaned from a brush and picked up out in the sun beneath the maple tree, or the pit cherry where the birds eat from the overladen, fertile branches until only the seeds remain on the trees.

I didn't know what kind of nest it was, or who had lived there. It didn't matter. I thought of the remnants of our lives carried up the hill that way and turned into shelter. That night, resting inside the walls of our home, the world outside weighed so heavily against the thin wood of the house. The sloped roof was the only thing between us and the universe. Everything outside of our wooden boundaries seemed so large. Filled with the night's citizens, it all came alive. The world opened in the thickets of the dark. The wild grapes would soon ripen on the vines. The burrowing ones were emerging. Horned owls sat in treetops. Mice scurried here and there. Skunks, fox, the slow and holy porcupine, all were passing by this way. The young of the solitary bees were feeding on the pollen in the dark. The whole world was a nest on its humble tilt, in the maze of the universe, holding us.

POSSIBILITIES FOR WRITING

1. How many different dwellings does Hogan include? Pick two that particularly engaged you or resonated for you. Why do you think Hogan included those? Explain what interests you most about her discussion of them.

2. What is implied by Hogan's story of the man who lived in a cave not far from her? What is conveyed by her story of Aldo Piacenzi, the man who built birdhouses? Explain the connections you see between these stories and at least one other that Hogan includes in her essay.

3. Write an essay about one of your dwellings—a place, house, room, or other space you value. In the process, identify and explain the connotations conveyed by the word "dwelling." How is that word, so frequently used by Hogan in this essay, different in connotation from others she might have used, such as "house," "home," "residence," "habitation," "abode," or "domicile"?

Michael Hogan (b. 1943) was born in Newport, Rhode Island. He is the author of fourteen books of fiction, poetry, and nonfiction, including Teaching from the Heart, *a collection of his essays and speeches, and the seminal work on the Irish Soldiers in the Mexican War of 1846–1848. His poetry and prose have been published in such literary magazines as the* Paris Review, *the* Harvard Review, *the* Iowa Review, *and the* American Poetry Review. *He is the recipient of numerous awards, including the NEA Creative Writing Fellowship and two Puschcart Prizes. He lives in Guadalajara, Mexico, with the well-known textile artist Lucinda Mayo.*

MICHAEL HOGAN

The Colonel

In "The Colonel," Michael Hogan describes his experiences in watching, learning, and playing tennis from his boyhood years into late middle age. Hogan's essay focuses on an army colonel, whose war stories induced the twelve-year-old Hogan to give up the pleasures of baseball, football, and basketball for the rigors of tennis. Colonel Flack taught the young Hogan not only the rudiments of the game but also important lessons about sportsmanship, competitiveness, courage, and grace.

Hogan conveys these and other lessons about the discipline of the game in a clear, direct, and graceful style, which echoes the way he plays the game. And he suggests that, played over a lifetime with diligence, passion, and attentive devotion, tennis can make a difference in a person's quality of life, a difference for which Hogan expresses "a sure sense of gratitude."

Tennis is so popular these days and so much a part of the average teenager's sports experience, that it is difficult for most of them to imagine a time when it was not. Yet, in the post–war period and the Fifties of my childhood, tennis was considered more a rich man's sport played at country clubs and exclusive resorts. Competitive singles was largely a sport of the male sex and, although women had been competing for years at Wimbledon and other international venues, most were amateurs and the few professionals who did compete got paid so little it was laughable. It wasn't until Billie Jean King's assertiveness in 1967 and the Virginia Slim tournaments of the 1970s that the sport opened up for generations of Chris Everts and Steffi Grafs, and finally grew to include million-dollar players like Venus Williams who changed the sport forever making it the dream of every athletic boy and girl.

The courts in my hometown of Newport, RI, were mostly off-limits to working class kids like me. The excellent grass center courts and the red clay courts of the private Newport Casino where the National Doubles Championships were held, were open only to wealthy members who paid a hefty annual fee. The courts at the Newport Country Club were restricted to those few rich families who were members, as were those at the even more exclusive Bailey's Beach. At the Brenton Village navy facility inside Fort Adams there were courts for officers and their dependents but these were not accessible to locals. Both composition and clay courts were available at Salve Regina College but only for registered students and faculty. So that left two casually-maintained asphalt courts at the city park on Carroll Avenue where during the summer, students home from college would bang away in lusty volleys and dominate the courts in rugged comradery.

A twelve-year-old working at a summer job, I had little interest in tennis. To me, pickup games of basketball and football were more fun and interesting. I played both at the Carroll Street Park and at the YMCA, and in the prolonged light of New England summer evenings practicing shots alone in the backyard with a hoop hung from the front of the garage. As fall approached and football season began, I'd play touch games with my friends and rougher tackle games with boys from uptown in the same park that abutted the tennis area. On occasion we might glance over at the courts if a particular cute coed was playing doubles. Sometimes we would head over to the water fountains close by to get a drink and watch a game or two. "Love-fifteen. Love-thirty. Deuce." We had no idea what this absurd scoring method could signify. It was remote from our experience, as were the crisp white shorts, the spotless tennis shoes, and the white sports shirts which were *de rigueur* in those days. We were ragamuffins, I suppose; heady youth, and tennis seemed effete, subtle, complex and sophisticated—more like an elaborate dance than a sport, a dance to which we would never be invited.

So, it came as a surprise to me when an Army colonel who lived up the street from us began talking about tennis one day with my Dad. "Does the boy play?" I heard him ask. "No," my Dad said, "but he loves sports and plays basketball, baseball, football." "Well," replied the Colonel, "if he ever wants a lesson tell him to stop by. I was an Army champion in my day."

Later my Dad would mention it, and when I replied that I thought it was a sissy game, he would begin to tell me of some of the great players of the day: Poncho Gonzalez, Jack Kramer, Ken Rosewell, but the names meant little to me. But I did like the old Colonel who had great stories to tell about the War which was not too distant in memory. My father's brother Harry had died in the forests of Belgium in 1944 during the last German push. A Little League baseball field in our neighborhood carried his name. War games in the local hills were still very much a part of our youthful pastimes. So, on a Saturday afternoon, home from a half day's labor at my summer job with a landscape company, I stopped by to talk to the Colonel. When the subject turned to tennis, his eyes lit up as he described the competition he faced in college and in the service. He regaled me with stories of tournaments, matches with famous players, games played at officer clubs in remote parts of the world. He said, "Tennis is the one game that, once you learn it, you will be able to play for the rest of your life. When your knees go out and you can't play football, when there is no gang of boys around for the pickup game of basketball or baseball, you can always find someone to play tennis with." So he convinced me. Or, perhaps it was his enthusiasm, my love for his stories and respect for his retired rank, his war experiences, or his genial personality and his enthusiasm, that I just felt I didn't want to disappoint. However it was, we agreed.

He loaned me one of his wooden rackets in its complicated screw-down press and the following day, right after early mass on a Sunday morning, he began teaching me the basics. In between suggestions about how to hold the racket and how to volley, he lectured me on the history of the sport, taught me how to score, how to adjust the net, how to anticipate the ball, how to refrain from cussing or displaying untoward emotional behavior. I think he probably bought me my first set of tennis whites that summer as well, although the first few games I'm sure I played in T-shirt and Levi cutoffs much to his distaste. That July was my thirteenth birthday and my father bought me my own racket, a Bancroft wood—expensive, highly polished and tightly strung with catgut and protected in a standard wooden press with butterfly screw-downs. The racket would be re-strung many times over the four years that I owned it. I would play with it in local matches, city tournaments, and even one memorable morning at the Newport Casino, where I got to volley with Poncho Gonzalez on the grass center court, courtesy of my father who owned a business next door and had persuaded the famous champion to trade a few strokes with his son.

The Colonel was, I suppose, in his mid-sixties which seemed ancient to me then. I could not imagine, as I improved in my tennis skills, and learned to volley deep, hit cross-court passing shots and top-spin lobs, that he would be able to keep up with me. Surely, the student would outplay the master any day now. But it never happened. Colonel Flack had a whole repertoire of moves; drop shots, slices, topspin backhands, corkscrew serves, and high-bouncing serves which just cut the end of the line. He knew the angles and limits of the court and, comfortable with these absorbed geometries, kept his young opponent racing from the net to the baseline, ragged and breathless.

As the summer passed, I improved, the muscles on my right forearm grew oversized, my lung capacity deepened, and my strokes improved from the gradual anticipation of the slides and twists that the ball would take as it came off the Colonel's racket. My service improved as well, so that I sometimes caught him wrong-footed and could come to the net quickly and put the ball away. I still didn't win a set but the games were closer and I noticed the Colonel was flushed and winded more and more often.

We played less the following year as I found new and younger competition among military dependants, boys from De La Salle Academy, and returning college players. I was often on the courts for hours each evening and on the weekends. With only two courts to play on, you had to win to keep the court and I was often a winner. Sometimes I would generously concede to play mixed doubles with couples who were waiting patiently on the sidelines.

Then one afternoon, shortly after my fourteenth birthday, all of that changed. A new boy appeared on the block; redheaded, cocky, with an easy confidence and grace and a powerful serve that could knock a poorly-gripped racket clear out of your hand. Tommy Gallagher was a compact, good-looking Irish boy who appeared from nowhere and had all the natural moves of a champion. I was blown off the court again and again in swift, blurred games of intense ferocity. I began to learn the difference between a "club player" as opposed to a "show player" or competitive athlete. Tommy played like he was born to it. There was nothing you could hit to him that he could not return. When I tried to play his game he beat me ruthlessly, contemptuously, as if I were wasting his time.

On one of those occasions, the semifinals of a citywide tournament, Colonel Flack was in the audience. Shamed by the 6–1, 6–0 defeat, I did not look him in the eye as I retreated back to the bench. "I'm not going to try and console you, Mike," he said. "You got sent to hell and back by that lad. And if you play him again, he'll beat you again. He's one of these kids who's a natural. But don't let him take away your pleasure in the game; don't let him do that to you. You're a club player and a decent one. Play your own game, take the shots you can, don't get caught up in his game. And don't be intimidated."

I was to play Tommy Gallagher several times over the next two years. He beat me, as he beat most of his competitors, but he won less easily as time went by, and never with the contemptuous indifference I had felt in that one semifinal. More importantly, losing to him did not take away from me the love of the game or my sense of myself as a player. Partly this was true because Colonel Flack and I returned to our early morning volleys interspersed with lessons. But now the lessons had more to do with eliminating distractions, watching the ball, and feeling the sun, the sweat on my skin, the slight breeze from the ocean, hearing the thwock of the perfectly hit ball coming off the strings. He taught me to be totally present in the moment, totally aware, totally focused.

He also trained me to go after every ball regardless of whether it seemed returnable or not. He taught me to play according to my skill level, placing shots carefully, not overhitting because of a desire to put it away like a pro, but stroking with the steady grace and pressure of a good club player who often tires out his more ambitious, more aggressive opponent.

Finally, he taught me that graciousness is what saves the game from savagery and ugliness. He instructed me not to give in to the temptation to call a ball out when it was in, to always give the opponent the benefit of the doubt, and that it was better to lose than to win unfairly. He reminded me to hold my temper in check, to always be polite, to return the balls in a single bounce to the server when there was no one to fetch balls.

But what he couldn't teach me and what I learned for myself over the years was that all of this was a gift. Tennis would change with the Australian 100 mph serves of Rod Laver, the aluminum and then titanium rackets, the oversized head rackets, with Wilson and Adidas logos covering every piece of equipment and raiment. Bad boys like John McEnroe would cuss out line judges and umpires, as aggressiveness had its day and then subsided . . . though never completely. Competitive tennis would be enshrined in every high school and university; tennis camps would groom a new generation of players like Pete Sampras and Andre Agassi intent on making millions as they made their mark in the sport. Still, I would go right on playing my 3.5 club-level game. I would play tennis in the dry heat of the Sonoran deserts of Tucson and on the mile-high courts of Denver. I would play in Argentina and Panama.

I would play after clearing the debris off a hurricane-littered court in Florida; I would hit the low-bounce ball while bundled in a jacket in up-state New York after sweeping off the snow-covered court, and—year after year—I would sweat through grueling sets in the tropical heat of May in Guadalajara. I would play through days of political unrest and assassination in my twenties, through the bitter, rancorous divorce in my thirties, through the crushing death of a beloved child in my forties, then through uncertain days of financial disasters and overseas currency devaluations in my fifties.

Now here I am in my sixties, approaching inexorably the age of my mentor, Colonel Flack, who on a summer morning took a skinny twelve-year old out to the concrete courts of a seaside town to give him the gift of lifelong victory. It is a way of maintaining both physical and psychological fitness, but also a way of moving through life with a focus, with grace and a sure sense of gratitude. One of those ineffable spiritual gifts which continue to give again and again when I walk on to a sun-speckled court, go over to measure the net with my "stick" (a Wilson H-26 titanium racket), and all the world narrows down to the clear geometries of the white lines, to the sound of the thwock as the ball hits the strings, as my muscles respond again in their dependable way to the known rhythms of the game, and everything is suddenly whole and perfect, and the world completely intelligible.

POSSIBILITIES FOR WRITING

1. Write a brief character sketch of Colonel Flack. Try to convey a sense of the colonel as a man and as a teacher.
2. Summarize the lessons Hogan learned from the colonel. To what extent do you think that these lessons are valuable for life as well as for tennis? Explain.
3. Write an essay about a sport, game, hobby, or other leisure pursuit for which you have a passion. Explain how you became involved in it and what values it holds for you.

Barbara Holland (b. 1925) is a freelance writer based in rural Virginia. She has written fiction, essays, and articles for a wide range of publications, including Cosmopolitan, Discovery, and Playboy. Among her books are Endangered Pleasures: In Defense of Naps, Bacon, Martinis, Profanity, and Other Indulgences (1995), Bingo Night at the Fire Halls (1998), and Wasn't the Grass Greener? (1999). Her memoir, When all the World was Young was published in 2005.

BARBARA HOLLAND

Naps

In "Naps," an essay from her book *Endangered Pleasures*, Barbara Holland makes a case for the importance of the daily nap. Holland notes that a nap forms part of the daily routine of people in many countries, especially throughout Europe. She notes further that human beings are naturally inclined to fall asleep in the middle of the afternoon—and do so when "deprived of daylight and their wristwatches."

Holland attributes Americans' avoidance of naps to a cultural bias against sleep coupled with a Puritanical strain that values hard work, which looks askance at pleasurable, seemingly nonproductive experiences such as naps. The afternoon nap, from this perspective, is considered "too luxurious, too sybaritic, too unproductive." It fails to meet the high Puritanical standard on both practical and moral grounds. Hence its absence in America.

In France, on a rented canal boat, my friends and I gazed in despair at the closed oaken gates of the lock. We'd come to them only seconds after the witching hour of noon, but we were too late. There was no one to open the lock for us; *l'éclusière* was at lunch, and after lunch she would lay herself down, close her eyes, and nap. At two, but not before, she would emerge refreshed from her square granite house and set the great cogs in motion.

We tied the boat up to a spindly bush beside the towpath and waited. And waited. It was high haying season, but the fields lay empty of farmers. The roads lay empty of trucks. France lunched, and then slept. So did Spain. So did much of the civilized world.

If we'd been differently nurtured we too would have taken a nap, but we were Americans, condemned from the age of four to trudge through our sleepless days. Americans are afraid of naps.

Napping is too luxurious, too sybaritic, too unproductive, and it's free; pleasures for which we don't pay make us anxious. Besides, it seems to be a natural inclination. Those who get paid to investigate such things have proved that people deprived of daylight and their wristwatches, with no notion of whether it was night or day, sink bliss-fully asleep in midafternoon as regular as clocks. Fighting off natural inclinations is a major Puritan virtue, and nothing that feels that good can be respectable.

They may have a point there. Certainly the process of falling asleep in the afternoon is quite different from bedtime sleep. Whether this is physi-ological or merely a by-product of guilt, it's a blatantly sensual experience, a voluptuous surrender, akin to the euphoric swoon of the heroine in a vampire movie. For the self-controlled, it's frightening—*how far down am I falling? will I ever climb back?* The sleep itself has a different texture. It's blacker, thicker, more intense, and works faster. Fifteen minutes later the napper pops back to the surface as from time travel, bewildered to find that it's only ten of two instead of centuries later.

Like skydiving, napping takes practice; the first few tries are scary.

The American nap is even scarier because it's unilateral. Sleeping Frenchmen are surrounded by sleeping compatriots, but Americans who lie down by day stiffen with the thought of the busy world rushing past. There we lie, visible and vulnerable on our daylit bed, ready to cut the strings and sink into the dark, swirling, almost sexual currents of the impending doze, but what will happen in our absence? Our stocks will fall; our employees will mutiny and seize the helm; our clients will tip-toe away to competitors. Even the housewife, taking advantage of the afternoon lull, knows at the deepest level of consciousness that the phone is about to ring.

And of course, for those of us with proper jobs, there's the problem of finding a bed. Some corporations, in their concern for their employ-ees' health and fitness, provide gym rooms where we can commit strenuous exercise at lunchtime, but where are our beds? In Japan, the productivity wonder of the industrialized world, properly run compa-nies maintain a nap room wherein the workers may refresh them-selves. Even in America, rumor has it, the costly CEOs of giant corporations work sequestered in private suites, guarded by watchper-sons, mainly so they can curl up unseen to sharpen their predatory powers with a quick snooze. A couple of recent presidents famous for their all-night energies kept up the pace by means of naps. Other pres-idents, less famous for energy, slept by day *and* night; woe to the unwary footstep that wakened Coolidge in the afternoon.

This leaves the rest of us lackeys bolt upright, toughing it out, try-ing to focus on the computer screen, from time to time snatching our chins up off our collarbones and glancing furtively around to see if we were noticed. The modern office isn't designed for privacy, and most of our cubicles have no doors to close, only gaps in the portable partitions. Lay our heads down on the desk at the appropriate hour and we're exposed to any passing snitch who strolls the halls enforcing alertness. It's a wonder they don't walk around ringing bells and blowing trumpets from one till three. American employers do not see the afternoon forty winks as refreshing the creative wellsprings of mere employees. They see it as goofing off.

Apparently most of us agree. Large numbers of us are, for one reason or another, home-bound, but do we indulge in the restorative nap? Mostly not. Even with no witness but ourselves, we're ashamed to. It would mean we weren't busy. We tell ourselves we have a million urgent things to do and our lives are so full and exciting we couldn't possibly lie down by daylight. Never mind that our heads are no particular use in midafternoon and half the work we do may need to be redone in the cold light of tomorrow morning. Oozing virtue and busyness, we flog ourselves on till evening.

In the evening, at least according to the cartoons, American men fall asleep on the couch, after dinner, a-flicker with light from the television screen. They are home from work, the day's toil accomplished, and they're free to doze, though if they'd napped at the biologically appointed time they wouldn't need to now, and at this hour it's not so much a nap as an awkward preview of the night's sleep, possibly leading to four-a.m. insomnia. Women, on the other hand, are never home from work unless it's someone else's home; home for them is simply different work, and naps are not an option.

It's time to rethink the nap from both the corporate and the personal viewpoint.

Those CEOs who find their own naps such an asset to productivity might consider what they'd do for the rest of us. They could hire consultants to conduct productivity studies, dividing us into teams of sleepers and wakers. When the results were in, they might even decide to mandate naps, as naps were mandated in nursery school, when we each unfolded a name-tagged blanket and spread it on the floor and lay down and shut up for a while. Granted we can't all have office suites, or even couches, and it would be unseemly to have us stacked up like firewood on the conference table, but we could use futons, stored discreetly under the desk, or folding cots, or sleeping bags. The phones could be left to their answering devices, the faxes could pile up in the hopper, and the sales reps could pound in vain on the door as they'd find themselves doing in France.

Those of us at home, with beds at hand, should take pleasure as well as productivity into account. Consider the cat. A perfectly healthy cat can nap through the entire month of February and wake feeling all the better for it. The house may be simply pattering with uncaught mice, but no twitch of guilt quivers the whiskers of the napping cat. In summer he stretches out to full length, preferably in a breezy doorway where he's rather in the way, and sometimes on his back, looking dead enough to alarm the chance visitor, and drapes his arm over his eyes. Swiftly and easily he lowers himself into sleep, sensuous, fur-lined sleep, the sleep of the untroubled conscience. Nothing tells him he ought to be rushing about his various occupations. Sleep, for a cat, is a worthy occupation in itself.

Let us consider the cat and go to bed. Bed the haven, the motherly lap, the downy nest. Bed, from which Earth with its fuss and fidgeting shrinks to the size of Pluto, visible only by telescope. We should loosen or remove some of our clothing, close the curtains, and lie down flat, allowing the vital forces to circulate through the brain and restore its muscle tone.

Bed is *not* a shameful, shiftless place to be by day, nor is it necessary to run a fever of 102 to deserve it. Bed can even be productive. The effortless horizontal body and the sensory deprivation of the quiet bedroom leave the mind free, even in sleep, to focus, to roam, sometimes to forge ahead. Knotty problems can unknot themselves as if by magic. Creative solutions can tiptoe across the coverlet and nestle onto the pillow of the napper, even while the black velvet paws of Morpheus lie closely over his eyes. He may wake half an hour later with the road ahead laid clear.

Creativity doesn't come a-running to those who toil and slave for her; she's as much the daughter of rest and play as of effort. Just because we're uncomfortable doesn't mean we're productive; just because we're comfortable doesn't mean we're lazy. Milton wrote *Paradise Lost* in bed. Winston Churchill, a prodigious producer, wrote all those large important histories in bed, brandy bottle at the ready. No doubt when inspiration flagged and his thoughts refused to marshal, he took a nip and a nap. Now, there was a man who knew a thing or two about a good day's work.

POSSIBILITIES FOR WRITING

1. What does "nap prejudice" represent for Holland? What does she see as its sources? Why does she think allowing for naps would be a good thing more generally? Do you tend to agree or disagree with her? Why?

2. What is your experience with naps, beginning in childhood and including your curent life? Who in your experience is most likely to nap? Why? What does this say about naps?
3. This essay comes from a book entitled *Endangered Pleasures.* Write an essay about what you consider an "endangered pleasure"—something you see as innocently enjoyable that is looked upon negatively by other people.

Langston Hughes (1902–1967) *was born in Joplin, Missouri, to a prominent African-American family. Interested in poetry from childhood, he attended Columbia University as an engineering major but dropped out after his first year to pursue his literary aspirations (he later graduated from Lincoln University). Spurred by the flourishing of black artists known as the Harlem Renaissance, he quickly found a distinctive voice that reflected the culture of everyday life, and he published his first works before he was out of his teens. Hughes is best known for his poetry, which often employs vernacular language and jazz-like rhythms, but he also wrote popular works of fiction, essays, plays, books for children, and several volumes of autobiography, including* The Big Sea *(1940), focusing on his childhood and teenage years.*

LANGSTON HUGHES

Salvation

In "Salvation," Hughes describes a memorable incident from his youth, one that had a decisive impact on his view of the world. In the span of just a few pages, Hughes tells a story of faith and doubt, of belief and disbelief, of how he was "saved from sin" when he was going on thirteen. "But not really saved." This paradoxical opening to "Salvation" establishes a tension that characterizes the essay, which culminates in an ironic reversal of expectations for the reader, and a life-altering realization for Hughes.

The power of Hughes's "Salvation" derives not only from its language, but also from the irony of its action, as well as its blend of humor and sadness, the humor of the child's literal understanding of what his aunt tells him to expect, and the sadness of his disappointed belief, which ironically, turns against itself. In restricting the point-of-view to that of a twelve-year-old child, Hughes enhances the credibility of his narrative and increases its dramatic power. His concluding paragraph is a quietly resounding tour-de-force of irony and epiphany.

I was saved from sin when I was going on thirteen. But not really saved. It happened like this. There was a big revival at my Auntie Reed's church. Every night for weeks there had been much preaching, singing, praying, and shouting, and some very hardened sinners had been brought to Christ, and the membership of the church had grown by leaps and bounds. Then just before the revival ended, they held a special meeting for children, "to bring the young lambs to the fold." My aunt spoke of it for days ahead. That night I was escorted to the front row and placed on the mourners' bench with all the other young sinners, who had not yet been brought to Jesus.

My aunt told me that when you were saved you saw a light, and something happened to you inside! And Jesus came into your life! And God was with you from then on! She said you could see and hear and feel Jesus in your soul. I believed her. I had heard a great many old people say the same thing and it seemed to me they ought to know. So I sat there calmly in the hot, crowded church, waiting for Jesus to come to me.

The preacher preached a wonderful rhythmical sermon, all moans and shouts and lonely cries and dire pictures of hell, and then he sang a song about the ninety and nine safe in the fold, but one little lamb was left out in the cold. Then he said: "Won't you come? Won't you come to Jesus? Young lambs, won't you come?" And he held out his arms to all us young sinners there on the mourners' bench. And the little girls cried. And some of them jumped up and went to Jesus right away. But most of us just sat there.

A great many old people came and knelt around us and prayed, old women with jet-black faces and braided hair, old men with work-gnarled hands. And the church sang a song about the lower lights are burning, some poor sinners to be saved. And the whole building rocked with prayer and song.

Still I kept waiting to *see* Jesus.

Finally all the young people had gone to the altar and were saved, but one boy and me. He was a rounder's son named Westley. Westley and I were surrounded by sisters and deacons praying. It was very hot in the church, and getting late now. Finally Westley said to me in a whisper: "God damn! I'm tired o' sitting here. Let's get up and be saved." So he got up and was saved.

Then I was left all alone on the mourners' bench. My aunt came and knelt at my knees and cried, while prayers and songs swirled all around me in the little church. The whole congregation prayed for me alone, in a mightly wail of moans and voices. And I kept waiting serenely for Jesus, waiting, waiting—but he didn't come. I wanted to see him, but nothing happened to me. Nothing! I wanted something to happen to me, but nothing happened.

I heard the songs and the minister saying: "Why don't you come? My dear child, why don't you come to Jesus? Jesus is waiting for you. He wants you. Why don't you come? Sister Reed, what is this child's name?"

"Langston," my aunt sobbed.

"Langston, why don't you come? Why don't you come and be saved? Oh, Lamb of God! Why don't you come?"

Now it was really getting late. I began to be ashamed of myself, holding everything up so long. I began to wonder what God thought about Westley, who certainly hadn't seen Jesus either, but who was now sitting proudly on the platform, swinging his knickerbockered legs and grinning down at me, surrounded by deacons and old women on their knees praying. God had not struck Westley dead for taking his name in vain or for lying in the temple. So I decided that maybe to save further trouble, I'd better lie, too, and say that Jesus had come, and get up and be saved.

So I got up.

Suddenly the whole room broke into a sea of shouting, as they saw me rise. Waves of rejoicing swept the place. Women leaped in the air. My aunt threw her arms around me. The minister took me by the hand and led me to the platform.

When things quieted down, in a hushed silence, punctuated by a few ecstatic "Amens," all the new young lambs were blessed in the name of God. Then joyous singing filled the room.

That night, for the last time in my life but one—for I was a big boy twelve years old—I cried. I cried, in bed alone, and couldn't stop. I buried my head under the quilts, but my aunt heard me. She woke up and told my uncle I was crying because the Holy Ghost had come into my life, and because I had seen Jesus. But I was really crying because I couldn't bear to tell her that I had lied, that I had deceived everybody in the church, and I hadn't seen Jesus, and that now I didn't believe there was a Jesus any more, since he didn't come to help me.

POSSIBILITIES FOR WRITING

1. Recall a time when, like Hughes, you did something you didn't really believe in because you found it easier to go along with the crowd. In an essay, narrate the experience, focusing on the situation, the other people involved, your feelings at the time, and the aftermath of the incident.

2. In this brief narration, Hughes does a great deal to re-create his experience vividly and concretely. Analyze Hughes's use of language—specific nouns, verbs, and adjectives—as well as his use of dialogue and repetition to add punch to his story.

3. Hughes ends his narration on a note of disillusionment: "now I didn't believe there was a Jesus any more, since he didn't come to help me." Have you ever been disillusioned about a deeply held and cherished belief? In an essay, explore that experience and its consequences in detail. How did you eventually cope with your disappointment?

Zora Neale Hurston (1891–1960) was born in Eatonville, Florida, where she spent her early years. She attended Howard University and in 1925 went to New York City, becoming involved in cultural activities in Harlem. There she met Langston Hughes, who, like Hurston, was interested in the folk elements of African-American culture, particularly as reflected in southern life. From 1925 through 1927 she attended Barnard College, studying anthropology with Dr. Franz Boas. She later did field research recording the folklore and ways of African-Americans, first in Harlem, then throughout the rural South. The fruits of this work appeared in her Mules and Men (1935). Hurston's best known words are Their Eyes Were Watering God (1937) and the autobiographical Dust Tracks on a Road (1942). These and other works were rediscovered as a result of the women's movement and in conjunction with an upsurge in the study of African-American literature, especially that of the Harlem Renaissance.

ZORA NEALE HURSTON

How It Feels To Be Colored Me

In "How It Feels To Be Colored Me." Hurston discusses her blackness as an aspect of race and of her cultural, social, and personal identity. The essay's tone is confident and upbeat, as Hurston celebrates herself as a modern African-American woman who knows her worth even when others do not.

The essay falls into four parts. In the first part, Hurston describes her childhood in Eatonville. Florida, and the change she underwent when she moved to Jacksonville and discovered she was no longer "everybody's Zora," but instead "a little colored girl." In the next two parts, Hurston describes two contrasting states of mind—feeling not at all "colored" on the one hand, and, on the other, feeling her racial difference from whites acutely. And in the last part, she describes how she came to terms proudly with who she is, a black American woman yet at the same time "the cosmic Zora."

I am colored but I offer nothing in the way of extenuating circumstances except the fact that I am the only Negro in the United States whose grandfather on the mother's side was *not* an Indian chief.

I remember the very day that I became colored. Up to my thirteenth year I lived in the little Negro town of Eatonville, Florida. It is exclusively a colored town. The only white people I knew passed through the town going to or coming from Orlando. The native whites rode dusty horses, the Northern tourists chugged down the sandy village road in automobiles. The town knew the Southerners and never stopped cane chewing when they passed. But the Northerners were something else again. They were peered at cautiously from behind curtains by the timid. The more venturesome would come out on the porch to watch them go past and got just as much pleasure out of the tourists as the tourists got out of the village.

The front porch might seem a daring place for the rest of the town, but it was a gallery seat to me. My favorite place was atop the gate-post. Proscenium box for a born first-nighter. Not only did I enjoy the show, but I didn't mind the actors knowing that I liked it. I usually spoke to them in passing. I'd wave at them and when they returned my salute, I would say something like this: "Howdy-do-well-I-thank-you-where-yoa-goin'?" Usually automobile or the horse paused at this, and after a queer exchange of compliments, I would probably "go a piece of the way" with them, as we say in farthest Florida. If one of my family happened to come to the front in time to see me, of course negotiations would be rudely broken off. But even so, it is clear that I was the first "welcome-to-our-state" Floridian, and I hope the Miami Chamber of Commerce will please take notice.

During this period, white people differed from colored to me only in that they rode through town and never lived there. They liked to hear me "speak pieces" and sing and wanted to see me dance the parse-me-la, and gave me generously of their small silver for doing these things, which seemed strange to me for I wanted to do them so much that I needed bribing to stop. Only they didn't know it. The colored people gave no dimes. They deplored any joyful tendencies in me, but I was their Zora nevertheless. I belonged to them, to the nearby hotels, to the county—everybody's Zora.

But changes came in the family when I was thirteen, and I was sent to school in Jacksonville. I left Eatonville, the town of the oleanders, as Zora. When I disembarked from the river-boat at Jacksonville, she was no more. It seemed that I had suffered a sea change. I was not Zora of Orange County any more, I was now a little colored girl. I found it out in certain ways. In my heart as well as in the mirror, I became a fast brown—warranted not to rub nor run.

But I am not tragically colored. There is no great sorrow dammed up in my soul, nor lurking behind my eyes. I do not mind at all. I do not belong to the sobbing school of Negrohood who hold that nature somehow has given them a lowdown dirty deal and whose feelings are all hurt about it. Even in the helter-skelter skirmish that is my life, I have seen that the world is to the strong regardless of a little pigmentation more or less. No, I do not weep at the world—I am too busy sharpening my oyster knife.

Someone is always at my elbow reminding me that I am the grand-daughter of slaves. It fails to register depression with me. Slavery is sixty years in the past. The operation was successful and the patient is doing well, thank you. The terrible struggle that made me an American out of a potential slave said "On the line!" The Reconstruction said "Get set!"; and the generation before said "Go!" I am off to a flying start and I must not halt in the stretch to look behind and weep. Slavery is the price I paid for civilization, and the choice was not with me. It is a bully adventure and worth all that I have paid through my ances-tors for it. No one on earth ever had a greater chance for glory. The world to be won and nothing to be lost. It is thrilling to think—to know that for any act of mine, I shall get twice as much praise or twice as much blame. It is quite exciting to hold the center of the national stage, with the spectators not knowing whether to laugh or to weep.

The position of my white neighbor is much more difficult. No brown specter pulls up a chair beside me when I sit down to eat. No dark ghost thrusts its leg against mine in bed. The game of keeping what one has is never so exciting as the game of getting.

I do not always feel colored. Even now I often achieve the uncon-scious Zora of Eatonville before the Hegira. I feel most colored when I am thrown against a sharp white background.

For instance at Barnard. "Beside the waters of the Hudson" I feel my race. Among the thousand white persons, I am a dark rock surged upon, overswept by a creamy sea. I am surged upon and overswept, but through it all, I remain myself. When covered by the waters, I am; and the ebb but reveals me again.

Sometimes it is the other way around. A white person is set down in our midst, but the contrast is just as sharp for me. For instance, when I sit in the drafty basement that is The New World Cabaret with a white person, my color comes. We enter chatting about any little nothing that we have in common and are seated by the jazz waiters. In the abrupt way that jazz orchestras have, this one plunges into a number. It loses no time in circumlocutions, but gets right down to business. It con-stricts the thorax and splits the heart with its tempo and narcotic har-monies. This orchestra grows rambunctious, rears on its hind legs and attacks the tonal veil with primitive fury, rending it, clawing it until it breaks through to the jungle beyond. I follow those heathen—follow them exultingly. I dance wildly inside myself; I yell within, I whoop; I shake my assegai above my head, I hurl it true to the mark *yeeeeooww!*

I am in the jungle and living in the jungle way. My face is painted red and yellow and my body is painted blue. My pulse is throbbing like a war drum. I want to slaughter something—give pain, give death to what, I do not know. But the piece ends. The men of the orchestra wipe their lips and rest their fingers. I creep back slowly to the veneer we call civilization with the last tone and find the white friend sitting motionless in his seat, smoking calmly.

"Good music they have here," he remarks, drumming the table with his fingertips.

Music! The great blobs of purple and red emotion have not touched him. He has only heard what I felt. He is far away and I see him but dimly across the ocean and the continent that have fallen between us. He is so pale with his whiteness then and I am so colored.

At certain times I have no race, I am *me*. When I set my hat at a certain angle and saunter down Seventh Avenue, Harlem City, feeling as snooty as the Lions in front of the Forty-Second Street Library, for instance. So far as my feelings are concerned, Peggy Hopkins Joyce on the Boule Mich with her gorgeous raiment, stately carriage, knees knocking together in a most aristocratic manner, has nothing on me. The cosmic Zora emerges. I belong to no race nor time. I am the eternal feminine with its string of beads.

I have no separate feeling about being an American citizen and colored. I am merely a fragment of the Great Soul that surges within the boundaries. My country, right or wrong.

Sometimes, I feel discriminated against, but it does not make me angry. It merely astonishes me. How *can* any deny themselves the pleasure of my company! It's beyond me.

But in the main, I feel like a brown bag of miscellany propped against a wall. Against a wall in company with other bags, white, red and yellow. Pour out the contents, and there is discovered a jumble of small things priceless and worthless. A first-water diamond, an empty spool, bits of broken glass, lengths of string, a key to a door long since crumbled away, a rusty knife-blade, old shoes saved for a road that never was and never will be, a nail bent under the weight of things too heavy for any nail, a dried flower or two, still a little fragrant. In your hand is the brown bag. On the ground before you is the jumble it held—so much like the jumble in the bags, could they be emptied, that all might be dumped in a single heap and the bags refilled without altering the content of any greatly. A bit of colored glass more or less would not matter. Perhaps that is how the Great Stuffer of Bags filled them in the first place—who knows?

POSSIBILITIES FOR WRITING

1. Hurston presents herself as happy with who she is, especially with her race. Do you think her experience and attitude are characteristic of most people? Why or why not? What does Hurston see as the advantages for her of being "colored"? Consider Hurston's presentation of herself from the standpoint of race. How does Hurston use her race to define herself, and how does she use race to convey her attitudes towards both others and towards herself?

2. Write an analysis of Hurston's essay. Consider its organization into four parts. Identify the focus and point of each part and the connections among the four parts leading to the essay's main idea. Identity and explain the key images Hurston uses to convey her main idea.

3. Write an essay in which you explore your identity in terms of gender, race, class, or ethnicity. Try to account for times when you feel especially acutely this aspect of your identity, and times when it seems to disappear or fade into near insignificance.

Pico Iyer (b. 1957) *was born in England to Indian parents, grew up in California, attended Eton and Oxford, and has lived in suburban Japan. Iyer is the author of half a dozen books along with essays and journalism that have appeared in* Time, Harper's, *the* New Yorker, *the* New York Review of Books, *and many other publications around the world. He has described himself as a "multinational soul on a multicultural globe," and his writing frequently probes the meaning of personal identity in a global context. His most recent books are* Sun after Dark: Flights into the Foreign (2004) *and* The Open Road: The Global Journey of the Fourteenth Dalai Lama (2008)

PICO IYER

Nowhere Man

In "Nowhere Man," Iyer describes an "entirely new breed of people" who do not live in a single place, but instead have multiple places of residences, often in different countries and continents. These individuals, many of them relatively young, find themselves learning about and living in quite different cultures, and thus become both multilingual and multicultural. Iyer describes both the up and down sides of such multiple cultural identities.

One of the more interesting features of "Nowhere Man" is Iyer's exploration of the consequences of being without a distinct national identity. Using himself as an example, Iyer highlights the advantages and drawbacks, the benefits and limitations of being a man without a country. Iyer's essay is distinctively modern in its references to technology, and how the new breed of rootless, international travelers he describes are connected to each other and to their far-flung quasi-residences via cell phones, faxes, and the Internet, while keeping abreast of world events via CNN, and eating in internationally franchised restaurants.

By the time I was nine, I was already used to going to school by plane, to sleeping in airports, to shuttling back and forth, three times a year, between my home in California and my boarding school in England. While I was growing up, I was never within six thousand miles of the nearest relative—and came, therefore, to learn how to define relations in nonfamilial ways. From the time I was a teenager, I took it for granted that I could take my budget vacation (as I did) in Bolivia and Tibet, China and Morocco. It never seemed strange to me that a girlfriend might be half a world (or ten hours flying time) away, that my closest friends might be on the other side of a continent or sea. It was only recently that I realized that all these habits of mind and life would scarcely have been imaginable in my parents' youth, that the very facts and facilities that shape my world are all distinctly new developments, and mark me as a modern type.

It was only recently, in fact, that I realized that I am an example, perhaps, of an entirely new breed of people, a transcontinental tribe of wanderers that is multiplying as fast as international telephone lines and frequent flier programs. We are the transit loungers, forever heading to the departure gate. We buy our interests duty-free, we eat our food on plastic plates, we watch the world through borrowed headphones. We pass through countries as through revolving doors, resident aliens of the world, impermanent residents of nowhere. Nothing is strange to us, and nowhere is foreign. We are visitors even in our own homes.

The modern world seems increasingly made for people like me. I can plop myself down anywhere and find myself in the same relation of familiarity and strangeness: Lusaka is scarcely more strange to me than the England in which I was born, the America where I am registered as an "alien," and the almost unvisited India that people tell me is my home. All have Holiday Inns, direct-dial phones, CNN, and DHL. All have sushi, Thai restaurants, and Kentucky Fried Chicken.

This kind of life offers an unprecedented sense of freedom and mobility: Tied down nowhere, we can pick and choose among locations. Ours is the first generation that can go off to visit Tibet for a week, or meet Tibetans down the street; ours is the first generation to be able to go to Nigeria for a holiday—to find our roots or to find that they are not there. At a superficial level, this new internationalism means that I can meet, in the Hilton coffee shop, an Indonesian businessman who is as conversant as I am with Magic Johnson and Madonna. At a deeper level, it means that I need never feel estranged. If all the world is alien to us, all the world is home.

And yet I sometimes think that this mobile way of life is as disquietingly novel as high-rises, or as the video monitors that are rewiring our consciousness. Even as we fret about the changes our progress wreaks in the air and on the airwaves, in forests and on streets, we hardly worry about the change it is working in ourselves, the new kind of soul that is being born out of a new kind of life. Yet this could be the most dangerous development of all, and the least examined.

For us in the transit lounge, disorientation is as alien as affiliation. We become professional observers, able to see the merits and deficiencies of anywhere, to balance our parents' viewpoints with their enemies' position. Yes, we say, of course it's terrible, but look at the situation from Saddam's point of view. I understand how you feel, but the Chinese had their own cultural reasons for Tiananmen Square. Fervor comes to seem to us the most foreign place of all.

Seasoned experts at dispassion, we are less good at involvement, or suspension of disbelief; at, in fact, the abolition of distance. We are masters of the aerial perspective, but touching down becomes more difficult. Unable to get stirred by the raising of a flag, we are sometimes unable to see how anyone could be stirred. I sometimes think that this is how Salman Rushdie, the great analyst of this condition, somehow became its victim. He had juggled homes for so long, so adroitly, that he forgot how the world looks to someone who is rooted—in country or in belief. He had chosen to live so far from affiliation that he could no longer see why people choose affiliation in the first place. Besides, being part of no society means one is accountable to no one, and need respect no laws outside one's own. If single-nation people can be fanatical as terrorists, we can end up ineffectual as peacekeepers.

We become, in fact, strangers to belief itself, unable to comprehend many of the rages and dogmas that animate (and unite) people. I could not begin to fathom why some Muslims would think of murder after hearing about *The Satanic Verses*; yet sometimes I force myself to recall that it is we, in our floating skepticism, who are the exceptions, that in China or Iran, in Korea or Peru, it is not so strange to give up one's life for a cause.

We end up, then, a little like nonaligned nations, confirming our reservations at every step. We tell ourselves, self-servingly, that nationalism breeds monsters, and choose to ignore the fact that internationalism breeds them too. Ours is the culpability not of the assassin, but of the bystander who takes a snapshot of the murder. Or, when the revolution catches fire, hops on the next plane out.

I wonder, sometimes, if this new kind of nonaffiliation may not be alien to something fundamental in the human state. Refugees at least harbor passionate feeling about the world they have left—and generally seek to return there. The exile at least is propelled by some kind of strong emotion away from the old country and toward the new; indifference is not an exile emotion. But what does the transit lounger feel? What are the issues that we would die for? What are the passions that we would live for?

Airports are among the only sites in public life where emotions are hugely sanctioned. We see people weep, shout, kiss in airports; we see them at the furthest edges of excitement and exhaustion. Airports are privileged spaces where we can see the primal states writ large—fear, recognition, hope. But there are some of us, perhaps, sitting at the departure gate, boarding passes in hand, who feel neither the pain of separation nor the exultation of wonder; who alight with the same emotions with which we embarked; who go down to the baggage carousel and watch our lives circling, circling, circling, waiting to be claimed.

POSSIBILITIES FOR WRITING

1. Discuss your perception of what Iyer describes as an "entirely new breed of people," the "nowhere man" of his title. What characterizes this new type of person? To what extent are you familiar with it? What consequences of "the transit lounge" syndrome does Iyer identify? Can you think of others?
2. Explain Iyer's remark that "being part of no society means one is accountable to no one." According to Iyer, what are the consequences of being rootless, of lacking a sense of being rooted in a particular place that one can call home? Do you agree with him? Why or why not?
3. The flip side of the rootlessness that Iyer describes is a strong sense of pride that people feel for their countries and for their nationalities. What dangers and what benefits does Iyer see as resulting from an intense pride in one's place of origin and/or residence? To what extent do you agree with his assessment? Explain.

Thomas Jefferson (1743–1826), the third president of the United States, was born in what is now Albemarle County, Virginia. He graduated from the College of William and Mary and later apprenticed as a lawyer. An early patriot leader, he forcefully argued in his 1774 pamphlet A Summary View of the Rights of British America *that the British government had no power over the American colonies and that colonial allegiance to the king was only voluntary. He drafted the Declaration of Independence in 1776, as a delegate to the Second Continental Congress, and he served as governor of Virginia during the final years of the Revolutionary War. He was elected vice president in 1793 and president in 1801, serving in the office until 1809. A man of great intellect, curiosity, and principle, he was also the founder of the University of Virginia.*

THOMAS JEFFERSON

The Declaration of Independence
Draft and Final Version

Thomas Jefferson is credited as the primary author of The Declaration of Independence, which he drafted together with John Adams, Benjamin Franklin, Roger Livingston, and Roger Sherman. It is instructive to compare the original draft, presented to Congress on June 28, 1776, with the final version, which was approved six days later on July 4th. In looking only at a single famous sentence, the one that begins "We hold these truths," it is immediately apparent how Jefferson streamlined the language, making the phrasing more balanced and cadenced, more pleasing to eye and ear, and, in doing so, made the language of the Declaration memorable.

The argument of the Declaration is based upon this first self-evident truth allied with two others. First, that governments are established to secure the inalienable rights of individuals. And second, that when a government destroys or refuses those rights, the people have a right to abolish it. With its careful reasoning, precise use of language, and logically developed argument, the Declaration of Independence is a model of clear, elegant, and cogent writing.

THOMAS JEFFERSON
Original Draft of The Declaration of Independence

A Declaration of the Representatives of the United States Of America, in General Congress Assembled

When in the course of human events it becomes necessary for a people to advance from that subordination in which they have hitherto remained, & to assume among the powers of the earth the equal & independant station to which the laws of nature & of nature's god entitle them, a decent respect to the opinions of mankind requires that they should declare the causes which impel them to the change.

We hold these truths to be sacred & undeniable; that all men are created equal & independant, that from that equal creation they derive rights inherent & inalienable, among which are the preservation of life, & liberty, & the spirit of happiness; that to secure these ends, governments are instituted among men, deriving their just powers from the consent of the governed; that whenever any form of government shall become destructive of these ends, it is the right of the people to alter or to abolish it, & to institute new government, laying its foundation on such principles & organising it's powers in such form, as to them shall seem most likely to effect their safety & happiness. prudence indeed will dictate that governments long established should not be changed for light & transient causes: and accordingly all experience hath shewn that mankind are more disposed to suffer while evils are sufferable, than to right themselves by abolishing the forms to which they are accustomed. but when a long train of abuses & usurpations, begun at a distinguished period, & pursuing invariably the same object, evinces a design to subject them to arbitrary power, it is their right, it is their duty, to throw off such government & to provide new guards for their future security. such has been the patient sufferance of these colonies; & such is now the necessity which constrains them to expunge their former systems of government. The history of his present majesty, is a history of unremitting injuries and usurpations, among which no one fact stands single or solitary to contradict the uniform tenor of the rest, all of which have in direct object the establishment of an absolute tyranny over these states. to prove this, let facts be submitted to a candid world, for the truth of which we pledge a faith yet unsullied by falsehood.

> he has refused his assent to laws the most wholesome and necessary for the public good:
>
> he has forbidden his governors to pass laws of immediate & pressing importance, unless suspended in their operation till his assent should be obtained: and when so suspended, he has neglected utterly to attend to them:
>
> he has refused to pass other laws for the accommodation of large districts of people unless those people would relinquish the right of representation, a right inestimable to them, & formidable to tyrants alone:
>
> he has dissolved Representative houses repeatedly & continually, for opposing with manly firmness his invasions on the rights of the people:
>
> he has refused for a long space of time to cause others to be elected, whereby the legislative powers, incapable of annihilation, have

returned to the people at large for their exercise, the state remaining in the mean time exposed to all the dangers of invasion from without, &, convulsions within:

he has suffered the administration of justice totally to cease in some of these colonies, refusing his assent to laws for establishing judiciary powers:

he has made our judges dependant on his will alone, for the tenure of their offices, and amount of their salaries:

he has erected a multitude of new offices by a self-assumed power, & sent hither swarms of officers to harrass our people & eat out their substance: he has kept among us in times of peace standing armies & ships of war:

he has affected to render the military, independent of & superior to the civil power:

he has combined with others to subject us to a jurisdiction foreign to our constitutions and unacknowledged by our laws; giving his assent to their pretended acts of legislation, for quartering large bodies of armed troops among us:

    for protecting them by a mock-trial from punishment for any murders they should commit on the inhabitants of these states;

    for cutting off our trade with all parts of the world:

    for imposing taxes on us without our consent:

    for depriving us of the benefits of trial by jury:

he has endeavored to prevent the population of these states; for that purpose obstructing the laws for naturalization of foreigners; refusing to pass others to encourage their migrations hither; & raising the conditions of new appropriations of lands:

    for transporting us beyond seas to be tried for pretended offences:

    for taking away our charters & altering fundamentally the forms of our governments:

    for suspending our own legislatures & declaring themselves invested with power to legislate for us in all cases whatsoever:

    he has abdicated government here, withdrawing his governors, & declaring us out of his allegiance & protection:

he has plundered our seas, ravaged our coasts, burnt our towns & destroyed the lives of our people:

he is at this time transporting large armies of foreign mercenaries to compleat the works of death, desolation & tyranny, already begun with circumstances of cruelty & perfidy unworthy the head of a civilized nation:

he has endeavored to bring on the inhabitants of our frontiers the merciless Indian savages, whose known rule of warfare is an undistinguished destruction of all ages, sexes, & conditions of existence:

he has incited treasonable insurrections of our fellow-citizens, with the allurements of forfeiture & confiscation of our property:

he has waged cruel war against human nature itself, violating it's most sacred rights of life & liberty in the persons of a distant people who never offended him, captivating & carrying them into slavery in another hemisphere, or to incur miserable death in their transportation thither. this piratical warfare, the opprobrium of infidel powers, is the warfare of the CHRISTIAN king of Great Britain, determined to keep open a market where MEN should be bought & sold; he has prostituted his negative for suppressing every legislative attempt to prohibit or to restrain this execrable commerce: and that this assemblage of horrors might want no fact of distinguished die, he is now exciting those very people to rise in arms among us, and to purchase that liberty of which he has deprived them, by murdering the people upon whom he also obtruded them; thus paying off former crimes committed against the liberties of one people, with crimes which he urges them to commit against the lives of another.

in every stage of these oppressions we have petitioned for redress in the most humble terms; our repeated petitions have been answered by repeated injury. a prince whose character is thus marked by every act which may define a tyrant, is unfit to be the ruler of a people who mean to be free. future ages will scarce believe that the hardiness of one man, adventured within the short compass of twelve years only, on so many acts of tyranny without a mask, over a people fostered & fixed in principles of liberty.

Nor have we been wanting in attentions to our British brethren. we have warned them from time to time of attempts by their legislature to extend a jurisdiction over these our states. we have reminded them of the circumstances of our emigration & settlement here, no one of which could warrant so strange a pretension: that these were effected at the expence of our own blood & treasure, unassisted by the wealth or the strength of Great Britain: that in constituting indeed our several forms of government, we had adopted one common king, thereby laying a foundation for perpetual league & amity with them; but that submission to their [Parliament, was no Part of our Constitution, nor ever in Idea, if History may be] credited: and we appealed to their native justice & magnanimity, as to the ties of our common kindred to disavow these usurpations which were likely to interrupt our correspondence & connection. they too have been deaf to the voice of justice & of consanguinity, & when occasions have been given them, by the regular course of their laws, of removing from their councils the disturbers of our harmony, they have by their free election re-established them in power. at this very time too they are permitting their chief magistrate to send over not only soldiers of our common blood, but Scotch & foreign mercenaries to invade & deluge us in blood. these facts have given the last stab to agonizing affection, and manly spirit bids us to renounce for ever these unfeeling brethren. we must endeavor to forget our former love for them, and to hold them as we hold the rest of mankind, enemies in war, in peace friends. we might have been a free & a great people together; but a communication of grandeur & of freedom it seems is below their dignity. be it so, since they will have it: the road to glory & happiness is open to us too; we will climb it in a separate state, and acquiesce in the necessity which pronounces our everlasting Adieu!

We therefore the representatives of the United States of America in General Congress assembled do, in the name & by authority of the good people of these states, reject and renounce all allegiance & subjection to the kings of Great Britain & all others who may hereafter claim by, through, or under them; we utterly dissolve & break off all political connection which may have heretofore subsisted between us & the people or parliament of Great Britain; and finally we do assert and declare these colonies to be free and independant states, and that as free & independant states they shall hereafter have power to levy war, conclude peace, contract alliances, establish commerce, & to do all other acts and things which independant states may of right do. And for the support of this declaration we mutually pledge to each other our lives, our fortunes, & our sacred honour.

THOMAS JEFFERSON AND OTHERS
The Declaration of Independence

In Congress, July 4, 1776

The Unanimous Declaration of The Thirteen United States of America

When in the Course of human events it becomes necessary for one people to dissolve the political bands which have connected them with another, and to assume among the powers of the earth, the separate and equal station to which the Laws of Nature and of Nature's God entitle them, a decent respect to the opinions of mankind requires that they should declare the causes which impel them to the separation.

We hold these truths to be self-evident, that all men are created equal, that they are endowed by their Creator with certain unalienable Rights, that among these are Life, Liberty and the pursuit of Happiness. That to secure these rights, Governments are instituted among Men, deriving their just powers from the consent of the governed. That whenever any Form of Government becomes destructive of these ends, it is the Right of the People to alter or to abolish it, and to institute new Government, laying its foundation on such principles and organizing its powers in such form, as to them shall seem most likely to effect their Safety and Happiness. Prudence, indeed, will dictate that Governments long established should not be changed for light and transient causes; and accordingly all experience hath shewn that mankind are more disposed to suffer, while evils are sufferable, than to right themselves by abolishing the forms to which they are accustomed. But when a long train of abuses and usurpations, pursuing invariably the same Object evinces a design to reduce them under absolute Despotism, it is their right, it is their duty, to throw off such Government, and to provide new Guards for their future security. Such has been the patient sufferance of these Colonies; and such is now the necessity which constrains them to alter their former Systems of Government. The history of the present King of Great Britain is a history of repeated injuries and usurpations, all having in direct object the establishment of an absolute Tyranny over these States. To prove this, let Facts be submitted to a candid world.

He has refused his Assent to Laws, the most wholesome and necessary for the public good.

He has forbidden his Government to pass laws of immediate and pressing importance, unless suspended in their operation till his Assent should be obtained; and when so suspended, he has utterly neglected to attend to them.

He has refused to pass other Laws for the accommodation of large districts of people, unless those people would relinquish the right of Representation in the Legislature, a right inestimable to them and formidable to tyrants only.

He has called together legislative bodies at places unusual, uncomfortable, and distant from the depository of their Public Records, for the sole purpose of fatiguing them into compliance with his measures.

He has dissolved Representative Houses repeatedly, for opposing with manly firmness his invasions on the rights of the people.

He has refused for a long time, after such dissolutions, to cause others to be elected; whereby the Legislative Powers, incapable of Annihilation, have returned to the People at large for their exercise; the State remaining in the mean time exposed to all the dangers of invasion from without, and convulsions within.

He has endeavored to prevent the population of these States; for that purpose obstructing the Laws for Naturalization of Foreigners; refusing to pass others to encourage their migration hither, and raising the conditions of new Appropriations of Lands.

He has obstructed the Administration of Justice, by refusing his Assent to Laws for establishing Judiciary Powers.

He has made Judges dependent on his Will alone, for the tenure of their offices, and the amount and payment of their salaries.

He has erected a multitude of New Offices, and sent hither swarms of Officers to harass our people, and eat out their substance.

He has kept among us, in times of peace, Standing Armies without the Consent of our legislatures.

He has affected to render the Military independent of and superior to the Civil Power.

He has combined with others to subject us to a jurisdiction foreign to our constitution, and unacknowledged by our laws; giving his Assent to their Acts of pretended Legislation: For quartering large bodies of armed troops among us: For protecting them, by a mock Trial, from punishment for any Murders which they should commit on the Inhabitants of these States: For cutting off our Trade with all parts of the world: For imposing Taxes on us without our Consent: For depriving us in many cases, of the benefits of Trial by Jury: For transporting us beyond Seas to be tried for pretended offenses: for abolishing the free System of English Laws in a neighboring Province, establishing therein an Arbitrary government, and enlarging its Boundaries so as to render it at once an example and fit instrument for introducing the same absolute rule into these Colonies: For taking away our Charters, abolishing our most valuable Laws and altering fundamentally the Forms of our Governments: For suspending our own Legislatures, and declaring themselves invested with power to legislate for us in all cases whatsoever.

He has abdicated Government here, by declaring us out of his Protection and waging War against us.

He has plundered our seas, ravaged our Coasts, burnt our towns, and destroyed the lives of our people.

He is at this time transporting large Armies of foreign Mercenaries to complete the works of death, desolation and tyranny, already begun with circumstances of Cruelty & Perfidy scarcely paralleled in the most barbarous ages, and totally unworthy the Head of a civilized nation.

He has constrained our fellow Citizens taken Captive on the high Seas to bear Arms against their Country, to become the executioners of their friends and Brethren, or to fall themselves by their Hands.

He has excited domestic insurrections amongst us, and has endeavored to bring on the inhabitants of our frontiers, the merciless Indian Savages, whose known rule of warfare, is an undistinguished destruction of all ages, sexes, and conditions.

In every stage of these Oppressions We have Petitioned for Redress in the most humble terms: Our repeated Petitions have been answered only by repeated injury. A Prince, whose character is thus marked by every act which may define a Tyrant, is unfit to be the ruler of a free people.

Nor have We been wanting in attention to our British brethren. We have warned them from time to time of attempts by their legislature to extend an unwarrantable jurisdiction over us. We have reminded them of the circumstances of our emigration and settlement here. We have appealed to their native justice and magnanimity, and we have conjured them by the ties of our common kindred to disavow these usurpations, which would inevitably interrupt our connections and correspondence. They too have been deaf to the voice of justice and of consanguinity. We must, therefore, acquiesce in the necessity, which denounces our Separation, and hold them, as we hold the rest of mankind, Enemies in War, in Peace Friends.

We, THEREFORE the Representatives of the UNITED STATES of AMERICA, in General Congress, Assembled, appealing to the Supreme Judge of the world for the rectitude of our intentions, do, in the Name, and by Authority of the good People of these Colonies, solemnly publish and declare, That these United Colonies are, and of Right ought to be FREE AND INDEPENDENT STATES; that they are Absolved from all Allegiance to the British Crown, and that all political connection between them and the State of Great Britain, is and ought to be totally dissolved; and that as Free and Independent States, they have full Power to levy War, conclude Peace, contract Alliances, establish Commerce, and to do all other

Acts and Things which Independent States may of right do. And for the support of this Declaration, with a firm reliance on the protection of Divine Providence, we mutually pledge to each other our Lives, our Fortunes, and our sacred Honor.

POSSIBILITIES OF WRITING

1. Compare the original draft with the final version of the Declaration. What would you point to as the most significant changes made by Jefferson? Do any of these alter the meaning of the document?

2. Focusing on the final version of the Declaration, consider the list of "repeated injuries and usurpations" charged against the King of England (paragraphs 3–21). Explain these, to the extent that you can, in language that is clear for a contemporary audience.

3. The opening sentence of the second paragraph of the Declaration in its final version ("We hold these truths to be self evident. . . .") is perhaps the most famous statement of the fundamental ideals of the United States as a nation. How do you respond to this statement? To what extent do you feel that the country has succeeded in embodying these ideals?

Yoshida Kenko (c1283–1350) *was a Buddhist monk who lived and wrote during the Muromachi and Kamakura periods. He is best known for his* Tsurezuregusa, *usually translated as "Essays in Idleness," but sometimes rendered as "Leisure Notes." Both translated titles testify to the occasional nature of Kenko's little essays. Both suggest the offhanded quality of his writing. His collection of short essays remains one of the most studied of Japanese literary works, and it is still a staple of the Japanese high school curriculum.*

YOSHIDA KENKO

189

In "Essay # 189," Kenko takes up the topic of how unexpected events interfere with our daily plans, how the unexpected alters our schedules and otherwise sabotages our efforts to exercise control over our lives. Kenko addresses his readers, as if he is speaking directly to us across the centuries and the oceans about everyday matters. His casual manner, nonetheless, provokes us to think about the role that uncertainty plays in our lives.

You may intend to do something today, only for pressing business to come up unexpectedly and take up all of your attention the rest of the day. Or a person you have been expecting is prevented from coming, or someone you hadn't expected comes calling. The thing you have counted on goes amiss, and the thing you had no hopes for is the only one to succeed. A matter which promised to be a nuisance passes off smoothly, and a matter which should have been easy proves a great hardship. Our daily experiences bear no resemblance to what we had anticipated. This is true throughout the year, and equally true for our entire lives. But if we decide that everything is bound to go contrary to our anticipations, we discover that naturally there are also some things which do not contradict expectations. This makes it all the harder to be definite about anything. The one thing you can be certain of is the truth that all is uncertainty.

POSSIBILITIES FOR WRITING

1. Summarize in a few sentences what you see as the central idea of Kenko's mini essay. Provide Essay #189 with a title, and explain the significance of Kenko's main point.

2. To what extent do you agree with Kenko about the way things often or almost always go contrary to our expectations? Explain what relevance this has to our lives.
3. Write an essay in which you describe a time when something happened that went contrary to your expectations. Explain what you expected, what actually happened, and why the difference between expectation and reality made a difference—why it mattered for you.

Jamaica Kincaid (b. 1949) grew up on the Caribbean island of Antigua, which was at the time a British colony. After graduating from the British equivalent of high school, she was sent to New York to work as a nanny for a wealthy white couple there and later studied at the New School for Social Research and Franconia College. After a series of odd jobs, she joined the staff of Ingenue magazine and went on to be a regular contributor to the New Yorker, where her writing first came to prominence. Most of her book-length work, whether fiction or nonfiction, is highly autobiographical and often focuses on her childhood and her family in Antigua; among these are Annie John *(1986),* A Small Place *(1988),* Lucy *(1990), and* My Brother *(1997). Among her more recent books are* Mr. Potter *(2002) and* Among Flowers: A walk in the Himalayas *(2005).*

JAMAICA KINCAID

On Seeing England
for the First Time

In "On Seeing England for the First Time," Jamaica Kincaid describes the influence England has had on her all her life, and how she feels and what she feels about it. She contrasts England with Antigua, where she was born and grew up, by describing differences in food and clothing. Although the traditional big English breakfast does not sit well in Antiguans' stomachs, they eat it anyway, as does the young Jamaica Kincaid, because it's what they do in England. And though the wide-brimmed felt hat her father wears out every six weeks is too hot for Antigua, he wears it anyway because it bears the mark of its English manufacturer.

Kincaid builds up her contrast and enlarges on her theme of England's influence, invoking the names of the English kings in a paragraph that peaks powerfully with Kincaid's description of the pace of English life. Accumulating details that contrast the two countries' climates and topographies, she reveals to her readers and to herself just how different her Antiguan world is from that of England, how alien, in fact, England really is to her. And this, even though she has been told all her life how important it is to live and act like the English, largely because as she comes to understand: "The world was theirs not mine; everything told me so."

When I saw England for the first time, I was a child in school sitting at a desk. The England I was looking at was laid out on a map gently, beautifully, delicately, a very special jewel; it lay on a bed of sky blue—the background of the map—its yellow form mysterious, because though it looked like a leg of mutton, it could not really look like anything so familiar as a leg of mutton because it was England—with shadings of pink and green, unlike any shadings of pink and green I had seen before, squiggly veins of red running in every direction. England was a special jewel all right, and only special people got to wear it. The people who got to wear England were English people. They wore it well and they wore it everywhere: in jungles, in deserts, on plains, on top of the highest mountains, on all the oceans, on all the seas, in places where they were not welcome, in places they should not have been. When my teacher had pinned this map up on the blackboard, she said, "This is England"—and she said it with authority, seriousness, and adoration, and we all sat up. It was as if she had said, "This is Jerusalem, the place you will go to when you die but only if you have been good." We understood then—we were meant to understand then—that England was to be our source of myth and the source from which we got our sense of reality, our sense of what was meaningful, our sense of what was meaningless—and much about our own lives and much about the very idea of us headed that last list.

At the time I was a child sitting at my desk seeing England for the first time, I was already very familiar with the greatness of it. Each morning before I left for school, I ate a breakfast of half a grapefruit, an egg, bread and butter and a slice of cheese, and a cup of cocoa; or half a grapefruit, a bowl of oat porridge, bread and butter and a slice of cheese, and a cup of cocoa. The can of cocoa was often left on the table in front of me. It had written on it the name of the company, the year the company was established, and the words "Made in England." Those words, "Made in England," were written on the box the oats came in too. They would also have been written on the box the shoes I was wearing came in; a bolt of gray linen cloth lying on the shelf of a store from which my mother had bought three yards to make the uniform that I was wearing had written along its edge those three words. The shoes I wore were made in England; so were my socks and cotton undergarments and the satin ribbons I wore tied at the end of two plaits of my hair. My father, who might have sat next to me at breakfast, was a carpenter and cabinet maker. The shoes he wore to work would have been made in England, as were his khaki shirt and trousers, his underpants and undershirt, his socks and brown felt hat. Felt was not the proper material from which a hat that was expected to provide shade from the hot sun should be made, but my father must have seen and admired a picture of an Englishman wearing such a hat in England, and this picture that he saw must have been so compelling that it caused him to wear the wrong hat for a hot climate most of his long life. And this hat—a brown felt hat—became so central to his character that it was the first thing he put on in the morning as he stepped out of bed and the last thing he took off before he stepped back into bed at night. As we sat at breakfast a car might go by. The car, a Hillman or a Zephyr, was made in England. The very idea of the meal itself, breakfast, and its substantial quality and quantity was an idea from England; we somehow knew that in England they began the day with this meal called breakfast and a proper breakfast was a big breakfast. No one I knew liked eating so much food so early in the day; it made us feel sleepy, tired. But this breakfast business was Made in England like almost everything else that surrounded us, the exceptions being the sea, the sky, and the air we breathed.

At the time I saw this map—seeing England for the first time—I did not say to myself, "Ah, so that's what it looks like," because there was no longing in me to put a shape to those three words that ran through every part of my life, no matter how small; for me to have had such a longing would have meant that I lived in a certain atmosphere, an atmosphere in which those three words were felt as a burden. But I did not live in such an atmosphere. My father's brown felt hat would develop a hole in its crown, the lining would separate from the hat itself and six weeks before he thought that he could not be seen wearing it—he was a very vain man—he would order another hat from England. And my mother taught me to eat my food in the English way: the knife in the right hand, the fork in the left, my elbows held still close to my side, the food carefully balanced on my fork and then brought up to my mouth. When I had finally mastered it, I overheard her saying to a friend, "Did you see how nicely she can eat?" But I knew then that I enjoyed my food more when I ate it with my bare hands, and I continued to do so when she wasn't looking. And when my teacher showed us the map, she asked us to study it carefully, because no test we would ever take would be complete without this statement: "Draw a map of England."

I did not know then that the statement "Draw a map of England" was something far worse than a declaration of war, for in fact a flat-out declaration of war would have put me on alert, and again in fact, there was no need for war—I had long ago been conquered. I did not know then that this statement was part of a process that would result in my erasure, not my physical erasure, but my erasure all the same. I did not know then that this statement was meant to make me feel in awe and small whenever I heard the word "England": awe at its existence, small because I was not from it. I did not know very much of anything then—certainly not what a blessing it was that I was unable to draw a map of England correctly.

After that there were many times of seeing England for the first time. I saw England in history. I knew the names of all the kings of England. I knew the names of their children, their wives, their disappointments, their triumphs, the names of people who betrayed them; I knew the dates on which they were born and the dates they died. I knew their conquests and was made to feel glad if I figured in them; I knew their defeats. I knew the details of the year 1066 (the Battle of Hastings, the end of the reign of the Anglo-Saxon Kings) before I knew the details of the year 1832 (the year slavery was abolished). It wasn't as bad as I make it sound now; it was worse. I did like so much hearing again and again how Alfred the Great, traveling in disguise, had been left to watch cakes, and because he wasn't used to this the cakes got burned, and Alfred burned his hands pulling them out of the fire, and the woman who had left him to watch the cakes screamed at him. I loved King Alfred. My grandfather was named after him; his son, my uncle, was named after King Alfred; my brother is named after King Alfred. And so there are three people in my family named after a man they have never met, a man who died over ten centuries ago. The first view I got of England then was not unlike the first view received by the person who named my grandfather.

This view, though—the naming of the kings, their deeds, their disappointments—was the vivid view, the forceful view. There were other views, subtler ones, softer, almost not there—but these were the ones that made the most lasting impression on me, these were the ones that made me really feel like nothing. "When morning touched the sky" was one phrase, for no morning touched the sky where I lived. The mornings where I lived came on abruptly, with a shock of heat and loud noises. "Evening approaches" was another, but the evenings where I lived did not approach; in fact, I had no evening—I had night and I had day and they came and went in a mechanical way: on, off; on, off. And then there were gentle mountains and low blue skies and moors over which people took walks for nothing but pleasure, when where I lived a walk was an act of labor, a burden, something only death or the automobile could relieve. And there were things that a small turn of a head could convey—entire worlds, whole lives would depend on this thing, a certain turn of a head. Everyday life could be quite tiring, more tiring than anything I was told not to do. I was told not to gossip, but they did that all the time. And they ate so much food, violating another of those rules they taught me: do not indulge in gluttony. And the foods they ate actually: if only sometime I could eat cold cuts after theater, cold cuts of lamb and mint sauce, and Yorkshire pudding and scones, and clotted cream, and sausages that came from up-country (imagine, "up-country"). And having troubling thoughts at twilight, a good time to have troubling thoughts, apparently; and servants who stole and left in the middle of a crisis, who were born with a limp or some other kind of deformity, not nourished properly in their mother's womb (that last part I figured out for myself; the point was, oh to have an untrustworthy servant); and wonderful cobbled streets onto which solid front doors opened; and people whose eyes were blue and who had fair skins and who smelled only of lavender, or sometimes sweet pea or primrose. And those flowers with those names: delphiniums, foxgloves, tulips, daffodils, floribunda, peonies; in bloom, a striking display, being cut and placed in large glass bowls, crystal, decorating rooms so large twenty families the size of mine could fit in comfortably but used only for passing through. And the weather was so remarkable because the rain fell gently always, only occasionally in deep gusts, and it colored the air various shades of gray, each an appealing shade for a dress to be worn when a portrait was being painted; and when it rained at twilight, wonderful things happened: people bumped into each other unexpectedly and that would lead to all sorts of turns of events—a plot, the mere weather caused plots. I saw that people rushed: they rushed to catch trains, they rushed toward each other and away from each other; they rushed and rushed and rushed. That word: rushed! I did not know what it was to do that. It was too hot to do that, and so I came to envy people who would rush, even though it had no meaning to me to do such a thing. But there they are again. They loved their children; their children were sent to their own rooms as a punishment, rooms larger than my entire house. They were special, everything about them said so, even their clothes; their clothes rustled, swished, soothed. The world was theirs, not mine; everything told me so.

If now as I speak of all this I give the impression of someone on the outside looking in, nose pressed up against a glass window, that is wrong. My nose was pressed up against a glass window all right, but there was an iron vise at the back of my neck forcing my head to stay in place. To avert my gaze was to fall back into something from which I had been rescued, a hole filled with nothing, and that was the word for everything about me, nothing. The reality of my life was conquests, subjugation, humiliation, enforced amnesia. I was forced to forget. Just for instance, this: I lived in a part of St. John's, Antigua, called Ovals. Ovals was made up of five streets, each of them named after a famous

English seaman—to be quite frank, an officially sanctioned criminal: Rodney Street (after George Rodney), Nelson Street (after Horatio Nelson), Drake Street (after Francis Drake), Hood Street, and Hawkins Street (after John Hawkins). But John Hawkins was knighted after a trip he made to Africa, opening up a new trade, the slave trade. He was then entitled to wear as his crest a Negro bound with a cord. Every single person living on Hawkins Street was descended from a slave. John Hawkins's ship, the one in which he transported the people he had bought and kidnapped, was called *The Jesus*. He later became the treasurer of the Royal Navy and rear admiral.

Again, the reality of my life, the life I led at the time I was being shown these views of England for the first time, for the second time, for the one-hundred-millionth time, was this: the sun shone with what sometimes seemed to be a deliberate cruelty; we must have done something to deserve that. My dresses did not rustle in the evening air as I strolled to the theater (I had no evening, I had no theater; my dresses were made of a cheap cotton, the weave of which would give way after not too many washings). I got up in the morning, I did my chores (fetched water from the public pipe for my mother, swept the yard), I washed myself, I went to a woman to have my hair combed freshly every day (because before we were allowed into our classroom our teachers would inspect us, and children who had not bathed that day, or had dirt under their fingernails, or whose hair had not been combed anew that day, might not be allowed to attend class). I ate that breakfast. I walked to school. At school we gathered in an auditorium and sang a hymn, "All Things Bright and Beautiful," and looking down on us as we sang were portraits of the Queen of England and her husband; they wore jewels and medals and they smiled. I was a Brownie. At each meeting we would form a little group around a flagpole, and after raising the Union Jack, we would say, "I promise to do my best, to do my duty to God and the Queen, to help other people every day and obey the scout's law."

Who were these people and why had I never seen them, I mean really seen them, in the place where they lived? I had never been to England. No one I knew had ever been to England, or I should say, no one I knew had ever been and returned to tell me about it. All the people I knew had gone to England had stayed there. Sometimes they left behind them their small children, never to see them again. England! I had seen England's representatives. I had seen the governor general at the public grounds at a ceremony celebrating the Queen's birthday.

I had seen an old princess and I had seen a young princess. They had both been extremely not beautiful, but who of us would have told them that? I had never seen England, really seen it, I had only met a representative, seen a picture, read books, memorized its history. I had never set foot, my own foot, in it.

The space between the idea of something and its reality is always wide and deep and dark. The longer they are kept apart—idea of thing, reality of thing—the wider the width, the deeper the depth, the thicker and darker the darkness. This space starts out empty, there is nothing in it, but it rapidly becomes filled up with obsession or desire or hatred or love—sometimes all of these things, sometimes some of these things, sometimes only one of these things. The existence of the world as I came to know it was a result of this: idea of thing over here, reality of thing way, way over there. There was Christopher Columbus, an unlikable man, an unpleasant man, a liar (and so, of course, a thief) surrounded by maps and schemes and plans, and there was the reality on the other side of that width, that depth, that darkness. He became obsessed, he became filled with desire, the hatred came later, love was never a part of it. Eventually, his idea met the longed for reality. That the idea of something and its reality are often two completely different things is something no one ever remembers; and so when they meet and find that they are not compatible, the weaker of the two, idea or reality, dies. That idea Christopher Columbus had was more powerful than the reality he met, and so the reality he met died.

And so finally, when I was a grown-up woman, the mother of two children, the wife of someone, a person who resides in a powerful country that takes up more than its fair share of a continent, the owner of a house with many rooms in it and of two automobiles, with the desire and will (which I very much act upon) to take from the world more than I give back to it, more than I deserve, more than I need, finally then, I saw England, the real England, not a picture, not a painting, not through a story in a book, but England, for the first time. In me, the space between the idea of it and its reality had become filled with hatred, and so when at last I saw it I wanted to take it into my hands and tear it into little pieces and then crumble it up as if it were clay, child's clay. That was impossible, and so I could only indulge in not-favorable opinions.

There were monuments everywhere; they commemorated victories, battles fought between them and the people who lived across the sea from them, all vile people, fought over which of them would have dominion over the people who looked like me. The monuments were useless to them now, people sat on them and ate their lunch. They were like markers on an old useless trail, like a piece of old string tied to a finger to jog the memory, like old decoration in an old house, dirty, useless, in the way. Their skins were so pale, it made them look so fragile, so weak, so ugly. What if I had the power to simply banish them from their land, send boat after boatload of them on a voyage that in fact had no destination, force them to live in a place where the sun's presence was a constant? This would rid them of their pale complexion and make them look more like me, make them look more like the people I love and treasure and hold dear, and more like the people who occupy the near and far reaches of my imagination, my history, my geography, and reduce them and everything they have ever known to figurines as evidence that I was in divine favor, what if all this was in my power? Could I resist it? No one ever has.

And they were rude, they were rude to each other. They didn't like each other very much. They didn't like each other in the way they didn't like me, and it occurred to me that their dislike for me was one of the few things they agreed on.

I was on a train in England with a friend, an English woman. Before we were in England she liked me very much. In England she didn't like me at all. She didn't like the claim I said I had on England, she didn't like the views I had of England. I didn't like England, she didn't like England, but she didn't like me not liking it too. She said, "I want to show you my England, I want to show you the England that I know and love." I had told her many times before that I knew England and I didn't want to love it anyway. She no longer lived in England; it was her own country, but it had not been kind to her, so she left. On the train, the conductor was rude to her; she asked something, and he responded in a rude way. She became ashamed. She was ashamed at the way he treated her; she was ashamed at the way he behaved. "This is the new England," she said. But I liked the conductor being rude; his behavior seemed quite appropriate. Earlier this had happened: we had gone to a store to buy a shirt for my husband; it was meant to be a special present, a special shirt to wear on special occasions. This was a store where the Prince of Wales has his shirts made, but the shirts sold in this store are beautiful all the same. I found a shirt I thought my husband would like and I wanted to buy him a tie to go with it. When I couldn't decide which one to choose, the salesman showed me a new set. He was very pleased with these, he said, because they bore the crest of the Prince of Wales, and the Prince of Wales had never allowed his crest to decorate an article of clothing before. There was something in the way he said it; his tone was slavish, reverential, awed. It made me feel angry; I wanted to hit him. I didn't do that. I said, my husband and I hate princes, my husband would never wear anything that had a prince's anything on it. My friend stiffened. The salesman stiffened. They both drew themselves in, away from me. My friend told me that the prince was a symbol of her Englishness, and I could see that I had caused offense. I looked at her. She was an English person, the sort of English person I used to know at home, the sort who was nobody in England but somebody when they came to live among the people like me. There were many people I could have seen England with; that I was seeing it with this particular person, a person who reminded me of the people who showed me England long ago as I sat in church or at my desk, made me feel silent and afraid, for I wondered if, all these years of our friendship, I had had a friend or had been in the thrall of a racial memory.

I went to Bath—we, my friend and I, did this, but though we were together, I was no longer with her. The landscape was almost as familiar as my own hand, but I had never been in this place before, so how could that be again? And the streets of Bath were familiar, too, but I had never walked on them before. It was all those years of reading, starting with Roman Britain. Why did I have to know about Roman Britain? It was of no real use to me, a person living on a hot, drought-ridden island, and it is of on use to me now, and yet my head is filled with this nonsense, Roman Britain. In Bath, I drank tea in a room I had read about in a novel written in the eighteenth century. In this very same room, young women wearing those dresses that rustled and so on danced and flirted and sometimes disgraced themselves with young men, soldiers, sailors, who were on their way to Bristol or someplace like that, so many places like that where so many adventures, the outcome of which was not good for me, began. Bristol, England. A sentence that began "That night the ship sailed from Bristol, England" would end not so good for me. And then I was driving through the countryside in an England motorcar, on narrow winding roads, and they were so familiar, through I had never been on them before; and through little villages the names of which I somehow knew so well though I had never been there before. And the countryside did have all those hedges and hedges, fields hedged in. I was marveling at all the toil of it, the planting of the hedges to begin with and then the care of it, all that clipping, year after year of clipping, and I wondered at the lives of the people who would have to do this, because wherever I see and feel the hands that hold up the world, I see and feel myself and all the people who look like me. And I said, "Those hedges" and my friend said that someone, a woman named Mrs. Rothchild, worried that the hedges weren't being taken care of properly; the farmers couldn't afford or find the help to keep up the hedges, and often they replaced them with wire fencing. I might have said to that, well if Mrs. Rothchild doesn't like the wire fencing, why doesn't she take care of the hedges herself, but I didn't. And then in those fields that were now hemmed in by wire fencing that a privileged woman didn't like was planted a vile yellow flowering bush that produced an oil, and my friend said that Mrs. Rothchild didn't like this either; it ruined the English countryside, it ruined the traditional look of the English countryside.

It was not at that moment that I wished every sentence, everything I knew, that began with England would end with "and then it all died; we don't know how, it just all died." At that moment, I was thinking, who are these people who forced me to think of them all the time, who forced me to think that the world I knew was incomplete, or without substance, or did not measure up because it was not England; that I was incomplete, or without substance, and did not measure up because I was not English. Who were these people? The person sitting next to me couldn't give me a clue; no one person could. In any case, if I had said to her, I find England ugly, I hate England; the weather is like a jail sentence, the English are a very ugly people, the food in England is like a jail sentence, the hair of English people is so straight, so dead looking, the English have an unbearable smell so different from the smell of people I know, real people of course, she would have said that I was a person full of prejudice. Apart from the fact that it is I—that is, the people who look like me—who made her aware of the unpleasantness of such a thing, the idea of such a thing, prejudice, she would have been only partly right, sort of right: I may be capable of prejudice, but my prejudices have no weight to them, my prejudices have no force behind them, my prejudices remain opinions, my prejudices remain my personal opinion. And a great feeling of rage and disappointment came over me as I looked at England, my head full of personal opinions that could not have public, my public, approval. The people I come from are powerless to do evil on grand scale.

The moment I wished every sentence, everything I knew, that began with England would end with "and then it all died, we don't know how, it just all died" was when I saw the white cliffs of Dover. I had sung hymns and recited poems that were about a longing to see the white cliffs of Dover again. At the time I sang the hymns and recited the poems, I could really long to see them again because I had never seen them at all, nor had anyone around me at the time. But there we were, groups of people longing for something we had never seen. And so there they were, the white cliffs, but they were not that pearly majestic thing I used to sing about, that thing that created such a feeling in these people that when they died in the place where I lived they had themselves buried facing a direction that would allow them to see the white cliffs of Dover when they were resurrected, as surely they would be. The white cliffs of Dover, when finally I saw them, were cliffs, but they were not white; you would only call them that if the word "white" meant something special to you; they were dirty and they were steep; they were so steep, the correct height from which all my views of England, starting with the map before me in my classroom and ending with the trip I had just taken, should jump and die and disappear forever.

POSSIBILITIES FOR WRITING

1. Why is Kincaid's view of England and the English so negative? Why does she claim that growing up surrounded by English culture on Antigua made her feel like "nothing"? In her next to last paragraph, she argues that, despite her hatred for England, she cannot accurately be accused of prejudice. Do you agree?

2. Throughout the essay, Kincaid presents concrete objects as having a larger symbolic significance—her father's felt hat, to name one of many examples. Find as many of these as you can; then, choose several that you think are particularly important to analyze in detail. What does this technique contribute to the overall meaning of the essay?

3. Kincaid writes that "the idea of something and its reality are often two completely different things . . . and so when they meet and find that they are not compatible, the weaker of the two, idea or reality, dies." Can you recall instances in your own life when your idea of something collided with its reality? In an essay explore the validity of Kincaid's statement.

Martin Luther King, Jr. (1929–1968), the most revered leader of the civil rights movement, was born in Atlanta, the son of a Baptist clergyman. A graduate of Morehouse College and Boston University, King was himself ordained in 1947 and became the minister at a church in Montgomery, Alabama, in 1954. There he spearheaded a year-long boycott of segregated city buses, which eventually resulted in the system's integration, and as head of the Southern Christian Leadership Conference, he took his crusade against segregation to other Southern cities. Noted for his commitment to peaceful demonstration and nonviolent resistance, King and those who protested with him often ended up in jail. An international figure by the 1960s, he was awarded a Nobel Peace Prize in 1964. King was assassinated in 1968 in Memphis, Tennessee.

MARTIN LUTHER KING, JR.

Letter from Birmingham Jail

King's "Letter" is a response to criticism made against his effort to use peaceful, nonviolent demonstrations as forms of public disruption to advance the cause of racial integration. King addresses his letter to an audience of clergymen, whom he assures from the start that he respects their sincerity and good will in presenting their criticism. But he quickly seizes the moral ground by explaining why he came to Birmingham, linking himself with the biblical prophets, who preached against social injustice. Developing his argument carefully, King answers their actual questions and anticipates their additional potential questions.

King takes up complex issues, including whether it is right to break a law to achieve a desired end, citing a roster of Christian and Jewish theologians and quoting the Roman Catholic theologian St. Augustine, who wrote that "an unjust law is no law at all." He also cites examples of revolutionary thinkers whose ideas and example changed history—from Socrates and Martin Luther to Thoreau and Mahatma Gandhi, whose civil disobedience in the form of nonviolent protest was politically effective.

My Dear Fellow Clergymen:

While confined here in the Birmingham city jail, I came across your recent statement calling my present activities "unwise and untimely." Seldom do I pause to answer criticism of my work and ideas. If I sought to answer all the criticisms that cross my desk, my secretaries would have little time for anything other than such correspondence in the course of the day, and I would have no time for constructive work. But since I feel that you are men of genuine good will and that your criticisms are sincerely set forth, I want to try to answer your statement in what I hope will be patient and reasonable terms.

I think I should indicate why I am here in Birmingham, since you have been influenced by the view which argues against "outsiders coming in." I have the honor of serving as president of the Southern Christian Leadership Conference, an organization operating in every southern state, with headquarters in Atlanta, Georgia. We have some eighty-five affiliated organizations across the South, and one of them is the Alabama Christian Movement for Human Rights. Frequently we share staff, educational, and financial resources with our affiliates. Several months ago the affiliate here in Birmingham asked us to be on call to engage in a nonviolent direct-action program if such were deemed necessary. We readily consented, and when the hour came we lived up to our promise. So I, along with several members of my staff, am here because I was invited here. I am here because I have organizational ties here.

But more basically, I am in Birmingham because injustice is here. Just as the prophets of the eighth century B.C. left their villages and carried their "thus saith the Lord" far beyond the boundaries of their home towns, and just as the Apostle Paul left his village of Tarsus and carried the gospel of Jesus Christ to the far corners of the Greco-Roman world, so am I compelled to carry the gospel of freedom beyond my own home town. Like Paul, I must constantly respond to the Macedonian call for aid.

Moreover, I am cognizant of the interrelatedness of all communities and states. I cannot sit idly by in Atlanta and not be concerned about what happens in Birmingham. Injustice anywhere is a threat to justice everywhere. We are caught in an inescapable network of mutuality, tied in a single garment of destiny. Whatever affects one directly, affects all indirectly. Never again can we afford to live with the narrow, provincial "outside agitator" idea. Anyone who lives inside the United States can never be considered an outsider anywhere within its bounds.

You deplore the demonstrations taking place in Birmingham. But your statement, I am sorry to say, fails to express a similar concern for the conditions that brought about the demonstrations. I am sure that none of you would want to rest content with the superficial kind of social analysis that deals merely with effects and does not grapple with underlying causes. It is unfortunate that demonstrations are taking place in Birmingham, but it is even more unfortunate that the city's white power structure left the Negro community with no alternative.

In any nonviolent campaign there are four basic steps: collection of the facts to determine whether injustices exist; negotiation;

self-purification; and direct action. We have gone through all these steps in Birmingham. There can be no gainsaying the fact that racial injustice engulfs this community. Birmingham is probably the most thoroughly segregated city in the United States. Its ugly record of brutality is widely known. Negroes have experienced grossly unjust treatment in the courts. There have been more unsolved bombings of Negro homes and churches in Birmingham than in any other city in the nation. These are the hard, brutal facts of the case. On the basis of these conditions, Negro leaders sought to negotiate with the city fathers. But the latter consistently refused to engage in good-faith negotiation.

Then, last September, came the opportunity to talk with leaders of Birmingham's economic community. In the course of the negotiations, certain promises were made by the merchants—for example, to remove the stores' humiliating racial signs. On the basis of these promises, the Reverend Fred Shuttlesworth and the leaders of the Alabama Christian Movement for Human Rights agreed to a moratorium on all demonstrations. As the weeks and months went by, we realized that we were the victims of a broken promise. A few signs, briefly removed, returned; the others remained.

As in so many past experiences, our hopes had been blasted, and the shadow of deep disappointment settled upon us. We had no alternative except to prepare for direct action, whereby we would present our very bodies as a means of laying our case before the conscience of the local and the national community. Mindful of the difficulties involved, we decided to undertake a process of self-purification. We began a series of workshops on nonviolence, and we repeatedly asked ourselves: "Are you able to accept blows without retaliating?" "Are you able to endure the ordeal of jail?" We decided to schedule our direct-action program for the Easter season, realizing that except for Christmas, this is the main shopping period of the year. Knowing that a strong economic-withdrawal program would be the by-product of direct action, we felt that this would be the best time to bring pressure to bear on the merchants for the needed change.

Then it occurred to us that Birmingham's mayoral election was coming up in March, and we speedily decided to postpone action until after election day. When we discovered that the Commissioner of Public Safety, Eugene "Bull" Connor, had piled up enough votes to be in the run-off, we decided again to postpone action until the day after the run-off so that the demonstrations could not be used to cloud the issues. Like many others, we wanted to see Mr. Connor defeated, and to this end we endured postponement after postponement. Having aided in this community need, we felt that our direct-action program could be delayed no longer.

You may well ask, "Why direct action? Why sit-ins, marches, and so forth? Isn't negotiation a better path?" You are quite right in calling for negotiation. Indeed, this is the very purpose of direct action. Nonviolent direct action seeks to create such a crisis and foster such a tension that a community which has constantly refused to negotiate is forced to confront the issue. It seeks so to dramatize the issue that it can no longer be ignored. My citing the creation of tension as part of the work of the nonviolent resister may sound rather shocking. But I must confess that I am not afraid of the word "tension." I have earnestly opposed violent tension, but there is a type of constructive, nonviolent tension which is necessary for growth. Just as Socrates felt that it was necessary to create a tension in the mind so that individuals could rise from the bondage of myths and half-truths to the unfettered realm of creative analysis and objective appraisal, so must we see the need for nonviolent gadflies to create the kind of tension in society that will help men rise from the dark depths of prejudice and racism to the majestic heights of understanding and brotherhood.

The purpose of our direct-action program is to create a situation so crisis-packed that it will inevitably open the door to negotiation. I therefore concur with you in your call for negotiation. Too long has our beloved Southland been bogged down in a tragic effort to live in monologue rather than dialogue.

One of the basic points in your statement is that the action that I and my associates have taken in Birmingham is untimely. Some have asked: "Why didn't you give the new city administration time to act?" The only answer that I can give to this query is that the new Birmingham administration must be prodded about as much as the outgoing one, before it will act. We are sadly mistaken if we feel that the election of Albert Boutwell as mayor will bring the millennium to Birmingham. While Mr. Boutwell is a much more gentle person than Mr. Connor, they are both segregationists, dedicated to maintenance of the status quo. I have hoped that Mr. Boutwell will be reasonable enough to see the futility of massive resistance to desegregation. But he will not see this without pressure from devotees of civil rights. My friends, I must say to you that we have not made a single gain in civil rights without determined legal and nonviolent pressure. Lamentably, it is an historical fact that privileged groups seldom give up their privileges voluntarily. Individuals may see the moral light and voluntarily give up their unjust posture, but, as Reinhold Niebuhr has reminded us, groups tend to be more immoral than individuals.

We know through painful experience that freedom is never voluntarily given by the oppressor; it must be demanded by the oppressed. Frankly, I have yet to engage in a direct-action campaign that was "well timed" in the view of those who have not suffered unduly from the disease of segregation. For years now I have heard the word "Wait!" It rings in the ear of every Negro with piercing familiarity. This "Wait" has almost always meant "Never." We must come to see, with one of our distinguished jurists, that "justice too long delayed is justice denied."

We have waited for more than 340 years for our constitutional and God-given rights. The nations of Asia and Africa are moving with jet-like speed toward gaining political independence, but we still creep at horse-and-buggy pace toward gaining a cup of coffee at a lunch counter. Perhaps it is easy for those who have never felt the stinging darts of segregation to say, "Wait." But when you have seen vicious mobs lynch your mothers and fathers at will and drown your sisters and brothers at whim; when you have seen hate-filled policemen curse, kick, and even kill your black brothers and sisters; when you see the vast majority of your twenty million Negro brothers smothering in an airtight cage of poverty in the midst of an affluent society; when you suddenly find your tongue twisted and your speech stammering as you seek to explain to your six-year-old daughter why she can't go to the public amusement park that has just been advertised on television, and see tears welling up in her eyes when she is told that Funtown is closed to colored children, and see ominous clouds of inferiority beginning to form in her little mental sky, and see her beginning to distort her personality by developing an unconscious bitterness toward white people; when you have to concoct an answer for a five-year-old son who is asking, "Daddy, why do white people treat colored people so mean?"; when you take a cross-country drive and find it necessary to sleep night after night in the uncomfortable corners of your automobile because no motel will accept you; when you are humiliated day in and day out by nagging signs reading "white" and "colored"; when your first name becomes "nigger," your middle name becomes "boy" (however old you are) and your last name becomes "John," and your wife and mother are never given the respected title "Mrs."; when you are harried by day and haunted by night by the fact that you are a

Negro, living constantly at tiptoe stance, never quite knowing what to expect next, and are plagued with inner fears and outer resentments; when you are forever fighting a degenerating sense of "nobodiness"— then you will understand why we find it difficult to wait. There comes a time when the cup of endurance runs over, and men are no longer willing to be plunged into the abyss of despair. I hope, sirs, you can understand our legitimate and unavoidable impatience.

You express a great deal of anxiety over our willingness to break laws. This is certainly a legitimate concern. Since we so diligently urge people to obey the Supreme Court's decision of 1954 outlawing segregation in the public schools, at first glance it may seem rather paradoxical for us consciously to break laws. One may well ask: "How can you advocate breaking some laws and obeying others?" The answer lies in the fact that there are two types of laws: just and unjust. I would be the first to advocate obeying just laws. One has not only a legal but a moral responsibility to obey just laws. Conversely, one has a moral responsibility to disobey unjust laws. I would agree with St. Augustine that "an unjust law is no law at all."

Now, what is the difference between the two? How does one determine whether a law is just or unjust? A just law is a man-made code that squares with the moral law or the law of God. An unjust law is a code that is out of harmony with the moral law. To put it in the terms of St. Thomas Aquinas: An unjust law is a human law that is not rooted in eternal law and natural law. Any law that uplifts human personality is just. Any law that degrades human personality is unjust. All segregation statutes are unjust because segregation distorts the soul and damages the personality. It gives the segregator a false sense of superiority and the segregated a false sense of inferiority. Segregation, to use the terminology of the Jewish philosopher Martin Buber, substitutes an "I-it" relationship for an "I-thou" relationship and ends up relegating persons to the status of things. Hence segregation is not only politically, economically, and sociologically unsound, it is morally wrong and sinful. Paul Tillich has said that sin is separation. Is not segregation an existential expression of man's tragic separation, his awful estrangement, his terrible sinfulness? Thus it is that I can urge men to obey the 1954 decision of the Supreme Court, for it is morally right; and I can urge them to disobey segregation ordinances, for they are morally wrong.

Let us consider a more concrete example of just and unjust laws. An unjust law is a code that a numerical or power majority group compels a minority group to obey but does not make binding on itself. This is *difference* made legal. By the same token, a just law is a code that a majority compels a minority to follow and that it is willing to follow itself. This is *sameness* made legal.

Let me give another explanation. A law is unjust if it is inflicted on a minority that, as a result of being denied the right to vote, had no part in enacting or devising the law. Who can say that the legislature of Alabama which set up that state's segregation laws was democratically elected? Throughout Alabama all sorts of devious methods are used to prevent Negroes from becoming registered voters, and there are some counties in which, even though Negroes constitute a majority of the population, not a single Negro is registered. Can any law enacted under such circumstances be considered democratically structured?

Sometimes a law is just on its face and unjust in its application. For instance, I have been arrested on a charge of parading without a permit. Now, there is nothing wrong in having an ordinance which requires a permit for a parade. But such an ordinance becomes unjust when it is used to maintain segregation and to deny citizens the First-Amendment privilege of peaceful assembly and protest.

I hope you are able to see the distinction I am trying to point out. In no sense do I advocate evading or defying the law, as would the rabid segregationist. That would lead to anarchy. One who breaks an unjust law must do so openly, lovingly, and with a willingness to accept the penalty. I submit that an individual who breaks a law that conscience tells him is unjust, and who willingly accepts the penalty of imprisonment in order to arouse the conscience of the community over its injustice, is in reality expressing the highest respect for law.

Of course, there is nothing new about this kind of civil disobedience. It was evidenced sublimely in the refusal of Shadrach, Meshach, and Abednego to obey the laws of Nebuchadnezzar, on the ground that a higher moral law was at stake. It was practiced superbly by the early Christians, who were willing to face hungry lions and the excruciating pain of chopping blocks rather than submit to certain unjust laws of the Roman Empire. To a degree, academic freedom is a reality today because Socrates practiced civil disobedience. In our own nation, the Boston Tea Party represented a massive act of civil disobedience.

We should never forget that everything Adolf Hitler did in Germany was "legal" and everything the Hungarian freedom fighters did in Hungary was "illegal." It was "illegal" to aid and comfort a Jew in Hitler's Germany. Even so, I am sure that, had I lived in Germany at the time,

I would have aided and comforted my Jewish brothers. If today I lived in a Communist country where certain principles dear to the Christian faith are suppressed, I would openly advocate disobeying that country's anti-religious laws.

I must make two honest confessions to you, my Christian and Jewish brothers. First, I must confess that over the past few years I have been gravely disappointed with the white moderate. I have almost reached the regrettable conclusion that the Negro's great stumbling block in his stride toward freedom is not the White Citizen's Counciler or the Ku Klux Klanner, but the white moderate, who is more devoted to "order" than to justice; who prefers a negative peace which is the absence of tension to a positive peace which is the presence of justice; who constantly says, "I agree with you in the goal you seek, but I cannot agree with your methods of direct action"; who paternalistically believes he can set the timetable for another man's freedom; who lives by a mythical concept of time and who constantly advises the Negro to wait for a "more convenient season." Shallow understanding from people of good will is more frustrating than absolute misunderstanding from people of ill will. Lukewarm acceptance is much more bewildering than outright rejection.

I had hoped that the white moderate would understand that law and order exist for the purpose of establishing justice and that when they fail in this purpose they become the dangerously structured dams that block the flow of social progress. I had hoped that the white moderate would understand that the present tension in the South is a necessary phase of the transition from an obnoxious negative peace, in which the Negro passively accepted his unjust plight, to a substantive and positive peace, in which all men will respect the dignity and worth of human personality. Actually, we who engage in nonviolent direct action are not the creators of tension. We merely bring to the surface the hidden tension that is already alive. We bring it out in the open, where it can be seen and dealt with. Like a boil that can never be cured so long as it is covered up but must be opened with all its ugliness to the natural medicines of air and light, injustice must be exposed, with all the tension its exposure creates, to the light of human conscience and the air of national opinion, before it can be cured.

In your statement you assert that our actions, even though peaceful, must be condemned because they precipitate violence. But is this a logical assertion? Isn't this like condemning a robbed man because his possession of money precipitated the evil act of robbery? Isn't this like condemning Socrates because his unswerving commitment to truth and his philosophical inquiries precipitated the act by the misguided populace in which they made him drink hemlock? Isn't this like condemning Jesus because his unique God-consciousness and never-ceasing devotion to God's will precipitated the evil act of crucifixion? We must come to see that, as the federal courts have consistently affirmed, it is wrong to urge an individual to cease his efforts to gain his basic constitutional rights because the quest may precipitate violence. Society must protect the robbed and punish the robber.

I had also hoped that the white moderate would reject the myth concerning time in relation to the struggle for freedom. I have just received a letter from a white brother in Texas. He writes: "All Christians know that the colored people will receive equal rights eventually, but it is possible that you are in too great a religious hurry. It has taken Christianity almost two thousand years to accomplish what it has. The teachings of Christ take time to come to earth." Such an attitude stems from a tragic misconception of time, from the strangely irrational notion that there is something in the very flow of time that will inevitably cure all ills. Actually, time itself is neutral; it can be used either destructively or constructively. More and more I feel that the people of ill will have used time much more effectively than have the people of good will. We will have to repent in this generation not merely for the hateful words and actions of the bad people, but for the appalling silence of the good people. Human progress never rolls in on wheels of inevitability; it comes through the tireless efforts of men willing to be co-workers with God, and without this hard work, time itself becomes an ally of the forces of social stagnation. We must use time creatively, in the knowledge that the time is always ripe to do right. Now is the time to make real the promise of democracy and transform our pending national elegy into a creative psalm of brotherhood. Now is the time to lift our national policy from the quicksand of racial injustice to the solid rock of human dignity.

You speak of our activity in Birmingham as extreme. At first I was rather disappointed that fellow clergymen would see my nonviolent efforts as those of an extremist. I began thinking about the fact that I stand in the middle of two opposing forces in the Negro community. One is a force of complacency, made up in part of Negroes who, as a result of long years of oppression, are so drained of self-respect and a sense of "somebodiness" that they have adjusted to segregation; and in part of a few middle-class Negroes who, because of a degree of academic and economic security and because in some ways they profit by segregation, have become insensitive to the problems of the masses. The other force is one of bitterness and hatred, and it comes perilously close to advocating violence. It is expressed in the various black nationalist groups that are springing up across the nation, the largest and best-known being Elijah Muhammad's Muslim movement. Nourished by the Negro's frustration over the continued existence of racial discrimination, this movement is made up of people who have lost faith in America, who have absolutely repudiated Christianity, and who have concluded that the white man is an incorrigible "devil."

I have tried to stand between these two forces, saying that we need emulate neither the "do-nothingism" of the complacent nor the hatred and despair of the black nationalist. For there is the more excellent way of love and nonviolent protest. I am grateful to God that, through the influence of the Negro church, the way of nonviolence became an integral part of our struggle.

If this philosophy had not emerged, by now many streets of the South would, I am convinced, be flowing with blood. And I am further convinced that if our white brothers dismiss as "rabblerousers" and "outside agitators" those of us who employ nonviolent direct action, and if they refuse to support our nonviolent efforts, millions of Negroes will, out of frustration and despair, seek solace and security in black-nationalist ideologies—a development that would inevitably lead to a frightening racial nightmare.

Oppressed people cannot remain oppressed forever. The yearning for freedom eventually manifests itself, and that is what has happened to the American Negro. Something within has reminded him of his birthright of freedom, and something without has reminded him that it can be gained. Consciously or unconsciously, he has been caught up by the *Zeitgeist,* and with his black brothers of Africa and his brown and yellow brothers of Asia, South America, and the Caribbean, the United States Negro is moving with a sense of great urgency toward the promised land of racial justice. If one recognizes this vital urge that has engulfed the Negro community, one should readily understand why public demonstrations are taking place. The Negro has many pent-up resentments and latent frustrations, and he must release them. So let him march; let him make prayer pilgrimages to the city hall; let him go on freedom rides—and try to understand why he must do so. If his repressed emotions are not released in nonviolent ways, they will seek expression through violence; this is not a threat but a fact of history. So I have not said to my people, "Get rid of your discontent." Rather, I have tried to say that this normal and healthy discontent can be channeled into the creative outlet of nonviolent direct action. And now this approach is being termed extremist.

But though I was initially disappointed at being categorized as an extremist, as I continued to think about the matter I gradually gained a measure of satisfaction from the label. Was not Jesus an extremist for love: "Love your enemies, bless them that curse you, do good to them that hate you, and pray for them which despitefully use you, and persecute you." Was not Amos an extremist for justice: "Let justice roll down like waters and righteousness like an ever-flowing stream." Was not Paul an extremist for the Christian gospel: "I bear in my body the marks of the Lord Jesus." Was not Martin Luther an extremist: "Here I stand; I cannot do otherwise, so help me God." And John Bunyan: "I will stay in jail to the end of my days before I make a butchery of my conscience." And Abraham Lincoln: "This nation cannot survive half slave and half free." And Thomas Jefferson: "We hold these truths to be self-evident, that all men are created equal. . . ." So the question is not whether we will be extremists, but what kind of extremists we will be. Will we be extremists for hate or for love? Will we be extremists for the preservation of injustice or for the extension of justice? In that dramatic scene on Calvary's hill three men were crucified. We must never forget that all three were crucified for the same crime—the crime of extremism. Two were extremists for immorality, and thus fell below their environment. The other, Jesus Christ, was an extremist for love, truth, and goodness, and thereby rose above his environment. Perhaps the South, the nation, and the world are in dire need of creative extremists.

I had hoped that the white moderate would see this need. Perhaps I was too optimistic; perhaps I expected too much. I suppose I should have realized that few members of the oppressor race can understand the deep groans and passionate yearnings of the oppressed race, and still fewer have the vision to see that injustice must be rooted out by strong, persistent, and determined action. I am thankful, however, that some of our white brothers in the South have grasped the meaning of this social revolution and committed themselves to it. They are still all too few in quantity, but they are big in quality. Some—such as Ralph McGill, Lillian Smith, Harry Golden, James McBride Dabbs, Ann Braden, and Sarah Patton Boyle—have written about our struggle in eloquent and prophetic terms. Others have marched with us down nameless streets of the South. They have languished in filthy, roach-infested jails, suffering the abuse and brutality of policemen who view them as "dirty nigger-lovers." Unlike so many of their moderate brothers and sisters, they have recognized the urgency of the moment and sensed the need for powerful "action" antidotes to combat the disease of segregation.

Let me take note of my other major disappointment. I have been so greatly disappointed with the white church and its leadership. Of course, there are some notable exceptions. I am not unmindful of the fact that each of you has taken some significant stands on this issue. I commend you, Reverend Stallings, for your Christian stand on this past Sunday, in welcoming Negroes to your worship service on a nonsegregated basis. I commend the Catholic leaders of this state for integrating Spring Hill College several years ago.

But despite these notable exceptions, I must honestly reiterate that I have been disappointed with the church. I do not say this as one of those negative critics who can always find something wrong with the church. I say this as a minister of the gospel, who loves the church; who was nurtured in its bosom; who has been sustained by its spiritual blessings and who will remain true to it as long as the cord of life shall lengthen.

When I was suddenly catapulted into the leadership of the bus protest in Montgomery, Alabama, a few years ago, I felt we would be supported by the white church. I felt that the white ministers, priests, and rabbis of the South would be among our strongest allies. Instead, some have been outright opponents, refusing to understand the freedom movement and misrepresenting its leaders; all too many others have been more cautious than courageous and have remained silent behind the anesthetizing security of stainedglass windows.

In spite of my shattered dreams, I came to Birmingham with the hope that the white religious leadership of this community would see the justice of our cause and, with deep moral concern, would serve as the channel through which our just grievances could reach the power structure. I had hoped that each of you would understand. But again I have been disappointed.

I have heard numerous southern religious leaders admonish their worshipers to comply with a desegregation decision because it is the law, but I have longed to hear white ministers declare: "Follow this decree because integration is morally right and because the Negro is your brother." In the midst of blatant injustices inflicted upon the

Negro, I have watched white churchmen stand on the sideline and mouth pious irrelevancies and sanctimonious trivialities. In the midst of a mighty struggle to rid our nation of racial and economic injustice, I have heard many ministers say: "Those are social issues, with which the gospel has no real concern." And I have watched many churches commit themselves to a completely otherworldly religion which makes a strange, un-Biblical distinction between body and soul, between the sacred and the secular.

I have traveled the length and breadth of Alabama, Mississippi, and all the other southern states. On sweltering summer days and crisp autumn mornings I have looked at the South's beautiful churches with their lofty spires pointing heavenward. I have beheld the impressive outlines of her massive religious-education buildings. Over and over I have found myself asking: "What kind of people worship here? Who is their God? Where were their voices when the lips of Governor Barnett dripped with words of interposition and nullification? Where were they when Governor Wallace gave a clarion call for defiance and hatred? Where were their voices of support when bruised and weary Negro men and women decided to rise from the dark dungeons of complacency to the bright hills of creative protest?"

Yes, these questions are still in my mind. In deep disappointment I have wept over the laxity of the church. But be assured that my tears have been tears of love. There can be no deep disappointment where there is not deep love. Yes, I love the church. How could I do otherwise? I am in the rather unique position of being the son, the grandson, and the great-grandson of preachers. Yes, I see the church as the body of Christ. But, oh! How we have blemished and scarred that body through social neglect and through fear of being nonconformists.

There was a time when the church was very powerful—in the time when the early Christians rejoiced at being deemed worthy to suffer for what they believed. In those days the church was not merely a thermometer that recorded the ideas and principles of popular opinion; it was a thermostat that transformed the mores of society. Whenever the early Christians entered a town, the people in power became disturbed and immediately sought to convict the Christians for being "disturbers of the peace" and "outside agitators." But the Christians pressed on, in the conviction that they were "a colony of heaven," called to obey God rather than man. Small in number, they were big in commitment. They were too God-intoxicated to be "astronomically intimidated." By their effort and example they brought an end to such ancient evils as infanticide and gladiatorial contests.

Things are different now. So often the contemporary church is a weak, ineffectual voice with an uncertain sound. So often it is an archdefender of the status quo. Far from being disturbed by the presence of the church, the power structure of the average community is consoled by the church's silent—and often even vocal—sanction of things as they are.

But the judgment of God is upon the church as never before. If today's church does not recapture the sacrificial spirit of the early church, it will lose its authenticity, forfeit the loyalty of millions, and be dismissed as an irrelevant social club with no meaning for the twentieth century. Every day I meet young people whose disappointment with the church has turned into outright disgust.

Perhaps I have once again been too optimistic. Is organized religion too inextricably bound to the status quo to save our nation and the world? Perhaps I must turn my faith to the inner spiritual church, the church within the church, as the true *ekklesia* and the hope of the world. But again I am thankful to God that some noble souls from the ranks of organized religion have broken loose from the paralyzing chains of conformity and joined us as active partners in the struggle for freedom. They have left their secure congregations and walked the streets of Albany, Georgia, with us. They have gone down the highways of the South on tortuous rides for freedom. Yes, they have gone to jail with us. Some have been dismissed from their churches, have lost the support of their bishops and fellow ministers. But they have acted in the faith that right defeated is stronger than evil triumphant. Their witness has been the spiritual salt that has preserved the true meaning of the gospel in these troubled times. They have carved a tunnel of hope through the dark mountain of disappointment.

I hope the church as a whole will meet the challenge of this decisive hour. But even if the church does not come to the aid of justice, I have no despair about the future. I have no fear about the outcome of our struggle in Birmingham, even if our motives are at present misunderstood. We will reach the goal of freedom in Birmingham and all over the nation, because the goal of America is freedom. Abused and scorned though we may be, our destiny is tied up with America's destiny. Before the pilgrims landed at Plymouth, we were here. Before the pen of Jefferson etched the majestic words of the Declaration of Independence across the pages of history, we were here. For more than two centuries our forebears labored in this country without wages: they made cotton king; they built the homes of their masters while suffering gross injustice and shameful humiliation—and yet out of a bottomless vitality they continued to thrive and develop. If the inexpressible cruelties of slavery could not stop us, the opposition we now face will surely fail. We will win our freedom because the sacred heritage of our nation and the eternal will of God are embodied in our echoing demands.

Before closing I feel impelled to mention one other point in your statement that has troubled me profoundly. You warmly commended the Birmingham police force for keeping "order" and "preventing violence." I doubt that you would have so warmly commended the police force if you had seen its dogs sinking their teeth into unarmed, nonviolent Negroes. I doubt that you would so quickly commend the policemen if you were to observe their ugly and inhumane treatment of Negroes here in the city jail; if you were to watch them push and curse old Negro women and young Negro girls; if you were to see them slap and kick old Negro men and young boys; if you were to observe them, as they did on two occasions, refuse to give us food because we wanted to sing our grace together. I cannot join you in your praise of the Birmingham police department.

It is true that the police have exercised a degree of discipline in handling the demonstrators. In this sense they have conducted themselves rather "nonviolently" in public. But for what purpose? To preserve the evil system of segregation. Over the past few years I have consistently preached that nonviolence demands that the means we use must be as pure as the ends we seek. I have tried to make clear that it is wrong to use immoral means to attain moral ends. But now I must affirm that it is just as wrong, or perhaps even more so, to use moral means to preserve immoral ends. Perhaps Mr. Connor and his policemen have been rather nonviolent in public, as was Chief Pritchett in Albany, Georgia, but they have used the moral means of nonviolence to maintain the immoral end of racial injustice. As T. S. Eliot has said. "The last temptation is the greatest treason: To do the right deed for the wrong reason."

I wish you had commended the Negro sit-inners and demonstrators of Birmingham for their sublime courage, their willingness to suffer, and their amazing discipline in the midst of great provocation. One day the South will recognize its real heroes. They will be the James

Merediths, with the noble sense of purpose that enables them to face jeering and hostile mobs, and with the agonizing loneliness that characterizes the life of the pioneer. They will be old, oppressed, battered Negro women, symbolized in a seventy-two-year-old woman in Montgomery, Alabama, who rose up with a sense of dignity and with her people decided not to ride segregated buses, and who responded with ungrammatical profundity to one who inquired about her weariness: "My feets is tired, but my soul is at rest." They will be the young high school and college students, the young ministers of the gospel and a host of their elders, courageously and nonviolently sitting in at lunch counters and willingly going to jail for conscience' sake. One day the South will know that when these disinherited children of God sat down at lunch counters, they were in reality standing up for what is best in the American dream and for the most sacred values in our Judaeo-Christian heritage, thereby bringing our nation back to those great wells of democracy which were dug deep by the founding fathers in their formulation of the Constitution and the Declaration of Independence.

Never before have I written so long a letter. I'm afraid it is much too long to take your precious time. I can assure you that it would have been much shorter if I had been writing from a comfortable desk, but what else can one do when he is alone in a narrow jail cell, other than write long letters, think long thoughts, and pray long prayers?

If I have said anything in this letter that overstates the truth and indicates an unreasonable impatience, I beg you to forgive me. If I have said anything that understates the truth and indicates my having a patience that allows me to settle for anything less than brotherhood, I beg God to forgive me.

I hope this letter finds you strong in the faith. I also hope that circumstances will soon make it possible for me to meet each of you, not as an integrationist or a civil-rights leader but as a fellow clergyman and a Christian brother. Let us all hope that the dark clouds of racial prejudice will soon pass away and the deep fog of misunderstanding will be lifted from our fear-drenched communities, and in some not too distant tomorrow the radiant stars of love and brotherhood will shine over our great nation with all their scintillating beauty.

Yours for the cause of Peace and Brotherhood,
MARTIN LUTHER KING, JR.

1. King's letter is a classic example of refutation, taking arguments made against one's opinions or actions and showing why they are wrong or incomplete. In an essay, note each point made in the statement condemning King's actions that King sets out to refute. How does he go about doing so? How do you respond to his arguments?

2. King is writing here to white moderates who say, in his words, "I agree with you in the goal you seek, but I cannot agree with your methods of direct action." In what ways has he tailored his arguments to such an audience? How does his tone reveal his understanding of this audience?

3. King makes a distinction between "just" and "unjust" laws. How does he define an "unjust" law? Do you agree with his definition? Point to any current examples of laws that you think are unjust, and explain why you feel as you do.

Stephen King (b. 1947) *grew up with his mother and brother in Portland, Maine. At an early age he began writing stories, with a particular interest in and fascination for science fiction and horror stories. Following his graduation from the University of Maine, as an English major, he began sending manuscripts to publishers. His novel* Carrie *was published in 1974, the first of more than thirty novels, including such successes as* The Shining *and* The Green Mile. *King has also produced five collections of short stories, nine screenplays and various works of nonfiction, including a book on writing. He recently edited* The Best American Short Stories, *2008. The following essay on horror movies appeared initially in* Playboy *magazine.*

STEPHEN KING

Why We Crave Horror Movies

In "Why We Crave Horror Movies," Stephen King analyzes the causes of people's fascination with the bizarre, the strange, and the macabre. He touches on a variety of factors from a wish to have fun to psychic release to a desire to watch people maimed and killed. And he considers the extravagant gestures of horror films and the crazy characters who inhabit them in light of normal human behavior and emotions.

King provides a number of examples in his essay, not only of horror films but also of popular culture and of historical horrors, such as the murders committed by Jack the Ripper. He reminds us that in addition to the "brotherhood of man," we also share an "insanity of man," with our interest in horror films reminding us of the worst, not the best of which we are capable.

I think that we're all mentally ill; those of us outside the asylums only hide it a little better—and maybe not all that much better, after all. We've all known people who talk to themselves, people who sometimes squinch their faces into horrible grimaces when they believe no one is watching, people who have some hysterical fear—of snakes, the dark, the tight place, the long drop . . . and, of course, those final worms and grubs that are waiting so patiently underground.

When we pay our four or five bucks and seat ourselves at tenth-row center in a theater showing a horror movie, we are daring the nightmare.

Why? Some of the reasons are simple and obvious. To show that we can, that we are not afraid, that we can ride this roller coaster. Which is not to say that a really good horror movie may not surprise a scream out of us at some point, the way we may scream when the roller coaster twists through a complete 360 or plows through a lake at the bottom of the drop. And horror movies, like roller coasters, have always been the special province of the young; by the time one turns 40 or 50, one's appetite for double twists or 360-degree loops may be considerably depleted.

We also go to re-establish our feelings of essential normality; the horror movie is innately conservative, even reactionary. Freda Jackson as the horrible melting woman in *Die, Monster, Die!* confirms for us that no matter how far we may be removed from the beauty of a Robert Redford or a Diana Ross, we are still light-years from true ugliness.

And we go to have fun.

Ah, but this is where the ground starts to slope away, isn't it? Because this is a very peculiar sort of fun indeed. The fun comes from seeing others menaced—sometimes killed. One critic has suggested that if pro football has become the voyeur's version of combat, then the horror film has become the modern version of the public lynching.

It is true that the mythic, "fairytale" horror film intends to take away the shades of gray. . . . It urges us to put away our more civilized and adult penchant for analysis and to become children again, seeing things in pure blacks and whites. It may be that horror movies provide psychic relief on this level because this invitation to lapse into simplicity, irrationality and even outright madness is extended so rarely. We are told we may allow our emotions a free rein . . . or no rein at all.

If we are all insane, then sanity becomes a matter of degree. If your insanity leads you to carve up women like Jack the Ripper or the Cleveland Torso Murderer, we clap you away in the funny farm (but neither of those two amateur-night surgeons was ever caught, heh-heh-heh); if, on the other hand your insanity leads you only to talk to yourself when you're under stress or to pick your nose on your morning bus, then you are left alone to go about your business . . . though it is doubtful that you will ever be invited to the best parties.

The potential lyncher is in almost all of us (excluding saints, past and present; but then, most saints have been crazy in their own ways), and every now and then, he had to be let loose to scream and roll around in the grass. Out emotions and our fears form their own body, and we recognize that it demands its own exercise to maintain proper muscle tone. Certain of these emotional muscles are accepted—even exalted—in civilized society; they are, of course, the emotions that tend to maintain the status quo of civilization itself. Love, friendship, loyalty, kindness— these are all the emotions that we applaud, emotions that have been immortalized in the couplets of Hallmark cards and in the verses (I don't care call it poetry) of Leonard Nimoy.

When we exhibit these emotions, society showers us with positive reinforcement; we learn this even before we get out of diapers. When, as children, we hug our rotten little puke of a sister and give her a kiss, all the aunts and uncles smile and twit and cry. "Isn't he the sweetest little thing?" Such covered treats as chocolate-covered graham crackers often follow. But if we deliberately slam the rotten little puke of a sister's fingers in the door, sanctions follow—angry remonstrance from parents, aunts and uncles; instead of a chocolate-covered graham cracker, a spanking.

But anticivilization emotions don't go away, and they demand periodic exercise. We have such "sick" jokes as, "What's the difference between a truckload of bowling balls and a truckload of dead babies? (You can't unload a truckload of bowling balls with a pitchfork . . . a joke, by the way, that I heard originally from a ten-year-old.) Such a joke may surprise a laugh or a grin out of us even as we recoil, a possibility that confirms the thesis: If we share a brotherhood of man, then we also share an insanity of man. None of which is intended as a defense of either the sick joke or insanity but merely as an explanation of why the best horror films, like the best fairy tales, manage to be reactionary, anarchistic, and revolutionary all at the same time.

The mythic horror movie, like the sick joke, has a dirty job to do. It deliberately appeals to all that is worst in us. It is morbidity unchained, our most base instincts let free, our nastiest fantasies realized . . . and it all happens, fittingly enough, in the dark. For those reasons, good liberals often shy away from horror films. For myself, I like to see the most aggressive of them—DAWN OF THE DEAD, for instance—as lifting a trap door in the civilized forebrain and throwing a basket of raw meat to the hungry alligators swimming around in that subterranean river beneath.

Why bother? Because it keeps them from getting out, man. It keeps them down there and me up here. It was Lennon and McCartney who said that all you need is love, and I would agree with that.

As long as you keep the gators fed.

POSSIBILITIES FOR WRITING

1. Identify the reasons King advances for our interest in and fascination with horror films. Which do you find the most unsettling? Which the most convincing? Why?

2. What has been your own experience watching horror films? Are they one of your favorite film genres, or do you avoid horror films? Identify one horror film and explain your response to it.

3. How does King begin and end his essay? How effective are the opening and closing? What comparisons and analogies does King make in the essay? Select one such comparison and explain what King says or shows through its use.

Maxine Hong Kingston (b. 1940) grew up in Stockton, California, the daughter of Chinese immigrants in a close-knit Asian community; her first language was a dialect of Chinese. She graduated from the University of California at Berkeley and went on to teach high school English in California and Hawaii. Her award-winning The Woman Warrior: Memoirs of a Childhood Among Ghosts *(1976) is an impressionistic remembrance of the stories she grew up with concerning women in her culture, both real and legendary. Its companion volume focusing on images of manhood,* China Men, *followed in 1980. Kingston has also published a novel,* Tripmaster Monkey: His Fake Book *(1989) and, more recently,* To Be the Poet *(2002) and* The Fifth Book of Peace *(2003). She was awarded a National Humanities Medal by the President Clinton in 1997.*

MAXINE HONG KINGSTON

On Discovery

"On Discovery" is an unusual piece of writing. An excerpt from Kingston's book *China Men*, "On Discovery" tells the story of a man who became a woman. Encased within Kingston's hybrid factual/fictional prose of the book, as a whole, is this parable about gender and identity. It's a prose piece that invites consideration of how gender identity is formed and why it is such a powerful cultural construct.

Tang Ao's odyssey takes him or her on a journey that could only be imagined, and one that ends with a shift in how Tang Ao imagines himself or herself. In Tang Ao's transformation from man to woman, Tang Ao undergoes as much an inner, psychological change as an external one.

In Tang Ao's case, the transformation was neither desired nor sought. But neither was it resisted when it was forced upon Tang Ao. It is a metamorphosis that Kingston's readers can hardly believe and certainly never forget.

Once upon a time, a man, named Tang Ao, looking for the Gold Mountain, crossed an ocean, and came upon the Land of Women. The women immediately captured him, not on guard against ladies. When they asked Tang Ao to come along, he followed; if he had had male companions, he would've winked over his shoulder.

"We have to prepare you to meet the queen," the women said. They locked him in a canopied apartment equipped with pots of makeup, mirrors, and a woman's clothes. "Let us help you off with your armor and boots," said the women. They slipped his coat off his shoulders, pulled it down his arms, and shackled his wrists behind him. The women who kneeled to take off his shoes chained his ankles together.

A door opened, and he expected to meet his match, but it was only two old women with sewing boxes in their hands. "The less you struggle, the less it'll hurt," one said, squinting a bright eye as she threaded her needle. Two captors sat on him while another held his head. He felt an old woman's dry fingers trace his ear; the long nail on her little finger scraped his neck. "What are you doing?" he asked. "Sewing your lips together," she joked, blackening needles in a candle flame. The ones who sat on him bounced with laughter. But the old woman did not sew his lips together. They pulled his earlobes taut and jabbed a needle through each of them. They had to poke and probe before puncturing the layers of skin correctly, the hole in the front of the lobe in line with one in back, the layers of skin sliding about so. They worked the needle through—a last jerk for the needle's wide eye ("needle's nose" in Chinese). They strung his raw flesh with silk threads; he could feel the fibers.

The women who sat on him turned to direct their attention to his feet. They bent his toes so far backward that his arched foot cracked. The old ladies squeezed each foot and broke many tiny bones along the sides. They gathered his toes, toes over and under one another like a knot of ginger root. Tang Ao wept with pain. As they wound the bandages tight and tighter around his feet, the women sang foot-binding songs to distract him: "Use aloe for binding feet and not for scholars."

During the months of a season, they fed him on women's food: the tea was thick with white chrysanthemums and stirred the cool female winds inside his body; chicken wings made his hair shine; vinegar soup improved his womb. They drew the loops of thread through the scabs that grew daily over the holes in his earlobes. One day they inserted gold hoops. Every night they unbound his feet, but his veins had shrunk, and the blood pumping through them hurt so much, he begged to have his feet rewrapped tight. They forced him to wash his used bandages, which were embroidered with flowers and smelled of rot and cheese. He hung the bandages up to dry, streamers that drooped and draped wall to wall. He felt embarrassed; the wrapping were like underwear, and they were his.

One day his attendants changed his gold hoops to jade studs and strapped his feet to shoes that curved like bridges. They plucked out each hair on his face, powdered him white, painted his eyebrows like a moth's wings, painted his cheeks and lips red. He served a meal at the queen's court. His hips swayed and his shoulders swiveled because of his shaped feet. "She's pretty, don't you agree?" the diners said, smacking their lips at his dainty feet as he bent to put dishes before them.

In the Women's Land there are no taxes and no wars. Some scholars say that that country was discovered during the reign of Empress Wu (A.D. 694–705), and some say earlier than that, A.D. 441, and it was in North America.

POSSIBILITIES FOR WRITING

1. What is Kingston's central idea in "On Discovery"? To what extent is this piece about gender switching? About gender roles? About power?

2. What ironies does Kingston play up in "On Discovery"? Consider both verbal irony and irony of situation—that is, ironic comments and ironic developments in the action.

3. Discuss the following comment by Simone de Beauvoir in relation to "On Discovery": "One is not born a woman; one becomes a woman."

August Kleinzahler (b. 1949) was born in Jersey City, New Jersey, and has lived much of his later life in San Francisco. Kleinzahler has been a taxi driver, a locksmith, a logger, and a building manager. He has been poet-in-residence at Brown University, has been named poet laureate of his hometown of Fort Lee, New Jersey, and has taught creative writing at the Iowa Writers' Workshop, at the University of California at Berkeley, and also to homeless veterans in the San Francisco Bay area. He is the author of seven books of poetry and is the recipient of numerous awards, including a National Book Critics Circle Award for Poetry and an Academy Award in Literature from the American Academy of Arts and Letters. In 2004 he published a collection of essays and meditations, Cutty, One Rock, from which "The Dog, The Family: A Household Tale," has been taken.

AUGUST KLEINZAHLER

The Dog, The Family: A Household Tale

In "The Dog, The Family: A Household Tale," August Kleinzahler describes the importance of his dog, called both Granny and Grand, in his life as a boy. Kleinzahler identifies the dog as a member of the household, one that was more influential in his upbringing, more important, and better looking than some other members of his family. Kleinzahler writes about Grand as if the dog were human, and he presents their relationship in fully human terms.

Kleinzahler also describes his and the dog's relationship with other family members. He uses humor to characterize these relationships, exaggerating, to some extent, their foibles and peculiarities, conveying, in the process, the flavor of his early life.

It was the dog who raised me. Oh, the others came and went with their nurturing gestures and concerns, but it was the dog on whose ear I teethed and who watched me through countless hours with the sagacity and bearing of a Ugandan tribal chief.

You can see him straining at the collar as my mother, dressed to the nines, first introduced him to me, freshly home from the hospital, lying across the nurse's lap, almost afloat, like an early Renaissance Christ child. You can see the muscles in his shoulders and neck. Perhaps he would have eaten me right then had I not been smelling of Mother, who I must say looks very pretty there in profile, probably about to head off to her Shakespeare club or into the city to see Paul Scofield in *Lear*, or something along those lines. Mother was very keen on Shakespeare, you see.

Going through the old photo albums you will find pictures of me in various stages of growing up, surrounded by the family: father, mother, sister, brother. But please notice, it is the dog at my side, seated upright, proudly displaying the musculature of his thick chest and the flame of white fur that ornamented it. I am his charge, the rest of them bit players. Not so much a Romulus-and-Remus situation as my having a guardian, a sort of dog uncle, rearing me in lieu of parents.

Actually, the dog looked very human, rather more so than one or two other members of the family. I had forgotten just how extreme was his facial resemblance to a human being until recently, when I showed my ladylove, Tarischa, an old photograph of the dog and me on the front stoop. Her eyes grew very large, then she began gagging.

We called him Granny or Grand, shortened from Twenty Grand, the famous racehorse after whom he was named. Father bought him on sale. He bought everything on sale. Grand was a boxer, purebred, but one of his ears was wrong; it didn't set up properly. And his right eye dripped. He also had a skin condition, something like mange but untreatable. Father got him for peanuts, really: a treasure, if you looked past certain cosmetic flaws.

Granny was a killer, but only when off the leash out of doors. He killed the chihuahua next door and Ernie Middelhauser's dog, Jo-Jo. He seldom attacked humans, only dogs, male dogs. Female dogs brought out his romantic side. You see, if you weren't careful when you opened the front or back door, he would shoot by you or between your legs and be gone for days. Eventually, he'd turn up hungry, looking a bit haggard. Father would kick him for a while until he tired of the exercise, and Granny would take it stoically, without growling or baring his teeth, only looking back at Father now and then with an ugly sneer.

I did miss him when he was off on one of his adventures, left alone with my toy soldiers and the cartoon shows of television's infancy. I recall one where a clown—I seem to remember his name was Cocoa—jumped out of an inkwell and made some difficulty for his creator. Cocoa was animated, the creator not: this provoked my imagination. After some difficulty, the creator always succeeded in getting Cocoa back in the bottle. There are certainly metaphors and allegories aplenty here if you go in for such things. Regardless, the dog would eventually return and we would pick up where we left off, no questions asked, no pouting or recriminations.

It's not as if the rest of the family weren't around. Father was at work, quite naturally, and Mother shopping, or perhaps at her Shakespeare club, which met on alternate Tuesdays. My brother would have been in the basement, at work on a model airplane, getting himself stoned senseless on glue fumes. Or if not in the basement, then in the apple tree, seeing how far he could get out on a limb before it snapped.

My sister lived in the attic. It was not such a bad thing to have her always up there, as she had Father's unpredictable disposition. Well, not always; she would occasionally come down to gnaw the meat off the steak bone we were ordered to save for her. Oh, and there were the suitors. My sister had an hourglass figure and a pixie hairdo. She favored very stupid boys with dodgy backgrounds and convertibles.

Otherwise, she read her Latin in the attic or, when saturated with Ovid, would play her rock-and-roll seventy-eights on her portable. She played "The Naughty Lady of Shady Lane" repeatedly, hundreds of times, for months on end. She would dance to this and other tunes: *thump, thump, thump.* No one in the family was particularly graceful, excepting the dog and, to a certain extent, me, having modeled my own movements on the dog's. My brother was not graceful but had a primitive athleticism, as I imagine the young Tecumseh or Cochise must have had, an athleticism given almost wholly over to mayhem. My brother was not unlike the dog in the behavior he evinced out of the house. Nor did Father receive my brother much differently from the dog when he'd stagger home at last with his assorted wounds and bills incurred.

My sister spent so much time in the attic with her Latin that she broke the record for A pluses at the local high school and went off to Smith College after her junior year to study Latin in the Big Leagues of American Higher Education. Such intellectual prowess was unheard of at this particular high school and my sister became a legend there, her name synonymous with braininess. The only other equivalent celebrity from that high school during that time was the fellow who wrote the hit song "Flying Purple People Eater," and there might even have been some challenge as to the song's *real* authorship.

Mother didn't like children, least of all her own, and me least among them. I was unplanned, an accident, a misfortune. You see, Mother and Father had taken the Fishblatts, their friends from around the corner, out to dinner, and everybody got quite drunk. That had been my parents' plan: to get the Fishblatts drunk. It seems the Fishblatts were making ready for a divorce, which signaled no more impromptu get-togethers only a hop, skip, and jump away. I suppose the plan was that when the appropriate level of drunkenness was achieved, there would be a series of ribald and stoical jokes about the imperfect union of marriage, hoots of exasperation, and unbridled guffaws, and the Fishblatts would stagger home, enjoy an amorous reconciliation of robust proportion, and resign themselves to being stuck with one another for the duration, a circumstance relieved from time to time by visits with my parents.

Well, now, it didn't turn out like that at all. The Fishblatts sobered up straightaway and got divorced. Mother became pregnant with me, years after she'd convinced herself she'd beaten that particular rap.

My appearance on the scene was unwelcome enough, but it turned out that I looked like the dog. I am not suggesting that Mother had been impregnated by Granny, not at all. You see, if Mother had only listened to her own mother and averted her eyes from the dog during the term of her pregnancy, it was said, this unhappy result might have been avoided. Nanny Farbisseneh, a tiny, dour creature originally from a bog outside of Kiev, who, when she spoke at all, issued terse commands in a broken English that drifted erratically into a goulash of Russian, Ukrainian, and Yiddish, held powerful, almost frightening influence over her three daughters, of whom Mother was the youngest. In the presence of Nanny, Mother and my two aunts were like zombified servant girls, oblivious of their own wants and those of their respective families.

Nanny Farbisseneh disapproved of dogs, and held a dim view of males of any species, so you see, a male dog, especially one with Granny's imperfections, could succeed only in eliciting her unalloyed revulsion. But despite Nanny Far's injunctions, Mother not only continued to look at the dog but gazed lovingly into his eyes (the right one caked with discharge) for hours on end. Mother, it turns out, loved four-legged creatures, both cloven and hoofed, and, without exception, even the most vicious and recalcitrant, they adored her, not least of all Grand. True, Mother fed the dog and saw to the removal of his feces, but Granny's love for Mother went far beyond this natural bond: the dog was in love with Mother, a situation that did not go unnoticed by Father, who routinely attacked the dog, either with his right foot or a rolled-up copy of *The Atlantic Monthly* brought down sharply on the dog's black, concertinaed snout.

So Mother, who seldom, if ever, disobeyed Nanny Far, in this instance made an egregious exception, one that she would rue and suffer to be daily reminded of for years and years. In fact, so considerable was her distress at having been delivered of this curious whelp that not a week after my birth both my parents disappeared to Guatemala for a fortnight, presumably to console one another, divert themselves with Mayan figurines, rain forests, cloudy fermented beverages made from tubers—whatever one does in such places. But in truth, knowing Father, Guatemala was probably that season's cheapest ticket. And Mother really, really wanted to get the hell out of Dodge.

My resemblance to the dog was not my only embarrassment to the family. I had a thick Czech accent as well, at least until the age of seven or so, when Father let our housekeeper, Christine, go. If memory serves, because she asked for a small raise after many years of devoted service.

Christine was a round, bosomy, gray-haired Czech woman, grandmotherly, if you will, but in the nice movie-and-storybook way as opposed to the Nanny Far way. Christine smelled of dough and fresh laundry. She loved me and had me entirely convinced I was the singular joy in her life, although I knew she had a son of her own. In the evenings, Christine would cook deep-fried potatoes, the smell of which was an enchantment. The memory of those potatoes stirs me to this day. It was an aroma of such pleasurable intensity that it seemed of another world and time, perhaps a subterranean wood-paneled beer hall–cum–restaurant somewhere in Bratislava, where officers, business leaders, and ladies of fashion would congregate a century earlier, taking refuge from the harsh elements and sustenance in the hearty, blissfully aromatic fare.

Then, after Christine had cleaned up, she would go home to her no-good, delinquent son, her three-room, cabbagey shithole, and watch *The Joe Franklin Show*, or some trash of that sort, like the ignorant bohunk she was. But to me, Christine was maternal beneficence, pleasure and abundance, my anti-Mother. Years later, as an adult, I would live with a young Czech woman, Canadian-Czech, and suck my thumb till it was raw as I watched her cook pierogi, chicken paprikash, her special Bohemian cookies. Then, when we were done eating, I'd lick her breasts while we copulated for hours, all the time thinking of Christine's tattersall apron and the smell of her fried potatoes from across the years.

When Christine had left, Mother took it into her head to take a more active role in the rearing of her youngest child, me. The dog was sent whimpering to the den. It was just Mother and me at the kitchen table.

I remember the moment very well, to this day. She clearly had plans for me, and her appraising, contemptuous look augured nothing good, at least insofar as I was concerned.

"It's back to the good ol' U.S. of A. for you, babykins," she said to me. "Let's lose the Kafka accent. It's giving your father and me the creeps, and your brother and sister are too embarrassed to bring home any of their friends. You're going to speak like an American child and act like an American child. And while you're at it, wipe the *schmutz* off your chin."

Had I forgotten what I told Mother at that particular point, her tittering rendition of it over the years would have been more than adequate in refreshing my memory: "I vont you should take a valk in dee voods and a beeg, bad volf eat you all whup!" That one really cracked her pits. "You really are the limit," she said mirthlessly, shaking her head in dismay. I could hear the dog whining piteously from behind the closed parlor doors.

Mother explained to me that if I didn't come around, and in a hurry, she'd make me take a job in Uncle Ja-Ja's factory, blocking hats. Uncle Ja-Ja was Nanny Far's little brother, although he, too, was ancient. He resembled an engorged frog with thick, black-rimmed glasses, and smelled of gherkins. Ja-Ja was always looking for cheap labor—child, adult, no matter—and surely would have jumped at the idea, but it was Great-Aunt Duhnny, the final authority among the Kiev bog contingent, who put her foot down. "Dog-boy go to school like ordinary child," she said, and that was that.

Father worked and read the paper. Children and child rearing, in his view, belonged to the realm of the female, and in my case the dog. The children were Mother's bailiwick. His job was to make money, then lose it, make it again, and so on, except when he was reading the paper, which was filled with information on how to make money, along with insights into the perils of how it might be lost.

Money and the record of its activity was not Father's only interest. He had a fascination with what he called "antiquities," or at least what they cost. In particular, he liked bodhisattvas, religious statuary from the Orient of sacred figures like Avalokitesvara, Manjusri, Kshitigarbha. Why a man of almost no formal education (having been repeatedly thrown out of school for antisocial behavior) should cotton to these small sculptures of holy beings who seek Buddhahood through the practice of perfect virtues, well . . . Regardless, the house looked like a Chinese souvenir shop, which was a terrible cross for Mother to bear.

A frightful snob about such things, Mother, who cherished a Todd Haynes look in domestic interiors, would sit there on the living-room sofa, smoking her Salems, and, regarding the clutter of sacred figures, say, "Just look at all that shit," shaking her head disconsolately.

Fortunately, or unfortunately, for Mother, Father, like those primeval forests that spontaneously autocombust every century or two to get rid of old growth and make room for new, every few months would go berserk and destroy everything in the house, invariably heading first for the bodhisattvas. I can only speculate in hindsight how many dozens of Avalokitesvaras (the bodhisattva of compassion, known as Kuan-yin in China) Father cracked over the mantelpiece.

As for the rest of us during these episodes, led by Mother, and with the dog bringing up the rear, we would retreat to the upstairs bathroom and lock ourselves in until it was evident the storm had blown itself out. It was not unpleasant to be in that small room with the rest of them for the fifteen or twenty minutes it took Father to "clear the brush out" downstairs. I seldom got to visit with my older siblings at such close quarters, and Mother seemed a veritable font of drolleries on these occasions. The dog was in good humor as well and relieved not to be on the other side of the door. When the crashing, grunts, and gargled imprecations subsided, we would proceed single file, in the exact order we had retreated, downstairs, where, inevitably, we'd find Father seated there in the living room, staring rather pensively at the rubble.

> *Years later, my psychologist girlfriend Clarissa would say to me, "Dog, has anyone ever suggested to you that you're rather, um,* labile*?"*
> *Fucking bitch . . . But turns out she didn't mean what I thought.*

The years passed. One day Father looked up from his paper and asked Mother where their two older children had gone; he hadn't seen them in a while. "They've been away at college for years, darling," she told him. The dog was getting on as well. I'd try to engage him in our customary frolic, but he'd only look up at me miserably, his dark jowls spread across the carpet.

In fact, Granny didn't age at all gracefully. He had never been what one would think of as a good-smelling creature, given as he was to flatulence and halitosis, along with an indefinable but distinctly unwholesome smell emanating from his diseased skin. It was not at all uncommon for the dog to puke up something he'd gotten into, and the house really was beginning to smell like a doggie vomitorium. Other than that, he slept, occasionally breaking wind or struggling to his feet to pee at the base of this chair or that. Toward the very end, he'd even gone off his horsemeat.

One day I came home from school to find Mother weeping at the foot of the hall stairs. It was a startling spectacle. I'd have been no less astonished if she'd taken wing and commenced doing the loop-the-loops over the house; or had I encountered Grand up on his hind legs singing "Que Sera, Sera" in a tremulous countertenor. Uh-oh, where was the dog? Even at this advanced stage in his decline he would probably have roused himself and staggered over. The dog would have found Mother's weeping no less peculiar and alarming than I.

So it was, staring at Mother with the curiosity and skepticism of an art historian or scientist dispatched by a museum to check out the phenomenon of "the weeping Madonna" in a dank little Italian church buried among the cypresses of some hill town, that I realized the dog was gone. Kaput. And with that realization came another: still a child, I was alone in the world; but far worse, alone with Mother and Father.

POSSIBILITIES FOR WRITING

1. What is the effect of Kleinzahler's opening sentence? Of his opening paragraph? How effective are these gambits as part of his four-paragraph introduction? Explain what this introduction accomplishes.
2. Identify the sources of humor in Kleinzahler's essay. To what extent did you find the essay funny? Compare Kleinzahler's humor with that of David Sedaris in "Me Talk Pretty One Day" (pp. 554–558).
3. Write an essay about an animal, perhaps a pet, that has been a part of your life. Or write an essay about why animals have not been a part of your life.

Robin Tolmach Lakoff (b. 1942) grew up in Brooklyn, New York, and received degrees from Radcliffe College, Indiana University, and Harvard. She has been a professor of linguistics at the University of California at Berkeley since 1972. Much of her work has focused on feminist issues and the degree to which traditional language usage has excluded or implicitly denigrated women. Lakoff's books include Language and Women's Place *(1975),* Talking Power: The Politics of Language in Our Lives *(1990), and* The Language War *(2000).*

ROBIN TOLMACH LAKOFF

You Are What You Say

In an essay first published in *Ms.* magazine in 1974, and later developed into a chapter in her book a decade later, *Language and Women's Place,* Robin Lakoff examines the ways women use language. She considers what women talk about and how they talk about what they do. Lakoff attributes the differences between men's and women's speech to culture, particularly to cultural biases that permit women to speak only in certain ways, and only of certain subjects.

Lacing her essay with examples from everyday speech situations, Lakoff demonstrates how women's lady-like language limits their effectiveness. She also explains the implications of women's linguistic habits. Both the language women use, and the language used to describe them, reveal women to be less important and less powerful than men.

Women's language is that pleasant (dainty?), euphemistic never-aggressive way of talking we learned as little girls. Cultural bias was built into the language we were allowed to speak, the subjects we were allowed to speak about, and the ways we were spoken of. Having learned our linguistic lesson well, we go out in the world, only to discover that we are communicative cripples—damned if we do, and damned if we don't.

If we refuse to talk "like a lady," we are ridiculed and criticized for being unfeminine. ("She thinks like a man" is, at best, a left-handed compliment.) If we do learn all the fuzzy-headed, unassertive language of our sex, we are ridiculed for being unable to think clearly, unable to take part in a serious discussion, and therefore unfit to hold a position of power.

It doesn't take much of this for a woman to begin feeling she deserves such treatment because of inadequacies in her own intelligence and education.

"Women's language" shows up in all levels of English. For example, women are encouraged and allowed to make far more precise discriminations in naming colors than men do. Words like *mauve, beige, ecru, aquamarine, lavender,* and so on, are unremarkable in a woman's active vocabulary, but largely absent from that of most men. I know of no evidence suggesting that women actually *see* a wider range of colors than men do. It is simply that fine discriminations of this sort are relevant to women's vocabularies, but not to men's; to men, who control most of the interesting affairs of the world, such distinctions are trivial—irrelevant.

In the area of syntax, we find similar gender-related peculiarities of speech. There is one construction, in particular, that women use conversationally far more than men: the tag question. A tag is midway between an outright statement and a yes-no question; it is less assertive than the former, but more confident than the latter.

A *flat statement* indicates confidence in the speaker's knowledge and is fairly certain to be believed; a *question* indicates a lack of knowledge on some point and implies that the gap in the speaker's knowledge can and will be remedied by an answer. For example, if, at a Little League game, I have had my glasses off, I can legitimately ask someone else: "Was the player out at third?" A *tag question,* being intermediate between statement and question, is used when the speaker is stating a claim, but lacks full confidence in the truth of that claim. So if I say, "Is Joan here?" I will probably not be surprised if my respondent answers "no"; but if I say, "Joan is here, isn't she?" instead, chances are I am already biased in favor of a positive answer, wanting only confirmation. I still want a response, but I have enough knowledge (or think I have) to predict that response. A tag question, then, might be thought of as a statement that doesn't demand to be believed by anyone but the speaker, a way of giving leeway, of not forcing the addressee to go along with the views of the speaker.

Another common use of the tag question is in small talk when the speaker is trying to elicit conversation: "Sure is hot here, isn't it?"

But in discussing personal feelings or opinions, only the speaker normally has any way of knowing the correct answer. Sentences such as "I have a headache, don't I?" are clearly ridiculous. But there are other examples where it is the speaker's opinions, rather than perceptions, for which corroboration is sought, as in "The situation in Southeast Asia is terrible, isn't it?"

While there are, of course, other possible interpretations of a sentence like this, one possibility is that the speaker has a particular answer in mind "yes" or "no"—but is reluctant to state it baldly. This sort of tag question is much more apt to be used by women than by men in conversation. Why is this the case?

The tag question allows a speaker to avoid commitment, and thereby avoid conflict with the addressee. The problem is that, by so doing, speakers may also give the impression of not really being sure of themselves, or looking to the addressee for confirmation of their views. This uncertainty is reinforced in more subliminal ways, too. There is a peculiar sentence-intonation pattern, used almost exclusively by women, as far as I know, which changes a declarative answer into a question. The effect of using the rising inflection typical of a yes-no question is to imply that the speaker is seeking confirmation, even though the speaker is clearly the only one who has the requisite information, which is why the question was put to her in the first place:

(Q) When will dinner be ready?
(A) Oh . . . around six o'clock . . . ?

It is as though the second speaker was saying, "Six o'clock—if that's okay with you, if you agree." The person being addressed is put in the position of having to provide confirmation. One likely consequence of this sort of speech pattern in a woman is that, often unbeknownst to herself, the speaker builds a reputation of tentativeness, and others will refrain from taking her seriously or trusting her with any real responsibilities, since she "can't make up her mind," and "isn't sure of herself."

Such idiosyncrasies may explain why women's language sounds much more "polite" than men's. It is polite to leave a decision open, not impose your mind, or views, or claims, or anyone else. So a tag question is a kind of polite statement, in that it does not force agreement or belief on the addressee. In the same way a request is a polite command, in that it does not force obedience on the addressee, but rather suggests something be done as a favor to the speaker. A clearly stated order implies a threat of certain consequences if it is not followed, and—even more impolite—implies that the speaker is in a superior position and able to enforce the order. By couching wishes in the form of a request, on the other hand, a speaker implies that if the request is not carried out, only the speaker will suffer; noncompliance cannot harm the addressee. So the decision is really left up to the addressee. The distinction becomes clear in these examples:

Close the door.
Please close the door.
Will you close the door?
Will you please close the door?
Won't you close the door?

In the same ways as words and speech patterns used *by* women undermine her image, those used to *describe* women make matters even worse. Often a word may be used of both men and women (and perhaps of things as well); but when it is applied to women, it assumes a special meaning that, by implication rather than outright assertion, is derogatory to women as a group.

The use of euphemisms has this effect. A euphemism is a substitute for a word that has acquired a bad connotation by association with something unpleasant or embarrassing. But almost as soon as the new word comes into common usage, it takes on the same old bad connotations, since feelings about the things or people referred to are not altered by a change of name; thus new euphemisms must be constantly found.

There is one euphemism for *woman* still very much alive. The word, of course, is *lady*. *Lady* has a masculine counterpart, namely *gentleman*, occasionally shortened to *gent*. But for some reason *lady* is very much commoner than *gent(leman)*.

The decision to use *lady* rather than *woman*, or vice versa, may considerably alter the sense of a sentence, as the following examples show:

a. A woman (lady) I know is a dean at Berkeley.
b. A woman (lady) I know makes amazing things out of shoelaces and old boxes.

The use of *lady* in (a) imparts a frivolous, or nonserious, tone to the sentence: the matter under discussion is not one of great moment. Similarly, in (b), using *lady* here would suggest that the speaker considered the "amazing things" not to be serious art, but merely a hobby or an aberration. If *woman* is used, she might be a serious sculptor. To say *lady doctor* is very condescending, since no one ever says *gentleman doctor* or even *man doctor*. For example, mention in the San Francisco *Chronicle* of January 31, 1972, of Madalyn Murray O'Hair as the *lady atheist* reduces her position to that of scatterbrained eccentric. Even *woman atheist* is scarcely defensible: sex is irrelevant to her philosophical position.

Many women argue that, on the other hand, *lady* carries with it overtones recalling the age of chivalry: conferring exalted stature on the person so referred to. This makes the term seem polite at first, but we must also remember that these implications are perilous: they suggest that a "lady" is helpless, and cannot do things by herself.

Lady can also be used to infer frivolousness, as in titles of organizations. Those that have a serious purpose (not merely that of enabling "the ladies" to spend time with one another) cannot use the word *lady* in their titles, but less serious ones may. Compare the *Ladies' Auxiliary* of a men's group, or the *Thursday Evening Ladies' Browning and Garden Society* with *Ladies' Liberation* or *Ladies' Strike for Peace*.

What is curious about this split is that *lady* is in origin a euphemism—a substitute that puts a better face on something people find uncomfortable—for *woman*. What kind of euphemism is it that subtly denigrates the people to whom it refers? Perhaps *lady* functions as a euphemism for *woman* because it does not contain the sexual implications present in *woman:* it is not "embarrassing" in that way. If this is so, we may expect that, in the future, *lady* will replace woman as the primary word for the human female, since *woman* will have become too blatantly sexual. That this distinction is already made in some contexts at least is shown in the following examples, where you can try replacing *woman* with *lady:*

a. She's only twelve, but she's already a woman.
b. After ten years in jail, Harry wanted to find a woman.
c. She's my woman, see, so don't mess around with her.

Another common substitute for *woman* is *girl*. One seldom hears a man past the age of adolescence referred to as a boy, save in expressions like "going out with the boys," which are meant to suggest an air of adolescent frivolity and irresponsibility. But women of all ages are "girls": one can have a man—not a boy—Friday, but only a girl—never a woman or even a lady—Friday; women have girlfriends, but men do not—in a nonsexual sense—have boyfriends. It may be that this use of *girl* is euphemistic in the same way the use of *lady* is: in stressing the idea of immaturity, it removes the sexual connotations lurking in *woman*. *Girl* brings to mind irresponsibility: you don't send a girl to do a woman's errand (or even, for that matter, a boy's errand). She is a person who is both too immature and too far from real life to be entrusted with responsibilities or with decisions of any serious or important nature.

Now let's take a pair of words which, in terms of the possible relationships in an earlier society, were simple male-female equivalents, analogous to *bull: cow*. Suppose we find that, for independent reasons, society has changed in such a way that the original meanings now are irrelevant. Yet the words have not been discarded, but have acquired new meanings, metaphorically related to their original senses. But suppose these new metaphorical uses are no longer parallel to each other.

By seeing where the parallelism breaks down, we discover something about the different roles played by men and women in this culture. One good example of such a divergence through time is found in the pair, *master: mistress*. Once used with reference to one's power over servants, these words have become unusable today in their original master-servant sense as the relationship has become less prevalent in our society. But the words are still common.

Unless used with reference to animals, *master* now generally refers to a man who has acquired consummate ability in some field, normally nonsexual. But its feminine counterpart cannot be used this way. It is practically restricted to its sexual sense of "paramour." We start out with two terms, both roughly paraphrasable as "one who has power over another." But the masculine form, once one person is no longer able to have absolute power over another, becomes usable metaphorically in the sense of "having power over *something*." *Master* requires as its object only the name of some activity, something inanimate and abstract. But *mistress* requires a masculine noun in the possessive to precede it. One cannot say: "Rhonda is a mistress." One must be *someone's* mistress. A man is defined by what he does, a woman by her sexuality, that is, in terms of one particular aspect of her relationship to men. It is one thing to be an *old master* like Hans Holbein, and another to be an *old mistress*.

The same is true of the words *spinster* and *bachelor*—gender words for "one who is not married." The resemblance ends with the definition. While *bachelor* is a neuter term, often used as a compliment, *spinster* normally is used pejoratively, with connotations of prissiness, fussiness, and so on. To be a bachelor implies that one has a choice of marrying or not, and this is what makes the idea of a bachelor existence attractive, in the popular literature. He has been pursued and has successfully eluded his pursuers. But a spinster is one who has not been pursued, or at least not seriously. She is old, unwanted goods. The metaphorical connotations of *bachelor* generally suggest sexual freedom; of *spinster*, puritanism or celibacy.

These examples could be multiplied. It is generally considered a *faux pas*, in society, to congratulate a woman on her engagement, while it is correct to congratulate her fiancé. Why is this? The reason seems to be that it is impolite to remind people of things that may be uncomfortable to them. To congratulate a woman on her engagement is really to say, "Thank goodness! You had a close call!" For the man, on the other hand, there was no such danger. His choosing to marry is viewed as a good thing, but not something essential.

The linguistic double standards holds throughout the life of the relationship. After marriage, bachelor and spinster become man and wife, not man and woman. The woman whose husband dies remains "John's widow"; John, however, is never "Mary's widower."

Finally, why is it that salesclerks and others are so quick to call women customers "dear," "honey," and other terms of endearment they really have no business using? A male customer would never put up with it. But women, like children, are supposed to enjoy these endearments, rather than being offended by them.

In more ways than one, it's time to speak up.

POSSIBILITIES FOR WRITING

1. How many of Lakoff's observations still hold true today? In what ways have things clearly changed? Can you cite some more contemporary examples of language differences between women and men?
2. Brainstorm a list of as many generic terms as you can think of that are used to name or describe women today, along with a similar list for men. What do these terms suggest about levels of gender-based power or authority in the early twenty-first century?
3. In what ways are other kinds of groups defined by language? What sorts of terms do such groups use to describe themselves? Are outsiders expected to use the same language or not? Why?

D. H. LAWRENCE

On Ben Franklin's Virtues

In the following excerpt from an essay on Ben Franklin from his book, *Studies in Classic American Literature,* D. H. Lawrence responds to Franklin's project for moral self-improvement. As a modernist romantic, Lawrence has little appreciation of Franklin's project and less patience with Franklin's pragmatic virtues.

Lawrence's tone throughout is irreverent. In treating Franklin's ideas comically and critically, Lawrence expresses a counter-ideal. He proposes a substitute rationale for how to live as a "moral animal" and not a "moral machine." And he offers an alternative set of precepts for acquiring the baker's dozen virtues that Franklin endorses.

The Perfectibility of Man! Ah heaven, what a dreary theme! The perfectibility of the Ford car! The perfectibility of which man? I am many men. Which of them are you going to perfect? I am not a mechanical contrivance.

Education! Which of the various me's do you propose to educate, and which do you propose to suppress?

Anyhow, I defy you. I defy you, oh society, to educate me or to suppress me, according to your dummy standards.

The ideal man! And which is he, if you please? Benjamin Franklin or Abraham Lincoln? The ideal man! Roosevelt or Porfirio Díaz?

There are other men in me, besides this patient ass who sits here in a tweed jacket. What am I doing, playing the patient ass in a tweed jacket? Who am I talking to? Who are you, at the other end of this patience?

Who are you? How many selves have you? And which of these selves do you want to be?

Is Yale College going to educate the self that is in the dark of you, or Harvard College?

The ideal self! Oh, but I have a strange and fugitive self shut out and howling like a wolf or a coyote under the ideal windows. See his red eyes in the dark? This is the self who is coming into his own.

The perfectibility of man, dear God! When every man as long as he remains alive is in himself a multitude of conflicting men. Which of these do you choose to perfect, at the expense of every other?

Old Daddy Franklin will tell you. He'll rig him up for you, the pattern American. Oh, Franklin was the first downright American. He knew what he was about, the sharp man. He set up the first dummy American.

At the beginning of his career this cunning little Benjamin drew up for himself a creed that should "satisfy the professors of every religion, but shock none.". . .

Man is a moral animal. All right. I am a moral animal. And I'm going to remain such. I'm not going to be turned into a virtuous little automaton as Benjamin would have me. "This is good, that is bad. Turn the little handle, and let the good tap flow," saith Benjamin, and all America with him. "But first of all extirpate those savages who are always turning on the bad tap."

I am a moral animal. But I am not a moral machine. I don't work with a little set of handles or levers. The Temperance-silence-order-resolution-frugality-industry-chastity-humility keyboard is not going to get me going. I'm really not just an automatic piano with a moral Benjamin getting tunes out of me.

Here's my creed, against Benjamin's. This is what I believe:

"That I am I."

"That my soul is a dark forest."

"That my known self will never be more than a little clearing in the forest."

"That gods, strange gods, come forth from the forest into the clearing of my known self, and then go back."

"That I must have the courage to let them come and go."

"That I will never let mankind put anything over me, but that I will try always to recognize and submit to the gods in me and the gods in other men and women."

There is my creed. He who runs may read. He who prefers to crawl, or to go by gasoline, can call it rot.

Then for a "list." It is rather fun to play at Benjamin.

1. **Temperance** Eat and carouse with Bacchus, or munch dry bread with Jesus, but don't sit down without one of the gods.
2. **Silence** Be still when you have nothing to say; when genuine passion moves you, say what you've got to say, and say it hot.
3. **Order** Know that you are responsible to the gods inside you and to the men in whom the gods are manifest. Recognize your superiors and your inferiors, according to the gods. This is the root of all order.
4. **Resolution** Resolve to abide by your own deepest promptings, and to sacrifice the smaller thing to the greater. Kill when you must, and be killed the same: the *must* coming from the gods inside you, or from the men in whom you recognize the Holy Ghost.
5. **Frugality** Demand nothing; accept what you see fit. Don't waste your pride or squander your emotion.
6. **Industry** Lose no time with ideals; serve the Holy Ghost; never serve mankind.
7. **Sincerity** To be sincere is to remember that I am I, and that the other man is not me.
8. **Justice** The only justice is to follow the sincere intuition of the soul, angry or gentle. Anger is just, and pity is just, but judgment is never just.
9. **Moderation** Beware of absolutes. There are many gods.
10. **Cleanliness** Don't be too clean. It impoverishes the blood.
11. **Tranquillity** The soul has many motions, many gods come and go. Try and find your deepest issue, in every confusion, and abide by that. Obey the man in whom you recognize the Holy Ghost; command when your honour comes to command.
12. **Chastity** Never "use" venery at all. Follow your passional impulse, if it be answered in the other being; but never have any motive in mind, neither offspring nor health nor even pleasure, nor even service. Only know that "venery" is of the great gods. An offering-up of yourself to the very great gods, the dark ones, and nothing else.
13. **Humility** See all men and women according to the Holy Ghost that is within them. Never yield before the barren.

There's my list. I have been trying dimly to realize it for a long time, and only America and old Benjamin have at last goaded me into trying to formulate it. . . .

POSSIBILITIES FOR WRITING

1. Lawrence argues the he is a "moral animal" but not a "virtuous little automaton." What does he mean? What difference is he referring to? How does the distinction here relate to his larger point?

2. Analyze Lawrence's descriptions of the thirteen "virtues" he names. What does this list suggest about Lawrence's personal system of values? Some research about Lawrence's personal moral code could be helpful here.

3. Compare Lawrence's essay with the Franklin essay "Arriving at Perfection" (pp. 230–233) on which it is based. Which one speaks more meaningfully to you? Why do you respond as you do?

Abraham Lincoln (1809–1865) was born in virtual poverty in rural Kentucky and spent most of his childhood in what is now Spencer County, Indiana. In 1827 he settled in New Salem, Illinois, where he worked in a general store and managed a mill. Almost completely self-educated, he spent much of his spare time during these years studying law and was elected to the state legislature in 1834, serving four terms. While in private practice as a lawyer, he ran unsuccessfully for national office several times, most notably a campaign for the Senate in which he emerged as a forceful opponent of the extension of slavery. Based on this, he was nominated for the Presidency by the Republican Party in 1860, winning with less than a majority of the popular vote. Commander and chief of the Northern forces during the Civil War, Lincoln was assassinated in its final year. His speeches are among the classics of American literature.

ABRAHAM LINCOLN

The Gettysburg Address

Abraham Lincoln's "Gettysburg Address," a little over two minutes long, was occasioned by the battle of Gettysburg, which took place the first three days of July, 1863, during the American Civil War. At the battle of Gettysburg, Union soldiers were victorious over their Confederate opponents. But both sides suffered heavy losses of life. Lincoln memorializes the soldiers who died at Gettysburg with language that is elevated, formal, and ceremonial. Each of Lincoln's sentences is carefully structured, with word balancing word, phrase balancing phrase, and clause balancing clause. Using contrast and repetition as well as balanced phrasing, Lincoln created a speech that is as memorable as it is beautiful.

Lincoln's speech begins with a formal phrase "Four score and seven years ago" that refers to an exalted moment in American history, 1776, the creation of the United States of America. His second sentence shifts to the present, to the country's immersion in the Civil War. It is followed by a few simple sentences that identify the occasion of Lincoln's presence and his remarks. These opening sentences set the stage for the glorious elaboration that follows, in which Lincoln celebrates the sacrifice made by those who gave their lives for the cause of freedom.

Four score and seven years ago our fathers brought forth on this continent, a new nation, conceived in Liberty, and dedicated to the proposition that all men are created equal.

Now we are engaged in a great civil war, testing whether that nation, or any nation so conceived and so dedicated, can long endure. We are met on a great battle-field of that war. We have come to dedicate a portion of that field, as a final resting place for those who here gave their lives that that nation might live. It is altogether fitting and proper that we should do this.

But, in a larger sense, we can not dedicate—we can not consecrate—we can not hallow—this ground. The brave men, living and dead, who struggled here, have consecrated it, far above our poor power to add or detract. The world will little note, nor long remember what we say here, but it can never forget what they did here. It is for us the living, rather, to be dedicated here to the unfinished work which they who fought here have thus far so nobly advanced. It is rather for us to be here dedicated to the great task remaining before us—that from these honored dead we take increased devotion to that cause for which they gave the last full measure of devotion—that we here highly resolve that these dead shall not have died in vain—that this nation, under God, shall have a new birth of freedom—and that government of the people, by the people, for the people, shall not perish from the earth.

POSSIBILITIES FOR WRITING

1. The Gettysburg Address was composed for a very specific occasion, yet it has come to be considered one of the most profound statements in American political history. What in the speech gives it weight beyond simply honoring those who were killed during the battle of Gettysburg? In what ways does it capture elements essential to the American ideal?
2. Analyze Lincoln's use of repetition, contrast, and balanced phrasing in the Gettysburg Address. Using examples of each from the text, explore their contributions to the overall effect of the speech.
3. Do some research about the composition of the Gettysburg address, initial public response to it, and how it was popularized. In an essay, report on the history of this document. You might wish to consult Gary Wills's book *Lincoln at Gettysburg.*

Niccolò Machiavelli (1469–1527), one of the major thinkers of the Italian Renaissance, was born in Florence, the son of a noble family fallen on hard times. After the Medicis fled the city in 1498, he joined the newly established republican government and became a highly trusted diplomat and secretary of defense. In 1513, after the return of Medici rule, he was accused of treason, suffering imprisonment and torture before being allowed to retire to his country estate. There he produced works of history, literature, and, most notably, political discourse. The most famous of these is The Prince *(written in 1513, but not published until 1531), a treatise in which Machiavelli explains that, in order to maintain power, princes must do anything necessary, however immoral. Read as a lesson in realpolitick, the book is seen as the first example of modern political theory.*

NICCOLÒ MACHIAVELLI

The Morals of the Prince

Niccolò Machiavelli wrote *The Prince* in 1513 as a guidebook for Guiliano de Medici, one of a family of Renaissance rulers of Florence. During the sixteenth century, Italy was a fragmented country, composed of various warring city-states all vying for power. Machiavelli believed that if the country were ever to be unified and brought to peace, it would take a strong ruler, an ideal prince, to do that. His book offered a prescription for creating such a successful monarch.

Machiavelli's advice to the ideal prince is designed to be effective in gaining and maintaining political power. For Machiavelli, power is the end or goal, and whatever means are necessary to acquire and preserve that power are entirely justified. The morals of the prince are not a consideration, any more than is his desire for popularity. The only concern is securing and staying in power. And if this requires pretense, so be it. Let the prince pretend to be whatever he needs to be—as long as he effectively maintains his position of power.

On the Reasons Why Men Are Praised or Blamed—Especially Princes

It remains now to be seen what style and principles a prince ought to adopt in dealing with his subjects and friends. I know the subject has been treated frequently before, and I'm afraid people will think me rash for trying to do so again, especially since I intend to differ in this discussion from what others have said. But since I intend to write something useful to an understanding reader, it seemed better to go after the real truth of the matter than to repeat what people have imagined. A great many men have imagined states and princedoms such as nobody ever saw or knew in the real world, for there's such a difference between the way we really live and the way we ought to live that the man who neglects the real to study the ideal will learn how to accomplish his ruin, not his salvation. Any man who tries to be good all the time is bound to come to ruin among the great number who are not good. Hence a prince who wants to keep his post must learn how not to be good, and use that knowledge, or refrain from using it, as necessity requires.

Putting aside, then, all the imaginary things that are said about princes, and getting down to the truth, let me say that whenever men are discussed (and especially princes because they are prominent), there are certain qualities that bring them either praise or blame. Thus some are considered generous, others stingy (I use a Tuscan term, since "greedy" in our speech means a man who wants to take other people's goods. We call a man "stingy" who clings to his own); some are givers, others grabbers: some cruel, others merciful; one man is treacherous, another faithful; one is feeble and effeminate, another fierce and spirited; one humane, another proud; one lustful, another chaste; one straightforward, another sly; one harsh, another gentle; one serious, another playful; one religious, another skeptical, and so on. I know everyone will agree that among these many qualities a prince certainly ought to have all those that are considered good. But since it is impossible to have and exercise them all, because the conditions of human life simply do not allow it, a prince must be shrewd enough to avoid the public disgrace of those vices that would lose him his state. If he possibly can, he should also guard against vices that will not lose him his state; but if he cannot prevent them, he should not be too worried about indulging them. And furthermore, he should not be too worried about incurring blame for any vice without which he would find it hard to save his state. For if you look at matters carefully, you will see that something resembling virtue, if you follow it, may be your ruin, while something else resembling vice will lead, if you follow it, to your security and well-being.

On Liberality and Stinginess

Let me begin, then, with the first of the qualities mentioned above, by saying that a reputation for liberality is doubtless very fine; but the generosity that earns you that reputation can do you great harm. For if you exercise your generosity in a really virtuous way, as you should, nobody will know of it, and you cannot escape the odium of the opposite vice. Hence if you wish to be widely known as a generous man, you must seize every opportunity to make a big display of your giving. A prince of this character is bound to use up his entire revenue in works of ostentation. Thus, in the end, if he wants to keep a name for generosity, he will have to load his people with exorbitant taxes and squeeze money out of them in every way he can. This is the first step in making him odious to his subjects; for when he is poor, nobody will respect him. Then, when his generosity has angered many and brought rewards to a few, the slightest difficulty will trouble him, and at the first approach of danger, down he goes. If by chance he foresees this, and tries to change his ways, he will immediately be labeled a miser.

Since a prince cannot use this virtue of liberality in such a way as to become known for it unless he harms his own security, he won't mind, if he judges prudently of things, being known as a miser. In due course he will be thought the more liberal man, when people see that his parsimony enables him to live on his income, to defend himself against his enemies, and to undertake major projects without burdening his people with taxes. Thus he will be acting liberally toward all those people from whom he takes nothing (and there are an immense number of them, and in a stingy way toward those people on whom he bestows nothing (and they are very few). In our times, we have seen great things being accomplished only by men who have had the name of misers; all the others have gone under. Pope Julius II, though he used his reputation as a generous man to gain the papacy, sacrificed it in order to be able to make war; the present king of France has waged many wars without levying a single extra tax on his people, simply because he could take care of the extra expenses out of the savings from his long parsimony. If the present king of Spain had a reputation for generosity, he would never have been able to undertake so many campaigns, or win so many of them.

Hence a prince who prefers not to rob his subjects, who wants to be able to defend himself, who wants to avoid poverty and contempt, and who doesn't want to become a plunderer, should not mind in the least if people consider him a miser; this is simply one of the vices that enable him to reign. Someone may object that Caesar used a reputation for generosity to become emperor, and many other people have also risen in the world, because they were generous or were supposed to be so. Well, I answer, either you are a prince already, or you are in the process of becoming one; in the first case, this reputation for generosity is harmful to you, in the second case it is very necessary. Caesar was one of those who wanted to become ruler in Rome; but after he had reached his goal, if he had lived, and had not cut down on his expenses, he would have ruined the empire itself. Someone may say: there have been plenty of princes, very successful in warfare, who have had a reputation for generosity. But I answer; either the prince is spending his own money and that of his subjects, or he is spending someone else's. In the first case, he ought to be sparing; in the second case, he ought to spend money like water. Any prince at the head of his army, which lives on loot, extortion, and plunder, disposes of other people's property, and is bound to be very generous; otherwise, his soldiers would desert him. You can always be a more generous giver when what you give is not yours or your subjects'; Cyrus, Caesar, and Alexander were generous in this way. Spending what belongs to other people does no harm to your reputation, rather it enhances it; only spending your own substance harms you. And there is nothing that wears out faster than generosity; even as you practice it, you lose the means of practicing it, and you become either poor and contemptible or (in the course of escaping poverty) rapacious and hateful. The thing above all against which a prince must protect himself is being contemptible and hateful; generosity leads to both. Thus, it's much wiser to put up with the reputation of being a miser, which brings you shame without hate, than to be forced—just because you want to appear generous—into a reputation for rapacity, which brings shame on you and hate along with it.

On Cruelty and Clemency: Whether It Is Better to Be Loved or Feared

Continuing now with our list of qualities, let me say that every prince should prefer to be considered merciful rather than cruel, yet he should be careful not to mismanage this clemency of his. People thought Cesare Borgia was cruel, but that cruelty of his reorganized the Romagna, united it, and established it in peace and loyalty. Anyone who views the matter realistically will see that this prince was much more merciful than the people of Florence who, to avoid the reputation of cruelty, allowed Pistoia to be destroyed. Thus, no prince should mind being called cruel for what he does to keep his subjects united and loyal; he may make examples of a very few, but he will be more merciful in reality than those who, in their tenderheartedness, allow disorders to occur, with their attendant murders and lootings. Such turbulence brings harm to an entire community, while the executions ordered by a prince affect only one individual at a time. A new prince, above all others, cannot possibly avoid a name for cruelty, since new states are always in danger. And Virgil, speaking through the mouth of Dido says:

> My cruel fate
> And doubts attending an unsettled state
> Force me to guard my coast from foreign foes.

Yet a prince should be slow to believe rumors and to commit himself to action on the basis of them. He should not be afraid of his own thoughts; he ought to proceed cautiously, moderating his conduct with prudence and humanity, allowing neither overconfidence to make him careless, nor overtimidity to make him intolerable.

Here the question arises: is it better to be loved than feared, or vice versa? I don't doubt that every prince would like to be both; but since it is hard to accommodate these qualities, if you have to make a choice, to be feared is much safer than to be loved. For it is a good general rule about men, that they are ungrateful, fickle, liars and deceivers, fearful of danger and greedy for gain. While you serve their welfare, they are all yours, offering their blood, their belongings, their lives, and their children's lives, as we noted above—so long as the danger is remote. But when the danger is close at hand, they turn against you. Then, any prince who has relied on their words and has made no other preparations will come to grief; because friendships that are bought at a price, and not with greatness and nobility of soul, may be paid for but they are not acquired, and they cannot be used in time of need. People are less concerned with offending a man who makes himself loved than one who makes himself feared: the reason is that love is a link of obligation which men, because they are rotten, will break any time they think doing so serves their advantage; but fear involves dread of punishment, from which they can never escape.

Still, a prince should make himself feared in such a way that, even if he gets no love, he gets no hate either; because it is perfectly possible to be feared and not hated, and this will be the result if only the prince will keep his hands off the property of his subjects or citizens, and off their women. When he does have to shed blood, he should be sure to have a strong justification and manifest cause; but above all, he should not confiscate people's property, because men are quicker to forget the death of a father than the loss of a patrimony. Besides, pretexts for confiscation are always plentiful, it never fails that a prince who starts living by plunder can find reasons to rob someone else. Excuses for proceeding against someone's life are much rarer and more quickly exhausted.

But a prince at the head of his armies and commanding a multitude of soldiers should not care a bit if he is considered cruel; without such a reputation, he could never hold his army together and ready for action. Among the marvelous deeds of Hannibal, this was prime: that, having an immense army, which included men of many different races and nations, and which he led to battle in distant countries, he never allowed them to fight among themselves or to rise against him, whether his fortune was good or bad. The reason for this could only be his inhuman cruelty, which, along with his countless other talents, made him an object of awe and terror to his soldiers; and without the cruelty, his other qualities would never have sufficed. The historians who pass snap judgments on these matters admire his accomplishments and at the same time condemn the cruelty which was their main cause.

When I say, "His other qualities would never have sufficed," we can see that this is true from the example of Scipio, an outstanding man not only among those of his own time, but in all recorded history; yet his armies revolted in Spain, for no other reason than his excessive leniency in allowing his soldiers more freedom than military discipline permits. Fabius Maximus rebuked him in the senate for this failing, calling him the corrupter of the Roman armies. When a lieutenant of Scipio's plundered the Locrians, he took no action in behalf of the people, and did nothing to discipline that insolent lieutenant; again, this was the result of his easygoing nature. Indeed, when someone in the senate wanted to excuse him on this occasion, he said there are many men who knew better how to avoid error themselves than how to correct error in others. Such a soft temper would in time have tarnished the fame and glory of Scipio, had he brought it to the office of emperor; but as he lived under the control of the senate, this harmful quality of his not only remained hidden but was considered creditable.

Returning to the question of being feared or loved, I conclude that since men love at their own inclination but can be made to fear at the inclination of the prince, a shrewd prince will lay his foundations on what is under his own control, not on what is controlled by others. He should simply take pains not to be hated, as I said.

The Way Princes Should Keep Their Word

How praiseworthy it is for a prince to keep his word and live with integrity rather than by craftiness, everyone understands; yet we see from recent experience that those princes have accomplished most who paid little heed to keeping their promises, but who knew how craftily to manipulate the minds of men. In the end, they won out over those who tried to act honestly.

You should consider then, that there are two ways of fighting, one with laws and the other with force. The first is properly a human method, the second belongs to beasts. But as the first method does not always suffice, you sometimes have to turn to the second. Thus a prince must know how to make good use of both the beast and the man. Ancient writers made subtle note of this fact when they wrote that Achilles and many other princes of antiquity were sent to be reared by Chiron the centaur, who trained them in his discipline. Having a teacher who is half man and half beast can only mean that a prince must know how to use both these two natures, and that one without the other has no lasting effect.

Since a prince must know how to use the character of beasts, he should pick for imitation the fox and the lion. As the lion cannot protect himself from traps, and the fox cannot defend himself from wolves, you have to be a fox in order to be wary of traps, and a lion to overawe the wolves. Those who try to live by the lion alone are badly mistaken. Thus a prudent prince cannot and should not keep his word when to do so would go against his interest, or when the reasons that made him pledge it no longer apply. Doubtless if all men were good, this rule would be bad; but since they are a sad lot, and keep no faith with you, you in your turn are under no obligation to keep it with them.

Besides, a prince will never lack for legitimate excuses to explain away his breaches of faith. Modern history will furnish innumerable examples of this behavior, showing how many treaties and promises have been made null and void by the faithlessness of princes, and how the man succeeded best who knew best how to play the fox. But it is a necessary part of this nature that you must conceal it carefully; you must be a great liar and hypocrite. Men are so simple of mind and so much dominated by their immediate needs, that a deceitful man will always find plenty who are ready to be deceived. One of many recent examples calls for mention. Alexander VI never did anything else, never had another thought, except to deceive men, and he always found fresh material to work on. Never was there a man more convincing in his assertions, who sealed his promises with more solemn oaths, and who observed them less. Yet his deceptions were always successful, because he knew exactly how to manage this sort of business.

In actual fact, a prince may not have all the admirable qualities we listed, but it is very necessary that he should seem to have them. Indeed, I will venture to say that when you have them and exercise them all the time, they are harmful to you; when you just seem to have them, they are useful. It is good to appear merciful, truthful, humane, sincere, and religious; it is good to be so in reality. But you must keep your mind so disposed that, in case of need, you can turn to the exact contrary. This has to be understood: a prince, and especially a new prince, cannot possibly exercise all those virtues for which men are called "good." To preserve the state, he often has to do things against his word, against charity, against humanity, against religion. Thus he has to have a mind ready to shift as the winds of fortune and the varying circumstances of life may dictate. And as I said above, he should not depart from the good if he can hold to it, but he should be ready to enter on evil if he has to.

Hence a prince should take great care never to drop a word that does not seem imbued with the five good qualities noted above; to anyone who sees or hears him, he should appear all compassion, all honor, all humanity, all integrity, all religion. Nothing is more necessary than to seem to have this last virtue. Men in general judge more by the sense of sight than by the sense of touch, because everyone can see but only a few can test by feeling. Everyone sees what you seem to be, few know what you really are; and those few do not dare take a stand against the general opinion, supported by the majesty of the government. In the actions of all men, and especially of princes who are not subject to a court of appeal, we must always look to the end. Let a prince, therefore, win victories and uphold his state; his methods will always be considered worthy, and everyone will praise them, because the masses are always impressed by the superficial appearance of things, and by the outcome of an enterprise. And the world consists of nothing but the masses; the few who have no influence when the many feel secure. A certain prince of our own time, whom it's just as well not to name, preaches nothing but peace and mutual trust, yet he is the determined enemy of both; and if on several different occasions he had observed either, he would have lost both his reputation and his throne.

POSSIBILITIES FOR WRITING

1. What seems to be Machiavelli's attitude toward those whom princes rule, and how does this factor into his advice? In developing your answer, cite specific passages from the text.

2. How do you respond to Machiavelli's characterization of morality here? In general, do you think that "moral" behavior is situational, that the morals one practices should depend on the situation one finds oneself in? Why or why not?

3. Consider what constitutes political power today—whether in a democracy such as the United States or under another political system with which you are familiar. To what extent does Machiavelli's advice apply under such a system, and to what extent does it not? Be as specific as possible in your use of examples.

Nancy Mairs (b. 1943) is a native of Long Beach. California, and attended Wheaton College and the University of Arizona, where she received her Ph.D. and later headed the women's studies program. Her earliest publications mere volumes of poetry; including Instead It Is Winter (1977), but it teas with the collection of autobiographical essays Plaintext (1956) that she began to receive wide attention as a writer. In these essays, admired for their sharp and unsentimental exploration of difficult personnel issues, Mairs often looks unflinchingly at the effects of her multiple sclerosis and the physical toll it takes on both herself and her family. Later collections include Carnal Arts (1990) and Waist-High in the World: Living Among the Nondisabled (1997). Mairs is also the author of Voice Lessons: On Becoming a (Woman) Writer (1996), and, most recently, A Dynamic God (2008).

NANCY MAIRS

On Being a Cripple

In "On Being a Cripple," Nancy Mairs writes about herself as a person who struggles on a daily basis with the consequences of multiple sclerosis (MS). Mairs has lived with MS so long and so intimately that she considers the disease as part of herself—as an aspect of her identity. Writing about the disease is a form of therapy for her.

Mairs writes with vigor and candor about what MS means for her and what it does to her. She is not embarrassed by her condition, though she admits to becoming angry and frustrated at times by her body's refusal to do what she wants it to do as a result of the disease. Mairs makes no apologies for herself, and she avoids either sentimentalizing her condition or assuming the role of victim. She accepts the MS that afflicts her because the disease is incurable. Instead of railing against the injustice of her affliction, Mairs chooses to live her life as fully as possible, all the while concentrating on how MS has opened and enriched her life.

To escape is nothing. Not to escape is nothing.

—LOUISE BOGAN

The other day I was thinking of writing an essay on being a cripple. I was thinking hard in one of the stalls of the women's room in my office building, as I was shoving my shirt into my jeans and tugging up my zipper. Preoccupied, I flushed, picked up my book bag, took my cane down from the hook, and unlatched the door. So many movements unbalanced me, and as I pulled the door open I fell over backward, landing fully clothed on the toilet seat with my legs splayed in front of me: the old beetle-on-its-back routine. Saturday afternoon, the building deserted, I was free to laugh aloud as I wriggled back to my feet, my voice bouncing off the yellowish tiles from all directions. Had anyone been there with me, I'd have been still and faint and hot with chagrin. I decided that it was high time to write the essay.

First, the matter of semantics. I am a cripple. I choose this word to name me. I choose from among several possibilities, the most common of which are "handicapped" and "disabled." I made the choice a number of years ago, without thinking, unaware of my motives for doing so. Even now, I'm not sure what those motives are, but I recognize that they are complex and not entirely flattering. People—crippled or not—wince at the word "cripple," as they do not at "handicapped" or "disabled." Perhaps I want them to wince. I want them to see me as a tough customer, one to whom the fates/gods/viruses have not been kind, but who can face the brutal truth of her existence squarely. As a cripple, I swagger.

But, to be fair to myself, a certain amount of honesty underlies my choice. "Cripple" seems to me a clean word, straightforward and precise. It has an honorable history, having made its first appearance in the Lindisfarne Gospel in the tenth century. As a lover of words, I like the accuracy with which it describes my condition: I have lost the full use of my limbs. "Disabled," by contrast, suggests any incapacity, physical or mental. And I certainly don't like "handicapped," which implies that I have deliberately been put at a disadvantage, by whom I can't imagine (my God is not a Handicapper General), in order to equalize chances in the great race of life. These words seem to me to be moving away from my condition, to be widening the gap between word and reality. Most remote is the recently coined euphemism "differently abled," which partakes of the same semantic hopefulness that transformed countries from "undeveloped" to "underdeveloped," then to "less developed," and finally to "developing" nations. People have continued to starve in those countries during the shift. Some realities do not obey the dictates of language.

Mine is one of them. Whatever you call me, I remain crippled. But I don't care what you call me, so long as it isn't "differently abled," which strikes me as pure verbal garbage designed, by its ability to describe anyone, to describe no one. I subscribe to George Orwell's thesis that "the slovenliness of our language makes it easier for us to have foolish thoughts." And I refuse to participate in the degeneration of the language to the extent that I deny that I have lost anything in the course of this calamitous disease; I refuse to pretend that the only differences between you and me are the various ordinary ones that distinguish any one person from another. But call me "disabled" or "handicapped" if you like. I have long since grown accustomed to them; and if they are vague, at least they hint at the truth. Moreover, I use them myself. Society is no readier to accept crippledness than to accept death, war, sex, sweat, or wrinkles. I would never refer to another person as a cripple. It is the word I use to name only myself.

I haven't always been crippled, a fact for which I am soundly grateful. To be whole of limb is, I know from experience, infinitely more pleasant and useful than to be crippled; and if that knowledge leaves one open to bitterness at my loss, the physical soundness I once enjoyed (though I did not enjoy it half enough) is well worth the occasional stab of regret. Though never any good at sports, I was a normally active child and young adult. I climbed trees, played hopscotch, jumped rope, skated, swam, rode my bicycle, sailed. I despised team sports, spending some of the wretchedest afternoons of my life, sweaty and humiliated, behind a field-hockey stick and under a basketball hoop. I tramped alone for miles along the bridle paths that webbed the woods behind the house I grew up in. I swayed through countless dim hours in the arms of one man or another under the scattered shot of light from mirrored balls, and gyrated through countless more as Tab Hunter and Johnny Mathis gave way to the Rolling Stones, Creedence Clearwater Revival, Cream. I walked down the aisle. I pushed baby carriages, changed tires in the rain, marched for peace.

When I was twenty-eight I started to trip and drop things. What at first seemed my natural clumsiness soon became too pronounced to shrug off. I consulted a neurologist, who told me that I had a brain tumor. A battery of tests, increasingly disagreeable, revealed no tumor. About a year and a half later I developed a blurred spot in one eye. I had, at last, the episodes "disseminated in space and time" requisite for a diagnosis: multiple sclerosis. I have never been sorry for the doctor's initial misdiagnosis, however. For almost a week, until the negative results of the tests were in, I thought that I was going to die right away. Every day for the past nearly ten years, then, has been a kind of gift. I accept all gifts.

Multiple sclerosis is a chronic degenerative disease of the central nervous system, in which the myelin that sheathes the nerves is somehow eaten away and scar tissue forms in its place, interrupting the nerves' signals. During its course, which is unpredictable and uncontrollable, one may lose vision, hearing, speech, the ability to walk, control of bladder and/or bowels, strength in any or all extremities, sensitivity to touch, vibration, and/or pain, potency, coordination of movements—the list of possibilities is lengthy and, yes horrifying. One may also lose one's sense of humor. That's the easiest to lose and the hardest to survive without.

In the past ten years, I have sustained some of these losses. Characteristic of MS are sudden attacks, called exacerbations, followed by remissions, and these I have not had. Instead, my disease has been slowly progressive. My left leg is now so weak that I walk with the aid of a brace and a cane; and for distances I use an Amigo, a variation on the electric wheelchair that looks rather like an electrified kiddie car. I no longer have much use of my left hand. Now my right side is weakening as well. I still have the blurred spot in my right eye. Overall, though, I've been lucky so far. My world has, of necessity, been circumscribed by my losses, but the terrain left me has been ample enough for me to continue many of the activities that absorb me: writing, teaching, raising children and cats and plants and snakes, reading, speaking publicly about MS and depression, even playing bridge with people patient and honorable enough to let me scatter cards every which way without sneaking a peek.

Lest I begin to sound like Pollyanna, however, let me say that I don't like having MS. I hate it. My life holds realities—harsh ones, some of them—that no right-minded human being ought to accept without grumbling. One of them is fatigue. I know of no one with MS who does not complain of bone-weariness; in a disease that presents an astonishing variety of symptoms, fatigue seems to be a common factor. I wake up in the morning feeling the way most people do at the end of a bad day, and I take it from there. As a result, I spend a lot of time in *extremis* and, impatient with limitation, I tend to ignore my fatigue until my body breaks down in some way and forces rest. Then I miss picnics, dinner parties, poetry readings, the brief visits of old friends from out of town. The offspring of a puritanical tradition of exceptional venerability, I cannot view these lapses without shame. My life often seems a series of small failures to do as I ought.

I lead, on the whole, an ordinary life, probably rather like the one I would have led had I not had MS. I am lucky that my predilections were already solitary, sedentary, and bookish—unlike the world-famous French cellist I have read about, or the young woman I talked with one long afternoon who wanted only to be a jockey. I had just begun graduate school when I found out something was wrong with me, and I have remained, interminably, a graduate student. Perhaps I would not have if I'd thought I had the stamina to return to a full-time job as a technical editor; but I've enjoyed my studies.

In addition to studying, I teach writing courses. I also teach medical students how to give neurological examinations. I pick up freelance editing jobs here and there. I have raised a foster son and sent him into the world, where he has made me two grandbabies, and I am still escorting my daughter and son through adolescence. I go to Mass every Saturday. I am a superb, if messy, cook. I am also an enthusiastic laundress, capable of sorting a hamper full of clothes into five subtly differentiated piles, but a terrible housekeeper. I can do italic writing and, in an emergency, bathe an oil-soaked cat. I play a fiendish game of Scrabble. When I have the time and the money, I like to sit on my front steps with my husband, drinking Amaretto and smoking a cigar, as we imagine our counterparts in Leningrad and make sure that the sun gets down once more behind the sharp childish scrawl of the Tucson Mountains.

This lively plenty has its bleak complement, of course, in all the things I can no longer do. I will never run again, except in dreams, and one day I may have to write that I will never walk again. I like to go camping, but I can't follow George and the children along the trails that wander out of a campsite through the desert or into the mountains. In fact, even on the level I've learned never to check the weather or try to hold a coherent conversation: I need all my attention for my wayward feet. Of late, I have begun to catch myself wondering how people can propel themselves without canes. With only one usable hand, I have to select my clothing with care not so much for style as for ease of ingress and egress, and even so, dressing can be laborious. I can no longer do fine stitchery, pick up babies, play the piano, braid my hair. I am immobilized by acute attacks of depression, which may or may not be physiologically related to MS but are certainly its logical concomitant.

These two elements, the plenty and the privation, are never pure, nor are the delight and wretchedness that accompany them. Almost every pickle that I get into as a result of my weakness and clumsiness—and I get into plenty—is funny as well as maddening and sometimes painful. I recall one May afternoon when a friend and I were going out for a drink after finishing up at school. As we were climbing into opposite sides of my car, chatting, I tripped and fell, flat and hard, onto the asphalt parking lot, my abrupt departure interrupting him in mid-sentence. "Where'd you go?" he called as he came around the back of the car to find me hauling myself up by the door frame. "Are you all right?" Yes, I told him, I was fine, just a bit rattly, and we drove off to find a shady patio and some beer. When I got home an hour or so later, my daughter greeted me with "What have you done to yourself?" I looked down. One elbow of my white turtleneck with the green froggies, one knee of my white trousers, one white kneesock were bloodsoaked. We peeled off the clothes and inspected the damage, which was nasty enough but not alarming. That part wasn't funny: The abrasions took a long time to heal, and one got a little infected. Even so, when I think of my friend talking earnestly, suddenly, to the hot thin air while I dropped from his view as though through a trap door, I find the image as silly as something from a Marx Brothers movie.

I may find it easier than other cripples to amuse myself because I live propped by the acceptance and the assistance and, sometimes, the amusement of those around me. Grocery clerks tear my checks out of my checkbook for me, and sales clerks find chairs to put into dressing rooms when I want to try on clothes. The people I work with make sure I teach at times when I am least likely to be fatigued, in places I can get to, with the materials I need. My students, with one anonymous exception (in an end-of-the-semester evaluation), have been unperturbed by my disability. Some even like it. One was immensely cheered by the information that I paint my own fingernails; she decided, she told me, that if I could go to such trouble over fine details, she could keep on writing essays. I suppose I became some sort of bright-fingered muse. She wrote good essays, too.

The most important struts in the framework of my existence, of course, are my husband and children. Dismayingly few marriages survive the MS test, and why should they? Most twenty-two- and nineteen-year-olds, like George and me, can vow in clear conscience, after a childhood of chicken pox and summer colds, to keep one another in sickness and in health so long as they both shall live. Not many are equipped for catastrophe: the dismay, the depression, the extra work, the boredom that a degenerative disease can insinuate into a relationship. And our society, with its emphasis on fun and its association of fun with physical performance, offers little encouragement for a whole spouse to stay with a crippled partner. Children experience similar stresses when faced with a crippled parent, and they are more helpless, since parents and children can't usually get divorced. They hate, of course, to be different from their peers, and the child whose mother is tacking down the aisle of a school auditorium packed with proud parents like a Cape Cod dinghy in a stiff breeze jolly well stands out in a crowd. Deprived of legal divorce, the child can at least deny the mother's disability, even her existence, forgetting to tell her about recitals and PTA meetings, refusing to accompany her to stores or church or the movies, never inviting friends to the house. Many do.

But I've been limping along for ten years now, and so far George and the children are still at my left elbow, holding tight. Anne and Matthew vacuum floors and dust furniture and haul trash and rake up dog droppings and button my cuffs and bake lasagna and Toll House cookies with just enough grumbling so I know that they don't have brain fever. And far from hiding me, they're forever dragging me by racks of fancy clothes or through teeming school corridors, or welcoming gaggles of friends while I'm wandering through the house in Anne's filmy pink babydoll pajamas. George generally calls before he brings someone home, but he does just as many dumb thankless chores as the children. And they all yell at me, laugh at some of my jokes, write me funny letters when we're apart—in short, treat me as an ordinary human being for whom they have some use. I think they like me. Unless they're faking. . . .

Faking. There's the rub. Tugging at the fringes of my consciousness always is the terror that people are kind to me only because I'm a cripple. My mother almost shattered me once, with that instinct mothers have—blind, I think, in this case, but unerring nonetheless—for striking blows along the fault-lines of their children's hearts, by telling me, in an attack on my selfishness. "We all have to make allowances for you, of course, because of the way you are." From the distance of a couple of years. I have to admit that I haven't any idea just what she meant, and I'm not sure that she knew either. She was awfully angry. But at the time, as the words thudded home, I felt my worst fear, suddenly realized. I could bear being called selfish: I am. But I couldn't bear the corroboration that those around me were doing in fact what I'd always suspected them of doing, professing fondness while silently putting up with me because of the way I am, A cripple. I've been a little cracked ever since.

Along with this fear that people are secretly accepting shoddy goods comes a relentless pressure to please—to prove myself worth the burdens I impose, I guess, or to build a substantial account of goodwill against which I may write drafts in times of need. Part of the pressure arises from social expectations. In our society, anyone who deviates from the norm had better find some way to compensate. Like fat people, who are expected to be jolly, cripples must bear their lot meekly and cheerfully. A grumpy cripple isn't playing by the rules. And much of pressure is self-generated. Early on I vowed that, if I had to have MS, by God I was going to do it well. This is a class act, ladies and gentlemen. No tears, no recriminations, no faint-heartedness.

One way and another, then, I wind up feeling like Tiny Tim, peering over the edge of the table at the Christmas goose, waving my crutch, piping down God's blessing on us all. Only sometimes I don't want to play Tiny Tim. I'd rather be Caliban, a most scurvy monster. Fortunately, at home no one much cares whether I'm a good cripple or a bad cripple as long as I make vichyssoise with fair regularity. One evening several years ago, Anne was reading at the dining-room table while I cooked dinner. As I opened a can of tomatoes, the can slipped in my left hand and juice spattered me and the counter with bloody spots. Fatigued and infuriated, I bellowed. "I'm so sick of being crippled!" Anne glanced at me over the top of her book. "There now," she said, "do you feel better?" "Yes." I said, "yes, I do. "She went back to her reading . I felt better. That's about all the attention my scurviness ever gets.

Because I hate being crippled, I sometimes hate myself for being a cripple. Over the years I have come to expect—even accept—attacks of violent self-loathing. Luckily, in general our society no longer connects deformity and disease directly with evil (though a charismatic once told me that I have MS because a devil is in me) and so I'm allowed to move largely at will, even among small children. But I'm not sure that this revision of attitude has been particularly helpful. Physical imperfection, even freed of moral disapprobation, still defies and violates the ideal, especially for women, whose confinement in their bodies as objects of desire is far from over. Each age, of course, has its ideal, and I doubt that ours is any better or worse than any other. Today's ideal woman, who lives on the glossy pages of dozens of magazines, seems to be between the ages of eighteen and twenty-five; her hair has body, her teeth flash white, her breath smells minty, her underarms are dry; she has a career but is still a fabulous cook, especially of meals that take less than twenty minutes to prepare; she does not ordinarily appear to have a husband or children; she is trim and deeply tanned; she jogs, swims, plays tennis, rides a bicycle, sails, but does not bowl; she travels widely, even to out-of-the-way places like Finland and Samoa, always in the company of the ideal man, who possesses a nearly identical set of characteristics. There are a few exceptions. Though usually white and often blonde, she may be black. Hispanic, Asian, or Native American, so long as she is unusually sleek. She may be old, provided she is selling a laxative or is Lauren Bacall. If she is selling a detergent, she may be married and have a flock of strikingly messy children. But she is never a cripple.

Like many women I know, I have always had an uneasy relationship with my body. I was not a popular child, largely, I think now, because I was peculiar: intelligent, intense, moody, shy, given to unexpected actions and inexplicable notions and emotions. But as I entered adolescence, I believed myself unpopular because I was homely: my breasts too flat, my mouth too wide, my hips too narrow, my clothing never quite right in fit or style. I was not, in fact, particularly ugly, old photographs inform me, though I was well off the ideal; but I carried this sense of self-alienation with me into adulthood, where it regenerated in response to the depredations of MS. Even with my brace I walk with a limp so pronounced that, seeing myself on the videotape of a television program on the disabled, I couldn't believe that anything but an inch-worm could make progress humping along like that. My shoulders droop and my pelvis thrusts forward as I try to balance myself upright, throwing my frame into a bony S. As a result of contractures, one shoulder is higher than the other and I carry one arm bent in front of me, the fingers curled into a claw. My left arm and leg have wasted into pipestems, and I try always to keep them covered. When I think about how my body must look to others, especially to men, to whom I have been trained to display myself, I feel ludicrous, even loathsome.

At my age, however, I don't spend much time thinking about my appearance. The burning egocentricity of adolescence, which assures one that all the world is looking all the time, has passed, thank God, and I'm generally too caught up in what I'm doing to step back, as I used to, and watch myself as though upon a stage. I'm also too old to believe in the accuracy of self-image. I know that I'm not a hideous crone, that in fact, when I'm rested, well dressed, and well made up, I look fine. The self-loathing I feel is neither physically nor intellectually substantial. What I hate is not me but a disease.

I am not a disease.

And a disease is not—at least not singlehandedly—going to determine who I am, though at first it seemed to be going to. Adjusting to a chronic incurable illness, I have moved through a process similar to that outlined by Elizabeth Kübler-Ross in *On Death and Dying*. The major difference—and it is far more significant than most people recognize—is that I can't be sure of the outcome, as the terminally ill cancer patient can. Research studies indicate that, with proper medical care, I may achieve a "normal" life span. And in our society, with its vision of death as the ultimate evil, worse even than decrepitude, the response to such news is, "Oh well, at least you're not going to *die.*" Are there worse things than dying? I think that there may be.

I think of two women I know, both with MS, both enough older than I to have served me as models. One took to her bed several years ago and has been there ever since. Although she can sit in a high-backed wheelchair, because she is incontinent she refuses to go out at all, even though incontinence pants, which are readily available at any pharmacy, could protect her from embarrassment. Instead, she stays at home and insists that her husband, a small quiet man, a retired civil servant, stay there with her except for a quick weekly foray to the supermarket. The other woman, whose illness was diagnosed when she was eighteen, a nursing student engaged to a young doctor, finished her training, married her doctor, accompanied him to Germany when he was in the service, bore three sons and a daughter, now grown and gone. When she can, she travels with her husband; she plays bridge, embroiders, swims regularly; she works, like me, as a symptomatic-patient instructor of medical students in neurology. Guess which woman I hope to be.

At the beginning, I thought about having MS almost incessantly. And because of the unpredictable course of the disease, my thoughts were always terrified. Each night I'd get into bed wondering whether I'd get out again the next morning, whether I'd be able to see, to speak, to hold a pen between my fingers. Knowing that the day might come when I'd be physically incapable of killing myself, I thought perhaps I ought to do so right away, while I still had the strength. Gradually I came to understand that the Nancy who might one day lie inert under a bedsheet, arms and legs paralyzed, unable to feed or bathe herself, unable to reach out for a gun, a bottle of pills, was not the Nancy I was at present, and that I could not presume to make decisions for that future Nancy, who might well not want in the least to die. Now the only provision I've made for the future Nancy is that when the time comes—and it is likely to come in the form of pneumonia, friend to the weak and the old—I am not to be treated with machines and medications. If she is unable to communicate by then, I hope she will be satisfied with these terms.

Thinking all the time about having MS grew tiresome and intrusive, especially in the large and tragic mode in which I was accustomed to considering my plight. Months and even years went by without catastrophe (at least without one related to MS), and really I was awfully busy, what with George and children and snakes and students and poems, and I hadn't the time, let alone the inclination, to devote myself to being a disease. Too, the richer my life became, the funnier it seemed, as though there were some connection between largesse and laughter, and so my tragic stance began to waver until, even with the aid of a brace and a cane, I couldn't hold it for very long at a time.

After several years I was satisfied with my adjustment. I had suffered my grief and fury and terror, I thought, but now I was at ease with my lot. Then one summer day I set out with George and the children across the desert for a vacation in California. Part way to Yuma I became aware that my right leg felt funny. "I think I've had an exacerbation," I told George, "What shall we do?" he asked. "I think we'd better get the hell to California." I said, "because I don't know whether I'll ever make it again." So we went on to San Diego and then to Orange, up the Pacific Coast Highway to Santa Cruz, across to Yosemite, down to Sequoia and Joshua Tree, and so back over the desert to home. It was a fine two-week trip, filled with friends and fair weather, and I wouldn't have missed it for the world, though I did in fact make it back to California two years later. Nor would there have been any point in missing it, since in MS, once the symptoms have appeared, the neurological damage has been done, and there's no way to predict or prevent that damage.

The incident spoiled my self-satisfaction, however. It renewed my grief and fury and terror, and I learned that one never finishes adjusting to MS. I don't know now why I thought one would. One does not, after all, finish adjusting to life, and MS is simply a fact of my life—not my favorite fact, of course—but as ordinary as my nose and my tropical fish and my yellow Mazda station wagon. It may at any time get worse, but no amount of worry, or anticipation can prepare me for a new loss. My life is a lesson in losses. I learn one at a time.

And I had best be patient in the learning, since I'll have to do it like it or not. As any rock fan knows, you can't always get what you want. Particularly when you have MS. You can't, for example, get cured. In recent years researchers and the organizations that fund research have started to pay MS some attention even though it isn't fatal; perhaps they have begun to see that life is something other than a quantitative phenomenon, that one may be very much alive for a very long time in a life that isn't worth living. The researchers have made some progress toward understanding the mechanism of the disease: It may well be an autoimmune reaction triggered by a slow-acting virus. But they are nowhere near its prevention, control, or cure. And most of us want to be cured. Some, unable to accept incurability, grasp at one treatment after another, no matter how bizarre: megavitamin therapy, gluten-free diet, injections of cobra venom, hypothermal suits, lymphocyto-pharesis, hyperbaric chambers. Many treatments are probably harmless enough, but none are curative.

The absence of a cure often makes MS patients bitter toward their doctors. Doctors are, after all, the priests of modern society, the new shamans, whose business is to heal, and many an MS patient roves from one to another, searching for the "good" doctor who will make him well. Doctors too think of themselves as healers, and for this reason many have trouble dealing with MS patients, whose disease in its intransigence defeats their aims and mocks their skills. Too few doctors, it is true, treat their patients as whole human beings, but the reverse is also true. I have always tried to be gentle with my doctors, who often have more at stake in terms of ego than I do. I may be frustrated, maddened, depressed by the incurability of my disease, but I am not diminished by it, and they are. When I push myself up from my seat in the waiting room and stumble toward them, I incarnate the limitation of their powers. The least I can do is refuse to press on their tenderest spots.

This gentleness is part of the reason that I'm not sorry to be a cripple. I didn't have it before. Perhaps I'd have developed it anyway—how could I know such a thing?—and I wish I had more of it, but I'm glad of what I have. It has opened and enriched my life enormously, this sense that my frailty and need must be mirrored in others, that in searching for and shaping a stable core in a life wrenched by change and loss, change and loss, I must recognize the same process, under individual conditions, in the lives around me. I do not deprecate such knowledge, however I've come by it.

All the same, if a cure were found, would I take it? In a minute, I may be a cripple, but I'm only occasionally a loony and never a saint. Anyway, in my brand of theology God doesn't give bonus points for a limp. I'd take a cure; I just don't need one. A friend who also has MS startled me once by asking. "Do you ever say to yourself. 'Why me, Lord?'" "No, Michael, I don't," I told him, "because whenever I try, the only response I can think of is 'Why not?'" If I could make a cosmic deal, who would I put in my place? What in my life would I give up in exchange for sound limbs and a thrilling rush of energy? No one.

Nothing, I might as well do the job myself. Now that I'm getting the hang of it.

POSSIBILITIES FOR WRITING

1. Mairs's essay exhibits a variety of shifts in tone, rellecting shifts in her own feelings about being crippled. Analyze "On Being a Cripple" to explore such shifts and their effect on your response to the essay as a whole.

2. The purpose of Mairs's essay is to provide first-hand insight into what it means to live with multiple sclerosis. What have you learned from her experiences and reflections? Explain what you find most intriguing, surprising, and moving about the life she presents.

3. If you are close to someone with a debilitating condition or disease, describe that person and how he or she copes with the difficulties and limitations that condition imposes. If you yourself have such a condition, focus on your own life. You may wish to compare the subject of your essay with Mairs as she presents herself in hers. Alternatively, you may imagine how a condition such as Mairs's would affect your life.

Karl Marx (1818–1883) was born in Germany, the son of a lawyer. Marx himself studied law for several years but then turned his attention to philosophy, earning a Ph.D from the University of Jena. Unable to secure an academic position, he turned to journalism, but his radical positions forced him to leave Germany in 1843. In Paris, Brussels, and finally London, he barely supported his large family with his work as a journalist and often relied on the generosity of friends, most notably his long-time associate Friedrich Engels (1820–1895). With Engels, Marx composed several important treatises that develop his theories of socialism and class struggle, including The Communist Manifesto *(1848) and* Das Kapital *(1867), which did a great deal to shape twentieth-century political history.*

KARL MARX AND FRIEDRICH ENGELS

The Communist Manifesto

In this excerpt from *The Communist Manifesto*, Karl Marx and Friedrich Engels present their vision of the ideal Communist social and economic revolution. Marx and Engels offer considerable analysis of class relations as a way to clarify the historical relationship between owners and workers. They accuse the capitalist owners of a kind of slavery in which the working classes labor for little more than the clothes on their backs and a barely adequate daily diet.

   The Communist Manifesto appealed to the many in Russia who were disillusioned with the tsarist regime. The Russian peasants and workers were quick to embrace its ideals. The authors' urgent tone was a call to action: "Let the ruling classes tremble at a Communistic revolution. The proletarians have nothing to lose but their chains." To conclude their manifesto, Marx and Engels provide a brief recapitulation of their main themes. They return to the urgent tone of the opening, and they emphasize the need for the workers of the world to "UNITE!"

I

*Bourgeois and Proletarians**

The history of all hitherto existing society is the history of class struggles.

   Freeman and slave, patrician and plebeian, lord and serf, guild-master[†] and journeyman, in a word, oppressor and oppressed, stood in constant opposition to one another, carried on an uninterrupted, now hidden, now open fight, a fight that each time ended, either in a

---

*By bourgeoisie is meant the class of modern Capitalists, owners of the means of social production and employers of wage-labour. By proletariat, the class of modern wage-labourers who, having no means of production of their own, are reduced to selling their labour-power in order to live [*Engels's note to the English edition of 1888*].

†Guild-master, that is, a full member of a guild, a master within, not a head of a guild [*Engels's note to the English edition of 1888*].

revolutionary re-constitution of society at large, or in the common ruin of the contending classes.

In the earlier epochs of history, we find almost everywhere a complicated arrangement of society into various orders, a manifold gradation of social rank. In ancient Rome we have patricians, knights, plebeians, slaves; in the Middle Ages, feudal lords, vassals, guild-masters, journeymen, apprentices, serfs; in almost all of these classes, again, subordinate gradations.

The modern bourgeois society that has sprouted from the ruins of feudal society has not done away with class antagonisms. It has but established new classes, new conditions of oppression, new forms of struggle in place of the old ones.

Our epoch, the epoch of the bourgeoisie, possesses, however, this distinctive feature: it has simplified the class antagonisms. Society as a whole is more and more splitting up into two great hostile camps, into two great classes directly facing each other: Bourgeoisie and Proletariat . . .

The bourgeoisie, historically, has played a most revolutionary part.

The bourgeoisie, wherever it has got the upper hand, has put an end to all feudal, patriarchal, idyllic relations. It has pitilessly torn asunder the motley feudal ties that bound man to his "natural superiors," and has left remaining no other nexus between man and man than naked self-interest, than callous "cash payment." It has drowned the most heavenly ecstasies of religious fervour, of chivalrous enthusiasm, of philistine sentimentalism, in the icy water of egotistical calculation. It has resolved personal worth into exchange value and in place of the numberless indefeasible chartered freedoms, has set up that single, unconscionable freedom—Free Trade. In one word, for exploitation, veiled by religious and political illusions, it has substituted naked, shameless, direct, brutal exploitation.

The bourgeoisie has stripped of its halo every occupation hitherto honoured and looked up to with reverent awe. It has converted the physician, the lawyer, the priest, the poet, the man of science, into its paid wage-labourers.

The bourgeoisie has torn away from the family its sentimental veil, and has reduced the family relation to a mere money relation.

The bourgeoisie has disclosed how it came to pass that the brutal display of vigour in the Middle Ages, which Reactionists so much admire, found its fitting complement in the most slothful indolence. It has been the first to show what man's activity can bring about. It has accomplished wonders far surpassing Egyptian pyramids, Roman aqueducts, and Gothic cathedrals; it has conducted expeditions that put in the shade all former Exoduses of nations and crusades.

The bourgeoisie cannot exist without constantly revolutionising the instruments of production, and thereby the relations of production, and with them the whole relations of society. Conservation of the old modes of production in unaltered form, was, on the contrary, the first condition of existence for all earlier industrial classes. Constant revolutionising of production, uninterrupted disturbance of all social conditions, everlasting uncertainty and agitation distinguish the bourgeois epoch from all earlier ones. All fixed, fast-frozen relations, with their train of ancient and venerable prejudices and opinions, are swept away, all new-formed ones become antiquated before they can ossify. All that is solid melts into air, all that is holy is profaned, and man is at last compelled to face with sober senses, his real conditions of life, and his relations with his kind.

The need of a constantly expanding market for its products chases the bourgeoisie over the whole surface of the globe. It must nestle everywhere, settle everywhere, establish connexions everywhere.

The bourgeoisie has through its exploitation of the world-market given a cosmopolitan character to production and consumption in every country. To the great chagrin of Reactionists, it has drawn from under the feet of industry the national ground on which it stood. All old-established national industries have been destroyed or are daily being destroyed. They are dislodged by new industries, whose introduction becomes a life and death question for all civilised nations, by industries that no longer work up indigenous raw material, but raw material drawn from the remotest zones; industries whose products are consumed, not only at home, but in every quarter of the globe. In place of the old wants, satisfied by the productions of the country, we find new wants, requiring for their satisfaction the products of distant lands and climes. In place of the old local and national seclusion and self-sufficiency, we have intercourse in every direction, universal interdependence of nations. And as in material, so also in intellectual production. The intellectual creations of individual nations become common property. National one-sidedness and narrow-mindedness become more and more impossible, and from the numerous national and local literatures, there arises a world literature.

The bourgeoisie, by the rapid improvement of all instruments of production, by the immensely facilitated means of communication, draws all, even the most barbarian, nations into civilisation. The cheap prices of its commodities are the heavy artillery with which it batters down all Chinese walls, with which it forces the barbarians' intensely obstinate hatred of foreigners to capitulate. It compels all nations, on pain of extinction, to adopt the bourgeois mode of production; it compels them to introduce what it calls civilisation into their midst, *i.e.,* to become bourgeois themselves. In one word, it creates a world after its own image.

The bourgeoisie has subjected the country to the rule of the towns. It has created enormous cities, has greatly increased the urban population as compared with the rural, and has thus rescued a considerable part of the population from the idiocy of rural life. Just as it has made the country dependent on the towns, so it has made barbarian and semi-barbarian countries dependent on the civilised ones, nations of peasants on nations of bourgeois, the East on the West.

The bourgeoisie keeps more and more doing away with the scattered state of the population, of the means of production, and of property. It has agglomerated population, centralised means of production, and has concentrated property in a few hands. The necessary consequence of this was political centralisation. Independent, or but loosely connected provinces, with separate interests, laws, governments and systems of taxation, became lumped together into one nation, with one government, one code of laws, one national class-interest, one frontier and one customs-tariff.

The bourgeoisie, during its rule of scarce one hundred years has created more massive and more colossal productive forces than have all preceding generations together. Subjection of Nature's forces to man, machinery, application of chemistry to industry and agriculture, steam-navigation, railways, electric telegraphs, clearing of whole continents for cultivation, canalisation of rivers, whole populations conjured out of the ground—what earlier century had even a presentiment that such productive forces slumbered in the lap of social labour? . . .

In proportion as the bourgeoisie, *i.e.,* capital, is developed, in the same proportion is the proletariat, the modern working class, developed—a class of labourers, who live only so long as they find work, and who find work only so long as their labour increases capital. These labourers, who must sell themselves piecemeal, are a commodity, like every other article of commerce, and are consequently exposed to all the vicissitudes of competition, to all the fluctuations of the market.

Owing to the extensive use of machinery and to division of labour, the work of the proletarians has lost all individual character, and, consequently, all charm for the workman. He becomes an appendage of the machine, and it is only the most simple, most monotonous, and most easily acquired knack, that is required of him. Hence, the cost of production of a workman is restricted, almost entirely, to the means of subsistence that he requires for his maintenance, and for the propagation of his race. But the price of a commodity, and therefore also of labour, is equal to its cost of production. In proportion, therefore, as the repulsiveness of the work increases, the wage decreases. Nay more, in proportion as the use of machinery and division of labour increases, in the same proportion the burden of toil also increases, whether by prolongation of the working hours, by increase of the work exacted in a given time or by increased speed of the machinery, etc.

Modern industry has converted the little workshop of the patriarchal master into the great factory of the industrial capitalist. Masses of labourers, crowded into the factory, are organised like soldiers. As privates of the industrial army they are placed under the command of a perfect hierarchy of officers and sergeants. Not only are they slaves of the bourgeois class, and of the bourgeois State; they are daily and hourly enslaved by the machine, by the overlooker, and, above all, by the individual bourgeois manufacturer himself. The more openly this despotism proclaims gain to be its end and aim, the more petty, the more hateful and the more embittering it is . . . .

Now and then the workers are victorious, but only for a time. The real fruit of their battles lies, not in the immediate result, but in the ever-expanding union of the workers. This union is helped on by the improved means of communication that are created by modern industry and that place the workers of different localities in contact with one another. It was just this contact that was needed to centralise the numerous local struggles, all of the same character, into one national struggle between classes. But every class struggle is a political struggle. And that union, to attain which the burghers of the Middle Ages, with their miserable highways, required centuries, the modern proletarians, thanks to railways, achieve in a few years.

This organisation of the proletarians into a class, and consequently into a political party, is continually being upset again by the competition between the workers themselves. But it ever rises up again, stronger, firmer, mightier. It compels legislative recognition of particular interests of the workers, by taking advantage of the divisions among the bourgeoisie itself. Thus the ten-hours' bill in England was carried.

Altogether collisions between the classes of the old society further, in many ways, the course of development of the proletariat. The bourgeoisie finds itself involved in a constant battle. At first with the aristocracy; later on, with those portions of the bourgeoisie itself, whose interests have become antagonistic to the progress of industry; at all times, with the bourgeoisie of foreign countries. In all these battles it sees itself compelled to appeal to the proletariat, to ask for its help, and thus, to drag it into the political arena. The bourgeoisie itself, therefore, supplies the proletariat with its own elements of political and general education, in other words, it furnishes the proletariat with weapons for fighting the bourgeoisie.

Further, as we have already seen, entire sections of the ruling classes are, by the advance of industry, precipitated into the proletariat, or are at least threatened in their conditions of existence. These also supply the proletariat with fresh elements of enlightenment and progress.

Finally, in times when the class struggle nears the decisive hour, the process of dissolution going on within the ruling class, in fact within the whole range of old society, assumes such a violent, glaring character, that a small section of the ruling class cuts itself adrift, and joins the revolutionary class, the class that holds the future in its hands. Just as, therefore, at an earlier period, a section of the nobility went over to the bourgeoisie, so now a portion of the bourgeoisie goes over to the proletariat, and in particular, a portion of the bourgeois ideologists, who have raised themselves to the level of comprehending theoretically the historical movement as a whole. . . .

In the conditions of the proletariat, those of old society at large are already virtually swamped. The proletarian is without property; his relation to his wife and children has no longer anything in common with the bourgeois family-relations; modern industrial labour, modern subjection to capital, the same in England as in France, in America as in Germany, has stripped him of every trace of national character. Law, morality, religion, are to him so many bourgeois prejudices, behind which lurk in ambush just as many bourgeois interests.

All the preceding classes that got the upper hand, sought to fortify their already acquired status by subjecting society at large to their conditions of appropriation. The proletarians cannot become masters of the productive forces of society, except by abolishing their own previous mode of appropriation, and thereby also every other previous mode of appropriation. They have nothing of their own to secure and to fortify, their mission is to destroy all previous securities for, and insurances of, individual property.

All previous historical movements were movements of minorities, or in the interests of minorities. The proletarian movement is the self-conscious independent movement of the immense majority, in the interests of the immense majority. The proletariat, the lowest stratum of our present society cannot stir, cannot raise itself up, without the whole superincumbent strata of official society being sprung into the air.

Though not in substance, yet in form, the struggle of the proletariat with the bourgeoisie is at first a national struggle. The proletariat of each country must, of course, first of all settle matters with its own bourgeoisie . . . .

IV

Position of the Communists in Relation to the Various Existing Opposition Parties

Section II has made clear the relations of the Communists to the existing working-class parties, such as the Chartists in England and the Agrarian Reformers in America.

The Communists fight for the attainment of the immediate aims, for the enforcement of the momentary interests of the working class; but in the movement of the present, they also represent and take care of the future of that movement. In France the Communists ally themselves with the Social-Democrats,* against the conservative and radical bourgeoisie, reserving, however, the right to take up a critical position in regard to phrases and illusions traditionally handed down from the great Revolution.

In Switzerland they support the Radicals, without losing sight of the fact that this party consists of antagonistic elements, partly of Democratic Socialists, in the French sense, partly of radical bourgeois.

In Poland they support the party that insists on an agrarian revolution as the prime condition for national emancipation, that party which fomented the insurrection of Cracow in 1846.

---

*The party then represented in Parliament by Ledru-Rollin, in literature by Louis Blanc, in the daily press by the *Réforme*. The name of Social Democracy signified, with these its inventors, a section of the Democratic or Republican party more or less tinged with Socialism [*Engels's note to the English edition of 1888*]. The party in France which at that time called itself Socialist-Democratic was represented in political life by Ledru-Rollin and in literature by Louis Blanc; thus it differed immeasurably from present-day German Social-Democracy [*Engels's note to the German edition of 1890*].

In Germany they fight with the bourgeoisie whenever it acts in a revolutionary way, against the absolute monarchy, the feudal squirearchy and the petty bourgeoisie.

But they never cease, for a single instant, to instil into the working class the clearest possible recognition of the hostile antagonism between bourgeoisie and proletariat, in order that the German workers may straightway use, as so many weapons against the bourgeoisie, the social and political conditions that the bourgeoisie must necessarily introduce along with its supremacy, and in order that, after the fall of the reactionary classes in Germany, the fight against the bourgeoisie itself may immediately begin.

The Communists turn their attention chiefly to Germany, because that country is on the eve of a bourgeois revolution that is bound to be carried out under more advanced conditions of European civilisation, and with a much more developed proletariat, than that of England was in the seventeenth, and of France in the eighteenth century, and because the bourgeois revolution in Germany will be but the prelude to an immediately following proletarian revolution.

In short, the Communists everywhere support every revolutionary movement against the existing social and political order of things.

In all these movements they bring to the front, as the leading question in each, the property question, no matter what its degree of development at the time.

Finally, they labour everywhere for the union and agreement of the democratic parties of all countries.

The Communists disdain to conceal their views and aims. They openly declare that their ends can be attained only by the forcible overthrow of all existing social conditions. Let the ruling classes tremble at a Communistic revolution. The proletarians have nothing to lose but their chains. They have a world to win.

WORKING MEN OF ALL COUNTRIES, UNITE!

POSSIBILITIES FOR WRITING

1. Trace Marx and Engels's argument, focusing specifically on five or six of their key terms.
2. What ideals are Marx and Engels espousing in the excerpt? How do you respond to their goals as they put them forth here?
3. How would you define and describe the political and economic classes that make up the United States today? Are there other classes to be included when you consider society internationally?

H(enry) L(ouis) Mencken (1880–1956) was born in Baltimore, Maryland, where he lived for most of his life. After studying at a polytechnic college, he began a career as a journalist, first at the Baltimore Herald, and then, from 1906 until his death, at the Baltimore Sun. He also edited the popular magazines Smart Set and the American Mercury, which he co-founded. A deliberate provocateur, Mencken aimed in much of his writing to shatter middle-class conventions and pin-prick any form of piety or sanctimoniousness. His columns were collected in six volumes, titled Prejudices (1919–1927), and he also published books on language and literature, as well as several autobiographical works.

H. L. MENCKEN

Portrait of an Ideal World

In "Portrait of an Ideal World," H. L. Mencken makes a case for how drinking alcohol in moderate quantities can have salutary effects on people throughout the world. Mencken presents his idea as a kind of "modest proposal," in which he argues that a couple of drinks to get people a little high would improve their disposition, their manners, and their overall feeling about their work and their lives.

Mencken is careful to distinguish his recommendation that people be kept in a state of mild inebriation from any suggestion of their being actually drunk. He proposes that people drink just enough to make them feel good, without impairing their ability to continue to perform their daily work and go about their everyday activities effectively. Mencken explains his proposal straightforwardly and clearly, providing reasons for why it is necessary and for how implementing it would make the world a better place to live.

That alcohol in dilute aqueous solution, when taken into the human organism, acts as a depressant, not as a stimulant, is now so much a commonplace of knowledge that even the more advanced varieties of physiologists are beginning to be aware of it. The intelligent layman no longer resorts to the jug when he has important business before him, whether intellectual or manual; he resorts to it after his business is done, and he desires to release his taut nerves and reduce the steam-pressure in his spleen. Alcohol, so to speak, unwinds us. It raises the threshold of sensation and makes us less sensitive to external stimuli, and particularly to those that are unpleasant. Putting a brake upon all the qualities which enable us to get on in the world and shine before our fellows—for example, combativeness, shrewdness, diligence, ambition—, it releases the qualities which mellow us and make our fellows love us—for example, amiability, generosity, toleration, humor, sympathy. A man who has taken aboard two or three cocktails is less competent than he was before to steer a battleship down the Ambrose Channel, or to cut off a leg, or to draw up a deed of trust, or to conduct Bach's B minor mass, but he is immensely more competent to entertain a dinner party, or to admire a pretty girl, or to *hear* Bach's B minor mass. The harsh, useful things of the world, from pulling teeth to digging potatoes, are best done by men who are as starkly sober as so many convicts in the death-house, but the lovely and useless things, the charming and exhilarating things, are best done by men with, as the phrase is, a few sheets in the wind. *Pithecanthropus erectus* was a teetotaler, but the angels, you may be sure, know what is proper at 5 p.m.

All this is so obvious that I marvel that no utopian has ever proposed to abolish all the sorrows of the world by the simple device of getting and keeping the whole human race gently stewed. I do not say drunk, remember; I say simply gently stewed—and apologize, as in duty bound, for not knowing how to describe the state in a more seemly phrase. The man who is in it is a man who has put all of his best qualities into his showcase. He is not only immensely more amiable than the cold sober man; he is immeasurably more decent. He reacts to all situations in an expansive, generous and humane manner. He has become more liberal, more tolerant, more kind. He is a better citizen, husband, father, friend. The enterprises that make human life on this earth uncomfortable and unsafe are never launched by such men. They are not makers of wars; they do not rob and oppress anyone. All the great villainies of history have been perpetrated by sober men, and chiefly by teetotalers. But all the charming and beautiful things, from the Song of Songs to terrapin *à la* Maryland, and from the nine Beethoven symphonies to the Martini cocktail, have been given to humanity by men who, when the hour came, turned from well water to something with color to it, and more in it than more oxygen and hydrogen.

I am well aware, of course, that getting the whole human race stewed and keeping it stewed, year in and year out, would present formidable technical difficulties. It would be hard to make the daily dose of each individual conform exactly to his private needs, and hard to get it to him at precisely the right time. On the one hand there would be the constant danger that large minorities might occasionally become cold sober, and so start wars, theological disputes, moral reforms, and other such unpleasantnesses. On the other hand, there would be danger that other minorities might proceed to actual intoxication, and so annoy us all with their fatuous bawling or maudlin tears. But such technical obstacles, of course, are by no means insurmountable. Perhaps they might be got around by abandoning the administration of alcohol *per ora* and distributing it instead by impregnating the air with it. I throw out the suggestion, and pass on. Such questions are for men skilled in therapeutics, government and business efficiency. They exist today and their enterprises often show a high ingenuity, but, being chiefly sober, they devote too much of their time to harassing the rest of us. Half-stewed, they would be ten times as genial, and perhaps at least half as efficient. Thousands of them, relieved of their present anti-social duties, would be idle, and eager for occupation. I trust to them in this small matter. If they didn't succeed completely, they would at least succeed partially.

The objection remains that even small doses of alcohol, if each followed upon the heels of its predecessor before the effects of the latter had worn off, would have a deleterious effect upon the physical health of the race—that the death-rate would increase, and whole categories of human beings would be exterminated. The answer here is that what I propose is not lengthening the span of life, but augmenting its joys. Suppose we assume that its duration is reduced 20%. My reply is that its delights will be increased at least 100%. Misled by statisticians, we fall only too often into the error of worshiping mere figures. To say that A will live to be eighty and B will die at forty is certainly not to argue plausibly that A is more to be envied than B. A, in point of fact, may have to spend all of his eighty years in Kansas or Arkansas, with nothing to eat save corn and hog-meat and nothing to drink save polluted river water, whereas B may put in his twenty years of discretion upon the Côte d'Azur, *wie Gott im Frankreich*. It is my contention that the world I picture, assuming the average duration of human life to be cut down even 50%, would be an infinitely happier and more charming world than that we live in today—that no intelligent human being, having once tasted its peace and joy, would go back voluntarily to the harsh brutalities and stupidities that we now suffer, and idiotically strive to prolong. If intelligent Americans, in these depressing days, still cling to life and try to stretch it out longer and longer, it is surely not logically, but only instinctively. It is the primeval brute in them that hangs on, not the man. The man knows only too well that ten years in a genuine civilized and happy country would be infinitely better than a geological epoch under the curses he must now face and endure every day.

Moreover, there is no need to admit that the moderate alcoholization of the whole race would materially reduce the duration of life.

A great many of us are moderately alcoholized already, and yet manage to survive quite as long as the bluenoses. As for the bluenoses themselves, who would repine if breathing alcohol-laden air brought them down with delirium tremens and so sterilized and exterminated them? The advantage to the race in general would be obvious and incalculable. All the worst strains—which now not only persist, but even prosper— would be stamped out in a few generations, and so the average human being would move appreciably away from, say, the norm of a Baptist clergyman in Georgia and toward the norm of Shakespeare, Mozart and Goethe. It would take aeons, of course, to go all the way, but there would be progress with every generation, slow but sure. Today, it must be manifest, we make no progress at all; instead we slip steadily backward. That the average civilized man of today is inferior to the average civilized man of two or three generations ago is too plain to need arguing. He has less enterprise and courage; he is less resourceful and various; he is more like a rabbit and less like a lion. Harsh oppressions have made him what he is. He is the victim of tyrants. Well, no man with two or three cocktails in him is a tyrant. He may be foolish, but he is not cruel. He may be noisy, but he is also tolerant, generous and kind. My proposal would restore Christianity to the world. It would rescue mankind from moralists, pedants and brutes.

POSSIBILITIES FOR WRITING

1. Mencken wrote this essay in the mid-1920s during Prohibition, when the sale of alcohol was essentially illegal in the United States (although people continued to obtain alcohol clandestinely). Evaluate his argument in terms of its potential effectiveness with readers who believe in banning alcohol.
2. Mencken plays down the idea of alcohol abuse. Read Scott Russell Sanders's "Under the Influence" (pp. 529–542). What might Sanders say to Mencken? How would you respond to both writers?
3. Today, drugs are more controversial than alcohol, although both are still subject to social and scientific debate. Explore your own thoughts about the availability of alcohol and drugs. Do you support a legal drinking age? Do you support laws against all drugs that are currently illegal? Why or why not?

Laura Miller is a journalist and critic living in New York. She is a co-founder of Salon.com, where she is currently a staff writer, and she is a regular contributor to the New York Times Book Review. Her work has appeared in the New Yorker, the Los Angeles Times, Time magazine, and other publications. She has also edited The Salon.com Reader's Guide to Contemporary Authors (2000).

LAURA MILLER

Cat People vs. Dog People

In "Cat People vs. Dog People," Laura Miller contrasts the behaviors of people who own dogs with those who own cats. She explains why "dog people" and "cat people" behave differently and the extent to which their behavior is influenced by the behavior of the animals they most love. She also explains why these two categories of people don't understand or trust each other.

Miller focuses her essay on three books that she summarizes and comments on—*The Feline Mystique,* which explores the relationship between women and their cats; *Dog Culture,* a collection of humorous essays about the behavior of dogs; and *Bones Would Rain from the Sky,* an exploration of the relationship between dogs and their owners. The three books provide her with an opportunity to exercise her critical faculties.

Of the questions that perplex humanity, some are eternal (What is the meaning of life? Do we have a spiritual essence that survives our material existence?) and some are ephemeral (Where is Osama bin Laden? Why does "Sex and the City" have a reputation for featuring fabulous clothes when most of the time poor Sarah Jessica Parker is dressed up like an organ grinder's monkey?). Still others are mundane, yet persistent. To the third category—joining that perennial earth-scorcher, "Which is better, Mac or PC?"—belongs the question at hand: Who are more annoying, cat people or dog people?

Only a noncombatant can judiciously address this one, and we often seem to be a vanishing breed; according to a 2001 survey by the American Pet Products Manufacturers Association, there are 68 million "owned dogs" and 73 million "owned cats" in America. For the record, though I should add that I like both dogs and cats and have lived with both, albeit not with either for years. When pressed to take sides, I've always leaned toward cats. I like the low-maintenance aspect of felines, and the fact that they don't smell—or not much, as long as the litter box isn't allowed to fester. Plus, all things considered, they're prettier. Admittedly, these are girly preferences, but they aren't very strong ones; I'm always up for petting a friendly pooch, too.

At any rate, the cats and dogs strike me as innocent parties to the dispute; when cat people are ragging on canines, it soon becomes obvious that the true objects of their scorn are dog owners, not the dogs themselves, and vice versa. These are discussions in which neither reason nor temperance flourish, but I'll try to summarize the essential critiques of each side in an effort to get them efficiently out of the way.

Dog people profess to be baffled by the cat person's affection for an animal that provides so little active amusement: Cats will not frolic with you in the surf or fetch sticks or point with their noses at a bird for you to shoot. Because cats can't be trained to do the same sorts of tricks that dogs do, they are considered to be less intelligent, and because they are not by nature as social as dogs, they are seen as comparatively aloof or indifferent to humans. Dog people think cat people are suckers for doting on sneaky, selfish creatures that only pretend to like people in order to get food and other goodies and that will never, say, jump into a raging, flood-swollen river to rescue a small child at the risk of their own lives, as the faithful hound supposedly will.

Cat people heap contempt on dog people for actually thinking a dog's devotion counts for much. A dog's love for its owner is, cat people say, entirely instinctual, indiscriminate and often unearned by its object; you are not loved for yourself but for the position you assume in the dog's life—anyone else would do as well. Therefore, dog owners must be so desperate for love as to be nearly undeserving of it. The willingness of dogs to learn tricks is a result not of their intelligence but of their dopey eagerness to please. That cats can't be bothered to sit or heel on command is, their partisans insist, a sign that they are more clever by half. Cats are also self-cleaning, slobber-free, handy when you've got a mouse problem and don't have to be walked.

You may notice—particularly if you are neither a cat person nor a dog person—that these arguments are boring. Through no choice of your own, you have heard them far too many times. They crop up around a dinner table or at a cocktail party, and the evening goes into a precipitous decline. But, I say, you don't know the half of it—not that is, unless you are an editor.

Some people think that an editor's primary responsibility is, when needed, to correct a writer's spelling and grammar, to gently request that a neglected aspect of the writer's topic be more fully explored, to rearrange paragraphs and suggest transitions so artfully that the writer's point emerges as a gleaming and unassailable truth. All these things are so, and yet there is more. Much of our work goes unsung.

I would argue, for example, that perhaps the editor's most uncelebrated task is to prevent writers from writing about their pets, or at the very least not to publish it when they do.

If this aspect of our sacred trust puzzles you, it is only because so many of us do our job so well. And so the public remains unaware of how often it's been saved from reading reams of fawning drivel about the noble doings of The Best Dog Ever or the droll antics The World's Sweetest Kitty. Even writers of formidably austere sensibility are prone to penning this sort of piffle when the subject is their own beloved pet. As for what the sentimental ones come up with—well, you just don't wanna know. Of course, we editors don't expect citations or to be praised for holding back the tidal wave of treacle that might otherwise roll forth and engulf the world's readers. That's not what we're about.

Unfortunately, however, we do sometimes nod. Or worse. For, just as millions of people inexplicably forked out their hard-earned cash for Robert James Waller's "The Bridges of Madison County," so are there many potential consumers of magazines and book products devoted to the slack-jawed adoration of pets. And editors need to make a living like everyone else. Hence, the three books that provide the pretext for this essay.

The first, "The Feline Mystique" by Clea Simon, purports to take as its subject the relationship between women and cats. The evidence to support this purportation consists of the usual factoids about ancient Egypt (they worshipped cats, you know) and T. S. Eliot, who was precisely the man I was thinking of when I mentioned writers of "austere sensibility" above. And then there is the inevitable reference to Colette (I read a few cat books in my preteen years, and they all go on about Colette). Mostly, though, this book concerns Simon, a journalist, her friends and various women she interviewed on the subject of their love for their cats.

If you could boil down the central message of "The Feline Mystique" to one sentence, it would read something like this: "I was a single woman with a cat and I know people say awful things about that, but I landed a man anyway, so neener neener neener." While, being single myself, I have some sympathy with Simon's frustration at finding herself part of a stigmatized group, the truth is that all this fretting over negative images and what people are probably saying about you behind your back is a mug's game. Writing a whole book to refute such notions—unless you're going to dish up some serious data along the lines of Susan Faludi's "Backlash"—strikes me as a prodigious waste of energy.

However, Simon is not one to let a grievance slide. At one point in "The Feline Mystique" she relates at some length a quarrel she had with a woman with whom she briefly shared a rental house 17 years ago. It was an argument over the proper use of the house's sewing room. Simon sees a subtext in which the dour, rigid, "unattached" roommate, tormented by "simmering jealousy" over Simon's giddy social life, lashed out at both the author and her new kitten—and furthermore, the roommate's own pet was an "extremely neurotic cat, overweight to the point of unhealthiness and unfriendly to anyone who was not her one person." This statement is tempered by a disclaimer about Simon's own "bias" in the matter (on the principle, I suppose, that it's actually charmingly forthright to be petty if you also kinda cop to it at the same time), but the real shock is that Simon even remembers this spat, let alone in such detail, let alone with the conviction that it's worth writing down.

"The Feline Mystique" goes on in this vein—meandering, defensive, self-regarding, affected (no one in this book lingers at a breakfast table when they can "tarry" instead, or sees a cat at the end of a hall when they can "espy" it) and wholly untroubled by any understanding of the difference between what is interesting and what is not, a discrimination that is more or less the stock in trade of good writers. There are many anecdotes and interviews with other cat-loving women, but these tend to be the kind of people who say things like, "To me, a baby would be a cat substitute," and think it witty and rather daring—along the lines of a T-shirt with "Chocoholic" printed on it. Anyone no-nonsense and intriguing, such as the tiger wrangler for the Ringling Brothers and Barnum Bailey Circus, gets a mere two pages before we're back to autobiographical stuff like "my kitty is no tiger . . . but he is fierce," followed by a fond story about how Simon's cat, Cyrus, once growled at the vet.

It is easier, though, to be hard on "The Feline Mystique"—and by extension, cat lovers—for its overweening tedium when you are relatively fresh to the task of pet-related reading. By the time you get through a book like "Dog Culture: Writers on the Character of Canines," you realize that, on the topic of their cats or dogs, almost everyone tends to say the some things over and over again. Most of the contributors to this anthology (edited by Ken Foster, a Salon contributor) are talented and genuinely funny. Foster himself even has the good sense to be sheepish about the book's premise, explaining that he initially asked contributors to "write about aspects of the dog world, but to avoid writing about their own dog. The last thing I wanted was a collection of otherwise intelligent people droning on and on about how their dog was different, more special than all the rest." Fat chance, Ken; that's like inviting an alcoholic to a wine tasting and expecting him to spit it out.

"Dog Culture" opens with one of its strongest essays, René Steinke's matter-of-fact account of how her initial disgust over her boyfriend's dog's eating habits (Coco chowed down on, among other things, a used tampon, birthday candles and "his own orange vomit"), morphed into affection as "day after day, the work of caring for Coco made me care about him." But, like many of the pieces in the book—and much writing about pets, especially dogs —it succumbs to a pedagogical imperative; dogs, it seems, are forever dispensing Lessons. You might think that most dogs are not gainfully employed, but in fact they are continuously occupied in teaching people how to embrace appetite, live in the moment, suffer in dignity, let go. And all for the price of a bow of kibble—they really ought to think about a union, or better yet, a development position at the Lifetime Channel.

Sometimes the perimeters of the Canine Campus expand to encompass an individual's entire life. That's the case with the dog trainer Suzanne Clothier, who has written "Bones Would Rain From the Sky: Deepening Our Relationships With Dogs." As a professional, Clothier might be expected to have absorbed more than the odd inspirational homily from her dogs (and other animals—she lives on a farm), and so she has; this book lays out her philosophy of life as it manifests in her training method. Or, at least, I think it does, for while I am in utter awe of Clothier as a moral being, as a writer she leaves something to be desired.

Clothier holds that it's possible to achieve a rapport with dogs so that their obedience can be obtained with a minimum of coercion and with no cruel or abusive treatment at all. It's an approach that requires almost infinite patience. Unfortunately, her approach to writing requires almost as much of the same, only on the part of her reader. She will take one of her admirable ideas, round up all the worst words that can be applied to it—abstraction, clichés, psychobabble, New Ageisms, managerial euphemisms—then proceed to rearrange these words in every possible configuration for pages.

The result is lots of sentences like this: "Only through what we learn in our most profound relationships can we find the completeness in ourselves." Even Clothier's anecdotes—which mostly involve confrontations with troublesome dogs and her indefatigable efforts to understand what's bothering the creatures—have a tendency to dissolve into a terminal vagueness (did the dog ever stop snapping?) that will probably frustrate anyone hoping to use the book as a guide. Alas, good writing is essentially a brutal, Darwinian enterprise, in which many tender young sentences are invited onto the page only to be coldly eliminated in the final draft. (It is no surprise that one of the profession's most hallowed maxims is "Kill your darlings.") Clothier is simply too generous, decent and kind for such ugly work.

If writing about cats is always in danger of sliding into narcissistic preciosity, the peril in dog writing is bathos. No one, it seems, can write very much about dogs without getting into man's inhumanity to animal, and while I don't doubt that all such stories (and worse) are true and I am as horrified by cruelty as the next person, there's something creepy about the retailing of such anecdotes and the voluptuous outrage they provoke. To her credit, Clothier seldom stoops to such melodrama. She is forever reminding her readers not to sentimentalize or idealize dogs, to remember that "this is not an end point, a place to rest in safety, free from the complications and grief that may attend our human relationships." All through "Bones Would Rain From the Sky," despite bouts of exasperation at the author's leaden prose, I was unfailingly impressed with Clothier's humility and her tireless determination to use her authority over these creatures wisely, to recognize their devotion as a responsibility and not just a gift.

I doubt that any cat book has a chapter on "leadership," as "Bones Would Rain From the Sky" does. Like us, dogs are fundamentally social animals and hard-wired for hierarchy. Cats, by contrast, are solitary by nature, and therefore, as Stephen Budiansky pointed out in the June 2002 issue of the *Atlantic Monthly,* all of their social behavior is learned. I suspect this is why, while most human-dog bonds are fairly similar, there seems to be so much variety in cat owners' relationships to their pets—every cat is a custom job. A cat may develop a personality that complements its owner's, but every dog speaks to every human being's need to be part of a pack; like us, they're political. Perhaps it's inevitable that anyone who spends a lifetime contemplating her relationships with dogs, as Clothier does, will keep returning to the same scouring quandaries that characterize our relationships to each other: how to listen, how to use the power we have justly, what we have a right to ask from others. Of course, most dog people don't seem to bother with this and are content instead to dote and regress. Still, the potential is there and so, I think the canine contingent has the edge. Just don't make me read about it ever again.

POSSIBILITIES FOR WRITING

1. Explain the characteristics of "cat people" and of "dog people" as Miller describes them. To what extent do you agree with what Miller says about them? Explain.

2. What characteristics of dogs and cats, and of the people who have them as pets, would you add to Miller's list? To what extent would you describe yourself as a dog or cat person? Do either of her characters apply to you? Why or why not?

3. Write your own essay in which you compare two different kinds of people by something they do or something they enjoy. For example: football fans and baseball fans (or basketball fans); soccer fans and tennis fans (or hockey fans); bird watchers and whale watchers; sitcom fans and reality TV fans—and so on.

HORACE MINER

Body Ritual Among the Nacirema

"Body Ritual Among the Nacirema" first appeared in the journal *American Anthropologist* in 1956. In his essay, Miner deploys his expertise as an anthropologist to study the behavior of a group of people that is simultaneously familiar and strange. The essay is something of an ethnographic study, as it looks closely at the customs of a familiar North American culture.

Because Miner's article was written for an academic professional journal, its tone is scientific and detached and its style formal and objective. The descriptive details he presents provide a close look at the culture at the middle of the twentieth century, and some of the behaviors Miner includes have changed.

The anthropologist has become so familiar with the diversity of ways in which different peoples behave in similar situations that he is not apt to be surprised by even the most exotic customs. In fact, if all of the logically possible combinations of behavior have not been found somewhere in the world, he is apt to suspect that they must be present in some yet undescribed tribe. This point has, in fact, been expressed with respect to clan organization by Murdock.[1] In this light, the magical beliefs and practices of the Nacirema present such unusual aspects that it seems desirable to describe them as an example of the extremes to which human behavior can go.

Professor Linton first brought the ritual of the Nacirema to the attention of anthropologists twenty years ago, but the culture of this people is still very poorly understood. They are a North American group living in the territory between the Canadian Cree, the Yaqui and Tarahumare of

---

[1]George Peter Murdock (1897–1985) was an anthropologist who identified and classified world cultures.—Eds.

Mexico, and the Carib and Arawak of the Antilles. Little is known of their origin, although tradition states that they came from the east. . . .

Nacirema culture is characterized by a highly developed market economy which has evolved in a rich natural habitat. While much of the people's time is devoted to economic pursuits, a large part of the fruits of these labors and a considerable portion of the day are spent in ritual activity. The focus of this activity is the human body, the appearance and health of which loom as a dominant concern in the ethos of the people. While such a concern is certainly not unusual, its ceremonial aspects and associated philosophy are unique.

The fundamental belief underlying the whole system appears to be that the human body is ugly and that its natural tendency is to debility and disease. Incarcerated in such a body, man's only hope is to avert these characteristics through the use of the powerful influences of ritual and ceremony. Every household has one or more shrines devoted to this purpose. The more powerful individuals in the society have several shrines in their houses and, in fact, the opulence of a house is often referred to in terms of the number of such ritual centers it possesses. Most houses are of wattle and daub construction, but the shrine rooms of the more wealthy are walled with stone. Poorer families imitate the rich by applying pottery plaques to their shrine walls.

While each family has at least one such shrine, the rituals associated with it are not family ceremonies but are private and secret. The rites are normally only discussed with children, and then only during the period when they are being initiated into these mysteries. I was able, however, to establish sufficient rapport with the natives to examine these shrines and to have the rituals described to me.

The focal point of the shrine is a box or chest which is built into the wall. In this chest are kept the many charms and magical potions without which no native believes he could live. These preparations are secured from a variety of specialized practitioners. The most powerful of these are the medicine men, whose assistance must be rewarded with substantial gifts. However, the medicine men do not provide the curative potions for their clients, but decide what the ingredients should be and then write them down in an ancient and secret language. This writing is understood only by the medicine men and by the herbalists who, for another gift, provide the required charm.

The charm is not disposed of after it has served its purpose, but is placed in the charm-box of the household shrine. As these magical materials are specific for certain ills, and the real or imagined maladies of the people are many, the charm-box is usually full to overflowing. The magical packets are so numerous that people forget what their purposes were and fear to use them again. While the natives are very vague on this point, we can only assume that the idea in retaining all the old magical materials is that their presence in the charm-box, before which the body rituals are conducted, will in some way protect the worshipper.

Beneath the charm-box is a small font. Each day every member of the family, in succession, enters the shrine room, bows his head before the charm-box, mingles different sorts of holy water in the font, and proceeds with a brief rite of ablution. The holy waters are secured from the Water Temple of the community, where the priests conduct elaborate ceremonies to make the liquid ritually pure.

In the hierarchy of magical practitioners, and below the medicine men in prestige, are specialists whose designation is best translated "holy-mouth-men." The Nacirema have an almost pathological horror of and fascination with the mouth, the condition of which is believed to have a supernatural influence on all social relationships. Were it not for the rituals of the mouth, they believe that their teeth would fall out, their gums bleed, their jaws shrink, their friends desert them, and their lovers reject them. They also believe that a strong relationship exists between oral and moral characteristics. For example, there is a ritual ablution of the mouth for children which is supposed to improve their moral fiber.

The daily body ritual performed by everyone includes a mouth-rite. Despite the fact that these people are so punctilious about care of the mouth, this rite involves a practice which strikes the uninitiated stranger as revolting. It was reported to me that the ritual consists of inserting a small bundle of hog hairs into the mouth, along with certain magical powders, and then moving the bundle in a highly formalized series of gestures.

In addition to the private mouth-rite, the people seek out a holy-mouth-man once or twice a year. These practitioners have an impressive set of paraphernalia, consisting of a variety of augers, awls, probes, and prods. The use of these objects in the exorcism of the evils of the mouth involves almost unbelievable ritual torture of the client. The holy-mouth-man opens the client's mouth and, using the above mentioned tools, enlarges any holes which decay may have created in the teeth. Magical materials are put into these holes. If there are not naturally occurring holes in the teeth, large sections of one or more teeth are gouged out so that the supernatural substance can be applied.

In the client's view, the purpose of these ministrations is to arrest decay and to draw friends. The extremely sacred and traditional character of the rite is evident in the fact that the natives return to the holy-mouth-men year after year, despite the fact that their teeth continue to decay.

It is to be hoped that, when a thorough study of the Nacirema is made, there will be careful inquiry into the personality structure of these people. One has but to watch the gleam in the eye of a holy-mouth-man, as he jabs an awl into an exposed nerve, to suspect that a certain amount of sadism is involved. If this can be established, a very interesting pattern emerges, for most of the population shows definite masochistic tendencies. It was to these that Professor Linton referred in discussing a distinctive part of the daily body ritual which is performed only by men. This part of the rite involves scraping and lacerating the surface of the face with a sharp instrument. Special women's rites are performed only four times during each lunar month, but what they lack in frequency is made up in barbarity. As part of this ceremony, women bake their heads in small ovens for about an hour. The theoretically interesting point is that what seems to be a preponderantly masochistic people have developed sadistic specialists.

The medicine men have an imposing temple, or *latipso*, in every community of any size. The more elaborate ceremonies required to treat very sick patients can only be performed at this temple. These ceremonies involve not only the thaumaturge but a permanent group of vestal maidens who move sedately about the temple chambers in distinctive costume and headdress.

The *latipso* ceremonies are so harsh that it is phenomenal that a fair proportion of the really sick natives who enter the temple ever recover. Small children whose indoctrination is still incomplete have been known to resist attempts to take them to the temple because "that is where you go to die." Despite this fact, sick adults are not only willing but eager to undergo the protracted ritual purification, if they can afford to do so. No matter how ill the supplicant or how grave the emergency, the guardians of many temples will not admit a client if he cannot give a rich gift to the custodian. Even after one has gained admission and survived the ceremonies, the guardians will not permit the neophyte to leave until he makes still another gift.

The supplicant entering the temple is first stripped of all his or her clothes. In everyday life the Nacirema avoids exposure of his body and its natural functions. Bathing and excretory acts are performed only in the secrecy of the household shrine, where they are ritualized as part of the body-rites. Psychological shock results from the fact that body secrecy is suddenly lost upon entry into the *latipso*. A man, whose own wife has never seen him in an excretory act, suddenly finds himself naked and assisted by a vestal maiden while he performs his natural functions into a sacred vessel. This sort of ceremonial treatment is necessitated by the fact that the excreta are used by a diviner to ascertain the course and nature of the client's sickness. Female clients, on the other hand, find their naked bodies are subjected to the scrutiny, manipulation and prodding of the medicine men.

Few supplicants in the temple are well enough to do anything but lie on their hard beds. The daily ceremonies, like the rites of the holy-mouth-man involve discomfort and torture. With ritual precision, the vestals awaken their miserable charges each dawn and roll them about on their beds of pain while performing ablutions, in the formal movements of which the maidens are highly trained. At other times they insert magic wands in the supplicant's mouth or force him to eat substances which are supposed to be healing. From time to time the medicine men come to their clients and jab magically treated needles into their flesh. The fact that these temple ceremonies may not cure, and may even kill the neophyte, in no way decreases the people's faith in the medicine men.

There remains one other kind of practitioner, known as a "listener." This witchdoctor has the power to exorcise the devils that lodge in the heads of people who have been bewitched. The Nacirema believe that parents bewitch their own children. Mothers are particularly suspected of putting a curse on children while teaching them the secret body rituals. The counter-magic of the witchdoctor is unusual in its lack of ritual. The patient simply tells the "listener" all his troubles and fears, beginning with the earliest difficulties he can remember. The memory displayed by the Nacirema in these exorcism sessions is truly remarkable. It is not uncommon for the patient to bemoan the rejection he felt upon being weaned as a babe, and a few individuals even see their troubles going back to the traumatic effects of their own birth.

In conclusion, mention must be made of certain practices which have their base in native esthetics but which depend upon the pervasive aversion to the natural body and its functions. There are ritual fasts to make fat people thin and ceremonial feasts to make thin people fat. Still other rites are used to make women's breasts larger if they are small, and smaller if they are large. General dissatisfaction with breast shape is symbolized in the fact that the ideal form is virtually outside the range of human variation. A few women afflicted with almost inhuman hyper-mammary development are so idolized that they make a handsome living by simply going from village to village and permitting the natives to stare at them for a fee.

Reference has already been made to the fact that excretory functions are ritualized, routinized, and relegated to secrecy. Natural reproductive functions are similarly distorted. Intercourse is taboo as a topic and scheduled as an act. Efforts are made to avoid pregnancy by the use of magical materials or by limiting intercourse to certain phases of the moon. Conception is actually very infrequent. When pregnant, women dress so as to hide their condition. Parturition takes place in secret, without friends or relatives to assist, and the majority of women do not nurse their infants.

Our review of the ritual life of the Nacirema has certainly shown them to be a magic-ridden people. It is hard to understand how they have managed to exist so long under the burdens which they have imposed upon themselves. But even such exotic customs as these take on real meaning when they are viewed with the insight provided by Malinowski[2] when he wrote:

> Looking from far and above, from our high places of safety in the developed civilization, it is easy to see all the crudity and irrelevance of magic. But without its power and guidance early man could not have mastered his practical difficulties as he has done, nor could man have advanced to the higher stages of civilization.

POSSIBILITIES FOR WRITING

1. At what point did you realize what Miner is up to in this piece? When did you discover just who the "Nacirema" are? Why do you think he describes the Nacirema as being a "magic-ridden" people? Do you agree with him? Why or why not?

2. Identify three social practices that Miner describes and explain how he satirizes each. What do the practices or behaviors have in common? How and why does Miner get us to view them in a fresh manner?

3. Try your hand at writing an essay that describes some familiar contemporary customs from the standpoint of an anthropologist, perhaps an anthropologist from another culture or world. You may wish to write about physical behavior and customs; social customs such as weddings; musical events such as rock concerts; or athletic contests such as the Super Bowl, the World Series, or the World Cup.

---

[2]Bronislaw Malinowski (1884–1942) was a Polish-born British anthropologist.

N. Scott Momaday (b. 1934) was born in Lawton, Oklahoma, of Kiowa ancestry and grew up on a reservation in New Mexico. A graduate of the University of New Mexico and of Stanford University, he won a Pulitzer Prize for his first novel, House Made of Dawn *(1968). Author of many genres in addition to fiction, Momaday has published volumes of poetry, including* The Gourd Dancer *(1976), and the memoirs* The Way to Rainy Mountain *(1969) and* The Names *(1976), as well as children's books, essay collections, and plays. He is also an artist whose work has been widely exhibited. For many years a professor at the University of Arizona, Momaday often takes as his subject the history and culture of Native Americans and, in particular, their relationship with the physical environment. His most recent book is* In the Bear's House *(1999).*

N. SCOTT MOMADAY

The Way to Rainy Mountain

In his autobiographical memoir, *The Way to Rainy Mountain*, N. Scott Momaday celebrates his Kiowa Native American heritage. Momaday describes both a place and a person in this essay from his memoir. He describes Rainy Mountain as a place saturated in the history of the Kiowa people. It is a place every aspect of which bears significance.

But it is not only place that is celebrated in Momaday's essay/memoir. He also memorializes his grandmother, who is, herself, a repository of Kiowa history and culture. Momaday's moving portrait captures her dignity and nobility as an individual and as a representative of her vanishing Kiowa world. In language at once reverential and wonderfully precise, Momaday describes the holy regard that his grandmother held for the sun, an awe and a reverence reflected in the sun dances of Kiowa cultural tradition.

A single knoll rises out of the plain in Oklahoma, north and west of the Wichita Range. For my people, the Kiowas, it is an old landmark, and they gave it the name Rainy Mountain. The hardest weather in the world is there. Winter brings blizzards, hot tornadic winds arise in the spring, and in summer the prairie is an anvil's edge. The grass turns brittle and brown, and it cracks beneath your feet. There are green belts along the rivers and creeks, linear groves of hickory and pecan, willow and witch hazel. At a distance in July or August the steaming foliage seems almost to writhe in fire. Great green and yellow grasshoppers are everywhere in the tall grass, popping up like corn to sting the flesh, and tortoises crawl about on the red earth, going nowhere in the plenty of time. Loneliness is an aspect of the land. All things in the plain are isolate; there is no confusion of objects in the eye, but *one* hill or *one* tree or *one* man. To look upon that landscape in the early morning, with the sun at your back, is to lose the sense of proportion. Your imagination comes to life, and this, you think, is where Creation was begun.

I returned to Rainy Mountain in July. My grandmother had died in the spring, and I wanted to be at her grave. She had lived to be very old and at last infirm. Her only living daughter was with her when she died, and I was told that in death her face was that of a child.

I like to think of her as a child. When she was born, the Kiowas were living the last great moment of their history. For more than a hundred years they had controlled the open range from the Smoky Hill River to the Red, from the headwaters of the Canadian to the fork of the Arkansas and Cimarron. In alliance with the Comanches, they had ruled the whole of the southern Plains. War was their sacred business, and they were among the finest horsemen the world has ever known. But warfare for the Kiowas was preeminently a matter of disposition rather than of survival, and they never understood the grim, unrelenting advance of the U.S. Cavalry. When at last, divided and ill-provisioned, they were driven onto the Staked Plains in the cold rains of autumn, they fell into panic. In Palo Duro Canyon they abandoned their crucial stores to pillage and had nothing then but their lives. In order to save themselves, they surrendered to the soldiers at Fort Sill and were imprisoned in the old stone corral that now stands as a military museum. My grandmother was spared the humiliation of those high gray walls by eight or ten years, but she must have known from birth the affliction of defeat, the dark brooding of old warriors.

Her name was Aho, and she belonged to the last culture to evolve in North America. Her forebears came down from the high country in western Montana nearly three centuries ago. They were a mountain people, a mysterious tribe of hunters whose language has never been positively classified in any major group. In the late seventeenth century they began a long migration to the south and east. It was a journey toward the dawn, and it led to a golden age. Along the way the Kiowas were befriended by the Crows, who gave them the culture and religion of the Plains. They acquired horses, and their ancient nomadic spirit was suddenly free of the ground. They acquired Tai-me, the sacred Sun Dance doll, from that moment the object and symbol of their worship, and so shared in the divinity of the sun. Not least, they acquired the sense of destiny, therefore courage and pride. When they entered upon the southern Plains they had been transformed. No longer were they slaves to the simple necessity of survival; they were a lordly and dangerous society of fighters and thieves, hunters and priests of the sun.

According to their origin myth, they entered the world through a hollow log. From one point of view, their migration was the fruit of an old prophecy, for indeed they emerged from a sunless world.

Although my grandmother lived out her long life in the shadow of Rainy Mountain, the immense landscape of the continental interior lay like memory in her blood. She could tell of the Crows, whom she had never seen, and of the Black Hills, where she had never been. I wanted to see in reality what she had seen more perfectly in the mind's eye, and traveled fifteen hundred miles to begin my pilgrimage.

Yellowstone, it seemed to me, was the top of the world, a region of deep lakes and dark timber, canyons and waterfalls. But, beautiful as it is, one might have the sense of confinement there. The skyline in all directions is close at hand, the high wall of the woods and deep cleavages of shade. There is a perfect freedom in the mountains, but it belongs to the eagle and the elk, the badger and the bear. The Kiowas reckoned their stature by the distance they could see, and they were bent and blind in the wilderness.

Descending eastward, the highland meadows are a stairway to the plain. In July the inland slope of the Rockies is luxuriant with flax and buckwheat, stonecrop and larkspur. The earth unfolds and the limit of the land recedes. Clusters of trees, and animals grazing far in the distance, cause the vision to reach away and wonder to build upon the mind. The sun follows a longer course in the day, and the sky is immense beyond all comparison. The great billowing clouds that sail upon it are the shadows that move upon the grain like water, dividing light. Farther down, in the land of the Crows and Blackfeet, the plain is yellow. Sweet clover takes hold of the hills and bends upon itself to cover and seal the soil. There the Kiowas paused on their way; they had come to the place where they must change their lives. The sun is at home on the plains. Precisely there does it have the certain character of a god. When the Kiowas came to the land of the Crows, they could see the dark lees of the hills at dawn across the Bighorn River, the profusion of light on the grain shelves, the oldest deity ranging after the solstices. Not yet would they veer southward to the caldron of the land that lay below; they must wean their blood from the northern winter and hold the mountains a while longer in their view. They bore Tai-me in procession to the east.

A dark mist lay over the Black Hills, and the land was like iron. At the top of a ridge I caught sight of Devil's Tower upthrust against the gray sky as if in the birth of time the core of the earth had broken through its crust and the motion of the world was begun. There are things in nature that engender an awful quiet in the heart of man; Devil's Tower is one of them. Two centuries ago, because they could not do otherwise, the Kiowas made a legend at the base of the rock. My grandmother said:

> *Eight children were there at play, seven sisters and their brother. Suddenly the boy was struck dumb; he trembled and began to run upon his hands and feet. His fingers became claws, and his body was covered with fur. Directly there was a bear where the boy had been. The sisters were terrified; they ran, and the bear after them. They came to the stump of a great tree, and the tree spoke to them. It bade them climb upon it, and as they did so it began to rise into the air. The bear came to kill them, but they were just beyond its reach. It reared against the tree and scored the bark all around with its claws. The seven sisters were borne into the sky, and they became the stars of the Big Dipper.*

From that moment, and so long as the legend lives, the Kiowas have kinsmen in the night sky. Whatever they were in the mountains, they could be no more. However tenuous their well-being, however much they had suffered and would suffer again, they had found a way out of the wilderness.

My grandmother had a reverence for the sun, a holy regard that now is all but gone out of mankind. There was a wariness in her, and an ancient awe. She was a Christian in her later years, but she had come a long way about, and she never forgot her birthright. As a child she had been to the Sun Dances; she had taken part in those annual rites, and by them she had learned the restoration of her people in the presence of Tai-me. She was about seven when the last Kiowa Sun Dance was held in 1887 on the Washita River above Rainy Mountain Creek. The buffalo were gone. In order to consummate the ancient sacrifice—to impale the head of a buffalo bull upon the medicine tree—a delegation of old men journeyed into Texas, there to beg and barter for an animal from the Goodnight herd. She was ten when the Kiowas came together for the last time as a living Sun Dance culture. They could find no buffalo; they had to hang an old hide from the sacred tree. Before the dance could begin, a company of soldiers rode out from Fort Sill under orders to disperse the tribe. Forbidden without cause the essential act of their faith, having seen the wild herds slaughtered and left to rot upon the ground, the Kiowas backed away forever from the medicine tree. That was July 20, 1890, at the great bend of the Washita. My grandmother was there. Without bitterness, and for as long as she lived, she bore a vision of deicide.

Now that I can have her only in memory, I see my grandmother in the several postures that were peculiar to her: standing at the wood stove on a winter morning and turning meat in a great iron skillet: sitting at the south window, bent above her beadwork, and afterwards, when her vision failed, looking down for a long time into the fold of her hands; going out upon a cane, very slowly as she did when the weight of age came upon her; praying. I remember her most often at prayer. She made long, rambling prayers out of suffering and hope, having seen many things. I was never sure that I had the right to hear, so exclusive were they of all mere custom and company. The last time I saw her she prayed standing by the side of her bed at night, naked to the waist, the light of a kerosene lamp moving upon her dark skin. Her long, black hair, always drawn and braided in the day, lay upon her shoulders and against her breasts like a shawl. I do not speak Kiowa, and I never understood her prayers, but there was something inherently sad in the sound, some merest hesitation upon the syllables of sorrow. She began in a high and descending pitch, exhausting her breath to silence; then again and again—and always the same intensity of effort, of something that is, and is not, like urgency in the human voice. Transported so in the dancing light among the shadows of her room, she seemed beyond the reach of time. But that was illusion; I think I knew then that I should not see her again.

Houses are like sentinels in the plain, old keepers of the weather watch. There, in a very little while, wood takes on the appearance of great age. All colors wear soon away in the wind and rain, and then the wood is burned gray and the grain appears and the nails turn red with rust. The windowpanes are black and opaque; you imagine there is nothing within, and indeed there are many ghosts, bones given up to the land. They stand here and there against the sky, and you approach them for a longer time than you expect. They belong in the distance; it is their domain.

Once there was a lot of sound in my grandmother's house, a lot of coming and going, feasting and talk. The summers there were full of excitement and reunion. The Kiowas are a summer people; they abide the cold and keep to themselves, but when the season turns and the land becomes warm and vital they cannot hold still; an old love of going returns upon them. The aged visitors who came to my grandmother's house when I was a child were made of lean and leather, and they bore themselves upright. They wore great black hats and bright ample shirts that shook in the wind. They rubbed fat upon their hair and wound their braids with strips of colored cloth. Some of them painted their faces and carried the scars of old and cherished enmities. They were an old council of warlords, come to remind and be reminded of who they were. Their wives and daughters served them well. The women might indulge themselves; gossip was at once the mark and compensation of their servitude. They made loud and elaborate talk among themselves, full of jest and gesture, fright and false alarm. They went abroad in fringed and flowered shawls, bright beadwork and German silver. They were at home in the kitchen, and they prepared meals that were banquets.

There were frequent prayer meetings, and great nocturnal feasts. When I was a child I played with my cousins outside, where the lamplight fell upon the ground and the singing of the old people rose up around us and carried away into the darkness. There were a lot of good things to eat, a lot of laughter and surprise. And afterwards, when the quiet returned, I lay down with my grandmother and could hear the frogs away by the river and feel the motion of the air.

Now there is a funeral silence in the rooms, the endless wake of some final word. The walls have closed in upon my grandmother's house. When I returned to it in mourning, I saw for the first time in my life how small it was. It was late at night, and there was a white moon, nearly full. I sat for a long time on the stone steps by the kitchen door. From there I could see out across the land; I could see the long row of trees by the creek, the low light upon the rolling plains, and the stars of the Big Dipper. Once I looked at the moon and caught sight of a strange thing. A cricket had perched upon the handrail, only a few inches away from me. My line of vision was such that the creature filled the moon like a fossil. It had gone there, I thought, to live and die, for there, of all places, was its small definition made whole and eternal. A warm wind rose up and purled like the longing within me.

The next morning I awoke at dawn and went out on the dirt road to Rainy Mountain. It was already hot, and the grasshoppers began to fill the air. Still, it was early in the morning, and the birds sang out of the shadows. The long yellow grass on the mountain shone in the bright light, and a scissortail hied above the land. There, where it ought to be, at the end of a long and legendary way, was my grandmother's grave. Here and there on the dark stones were ancestral names. Looking back once, I saw the mountain and came away.

POSSIBILITIES FOR WRITING

1. Momaday traces the migration of the Kiowa from Montana to the Great Plains in terms of both physical landscape and of spiritual development. For him, how are the two related in the rise and fall of Kiowa history and culture? What is the significance of his ending the story of his journey at his grandmother's grave?

2. What does his grandmother represent for Momaday? Why, for example, does he begin his pilgrimage to her grave from Yellowstone, fifteen hundred miles away? How do his memories of her, as he describes them, help develop this image?

3. Explore the ways in which a grandparent or other older relative provides you with ties to your history and culture. Like Momaday, you may wish to develop the influence of a particular place associated with that person as well.

Michel de Montaigne (1533–1592), *the father of the modern essay, was born in Perigord, France, to a family of wealthy landowners. He studied law at the University of Guyenne in Bordeaux and during his career served as a local magistrate and later as mayor of Bordeaux. In 1580 he published the first of his collected Essais, which were revised and added to in 1588. These "attempts" or "trials," as he termed them, dealt with a wide range of subjects and were intended as personal, but at the same time universal, reflections on the human condition. Intensely intellectual, the essais are nonetheless written in concrete, everyday language and marked by a great deal of humor. His works were highly influential throughout Europe, not only in terms of their subject matter but also as exemplars of this unique literary form.*

MICHEL DE MONTAIGNE

Of Smells

Michel de Montaigne originated a unique style that is at once both personal and reflective. Montaigne's "Of Smells," though one of his shortest essays, exemplifies his characteristic method. It begins with a few general thoughts on the nature of odors that human beings give off. It moves quickly to a series of quotations from Montaigne's reading in classic writers from the past. And it includes a number of observations based on Montaigne's experience—his autobiographical perspective on what he himself has noticed about the way people smell, including the way he himself smells.

The unpretentiousness of this little essay is part of its charm. "Of Smells" wears its learning lightly. And it leans lightly, too, on what Montaigne has experienced in the realm of the olfactory. It never pretends to be anything more than a brief set of notes on what is noteworthy about smell. Montaigne's essay is suggestive without being insistent. It presents opportunities for readers to notice what Montaigne himself has noticed. But it doesn't force the issue; it doesn't argue in any systematic or methodical way. Nonetheless, "Of Smells" makes a good case for the influence of smell in our everyday lives.

It is said of some, as of Alexander the Great, that their sweat emitted a sweet odor, owing to some rare and extraordinary constitution of theirs, of which Plutarch and others seek the cause. But the common make-up of bodies is the opposite, and the best condition they may have is to be free of smell. The sweetness even of the purest breath has nothing more excellent about it than to be without any odor that offends us, as is that of very healthy children. That is why, says Plautus,

> A woman smells good when she does not smell.

The most perfect smell for a woman is to smell of nothing, as they say that her actions smell best when they are imperceptible and mute, And perfumes are rightly considered suspicious in those who use them, and thought to be used to cover up some natural defect in that quarter. Whence arise these nice sayings of the ancient poets: To smell good is to stink:

> You laugh at us because we do not smell.
> I'd rather smell of nothing than smell sweet.
>
> MARTIAL

And elsewhere:

> Men who smell always sweet, Posthumus, don't smell good.
>
> MARTIAL

However, I like very much to be surrounded with good smells, and I hate bad ones beyond measure, and detect them from further off than anyone else:

> My scent will sooner be aware
> Where goat-smells, Polypus, in hairy arm-pits lurk,
> Than keen hounds scent a wild boar's lair.
>
> HORACE

The simplest and most natural smells seem to me the most agreeable. And this concern chiefly affects the ladies. Amid the densest barbarism, the Scythian women, after washing, powder and plaster their whole body and face with a certain odoriferous drug that is native to their soil; and having removed this paint to approach the men, they find themselves both sleek and perfumed.

Whatever the odor is, it is a marvel how it clings to me and how apt my skin is to imbibe it. He who complains of nature that she has left man without an instrument to convey smells to his nose is wrong, for they convey themselves. But in my particular case my mustache, which is thick, performs that service. If I bring my gloves or my handkerchief near it, the smell will stay there a whole day. It betrays the place I come from. The close kisses of youth, savory, greedy, and sticky, once used to adhere to it and stay there for several hours after. And yet, for all that, I find myself little subject to epidemics, which are caught by communication and bred by the contagion of the air; and I have escaped those of my time, of which there have been many sorts in our cities and our armies. We read of Socrates that though he never left Athens during many recurrences of the plague which so many times tormented that city, he alone never found himself the worse for it.

The doctors might, I believe, derive more use from odors than they do; for I have often noticed that they make a change in me and work upon my spirits according to their properties; which makes me approve of the idea that the use of incense and perfumes in churches, so ancient and widespread in all nations and religions, was intended to delight us and arouse and purify our senses to make us more fit for contemplation.

I should like, in order to judge of it, to have shared the art of those cooks who know how to add a seasoning of foreign odors to the savor of foods, as was particularly remarked in the service of the king of Tunis, who in our time landed at Naples to confer with the Emperor Charles. They stuffed his foods with aromatic substances, so sumptuously that one peacock and two pheasants came to a hundred ducats to dress them in that manner; and when they were carved, they filled not only the dining hall but all the rooms in his palace, and even the neighboring houses, with sweet fumes which did not vanish for some time.

The principal care I take in my lodgings is to avoid heavy, stinking air. Those beautiful cities Venice and Paris weaken my fondness for them by the acrid smell of the marshes of the one and of the mud of the other.

POSSIBILITIES FOR WRITING

1. Trace closely the arc of this brief essay, exploring the sequence of thoughts from beginning to end. Do you find a coherent pattern here? If so, explain the pattern you find. If not, how does this fact affect your reading of the essay?

2. Write an essay of your own titled "Of Smells." Focus on your personal responses to the odors you encounter at home, in public, and in man-made and natural settings, as well as on how our culture seems to define good and bad smells. Don't be afraid to be whimsical.

3. Using Montaigne as a model, write an impressionistic essay on a topic that is common to everyone's experience but that would not normally be thought of as the subject of an essay: hands or feet, say, or tears, or refrigerators, or dust. Use your imagination. Incorporate quotations as you may find them.

Bharati Mukherjee (b. 1940) was born in Calcutta, India, and describes herself as an American writer of Indian origin, having lived most of her life in the United States. She is the author of a number of novels, including Desirable Daughters *(2002), several works of nonfiction, and a few collections of short stories. A professor of English at the University of California, Mukherjee has received a number of awards for her work, including a National Books Circle Award.*

BHARATI MUKHERJEE

Imagining Homelands

In "Imagining Homelands," Mukherjee investigates the immigrant experience, which she classifies according to four aspects: "expatriation, exile, immigration, and repatriation." She distinguishes among these terms and the experiences and implications associated with them. Along the way, she raises a series of fundamental questions about identity, including both personal and national identity.

This essay is about four narratives, those of expatriation, exile, immigration, and repatriation. From those subnarratives, I hope to weave a revisionist theory for contemporary residency and citizenship, or at least to suggest new terms in the unresolved debate that threatens to grow louder and more rancorous in years to come.

The question, as always, is, What is America? Is it a place or an idea, is it a patchwork of diverse communities, or a nuanced, accented, multi-colored myth of shared values? Are we heading, in these final years of the millennium, toward the ancient dream of unity through diversity—*e pluribus unum*—or have we already taken the first steps down the long slope to chaos? Far from unity, we can't seem to find consensus on anything these days, not on affirmative action, on national educational standards, on needle exchanges, on family values, a drug policy, a trade policy, Most-Favored-Nation status for China, environmental protection, medical care, bilingual education, or even the designated hitter rule.

Both tendencies, chaos and unity, have attended our history. We are both a liberal experiment and a bulwark of reaction. De Tocqueville saw both tendencies, as did Lincoln, Faulkner, Melville and Emerson, and W. E. B. Du Bois, Frederick Douglass, and Martin Luther King, Jr.

I'm not a historian, only a fiction writer born and raised on a different continent who did not even become an American citizen until a dozen years ago. My work is set almost entirely within "immigrant communities," as they are so designated, although seen from the inside there is little that is communal about them, and only a minority of their inhabitants are even immigrants. Nevertheless, it is the reality of transplantation and psychological metamorphosis that is my material, not the world I left behind. I call myself an American writer, not an Indian one. I do not do this for material advantage (as Indian critics often assume), for there is far more commercial interest in the West in the India of tropical languor, dowry-death, and caste-strife than in scraped-knuckled, bruised-elbow immigration. I do it because I see in the process of immigration (in its widest sense, including at least three stages that have very little to do with changing citizenship) the stage, and the battleground, for the most exciting dramas of our time. A neighborhood like Jackson Heights, Queens, is on a par with Renaissance Venice for its richness of character and depth of intrigue. The same is true of my current home of San Francisco, my teaching campus of Berkeley, of Miami and Brooklyn, San Antonio and Detroit.

The national myth of immigration, the heart-warming saga of babushka-clad refugees climbing to the deck of the tramp steamer for a glimpse of the Statue of Liberty ("Look, Mama, just like the pictures we saw in Minsk, or Abruzzi, or Crete"), is just that, an image out of aging newspapers or our collective pop-memory banks. Today's arrivals are more likely to be discharged on a beach and told to swim ashore, be dropped in a desert and told to run, if they survive at all. Immigration, as I experience it, is made up of several conflicting parts. For my purposes here, *immigration* refers to the act of adopting new citizenship, of going the full nine yards of transformation. As such, it is but one option to be exercised by noncitizens living in this country.

Definitions seem to be in order. *Expatriation* is an act of sustained self-removal from one's native culture, balanced by a conscious resistance to total inclusion in the new host society. The motives for expatriation are as numerous as the expatriates themselves: aesthetic and intellectual affinity, a better job, a more interesting or less hassled life, greater freedom or simple tax relief, just as the motives for non-integration may range from principle, to nostalgia, to laziness or fear. The roster of notable expatriates in the realm of literature alone is immensely long, rich in honors and deep in respect: Henry James, T. S. Eliot, Joseph Conrad, V. S. Naipaul (before their formal acceptance of British citizenship), Vladimir Nabokov, James Joyce, Samuel Beckett, Paul Bowles, Mavis Gallant, Gabriel Garcia Márquez, Witold Gombrowicz, Anthony Burgess, Graham Greene, Derek Walcott, Malcolm Lowry,

Wilson Harris—names, even with a few glaring omissions that any literate audience can fill in, that we'd all agree rise to the top of any listing of the twentieth century's most notable literary achievements.

They are, in fact, our great voices of modernism as well as a few of postmodernism; their works are encyclopedic, their visions ironic and penetrating, their analyses detached and scrupulous, their styles experimental yet crystalline. If the ultimate goal of literature is to achieve universality and a kind of god-like omniscience, expatriation—the escape from small-mindedness, from niggling irritations—might well be a contributing factor.

The expatriate is the ultimate self-made artist, even the chooser of a language in which to operate, as Conrad, Beckett, Kundera, and Nabokov testify, an almost literal exponent of Joyce's dream of self-forging in the smithy of his soul. It is possible, in expatriation, to step out of the constraints into which one has been born and to exercise to the fullest the dual vision of the detached outsider. The expatriate Hungarian, Czech, or Pole of an earlier era, or today's Yugoslav or Bangladeshi, Algerian or Palestinian expatriate, asks only that the host culture permit him or her to retain an alien core that will not be compromised or surrendered. The bargain is thus struck: I will be a model resident. In return for your tolerance and noninterference, I will not attack the fundamental flaws of your society with anything like the zeal I bring to the dissection of my own people. I will imagine a new homeland built on reclaimed land.

I confess, it is an attractive bargain, one which I entertained myself, many years ago.

In the case of *exile*, the comparative luxury of self-removal is replaced by harsh compulsion. The spectrum of choice is gravely narrowed; the alternatives may be no more subtle than death, imprisonment, or a one-way ticket to oblivion. We all cheered the arrival of Aleksandr Solzhenitsyn in America, thinking we would gain a new voice in our literature as we did with Auden and Isherwood, or a new superstar as we have with so many singers and actors, or sensational tennis players. The list of twentieth-century exiles is an alternate Who's Who of Nobel listings in the sciences and literature, as well as an honor roll of world-class painters, dancers, performers, and composers. In some cases, the urgency of exile may, in time, blend into the serendipity of expatriation—Milan Kundera in Paris, Picasso in Arles, Chaplin in Switzerland—but for the most part, the exile does not achieve the same Olympian detachment enjoyed by the expatriate.

The exile is still tied to a mother country and a major cause that are the source of his wounding, and he may or may not choose, or have the option of choosing, to translate his passions or his words. The United States at present is home to dozens of exiles writing in their native Spanish and Russian and Arabic, in Chinese and Burmese, in Tamil and Aramaic, publishing in their own form of *samizdat* or exile presses, interviewed on ethnic radio and reviewed in the ethnic press, and few of us will ever have the good fortune to read their work or know of their existence. Similar, if not larger, populations cluster in Paris, Toronto, and London, in Berlin and Mexico City, in Amsterdam and Barcelona.[1]

Exile lacks the grandeur, the majesty of expatriation. The expatriate, at least, is validated by a host culture which extends the hospitality, and he often returns it in civic dutifulness. But the exile is a petitioner. He brings with him the guilty reminders of suffering, his stay is provisional and easily revoked, and he is often consigned to the underworld of ethnic intrigue, outside the purview of the law or of the press. If expatriation is the route of cool detachment, exile is for some that of furious engagement.

I must confess my own years of furious engagement, not in this country, but in my husband's Canada. When we lived in the Greek neighborhoods of Montreal, we were brought into daily contact with the passions of pro- and anti- "Colonels" Greek immigrants, the threats of arson by pro-junta Greeks on anti-junta businesses. In Toronto and Vancouver, the early years of the Punjab civil war were playing themselves out on the streets of various Little Indias. In all cases, police response, despite appeals for protection by what are called in Canada "visible minorities," and by simple Canadian citizens such as myself,

BHARATI MUKHERJEE

432

---

[1]Exile may become the subject of great literature, but it does not encourage the conditions for its production. For every Solzhenitsyn or Thomas Mann, every Freud, Kundera, or Skvorecky, every Ngugi wa Thiong'o or Wole Soyinka, every Liu Binyan, there are still today's Isaac Babels trapped behind the lines of their own despotisms. Read the heartbreaking reports of Amnesty International or of PEN'S Freedom to Write committee and you will learn that the free world is still comparatively blind and deaf to the fate of Algerian, Turkish, Iranian, Malaysian, Indonesian, Cuban, Chinese, Burmese, Siorra Leonean, Nigerian, Egyptian, Cambodian, Tamil, and Sinhalese dissidents. Their names are not known, their causes are not sexy, their languages are not in wide distribution in the West, and for these reasons, along with those of trade and political influence, their lives, their bravery, and their work go unvalidated.

It makes you wonder, sometimes, if anyone stays at home. Is same sort of major disruption essential for great writing? Of course that's not the truth, as even a moment's reflection can show, but the list of expatriate and exiled writers is nevertheless a daunting one to contemplate. It might be truer to say that all writers are expatriates to one degree or another, or they are internal exiles; certainty William Faulkner or Flannery O'Connor, Bernard Malamud or Cynthia Ozick, hail from a country without a passport. [All notes are Mukherjee's.]

harassed on the streets and in public transportation by white youths, was a variant of "It's not our [meaning white, Canadian] problem. You guys"—or more likely, *you little people*— "settle it among yourselves."[2]

In November 1996, the *New York Times* asked me to contribute an op-ed piece inspired by the so-called immigration debate that was then raging on both sides during the election battle. Are we "all immigrants," as the pietistic national myth would have it, therefore duty-bound to support immigration as an apple pie or motherhood issue, or are most new immigrants cheats and rip-off artists, as many nativists seem to believe?

I chose to write of my older sister and myself, two Calcutta-born women from identical backgrounds with the same Cambridge-tested accent, the same convent education, who had been in the United States for over thirty-five years. My sister married an Indian student in Detroit and has remained in the same job and the same house, wearing saris, cooking familiar food, guarding the accent, for the past thirty years. She holds the much-valued U.S. green card but feels her home is still India, where she intends to retire in the next few years. I, too, married a fellow student in the Writers' Workshop at the University of Iowa, an American of Canadian parentage, and we have lived in Canada and in several parts of the United States, moving at least twenty times, and have often been obliged by professional circumstances to live many years apart. I am a U.S. citizen and could not imagine returning to India for other than family visits and relaxed vacations. My accent is an amalgam of the places I've lived, my wardrobe is a similar hodgepodge, and so is our daily menu.

The question I meant to raise was simply this: Which one of us is the freak? Someone who retains the food, the clothes, the accent of expatriation, or her T-shirted, blue-jeaned sister? The answer is by no means clear.

That little article, anecdotal in nature, aroused more passions than many of my novels. When I give readings or interviews in India, it becomes a lead-question (the article was reprinted in several Indian newspapers), and the questioners are often anything but cordial. Conversely, the article has been celebrated by the liberal mainstream in

---

[2] I should add that it very much as a "white, Canadian" problem. The eventual outcome of such racist smugness was the bloodiest terrorist act of modern times, the blowing up, by a small group of Sikh extremists, of an Air India 747 over the coast of Ireland, with the loss of 329 Canadian lives. If you can find a copy of the book. *The Sorrow and the Terror*, which my husband and I co-authored in 1987, you'll understand some of the urgency that has motivated both of our writings since that tragic event.

this country as a bold statement of faith in the American experiment, warts and all. Neither reaction is entirely satisfactory.

Among some Indian intellectuals it is read as a polarizing document, an implicit rejection of the worth of hundreds of thousands of law-abiding, tax-paying, communally and religiously conservative, contributing Indian nationals, like my sister, working and residing overseas. At its fringes, that interpretation tends to bracket my pro-immigration, let-it-go stance with those of some unsavory company, English-only, "American First"-ers of a stripe with Enoch Powell or the current crop of French and Austrian race-baiters who even propose cleansing the various European motherlands of Turks, Gypsies, North Africans, Kurds, and Bosnian/Kosovo refugees. We all know the end-point of such appeals to purity, especially in Europe.

Given my presumed respectability in the United States as a member of a prominent minority community, and my access to mainstream media, I try at every opportunity to distinguish my position from those of ill-disposed, anti-immigrant Americans as well as of instinctive Americaphobes, a large number of whom, unfortunately, can be found among India-born academics in American universities. I know I'm not the only person from a minority community who weighs American promise against American history on a daily basis and who still finds a positive balance, but it still seems necessary to emphasize my basic position. I am an integrationist and, to use a deliberately ugly word, a mongrelizer. My sister, like most expatriates or exiles, is not. Mongrels lose a lot of prestige and pedigree in their travels, they're not as classically proportioned or predictably behaved as purebred, and, more to the point, their presence crease a third, unpredictable, sometimes undesirable, and often untrainable mutt. Because I am here, I am changed totally by you and by my commitment to this country and its problems, but so are you. You are now implicated in my life; you probably entrust your health, or aspects of it, to Indian doctors or dentists, you can now eat my food in nearly any town, run India-designed software on your India-designed computer. I'm just as mainstream as anyone else. I am also a proud India-born, Bengali-speaking Hindu. These positions need not be antithetical.

Like my academic colleagues with whom I have conducted many public quarrels, I too grew up in a British-centered universe in India. As a college student I too would have snickered at the pretense of an American culture, of an American literature. To declare my American-ness, and not to retain the genteel expatriation of an upper-class

Bengali Brahmin, is, in their minds, to be linked with and to share the historical guilt of slavery, segregation, extermination of Native Americans, the CIA, Vietnam, and to be linked with the hypocrisy of supporting both freedom and dictatorships, and with a generally vulgar "Coca-Cola" and "McDonald's" culture.

That is a far less comforting heritage than that of my forebears, at least as it was communicated to me. My city, my religion, my caste, were always the innocent victims of foreign invaders. We were the colonized, the humiliated, the despised. History had cleansed us of all ancestral sins. Many of my colleagues apparently still believe in the myth of national innocence, and will do anything to maintain it.

The tale of two sisters of course suggests larger narratives, those of expatriation and those of immigration. The narrative of expatriation calls to mind villas in the south of France, on the shores of Lake Geneva, apartments in Paris, but it is no stranger to Detroit as well. The narrative of expatriation fairly drips with respectability, or at least with privilege, but the narrative of immigration calls to mind crowded tenements, Ellis Island, sweatshops, accents, strange foods, taxicab drivers, bizarre holidays, strange religions, unseemly ethnic passions.

And it must be admitted, especially in New York City, that the narrative of immigration is a scripted cliché. Little Italy, the Lower East Side, Chinatown, Brighton Beach, Yorkville, Harlem, the South Bronx, and the Upper East Side, the Upper West Side—we can almost populate those neighborhoods from central casting, from war movies, B-movies, TV dramas, sitcoms, and musicals. It is a cliché because it is the story of the parents and grandparents of second- and third-generation Americans and it's been handed over to *me* and to millions like me, unchanged. The narrative turned out happily, in general; the poor became middle class, the foreign became more American than Americans, traditional national values were not deeply challenged, but were even upheld and strengthened. (For those who didn't fit in, and there were many, things turned out differently. Sacco and Vanzetti were executed, so was Bruno Hauptmann, so were the Rosenbergs.) It's a cliché because the language has not been updated.

Central-casting immigration is European, white, Christian and Jewish. The distance between America and Europe a hundred years ago seemed vast, unimaginable; the linguistic, cultural, and religious differences tested the very limits of contemporary assimilation. Of course, more alien populations were simply barred from any thought of immigration, Asians were "sojourners" whose wives were not admitted; African Americans were denied the vote; Latinos and French-Canadians (who were called "blue-eyed Chinese") clustered in enclaves near their borders; they were considered unassimilable.

The immigration narrative changed with the end of colonialism. Vast populations were no longer hemmed in by colonial legislation. The old European-favored quota system was challenged; talent, merit, and family unification became an aim of immigration policy. The new arrivals were no longer populating an empty landscape or providing muscle for labor-intensive heavy industry.

We Americans fought bitter wars in alien areas, we disrupted civilizations and admitted some of the survivors. The cold war sent its refugees to Florida, to Brooklyn, to Minneapolis. We wanted professionals, we needed doctors, engineers, researchers, and entrepreneurs. We educated the Third World's brightest in our schools and then we kept them. They brought in their parents, their cousins, they sponsored others. Immigrant communities grew from a dozen epicenters, from Queens to Glendale, Miami to Minnesota, and each community became self-sustaining. Dithering and cynical politics allowed uncountable millions of undocumented workers to enter, and while their net value to the economy is not really in dispute, their likely contribution to a broadening of American democracy certainly is, especially if they are kept underground, not permitted to educate their children or to enjoy some semblance of public acceptance. In California, we can already see how we've permitted the situation to coarsen the public dialogue.

There are now Little Indias, Koreas, Jamaicas, Colombias, Saigons, Moscows, Mexicos, Vientianes, Manilas, Chinas, in cities that had never experienced immigration communities in earlier waves. My concern is definitely not with their presence here, it is with our ability to *adjust* to their presence and to make it a productive, that is, a mongrelizing encounter. If five million undocumented aliens are now in the country, living in slums and barrios, working at odd jobs, hiding from authorities, sending money home, neglecting their children, engaging in criminal activity (my New York apartment was ransacked by that most innocent, icon of Manhattan life, the Chinese take-out delivery man, whose hotbox contained an acetylene torch for cutting through my firedoor), we may never encounter one another except in figurative dark alleys—and that is an immigration tragedy.

Immigration may be an uplifting narrative, but it's not pretty and certainly not elegant, like expatriation. It's low-tech. I am an immigrant, and to achieve that honor, I gave up status that I'll never be able to achieve in the New World. I became this thing new to U.S. history, someone who had never existed before me and hundreds of thousands like me: an Indo-American. As a writer, I had to decide how to describe myself—Asian-American, Indo-American, unhyphenated American? I claim myself as an American in the immigrant tradition of writers I most admire, Henry Roth and Bernard Malamud; yet it is still, after fifteen years of aggressive correction, a rare literary notice that does not identify me as "Indian." It's apparently easier for Monica Seles to be accepted as American than me, and I wonder why that might be.

We are still fighting the tradition of nineteenth-century exclusivism, the branding of the "visibly foreign" or the non-Judeo/Christian as unsuited for naturalization. It was the price paid by native-born Japanese-Americans in World War II, by the Latino-appearing in Los Angeles, by Asians just about anywhere; accepted as "sojourners" doing dirty and underpaid work, but not as Americans altering the appearance, eventually, of us all.

There is a fourth narrative, not often mentioned, but one which complicates even the murkier aspects of immigration. I think of it as *repatriation,* a repopulation of formerly Spanish lands, formerly French lands, formerly Native American lands, which involves the undocumented movement of millions over borders that we may think of as unviolable but which others have long considered mere extensions of their homeland. When my husband, Clark Blaise, was researching a book about his French-Canadian father, he was struck by the fact that Léo Blais's native village of Quebec was part of the same parish that reached into Maine, that family members were buried on both sides of the border, that my father-in-law could emigrate from Canada in 1912 and arrive in Manchester, New Hampshire, work in the mills and go to school and never learn a word of English. What was true in New England ninety years ago has always been true in the Rio Grande Valley and East Los Angeles; it has become the rule in South Florida, and East Harlem and the South Bronx. If we speak seriously of the Pacific Rim, and of profiting from its markets and asserting our influence upon it, we are implicitly inviting all Asia to our shores—particularly if our history also includes a significant amount of historical "collateral damage," as in the case of the Philippines and Vietnam. It's America's own version of Israel's Law of Return. Immigrant groups are reclaiming their lands and feel no need to make apologies or accommodations to the latest landlords. Geography is once again dictating destiny. (Anyone who doubts it should take a look at Vancouver, British Columbia, now a virtual extension of Hong Kong.) We English-speakers are a minority in the New World; we are integrating our economies, and the implication is that we must adjust to the free movement of workers in much the way Europe does today.

Expatriation, exile, immigration, and 30 repatriation, four ways of accommodating the modern restlessness, the modern dislocations, the abuses of history, the hopes of affluence. It seems to me we have entered a supranational age, in which traditional citizenship is likely to be a murky identification and where technical proficiency is the true passport to acceptance. Somehow, we must find a way of integrating all four modes of entry into our narrative of Americanism, for the cruelties of history itself have imposed too heavy a burden on the normal channels of transformation.

With the pietistic formula "we are all immigrants," I have to disagree. We are not, and never were. We have reinvented the myths of our founding so many times, and for so many audiences, that we've probably lost all trace of a unifying narrative. Many never had the chance to immigrate; many never wanted to. Did we come seeking religious freedom? I didn't. Did we come to escape oppression, the shackles of dictatorship? I didn't. Did we rejoin the remnants of our scattered family? I didn't. Have we come seeking happiness and fortune?—for both, I should have stayed where I was. We are expatriates, exiles, slaves, and dispossessed, we are conquerors, plunderers, refugees, and amnesty-seekers, we are temporary workers, undocumented workers, visitors, students, tourists, we are joy-seekers, claim-jumpers, parole-violators.

While it would not work for me, and I do feel the process of classic immigration has liberated me in ways that expatriation never could, I must be prepared to accept the validity of my sister Mira's narrative of expatriation and those of others like her. Their voices are hidden inside me, I have written some of their stories, and I grieve for them far more than I resent them—it's a reaction curiously similar to that of most Third World writers toward the work of V. S. Naipaul. "Damn him," I want to shout, damn his superior airs, damn his cold detachment, damn his vast talent, damn his crystalline sentences. I want him to manifest love, for just a paragraph or two, to cut loose. This does not affect my respect for his work. I want my sister to feel love for this country that she, in the depths of her heart, cannot. This does not affect the contribution she makes to school children in Detroit.

I have met the undocumented and I have written about them; I too want them to know some of our freedoms, I want them to know relief from poverty, from fear of deportation, from exploitation, but I realize America will never be more for them than a chance to work, to pocket a little money and snatch a little fun. It was their country and we were the interlopers, and in their hearts and in their history it is still their land. For us to call them aliens in those strings of mission-named California cities, we must surrender a bit of our own sanity.

We must be prepared to accept the bitter, exiled discourse, whether it comes from the Cuban-Americans of Miami, the Vietnamese of California, or the Russian Jews of Brighton Beach and Los Angeles, their tight defensiveness, their aggressiveness, their blinkered vision. And what of the vast minority discourse in this country, the African-American expressions with their anti-Semitic and anti-Asian notes, their own internal dispute with the world that brought them here, that refused to integrate them but then stole every degree of their self-expression?

And beyond that, we must understand, and truly accept, that the United States for all its power is only a minority state. It must accommodate itself to the preponderance of Latin Americans in this hemisphere, and it must understand that part of its core is the acceptance of the cruel fact of its minority status.

POSSIBILITIES FOR WRITING

1. Explain the difference between Mukherjee's immigrant experience and that of her sister. What does the author mean by calling herself a "mongrelizer" and an "integrationist"?
2. Develop a brief argument on whether America is, in Mukherjee's words, "a place or an idea," "a patchwork of diverse communication" or a "nuanced, accented, multicolored myth of shared values."
3. Write an essay in which you explore your own cultural identity. Consider your heritage and the extent to which your ancestry affects your Americanness. You may wish to use one or another of Mukherjee's four categories as part of your analysis of your own cultural identity.

NUALA O'FAOLAIN

Are You Somebody?

In "Are You Somebody," the introduction to Nuala O'Faolain's memoir of the same title, the author introduces the themes and identifies the question that serves as a catalyst for her book. O'Faolain's goal was to identify the person behind the author of the columns she wrote for the *Irish Times*, to let her readers know who she was and what she was like. First identifying herself as a "nobody," a girl who became a woman in a country where men were the measure of all things important, she resisted this definition with a pressing sense of individuality and selfhood.

O'Faolain's style is honest and direct and her tone absent of sentimentality. Paradoxically, in writing about herself and her sense of her individual self, her stories transcend her personal experience to resonate with the lives of her readers.

I was born in a Dublin that was much more like something from an earlier century than like the present day. I was one of nine children, when nine was not even thought of as a big family, among the teeming, penniless, anonymous Irish of the day. I was typical: a nobody, who came of an unrecorded line of nobodies. In a conservative Catholic country, which feared sexuality and forbade me even information about my body, I could expect difficulty in getting through my life as a girl and a woman. But at least—it would have been assumed—I wouldn't have the burden of having to earn a good wage. Eventually some man would marry me and keep me.

But there are no typical people. And places don't stay the same. The world changed around Ireland, and even Ireland changed, and I was to be both an agent of change and a beneficiary of it. I didn't see that, until I wrote out my story. I was immured in the experience of my own life. Most of the time I just went blindly from day to day, and though what I was doing must have looked ordinary enough—growing up in the countryside, getting through school, falling in love, discovering lust, learning, working, travelling, moving in and out of health and happiness—to myself I was usually barely hanging on. I never stood back and looked at myself and what I was doing. I didn't value myself enough—take myself seriously enough—to reflect even privately on whether my existence had any pattern, any meaning. I took it for granted that like most of the billions of people who are born and die on this planet I was just an accident. There was no reason for me.

Yet my life burned inside me. Even such as it was, it was the only record of me, and it was my only creation, and something in me would not accept that it was insignificant. Something in me must have been waiting to stand up and demand to be counted. Because eventually, when I was presented with an opportunity to talk about myself, I grasped at it. I'm on my own anyway, I thought. What have I to lose? But I needed to speak, too. I needed to howl.

What happened was that in my forties, back in the Dublin of my birth, I began working for the most respected newspaper in the country—*The Irish Times*—as an opinion columnist. This was a wonderful job to have, and a quite unexpected one. The very idea of an Irishwoman opinion columnist would have been unthinkable for most of my life. The columns were usually about politics or social questions or moments in popular culture—they weren't personal at all. They used a confident, public voice. My readers probably thought I was as confident as that all the time, but I knew the truth. My private life was solitary. My private voice was apologetic. In terms of national influence I mattered, in Ireland. But I possessed nothing of what has traditionally mattered to women and what had mattered to me during most of my life. I had no lover, no child. It seemed to me that I had nothing to look back on but failure.

But when I'd been writing my columns for ten years or so, a publisher came to me and asked whether he could put some of them together in book form. I said that was fine. No one would track my work through the back numbers of the newspaper, but a book gets around. It might be the only thing to read in a trekker's hut in Nepal. It would be catalogued in the National Library. It would be there for my grandniece, who is only a baby now. But I wasn't interested in the old columns. I was interested in what I would say in the personal introduction I'd promised to write. What would I say about myself, the person who *wrote* the columns? Now that I had the opportunity, how would I introduce myself?

I'm fairly well known in Ireland. I've been on television a lot, and there's a photo of me in the paper, at the top of my column. But I'm no star. People have to look at me twice or three times to put a name on me. Sometimes when I'm drinking in a lounge bar, a group of women, say, across the room, may look at me and send one of their number over to me, or when I'm in the grocery store someone who has just passed me by turns back and comes right up to me and scrutinises my face. "Are you somebody?" they ask. Well—am I somebody? I'm not anybody in terms of the world, but then, who decides what a somebody is? How is a somebody made? I've never done anything remarkable; neither have most people. Yet most people, like me, feel remarkable. That self-importance welled up inside me. I had the desire to give an account of my life. I was finished with furtiveness. I sat down to write the introduction, and I summoned my pride. I turned it into a memoir.

I imagined the hostile response I'd get in my little Irish world. "Who does she think she is?" I could hear the reviewers saying. But it turned out not to be like that at all. The world my story went out to turned out to be much, much bigger than I'd ever thought. And it turned out to be full of people who knew me, who were sisters and brothers although we had never met, who were there to welcome me coming out of the shadows, and who wanted to throw off the shadows that obscured their own lives, too. My small voice was answered by a rich chorus of voices: my voice, which had once been mute! Of all the places where my story might start, even, it started itself at a point in my life when I could not speak at all. . . .

POSSIBILITIES FOR WRITING

1. O'Faolain calls herself a "nobody" and says that she is "typical." How does she use these terms to set up her piece? To what extent are these terms effective ones for her purpose? What other words and phrases echo and support these?

2. What motivated O'Faolain to write "Are You Somebody?"? What motivated her to write her newspaper columns? From the evidence of this short piece, to what extent does O'Faolain consider herself a writer? What kind of writer?

3. Imagine that you were invited to write your autobiography—a memoir of your life so far. Write the introduction, or preliminary setup chapter, using O'Faolain's "Are You Somebody?" as a model.

George Orwell (1903–1950) was born Eric Blair in Bengal, India, where his father was a minor functionary in the British colonial government. Schooled in England, he chose not to attend university and instead joined the Indian Imperial Police in Burma. After five years, however, he became disillusioned with the whole notion of colonial rule and returned to England to pursue a career as a writer. His first book, Down and Out in Paris and London *(1933), chronicled his experiences living a self-imposed hand-to-mouth existence among the poor of the two cities and established what would become one of his principle themes: the exploitation of the working classes and the injustice inherent in modern societies and governments. In addition to his many works of nonfiction, Orwell is known for his scathing political novels* Animal Farm *(1945) and* 1984 *(1949).*

GEORGE ORWELL

Politics and the English Language

In "Politics and the English Language," George Orwell makes a plea for using language with clarity, honesty, and directness. He argues that far too much published writing, especially academic prose, suffers from vagueness, obscurity, and sheer ugliness. He argues, further, that confused writing reflects confused thinking, and that the way to begin thinking more clearly is to attend carefully to the clarity of writing.

To make his case, Orwell accumulates examples from newspapers, magazines, books, and professional journals. He analyzes his samples, pointing out their flaws of language and thought. And he concludes by making a list of bad writing habits to avoid. One of the special fascinations of the essay is that Orwell himself violates his rules a bit. But he covers himself in his guidelines when he suggests that writers follow them, except in cases where following the rules would lead them to say something "barbarous."

Most people who bother with the matter at all would admit that the English language is in a bad way, but it is generally assumed that we cannot by conscious action do anything about it. Our civilization is decadent and our language—so the argument runs—must inevitably share in the general collapse. It follows that any struggle against the abuse of language is a sentimental archaism, like preferring candles to electric light or hansom cabs to aeroplanes. Underneath this lies the half-conscious belief that language is a natural growth and not an instrument which we shape for our own purposes.

Now, it is clear that the decline of a language must ultimately have political and economic causes: it is not due simply to the bad influence of this or that individual writer. But an effect can become a cause, reinforcing the original cause and producing the same effect in an intensified form, and so on indefinitely. A man may take to drink because he feels himself to be a failure, and then fail all the more completely because he drinks. It is rather the same thing that is happening to the English language. It becomes ugly and inaccurate because our thoughts are foolish, but the slovenliness of our language makes it easier for us to have foolish thoughts. The point is that the process is reversible. Modern English, especially written English, is full of bad habits which spread by imitation and which can be avoided if one is willing to take the necessary trouble. If one gets rid of these habits one can think more clearly, and to think clearly is a necessary first step towards political regeneration: so that the fight against bad English is not frivolous and is not the exclusive concern of professional writers. I will come back to this presently, and I hope that by that time the meaning of what I have said here will have become clearer. Meanwhile, here are five specimens of the English language as it is now habitually written.

These five passages have not been picked out because they are especially bad—I could have quoted far worse if I had chosen—but because they illustrate various of the mental vices from which we now suffer. They are a little below the average, but are fairly representative samples. I number them so that I can refer back to them when necessary:

"(1) I am not, indeed, sure whether it is not true to say that the Milton who once seemed not unlike a seventeenth-century Shelley had not become, out of an experience ever more bitter in each year, more alien [sic] to the founder of that Jesuit sect which nothing could induce him to tolerate."

PROFESSOR HAROLD LASKI (*ESSAY IN* FREEDOM OF EXPRESSION)

"(2) Above all, we cannot play ducks and drakes with a native battery of idioms which prescribes such egregious collocations of vocables as the Basic put up with for tolerate or put at a loss for bewilder."

PROFESSOR LANCELOT HOGBEN (INTERGLOSSA)

"(3) On the one side we have the free personality: by definition it is not neurotic, for it has neither conflict nor dream. Its desires, such as they are, are transparent, for they are just what institutional approval keeps in the forefront of consciousness; another institutional pattern would alter their number and intensity; there is little in them that is natural, irreducible, or culturally dangerous. But on the other side, the social bond itself is nothing but the mutual reflection of these self-secure

integrities. Recall the definition of love. Is not this the very picture of a small academic? Where is there a place in this hall of mirrors for either personality or fraternity?"

ESSAY ON PSYCHOLOGY IN POLITICS (NEW YORK)

"(4) All the 'best people' from the gentlemen's clubs, and all the frantic fascist captains, united in common hatred of Socialism and bestial horror of the rising tide of the mass revolutionary movement, have turned to acts of provocation, to foul incendiarism, to medieval legends of poisoned wells, to legalize their own destruction of proletarian organizations, and rouse the agitated petty-bourgeoisie to chauvinistic fervour on behalf of the fight against the revolutionary way out of the crisis."

COMMUNIST PAMPHLET

"(5) If a new spirit is to be refused into this old country, there is one thorny and contentious reform which must be tackled, and that is the humanization and galvanization of the B.B.C. Timidity here will bespeak cancer and atrophy of the soul. The heart of Britain may be sound and of strong beat, for instance, but the British lion's roar at present is like that of Bottom in Shakespeare's Midsummer Night's Dream—*as gentle as any sucking dove. A virile new Britain cannot continue indefinitely to be traduced in the eyes or rather ears, of the world by the effete languors of Langham Place, brazenly masquerading as 'standard English'. When the Voice of Britain is heard at nine o'clock, better far and infinitely less ludicrous to hear aitches honestly dropped than the present priggish, inflated, inhibited, school-ma'amish arch braying of blameless bashful mewing maidens!"*

LETTER IN TRIBUNE

Each of these passages has faults of its own, but, quite apart from avoidable ugliness, two qualities are common to all of them. The first is staleness of imagery: the other is lack of precision. The writer either has a meaning and cannot express it, or he inadvertently says something else, or he is almost indifferent as to whether his words mean anything or not. This mixture of vagueness and sheer incompetence is the most marked characteristic of modern English prose, and especially of any kind of political writing. As soon as certain topics are raised, the concrete melts into the abstract and no one seems able to think of turns of speech that are not hackneyed: prose consists less and less of *words* chosen for the sake of their meaning, and more and more of *phrases* tacked together like the sections of a prefabricated hen-house. I list below, with notes and examples, various of the tricks by means of which the work of prose-construction is habitually dodged:

Dying Metaphors

A newly invented metaphor assists thought by evoking a visual image, while on the other hand a metaphor which is technically "dead" (e.g. *iron resolution*) has in effect reverted to being an ordinary word and can generally be used without loss of vividness. But in between these two classes there is a huge dump of worn-out metaphors which have lost all evocative power and are merely used because they save people the trouble of inventing phrases for themselves. Examples are: *Ring the changes on, take up the cudgels for, toe the line, ride roughshod over, stand shoulder to shoulder with, play into the hands of, no axe to grind, grist to the mill, fishing in troubled waters, on the order of the day, Achilles heel, swan song, hotbed.* Many of these are used without knowledge of their meaning (what is a "rift," for instance?), and incompatible metaphors are frequently mixed, a sure sign that the writer is not interested in what he is saying. Some metaphors now current have been twisted out of their original meaning without those who use them even being aware of the fact. For example, *toe the line* is sometimes written *tow the line.* Another example is *the hammer and the anvil,* now always used with the implication that the anvil gets the worst of it. In real life it is always the anvil that breaks the hammer, never the other way about: a writer who stopped to think what he was saying would be aware of this, and would avoid perverting the original phrase.

Operators or Verbal False Limbs

These save the trouble of picking out appropriate verbs and nouns, and at the same time pad each sentence with extra syllables which give it an appearance of symmetry. Characteristic phrases are: *render inoperative, militate against, make contact with, be subjected to, give rise to, give grounds for, have the effect of, play a leading part (role) in, make itself felt, take effect, exhibit a tendency to, serve the purpose of,* etc., etc. The keynote is the elimination of simple verbs. Instead of being a single word, such as *break, stop, spoil, mend, kill,* a verb becomes a *phrase,* made up of a noun or adjective tacked on to some general-purposes verb such as *prove, serve, form, play, render.* In addition, the passive voice is wherever possible used in preference to the active, and noun constructions are used instead of gerunds (*by examination of* instead of *by examining*). The range of verbs is further cut down by means of the *-ize* and *de-* formation, and the banal statements are given an appearance of profundity by means of the *not un-* formation. Simple conjunctions and prepositions are replaced by such phrases as *with respect to, having regard to, the fact that, by dint of, in view of, in the interest of, on the hypothesis that;* and the ends of sentences are saved from anticlimax by such resounding commonplaces as *greatly to be desired, cannot be left out of account, a development to be expected in the near future, deserving of serious consideration, brought to a satisfactory conclusion,* and so on and so forth.

Pretentious Diction

Words like *phenomenon, element, individual* (as noun), *objective, categorical, effective, virtual, basic, primary, promote, constitute, exhibit, exploit, utilize, eliminate, liquidate,* are used to dress up simple statements and give an air of scientific impartiality to biased judgments. Adjectives like *epoch-making, epic, historic, unforgettable, triumphant, age-old, inevitable, inexorable, veritable,* are used to dignify the sordid processes of international politics, while writing that aims at glorifying war usually takes on an archaic colour, its characteristic words being: *realm, throne, chariot, mailed fist, trident, sword, shield, buckler, banner, jackboot, clarion.* Foreign words and expressions such as *cul de sac, ancien régime, deus ex machina, mutatis mutandis, status quo, gleichschaltung, weltanschauung,* are used to give an air of culture and elegance. Except for the useful abbreviations *i.e., e.g.,* and *etc.,* there is no real need for any of the hundreds of foreign phrases now current in English. Bad writers, and especially scientific, political and sociological writers, are nearly aways haunted by the notion that Latin or Greek words are grander than Saxon ones, and unnecessary words like *expedite, ameliorate, predict, extraneous, deracinated, clandestine, subagueous* and hundreds of others constantly gain ground from their Anglo-Saxon opposite numbers.[1] The jargon peculiar to Marxist writing (*hyena, hangman, cannibal, petty bourgeois, these gentry, lacquey, flunkey, mad dog, White Guard,* etc., consists largely of

---

[1]An interesting illustration of this is the way in which the English flower names which were in use till very recently are being ousted by Greek ones, *snapdragon* becoming *antirrhinum, forget-me-not* becoming *myosotis,* etc. It is hard to see any practical reason for this change of fashion: it is probably due to an instinctive turning-away from the more homely word and a vague feeling that the Greek word is scientific [Orwell's note].

words and phrases translated from Russian, German or French; but the normal way of coining a new word is to use a Latin or Greek root with the appropriate affix and, where necessary, the -ize formation. It is often easier to make up words of this kind (*deregionalize, impermissible, extramarital, nonfragmentatory* and so forth) than to think up the English words that will cover one's meaning. The result, in general, is an increase in slovenliness and vagueness.

Meaningless Words

In certain kinds of writing, particularly in art criticism and literary criticism, it is normal to come across long passages which are almost completely lacking in meaning.[2] Words like *romantic, plastic, values, human, dead, sentimental, natural, vitality*, as used in art criticism, are strictly meaningless in the sense that they not only do not point to any discoverable object, but are hardly ever expected to do so by the reader. When one critic writes, "The outstanding feature of Mr. X's work is its living quality," while another writes, "The immediately striking thing about Mr. X's work is its peculiar deadness," the reader accepts this as a simple difference of opinion. If words like *black* and *white* were involved, instead of the jargon words *dead* and *living*, he would see at once that language was being used in an improper way. Many political words are similarly abused. The word *Fascism* has now no meaning except in so far as it signifies "something not desirable." The words *democracy, socialism, freedom, patriotic, realistic, justice*, have each of them several different meanings which cannot be reconciled with one another. In the case of a word like *democracy*, not only is there no agreed definition, but the attempt to make one is resisted from all sides. It is almost universally felt that when we call a country democratic we are praising it: consequently the defenders of every kind of régime claim that it is a democracy, and fear that they might have to stop using the word if it were tied down to any one meaning. Words of this kind are often used in a consciously dishonest way. That is, the person who uses them has his own private definition, but allows his hearer to think he means something quite different. Statements like *Marshal Pétain was a true*

GEORGE ORWELL

448

[2]Example: "Comfort's catholicity of perception and image, strangely Whitmanesque in range, almost the exact opposite in aesthetic compulsion, continues to evoke that trembling atmospheric accumulative hinting at a cruel, an inexorably serene timelessness . . . . Wrey Gardiner scores by aiming at simple bull's-eyes with precision. Only they are not so simple, and through this contented sadness runs more than the surface bittersweet of resignation" (*Poetry Quarterly*) [Orwell's note].

patriot, *The Soviet Press is the freest in the world*, *The Catholic Church is opposed to persecution*, are almost always made with intent to deceive. Other words used in variable meanings, in most cases more or less dishonestly, are: *class, totalitarian, science, progressive, reactionary, bourgeois, equality.*

Now that I have made this catalogue of swindles and perversions, let me give another example of the kind of writing that they lead to. This time it must of its nature be an imaginary one. I am going to translate a passage of good English into modern English of the worst sort. Here is a well-known verse from *Ecclesiastes:*

> *"I returned and saw under the sun, that the race is not to the swift, nor the battle to the strong, neither yet bread to the wise, nor yet riches to men of understanding, nor yet favour to men of skill; but time and chance happeneth to them all."*

Here it is in modern English:

> *"Objective consideration of contemporary phenomena compels the conclusion that success or failure in competitive activities exhibits no tendency to be commensurate with innate capacity, but that a considerable element of the unpredictable must invariably be taken into account."*

This is a parody, but not a very gross one. Exhibit (3), above, for instance, contains several patches of the same kind of English. It will be seen that I have not made a full translation. The beginning and ending of the sentence follow the original meaning fairly closely, but in the middle the concrete illustrations—race, battle, bread—dissolve into the vague phrase "success or failure in competitive activities." This had to be so, because no modern writer of the kind I am discussing—no one capable of using phrases like "objective consideration of contemporary phenomena"—would ever tabulate his thoughts in that precise and detailed way. The whole tendency of modern prose is away from concreteness. Now analyse these two sentences a little more closely. The first contains forty-nine words but only sixty syllables, and all its words are those of everyday life. The second contains thirty-eight words of ninety syllables: eighteen of its words are from Latin roots, and one from Greek. The first sentence contains six vivid images, and only one phrase ("time and chance") that could be called vague. The second contains not a single fresh, arresting phrase, and in spite of its ninety syllables it gives only a shortened version of the meaning contained in the first. Yet without a doubt it is the second kind of sentence that is gaining ground in modern English. I do not want to exaggerate. This kind of writing is not yet universal, and outcrops of simplicity will occur here and there in the worst-written page. Still, if you or I were told to write a few lines on the uncertainty of human fortunes, we should probably come much nearer to my imaginary sentence than to the one from *Ecclesiastes.*

As I have tried to show, modern writing at its worst does not consist in picking out words for the sake of their meaning and inventing images in order to make the meaning clearer. It consists in gumming together long strips of words which have already been set in order by someone else, and making the results presentable by sheer humbug. The attraction of this way of writing is that it is easy. It is easier—even quicker, once you have the habit—to say *In my opinion it is a not unjustifiable assumption that* than to say *I think.* If you use ready-made phrases, you not only don't have to hunt about for words; you also don't have to bother with the rhythms of your sentences, since these phrases are generally so arranged as to be more or less euphonious. When you are composing in a hurry—when you are dictating to a stenographer, for instance, or making a public speech—it is natural to fall into a pretentious, Latinized style. Tags like *a consideration which we should do well to bear in mind* or *a conclusion to which all of us would readily assent* will save many a sentence from coming down with a bump. By using stale metaphors, similes and idioms, you save much mental effort, at the cost of leaving your meaning vague, not only for your reader but for yourself. This is the significance of mixed metaphors. The sole aim of a metaphor is to call up a visual image. When these images clash— as in *The Fascist octopus has sung its swan song, the jackboot is thrown into the melting pot*—it can be taken as certain that the writer is not seeing a mental image of the objects he is naming; in other words he is not really thinking. Look again at the examples I gave at the beginning of this essay. Professor Laski (1) uses five negatives in fifty-three words. One of these is superfluous, making nonsense of the whole passage, and in addition there is the slip *alien* for akin, making further nonsense, and several avoidable pieces of clumsiness which increase the general vagueness. Professor Hogben (2) plays ducks and drakes with a battery which is able to write prescriptions, and, while disapproving of the everyday phrase *put up with,* is unwilling to look *egregious* up in the dictionary and see what it means. (3), if one takes an uncharitable attitude towards it, is simply meaningless: probably one could work out its intended meaning by reading the whole of the article in which it occurs. In (4), the writer knows more or less what he wants to say, but an accumulation of stale phrases chokes him like tea leaves blocking a sink. In (5), words and meaning have almost parted company. People who write in this manner usually have a general emotional meaning—they dislike one thing and want to express solidarity with another—but they are not interested in the detail of what they are saying. A scrupulous writer, in every sentence that he writes, will ask himself at least four questions, thus: What am I trying to say? What words will express it? What image or idiom will make it clearer? Is this image fresh enough to have an effect? And he will probably ask himself two more: Could I put it more shortly? Have I said anything that is avoidably ugly? But you are not obliged to go to all this trouble. You can shirk it by simply throwing your mind open and letting the ready-made phrases come crowding in. They will construct your sentences for you—even think your thoughts for you, to a certain extent—and at need they will perform the important service of partially concealing your meaning even from yourself. It is at this point that the special connection between politics and the debasement of language becomes clear.

In our time it is broadly true that political writing is bad writing. Where it is not true, it will generally be found that the writer is some kind of rebel, expressing his private opinions and not a "party line." Orthodoxy, of whatever colour, seems to demand a lifeless, imitative style. The political dialects to be found in pamphlets, leading articles, manifestos, White Papers and the speeches of under-secretaries do, of course, vary from party to party, but they are all alike in that one almost never finds in them a fresh, vivid, homemade turn of speech. When one watches some tired hack on the platform mechanically repeating the familiar phrases—*bestial atrocities, iron heel, bloodstained tyranny, free peoples of the world, stand shoulder to shoulder*—one often has a curious feeling that one is not watching a live human being but some kind of dummy: a feeling which suddenly becomes stronger at moments when the light catches the speaker's spectacles and turns them into blank discs which seem to have no eyes behind them. And this is not altogether fanciful. A speaker who uses that kind of phraseology has gone some distance towards turning himself into a machine. The appropriate noises are coming out of his larynx, but his brain is not involved as it would be if he were choosing his words for himself. If the speech he is making is one that he is accustomed to make over and over again, he may be almost unconscious of what he is saying, as one is when one utters the responses in church. And this reduced state of consciousness, if not indispensable, is at any rate favourable to political conformity.

In our time, political speech and writing are largely the defence of the indefensible. Things like the continuance of British rule in India, the Russian purges and deportations, the dropping of the atom bombs on Japan, can indeed be defended, but only by arguments which are too brutal for most people to face, and which do not square with the professed aims of political parties. Thus political language has to consist largely of euphemism, question-begging and sheer cloudy vagueness. Defenceless villages are bombarded from the air, the inhabitants driven out into the countryside, the cattle machine-gunned, the huts set on fire with incendiary bullets: this is called *pacification*. Millions of peasants are robbed of their farms and sent trudging along the roads with no more than they can carry: this is called *transfer of population* or *rectification of frontiers*. People are imprisoned for years without trial, or shot in the back of the neck or sent to die of scurvy in Arctic lumber camps: this is called *elimination of unreliable elements*. Such phraseology is needed if one wants to name things without calling up mental pictures of them. Consider for instance some comfortable English professor defending Russian totalitarianism. He cannot say outright, "I believe in killing off your opponents when you can get good results by doing so." Probably, therefore, he will say something like this:

"While freely conceding that the Soviet régime exhibits certain features which the humanitarian may be inclined to deplore, we must, I think, agree that a certain curtailment of the right to political opposition is an unavoidable concomitant of transitional periods, and that the rigors which the Russian people have been called upon to undergo have been amply justified in the sphere of concrete achievement."

The inflated style is itself a kind of euphemism. A mass of Latin words falls upon the facts like soft snow, blurring the outlines and covering up all the details. The great enemy of clear language is insincerity. When there is a gap between one's real and one's declared aims, one turns as it were instinctively to long words and exhausted idioms, like a cuttlefish squirting out ink. In our age there is no such thing as "keeping out of politics." All issues are political issues, and politics itself is a mass of lies, evasions, folly, hatred and schizophrenia. When the general atmosphere is bad, language must suffer. I should expect to find—this is a guess which I have not sufficient knowledge to verify—that the German, Russian and Italian languages have all deteriorated in the last ten or fifteen years, as a result of dictatorship.

But if thought corrupts language, language can also corrupt thought. A bad usage can spread by tradition and imitation, even among people who should and do know better. The debased language that I have been discussing is in some ways very convenient. Phrases like *a not unjustifiable assumption, leaves much to be desired, would serve no good purpose, a consideration which we should do well to bear in mind,* are a continuous temptation, a packet of aspirins always at one's elbow. Look back through this essay, and for certain you will find that I have again and again committed the very faults I am protesting against. By this morning's post I have received a pamphlet dealing with conditions in Germany. The author tells me that he "felt impelled" to write it. I open it at random, and here is almost the first sentence that I see: "(The Allies) have an opportunity not only of achieving a radical transformation of Germany's social and political structure in such a way as to avoid a nationalistic reaction in Germany itself, but at the same time of laying the foundations of a co-operative and unified Europe." You see, he "feels impelled" to write—feels, presumably, that he has something new to say—and yet his words, like cavalry horses answering the bugle, group themselves automatically into the familiar dreary pattern. This invasion of one's mind by ready-made phrases (*lay the foundations, achieve a radical transformation*) can only be prevented if one is constantly on guard against them, and every such phrase anaesthetizes a portion of one's brain.

I said earlier that the decadence of our language is probably curable. Those who deny this would argue, if they produced an argument at all, that language merely reflects existing social conditions, and that we cannot influence its development by any direct tinkering with words and constructions. So far as the general tone or spirit of a language goes, this may be true, but it is not true in detail. Silly words and expressions have often disappeared, not through any evolutionary process but owing to the conscious action of a minority. Two recent examples were *explore every avenue* and *leave no stone unturned,* which were killed by the jeers of a few journalists. There is a long list of fly-blown metaphors which could similarly be got rid of if enough people would interest themselves in the job; and it should also be possible to laugh the *not un-* formation out of existence,[3] to reduce the amount of Latin and Greek in the average sentence, to drive out foreign phrases

[3]One can cure oneself of the *not un-* formation by memorizing this sentence: *A not unblack dog was chasing a not unsmall rabbit across a not ungreen field* [Orwell's note].

and strayed scientific words, and, in general, to make pretentiousness unfashionable. But all these are minor points. The defence of the English language implies more than this, and perhaps it is best to start by saying what it does *not* imply.

To begin with it has nothing to do with archaism, with the salvaging of obsolete words and turns of speech, or with the setting up of a "standard English" which must never be departed from. On the contrary, it is especially concerned with the scrapping of every word or idiom which has outworn its usefulness. It has nothing to do with correct grammar and syntax, which are of no importance so long as one makes one's meaning clear, or with the avoidance of Americanisms, or with having what is called a "good prose style." On the other hand it is not concerned with fake simplicity and the attempt to make written English colloquial. Nor does it even imply in every case preferring the Saxon word to the Latin one, though it does imply using the fewest and shortest words that will cover one's meaning. What is above all needed is to let the meaning choose the word, and not the other way about. In prose, the worst thing one can do with words is to surrender to them. When you think of a concrete object, you think wordlessly, and then, if you want to describe the thing you have been visualizing you probably hunt about till you find the exact words that seem to fit. When you think of something abstract you are more inclined to use words from the start, and unless you make a conscious effort to prevent it, the existing dialect will come rushing in and do the job for you, at the expense of blurring or even changing your meaning. Probably it is better to put off using words as long as possible and get one's meaning as clear as one can through pictures or sensations. Afterwards one can choose—not simply *accept*—the phrases that will best cover the meaning, and then switch round and decide what impression one's words are likely to make on another person. This last effort of the mind cuts out all stale or mixed images, all prefabricated phrases, needless repetitions, and humbug and vagueness generally. But one can often be in doubt about the effect of a word or a phrase, and one needs rules that one can rely on when instinct fails. I think the following rules will cover most cases:

i. Never use a metaphor, simile or other figure of speech which you are used to seeing in print.
ii. Never use a long word where a short one will do.
iii. If it is possible to cut a word out, always cut it out.
iv. Never use the passive where you can use the active.

v. Never use a foreign phrase, a scientific word or a jargon word if you can think of an everyday English equivalent.

vi. Break any of these rules sooner than say anything outright barbarous.

These rules sound elementary, and so they are, but they demand a deep change of attitude in anyone who has grown used to writing in the style now fashionable. One could keep all of them and still write bad English, but one could not write the kind of stuff that I quoted in those five specimens at the beginning of this article.

I have not here been considering the literary use of language, but merely language as an instrument for expressing and not for concealing or preventing thought. Stuart Chase and others have come near to claiming that all abstract words are meaningless, and have used this as a pretext for advocating a kind of political quietism. Since you don't know what Fascism is, how can you struggle against Fascism? One need not swallow such absurdities as this, but one ought to recognize that the present political chaos is connected with the decay of language, and that one can probably bring about some improvement by starting at the verbal end. If you simplify your English, you are freed from the worst follies of orthodoxy. You cannot speak any of the necessary dialects, and when you make a stupid remark its stupidity will be obvious, even to yourself. Political language—and with variations this is true of all political parties, from Conservatives to Anarchists—is designed to make lies sound truthful and murder respectable, and to give an appearance of solidity to pure wind. One cannot change this all in a moment, but one can at least change one's own habits, and from time to time one can even, if one jeers loudly enough, send some worn-out and useless phrase—some *jackboot, Achilles' heel, hotbed, melting pot, acid test, veritable inferno* or other lump of verbal refuse—into the dustbin where it belongs.

POSSIBILITIES FOR WRITING

1. Why is Orwell so concerned over the state of the English language? Why does he think it has degenerated so? What differences does he see his suggested reforms making?

2. Despite the difficulties you may have understanding specific allusions, what advice from Orwell can you apply to your own writing? To your reading?

3. Examine several current examples of political or sociological writing—published political speeches, for example, or essays in a current sociological journal. Analyze the examples for the kinds of "tricks" Orwell lambastes.

Shooting an Elephant

George Orwell's "Shooting an Elephant," one of the most frequently anthologized and analyzed of all essays, has achieved the status of a classic. The essay describes Orwell's experience in Burma, when he served as a sub-divisional police officer for Burma's colonial master, England. Through an incident that involved his shooting of an elephant, Orwell conveys his ambivalence about the people he supervises and the country he serves.

At the climactic moment of the essay, Orwell describes in harrowing detail the agony of the elephant in its death throes. At this point Orwell has so slowed the pace of the essay as to create a cinematic effect of slow motion, which highlights the elephant's agony and intensifies the emotional effect upon the reader. Then with the narrative drive halted and the harrowing description over, Orwell speculates on the larger significance of this most unusual experience.

In Moulmein, in Lower Burma, I was hated by large numbers of people—the only time in my life that I have been important enough for this to happen to me. I was sub-divisional police officer of the town, and in an aimless, petty kind of way anti-European feeling was very bitter. No one had the guts to raise a riot, but if a European woman went through the bazaars alone somebody would probably spit betel juice over her dress. As a police officer I was an obvious target and was baited whenever it seemed safe to do so. When a nimble Burman tripped me up on the football field and the referee (another Burman) looked the other way, the crowd yelled with hideous laughter. This happened more than once. In the end the sneering yellow faces of young men that met me everywhere, the insults hooted after me when I was at a safe distance, got badly on my nerves. The young Buddhist priests were the worst of all. There were several thousands of them in the town and none of them seemed to have anything to do except stand on street corners and jeer at Europeans.

All this was perplexing and upsetting. For at that time I had already made up my mind that imperialism was an evil thing and the sooner I chucked up my job and got out of it the better. Theoretically—and secretly, of course—I was all for the Burmese and all against their oppressors, the British. As for the job I was doing, I hated it more bitterly than I can perhaps make clear. In a job like that you see the dirty work of Empire at close quarters. The wretched prisoners huddling in the stinking cages of the lock-ups, the grey, cowed faces of the long-term convicts, the scarred buttocks of the men who had been flogged with bamboos—all these oppressed me with an intolerable sense of guilt. But I could get nothing into perspective. I was young and ill-educated and I had had to think out my problems in the utter silence that is imposed on every Englishman in the East. I did not even know that the British Empire is dying, still less did I know that it is a great deal better than the younger empires that are going to supplant it. All I knew was that I was stuck between my hatred of the empire I served and my rage against the evil-spirited little beasts who tried to make my job impossible. With one part of my mind I thought of the British Raj as an unbreakable tyranny, as something clamped down, in *saecula saeculorum* upon the will of prostrate peoples; with another part I thought that the greatest joy in the world would be to drive a bayonet into a Buddhist priest's guts. Feelings like these are the normal by-products of imperialism; ask any Anglo-Indian official, if you can catch him off duty.

One day something happened which in a roundabout way was enlightening. It was a tiny incident in itself, but it gave me a better glimpse than I had had before of the real nature of imperialism—the real motives for which despotic governments act. Early one morning the sub-inspector at a police station the other end of the town rang me up on the 'phone and said that an elephant was ravaging the bazaar. Would I please come and do something about it? I did not know what I could do, but I wanted to see what was happening and I got on to a pony and started out. I took my rifle, an old .44 Winchester and much too small to kill an elephant, but I thought the noise might be useful *in terrorem*. Various Burmans stopped me on the way and told me about the elephant's doings. It was not, of course, a wild elephant, but a tame one which had gone "must." It had been chained up, as tame elephants always are when their attack of "must" is due, but on the previous night it had broken its chain and escaped. Its mahout, the only person who could manage it when it was in that state, had set out in pursuit, but had taken the wrong direction and was now twelve hours' journey away, and in the morning the elephant had suddenly reappeared in the town. The Burmese population had no weapons and were quite helpless against it. It had already destroyed somebody's bamboo hut, killed a cow and raided some fruit-stalls and devoured the stock; also it had met the municipal rubbish van and, when the driver jumped out and took to his heels, had turned the van over and inflicted violences upon it.

The Burmese sub-inspector and some Indian constables were waiting for me in the quarter where the elephant had been seen. It was a very poor quarter, a labyrinth of squalid bamboo huts, thatched with palm-leaf, winding all over a steep hillside. I remember that it was a cloudy, stuffy morning at the beginning of the rains. We began questioning the people as to where the elephant had gone and, as usual, failed to get any definite information. That is invariably the case in the East; a story always sounds clear enough at a distance, but the nearer you get to the scene of events the vaguer it becomes. Some of the people said that the elephant had gone in one direction, some said that he had gone in another, some professed not even to have heard of any elephant. I had almost made up my mind that the whole story was a pack of lies, when we heard yells a little distance away. There was a loud, scandalized cry of "Go away, child! Go away this instant!" and an old woman with a switch in her hand came round the corner of a hut, violently shooing away a crowd of naked children. Some more women followed, clicking their tongues and exclaiming; evidently there was something that the children ought not to have seen. I rounded the hut and saw a man's dead body sprawling in the mud. He was an Indian, a black Dravidian coolie, almost naked, and he could not have been dead many minutes. The people said that the elephant had come suddenly upon him round the corner of the hut, caught him with its trunk, put its foot on his back and ground him into the earth. This was the rainy season and the ground was soft, and his face had scored a trench a foot deep and a couple of yards long. He was lying on his belly with arms crucified and head sharply twisted to one side. His face was coated with mud, the eyes wide open, the teeth bared and grinning with an expression of unendurable agony. (Never tell me, by the way, that the dead look peaceful. Most of the corpses I have seen looked devilish.) The friction of the great beast's foot had stripped the skin from his back as neatly as one skins a rabbit. As soon as I saw the dead man I sent an orderly to a friend's house nearby to borrow an elephant rifle. I had already sent back the pony, not wanting it to go mad with fright and throw me if it smelt the elephant.

The orderly came back in a few minutes with a rifle and five cartridges, and meanwhile some Burmans had arrived and told us that the elephant was in the paddy fields below, only a few hundred yards away. As I started forward practically the whole population of the quarter flocked out of the houses and followed me. They had seen the rifle and were all shouting excitedly that I was going to shoot the elephant. They had not shown much interest in the elephant when he was merely ravaging their homes, but it was different now that he was going to be shot. It was a bit of fun to them, as it would be to an English crowd; besides they wanted the meat. It made me vaguely uneasy. I had no intention of shooting the elephant—I had merely sent for the rifle to defend myself if necessary—and it is always unnerving to have a crowd following you. I marched down the hill, looking and feeling a fool, with the rifle over my shoulder and an ever-growing army of people jostling at my heels. At the bottom, when you got away from the huts, there was a metalled road and beyond that a miry waste of paddy fields a thousand yards across, not yet ploughed but soggy from the first rains and dotted with coarse grass. The elephant was standing eight yards from the road, his left side towards us. He took not the slightest notice of the crowd's approach. He was tearing up bunches of grass, beating them against his knees to clean them and stuffing them into his mouth.

I had halted on the road. As soon as I saw the elephant I knew with perfect certainty that I ought not to shoot him. It is a serious matter to shoot a working elephant—it is comparable to destroying a huge and costly piece of machinery—and obviously one ought not to do it if it can possibly be avoided. And at that distance, peacefully eating, the elephant looked no more dangerous than a cow. I thought then and I think now that his attack of "must" was already passing off; in which case he would merely wander harmlessly about until the mahout came back and caught him. Moreover, I did not in the least want to shoot him. I decided that I would watch him for a little while to make sure that he did not turn savage again, and then go home.

But at that moment I glanced round at the crowd that had followed me. It was an immense crowd, two thousand at the least and growing every minute. It blocked the road for a long distance on either side. I looked at the sea of yellow faces above the garish clothes—faces all happy and excited over this bit of fun, all certain that the elephant was going to be shot. They were watching me as they would watch a conjurer about to perform a trick. They did not like me, but with the magical rifle in my hands I was momentarily worth watching. And suddenly I realized that I should have to shoot the elephant after all. The people expected it of me and I had got to do it; I could feel their two thousand wills pressing me forward, irresistibly. And it was at this moment, as I stood there with the rifle in my hands, that I first grasped the hollowness, the futility of the white man's dominion in the East. Here was I, the white man with his gun, standing in front of the unarmed native crowd—seemingly the leading actor of the piece; but in reality I was only an absurd puppet pushed to and fro by the will of those yellow faces behind. I perceived in this moment that when the white man turns tyrant it is his own freedom that he destroys. He becomes a sort of hollow, posing dummy, the conventionalized figure of a sahib. For it is the condition of his rule that he shall spend his life in trying to impress the "natives," and so in every crisis he has got to do what the "natives" expect of him. He wears a mask, and his face grows to fit it. I had got to shoot the elephant. I had committed myself to doing it when I sent for the rifle. A sahib has got to act like a sahib; he has got to appear resolute, to know his own mind and do definite things. To come all that way, rifle in hand, with two thousand people marching at my heels, and then to trail feebly away, having done nothing—no, that was impossible. The crowd would laugh at me. And my whole life, every white man's life in the East, was one long struggle not to be laughed at.

But I did not want to shoot the elephant. I watched him beating his bunch of grass against his knees, with that preoccupied grandmotherly air that elephants have. It seemed to me that it would be murder to shoot him. At that age I was not squeamish about killing animals, but I had never shot an elephant and never wanted to. (Somehow it always seems worse to kill a *large* animal.) Besides, there was the beast's owner to be considered. Alive, the elephant was worth at least a hundred pounds; dead, he would only be worth the value of his tusks, five pounds, possibly. But I had got to act quickly. I turned to some experienced-looking Burmans who had been there when we arrived, and asked them how the elephant had been behaving. They all said the same thing: he took no notice of you if you left him alone, but he might charge if you went too close to him.

It was perfectly clear to me what I ought to do. I ought to walk up to within, say, twenty-five yards of the elephant and test his behavior. If he charged, I could shoot; if he took no notice of me, it would be safe to leave him until the mahout came back. But also I knew that I was going to do no such thing. I was a poor shot with a rifle and the ground was soft mud into which one would sink at every step. If the elephant charged and I missed him, I should have about as much chance as a toad under a steam-roller. But even then I was not thinking particularly of my own skin, only of the watchful yellow faces behind. For at that moment, with the crowd watching me, I was not afraid in the ordinary sense, as I would have been if I had been alone. A white man mustn't be frightened in front of "natives"; and so, in general, he isn't frightened. The sole thought in my mind was that if anything went wrong those two thousand Burmans would see me pursued, caught, trampled on and reduced to a grinning corpse like that Indian up the hill. And if that happened it was quite probable that some of them would laugh. That would never do. There was only one alternative. I shoved the cartridges into the magazine and lay down on the road to get a better aim.

The crowd grew very still, and a deep, low, happy sigh, as of people who see the theatre curtain go up at last, breathed from innumerable throats. They were going to have their bit of fun after all. The rifle was a beautiful German thing with cross-hair sights. I did not then know that in shooting an elephant one would shoot to cut an imaginary bar running from ear-hole to ear-hole. I ought, therefore, as the elephant was sideways on, to have aimed straight at his ear-hole; actually I aimed several inches in front of this, thinking the brain would be further forward.

When I pulled the trigger I did not hear the bang or feel the kick—one never does when a shot goes home—but I heard the devilish roar of glee that went up from the crowd. In that instant, in too short a time, one would have thought, even for the bullet to get there, a mysterious, terrible change had come over the elephant. He neither stirred nor fell, but every line of his body had altered. He looked suddenly stricken, shrunken, immensely old, as though the frightful impact of the bullet had paralysed him without knocking him down. At last, after what seemed a long time—it might have been five seconds, I dare say—he sagged flabbily to his knees. His mouth slobbered. An enormous senility seemed to have settled upon him. One could have imagined him thousands of years old. I fired again into the same spot. At the second shot he did not collapse but climbed with desperate slowness to his feet and stood weakly upright, with legs sagging and head drooping. I fired a third time. That was the shot that did for him. You could see the agony of it jolt his whole body and knock the last remnant of strength from his legs. But in falling he seemed for a moment to rise, for as his hind legs collapsed beneath him he seemed to tower upward like a huge rock toppling, his trunk reaching skywards like a tree. He trumpeted, for the first and only time. And then down he came, his belly towards me, with a crash that seemed to shake the ground even where I lay.

I got up. The Burmans were already racing past me across the mud. It was obvious that the elephant would never rise again, but he was not dead. He was breathing very rhythmically with long rattling gasps, his great mound of a side painfully rising and falling. His mouth was wide open—I could see far down into caverns of pale pink throat. I waited a long time for him to die, but his breathing did not weaken. Finally I fired my two remaining shots into the spot where I thought his heart must be. The thick blood welled out of him like red velvet, but still he did not die. His body did not even jerk when the shots hit him, the tortured breathing continued without a pause. He was dying, very slowly and in great agony, but in some world remote from me where not even a bullet could damage him further. I felt that I had got to put an end to that dreadful noise. It seemed dreadful to see the great beast lying there, powerless to move and yet powerless to die, and not even to be able to finish him. I sent back for my small rifle and poured shot after shot into his heart and down his throat. They seemed to make no impression. The tortured gasps continued as steadily as the ticking of a clock.

In the end I could not stand it any longer and went away. I heard later that it took him half an hour to die. Burmans were bringing dahs and baskets even before I left, and I was told they had stripped his body almost to the bones by the afternoon.

Afterwards, of course, there were endless discussions about the shooting of the elephant. The owner was furious, but he was only an Indian and could do nothing. Besides, legally I had done the right thing, for a mad elephant has to be killed, like a mad dog, if its owner fails to control it. Among the Europeans opinion was divided. The older men said I was right, the younger men said it was a damn shame to shoot an elephant for killing a coolie, because an elephant was worth more than any damn Coringhee coolie. And afterwards I was very glad that the coolie had been killed; it put me legally in the right and it gave me a sufficient pretext for shooting the elephant. I often wondered whether any of the others grasped that I had done it solely to avoid looking a fool.

POSSIBILITIES FOR WRITING

1. Orwell makes the point in his second paragraph that he had come to believe that "imperialism was an evil thing," and he goes on to explain why he believes this both explicitly, through his own thoughts, and implicitly, through the circumstances of the story he tells. In an essay, examine Orwell's views of the evils of imperialism, both for the natives and for the colonizers.

2. Analyze Orwell's essay to consider the sense of ambivalence he felt in his position as part of the imperial police force. What does this ambivalence contribute to the tone of the essay and to Orwell's central point?
3. Orwell describes acting against his better judgment "solely to avoid looking like a fool." Have you ever done anything you believed to be wrong in order to save face, to avoid looking like a fool? Describe such an experience and what it led you to understand about yourself and about the pressure to save face.

Cynthia Ozick (b. 1928) was born in New York City and grew up in Brooklyn. She received degrees from New York University and Ohio State University and began her career as an advertising copywriter. Her first novel, Trust *(1966), brought immediate critical attention, and her other works of fiction include* Bloodshed and Three Novellas *(1976),* The Messiah of Stockholm *(1987), and* The Puttermesser Papers *(1997). However, Ozick is probably best known for her many critical and autobiographical essays collected in* Art and Ardor *(1983).* Metaphor and Memory *(1989),* Quarrels and Quandaries *(2000), and* The Din in the Head *(2006) among others. Her most recent book is* Dictation, *a collection of four fictional pieces, She is noted for her brilliant style, her incisive powers of observation, and her intensely ethical concerns.*

CYNTHIA OZICK

The Seam of the Snail

Cynthia Ozick's essay, "The Seam of the Snail" has also appeared under an alternate title, "Excellence." The present title has the virtue of highlighting an image Ozick uses at the end: an image that suggests her own way of writing and being. The image also suggests another kind of "seam," the seam of sewn objects, which Ozick says that her mother made imperfectly and hid them where they wouldn't be seen. The more general alternative title has the virtue of providing an umbrella concept that encompasses the two contrasting styles of excellence exemplified by Ozick and her mother.

Ozick, in fact, uses contrast throughout the essay, setting off her mother's way of doing things against the way she does them. In the process of working out this contrast, Ozick presents a portrait of her mother that acknowledges her mother's exuberant skill and her numerous accomplishments without ignoring her imperfections. Through her use of images of growth and flowering, Ozick describes her mother's "lavish" excellence as a "comedy of prodigality."

Ozick describes herself with another set of images, those that suggest confinement and restraint. She calls herself a self-styled "pinched perfectionist" who attends to "crabbed minutiae." And she compares herself to a snail, which not only moves very slowly, but also depletes its body a little at a time, oozing an inky stain. This Ozick sees as an analogue to her "exacting perfectionism" as a writer who ekes out sentences painstakingly and scrupulously in contrast to her mother's unconscious easy, prodigality.

In my Depression childhood, whenever I had a new dress, my cousin Sarah would get suspicious. The nicer the dress was, and especially the more expensive it looked, the more suspicious she would get. Finally she would lift the hem and check the seams. This was to see if the dress had been bought or if my mother had sewed it. Sarah could always tell. My mother's sewing had elegant outsides, but there was something catch-as-catch-can about the insides. Sarah's sewing, by contrast, was as impeccably finished inside as out; not one stray thread dangled.

My uncle Jake built meticulous grandfather clocks out of rosewood; he was a perfectionist, and sent to England for the clockworks. My mother built serviceable radiator covers and a serviceable cabinet, with hinged doors, for the pantry. She built a pair of bookcases for the living room. Once, after I was grown and in a house of my own, she fixed the sewer pipe. She painted ceilings, and also landscapes; she reupholstered chairs. One summer she planted a whole yard of tall corn. She thought herself capable of doing anything, and did everything she imagined. But nothing was perfect. There was always some clear flaw, never visible head-on. You had to look underneath where the seams were. The corn thrived, though not in rows. The stalks elbowed one another like gossips in a dense little village.

"Miss Brrrrooobaker," my mother used to mock, rolling her Russian *r*s, whenever I crossed a *l* she had left uncrossed, or corrected a word she had misspelled, or became impatient with a *v* that had tangled itself up with a *w* in her speech. ("*Vv*ventriloquist," I would say. "*Vv*ventriloquist," she would obediently repeat. And the next time it would come out "wiolinist.") Miss Brubaker was my high school English teacher, and my mother invoked her name as an emblem of raging finical obsession. "Miss Brrrrooobaker," my mother's voice hoots at me down the years, as I go on casting and recasting sentences in a tiny handwriting on monomoniacally uniform paper. The loops of my mother's handwriting—it was the Palmer Method—were as big as hoops, spilling generous splashy ebullience. She could pull off, at five minutes' notice, a satisfying dinner for 10 concocted out of nothing more than originality and panache. But the napkin would be folded a little off-center, and the spoon might be on the wrong side of the knife. She was an optimist who ignored trifles; for her, God was not in the details but in the intent. And all these culinary and agricultural efflorescences were extracurricular, accomplished in the crevices and niches of a 14-hour business day. When she scribbled out her family memoirs, in heaps of dog-eared note-books, or on the backs of old bills, or on the margins of last year's calendar, I would resist typing them: in the speed of the chase she often omitted words like "the," "and," "will." The same flashing and bountiful hand fashioned and fired ceramic pots, and painted brilliant autumn views and vases of imaginary flowers and ferns, and decorated ordinary Woolworth platters with lavish enameled gardens. But bits of the painted petals would chip away.

Lavish: my mother was as lavish as nature. She woke early and saturated the hours with work and inventiveness, and read late into the night. She was all profusion, abundance, fabrication. Angry at her children, she would run after us whirling the cord of the electric iron, like a lasso or a whip; but she never caught us. When, in the seventh grade, I was afraid of failing the Music Appreciation final exam because I could not tell the difference between "To a Wild Rose" and "Barcarolle," she got the idea of sending me to school with a gauze sling rigged up on my writing arm, and an explanatory note that was purest fiction. But the sling kept slipping off. My mother gave advice like mad—she boiled over with so much passion for the predicaments of strangers that they turned into permanent cronies. She told intimate stories about people I had never heard of.

Despite the gargantuan Palmer loops (or possibly because of them), I have always known that my mother's was a life of—intricately abashing word!—excellence: insofar as excellence means ripe generosity. She burgeoned, she proliferated; she was endlessly leafy and flowering. She wore red hats, and called herself a gypsy. In her girlhood she marched with the suffragettes and for Margaret Sanger and called herself a Red. She made me laugh, she was so varied: like a tree on which lemons, pomegranates, and prickly pears absurdly all hang together. She had the comedy of prodigality.

My own way is a thousand times more confined. I am a pinched perfectionist, the ultimate fruition of Miss Brubaker; I attend to crabbed minutiae and am self-trammeled through taking pains. I am a kind of human snail, locked in and condemned by my own nature. The ancients believed that the moist track left by the snail as it crept was the snail's own essence, depleting its body little by little; the farther the snail toiled, the smaller it became, until it finally rubbed itself out. That is how perfectionists are. Say to us Excellence, and we will show you how we use up our substance and wear ourselves away, while making scarcely any progress at all. The fact that I am an exacting perfectionist in a narrow strait only, and nowhere else, is hardly to the point, since nothing matters to me so much as a comely and muscular sentence. It is my narrow strait, this snail's road: the track of the sentence I am writing now: and when I have eked out the wet substance, ink or blood, that is its mark. I will begin the next sentence. Only in reading out sentences am I perfectionist; but then there is nothing else I know how to do, or take much interest in. I miter every pair of abutting sentences as scrupulously as Uncle Jake fitted one strip or rosewood against another. My mother's worldly and bountiful hand has escaped me. The sentence I am writing is my cabin and my shell, compact, self-sufficient. It is the burnished horizon—a merciless planet where flawlessness is the single standard, where even the inmost seams, however hidden from a laxer eye, must meet perfection. Here "excellence" is not strewn casually from a tipped cornucopia, here disorder does not account for charm, here trifles rule like tyrants.

I measure my life in sentences, and my sentences are superior to my mother's, pressed out, line by line, like the lustrous ooze on the underside of the snail, the snail's secret open seam, its wound, leaking attar. My mother was too mettlesome to feel the force of a comma. She scorned minutiae. She measured her life according to what poured from the horn of plenty, which was her ample, cascading, elastic, susceptible, inexact heart. My narrower heart rides between the tiny horns of the snail, dwindling as it goes.

And out of this thinnest thread, this ink-wet line of words, must rise a visionary fog, a mist, a smoke, forging cities, histories, sorrows, quagmires, entanglements, lives of sinners, even the life of my furnace-hearted mother; so much wilderness, waywardness, plentitude on the head of the precise and impeccable snail, between the horns.

POSSIBILITIES FOR WRITING

1. Consider Ozick's diction here, the words and images she uses in describing her mother and herself. How does she use specific language to develop the sense of contrast between the two?
2. In this essay Ozick describes two different kinds of excellence—one of "ripe generosity" and one of narrow perfectionism. Can you find examples of these two kinds of excellence in your own experience? Write an essay in which you explore the contrasts between these two kinds of excellence in broader detail.
3. Write an essay describing a larger than life character in your own life. You may, if you wish, also contrast this person with yourself or with someone else your subject is close to.

Plato (c.427–347 BCE) is today the most widely read of the ancient Greek philosophers. A student of the martyred philosopher Socrates, he cast much of his philosophical writing as dialogues between Socrates and other real or imagined speakers. The point in his earlier dialogues is often not so much to resolve a question as to suggest the limits of what can be known. In his later work, Plato went further toward trying to define a universal vision of the cosmos and of a hierarchy of ideas. His most famous work, The Republic, *is an attempt to define the ideal state based on the idea of the Good, which, in his view, existed (as do all ideas, ultimately) as an independent reality. It is to this highest good, Plato noted throughout his work, that the philosopher and indeed all human beings, should aspire.*

PLATO

The Allegory of the Cave

In "The Allegory of the Cave" from the *Republic,* Plato famously describes the state of knowledge (or ignorance) in which human beings find themselves. Plato puts the explanation of humanity's lack of true knowledge in the mouth of Socrates, who employs a grand analogy to convey Plato's central idea about human ignorance. Socrates' interlocutor is Glaucon, who responds by acknowledging that he understands the philosopher's explanation, and by asking questions, to which Socrates responds as a teacher instructing a pupil.

"The Allegory of the Cave" illustrates Plato's distinction between true knowledge of reality and the illusion of appearances. Plato's use of the imagery of light to represent knowledge and darkness to symbolize ignorance has become a common way to represent truth. His use of the dialogue form humanizes his abstract concepts, bringing abstract philosophical speculation down to earth. Taken together, the dialogue form, the imagery of light and darkness, and the use of an allegorical story with a symbolic meaning make Plato's essay on knowledge and ignorance both accessible and memorable.

And now, I said, let me show in a figure how far our nature is enlightened or unenlightened: Behold! human beings living in an underground den, which has a mouth open toward the light and reaching all along the den; here they have been from their childhood, and have their legs and necks chained so that they cannot move, and can only see before them, being prevented by the chains from turning round their heads. Above and behind them a fire is blazing at a distance, and between the fire and the prisoners there is a raised way; and you will see, if you look, a low wall built along the way, like the screen which marionette players have in front of them, over which they show the puppets.

I see.

And do you see, I said, men passing along the wall carrying all sorts of vessels, and statues and figures of animals made of wood and stone and various materials, which appear over the wall? Some of them are talking, others silent.

You have shown me a strange image, and they are strange prisoners.

Like ourselves, I replied; and they see only their own shadows, or the shadows of one another, which the fire throws on the opposite wall of the cave?

True, he said; how could they see anything but the shadows if they were never allowed to move their heads?

And of the objects which are being carried in like manner they would only see the shadows?

Yes, he said.

And if they were able to converse with one another, would they not suppose that they were naming what was actually before them?

Very true.

And suppose further that the prison had an echo which came from the other side, would they not be sure to fancy when one of the passersby spoke that the voice which they heard came from the passing shadow?

No question, he replied.

To them, I said, the truth would be literally nothing but the shadows of the images.

That is certain.

And now look again, and see what will naturally follow if the prisoners are released and disabused of their error. At first, when any of them is liberated and compelled suddenly to stand up and turn his neck round and walk and look toward the light, he will suffer sharp pains; the glare will distress him and he will be unable to see the realities of which in his former state he had seen the shadows; and then conceive some one saying to him, that what he saw before was an illusion, but that now, when he is approaching nearer to being and his eye is turned toward more real existence, he has a clearer vision—what will be his reply? And you may further imagine that his instructor is pointing to the objects as they pass and requiring him to name them—will he not be perplexed? Will he not fancy that the shadows which he formerly saw are truer than the objects which are now shown to him?

Far truer.

And if he is compelled to look straight at the light, will he not have a pain in his eyes which will make him turn away to take refuge in the objects of vision which he can see, and which he will conceive to be in reality clearer than the things which are now being shown to him?

True, he said.

And suppose once more, that he is reluctantly dragged up a steep and rugged ascent, and held fast until he is forced into the presence of the sun himself, is he not likely to be pained and irritated? When he approaches the light his eyes will be dazzled and he will not be able to see anything at all of what are now called realities.

Not all in a moment, he said.

He will require to grow accustomed to the sight of the upper world. And first he will see the shadows best, next the reflections of men and other objects in the water, and then the objects themselves; then he will gaze upon the light of the moon and the stars and the spangled heaven; and he will see the sky and the stars by night better than the sun or the light of the sun by day?

Certainly.

Last of all he will be able to see the sun, and not mere reflections of him in the water, but he will see him in his own proper place, and not in another; and he will contemplate him as he is.

Certainly.

He will then proceed to argue that this is he who gives the season and the years, and is the guardian of all that is in the visible world, and in a certain way the cause of all things which he and his fellows have been accustomed to behold?

Clearly, he said, he would first see the sun and then reason about him. And when he remembered his old habitation, and the wisdom of the den and his fellow-prisoners, do you not suppose that he would felicitate himself on the change, and pity them?

Certainly, he would.

And if they were in the habit of conferring honors among themselves on those who were quickest to observe the passing shadows and to remark which of them went before, and which followed after, and which were together; and who were therefore best able to draw conclusions as to the future, do you think that he would care for such honors and glories, or envy the possessors of them? Would he not say with Homer,

> Better to be the poor servant of a poor master,

and to endure anything, rather than think as they do and live after their manner?

Yes, he said, I think that he would rather suffer anything than entertain these false notions and live in this miserable manner.

Imagine once more, I said, such as one coming suddenly out of the sun to be replaced in his old situation; would he not be certain to have his eyes full of darkness?

To be sure, he said.

And if there were a contest, and he had to compete in measuring the shadows with the prisoners who had never moved out of the den, while his sight was still weak, and before his eyes had become steady (and the time which would be needed to acquire this new habit of sight might be very considerable) would he not be ridiculous? Men would say of him that up he went and down he came without his eyes; and that it was better not even to think of ascending; and if any one tried to loose another and lead him up to the light, let them only catch the offender, and they would put him to death.

No question, he said.

This entire allegory, I said, you may now append, dear Glaucon, to the previous argument; the prison-house is the world of sight, the light of the fire is the sun, and you will not misapprehend me if you interpret the journey upwards to be the ascent of the soul into the intellectual world according to my poor belief, which, at your desire, I have expressed—whether rightly or wrongly God knows. But, whether true or false, my opinion is that in the world of knowledge the idea of good appears last of all, and is seen only with an effort; and, when seen, is also inferred to be the universal author of all things beautiful and right, parent of light and of the lord of light in this visible world, and the immediate source of reason and truth in the intellectual; and that this is the power upon which he who would act rationally either in public or private life must have his eye fixed.

I agree, he said, as far as I am able to understand you.

Moreover, I said, you must not wonder that those who attain to this beatific vision are unwilling to descend to human affairs; for their souls are ever hastening into the upper world where they desire to dwell; which desire of theirs is very natural, if our allegory may be trusted.

Yes, very natural.

And is there anything surprising in one who passes from divine contemplations to the evil state of man, misbehaving himself in a ridiculous manner; if, while his eyes are blinking and before he has become accustomed to the surrounding darkness, he is compelled to fight in courts of law, or in other places, about the images or the shadows of images of justice, and is endeavoring to meet the conceptions of those who have never yet seen absolute justice?

Anything but surprising, he replied.

Any one who has common sense will remember that the bewilderments of the eyes are of two kinds, and arise from two causes, either from coming out of the light or from going into the light, which is true of the mind's eye, quite as much as of the bodily eye; and he who remembers this when he sees any one whose vision is perplexed and weak, will not be too ready to laugh; he will first ask whether that soul of man has come out of the brighter life, and is unable to see because unaccustomed to the dark, or having turned from darkness to the day is dazzled by excess of light. And he will count the one happy in his condition and state of being, and he will pity the other; or, if he have a mind to laugh at the soul which comes from below into the light, there will be more reason in this than in the laugh which greets him who returns from above out of the light into the den.

That, he said, is a very just distinction.

POSSIBILITIES FOR WRITING

1. Analyze Plato's allegory carefully, then interpret it in your own words. What do the various elements of the allegory represent?
2. Near the end Plato refers to "shadows of images of justice" and "absolute justice." What does he mean? How do you respond to such images of "absolutes"?
3. Write an allegory of your own about perception and reality or another philosophical or psychological distinction that intrigues you.

Katherine Anne Porter (1890–1980) *was born in Indian Creek, Texas, and raised by her grandmother after her mother died. She married and divorced while she was in her teens, then left Texas to work as a journalist in Chicago and other cities before settling in New York. She didn't publish her first collection of stories until she was forty, but* Flowering Judas (1930) *was an immediate critical success. This was followed by* Pale Horse, Pale Rider (1939) *and* The Leaning Tower (1944) *and finally by* Ship of Fools (1962), *her only full-length novel. Her output was relatively small, but marked by meticulous craftsmanship, and her* Collected Stories (1965) *won the Pulitzer Prize and the National Book Award. The* Days Before, *a collection of essays, appeared in 1952, and* Collected Essays and Occasional Writings *in 1971.*

KATHERINE ANNE PORTER

The Necessary Enemy

In "The Necessary Enemy," Katherine Anne Porter provides an incisive analysis of romantic love. Porter presents a case study in a penetrating psychological analysis of the relationship between love and hatred in the heart of a prototypical young married woman. Porter enriches and complicates the psychological portrait by drawing on the young woman's childhood feelings of love and hate, and by including brief comments on the love-hate expressed by the woman's parents toward her and toward each other.

Porter, however, is not entirely opposed to the idea of romantic love. She argues that it should be retained, but that it must be tempered by a strong dose of reality. And for this, Porter suggests that hatred is inevitable as a "necessary enemy and ally" of love. It's a tough-minded notion that concludes a brutally honest essay.

She is a frank, charming, fresh-hearted young woman who married for love. She and her husband are one of those gay, good-looking young pairs who ornament this modern scene rather more in profusion perhaps than ever before in our history. They are handsome, with a talent for finding their way in their world, they work at things that interest them, their tastes agree and their hopes. They intend in all good faith to spend their lives together, to have children and do well by them and each other—to be happy, in fact, which for them is the whole point of their marriage. And all in stride, keeping their wits about them. Nothing romantic, mind you; their feet are on the ground.

Unless they were this sort of person, there would be not much point to what I wish to say; for they would seem to be an example of the high-spirited, right-minded young whom the critics are always invoking to come forth and do their duty and practice all those sterling old-fashioned virtues which in every generation seem to be falling into disrepair. As for virtues, these young people are more or less on their own, like most of their kind; they get very little moral or other aid from their society; but after three years of marriage this very contemporary young woman finds herself facing the oldest and ugliest dilemma of marriage.

She is dismayed, horrified, full of guilt and forebodings because she is finding out little by little that she is capable of hating her husband, whom she loves faithfully. She can hate him at times as fiercely and mysteriously, indeed in terribly much the same way, as often she hated her parents, her brothers and sisters, whom she loves, when she was a child. Even then it had seemed to her a kind of black treacherousness in her, her private wickedness that, just the same, gave her her only private life. That was one thing her parents never knew about her, never seemed to suspect. For it was never given a name. They did and said hateful things to her and to each other as if by right, as if in them it was a kind of virtue. But when they said to her, "Control your feelings," it was never when she was amiable and obedient, only in the black times of her hate. So it was her secret, a shameful one. When they punished her, sometimes for the strangest reasons, it was, they said, only because they loved her—it was for her good. She did not believe this, but she thought herself guilty of something worse than ever they had punished her for. None of this really frightened her: the real fright came when she discovered that at times her father and mother hated each other; this was like standing on the doorsill of a familiar room and seeing in a lightning flash that the floor was gone, you were on the edge of a bottomless pit. Sometimes she felt that both of them hated her, but that passed, it was simply not a thing to be thought of, much less believed. She thought she had outgrown all this, but here it was again, an element in her own nature she could not control, or feared she could not. She would have to hide from her husband, if she could, the same spot in her feelings she had hidden from her parents, and for the same no doubt disreputable, selfish reason: she wants to keep his love.

Above all, she wants him to be absolutely confident that she loves him, for that is the real truth, no matter how unreasonable it sounds, and no matter how her own feelings betray them both at times. She depends recklessly on his love; yet while she is hating him, he might very well be hating her as much or even more, and it would serve her right. But she does not want to be served right, she wants to be loved and forgiven—that is, to be sure he would forgive her anything, if he had any notion of what she had done. But best of all she would like not to have anything in her love that should ask forgiveness. She doesn't mean about their quarrels—they are not so bad. Her feelings are out of proportion, perhaps. She knows it is perfectly natural for people to disagree, have fits of temper, fight it out; they learn quite a lot about each other that way, and not all of it disappointing either. When it passes, her hatred seems quite unreal. It always did.

Love. We are early taught to say it. I love you. We are trained to the thought of it as if there were nothing else, or nothing else worth having without it, or nothing worth having which it could not bring with it. Love is taught, always by precept, sometimes by example. Then hate, which no one meant to teach us, comes of itself. It is true that if we say I love you, it may be received with doubt, for there are times when it is hard to believe. Say I hate you, and the one spoken to believes it instantly, once for all.

Say I love you a thousand times to that person afterward and mean it every time, and still it does not change the fact that once we said I hate you, and meant that too. It leaves a mark on that surface love had worn so smooth with its eternal caresses. Love must be learned, and learned again and again; there is no end to it. Hate needs no instruction, but waits only to be provoked . . . hate, the unspoken word, the unacknowledged presence in the house, that faint smell of brimstone among the roses, that invisible tongue-tripper, that unkempt finger in every pie, that sudden oh-so-curiously *chilling* look—could it be boredom?—on your dear one's features, making them quite ugly. Be careful: love, perfect love, is in danger.

If it is not perfect, it is not love, and if it is not love, it is bound to be hate sooner or later. This is perhaps a not too exaggerated statement of the extreme position of Romantic Love, more especially in America, where we are all brought up on it, whether we know it or not. Romantic Love is changeless, faithful, passionate, and its sole end is to render the two lovers happy. It has no obstacles save those provided by the hazards of fate (that is to say, society), and such sufferings as the lovers may cause each other are only another word for delight: exciting jealousies, thrilling uncertainties, the ritual dance of courtship within the charmed closed circle of their secret alliance; all *real* troubles come from without, they face them unitedly in perfect confidence. Marriage is not the end but only the beginning of true happiness, cloudless, changeless to the end. That the candidates for this blissful condition have never seen an example of it, nor ever knew anyone who had, makes no difference. That is the ideal and they will achieve it.

How did Romantic Love manage to get into marriage at last, where it was most certainly never intended to be? At its highest it was tragic: the love of Héloïse and Abélard. At its most graceful, it was the homage of the trouv ère for his lady. In its most popular form, the adulterous strayings of solidly married couples who meant to stray for their own good reasons, but at the same time do nothing to upset the property settlements or the line of legitimacy; at its most trivial, the pretty trifling of shepherd and shepherdess.

This was generally condemned by church and state and a word of fear to honest wives whose mortal enemy it was. Love within the sober, sacred realities of marriage was a matter of personal luck, but in any case, private feelings were strictly a private affair having, at least in theory, no bearing whatever on the fixed practice of the rules of an institution never intended as a recreation ground for either sex. If the couple discharged their religious and social obligations, furnished forth a copious progeny, kept their troubles to themselves, maintained public civility and died under the same roof, even if not always on speaking terms, it was rightly regarded as a successful marriage. Apparently this testing ground was too severe for all but the stoutest spirits; it too was based on an ideal, as impossible in its way as the ideal Romantic Love. One good thing to be said for it is that society took responsibility for the conditions of marriage, and the sufferers within its bonds could always blame the system, not themselves. But Romantic Love crept into the marriage bed, very stealthily, by centuries, bringing its absurd notions about love as eternal springtime and marriage as a personal adventure meant to provide personal happiness. To a Western romantic such as I, though my views have been much modified by painful experience, it still seems to me a charming work of the human imagination, and it is a pity its central notion has been taken too literally and has hardened into a convention as cramping and enslaving as the older one. The refusal to acknowledge the evils in ourselves which therefore are implicit in any human situation is as extreme and unworkable a proposition as the doctrine of total depravity; but somewhere between them, or maybe beyond them, there does exist a possibility for reconciliation between our desires for impossible satisfactions and the simple unalterable fact that we also desire to be unhappy and that we create our own sufferings; and out of these sufferings we salvage our fragments of happiness.

Our young woman who has been taught that an important part of her human nature is not real because it makes trouble and interferes with her peace of mind and shakes her self-love, has been very badly taught; but she has arrived at a most important stage of her re-education. She is afraid her marriage is going to fail because she has not love enough to face its difficulties; and this because at times she feels a painful hostility toward her husband, and cannot admit its reality because such an admission would damage in her own eyes her view of what love should be, an absurd view, based on her vanity of power. Her hatred is real as her love is real, but her hatred has the advantage at present because it works on a blind instinctual level, it is lawless; and her love is subjected to a code of ideal conditions, impossible by their very nature of fulfillment, which prevents its free growth and deprives it of its right to recognize its human limitations and come to grips with them. Hatred is natural in a sense that love, as she conceives it, a young person brought up in the tradition of Romantic Love, is not natural at all. Yet it did not come by hazard, it is the very imperfect expression of the need of the human imagination to create beauty and harmony out of chaos, no matter how mistaken its notion of these things may be, nor how clumsy its methods. It has conjured love out of the air, and seeks to preserve it by incantations; when she spoke a vow to love and honor her husband until death, she did a very reckless thing, for it is not possible by an act of the will to fulfill such an engagement. But it was the necessary act of faith performed in defense of a mode of feeling, the statement of honorable intention to practice as well as she is able the noble, acquired faculty of love, that very mysterious overtone to sex which is the best thing in it. Her hatred is part of it, the necessary enemy and ally.

POSSIBILITIES FOR WRITING

1. Explain what Porter means by love, "Romantic Love," and hate. Why does she believe that hate is a "necessary evil"?

2. Near the end Porter writes, "The refusal to acknowledge the evils in ourselves which therefore are implicit in any human situation is as extreme and unworkable a proposition as the doctrine of total depravity; but somewhere between them, or maybe beyond them, there does exist a possibility for reconciliation between our desires for impossible satisfactions and the simple unalterable fact that we also desire to be unhappy and that we create our own sufferings; and out of the sufferings we salvage our fragments of happiness." How do you interpret this passage? How do you respond to it?

3. This essay was written at a time when divorce was becoming more common but not nearly so prevalent as it is today, when many experts are decrying its effects. What are your thoughts on marriage and divorce? Have your thoughts been influenced by Porter in any way? Why or why not?

Anna Quindlen (b. 1952) wrote a column for the New York Times *op-ed page during the early 1990s. She resigned her position in 1994 to devote more time to writing fiction. Since then she has published three novels,* One True Thing *(1994),* Black and Blue *(1998), and* Blessings *(2002). Her most recent book is* Good Dog. Stay *(2007), a work of nonfiction. In her work as both a columnist and a writer of fiction and nonfiction books, Quindlen's focus remains on social issues, especially the role and experience of women, and on family life. Her writing is down to earth and close to home. "Between the Sexes, A Great Divide" reveals Quindlen's wit and warmth as a writer and as a person.*

ANNA QUINDLEN

Between the Sexes, A Great Divide

In "Between the Sexes, A Great Divide," Anna Quindlen describes the gulf that separates boys and girls, men and women. She begins with the image of the empty space in the middle of a junior high school dance floor, girls huddled together on one side of the room, boys clustered on the other. Quindlen returns to this image later in the essay, using it to suggest the ways men and women live in separate and differentiated mental and emotional spaces.

Although Quindlen plays up the ways that men and women, girls and boys are divided from one another, she finds a way to reconcile their gender differences. Quindlen suggests that the two sexes do indeed eventually come together as partners, first on their school dance floor and later as married couples. And it is the dances both literal and figurative, she observes, not the differences, that matter.

Perhaps we all have the same memory of the first boy-girl party we attended. The floors were waxed, the music loud, the air thick with the smell of cologne. The boys stood on one side of the room and the girls on the other, each affecting a nonchalance belied by the shuffling male loafers and the occasional high birdlike sound of a female giggle.

Eventually, one of the taller, better-looking boys, perhaps dogged by two slightly shorter, squeakier acolytes, would make the big move across the chasm to ask the cutest girl to dance. Eventually, one of the girls would brave the divide to start a conversation on the other side. We would immediately develop a certain opinion of that girl, so that for the rest of our school years together, pajama parties would fairly crackle when she was not there.

None of us would consciously know it then, but what we were see-ing, that great empty space in the center of the floor as fearful as a trapdoor, was the great division between the sexes. It was wonderful to think of the time when it would no longer be there, when the school gym would be a great meeting ground in which we would mingle freely, girl and boy, boy and girl, person to person, all alike. And maybe that's going to happen sometime in my lifetime, but I can't say I know when.

I've thought about this for some time, because I've written some loving things about men, and some nasty things too, and I meant them all. And I've always been a feminist, and I've been one of the boys as well, and I've given both sides a pretty good shot. I've spent a lot of time telling myself that men and women are fundamentally alike, mainly in the service of arguing that women should not only be permitted but be welcomed into a variety of positions and roles that only men occupied.

And then something happens, a little thing usually, and all I can see is that great shiny space in the middle of the dance floor where no one ever meets. "I swear to God we are a different species," one of my friends said on the telephone recently. I can't remember whether the occasion was a fight with her husband, a scene at work or a con-tretemps with a mutual male friend of ours. No matter. She's said it before and she'll say it again, just like all my other friends have said it to me, and I to them. Men are the other.

We are the other, too, of course. That's why we want to believe so badly that there are no others at all, because over the course of human history being other has meant being symbols of divinity, evil, carnal degeneration, perfect love, fertility and death, to name a few. And any-body who has ever been a symbol knows that it's about as relaxing as sitting on a piece of Louis XV furniture. It is also true that over the course of history, we have been subordinate to others, symbols of weakness, dependency and emotions run amok.

Yet isn't it odd that I feel that the prejudice is somehow easier to deal with than the simple difference? Prejudice is evil and can be fought, while difference simply is. I live with three males, one husband and two sons, and occasionally I realize with great clarity that they are gazing across a divide at me, not because of big differences among us, but because of small ones.

The amaryllis bulb haunts me. "Why did you put an onion in a pot in the bathroom?" my elder son asked several months ago. I explained that it was not an onion but an amaryllis bulb and that soon it would grow into fabulous flowers. "What is that thing in the bathroom?" his father said later the same day. Impatiently I explained again. A look flashed between them, and then the littlest boy, too. Mom. Weird. Women.

Once I would have felt anger flame inside me at that. But I've done the same so many times now. On the telephone a friend and I will be commiserating about the failure of our husbands to listen when we talk, or their inexorable linear thinking, or their total blindness to the use and necessity of things like amaryllis bulbs. One of us will sigh, and the other will know what the sigh means. Husband. Strange. Men. Is it any wonder that our relationships are so often riddled with misunderstandings and disappointments?

In the children you can see the beginnings, even though we raise them in households in which mothers do things fathers once did, and vice versa. Children try to nail down the world, and themselves, early on and in a very primitive and real way. I remember a stage with my elder son in which, going through the supermarket or walking down the street, he would pin me down on each person walking by, and on such disparate cultural influences as Vanna White and Captain Kangaroo, by demanding that I tell him which genitalia category they fell in. Very soon, he got the idea: us and them, him and her. It was all very well to say that all people are the same inside (even if I had believed it) but he thought the outside was very important, too, and it helped him classify the world.

I must never forget, I suppose, that even in the gym, with all that space between us, we still managed to pick partners and dance. It's the dance that's important, not the difference. (I shouldn't leave out who leads and who follows. But I speak to that from a strange perspective, since any man who has ever danced with me can attest to the fact that I have never learned to follow.)

I have just met the dance downstairs. My elder son has one of his best friends over, and he does not care that she is a girl, and she does not care that he is a boy. But she is complaining that he is chasing her with the plastic spider and making her scream, and he is grinning maniacally because that is just exactly the response he is looking for, and they are both having a great time. Two children, raised in egalitarian households in the 1980s. Between them the floor already stretches, an ocean to cross before they can dance uneasily in one another's arms.

POSSIBILITIES FOR WRITING

1. To what extent do you find Quindlen's argument about the divide between the sexes persuasive? Do you find her images and examples compelling? Why or why not?

2. If women are indeed the "other" to men, and vice versa, then how does this otherness of each gender affect their ability to work together? What do women's and men's sexual differences mean for women being, as Quindlen argues, "not only permitted but welcomed into a variety of positions and roles that only men occupied"?

3. Write your own essay about the divide (or lack of one) between women and men. You may wish to use examples from your own experience to show how men and women misunderstand each other, or how they approach things in different ways. Or you may wish to use Quindlen's essay as the basis for a persuasive essay in which you agree, disagree, or qualify what Quindlen says about the great divide between the sexes.

Clotaire Rapaille (b. 1941) is a French-born American market researcher and author of The Culture Code, 7 Secrets of Marketing in a Multi-Cultural World. *His marketing work is based on his background as a psychiatrist and medical anthropologist. Rapaille received a masters of political science, a masters of psychology, and a doctorate of medical anthropology from the University of Paris–Sorbonne. In addition to his books, he is known for advising politicians and advertisers on how to influence people's unconscious decision making. Rapaille claims that the majority of decision making is unconscious and therefore that is where advertisers should target their advertising messages.*

CLOTAIRE RAPAILLE

Working for a Living: The Codes for Work and Money

In "Working for a Living: The Codes for Work and Money," a chapter from his book, *The Culture Code*, Rapaille explains the underlying reasons people value work and money. He identifies what he sees as the hidden assumptions behind people's behavior as it relates to work and money. And he highlights the cultural and social implications of that work-related and money-related behavior.

Rapaille bases his ideas about work and money on an analysis of comments made by members of focus groups in sessions Rapaille himself conducted. He couples this analysis with his long-standing experience as a consultant to corporations on devising strategies for marketing their products successfully. His explanation of how Americans value their jobs and their incomes emphasizes both social and psychological aspects of their behavior.

"What do you do?"

When someone asks you that question, you could offer any number of answers. You might discuss your role as a parent. Or you could talk about the various things you do to maintain your household. You might respond with a list of your hobbies. In America, though, the question really means "What *job* do you do?" and the only expected answer involves your work.

There is something very powerful and revealing about the way we ask "What do you do?" in American culture. It's another way of asking "What is your purpose?" as though one were looking at an unfamiliar machine and asking "What is it for?" We usually ask it almost as soon as we meet someone. "Where do you come from?" is the first question, followed by "What do you do?" The answers enable us to size someone up, as well as providing an evening's worth of small talk.

In several other cultures, one's work is not nearly the passion and preoccupation it is in ours. Stendhal's classic novel *The Red and the Black* defined a French culture in which one's life had value only if one served the country (as part of the military—the red) or God (as one of the clergy—the black). All other occupations were vulgar, best left to peasants. This attitude still pervades French culture and leads to a system in which the unemployed receive more money than many service employees receive. A major best-seller in France is *Bonjour Paresse*, whose title translates as "Hello Laziness."

Most of my European friends are baffled that I continue to work so hard long after I've made enough money to keep me comfortable the rest of my life. To them, the concept of continuing at one's job because one loves one's work is unfathomable. Europeans usually take six weeks of vacation every year. Here, two weeks is the norm, and many people take their work on vacation with them, or even go years without a vacation while they are building their careers.

This has been the American approach to work from the very beginning of our culture. When our forefathers came to America and discovered a huge undeveloped land, their first thought wasn't "Let's have some tea." It was "Let's get to work." There was a New World to create, and it wasn't going to create itself. Towns needed building. The West needed opening. The rudiments of a bold political experiment needed to be put in place. There wasn't time for leisure then, and in a very real way, we still believe there isn't time for it now. Americans work longer hours than the people of any other culture.

Americans celebrate work and turn successful businesspeople into celebrities. Donald Trump and Bill Gates are pop stars. Stephen R. Covey, Jack Welch, and Lee Iacocca are mega-selling authors. Instead of *Bonjour Paresse*, our best-sellers include *The Seven Habits of Highly Effective People* and *Good to Great*. Billionaire owners of sports teams, like George Steinbrenner and Mark Cuban, make the headlines as often as the athletes they employ.

Why does work mean so much to us?
Why do we need to love our jobs?
Why is it so important to us to have a strong work ethic?

When I set out to discover the Code for work in America, I was able to play my role of "visitor from another planet" with unusual credibility. While I myself had an extremely positive attitude toward work and a huge amount of passion for what I did, I grew up surrounded by those who embraced the French attitude. I already knew that Americans took a very different approach to work, but I was curious about how they imprinted this and what it meant to them at an unconscious level.

The "bad focus group" conversations of the first hour of the discovery sessions varied widely. While some participants spoke with excitement and optimism about their jobs, others complained about long hours, low pay, and difficult employers. And while all seemed to agree that work was something you "had to do," their attitudes about this obligation ranged. When we got to the third hour, however, and I asked participants to recall their first imprint of work, a very clear pattern emerged.

I had a paper route when I was a teenager. There were days when I dreaded it—snow was the worst—but for the most part, I had fun with it. I liked collection days, and not only because I got tips. I liked talking to the customers and getting to know them.—a forty-five-year-old man

My most powerful memory was just a couple of weeks ago. I'm a camp counselor and I ran into one of my kids at the video store. She saw me and ran into my arms and brought me over to meet her father. When she said, "Dad, this is my counselor," she said it like I was a queen or something.—an eighteen-year-old woman

I work three jobs to keep my family going. It seems that the only thing I do is work all the time.—a forty-seven-year-old man

I remember my first grown-up job. I worked during the summer in high school and college, but this was totally different. This was a career. I liked having colleagues and taking on assignments and planning out my future. I got a promotion after only six months and I felt like I was on the map.—a thirty-two-year old woman

I worked for the same company for twenty-three years. One day, a bigger company bought them and suddenly I was out on the street. For six months, I kept trying to find a new job and kept getting nowhere. When I wasn't looking for a job, I felt like I had nothing to do. My wife and kids had their lives, but I had nothing. I finally got a new job for much less than I used to make. It doesn't feel the same, and I don't feel the same.—a forty-seven-year-old man

My first paying gig changed my life. This was it. I had arrived. I was a professional musician!—a twenty-nine-year-old man

My first memory of work was watching my mother break her back lugging boxes of fruit for her fruit stand. It seemed to me that she was struggling all the time, but she never complained about it. I know she didn't like the long hours and the hard labor, but she liked talking to customers. Everyone knew who she was—she was the fruit stand lady.—a sixty-nine-year-old woman

The tone of the stories ran the gamut—people were happy with their work, they hated it, they fell invigorated, disappointed, or overwhelmed—but the energy of the stories moved in a very specific direction. Work put you in a position to get to know people, excite children, keep your family going, or plan your future. Work could make you feel that you were like a queen, that you were on the map, or that you had arrived; work could make you feel that it was all you did; if you lost your work, you could feel that you had nothing.

Though participants might have suggested otherwise in the first hour of our sessions, their third-hour stories gave them away. For Americans, work wasn't simply something you did to make a living or because you had to do it. Even if you didn't like your work, it had a much more powerful dimension, a life-defining dimension.

The American Culture Code for work is WHO YOU ARE.

When we are wearing the new glasses provided by the Culture Code, the question "What do you do?" takes on added meaning. In essence, when we ask someone what she does for a living, we ask her who she is, Americans very strongly believe that they are what they do in their jobs. Why are unemployed people often depressed by the loss of their jobs? Because they are unsure of how they will pay the bills? Certainly. At a deeper level, though, it is because they believe that if they are "doing" nothing, then they are nobodies.

If work means "who we are," then it is perfectly understandable that we seek so much meaning in our jobs. If our jobs feel meaningless, then "who we are" is meaningless as well. If we feel inspired, if we believe that our jobs have genuine value to the company we work for (even if that "company" is ourselves) and that we are doing something worthwhile in our work, that belief bolsters our sense of identity. This is perhaps the most fundamental reason why it is important for employers to keep their employees content and motivated. A company operated by people with a negative sense of identity can't possibly run well.

Ritz-Carlton does an excellent job of giving its staff a positive sense of who they are. The company calls its employees "ladies and gentlemen serving ladies and gentlemen." Their goal is to give their guests the best hotel experience of their lives, and their employees' job is to provide that experience. Ritz-Carlton understands that if they want to create a culture of sophistication for their guests, they need to do the same for those who work there. They treat their staff like adults and give them a strong sense of empowerment. If a cleaning person encounters a guest with a problem and the guest complains to her, that cleaning person has the power to improve his experience by giving him a free meal or even a free night in a room. This gives the cleaning person a strong sense of motivation, the belief that she is part of the corporate mission.

Another component of the Ritz-Carlton management approach is that they refuse to burden their staff with the motto that "The customer is always right." Understanding how humiliating it can be to live by that precept, the president of Ritz-Carlton tells his employees that if someone gets out of hand, to let him or someone else in management know and they will take care of it. Again, this approach fortifies the employees' sense of who they are. It is much easier to treat the guests like "ladies and gentlemen" when you are treated like a lady or a gentleman yourself. Ritz-Carlton employees tend to be very loyal and very proud of what they do.

Effective employee relations in other cultures reflect that culture's attitude about work. In France, work takes a backseat to the pursuit of pleasure. If a job isn't entertaining, most French workers would prefer unemployment. Gerard Blitz adopted this French approach to staff management when he founded Club Med. One of the first things he did was change job titles—for instance, the manager of a Club Med is the *chef du village* (chief of the village). Then he instituted nightly shows at which employees entertained guests. Any member of the staff could go up on stage if he or she had the guts. In addition, when Club Med opened its doors, it positioned itself as a welcome place for willing and adventurous singles. In such a sexually charged environment, the personnel had an excellent chance of sharing in the fun. This camplike atmosphere in a resort setting made work pleasurable for the staff—so much so that Club Med regularly gets away with paying their employees less than the competition.

Always on the Job

Americans rarely accept a dead end in their jobs without a fight, and they strongly believe that you are only as good as your last deal. A billionaire still works sixty hours a week because he needs constant affirmation of who he is. A recently promoted middle manager ratchets up her work energy because she already has the next promotion in her sights. Our work ethic is so strong because at the unconscious level, we equate work with who we are and we believe that if we work hard and improve our professional standing, we become better people. Remember, the American Code for health is movement; this extends to professional health as well. It is possible to be happy doing the same job for thirty years, but only if that job provides consistent new challenges. Otherwise, we think of ourselves as "stuck in a rut" or "going nowhere." How many people do you know who are thrilled to do the same job on an assembly line or as an office functionary indefinitely?

We're always seeking the next promotion, the next opportunity, the next chance for something big. If you talk to a cabdriver in Manhattan, you're more likely to find that he's going to school to get a better job than that he plans to drive a cab the rest of his life. If you meet a waitress in Southern California, she's likely to tell you that she has an audition for a movie next week. The cabdriver might never get out of his cab and the waitress might be performing a recitation of daily specials for the next twenty years, but the sense that they're moving toward something more glamorous is very much on Code. On the other hand, those who fail to act, who accept the limitations of their work with barely a grumble, are likely to feel miserable about their lives. The hopelessness of their jobs has done critical damage to their identities.

Our new glasses also help explain why we celebrate hugely successful businesspeople. We love the story of Bill Gates laboring away in his garage, coming up with a great idea, and becoming the richest person in the world. Why? Because it reinforces the notion that "who we are" has endless room for growth. The self-made millionaire (or, in Gates's case, "fifty-billionaire") is an inspirational symbol for us because it proves that all of us can work hard, find the thing that we do superbly, and forge an extraordinary identity. Similarly, stories like those of Tom Clancy (a middle-aged insurance salesman who became an enormously popular novelist) and Grandma Moses (a woman who started painting when she was in her seventies and became a legendary folk artist) show us that we always have the opportunity for greatness.

Deep down, we believe that you never have to be stuck in what you do. Self-reinvention is definitely on Code. If your work no longer provides you with the sense of who you are that you desire, it is not only acceptable but also preferable to seek something new. Americans champion entrepreneurs because they are our most aggressive identity-seekers. They don't wait for someone to tell them what to be, but rather take significant risks to become what they believe they should be.

Entrepreneurs are inspirational to us because they set their own course for identity evolution. We all want to believe that we are headed somewhere in our work, that we aren't going to stay in the same place for the rest of our lives. Most of us have an ideal job in mind, and it usually involves movement of some sort from our current place (bigger office, bigger staff, being the boss, being able to quit that second job). Since work suggests who we are to us, we put significant stock into this progression. None of us want to feel that we are "done," that who we are will remain stagnant for the remainder of our lives. Retirees, after decades of work, seek new jobs in retirement, even when money isn't an object. We saw earlier that they do so in part because they dread immobility, which is equivalent to death. It is significant, though, that the activity they choose is work. They don't work because they need the income; they work because they so strongly connect their identities with the work they do that they feel the need to keep working in order to feel that they still exist.

So what does one do with knowledge of the Code? From an employer's perspective, the Code offers a path to making the most of employee relations, as Ritz-Carlton has. The understanding that employees connect their jobs with who they are makes it clear that employers should put a premium on keeping staff inspired. Calling regular staff meetings to solicit input on how to improve a company is on Code. Involving staff in the direction of the company gives them an elevated sense of identity, the feeling that they are integral to the company's success.

Similarly, helping employees understand their career paths is on Code. If someone can see that a clerical position leads to a position with greater responsibility, which leads to a management position, a middle management position, and ultimately an executive position, she can see that she is going somewhere, and that heightens her sense of who she is.

Employees always expect monetary rewards to accompany promotions, but an on-Code employer takes rewards further. Promotions should come with new responsibilities and especially with new tools to help the employee do a more effective job (a better computer, access to an expense account, operation of machinery that is more powerful). In addition to giving him a way to do his job better, such changes give him a visceral sense that his identity is expanding.

One of the common mistakes that employers make is looking at a team of employees (for instance a sales force or a marketing staff) as a homogenous group that rises and falls together. Offering incentives (a group bonus or a vacation trip) to a team as a whole is off Code because it fails to acknowledge who an individual is. While teamwork is important within a corporation, the team should be regarded as a support group that allows individuals to become champions. Think of a jazz band. The band lays down a basic musical structure that allows each soloist to shine. When a saxophonist plays a stirring solo, he receives individual recognition (applause after the solo) above the other members of the band (who will get the chance for recognition during their own solos later in the song). Sending an entire team to the Bahamas for a job well done actually blunts an employee's efforts to do his best work. He only needs to perform well enough to help achieve the team objective. If, on the other hand, the employee knew that individual rewards were possible, he would be more likely to strive to outperform expectations.

"Show me the Money"

Ask most people why they work and they're likely to answer "To make money." The Culture Code shows us that this isn't actually true, but there *is* a very strong connection between work and money in this culture.

The Code for money offers a very powerful tool for understanding America. People around the world perceive us as being concerned only with money. This huge misconception is one of the reasons so many of them fail to see what really does motivate us. At the same time, though, Americans themselves perceive this preoccupation with money and think it suggests that we are greedy at heart or that we prize material goods over enhancement of the spirit. This, too, is a misconception, one that gives us much less credit than we deserve.

There is very little "old money" in America. The overwhelming preponderance of the wealth in this country belongs to the person who originally earned it. Our culture is filled with "self-made" people, and in some very real way, we all have the same starting point with regard to wealth—we all began poor. We came here with no money and established the goal of making life better for our children. Some succeeded in extraordinary ways immediately, while others simply improved the situation slightly for the next generation. Regardless, the notion that we "come from nothing" pervades America. In a sense, we have the poorest rich people in the world, because even those who accumulate huge sums of money think like poor people. They continue to work hard, they continue to focus on cash flow and expenses, and they continue to struggle to earn more.

A discovery undertaken for J. P. Morgan and Citibank revealed why. Listen to the third-hour stories:

I still have the first dollar I received when I opened the doors at my dry-cleaning business. It's in a frame in my office in the back of the store. I look at it every morning to remind me that my business is a good one.—a sixty-two-year-old man

My dad got injured one spring when I was a teenager, so he asked me to turn over the vegetable garden for him and put in new plants. This was much harder work than anything I ever did before and there were a couple of times when I thought about quitting. I kept going, though, because I knew my father needed me to do it. When I finished, he gave me twenty bucks, which was a decent amount of cash at the time. I wound up getting a radio I really wanted with it. I held on to that radio for a long time because I worked so hard to get it.—a man in his fifties

My first, most powerful, and most recent memory of money is that I don't have any. Whatever I make goes to pay the bills. I never expected it to be like this after all these years. I don't know how I'll ever get out of this hole.—a forty-three-year-old man

We never had money when I was growing up and I had to take out a lot of loans to pay for college. That felt like a huge burden when I graduated. Fortunately, I got a good job right away and after some quick promotions, I was making good money. One of the first things I did was pay off my student loans. I loved that I could do that and still have plenty of money left over.—a thirty-two-year-old woman

My most powerful memory is going in and asking my boss for a raise for the first time. I was doing okay and I didn't need the money all that much, but I also knew I was making a lot of money for him and that I deserved it. He gave me a hard time at first, but then he gave in. It felt great to know that he appreciated me enough to pay me more.—a thirty-five-year-old man

I was the fifth of five kids in my family, and all of my siblings were significantly older than me. Whenever we went out together, one of them always paid my way, which was necessary because I didn't have much

*money, but always made me feel a little bad. One night—this is my most powerful memory—we all went out to dinner at an Italian restaurant. The food was great and we all had a really good time. When the check came, I reached across the table and grabbed it. They tried to argue with me, but I told them I'd just gotten a little bonus at work and wanted to treat everyone. They were very proud of me and I felt like I had a different place in the family after that.—*a woman in her thirties

*This whole session has been difficult for me. I try not to think too much about money. I'm up to my neck in bills and I don't have a clue how I'm going to pay them off. Most of my friends have more money than I do and I try to fake it and keep up with them when we're out. I know I can't keep up, though, and it's gonna kill me if I don't stop.—*a twenty-four-year-old man

Clearly, money signifies more to Americans than the means to buy things. It shows us how we're doing, tells us how far we've come from impoverished poor roots. Money reminds you that your "business is a good one," that you've worked hard to get something, that you can carry your burdens, that you are appreciated, and that you are moving up to the next level. Not having money makes you feel as if you are "in a hole"; you may feel that "it's gonna kill me."

The American culture has no titles of nobility to show us who the big winners are. Without them, we need something that performs a similar function. Participants tell us through their third-hour stories that that thing is money.

The American Culture Code for money is PROOF.

In spite of what people from other cultures—and many from our own—say about our attitude toward money, the Code shows that money isn't a goal in and of itself for most Americans. We rely on it to show us that we are good, that we have true value in the world. An American can't be knighted for his deeds or become a baroness, as Margaret Thatcher has. American accolades are relative and ephemeral. We can prove what we've accomplished only by making as much money as possible.

Money is our barometer of success. Most Americans find it impossible to feel successful if they feel they are underpaid. Money is a scorecard. If someone is doing a job similar to yours and making more money, you unconsciously believe that he or she is doing a better job.

Being paid for a job imbues it with instant credibility. I spoke with someone recently who told me about his early struggles to become a professional writer after leaving a corporate career. For two years, even though he was doing high-quality work, he failed to make any money at it. "I felt unemployed," he told me, "even though I was working ten hours a day." A publishing contract changed his attitude about his accomplishments instantly. Suddenly the previous two years gained validity. The money the publisher paid him was proof.

Because we believe money is proof, we see a very strong connection between money and work. Money earned via hard work is admirable, proof that you are a good person. We have little respect, however, for those who inherit money rather than making it on their own. We might be fascinated by the exploits of someone like Paris Hilton, but we don't feel that she's proven anything, because she was born rich and her celebrity stems exclusively from her wealth. We attribute Patty Hearst's early difficulties to her growing up an heiress, and we consider the ongoing problems of the Getty children to be the product of old money. We love it that Bill Gates has more money than the Queen of England, because he earned every penny of it himself.

While we don't have much respect for trust fund babies who live off the family fortune, we have completely different feelings about those who build on their inherited legacy and establish substantial careers of their own. Robert Wood Johnson worked hard to take Johnson & Johnson to new levels of growth and profitability William Clay Ford Jr. did the same with the Ford Motor Company. These people, while starting from a very different place from most Americans, prove themselves by making their own money and increasing the family fortune. Wealthy American businesspeople will say that they want their children to establish themselves. They will of course provide access and connections (and they might underestimate the extent to which this makes a difference), but they won't give their children a "free ride." Making every generation prove itself anew is definitely on Code.

Even if we work very hard, we can find this good money/bad money dichotomy in our own lives. One of the things revealed by the study I did for Morgan and Citibank is that Americans see interest income and capital gains as "bad money" because they didn't earn it themselves. Investors who took a very active role in managing their stock portfolios felt they "made" this money, while those who simply followed the advice of their brokers did not. Banks and investment firms that tell their customers "Give us your money, and we'll make it work for you" are totally off Code. On-Code firms portray themselves as facilitators who provide their clients with tools for generating more money.

Many European cultures have a different view of money and its function. At a certain point, if one earns a great deal of money in these cultures, one simply settles back on the estate, leaving the world of commerce behind. Here, of course, we believe we're only as good as our last deal, and even when we've made billions we want to make billions more to prove how good we are. In America, we can dream about having no limits, about striking it rich regardless of how little we had at birth. In Europe, you might start out with a bit of money, but it is considerably more difficult to grow out of your station (a French book published a few years ago whose title can be translated as "The Heirs" showed that there was very little economic movement in that country: the children of doctors became doctors, the children of bankers became bankers, and it was very difficult to move into these classes or beyond them). Hence, money in France isn't a form of proof, but an unpleasant fact.

In France, a common topic at elegant dinner parties is sex. The French consider it entirely acceptable to discuss sexual positions, multiple partners, and different kinds of lingerie while entertaining guests. They consider the topic of money, however, to be vulgar; it is exceedingly impolite to ask how much money someone makes or how much he or she paid for something. Here, of course, we would be appalled by an explicit sexual discussion at dinner, but we can talk about money all night long. Different Culture Codes lead to different behaviors.

It has been said that Americans consider money their religion. While this is often meant critically, it has an element of truth that doesn't have a negative dimension. The "proof" that we derive from money is the proof of our goodness—not only of the quality of our work at our chosen professions, but also of our quality as people. We truly believe there is a link between goodness and monetary success and that those who cheat and lie their way to the top ultimately meet their comeuppance on both the spiritual and financial planes. Consistent with this mind-set is the American attitude toward charitable donations. There is no luggage rack on a hearse, and since you cannot take your possessions and money into the afterlife with you, Americans (not just dying ones) choose to give a significant amount of it away to those in need. Studies show that Americans are the most charitable people in the world. Even people who barely scrape by tend to be generous with the money they share with others. The rich even appear to compete over who makes the largest donations. While the generosity seems to be heartfelt, there is a strong sense of obligation that comes with being wealthy in this culture. Americans expect their most fortunate to share what they've earned, and we have an entire system of laws in place for giving one's money away.

The new glasses of the Culture Code offer us strong, even counter-intuitive, insights into dealing with money in America. It is off Code, for example, to preach profitability to one's employees. Money is the proof of goodness, not in itself the goal. Instead, a company's management must inspire employees to be the best they can possibly be and to make the company as strong as it can possibly be. This is on Code for both work and money and, if done effectively, leads to profitability.

The two Codes together lead to another surprising conclusion: money alone is the worst reward for an American employee. It doesn't last and it is never sufficient. Yes, money is proof, and as such, it is a critical component of any reward system. But the most on-Code approach is to use money as a global positioning system that shows the employee where he is on his career path. At every promotion, the employee should be shown a visual representation of the income curve that he or she is on. The angle at which one's salary is climbing is a powerful symbol of growth. It is visual proof. A tangible award of some sort presented at the same time as the promotion gives the employee a tactile experience of his enhanced sense of who he is. Maybe it is a plaque of some sort. Maybe it is a new office, or a new accessory for the office. These tangible symbols last much longer than money, though they admittedly mean very little without it.

Work and Money: An American Marriage Built to Last

The Codes show that Americans draw a very strong connection between work and money. The sense of "who you are" derived from work is intertwined with the "proof" provided by the money one earns. We are suspicious, and even dismissive, of money gained without hard work. For instance, we have little respect for those who gain sudden wealth through the lottery. Americans don't regard this as "real" money because it isn't earned. A lottery winner *proves* nothing by winning the lottery, except that he or she was very fortunate. Lottery winners themselves seem to share some of this sensibility. Their instant wealth makes them anomalies: they don't truly belong with the rich, because they didn't work their way into that world, nor do they fit any longer among their peers, because their money separates them. We tend to forget the names of lottery winners within a day or so and never hear from them again.

Interestingly, we look at game show winners differently. Of course, this is on Code. When Ken Jennings won seventy-four consecutive rounds of the quiz show *jeopardy!* (acquiring more than $2.5 million in the process), he became an instant celebrity. Unlike a lottery winner's, however, Jennings's star didn't fade immediately. He received endorsement deals, speaking engagements, and a place in television history. Ken Jennings earned his money by battling and beating contestants for months; he *proved* himself repeatedly.

Ken Jennings received an opportunity and he made the most of it. This is what we really want as Americans. We may dream of winning the lottery and escaping the rat race. What the Codes for work and money show, though, is that work is an essential part of who we are and that we just want a chance to prove ourselves and receive tangible evidence that we have succeeded.

POSSIBILITIES FOR WRITING

1. What, according, to Rapaille, is the hidden reason—the "code"—for work? What does Rapaille identify as the code for money? And to what extent do you agree with what he claims are the real drivers and motivators—the real meanings behind work and money? Explain.

2. Why are you, personally, interested in work for yourself—and what kind(s) of work do you plan to or hope to pursue? What kinds of work are your friends interested in—or what kinds of work are they involved in? Why? To what extent are work and money linked? To what extent do you see them as separate entities and concerns? How do you think Rapaille sees the link between work and money?

3. Write an essay about either work or money (or the link between them). Consider the values you ascribe to work and/or money. You may wish to consider, as well, what Rapaille says about them—and whether you wish to endorse, qualify, or contest his ideas.

Richard Rodriguez (b. 1944) is a native of San Francisco, the son of Mexican-American immigrants. A self-described "scholarship boy," he attended Catholic schools as a child and later Stanford and Columbia universities; he received undergraduate and graduate degrees in English from the University of California at Berkeley. Rodriguez currently works primarily as a journalist: he is an editor for the Pacific News Service, and he contributes to such periodicals as Harper's *and* U.S. News and World Report, *as well as writing columns for the* Los Angeles Times. *His commentary about American life and Hispanic culture on PBS's* NewsHour *won him the prestigious Peabody Award in 1997. His best known publication, however, is* Hunger of Memory: The Education of Richard Rodriguez, *his 1982 collection of autobiographical essays exploring his growing up as the son of immigrant parents.*

RICHARD RODRIGUEZ

Aria: A Memoir of a Bilingual Childhood

"Aria: A Memoir of a Bilingual Childhood" was originally published in the *American Scholar* (1980/1981) and later served as the opening chapter of Rodriguez's intellectual autobiography, *Hunger of Memory.* In "Aria," Rodriguez describes growing up in a bilingual and a bicultural world, the son of Mexican immigrants who lived in a mixed-race neighborhood in Sacramento, California.

In this essay, Rodriguez reflects on the tensions he experienced at school and at home between the Spanish-language world of his parents and his past, and the English-language world of his school and his adopted country. Rodriguez describes what is gained and what is lost as he makes the transition from Spanish to English, and between the different social and cultural contexts associated with each.

I remember, to start with, that day in Sacramento, in a California now nearly thirty years past, when I first entered a classroom—able to understand about fifty stray English words. The third of four children, I had been preceded by my older brother and sister to a neighborhood Roman Catholic school. But neither of them had revealed very much about their classroom experiences. They left each morning and returned each afternoon, always together, speaking Spanish as they climbed the five steps to the porch. And their mysterious books, wrapped in brown shopping-bag paper, remained on the table next to the door, closed firmly behind them.

An accident of geography sent me to a school where all my class-mates were white and many were the children of doctors and lawyers and business executives. On that first day of school, my classmates must certainly have been uneasy to find themselves apart from their families, in the first institution of their lives. But I was astonished. I was fated to be the "problem student" in class.

The nun said, in a friendly but oddly impersonal voice: "Boys and girls, this is Richard Rodriguez." (I heard her sound it out: *Rich-heard Road-ree-guess.*) It was the first time I had heard anyone say my name in English. "Richard," the nun repeated more slowly, writing my name down in her book. Quickly I turned to see my mother's face dissolve in a watery blur behind the pebbled-glass door.

Now, many years later, I hear of something called "bilingual education"—a scheme proposed in the late 1960s by Hispanic-American social activists, later endorsed by a congressional vote. It is a program that seeks to permit non-English-speaking children (many from lower class homes) to use their "family language" as the language of school. Such, at least, is the aim its supporters announce. I hear them, and am forced to say no: It is not possible for a child, any child, ever to use his family's language in school. Not to understand this is to misunderstand the public uses of schooling and to trivialize the nature of intimate life.

Memory teaches me what I know of these matters. The boy reminds the adult. I was a bilingual child, but of a certain kind: "socially disadvantaged," the son of working-class parents, both Mexican immigrants.

In the early years of my boyhood, my parents coped very well in America. My father had steady work. My mother managed at home. They were nobody's victims. When we moved to a house many blocks from the Mexican-American section of town, they were not intimidated by those two or three neighbors who initially tried to make us unwelcome. ("Keep your brats away from my sidewalk!") But despite all they achieved, or perhaps because they had so much to achieve, they lacked any deep feeling of ease, of belonging in public. They regarded the people at work or in crowds as being very distant from us. Those were the others, *los gringos.* That term was interchangeable in their speech with another, even more telling: *los americanos.*

I grew up in a house where the only regular guests were my relations. On a certain day, enormous families of relatives would visit us, and there would be so many people that the noise and the bodies would spill out to the backyard and onto the front porch. Then for weeks no one would come. (If the doorbell rang, it was usually a salesman.) Our house stood apart—gaudy yellow in a row of white bungalows. We were the people with the noisy dog, the people who raised chickens. We were the foreigners on the block. A few neighbors would smile and wave at us. We waved back. But until I was seven years old, I did not know the name of the old couple living next door or the names of the kids living across the street.

In public, my father and mother spoke a hesitant, accented, and not always grammatical English. And then they would have to strain, their bodies tense, to catch the sense of what was rapidly said by *los gringos*. At home, they returned to Spanish. The language of their Mexican past sounded in counterpoint to the English spoken in public. The words would come quickly, with ease. Conveyed through those sounds was the pleasing, soothing, consoling reminder that one was at home.

During those years when I was first learning to speak, my mother and father addressed me only in Spanish; in Spanish I learned to reply. By contrast, English (*inglés*) was the language I came to associate with gringos, rarely heard in the house. I learned my first words of English over-hearing my parents speaking to strangers. At six years of age, I knew just enough words for my mother to trust me on errands to stores one block away—but no more.

I was then a listening child, careful to hear the very different sounds of Spanish and English. Wide-eyed with hearing, I'd listen to sounds more than to words. First, there were English (gringo) sounds. So many words still were unknown to me that when the butcher or the lady at the drugstore said something, exotic polysyllabic sounds would bloom in the midst of their sentences. Often the speech of people in public seemed to me very loud, booming with confidence. The man behind the counter would literally ask, "What can I do for you?" But by being so firm and clear, the sound of his voice said that he was a gringo; he belonged in public society. There were also the high, nasal notes of middle-class American speech—which I rarely am conscious of hearing today because I hear them so often, but could not stop hearing when I was a boy. Crowds at Safeway or at bus stops were noisy with the birdlike sounds of *los gringos*. I'd move away from them all—all the chirping chatter above me.

My own sounds I was unable to hear, but I knew that I spoke English poorly. My words could not extend to form complete thoughts. And the words I did speak I didn't know well enough to make distinct sounds. (Listeners would usually lower their heads to hear better what

RICHARD RODRIGUEZ

I was trying to say.) But it was one thing for *me* to speak English with difficulty; it was more troubling to hear my parents speaking in public: their high-whining vowels and guttural consonants; their sentences that got stuck with "eh" and "ah" sounds; the confused syntax; the hesitant rhythm of sounds so different from the way gringos spoke. I'd notice, moreover, that my parents' voices were softer than those of gringos we would meet.

I am tempted to say now that none of this mattered. (In adulthood I am embarrassed by childhood fears.) And, in a way, it didn't matter very much that my parents could not speak English with ease. Their linguistic difficulties had no serious consequences. My mother and father made themselves understood at the county hospital clinic and at government offices. And yet, in another way, it mattered very much. It was unsettling to hear my parents struggle with English. Hearing them, I'd grow nervous, and my clutching trust in their protection and power would be weakened.

There were many times like the night at a brightly lit gasoline station (a blaring white memory) when I stood uneasily hearing my father talk to a teenage attendant. I do not recall what they were saying, but I cannot forget the sounds my father made as he spoke. At one point his words slid together to form one long word—sounds as confused as the threads of blue and green oil in the puddle next to my shoes. His voice rushed through what he had left to say. Toward the end, he reached falsetto notes, appealing to his listener's understanding. I looked away at the lights of passing automobiles. I tried not to hear any more. But I heard only too well the attendant's reply, his calm, easy tones. Shortly afterward, headed for home, I shivered when my father put his hand on my shoulder. The very first chance that I got, I evaded his grasp and ran on ahead into the dark, skipping with feigned boyish exuberance.

But then there was Spanish: *español*, the language rarely heard away from the house; *español*, the language which seemed to me therefore a private language, my family's language. To hear its sounds was to feel myself specially recognized as one of the family, apart from *los otros*. A simple remark, an inconsequential comment could convey that assurance. My parents would say something to me and I would feel embraced by the sounds of their words. Those sounds said: *I am speaking with ease in Spanish. I am addressing you in words I never use with los gringos. I recognize you as someone special, close, like no one outside. You belong with us. In the family. Ricardo.*

At the age of six, well past the time when most middle-class children no longer notice the difference between sounds uttered at home and words spoken in public, I had a different experience. I lived in a world compounded of sounds. I was a child longer than most. I lived in a magical world, surrounded by sounds both pleasing and fearful. I shared with my family a language enchantingly private—different from that used in the city around us.

Just opening or closing the screen door behind me was an important experience. I'd rarely leave home all alone or without feeling reluctance. Walking down the sidewalk, under the canopy of tall trees, I'd warily notice the (suddenly) silent neighborhood kids who stood warily watching me. Nervously, I'd arrive at the grocery store to hear there the sounds of the gringo, reminding me that in this so-big world I was a foreigner. But if leaving home was never routine, neither was coming back. Walking toward our house, climbing the steps from the sidewalk, in summer when the front door was open, I'd hear voices beyond the screen door talking in Spanish. For a second or two I'd stay, linger there listening. Smiling, I'd hear my mother call out, saying in Spanish, "Is that you, Richard?" Those were her words, but all the while her sounds would assure me: *You are home now. Come closer inside. With us.* "*Sí,*" I'd reply.

Once more inside the house, I would resume my place in the family. The sounds would grow harder to hear. Once more at home, I would grow less conscious of them. It required, however, no more than the blurt of the doorbell to alert me all over again to listen to sounds. The house would turn instantly quiet while my mother went to the door. I'd hear her hard English sounds. I'd wait to hear her voice turn to soft-sounding Spanish, which assured me, as surely as did the clicking tongue of the lock on the door, that the stranger was gone.

Plainly it is not healthy to hear such sounds so often. It is not healthy to distinguish public from private sounds so easily. I remained cloistered by sounds, timid and shy in public, too dependent on the voices at home. And yet I was a very happy child when I was at home. I remember many nights when my father would come back from work, and I'd hear him call out to my mother in Spanish, sounding relieved. In Spanish, his voice would sound the light and free notes that he never could manage in English. Some nights I'd jump up just hearing his voice. My brother and I would come running into the room where he was with our mother. Our laughing (so deep was the pleasure!) became screaming. Like others who feel the pain of public alienation, we transformed the knowledge of our public separateness into a consoling reminder of our intimacy. Excited, our voices joined in a celebration of sounds. *We are speaking now the way we never speak out in public—we are together,* the sounds told me. Some nights no one seemed willing to loosen the hold that sounds had on us. At dinner we invented new words that sounded Spanish, but made sense only to us. We pieced together new words by taking, say, an English verb and giving it Spanish endings. My mother's instructions at bedtime would be lacquered with mock-urgent tones. Or a word like *sí*, sounded in several notes, would convey added measures of feeling. Tongues lingered around the edges of words, especially fat vowels. And we happily sounded that military drum roll, the twirling roar of the Spanish *r.* Family language, my family's sounds: the voices of my parents and sisters and brother. Their voices insisting: *You belong here. We are family members. Related. Special to one another. Listen!* Voices singing and sighing, rising and straining, then surging, teeming with pleasure which burst syllables into fragments of laughter. At times it seemed there was steady quiet only when, from another room, the rustling whispers of my parents faded and I edged closer to sleep.

Supporters of bilingual education imply today that students like me miss a great deal by not being taught in their family's language. What they seem not to recognize is that, as a socially disadvantaged child, I regarded Spanish as a private language. It was a ghetto language that deepened and strengthened my feeling of public separateness. What I needed to learn in school was that I had the right, and the obligation, to speak the public language. The odd truth is that my first-grade classmates could have become bilingual, in the conventional sense of the word, more easily than I. Had they been taught early (as upper middle-class children often are taught) a "second language" like Spanish or French, they could have regarded it simply as another public language. In my case, such bilingualism could not have been so quickly achieved. What I did not believe was that I could speak a single public language.

Without question, it would have pleased me to have heard my teachers address me in Spanish when I entered the classroom. I would have felt much less afraid. I would have imagined that my instructors were somehow "related" to me; I would indeed have heard their Spanish as my family's language. I would have trusted them and responded with ease. But I would have delayed—postponed for how long?—having to learn the language of public society. I would have evaded—and for how long?—learning the great lesson of school: that I had a public identity.

Fortunately, my teachers were unsentimental about their responsibility. What they understood was that I needed to speak public English. So their voices would search me out, asking me questions. Each time I heard them I'd look up in surprise to see a nun's face frowning at me. I'd mumble, not really meaning to answer. The nun would persist. "Richard, stand up. Don't look at the floor. Speak up. Speak to the entire class, not just to me!" But I couldn't believe English could be my language to use. (In part, I did not want to believe it.) I continued to mumble. I resisted the teacher's demands. (Did I somehow suspect that once I learned this public language my family life would be changed?) Silent, waiting for the bell to sound, I remained dazed, diffident, afraid.

Because I wrongly imagined that English was intrinsically a public language and Spanish was intrinsically private, I easily noted the difference between classroom language and the language of home. At school, words were directed to a general audience of listeners. ("Boys and girls . . .") Words were meaningfully ordered. And the point was not self-expression alone, but to make oneself understood by many others. The teacher quizzed: "Boys and girls, why do we use that word in this sentence? Could we think of a better word to use there? Would the sentence change its meaning if the words were differently arranged? Isn't there a better way of saying much the same thing?" (I couldn't say. I wouldn't try to say.)

Three months passed. Five. A half year. Unsmiling, ever watchful, my teachers noted my silence. They began to connect my behavior with the slow progress my brother and sisters were making. Until, one Saturday morning, three nuns arrived at the house to talk to our parents. Stiffly they sat on the blue living-room sofa. From the doorway of another room, spying on the visitors, I noted the incongruity, the clash of two worlds, the faces and voices of school intruding upon the familiar setting of home. I overheard one voice gently wondering, "Do your children speak only Spanish at home, Mrs. Rodriguez?" While another voice added, "That Richard especially seems so timid and shy."

That Rich-heard!

With great tact, the visitors continued, "Is it possible for you and your husband to encourage your children to practice their English when they are home?" Of course my parents complied. What would they not do for their children's well-being? And how could they question the Church's authority which those women represented? In an instant they agreed to give up the language (the sounds) which had revealed and accentuated our family's closeness. The moment after the visitors left, the change was observed. *"Ahora,* speak to us only *en inglés,"* my father and mother told us.

At first, it seemed a kind of game. After dinner each night, the family gathered together to practice "our" English. It was still then *inglés,* a language foreign to us, so we felt drawn to it as strangers. Laughing, we would try to define words we could not pronounce. We played with strange English sounds, often over-anglicizing our pronunciations. And we filled the smiling gaps of our sentences with familiar Spanish sounds. But that was cheating, somebody shouted, and everyone laughed.

In school, meanwhile, like my brother and sisters, I was required to attend a daily tutoring session. I needed a full year of this special work. I also needed my teachers to keep my attention from straying in class by calling out, *"Rich-heard!"*—their English voices slowly loosening the ties to my other name, with its three notes, *Ri-car-do.* Most of all, I needed to hear my mother and father speak to me in a moment of seriousness in "broken"—suddenly heartbreaking—English. This scene was inevitable. One Saturday morning I entered the kitchen where my parents were talking, but I did not realize that they were talking in Spanish until, the moment they saw me, their voices changed and they began speaking English. The gringo sounds they uttered startled me. Pushed me away. In that moment of trivial misunderstanding and profound insight, I felt my throat twisted by unsounded grief. I simply turned and left the room. But I had no place to escape to where I could grieve in Spanish. My brother and sisters were speaking English in another part of the house.

Again and again in the days following, as I grew increasingly angry, I was obliged to hear my mother and father encouraging me: "Speak to us *en inglés."* Only then did I determine to learn classroom English. Thus, sometime afterward it happened: one day in school, I raised my hand to volunteer an answer to a question. I spoke out in a loud voice and I did not think it remarkable when the entire class understood. That day I moved very far from being the disadvantaged child I had been only days earlier. Taken hold at last was the belief, the calming assurance, that I *belonged* in public.

Shortly after, I stopped hearing the high, troubling sounds of *los gringos.* A more and more confident speaker of English, I didn't listen to how strangers sounded when they talked to me. With so many

English-speaking people around me, I no longer heard American accents. Conversations quickened. Listening to persons whose voices sounded eccentrically pitched, I might note their sounds for a few seconds, but then I'd concentrate on what they were saying. Now when I heard someone's tone of voice—angry or questioning or sarcastic or happy or sad—I didn't distinguish it from the words it expressed. Sound and word were thus tightly wedded. At the end of each day I was often bemused, and always relieved, to realize how "soundless," though crowded with words, my day in public had been. An eight-year-old boy, I finally came to accept what had been technically true since my birth: I was an American citizen.

But diminished by then was the special feeling of closeness at home. Gone was the desperate, urgent, intense feeling of being at home among those with whom I felt intimate. Our family remained a loving family, but one greatly changed. We were no longer so close, no longer bound tightly together by the knowledge of our separateness from *los gringos*. Neither my older brother nor my sisters rushed home after school any more. Nor did I. When I arrived home, often there would be neighborhood kids in the house. Or the house would be empty of sounds.

Following the dramatic Americanization of their children, even my parents grew more publicly confident—especially my mother. First she learned the names of all the people on the block. Then she decided we needed to have a telephone in our house. My father, for his part, continued to use the word *gringo*, but it was no longer charged with bitterness or distrust. Stripped of any emotional content, the word simply became a name for those Americans not of Hispanic descent. Hearing him, sometimes, I wasn't sure if he was pronouncing the Spanish word *gringo*, or saying gringo in English.

There was a new silence at home. As we children learned more and more English, we shared fewer and fewer words with our parents. Sentences needed to be spoken slowly when one of us addressed our mother or father. Often the parent wouldn't understand. The child would need to repeat himself. Still the parent misunderstood. The young voice, frustrated, would end up saying, "Never mind"—the subject was closed. Dinners would be noisy with the clinking of knives and forks against dishes. My mother would smile softly between her remarks; my father, at the other end of the table, would chew and chew his food while he stared over the heads of his children.

My mother! My father! After English became my primary language, I no longer knew what words to use in addressing my parents. The old

Spanish words (those tender accents of sound) I had earlier used—
mamá and *papá*—I couldn't use any more. They would have been all-
too-painful reminders of how much had changed in my life. On the
other hand, the words I heard neighborhood kids call their parents
seemed equally unsatisfactory. "Mother" and "father," "ma," "papa," "pa,"
"dad," "pop" (how I hated the all-American sound of that last word)—all
these I felt were unsuitable terms of address for *my* parents. As a result,
I never used them at home. Whenever I'd speak to my parents, I would
try to get their attention by looking at them. In public conversations, I'd
refer to them as my "parents" or my "mother" and "father."

My mother and father, for their part, responded differently, as their
children spoke to them less. My mother grew restless, seemed troubled
and anxious at the scarceness of words exchanged in the house. She
would question me about my day when I came home from school. She
smiled at my small talk. She pried at the edges of my sentences to get
me to say something more. ("What . . . ?") She'd join conversations she
overheard, but her intrusions often stopped her children's talking. By
contrast, my father seemed to grow reconciled to the new quiet.
Though his English somewhat improved, he tended more and more to
retire into silence. At dinner he spoke very little. One night his children
and even his wife helplessly giggled at his garbled English pronunciation of the Catholic "Grace Before Meals." Thereafter he made his wife
recite the prayer at the start of each meal, even on formal occasions
when there were guests in the house.

Hers became the public voice of the family. On official business it
was she, not my father, who would usually talk to strangers on the
phone or in stores. We children grew so accustomed to his silence that
years later we would routinely refer to his "shyness." (My mother often
tried to explain: Both of his parents died when he was eight. He was
raised by an uncle who treated him as little more than a menial servant. He was never encouraged to speak. He grew up alone—a man of
few words.) But I realized my father was not shy whenever I'd watch
him speaking Spanish with relatives. Using Spanish, he was quickly
effusive. Especially when talking with other men, his voice would
spark, flicker, flare alive with varied sounds. In Spanish he expressed
ideas and feelings he rarely revealed when speaking English. With firm
Spanish sounds he conveyed a confidence and authority that English
would never allow him.

The silence at home, however, was not simply the result of fewer
words passing between parents and children. More profound for me

was the silence created by my inattention to sounds. At about the time I no longer bothered to listen with care to the sounds of English in public, I grew careless about listening to the sounds made by the family when they spoke. Most of the time I would hear someone speaking at home and didn't distinguish his sounds from the words people uttered in public. I didn't even pay much attention to my parents' accented and ungrammatical speech—at least not at home. Only when I was with them in public would I become alert to their accents. But even then their sounds caused me less and less concern. For I was growing increasingly confident of my own public identity.

I would have been happier about my public success had I not recalled, sometimes, what it had been like earlier, when my family conveyed its intimacy through a set of conveniently private sounds. Sometimes in public, hearing a stranger, I'd hark back to my lost past. A Mexican farm worker approached me one day downtown. He wanted directions to some place. "*Hijito*, . . ." he said. And his voice stirred old longings. Another time I was standing beside my mother in the visiting room of a Carmelite convent, before the dense screen which rendered the nuns shadowy figures. I heard several of them speaking Spanish in their busy, singsong, overlapping voices, assuring my mother that, yes, yes, we were remembered, all our family was remembered, in their prayers. Those voices echoed faraway family sounds. Another day a dark-faced old woman touched my shoulder lightly to steady herself as she boarded a bus. She murmured something to me I couldn't quite comprehend. Her Spanish voice came near, like the face of a never-before-seen relative in the instant before I was kissed. That voice, like so many of the Spanish voices I'd hear in public, recalled the golden age of my childhood.

Bilingual educators say today that children lose a degree of "individuality" by becoming assimilated into public society. (Bilingual schooling is a program popularized in the seventies, that decade when middle-class "ethnics" began to resist the process of assimilation—the "American melting pot.") But the bilingualists oversimplify when they scorn the value and necessity of assimilation. They do not seem to realize that a person is individualized in two ways. So they do not realize that, while one suffers a diminished sense of *private* individuality by being assimilated into public society, such assimilation makes possible the achievement of *public* individuality.

Simplistically again, the bilingualists insist that a student should be reminded of his difference from others in mass society, of his "heritage."

But they equate mere separateness with individuality. The fact is that only in private—with intimates—is separateness from the crowd a prerequisite for individuality; an intimate "tells" me that I am unique, unlike all others, apart from the crowd. In public, by contrast, full individuality is achieved, paradoxically, by those who are able to consider themselves members of the crowd. Thus it happened for me. Only when I was able to think of myself as an American, no longer an alien in gringo society, could I seek the rights and opportunities necessary for full public individuality. The social and political advantages I enjoy as a man began on the day I came to believe that my name is indeed *Rich-heard Road-ree-guess.* It is true that my public society today is often impersonal; in fact, my public society is usually mass society. But despite the anonymity of the crowd, and despite the fact that the individuality I achieve in public is often tenuous—because it depends on my being one in a crowd—I celebrate the day I acquired my new name. Those middle-class ethnics who scorn assimilation seem to me filled with decadent self-pity, obsessed by the burden of public life. Dangerously, they romanticize public separateness and trivialize the dilemma of those who are truly socially disadvantaged.

If I rehearse here the changes in my private life after my Americanization, it is finally to emphasize a public gain. The loss implies the gain. The house I returned to each afternoon was quiet. Intimate sounds no longer greeted me at the door. Inside there were other noises. The telephone rang. Neighborhood kids ran past the door of the bedroom where I was reading my schoolbooks—covered with brown shopping-bag paper. Once I learned the public language, it would never again be easy for me to hear intimate family voices. More and more of my day was spent hearing words, not sounds. But that may only be a way of saying that on the day I raised my hand in class and spoke loudly to an entire roomful of faces, my childhood started to end.

I grew up the victim of a disconcerting confusion. As I became fluent in English, I could no longer speak Spanish with confidence. I continued to understand spoken Spanish, and in high school I learned how to read and write Spanish. But for many years I could not pronounce it. A powerful guilt blocked my spoken words; an essential glue was missing whenever I would try to connect words to form sentences. I would be unable to break a barrier of sound, to speak freely. I would speak, or try to speak, Spanish, and I would manage to utter halting, hiccuping sounds which betrayed my unease. (Even today I speak Spanish very slowly, at best.)

When relatives and Spanish-speaking friends of my parents came to the house, my brother and sisters would usually manage to say a few words before being excused. I never managed so gracefully. Each time I'd hear myself addressed in Spanish, I couldn't respond with any success. I'd know the words I wanted to say, but I couldn't say them. I would try to speak, but everything I said seemed to me horribly anglicized. My mouth wouldn't form the sounds right. My jaw would tremble. After a phrase or two, I'd stutter, cough up a warm, silvery sound, and stop.

My listeners were surprised to hear me. They'd lower their heads to grasp better what I was trying to say. They would repeat their questions in gentle, affectionate voices. But then I would answer in English. No, no, they would say, we want you to speak to us in Spanish ("*en español*"). But I couldn't do it. Then they would call me *Pocho*. Sometimes playfully, teasing, using the tender diminutive—*mi pochito*. Sometimes not so playfully but mockingly, *pocho*. (A Spanish dictionary defines that word as an adjective meaning "colorless" or "bland." But I heard it as a noun, naming the Mexican-American who, in becoming an American, forgets his native society.) "*¡Pocho!*" my mother's best friend muttered, shaking her head. And my mother laughed, somewhere behind me. She said that her children didn't want to practice "our Spanish" after they started going to school. My mother's smiling voice made me suspect that the lady who faced me was not really angry at me. But searching her face, I couldn't find the hint of a smile.

Embarrassed, my parents would often need to explain their children's inability to speak fluent Spanish during those years. My mother encountered the wrath of her brother, her only brother, when he came up from Mexico one summer with his family and saw his nieces and nephews for the very first time. After listening to me, he looked away and said what a disgrace it was that my siblings and I couldn't speak Spanish, "*su propria idioma.*" He made that remark to my mother, but I noticed that he stared at my father.

One other visitor from those years I clearly remember: a long-time friend of my father from San Francisco who came to stay with us for several days in late August. He took great interest in me after he realized that I couldn't answer his questions in Spanish. He would grab me, as I started to leave the kitchen. He would ask me something. Usually he wouldn't bother to wait for my mumbled response. Knowingly, he'd murmur, "*¿Ay pocho, pocho, donde vas?*" And he would press his thumbs into the upper part of my arms, making me squirm with pain. Dumbly

I'd stand there, waiting for his wife to notice us and call him off with a benign smile. I'd giggle, hoping to deflate the tension between us, pretending that I hadn't seen the glittering scorn in his glance.

I recount such incidents only because they suggest the fierce power that Spanish had over many people I met at home, how strongly Spanish was associated with closeness. Most of those people who called me a *pocho* could have spoken English to me, but many wouldn't. They seemed to think that Spanish was the only language we could use among ourselves, that Spanish alone permitted our association. (Such persons are always vulnerable to the ghetto merchant and the politician who have learned the value of speaking their clients' "family language" so as to gain immediate trust.) For my part, I felt that by learning English I had somehow committed a sin of betrayal. But betrayal against whom? Not exactly against the visitors to the house. Rather, I felt I had betrayed my immediate family. I knew that my parents had encouraged me to learn English. I knew that I had turned to English with angry reluctance. But once I spoke English with ease, I came to feel guilty. I sensed that I had broken the spell of intimacy which had once held the family so close together. It was this original sin against my family that I recalled whenever anyone addressed me in Spanish and I responded, confounded.

Yet even during those years of guilt, I was coming to grasp certain consoling truths about language and intimacy—truths that I learned gradually. Once, I remember playing with a friend in the backyard when my grandmother appeared at the window. Her face was stern with suspicion when she saw the boy (the *gringo* boy) I was with. She called out to me in Spanish, sounding the whistle of her ancient breath. My companion looked up and watched her intently as she lowered the window and moved (still visible) behind the light curtain, watching us both. He wanted to know what she had said. I started to tell him, to translate her Spanish words into English. The problem was, however, that though I knew how to translate exactly what she had told me, I realized that any translation would distort the deepest meaning of her message: it had been directed only to me. This message of intimacy could never be translated because it did not lie in the actual words she had used but passed through them. So any translation would have seemed wrong; the words would have been stripped of an essential meaning. Finally I decided not to tell my friend anything—just that I didn't hear all she had said.

This insight was unfolded in time. As I made more and more friends outside my house, I began to recognize intimate messages spoken in English in a close friend's confidential tone or secretive whisper. Even more remarkable were those instances when, apparently for no special reason, I'd become conscious of the fact that my companion was speaking *only to me.* I'd marvel then, just hearing his voice. It was a stunning event to be able to break through the barrier of public silence, to be able to hear the voice of the other, to realize that it was directed just to me. After such moments of intimacy outside the house, I began to trust what I heard intimately conveyed through my family's English. Voices at home at last punctured sad confusion. I'd hear myself addressed as an intimate—in English. Such moments were never as raucous with sound as in past times, when we had used our "private" Spanish. (Our English-sounding house was never to be as noisy as our Spanish-sounding house had been.) Intimate moments were usually moments of soft sound. My mother would be ironing in the dining room while I did my homework nearby. She would look over at me, smile, and her voice sounded to tell me that I was her son. *Richard.*

Intimacy thus continued at home; intimacy was not stilled by English. Though there were fewer occasions for it—a change in my life that I would never forget—there were also times when I sensed the deep truth about language and intimacy: *Intimacy is not created by a particular language; it is created by intimates.* Thus the great change in my life was not linguistic but social. If, after becoming a successful student, I no longer heard intimate voices as often as I had earlier, it was not because I spoke English instead of Spanish. It was because I spoke public language for most of my day. I moved easily at last, a citizen in a crowded city of words.

As a man I spend most of my day in public, in a world largely devoid of speech sounds. So I am quickly attracted by the glamorous quality of certain alien voices. I still am gripped with excitement when someone passes me on the street, speaking in Spanish. I have not moved beyond the range of the nostalgic pull of those sounds. And there is something very compelling about the sounds of lower-class blacks. Of all the accented versions of English that I hear in public, I hear theirs most intently. The Japanese tourist stops me downtown to ask me a question and I inch my way past his accent to concentrate on what he is saying. The eastern European immigrant in the neighborhood delicatessen speaks to me and, again, I do not pay much attention to his sounds, nor to the Texas accent of one of my neighbors or the Chicago accent of the woman who lives in the apartment below me. But when the ghetto black teenagers get on the city bus, I hear them. Their sounds in my society are the sounds of the outsider. Their voices annoy me for being so loud—so self-sufficient and unconcerned by my presence, but for the same reason they are glamorous: a romantic gesture against public acceptance. And as I listen to their shouted laughter, I realize my own quietness. I feel envious of them—envious of their brazen intimacy.

I warn myself away from such envy, however. Overhearing those teenagers, I think of the black political activists who lately have argued in favor of using black English in public schools—an argument that varies only slightly from that of foreign-language bilingualists. I have heard "radical" linguists make the point that black English is a complex and intricate version of English. And I do not doubt it. But neither do I think that black English should be a language of public instruction. What makes it inappropriate in classrooms is not something in the language itself but, rather, what lower-class speakers make of it. Just as Spanish would have been a dangerous language for me to have used at the start of my education, so black English would be a dangerous language to use in the schooling of teenagers for whom it reinforces feelings of public separateness.

This seems to me an obvious point to make, and yet it must be said. In recent years there have been many attempts to make the language of the alien a public language. "Bilingual education, two ways to understand..." television and radio commercials glibly announce. Propo-nents of bilingual education are careful to say that above all they want every student to acquire a good education. Their argument goes something like this: Children permitted to use their family language will not be so alienated and will be better able to match the progress of English-speaking students in the crucial first months of schooling. Increasingly confident of their ability, such children will be more inclined to apply themselves to their studies in the future. But then the bilingualists also claim another very different goal. They say that children who use their family language in school will retain a sense of their ethnic heritage and their family ties. Thus the support-ers of bilingual education want it both ways. They propose bilingual schooling as a way of helping students acquire the classroom skills crucial for public success. But they likewise insist that bilingual instruction will give students a sense of their identity apart from the English-speaking public.

Behind this scheme gleams a bright promise for the alien child: One can become a public person while still remaining a private person. Who would not want to believe such an appealing idea? Who can be surprised that the scheme has the support of so many middle-class ethnic Americans? If the barrio or ghetto child can retain his separateness even while being publicly educated, then it is almost possible to believe that no private cost need be paid for public success. This is the consolation offered by any of the number of current bilingual programs. Consider, for example, the bilingual voter's ballot. In some American cities one can cast a ballot printed in several languages. Such a document implies that it is possible for one to exercise that most public of rights—the right to vote—while still keeping oneself apart, unassimilated in public life.

It is not enough to say that such schemes are foolish and certainly doomed. Middle-class supporters of public bilingualism toy with the confusion of those Americans who cannot speak standard English as well as they do. Moreover, bilingual enthusiasts sin against intimacy. A Hispanic-American tells me, "I will never give up my family language," and he clutches a group of words as though they were the source of his family ties. He credits to language what he should credit to family members. This is a convenient mistake, for as long as he holds on to certain familiar words, he can ignore how much else has actually changed in his life.

It has happened before. In earlier decades, persons ambitious for social mobility, and newly successful, similarly seized upon certain "family words." Workingmen attempting to gain political power, for example, took to calling one another "brother." The word as they used it, however, could never resemble the word (the sound) "brother" exchanged by two people in intimate greeting. The context of its public delivery made it at best a metaphor; with repetition it was only a vague echo of the intimate sound. Context forced the change. Context could not be overruled. Context will always protect the realm of the intimate from public misuse. Today middle-class white Americans continue to prove the importance of context as they try to ignore it. They seize upon idioms of the black ghetto, but their attempt to appropriate such expressions invariably changes the meaning. As it becomes a public expression, the ghetto idiom loses its sound, its message of public separateness and strident intimacy. With public repetition it becomes a series of words, increasingly lifeless.

The mystery of intimate utterance remains. The communication of intimacy passes through the word and enlivens its sound, but it cannot be held by the word. It cannot be retained or ever quoted because it is too fluid. It depends not on words but on persons.

My grandmother! She stood among my other relations mocking me when I no longer spoke Spanish. *Pocho*, she said. But then it made no difference. She'd laugh, and our relationship continued because language was never its source. She was a woman in her eighties during the first decade of my life—a mysterious woman to me, my only living grandparent, a woman of Mexico in a long black dress that reached down to her shoes. She was the one relative of mine who spoke no word of English. She had no interest in gringo society and remained completely aloof from the public. She was protected by her daughters, protected even by me when we went to Safeway together and I needed to act as her translator. An eccentric woman. Hard. Soft.

When my family visited my aunt's house in San Francisco, my grandmother would search for me among my many cousins. When she found me, she'd chase them away. Pinching her granddaughters, she would warn them away from me. Then she'd take me to her room, where she had prepared for my coming. There would be a chair next to the bed, a dusty jellied candy nearby, and a copy of *Life en Español* for me to examine. "There," she'd say. And I'd sit content, a boy of eight. *Pocho*, her favorite. I'd sift through the pictures of earthquake-destroyed Latin-American cities and blonde-wigged Mexican movie stars. And all the while I'd listen to the sound of my grandmother's voice. She'd pace around the room, telling me stories of her life. Her past. They were stories so familiar that I couldn't remember when I'd heard them for the first time. I'd look up sometimes to listen. Other times she'd look over at me, but she never expected a response. Sometimes I'd smile or nod. (I understood exactly what she was saying.) But it never seemed to matter to her one way or the other. It was enough that I was there. The words she spoke were almost irrelevant to that fact. We were content. And the great mystery remained: intimate utterance.

I learn nothing about language and intimacy listening to those social activists who propose using one's family language in public life. I learn much more simply by listening to songs on a radio, or hearing a great voice at the opera, or overhearing the woman downstairs at an open window singing to herself. Singers celebrate the human voice. Their lyrics are words, but, animated by voice, those words are subsumed into sounds. (This suggests a central truth about language: All words are capable of becoming sounds as we fill them with the "music" of our life.) With excitement I hear the words yielding their enormous power to sound, even though their meaning is never totally obliterated. In most songs, the drama or tension results from the way that the singer moves between words (sense) and notes (song). At one moment the song simply "says" something; at another moment the voice stretches out the words and moves to the realm of pure sound. Most songs are about love: lost love, celebrations of loving, pleas. By simply being occasions when sounds soar through words, however, songs put me in mind of the most intimate moments of life.

Finally, among all types of music, I find songs created by lyric poets most compelling. On no other public occasion is sound so important for me. Written poems on a page seem at first glance a mere collection of words. And yet, without musical accompaniment, the poet leads me to hear the sounds of the words that I read. As song, a poem moves between the levels of sound and sense, never limited to one realm or the other. As a public artifact, the poem can never offer truly intimate sound, but it helps me to recall the intimate times of my life. As I read in my room, I grow deeply conscious of being alone, sounding my voice in search of another. The poem serves, then, as a memory device; it forces remembrance. And it refreshes; it reminds me of the possibility of escaping public words, the possibility that awaits me in intimate meetings.

The child reminds the adult: To seek intimate sounds is to seek the company of intimates. I do not expect to hear those sounds in public. I would dishonor those I have loved, and those I love now, to claim anything else. I would dishonor our intimacy by holding on to a particular language and calling it my family language. Intimacy cannot be trapped within words; it passes through words. It passes. Intimates leave the room. Doors close. Faces move away from the window. Time passes, and voices recede into the dark. Death finally quiets the voice. There is no way to deny it, no way to stand in the crowd claiming to utter one's family language.

The last time I saw my grandmother I was nine years old. I can tell you some of the things she said to me as I stood by her bed, but I cannot quote the message of intimacy she conveyed with her voice. She laughed, holding my hand. Her voice illumined disjointed memories as it passed them again. She remembered her husband—his green eyes, his magic name of Narcissio, his early death. She remembered the farm in Mexico, the eucalyptus trees nearby (their scent, she remembered, like incense). She remembered the family cow, the bell around its neck heard miles away. A dog. She remembered working as a seamstress, how she'd leave her daughters and son for long hours to go into Guadalajara to work. And how my mother would come running toward her in the sun—in her bright yellow dress—on her return. "MMMAAAAMMMMÁÁÁÁÁ," the old lady mimicked her daughter (my mother) to her daughter's son. She laughed. There was the snap of a cough. An aunt came into the room and told me it was time I should leave. "You can see her tomorrow," she promised. So I kissed my grandmother's cracked face. And the last thing I saw was her thin, oddly youthful thigh, as my aunt rearranged the sheet on the bed.

At the funeral parlor a few days after, I remember kneeling with my relatives during the rosary. Among their voices I traced, then lost, the sounds of individual aunts in the surge of the common prayer. And I heard at that moment what since I have heard very often—the sound the women in my family make when they are praying in sadness. When I went up to look at my grandmother, I saw her through the haze of a veil draped over the open lid of the casket. Her face looked calm—but distant and unyielding to love. It was not the face I remembered seeing most often. It was the face she made in public when the clerk at Safeway asked her some question and I would need to respond. It was her public face that the mortician had designed with his dubious art.

POSSIBILITIES FOR WRITING

1. Discuss the drawbacks and benefits for Rodriguez and his family as he makes the transition from using Spanish as his only language to giving English primacy. Consider how Rodriguez characterizes each language, along with the personal associations Spanish and English have for him.

2. Discuss Rodriguez's arguments against bilingual education—or at least against some forms of it, as he explains in this essay. Explain his reasons for opposing using students' native language and instead immersing them in English.

3. Write an essay about your own experience with language—particularly if you speak more than one. Reflect on experiences you have had at home, in school, or at work, in which your use(s) of language had important ramifications for you personally, and perhaps beyond yourself as well.

Judy Ruiz (b. 1944) *earned a Master of Fine Arts in poetry from the University of Arkansas in 1988, and she won an Arkansas Arts Fellowship shortly afterward. Ruiz has published poems in a wide variety of journals, with her first book of poems,* Talking Razzmatazz, *published in 1991. In addition to poetry, Ruiz has published nonfiction, which has been included in* Surviving Crisis (1997) *and* Connecting (1998). *"Oranges and Sweet Sister Boy" originally appeared in* Iowa Woman *magazine in 1988. It was included in* The Best American Essays (1989).

JUDY RUIZ

Oranges and Sweet Sister Boy

In "Oranges and Sweet Sister Boy," Judy Ruiz describes the sexual transformation of her brother. Ruiz explains her brother's emotional and psychological reasons for the sex change operation he chooses to undergo, and she includes the impact the transformation had on her and on other members of her family.

Ruiz pulls no punches in her essay in talking about herself, her brother, or her parents. She raises a series of questions about sexual identity that emerge out of her thinking about her brother's sexual identity and her own. And she shows how complicated it is to get our minds around a transformation of sexual identity by the challenges she confronts in what to call her brother after the operation and how to refer to him or her.

I am sleeping, hard, when the telephone rings. It's my brother, and he's calling to say that he is now my sister. I feel something fry a little, deep behind my eyes. Knowing how sometimes dreams get mixed up with not-dreams, I decide to do a reality test at once. "Let me get a cigarette," I say, knowing that if I reach for a Marlboro and it turns into a trombone or a snake or anything else on the way to my lips that I'm still out in the large world of dreams.

The cigarette stays a cigarette. I light it. I ask my brother to run that stuff by me again.

It is the Texas Zephyr at midnight—the woman in a white suit, the man in a blue uniform; she carries flowers—I know they are flowers. The petals spill and spill into the aisle, and a child goes past this couple who have just come from their own wedding—goes past them and past them, going always to the toilet but really just going past them; and the child could be a horse or she could be the police and they'd not notice her any more than they do, which is not at all—the man's hands high up on the woman's legs, her skirt up, her stockings and garters, the petals and finally all the flowers spilling out into the aisle and his

mouth open on her. My mother, My father, I am conceived near Dallas
in the dark white a child passes, a young girl who knows and doesn't
know, who witnesses, in glimpses, the creation of the universe, who
feels an odd hurt as her own mother, fat and empty, snores with her
mouth open, her false teeth slipping down, snores and snores just two
seats behind the Creators.

News can make a person stupid. It can make you think you can do
something. So I ask The Blade question, thinking that if he hasn't had
the operation yet that I can fly to him, rent a cabin out on Puget Sound.
That we can talk. That I can get him to touch base with reality.

"Begin with an orange," I would tell him. "Because oranges are
mildly intrusive by nature, put the orange somewhere so that it will not
bother you—in the cupboard, in a drawer, even a pocket or a handbag
will do. The orange, being a patient fruit, will wait for you much longer
than say a banana or a peach."

I would hold an orange out to him. I would say. "This is the one
that will save your life." And I would tell him about the woman I saw in
a bus station who bit right into her orange like it was an apple. She was
wild looking, as if she'd been outside for too long in a wind that blew
the same way all the time. One of the dregs of humanity, our mother
would have called her, the same mother who never brought fruit into
the house except in cans. My children used to ask me to "start" their
oranges for them. That meant to make a hole in the orange so they
could peel the rind away, and their small hands weren't equipped with
fingernails that were long enough or strong enough to do the job.
Sometimes they would suck the juice out of the hole my thumbnail
had made, leaving the orange flat and sad.

The earrings are as big as dessert plates, filigree gold-plated with thin
dangles hanging down that touch her bare shoulders. She stands in
front of the Alamo while a bald man takes her picture. The sun is
absorbed by the earrings so quickly that by the time she feels the heat,
it in too late. The hanging dangles make small blisters on her
shoulders, as if a centipede had traveled there. She takes the famous
river walk in spiked heels, rides in a boat, eats some Italian noodles,
returns to the motel room, soaks her feet, and applies small band-aids
to her toes. She is briefly concerned about the gun on the nightstand.
The toilet flushes. She pretends to be sleeping. The gun is just large and
heavy. A .45? A .357 magnum? She's never been good with names. She
hopes he doesn't try to. Or that if he does, that it's not loaded. But he'll

say it's loaded just for fun. Or he'll pull the trigger and the bullet will lodge in her medulla oblongata, ripping through her womb first, taking everything else vital on the way.

In the magazine articles, you don't see this: "Well, yes. The testicles have to come out. And yes. The penis is cut off." What you get is tonsils. So-and-so has had a "sex change" operation. A sex change operation. How precious. How benign. Doctor, just what do you people do with those penises?

News can make a person a little crazy also. News like, "We regret to inform you that you have failed your sanity hearing."

The bracelet on my wrist bears the necessary information about me, but there is one small error. The receptionist typing the information asked me my religious preference. I said, "None." She typed, "Neon."

Pearl doesn't have any teeth and her tongue looks weird. She says "Pumpkin pie." That's all she says. Sometimes she runs her hands over my bed sheets and says pumpkin pie. Sometimes I am under the sheets. Marsha got stabbed in the chest, but she tells everyone she fell on a knife. Elizabeth—she's the one who thinks her shoe is a baby—hit me in the back with a tray right after one of the cooks gave me extra toast. There's a note on the bulletin board about a class for the nurses: "How Putting A Towel On Someone's Face Makes Them Stop Banging Their Spoon/OR Reduction of Disruptive Mealtime Behavior By Facial Screening—7 P.M.—Conference Room." Another note announces the topic for remotivation class: "COWS." All the paranoid schizophrenics will be there.

Here, in the place for the permanently bewildered, I fit right in. Not because I stood at the window that first night and listened to the trains. Not because I imagined those trains were bracelets, the jewelry of earth. Not even because I imagined that one of those bracelets was on my own arm and was the Texas Zephyr where a young couple made love and conceived me. I am eighteen and beautiful and committed to the state hospital by a district court judge for a period of one day to life. Because I am a paranoid schizophrenic.

I will learn about cows.

So I'm being very quiet in the back of the classroom, and I'm peeling an orange. It's the smell that makes the others begin to turn around, that mildly intrusive nature. The course is called "Women and Modern Literature," and the diaries of Virginia Woolf are up for discussion except nobody has anything to say. I, of course, am making a mess with the orange; and I'm wanting to say that my brother is now my sister.

Later, with my hands still orangey, I wander in to leave something on a desk in a professor's office, and he's reading so I'm being very quiet, and then he says, sort of out of nowhere, "Emily Dickinson up there in her room making poems while her brother was making love to her best friend right downstairs on the dining room table. A regular thing. Think of it. And Walt Whitman out sniffing around the boys. Our two great American poets," And I want to grab this professor's arm and say, "Listen. My brother called me and now he's my sister, and I'm having trouble making sense out of my life right now, so would you mind not telling me any more stuff about sex." And I want my knuckles to turn white while the pressure of my fingers leaves imprints right through his jacket, little indentations he can interpret as urgent. But I don't say anything. And I don't grab his arm. I go read a magazine. I find this:

> *"I've never found an explanation for why the human race has so many languages. When the brain became a language brain, it obviously needed to develop an intense degree of plasticity. Such plasticity allows languages to be logical, coherent systems and yet be extremely variable. The same brain that thinks in words and symbols is also a brain that has to be freed up with regard to sexual turn-on and partnering. God knows why sex attitudes have not been subject to the corresponding degrees of modification and variety as language. I suspect there's a close parallel between the two. The brain doesn't seem incredibly efficient with regard to sex."*

John Money said that. The same John Money who, with surgeon Howard W. Jones, performed the first sex change operation in the United States in 1965 at Johns Hopkins University and Hospital in Baltimore.

Money also tells about the *hijra* of India who disgrace their families because they are too effeminate: "The ultimate stage of the *hijra* is to get up the courage to go through the amputation of penis and testicles. They had no anesthetic." Money also answers anyone who might think that "heartless members of the medical profession are forcing these poor darlings to go and get themselves cut up and mutilated," or who think the medical profession should leave them alone. "You'd have lots of patient willing to get a gun and blow off their own genitals if you don't do it. I've had several who got knives and cut themselves trying to get rid of their sex organs. That's their obsession!"

Perhaps better than all else, I understand obsession. It is of the mind. And it is language-bound. Sex is of the body. It has no words. I am stunned to learn that someone with an obsession of the mind can have parts of the body surgically removed. This is my brother I speak of. Thus is not some lunatic named Carl who becomes Carlene. This is my brother.

So while we're out in that cabin on Puget Sound, I'll tell him about LuAnn. She is the sort of woman who orders the in-season fruit and a little cottage cheese. I am the sort of woman who orders a double cheeseburger and fries. LuAnn and I are sitting in her car. She has a huge orange, and she peels it so the peel falls off in one neat strip. I have a sack of oranges, the small ones. The peel of my orange comes off in hunks about the size of a baby's nail. "Oh, you bought the *juice* oranges," LuAnn says to me. Her emphasis on the word "juice" makes me want to die or something. I lack the courage to admit my ignorance, so I smile and breathe "yes," as if I know some secret, when I'm wanting to scream at her about how my mother didn't teach me about fruit and my own blood pounds in my head wanting out, out.

There is a pattern to this thought as there is a pattern for a jumpsuit. Sew the sleeve to the leg, sew the leg to the collar. Put the garment on. Sew the mouth shut. This is how I tell about being quiet because I am bad, and because I cannot stand it when he beats me or my brother.

"The first time I got caught in your clothes was when I was four years old and you were over at Sarah what's-her-name's babysitting. Dad beat me so hard I thought I was going to die. I really thought I was going to die. That was the day I made up my mind I would *never* get caught again. And I never got caught again." My brother goes on to say he continued to go through my things until I was hospitalized. A mystery is solved.

He wore my clothes. He played in my makeup. I kept saying, back then, that someone was going through my stuff. I kept saying it and saying it. I told the counselor at school. "Someone goes in my room when I'm not there, and I *know* it—goes in there and wears my clothes and goes through my stuff." I was assured by the counselor that this was not so. I was assured by my mother that this was not so. I thought my mother was doing it, snooping around for clues like mothers do. It made me a little crazy, so I started deliberately leaving things in a certain order so that I would be able to prove to myself that someone, indeed, was going through my belongings. No one, not one person, ever believed that my room was being ransacked; I was accused of just making it up. A paranoid fixation.

And all the time it was old Goldilocks.

So I tell my brother to promise me he'll see someone who counsels adult children from dysfunctional families. I tell him he needs to deal with the fact that he was physically abused on a daily basis. He tells me he doesn't remember being beaten except on three occasions. He wants me to get into a support group for families of people who are having a sex change. Support groups are people who are in the same boat. Except no one has any oars in the water.

I tell him I know how it feels to think you are in the wrong body. I tell him how I wanted my boyfriend to put a gun up inside me and blow the woman out, how I thought wearing spiked heels and low-cut dresses would somehow help my crisis, that putting on an ultra-feminine outside would mask the maleness I felt needed hiding. I tell him it's the rule, rather than the exception, that people from families like ours have very spooky sexual identity problems. He tells me that his sexuality is a birth defect. I recognize the lingo. It's support-group-for-transsexuals lingo. He tells me he sits down to pee. He told his therapist that he used to wet all over the floor. His therapist said, "You can't aim the bullets if you don't touch the gun." Lingo. My brother is hell-bent for castration, the castration that started before he had language: the castration of abuse. He will simply finish what was set in motion long ago.

I will tell my brother about the time I took ten sacks of oranges into a school so that I could teach metaphor. The school was for special students—those who were socially or intellectually impaired. I had planned to have them peel the oranges as I spoke about how much the world is like the orange. I handed out the oranges. The students refused to peel them, not because they wanted to make life difficult for me— they were enchanted with the gift. One child asked if he could have an orange to take home to his little brother. Another said he would bring me ten dollars the next day if I would give him a sack of oranges. And I knew I was at home, that these children and I shared something that *makes* the leap of mind the metaphor attempts. And something in me healed.

A neighbor of mine takes pantyhose and cuts them up and sews them up after stuffing them. Then she puts these things into Mason jars and sells them, you know, to put out on the mantel for conversation. They are little penises and little scrotums, complete with hair. She calls them "Pickled Peters."

A friend of mine had a sister who had a sex change operation. This young woman had her breasts removed and ran around the house with no shirt on before the stitches were taken out. She answered the door one evening. A young man had come to call on my friend. The sex-changed sister invited him in and offered him some black bean soup as if she were perfectly normal with her red surgical wounds and her black stitches. The young man left and never went back. A couple years later, my friend's sister/brother died when s/he ran a car into a concrete bridge railing. I hope for a happier ending. For my brother, for myself, for all of us.

My brother calls. He's done his toenails: Shimmering Cinnamon. And he's left his wife and children and purchased some nightgowns at a yard sale. His hair is getting longer. He wears a special bra. Most of the people he works with know about the changes in his life. His voice is not the same voice I've heard for years; he sounds happy.

My brother calls. He's always envied me, my woman's body. The same body I live in and have cursed for its softness. He asks me how I feel about myself. He says, "You know, you are really our father's first-born son." He tells me he used to want to be me because I was the only person our father almost loved.

The drama of life. After I saw that woman in the bus station eat an orange as if it were an apple, I went out into the street and smoked a joint with some guy I'd met on the bus. Then I hailed a cab and went to a tattoo parlor. The tattoo artist tried to talk me into getting a nice bird or butterfly design; I had chosen a design on his wall that appealed to me—a symbol I didn't know the meaning of. It is the Yin-Yang, and it's tattooed above my right ankle bone. I supposed my drugged, crazed consciousness knew more than I knew: that yin combines with yang to produce all that comes to be. I am drawn to androgyny.

Of course there is the nagging possibility that my brother's dilemma is genetic. Our father used to dress in drag on Halloween, and he made a beautiful woman. One year, the year my mother cut my brother's blond curls off, my father taped those curls to his own head and tied a silk scarf over the tape. Even his close friends didn't know it was him. And my youngest daughter was a body builder for a while, her lean body as muscular as a man's. And my sons are beautiful, not handsome: they look androgynous.

Then there's my grandson. I saw him when he was less than an hour old. He was naked and had hiccups. I watched as he had his first bath, and I heard him cry. He had not been named yet, but his little crib had a blue card affixed to it with tape. And on the card were the words "Baby Boy." There was no doubt in me that the words were true.

When my brother was born, my father was off flying jets in Korea. I went to the hospital with my grandfather to get my mother and this new brother. I remember how I wanted a sister, and I remember looking at him as my mother held him in the front seat of the car. I was certain he was a sister, certain that my mother was joking. She removed his diaper to show me that he was a boy. I still didn't believe her. Considering what has happened lately, I wonder if my child-skewed consciouaness knew more than the anatomical proof suggested.

I try to make peace with myself. I try to understand his decision to alter himself. I try to think of him as her. I write his woman name, and I feel like I'm betraying myself. I try to be open-minded, but something in me shuts down. I think we humans are in big trouble, that many of us don't really have a clue as to what acceptable human behavior is. Something in me says no to all this, that this surgery business is the ultimate betrayal of the self. And yet, I want my brother to be happy.

It was in the city of San Antonio that my father had his surgery. I rode the bus from Kansas to Texas, and arrived at the hospital two days after the operation to find my father sitting in the solarium playing solitaire. He had a type of cancer that particularly thrived on testosterone. And so he was castrated in order to ease his pain and to stop the growth of tumors. He died six months later.

Back in the sleep of the large world of dreams, I have done surgeries under water in which I float my father's testicles back into him, and he—the brutal man he was—emerges from the pool a tan and smiling man, parting the surface of the water with his perfect head. He loves all the grief away.

I will tell my brother all I know of oranges, that if you squeeze the orange peel into a flame, small fires happen because of the volatile oil in the peel. Also, if you squeeze the peel and it gets into your cat's eyes, the cat will blink and blink. I will tell him there is no perfect rhyme for the word "orange," and that if we can just make up a good word we can be immortal. We will become obsessed with finding the right word, and I will be joyous at our legitimate pursuit.

I have purchased a black camisole with lace to send to my new sister. And a card. On the outside of the card there's a drawing of a woman sitting by a pond and a zebra is off to the left. Inside are these words: "The past is ended. Be happy." And I have asked my companions to hold me and I have cried. My self is wet and small. But it is not dark. Sometimes, if no one touches me, I will die.

Sister, you are the best craziness of the family. Brother, love what you love.

POSSIBILITIES FOR WRITING

1. Write a letter to Ruiz responding to her essay. Single out two or three sections in particular that interest you, puzzle you, shock or astonish you, or otherwise engage you.
2. Describe your experience of reading Ruiz's essay. How did you respond to the first two sentences? The first two paragraphs? The ending? Did your feelings or reactions change during your reading?
3. Write an essay about your sexual identity. What does it mean for you to be a man or woman? Identify a few key features of masculinity and/or femininity, as you understand them, and perhaps experience them.

Nicola Sacco (1891–1927) was an Italian immigrant shoemaker from Italy. His name is forever linked with that of Bartolomeo Vanzetti (1888–1927), who, like Sacco, was an Italian-American anarchist who was arrested, tried, convicted, and executed in Massachusetts. Sacco and Vanzetti were accused of murdering two people at a shoe factory and with stealing a little more than $15,700. Many historians believe that Sacco and Vanzetti were denied their civil liberties and that they were victims of anti-Italian prejudice. Their case, which has been debated for more than three quarters of a century, inspired and influenced many writers and artists, such as novelist Upton Sinclair, poet Carl Sandburg, playwright Maxwell Anderson, film director Giuliano Montaldo, and folksingers Pete Seeger and Woody Guthrie, who set to music some words from one of Sacco's letters to his son, Dante.

NICOLA SACCO

Letter to His Son

In "Letter to His Son," Nicola Sacco writes to his son, Dante, just before being executed. His letter is eloquent in its simplicity and emotionally stirring even though its English is less than perfect. Sacco gives advice to his son about what to value in life and about how to live, especially about how to be strong in the face of adversity and to help the weak and the powerless. On one hand, Sacco wants his son to understand the sacrifices made by Sacco and his comrades in the opposition movement; on the other hand, Sacco wants his son to appreciate how as a father he misses a normal family life with his son, his daughter, and his wife.

August 18, 1927. Charlestown State Prison

My Dear Son and Companion:

Since the day I saw you last I had always the idea to write you this letter, but the length of my hunger strike and the thought I might not be able to explain myself, made me put it off all this time.

The other day, I ended my hunger strike and just as soon as I did that I thought of you to write to you, but I find that I did not have enough strength and I cannot finish it at one time. However, I want to get it down in any way before they take us again to the death-house, because it is my conviction that just as soon as the court refuses a new trial to us they will take us there. And between Friday and Monday, if nothing happens, they will electrocute us right after midnight, on August 22nd. Therefore, here I am, right with you with love and with open heart as ever I was yesterday.

I never thought that our inseparable life could be separated, but the thought of seven dolorous years makes it seem it did come, but then it has not changed really the unrest and the heart-beat of affection. That has remained as it was. More, I say that our ineffable affection reciprocal, is today more than any other time, of course. That is not only a great deal but it is grand because you can see the real brotherly love, not only in joy but also and more in the struggle of suffering. Remember this, Dante. We have demonstrated this, and modesty apart, we are proud of it.

Much we have suffered during this long Calvary. We protest today as we protested yesterday. We protest always for our freedom.

If I stopped hunger strike the other day, it was because there was no more sign of life in me. Because I protested with my hunger strike yesterday as today I protest for life and not for death.

I sacrificed because I wanted to come back to the embrace of your dear little sister Ines and your mother and all the beloved friends and comrades of life and not death. So Son, today life begins to revive slow and calm, but yet without horizon and always with sadness and visions of death.

Well, my dear boy, after your mother had talked to me so much and I had dreamed of you day and night, how joyful it was to see you at last. To have talked with you like we used to in the days—in those days. Much I told you on that visit and more I wanted to say, but I saw that you will remain the same affectionate boy, faithful to your mother who loves you so much, and I did not want to hurt your sensibilities any longer, because I am sure that you will continue to be the same boy and remember what I have told you. I knew that and what here I am going to tell you will touch your sensibilities, but don't cry Dante, because many tears have been wasted, as your mother's have been wasted for seven years, and never did any good. So, Son, instead of crying, be strong, so as to be able to comfort your mother, and when you want to distract your mother from the discouraging soulness, I will tell you what I used to do. To take her for a long walk in the quiet country, gathering wild flowers here and there, resting under the shade of trees, between the harmony of the vivid stream and the gentle tranquility of the mothernature, and I am sure that she will enjoy this very much, as you surely would be happy for it. But remember always, Dante, in the play of happiness, don't you use all for yourself only, but down yourself just one step, at your side and help the weak ones that cry for help, help the prosecuted and the victim, because they are your better friends; they are the comrades that fight and fall as your father and Bartolo fought and fell yesterday for the conquest of the joy of freedom for all and the poor workers. In this struggle of life you will find more love and you will be loved.

I am sure that from what your mother told me about what you said during these last terrible days when I was lying in the iniquitous death-house—that description gave me happiness because it showed you will be the beloved boy I had always dreamed.

Therefore whatever should happen tomorrow, nobody knows, but if they should kill us, you must not forget to look at your friends and comrades with the smiling gaze of gratitude as you look at your beloved ones, because they love you as they love every one of the fallen persecuted comrades. I tell you, your father that is all the life to you, your father that loved you and saw them, and knows their noble faith (that is mine) their supreme sacrifice that they are still doing for our freedom, for I have fought with them, and they are the ones that still hold the last of our hope that today they can still save us from electrocution, it is the struggle and fight between the rich and the poor for safety and freedom, Son, which you will understand in the future of your years to come, of this unrest and struggle of life's death.

Much I thought of you when I was lying in the death-house—the singing, the kind tender voices of the children from the playground, where there was all the life and the joy of liberty—just one step from the wall which contains the buried agony of three buried souls. It would remind me so often of you and your sister Ines, and I wish I could see you every moment. But I feel better that you did not come to the death-house so that you could not see the horrible picture of three lying in agony waiting to be electrocuted, because I do not know what effect it would have on your young age. But then, in another way if you were not so sensitive it would be very useful to you tomorrow when you could use this horrible memory to hold up to the world the shame of the country in this cruel persecution and unjust death. Yes, Dante, they can crucify our bodies today as they are doing, but they cannot destroy our ideas, that will remain for the youth of the future to come.

Dante, when I said three human lives buried, I meant to say that with us there is another young man by the name of Celestino Maderios that is to be electrocuted at the same time with us. He has been twice before in that horrible death-house, that should be destroyed with the hammers of real progress—that horrible house that will shame forever the future of the citizens of Massachusetts. They should destroy that house and put up a factory or school, to teach many of the hundreds of the poor orphan boys of the world.

Dante, I say once more to love and be nearest to your mother and the beloved ones in these sad days, and I am sure that with your brave heart and kind goodness they will feel less discomfort. And you will also not forget to love me a little for I do—O, Sonny! thinking so much and so often of you.

Best fraternal greetings to all the beloved ones, love and kisses to your little Ines and mother. Most hearty affectionate embrace.

Your Father and Companion
Nicola Sacco

POSSIBILITIES FOR WRITING

1. Write a personal response to Nicola Sacco's letter to his son. How do you respond to what Sacco says to his son in this letter? Single out one or two moments for special consideration.
2. Compare Sacco's letter to his son, Dante, with that of Lord Chesterfield to his son, Philip (pp. 118–119). What kind of relationship does each father seem to have with his son, as evidenced by the details of their respective letters?
3. Write a letter to someone important in your life—a child, parent, sibling, grandparent, or other relative—or to a friend. Use your letter to give advice about what you think is important for the future.

Scott Russell Sanders (b. 1945) *was born into a working class family in Memphis and received scholarships to Brown and to Cambridge University in England. He has published books in many genres: novels, poetry, children's stories, science fiction, nature writing, and personal essays. These essays, noted for their sincerity and subtle grace, have been collected in* The Paradise of Bombs (1988), Secrets of the Universe (1991), *and* Writing from the Center (1995), *among others. Among Sanders latest books for adult readers are* A Private History of Awe (2006), *and* A Conservationist Manifesto (2009). *He is a professor of English and creative writing at Indiana University.*

SCOTT RUSSELL SANDERS

Under the Influence

In "Under the Influence," Scott Russell Sanders explains why he doesn't drink alcohol. Sanders's title refers to the influence that alcohol had on his father, who drank heavily, nearly constantly, and whose drinking not only harmed his family, but also left an indelible impression on his son. Sanders describes the self-deception his father engaged in along with the deception of others, who played along and pretended with him that his drinking was not a serious problem either for him or for them. And Sanders describes unflinchingly what he calls "the corrosive mixture of helplessness, responsibility, and shame" that he felt "as the son of an alcoholic."

Sanders's essay, however, is not only about his father. It is also about himself—about how, in important ways, he remains "under the influence" of his father. Not as a drinker, since he only "sips warily," drinking perhaps a glass of wine or beer a week—nothing more and nothing stronger. Sanders drinks little alcohol and drinks warily out of fear and out of knowledge, a knowledge and a fear that as the child of an alcoholic he is four times more likely than others to become an alcoholic himself.

My father drank. He drank as a gut-punched boxer gasps for breath, as a starving dog gobbles food—compulsively, secretly, in pain and trembling. I use the past tense not because he ever quit drinking but because he quit living. That is how the story ends for my father, age sixty-four, heart bursting, body cooling and forsaken on the linoleum of my brother's trailer. The story continues for my brother, my sister, my mother, and me, and will continue so long as memory holds.

In the perennial present of memory, I slip into the garage or barn to see my father tipping back the flat green bottles of wine, the brown cylinders of whiskey, the cans of beer disguised in paper bags. His Adam's apple bobs, the liquid gurgles, he wipes the sandy-haired back of a hand over his lips, and then, his bloodshot gaze bumping into me, he stashes the bottle or can inside his jacket, under the workbench, between two bales of hay, and we both pretend the moment has not occurred.

"What's up, buddy?" he says, thick-tongued and edgy.

"Sky's up," I answer, playing along.

"And don't forget prices," he grumbles. "Prices are always up. And taxes."

In memory, his white 1951 Pontiac with the stripes down the hood and the Indian head on the snout jounces to a stop in the driveway; or it is the 1956 Ford station wagon, or the 1963 Rambler shaped like a toad, or the sleek 1969 Bonneville that will do 120 miles per hour on straightaways; or it is the robin's-egg blue pickup, new in 1980, battered in 1981, the year of his death. He climbs out, grinning dangerously, unsteady on his legs, and we children interrupt our game of catch, our building of snow forts, our picking of plums, to watch in silence as he weaves past into the house, where he slumps into his overstuffed chair and falls asleep. Shaking her head, our mother stubs out the cigarette he has left smoldering in the ashtray. All evening, until our bedtimes, we tiptoe past him, as past a snoring dragon. Then we curl in our fearful sheets, listening. Eventually he wakes with a grunt, Mother slings accusations at him, he snarls back, she yells, he growls, their voices clashing. Before long, she retreats to their bedroom, sobbing—not from the blows of fists, for he never strikes her, but from the force of words.

Left alone, our father prowls the house, thumping into furniture, rummaging in the kitchen, slamming doors, turning the pages of the newspaper with a savage crackle, muttering back at the late-night drivel from television. The roof might fly off, the walls might buckle from the pressure of his rage. Whatever my brother and sister and mother may be thinking on their own rumpled pillows, I lie there hating him, loving him, fearing him, knowing I have failed him. I tell myself he drinks to ease an ache that gnaws at his belly, an ache I must have caused by disappointing him somehow, a murderous ache I should be able to relieve by doing all my chores, earning A's in school, winning baseball games, fixing the broken washer and the burst pipes, bringing in money to fill his empty wallet. He would not hide the green bottles in his tool box, would not sneak off to the barn with a lump under his coat, would not fall asleep in the daylight, would not roar and fume, would not drink himself to death, if only I were perfect.

I am forty-two as I write these words, and I know full well now that my father was an alcoholic, a man consumed by disease rather than by disappointment. What had seemed to me a private grief is in fact a public scourge. In the United States alone some ten or fifteen million people share his ailment, and behind the doors they slam in fury or disgrace, countless other children tremble. I comfort myself with such knowledge, holding it against the throb of memory like an ice pack against a bruise. There are keener sources of grief: poverty, racism, rape, war. I do not wish to compete for a trophy in suffering. I am only trying to understand the corrosive mixture of helplessness, responsibility, and shame that I learned to feel as the son of an alcoholic. I realize now that I did not cause my father's illness, nor could I have cured it. Yet for all this grown-up knowledge, I am still ten years old, my own son's age, and as that boy I struggle in guilt and confusion to save my father from pain.

Consider a few of our synonyms for *drunk*: tipsy, tight, pickled, soused, and plowed; stoned and stewed, lubricated and inebriated, juiced and sluiced; three sheets to the wind, in your cups, out of your mind, under the table; lit up, tanked up, wiped out; besotted, blotto, bombed, and buzzed; plastered, polluted, putrified; loaded or looped, boozy, woozy, fuddled, or smashed; crocked and shit-faced, corked and pissed, snockered and sloshed.

It is a mostly humorous lexicon, as the lore that deals with drunks—in jokes and cartoons, in plays, films, and television skits—is largely comic. Aunt Matilda nips elderberry wine from the sideboard and burps politely during supper. Uncle Fred slouches to the table glassy-eyed, wearing a lamp shade for a hat and murmuring, "Candy is dandy but liquor is quicker." Inspired by cocktails, Mrs. Somebody recounts the events of her day in a fuzzy dialect, while Mr. Somebody nibbles her ear and croons a bawdy song. On the sofa with Boyfriend, Daughter giggles, licking gin from her lips, and loosens the bows in her hair. Junior knocks back some brews with his chums at the Leopard Lounge and stumbles home to the wrong house, wonders foggily why he cannot locate his pajamas, and crawls naked into bed with the ugliest girl in school. The family dog slurps from a neglected martini and wobbles to the nursery, where he vomits in Baby's shoe.

It is all great fun. But if in the audience you notice a few laughing faces turn grim when the drunk lurches on stage, don't be surprised, for these are the children of alcoholics. Over the grinning mask of Dionysus, the leering mask of Bacchus, these children cannot help seeing the bloated features of their own parents. Instead of laughing, they wince, they mourn. Instead of celebrating the drunk as one freed from constraints, they pity him as one enslaved. They refuse to believe *in vino veritas*, having seen their befuddled parents skid away from truth toward folly and oblivion. And so these children bite their lips until the lush staggers into the wings.

My father, when drunk, was neither funny nor honest; he was pathetic, frightening, deceitful. There seemed to be a leak in him somewhere, and he poured in booze to keep from draining dry. Like a torture victim who refuses to squeal, he would never admit that he had touched a drop, not even in his last year, when he seemed to be dissolving in alcohol before our very eyes. I never knew him to lie about anything, ever, except about this one ruinous fact. Drowsy, clumsy, unable to fix a bicycle tire, throw a baseball, balance a grocery sack, or walk across the room, he was stripped of his true self by drink. In a matter of minutes, the contents of a bottle could transform a brave man into a coward, a buddy into a bully, a gifted athlete and skilled carpenter and shrewd businessman into a bumbler. No dictionary of synonyms for *drunk* would soften the anguish of watching our prince turn into a frog.

Father's drinking became the family secret. While growing up, we children never breathed a word of it beyond the four walls of our house. To this day, my brother and sister rarely mention it, and then only when I press them. I did not confess the ugly, bewildering fact to my wife until his wavering walk and slurred speech forced me to. Recently, on the seventh anniversary of my father's death, I asked my mother if she ever spoke of his drinking to friends. "No, no, never," she replied hastily. "I couldn't bear for anyone to know."

The secret bores under the skin, gets in the blood, into the bone, and stays there. Long after you have supposedly been cured of malaria, the fever can flare up, the tremors can shake you. So it is with the fevers of shame. You swallow the bitter quinine of knowledge, and you learn to feel pity and compassion toward the drinker. Yet the shame lingers in your marrow, and, because of the shame, anger.

For a long stretch of my childhood we lived on a military reservation in Ohio, an arsenal where bombs were stored underground in bunkers, vintage airplanes burst into flames, and unstable artillery shells boomed nightly at the dump. We had the feeling, as children, that we played in a mine field, where a heedless footfall could trigger an explosion. When Father was drinking, the house, too, became a mine field. The least bump could set off either parent.

The more he drank, the more obsessed Mother became with stopping him. She hunted for bottles, counted the cash in his wallet, sniffed at his breath. Without meaning to snoop, we children blundered left and right into damning evidence. On afternoons when he came home from work sober, we flung ourselves at him for hugs, and felt against our ribs the telltale lump in his coat. In the barn we tumbled on the hay and heard beneath our sneakers the crunch of buried glass. We tugged open a drawer in his workbench, looking for screwdrivers or crescent wrenches, and spied a gleaming six-pack among the tools. Playing tag, we darted around the house just in time to see him sway on the rear stoop and heave a finished bottle into the woods. In his good night kiss we smelled the cloying sweetness of Clorets, the mints he chewed to camouflage his dragon's breath.

I can summon up that kiss right now by recalling Theodore Roethke's lines about his own father in "My Papa's Waltz":

> The whiskey on your breath
> Could make a small boy dizzy;
> But I hung on like death:
> Such waltzing was not easy.

Such waltzing was hard, terribly hard, for with a boy's scrawny arms I was trying to hold my tipsy father upright.

For years, the chief source of those incriminating bottles and cans was a grimy store a mile from us, a cinder block place called Sly's, with two gas pumps outside and a moth-eaten dog asleep in the window. A strip of flypaper, speckled the year round with black bodies, coiled in the doorway. Inside, on rusty metal shelves or in wheezing coolers, you could find pop and Popsicles, cigarettes, potato chips, canned soup, raunchy postcards, fishing gear, Twinkies, wine, and beer. When Father drove anywhere on errands, Mother would send us kids along as guards, warning us not to let him out of our sight. And so with one or more of us on board, Father would cruise up to Sly's, pump a dollar's worth of gas or pump the tires with air, and then, telling us to wait in the car, he would head for that fly-spangled doorway.

Dutiful and panicky, we cried, "Let us go in with you!"

"No," he answered. "I'll be back in two shakes."

"Please!"

"No!" he roared. "Don't you budge, or I'll jerk a knot in your tails!"

So we stayed put, kicking the seats, while he ducked inside. Often, when he had parked the car at a careless angle, we gazed in through the window and saw Mr. Sly fetching down from a shelf behind the cash register two green pints of Gallo wine. Father swigged one of them right there at the counter, stuffed the other in his pocket, and then out he came, a bulge in his coat, a flustered look on his red face.

Because the Mom and Pop who ran the dump were neighbors of ours, living just down the tar-blistered road, I hated them all the more for poisoning my father. I wanted to sneak in their store and smash the bottles and set fire to the place. I also hated the Gallo brothers, Ernest and Julio, whose jovial faces shone from the labels of their wine, labels I would find, torn and curled, when I burned the trash. I noted the Gallo brothers' address, in California, and I studied the road atlas to see how far that was from Ohio, because I meant to go out there and tell Ernest and Julio what they were doing to my father, and then, if they showed no mercy, I would kill them.

While growing up on the back roads and in the country schools and cramped Methodist churches of Ohio and Tennessee, I never heard the word *alcoholism*, never happened across it in books or magazines. In the nearby towns, there were no addiction treatment programs, no community mental health centers, no Alcoholics Anonymous chapters, no therapists. Left alone with our grievous secret, we had no way of understanding Father's drinking except as an act of will, a deliberate folly or cruelty, a moral weakness, a sin. He drank because he chose to, pure and simple. Why our father, so playful and competent and kind when sober, would choose to ruin himself and punish his family, we could not fathom.

Our neighborhood was high on the Bible, and the Bible was hard on drunkards. "Woe to those who are heroes at drinking wine, and valiant men in mixing strong drink," wrote Isaiah. "The priest and the prophet reel with strong drink, they are confused with wine, they err in vision, they stumble in giving judgment. For all tables are full of vomit, no place is without filthiness." We children had seen those fouled tables at the local truck stop where the notorious boozers hung out, our father occasionally among them. "Wine and new wine take away the understanding," declared the prophet Hosea. We had also seen evidence of that in our father, who could multiply seven-digit numbers in his head when sober, but when drunk could not help us with fourth-grade math. Proverbs warned: "Do not look at wine when it is red, when it sparkles in the cup and goes down smoothly. At the last it bites like a serpent, and stings like an adder. Your eyes will see strange things, and your mind utter perverse things." Woe, woe.

Dismayingly often, these biblical drunkards stirred up trouble for their own kids. Noah made fresh wine after the flood, drank too much of it, fell asleep without any clothes on, and was glimpsed in the buff by his son Ham, whom Noah promptly cursed. In one passage—it was so shocking we had to read it under our blankets with flashlights—the patriarch Lot fell down drunk and slept with his daughters. The sins of the fathers set their children's teeth on edge.

Our ministers were fond of quoting St. Paul's pronouncement that drunkards would not inherit the kingdom of God. These grave preachers assured us that the wine referred to during the Last Supper was in fact grape juice. Bible and sermons and hymns combined to give us the impression that Moses should have brought down from the mountain another stone tablet, bearing the Eleventh Commandment: Thou shalt not drink.

The scariest and most illuminating Bible story apropos of drunkards was the one about the lunatic and the swine. Matthew, Mark, and Luke each told a version of the tale. We knew it by heart: When Jesus climbed out of his boat one day, this lunatic came charging up from the graveyard, stark naked and filthy, frothing at the mouth, so violent that he broke the strongest chains. Nobody would go near him. Night and day for years this madman had been wailing among the tombs and bruising himself with stones. Jesus took one look at him and said, "Come out of the man, you unclean spirits!" for he could see that the lunatic was possessed by demons. Meanwhile, some hogs were conveniently rooting nearby. "If we have to come out," begged the demons, "at least let us go into those swine." Jesus agreed. The unclean spirits entered the hogs, and the hogs rushed straight off a cliff and plunged into a lake. Hearing the story in Sunday school, my friends thought mainly of the pigs. (How big a splash did they make? Who paid for the lost pork?) But I thought of the redeemed lunatic, who bathed himself and put on clothes and calmly sat at the feet of Jesus, restored—so the Bible said—to "his right mind."

When drunk, our father was clearly in his wrong mind. He became a stranger, as fearful to us as any graveyard lunatic, not quite frothing at the mouth but fierce enough, quick-tempered, explosive; or else he grew maudlin and weepy, which frightened us nearly as much. In my boyhood despair, I reasoned that maybe he wasn't to blame for turning into an ogre. Maybe, like the lunatic, he was possessed by demons.

I found support for my theory when I heard liquor referred to as "spirits," when the newspapers reported that somebody had been arrested for "driving under the influence," and when church ladies railed against that "demon drink."

If my father was indeed possessed, who would exorcise him? If he was a sinner, who would save him? If he was ill, who would cure him? If he suffered, who would ease his pain? Not ministers or doctors, for we could not bring ourselves to confide in them; not the neighbors, for we pretended they had never seen him drunk; not Mother, who fussed and pleaded but could not budge him; not my brother and sister, who were only kids. That left me. It did not matter that I, too, was only a child, and a bewildered one at that. I could not excuse myself.

On first reading a description of delirium tremens—in a book on alcoholism I smuggled from the library—I thought immediately of the frothing lunatic and the frenzied swine. When I read stories or watched films about grisly metamorphoses—Dr. Jekyll becoming Mr. Hyde, the mild husband changing into a werewolf, the kindly neighbor taken over by a brutal alien—I could not help seeing my own father's mutation from sober to drunk. Even today, knowing better, I am attracted by the demonic theory of drink, for when I recall my father's transformation, the emergence of his ugly second self, I find it easy to believe in possession by unclean spirits. We never knew which version of Father would come home from work, the true or the tainted, nor could we guess how far down the slope toward cruelty he would slide.

How far a man *could* slide we gauged by observing our back-road neighbors—the out-of-work miners who had dragged their families to our corner of Ohio from the desolate hollows of Appalachia, the tight-fisted farmers, the surly mechanics, the balked and broken men. There was, for example, whiskey-soaked Mr. Jenkins, who beat his wife and kids so hard we could hear their screams from the road. There was Mr. Lavo the wino, who fell asleep smoking time and again, until one night his disgusted wife bundled up the children and went outside and left him in his easy chair to burn; he awoke on his own, staggered out coughing into the yard, and pounded her flat while the children looked on and the shack turned to ash. There was the truck driver, Mr. Sampson, who tripped over his son's tricycle one night while drunk and got so mad that he jumped into his semi and drove away, shifting through the dozen gears, and never came back. We saw the bruised children of these fathers clump onto our school bus, we saw the abandoned children huddle in the pews at church, we saw the stunned and battered mothers begging for help at our doors.

Our own father never beat us, and I don't think he ever beat Mother, but he threatened often. The Old Testament Yahweh was not more terrible in his wrath. Eyes blazing, voice booming, Father would pull out his belt and swear to give us a whipping, but he never followed through, never needed to, because we could imagine it so vividly. He shoved us, pawed us with the back of his hand, as an irked bear might smack a cub, not to injure, just to clear a space. I can see him grabbing Mother by the hair as she cowers on a chair during a nightly quarrel. He twists her neck back until she gapes up at him, and then he lifts over her skull a glass quart bottle of milk, the milk running down his forearm, and he yells at her, "Say just one more word, one goddamn word, and I'll shut you up!" I fear she will prick him with her sharp tongue, but she is terrified into silence, and so am I, and the leaking bottle quivers in the air, and milk slithers through the red hair of my father's uplifted arm, and the entire scene is there to this moment, the head jerked back, the club raised.

When the drink made him weepy, Father would pack a bag and kiss each of us children on the head, and announce from the front door that he was moving out. "Where to?" we demanded, fearful each time that he would leave for good, as Mr. Sampson had roared away for good in his diesel truck. "Someplace where I won't get hounded every minute," Father would answer, his jaw quivering. He stabbed a look at Mother, who might say, "Don't run into the ditch before you get there," or, "Good riddance," and then he would slink away. Mother watched him go with arms crossed over her chest, her face closed like the lid on a box of snakes. We children bawled. Where could he go? To the truck stop, that den of iniquity? To one of those dark, ratty flophouses in town? Would he wind up sleeping under a railroad bridge or on a park bench or in a cardboard box, mummied in rags, like the bums we had seen on our trips to Cleveland and Chicago? We bawled and bawled, wondering if he would ever come back.

He always did come back, a day or a week later, but each time there was a sliver less of him.

In Kafka's *The Metamorphosis*, which opens famously with Gregor Samsa waking up from uneasy dreams to find himself transformed into an insect, Gregor's family keep reassuring themselves that things will be just fine again, "When he comes back to us." Each time alcohol transformed our father, we held out the same hope, that he would really and truly come back to us, our authentic father, the tender and playful and competent man, and then all things would be fine. We had grounds for such hope. After his weepy departures and chapfallen returns, he would sometimes go weeks, even months without drinking. Those were glad times. Joy banged inside my ribs. Every day without the furtive glint of bottles, every meal without a fight, every bedtime without sobs encouraged us to believe that such bliss might go on forever.

Mother was fooled by just such a hope all during the forty-odd years she knew this Greeley Ray Sanders. Soon after she met him in a Chicago delicatessen on the eve of World War II, and fell for his butter-melting Mississippi drawl and his wavy red hair, she learned that he drank heavily. But then so did a lot of men. She would soon coax or scold him into breaking the nasty habit. She would point out to him how ugly and foolish it was, this bleary drinking, and then he would quit. He refused to quit during their engagement, however, still refused during the first years of marriage, refused until my sister came along. The shock of fatherhood sobered him, and he remained sober through my birth at the end of the war and right on through until we moved in 1951 to the Ohio arsenal, that paradise of bombs. Like all places that make a business of death, the arsenal had more than its share of alcoholics and drug addicts and other varieties of escape artists. There I turned six and started school and woke into a child's flickering awareness, just in time to see my father begin sneaking swigs in the garage.

He sobered up again for most of a year at the height of the Korean War, to celebrate the birth of my brother. But aside from that dry spell, his only breaks from drinking before I graduated from high school were just long enough to raise and then dash our hopes. Then during the fall of my senior year—the time of the Cuban missile crisis, when it seemed that the nightly explosions at the munitions dump and the nightly rages in our household might spread to engulf the globe—Father collapsed. His liver, kidneys, and heart all conked out. The doctors saved him, but only by a hair. He stayed in the hospital for weeks, going through a withdrawal so terrible that Mother would not let us visit him. If he wanted to kill himself, the doctors solemnly warned him, all he had to do was hit the bottle again. One binge would finish him.

Father must have believed them, for he stayed dry the next fifteen years. It was an answer to prayer, Mother said, it was a miracle. I believe it was a reflex of fear, which he sustained over the years through courage and pride. He knew a man could die from drink, for his brother Roscoe had. We children never laid eyes on doomed Uncle Roscoe, but in the stories Mother told us he became a fairy-tale figure, like a boy who took the wrong turning in the woods and was gobbled up by the wolf.

The fifteen-year dry spell came to an end with Father's retirement in the spring of 1978. Like many men, he gave up his identity along with his job. One day he was a boss at the factory, with a brass plate on his door and a reputation to uphold; the next day he was a nobody at home. He and Mother were leaving Ontario, the last of the many places to which his job had carried them, and they were moving to a new house in Mississippi, his childhood stomping grounds. As a boy in Mississippi, Father sold Coca-Cola during dances while the moonshiners peddled their brew in the parking lot; as a young blade, he fought in bars and in the ring, seeking a state Golden Gloves championship; he gambled at poker, hunted pheasants, raced motorcycles and cars, played semiprofessional baseball, and, along with all his buddies—in the Black Cat Saloon, behind the cotton gin, in the wood—he drank. It was a perilous youth to dream of recovering.

After his final day of work, Mother drove on ahead with a car full of begonias and violets, while Father stayed behind to oversee the packing. When the van was loaded, the sweaty movers broke open a six-pack and offered him a beer.

"Let's drink to retirement!" they crowed. "Let's drink to freedom! to fishing! hunting! loafing! Let's drink to a guy who's going home!"

At least I imagine some such words, for that is all I can do, imagine, and I see Father's hand trembling in midair as he thinks about the fifteen sober years and about the doctors' warning, and he tells himself *Goddamnit, I am a free man,* and *Why can't a free man drink one beer after a lifetime of hard work?* and I see his arm reaching, his fingers closing, the can tilting to his lips. I even supply a label for the beer, a swaggering brand that promises on television to deliver the essence of life. I watch the amber liquid pour down his throat, the alcohol steal into his blood, the key turn in his brain.

Soon after my parents moved back to Father's treacherous stomping ground, my wife and I visited them in Mississippi with our five-year-old daughter. Mother had been too distraught to warn me about the return of the demons. So when I climbed out of the car that bright July morning and saw my father napping in the hammock, I felt uneasy, for in all his sober years I had never known him to sleep in daylight. Then he lurched upright, blinked his bloodshot eyes, and greeted us in a syrupy voice. I was hurled back helpless into childhood.

"What's the matter with Papaw?" our daughter asked.

"Nothing," I said. "Nothing!"

Like a child again, I pretended not to see him in his stupor, and behind my phony smile I grieved. On that visit and on the few that remained before his death, once again I found bottles in the work-bench, bottles in the woods. Again his hands shook too much for him to run a saw, to make his precious miniature furniture, to drive straight down back roads. Again he wound up in the ditch, in the hospital, in jail, in treatment centers. Again he shouted and wept. Again he lied. "I never touched a drop," he swore. "Your mother's making it up."

I no longer fancied I could reason with the men whose names I found on the bottles—Jim Beam, Jack Daniels—nor did I hope to save my father by burning down a store. I was able now to press the cold statistics about alcoholism against the ache of memory: ten million victims, fifteen million, twenty. And yet, in spite of my age, I reacted in the same blind way as I had in childhood, ignoring biology, forgetting numbers, vainly seeking to erase through my efforts whatever drove him to drink. I worked on their place twelve and sixteen hours a day, in the swelter of Mississippi summers, digging ditches, running electrical wires, planting trees, mowing grass, building sheds, as though what nagged at him was some list of chores, as though by taking his worries on my shoulders I could redeem him. I was flung back into boyhood, acting as though my father would not drink himself to death if only I were perfect.

I failed of perfection; he succeeded in dying. To the end, he considered himself not sick but sinful. "Do you want to kill yourself?" I asked him. "Why not?" he answered. "Why the hell not? What's there to save?" To the end, he would not speak about his feelings, would not or could not give a name to the beast that was devouring him.

In silence, he went rushing off the cliff. Unlike the biblical swine, however, he left behind a few of the demons to haunt his children. Life with him and the loss of him twisted us into shapes that will be familiar to other sons and daughters of alcoholics. My brother became a rebel, my sister retreated into shyness, I played the stalwart and dutiful son who would hold the family together. If my father was unstable, I would be a rock. If he squandered money on drink, I would pinch every penny. If he wept when drunk—and only when drunk—I would not let myself weep at all. If he roared at the Little League umpire for calling my pitches balls, I would throw nothing but strikes. Watching him flounder and rage, I came to dread the loss of control. I would go through life without making anyone mad. I vowed never to put in my mouth or veins any chemical that would banish my everyday self. I would never make a scene, never lash out at the ones I loved, never hurt a soul. Through hard work, relentless work, I would achieve something dazzling—in the classroom, on the basketball floor, in the science lab, in the pages of books—and my achievement would distract the world's eyes from his humiliation. I would become a worthy sacrifice, and the smoke of my burning would please God.

It is far easier to recognize these twists in my character than to undo them. Work has become an addiction for me, as drink was an addiction for my father. Knowing this, my daughter gave me a placard for the wall: WORKAHOLIC. The labor is endless and futile, for I can no more redeem myself through work than I could redeem my father. I still panic in the face of other people's anger, because his drunken temper was so terrible. I shrink from causing sadness or disappointment even to strangers, as though I were still concealing the family shame. I still notice every twitch of emotion in the faces around me, having learned as a child to read the weather in faces, and I blame myself for their least pang of unhappiness or anger. In certain moods I blame myself for everything. Guilt burns like acid in my veins.

I am moved to write these pages now because my own son, at the age of ten, is taking on himself the griefs of the world, and in particular the griefs of his father. He tells me that when I am gripped by sadness he feels responsible; he feels there must be something he can do to spring me from depression, to fix my life. And that crushing sense of responsibility is exactly what I felt at the age of ten in the face of my father's drinking. My son wonders if I, too, am possessed. I write, therefore, to drag into the light what eats at me—the fear, the guilt, the shame—so that my own children may be spared.

I still shy away from nightclubs, from bars, from parties where the solvent is alcohol. My friends puzzle over this, but it is no more peculiar than for a man to shy away from the lions' den after seeing his father torn apart. I took my own first drink at the age of twenty-one, half a glass of burgundy. I knew the odds of my becoming an alcoholic were four times higher than for the sons of nonalcoholic fathers. So I sipped warily.

I still do—once a week, perhaps, a glass of wine, a can of beer, nothing stronger, nothing more. I listen for the turning of a key in my brain.

POSSIBILITIES FOR WRITING

1. Despite his harrowing depiction of his father's drunkenness, do you think Sanders manages to create any sympathy for the man? If so, how does he do this? If not, how do you respond to Sanders's sense of caring for his father?

2. Throughout, the essay is characterized by numerous biblical references. Find as many of these as you can and analyze them, discussing what they contribute to the essay's overall meaning and impact.

3. Write an essay about your own experiences with alcohol, though not necessarily as a drinker yourself; you may focus on how alcohol has affected people you know.

Luc Sante (b. 1954) was born in Verviers, Belgium, and emigrated to the United States in 1963. He attended Columbia University and since 1984 has been a full-time writer. A book critic for New York magazine and a frequent contributor to the New York Review of Books, he is also a senior contributor to the Internet magazine Slate. Sante has written about art, films, books, photography, and various cultural issues for many other periodicals. He received a Whiting Writer's Award in 1989, a Guggenheim Fellowship in 1992, and, in 1997, a Literature Award from the American Academy of Arts and Letters. Author of five books—Low Life (1991), Evidence (1992), and The Factory of Facts (1998)—Sante's most recent book is No Smoking, a collection of ads, photos, art, and quotations about tobacco and its uses, and Kill all Your Darlings (2007).

LUC SANTE

What Secrets Tell

In "What Secrets Tell," Luc Sante considers the recent phenomenon of the wholesale unveiling of secrets, the ways in which what had previously been undisclosed and hidden is now becoming more and better known to ever larger numbers of people. Sante considers both the kinds of public secrets held by governments and the more personal secrets of private individuals. His emphasis is on why people are revealing secrets more than they used to—why confessional writing and TV have become popular forms of disclosure and why they continue to remain so.

Sante organizes his essay into two major parts. In the first part, he considers different types of secrets, including personal secrets, romantic secrets, trade secrets, state secrets, and mystical secrets, as well as secret formulas and secret societies. In the second part he considers the reasons people need secrets and why they, by turns, conceal and reveal them.

Once, it was believed that a wholesale revelation of secrets would not occur until the Day of Judgment, when graves would be opened and the tongues of the dead at last loosened. Nowadays you might almost get the impression that the time had arrived, so profuse has been the unsealing of lips, the unlocking of vaults, the uncovering of caches. Secrets, some of them moss-covered with age, have one after another been stripped naked in public. There are two major catalysts for this phenomenon. The dissolution of the Soviet empire, first of all, opened a tremendous number of lead-lined rooms. We now know where various bodies are buried, who spied and for whom, and what they transmitted. Because to Westerners the USSR was for more than seventy years the No. 1 sphinx, the serial release of KGB documents over the past decade has solved whole shelves' worth of longstanding mysteries and promoted an atmosphere of real or imaginary worldwide openness.

And then there is the Internet, which has proved a nemesis to secrecy official and unofficial at home. Nothing of major importance, it would seem, can remain hidden for long before someone in on the deal feels the urge to post the details online. The Web is the universal souk, where fans, zealots, voyeurs, lonely crusaders, congenital meddlers, dirt brokers, disgruntled ex-employees, and the idly curious can trade facts, as well as rumors and fantasies posing as facts, in relative safety and anonymity. A secret posted on the Web can reach an astonishing number of eyes in no time at all; deniability doesn't count for much when you've got a few million eager witnesses. The secret, once an important, gold-backed currency, appears in danger of rapid devaluation as the screens of the world are flooded with industrial quantities of the skinny.

A third factor, meanwhile, has been coursing through American culture since before either of the other two became relevant. The urge to confess one's hidden transgressions before an audience of strangers, a peculiar phenomenon that came to our attention in the 1980s, has wildly miscellaneous roots: revival-tent epiphanies, Alcoholics Anonymous, psychotherapy and its many cousins, televised trials and certain odd game shows of the past, the poetry of Robert Lowell and Sylvia Plath, the memoirs of Mafiosi and Hollywood lechers and Watergate spear-carriers. Baring all in public attracts attention and at least used to assure forgiveness. Today it's all about entertainment value, with maybe some cathartic relief thrown in, and the secrets revealed have become more inconsequential even as they have become more sordid. The taboo-busting memoir, which was the intellectuals' outlet, seems to have dried up recently, but the TV confession shows are still strong after more than a decade—television thrives on repetition. Anyway, the phenomenon builds momentum, and the measure of normality is subject to continual revision: the more rubber fetishists reveal all before a live studio audience, the more additional rubber fetishists will feel impelled to do the same. At this rate, the last living American with a hidden vice will surrender to Jerry Springer in about eight years.

So are we in the midst of a new era of candor? Not likely. We need secrets far too much to jettison them. Just as it is possible that today secrets are being manufactured for the express purpose of revealing them amid trumpet flourishes, so it has happened and will happen again that secrets are constructed simply to answer a pressing need for secrets. Secrets are a permanent feature of the human condition. We need secrets the way we need black holes, for their mystery; the way we need land-speed records, for their enlargement of scale; the way we need sexy models in advertisements, for their seductively false promises; the way we need lotteries, for their vague possibility. We also need them the way we need bank vaults and sock drawers and glove compartments. Anybody who doesn't carry around one or two secrets probably has all the depth of a place mat.

But then the word "secret" conceals under its mantle a teeming and motley population of types. Secrets cater to the entire range of human susceptibilities, from the laughably trivial to the terrifyingly fundamental. Principal landmarks along the way include:

Personal Secrets. In other words, those secrets that are chiefly of interest to the persons who carry them around. You know the sort: you pick your nose when no one's looking; your real first name is Eustace; you wear a truss for nonmedical reasons. If such things were revealed, your ego might take a beating and your intimates could gain a weapon for use in squabbles or extortions, but the foundations of your house would not be shaken.

Romantic Secrets. They run the gamut. That interval of passion you once shared with your dentist when the two of you were stuck in an elevator with a bottle of Cherry Kijafa may remain swathed in gauze for all eternity, although your partner might eventually demand to know the identity of this "Shirley" whose name you utter in your sleep. That you enjoy above all the erotic sensation of being pinched with tweezers until you bleed might not matter a whole lot to anyone, unless you decide to run for office, and then you will find yourself sending discreet sums of money to people you haven't thought of in years. Couples often tacitly erect a whole edifice of secrets, based on real or imagined causes for jealousy. This can be relatively harmless, or it can be a symptom of the relationship's becoming a regime.

Secrets in Gossip. That is, the wheat left over when gossip's chaff is sifted out. Secrets that surface as gossip are usually of the mildest sort, personal eccentricities and romantic peccadilloes not of much interest outside a closed circle. (It is understood that there is a direct correlation between the degree of triviality of the secret transmitted as gossip and the rank of the gossip's subject within that circle.) Gossip, though, demonstrates how secrets can become currency, as the teller invests the hearer with power in exchange for esteem. The possession of a secret concerning another is, like all forms of power, something of a burden, a weight pressing one's lips together, which can be relieved only by telling someone else. This, added to a hunger for knowledge on the part of all within the gossip circle, keeps the wheel of the secret-fueled gossip economy turning.

Trade Secrets. The monetary economy, meanwhile, revolves around a wide and diverse range of secrets. A business strategy is a secret until it becomes a *fait accompli.* The details of the financial health of a company are kept as secret as the law allows. Anyone with a degree of power in the market is continually keeping secrets—from competitors, from the press, from anyone who is an outsider, including friends and family, but sometimes from colleagues and office mates. The reasons are obvious: everyone is naked in a cutthroat world, and secrets are clothing. It goes without saying that secrets protect innovations and that they also hide various extralegal undertakings—the ostensibly respectable bank that takes in laundry on the side, for example. Business also employs secrets strategically, as secrets qua secrets, usually painting the word "secret" in letters 10 stories tall. Naturally the new car model will differ little from the previous year's, but a bit of cloak-and-dagger about it will increase public interest. The "secret recipe" is on a par with "new and improved" as a carny barker's hook. The cake mix or soft drink or laundry soap may, of course, actually include a secret ingredient, known only to staff chemists and highly placed executives, but very often a "secret ingredient" is rumored or bruited about primarily as a lure to the gulls of the public.

Secret Formulas. The public hunger for secrets is primordial. It is first and foremost a matter of curiosity, but it also springs from a painful awareness of rank and a belief that things are different upstairs, with a more or less fanciful idea of the specifics. These days, with fortune-building running at a pitch not seen since the 1920s, there is widespread demand for financial folklore. You can make a lot of money catering to the suspicion that there exist shortcuts known only to a few. That some people are richer, thinner, more charismatic, or whiter of teeth may be a result of a variety of imponderable factors, but for everyone who in moments of desperation has imagined that there must be some simple trick, some formula or high sign or investment routine or hidden spa, there is an author with a book aimed at the exact combination of vulnerability and prurient imagination. Such publications run along the entire span of implied legitimacy based upon demographics, from the crudities aimed at the supermarket-tabloid constituency (diets centered on junk food named in the Bible, for instance) to the overpriced hard-cover pamphlets catering to the anxieties of the managerial class by dressing up received ideas with slogans and numbered lists. For centuries, the secret has been a sure-fire sales gimmick. All you have to do is combine the banal and the esoteric.

Secret Societies. There are probably a lot fewer than there once were, but somewhere in America, no doubt, insurance adjusters and trophy engravers still gather once a month in acrylic gowns and button-flap underwear to exchange phrases in pseudobiblical Double Dutch and then get down to the business of drinking beer. It helps them feel special to be the only ones in town who know the three-finger handshake. The setup descends from the heresies of the Middle Ages by way of the pecking order of the playground. We can laugh at them, now that they are so enfeebled, but there was a time not long ago when they dominated the social life of male middle-class America, and in many ways their pretensions are not so far removed from those of the Mafia or the CIA.

Mystical Secrets. The secret is bait. The secret leads votaries by the nose through a maze of connected chambers, in each of which they must ante up. Only when they have finally tumbled to there being no secret (and they have run through the better part of their inheritances) can they truly be counted as initiates. But few have the stamina to get that far, and most instead spend their spare afternoons consuming one tome after another promoting the secrets of, variously, the pyramids, the Templars, the ascended masters, the elders of Mu, the Essene scrolls, and so on through greater and lesser degrees of perceived legitimacy, all of which flutter around the edges of the secret, none of which make so bold as to suggest what it might consist of.

State Secrets. "Our laws are not generally known; they are kept secret by the small group of nobles who rule us," wrote Kafka in one of his miniature stories. "We are convinced that these ancient laws are scrupulously administered; nevertheless it is an extremely painful thing to be ruled by laws that one does not know." This is the essence of state secrets. A government does not have to be totalitarian, particularly, to possess a stratum of laws whose existence cannot be generally known because they describe the limits of the knowable. It is forbidden for unauthorized persons to possess certain kinds of information. What kinds of information? Well, that's the trouble; if you knew that, you would already know too much. State secrets range all the way from banal prohibitions on photographing customs booths and power plants to the highest levels of technical esoterica.

Atomic Secrets. "Stop me if you've heard this atomic secret," cracked William Burroughs in *Naked Lunch*. Atomic secrets may be the world's most famous class of secret, an oxymoron, surely, but for the fact that few enough people would recognize or understand an atomic secret if it landed in their mailboxes. The workaday state secret may be a matter of mere protocol or protection of resources, not unlike industries safeguarding the peculiarities of their production methods. The atomic secret, however, ascends to the level of the sacred because it manifests in concrete form the terror that mystics can only suggest: the end of the world. The secret of life may be an empty proposition, but the secret of death is actually legible to those who possess the language and the tools.

The existence of the Internet, too, has increased the fluidity of secrets. Suddenly no one knows the difference between fact and folklore. Maybe secrets are posted all the time on fixed or fleeting sites, or maybe those are just clever counterfeits of secrets. Maybe the real deal is available on some site no one has thought to access yet. The Web, after all, offers the possibility that every iota of information in the world will sooner or later appear, but it may be that, like Jorge Luis Borges's library of Babel, the Web will eventually serve up every possible combination of words, so that finally no one at all will be able to tell a secret from its chance approximation.

Confessional culture further devalues the secret. It may be a big deal to the one making a clean breast of things, but to the audience it's *Grand Guignol*, rated on its novelty quotient or on how much carnage it inspires on the set. Secrets are loose change—celebrities keep bagfuls in the storm cellar for when they need to score some publicity by leaking a few to the tabs. The daytime-TV guests each have one, but each greatly resembles others previously broadcast by other guests, and there is a limitless supply of new guests eating doughnuts in the greenroom. Anyway, whole classes of lifestyle deviations that used to be secret are now strictly ho-hum, will inspire yawns, have support groups devoted to them right down the street. That truly private shame of yours, meanwhile, probably requires too much context to be particularly negotiable, and the only three people who will care enough are not very likely to derive much entertainment from it. And what good is a secret then? That kind of secret will remain impervious to trends.

There is a deep human need for secrets that transcends all rational explanations. The revelation of a secret can be liberating, even intoxicating, at least at first, but to those on the receiving end, it is finally disappointing. This is in part because few secrets can live up to their packaging. Secrets need to mature some to be truly effective—a point too often missed in today's climate—but secrets known of long before they are divulged are especially susceptible to anticlimax. Witness the recent publication by the Catholic Church of the final prophecy of Fatima. It fell with a thud, especially because its revelation was way ex post facto—the papal assassination attempt, nearly twenty years stone cold! Holy secrets have an obligation to lie beyond human understanding and, if unveiled, to produce a physically overwhelming effect.

People need secrets because they need the assurance that there is something left to discover, that they have not exhausted the limits of their environment, that a prize might lie in wait like money in the pocket of an old jacket, that the existence of things beyond their ken might propose as a corollary that their own minds contain unsuspected corridors. People need uncertainty and destabilization the way they need comfort and security. It's not that secrets make them feel small but that they make the world seem bigger—a major necessity these days, when sensations need to be extreme to register at all. Secrets reawaken that feeling from childhood that the ways of the world were infinitely mysterious, unpredictable, and densely packed, and that someday you might come to know and master them. Secrets purvey affordable glamour, suggest danger without presenting an actual threat. If there were no more secrets, an important motor of life would be stopped, and the days would merge into a continuous blur. Secrets hold out the promise, false but necessary, that death will be deferred until their unveiling.

POSSIBILITIES FOR WRITING

1. How many types of secrets does Sante identify? What other kinds of secrets can you think of besides those Sante mentions? Do you agree with the reasons Sante cites for the breakdown of secrecy? Why or why not?
2. Describe a time an important secret was kept from you and/or a time when you kept an important secret from someone else. In either or both cases, explain why the secrets were kept and what the results of the secrecy were.
3. Write an essay about the attractions of secrecy, both keeping secrets and learning them. Consider secrecy's benefits and drawbacks in both the personal realm and in the public world.

Chief Seattle (c. 1786–1866), the son of a chief of the Suquamish tribe in the Northwest United States, himself became chief of a confederation of tribes in 1810. With the arrival of white settlers to the area, he was instrumental in establishing peaceful relations, well aware that the superior weapons of the newcomers inevitably gave them the upper hand. The Washington city of Seattle was named in his honor (though his name in the Salish language was Sealth, its pronunciation was corrupted by those who wished to honor him).

CHIEF SEATTLE

Speech on the Signing of the Treaty of Port Elliott

The following speech, given by Chief Seattle (Sealth) of the Suquamish tribe of Native American Indians, was a reply to Governor Isaac Stevens, Commissioner of Indian Affairs for the Washington Territory. Although presented in his native language, Chief Seattle's speech was recorded and translated by Henry A. Smith, who was fluent in a number of Native American languages. Contemporary sources also report that Chief Seattle presented his speech with his hand on the head of Governor Stevens, the Chief being a foot taller than the governor.

Chief Seattle's speech is noteworthy for its formal style—for its seriousness of purpose, its grave dignity of tone and feeling. It is noteworthy, too, for its references to nature, especially in its metaphors for the sacredness of the natural world. The speech is noble, eloquent, and wise, a fitting and memorable tribute to the people that Chief Seattle memorializes.

Yonder sky that has wept tears of compassion upon my people for centuries untold, and which to us appears changeless and eternal, may change. Today is fair. Tomorrow may be overcast with clouds. My words are like the stars that never change. Whatever Seattle says the great chief at Washington can rely upon with as much certainty as he can upon the return of the sun or the seasons. The White Chief says that Big Chief at Washington sends us greetings of friendship and goodwill. That is kind of him for we know he has little need of our friendship in return. His people are many. They are like the grass that covers vast prairies. My people are few. They resemble the scattering trees of a storm-swept plain. The great, and—I presume— good, White Chief sends us word that he wishes to buy our lands but is willing to allow us enough to live comfortably. This indeed appears just, even generous, for the Red Man no longer has rights that he need respect, and the offer may be wise also, as we are no longer in need of an extensive country. . . . I will not dwell on, nor mourn over, our untimely decay, nor reproach our paleface brothers with hastening it, as we too may have been somewhat to blame.

Youth is impulsive. When our young men grow angry at some real or imaginary wrong, and disfigure their faces with black paint, it denotes that their hearts are black, and then they are often cruel and relentless, and our old men and old women are unable to restrain them. Thus it has ever been. Thus it was when the white men first began to push our forefathers further westward. But let us hope that the hostilities between us may never return. We would have everything to lose and nothing to gain. Revenge by young men is considered gain, even at the cost of their own lives, but old men who stay at home in times of war, and mothers who have sons to lose, know better.

Our good father at Washington—for I presume he is now our father as well as yours, since King George has moved his boundaries further north—our great good father, I say, sends us word that if we do as he desires he will protect us. His brave warriors will be to us a bristling wall of strength, and his wonderful ships of war will fill our harbors so that our ancient enemies far to the northward—the Hydas and Tsimpsians—will cease to frighten our women, children, and old men. Then in reality will he be our father and we his children. But can that ever be? Your God is not our God! Your God loves your people and hates mine. He folds his strong and protecting arms lovingly about the paleface and leads him by the hand as a father leads his infant son— but He has forsaken His red children—if they really are his. Our God, the Great Spirit, seems also to have forsaken us. Your God makes your people wax strong every day. Soon they will fill the land. Our people are ebbing away like a rapidly receding tide that will never return. The white man's God cannot love our people or He would protect them. They seem to be orphans who can look nowhere for help. How then can we be brothers? How can your God become our God and renew our prosperity and awaken in us dreams of returning greatness? If we have a common heavenly father He must be partial—for He came to his paleface children. We never saw Him. He gave you laws but He had no word for His red children whose teeming multitudes once filled this vast continent as stars fill the firmament. No; we are two distinct races with separate origins and separate destinies. There is little in common between us.

To us the ashes of our ancestors are sacred and their resting place is hallowed ground. You wander far from the graves of your ancestors and seemingly without regret. Your religion was written upon tables of stone by the iron finger of your God so that you could not forget. The Red Man could never comprehend nor remember it. Our religion is the traditions of our ancestors—the dreams of our old men, given them in solemn hours of night by the Great Spirit; and the visions of our sachems; and it is written in the hearts of our people.

Your dead cease to love you and the land of their nativity as soon as they pass the portals of the tomb and wander way beyond the stars. They are soon forgotten and never return. Our dead never forget the beautiful world that gave them being.

Day and night cannot dwell together. The Red Man has ever fled the approach of the White Man, as the morning mist flees before the morning sun. However, your proposition seems fair and I think that my people will accept it and will retire to the reservation you offer them. Then we will dwell apart in peace, for the words of the Great White Chief seem to be the words of nature speaking to my people out of dense darkness.

It matters little where we pass the remnant of our days. They will not be many. A few more moons; a few more winters—and not one of the descendants of the mighty hosts that once moved over this broad land or lived in happy homes, protected by the Great Spirit, will remain to mourn over the graves of a people once more powerful and hopeful than yours. But why should I mourn at the untimely fate of my people? Tribe follows tribe, and nation follows nation, like the waves of the sea. It is the order of nature, and regret is useless. Your time of decay may be distant, but it will surely come, for even the White Man whose God walked and talked with him as friend with friend, cannot be exempt from the common destiny. We may be brothers after all. We will see.

We will ponder your proposition, and when we decide we will let you know. But should we accept it, I here and now make this condition that we will not be denied the privilege without molestation of visiting at any time the tombs of our ancestors, friends and children. Every part of this soil is sacred in the estimation of my people. Every hillside, every valley, every plain and grove, has been hallowed by some sad or happy event in days long vanished. . . . The very dust upon which you now stand responds more lovingly to their footsteps than to yours, because it is rich with the blood of our ancestors and our bare feet are conscious of the sympathetic touch. . . . Even the little children who lived here and rejoiced here for a brief season will love these somber solitudes and at eventide they greet shadowy returning spirits.

And when the last Red Man shall have perished, and the memory of my tribe shall have become a myth among the White Men, these shores will swarm with the invisible dead of my tribe, and when your children's children think themselves alone in the field, the store, the shop, upon the highway, or in the silence of the pathless woods, they will not be alone. . . . At night when the streets of your cities and villages are silent and you think them deserted, they will throng with the returning hosts that once filled and still love this beautiful land. The White Man will never be alone.

Let him be just and deal kindly with my people, for the dead are not powerless. Dead, did I say? There is no death, only a change of worlds.

POSSIBILITIES FOR WRITING

1. What does Chief Seattle suggest are the differences between Native peoples and European? What are their commonalities? How do these differences and similarities contribute to his larger point?
2. Trace your personal response to the speech from its opening to its conclusion. Are your feelings conflicted in any way? If so, what might be the source of these conflicts?
3. This is basically a speech of surrender. How does Chief Seattle maintain a sense of dignity, even triumph? Cite specific passages from the text.

David Sedaris (b. 1956) was born in Johnson City, New York, and raised in
Raleigh, North Carolina. Sedaris launched his career as a humorist on the
National Public Radio show "Morning Edition." His plays, one of which won an
Obie Award, have been produced at La Mama and at Lincoln Center, among other
theatrical venues. A number of his books, collections of essays, and stories, have
been best-sellers, including Barrel Fever (1994), Naked (1997), Holiday on Ice
(1997), Dress Your Family in Corduroy and Denim (2004), When You are
Engulfed in Flames (2009), and Me Talk Pretty One Day (2000), *from which the
essay of that title has been taken. An essayist whose work appears regularly in the
New Yorker and Esquire, Sedaris was named Humorist of the Year by* Time
magazine in 2001, when he also received the Thurber Prize for American Humor.

DAVID SEDARIS

Me Talk Pretty One Day

In "Me Talk Pretty One Day," David Sedaris describes his experience learning
French at the age of forty-one. With his title serving as a clue to the difficulties
he encounters, Sedaris conveys with wit and insight what it is like to begin
learning a foreign language. He also conveys what it's like to suffer at the
hands of a harsh teacher, though Sedaris exaggerates the teacher's harshness
to achieve his comic purpose.

One of the pleasures of Sedaris's essay is the way it uses surprise and
the unpredictable, including the unpredictable behavior of the teacher. The
fear she strikes in her students leads one of them at least to make enough
progress that he comes to understand spoken French pretty well, even when,
or especially when, the teacher severely criticizes him. But as successful as
that achievement in understanding may be, it's a long way from that to
grammatically accurate mature speech in the language.

At the age of forty-one, I am returning to school and have to think of
myself as what my French textbook calls "a true debutant." After paying
my tuition, I was issued a student ID, which allows me a discounted
entry fee at movie theaters, puppet shows, and Festyland, a far-flung
amusement park that advertises with billboards picturing a cartoon
stegosaurus sitting in a canoe and eating what appears to be a ham
sandwich.

I've moved to Paris with hopes of learning the language. My school
is an easy ten-minute walk from my apartment, and on the first day of
class I arrived early, watching as the returning students greeted one
another in the school lobby. Vacations were recounted, and questions
were raised concerning mutual friends with names like Kang and
Vlatnya. Regardless of their nationalities, everyone spoke in what
sounded to me like excellent French. Some accents were better than
others, but the students exhibited an ease and confidence I found

intimidating. As an added discomfort, they were all young, attractive, and well dressed, causing me to feel not unlike Pa Kettle trapped backstage after a fashion show.

The first day of class was nerve-racking because I knew I'd be expected to perform. That's the way they do it here—it's everybody into the language pool, sink or swim. The teacher marched in, deeply tanned from a recent vacation, and proceeded to rattle off a series of administrative announcements. I've spent quite a few summers in Normandy, and I took a monthlong French class before leaving New York. I'm not completely in the dark, yet I understood only half of what this woman was saying.

"If you have not *meimslsxp* or *lgpdmurct* by this time, then you should not be in this room. Has everyone *apzkiubjxow*? Everyone? Good, we shall begin." She spread out her lesson plan and sighed, saying, "All right, then, who knows the alphabet?"

It was startling because (a) I hadn't been asked that question in a while and (b) I realized, while laughing, that I myself did *not* know the alphabet. They're the same letters, but in France they're pronounced differently. I know the shape of the alphabet but had no idea what it actually sounded like.

"Ahh." The teacher went to the board and sketched the letter *a*. "Do we have anyone in the room whose first name commences with an *ahh*?"

Two Polish Annas raised their hands, and the teacher instructed them to present themselves by stating their names, nationalities, occupations, and a brief list of things they liked and disliked in this world. The first Anna hailed from an industrial town outside of Warsaw and had front teeth the size of tombstones. She worked as a seamstress, enjoyed quiet times with friends, and hated the mosquito.

"Oh, really," the teacher said. "How very interesting. I thought that everyone loved the mosquito, but here, in front of all the world, you claim to detest him. How is it that we've been blessed with someone as unique and original as you? Tell us, please."

The seamstress did not understand what was being said but knew that this was an occasion for shame. Her rabbity mouth huffed for breath, and she stared down at her lap as though the appropriate comeback were stitched somewhere alongside the zipper of her slacks.

The second Anna learned from the first and claimed to love sunshine and detest lies. It sounded like a translation of one of those Playmate of the Month data sheets, the answers always written in the same loopy handwriting: "Turn-ons: Mom's famous five-alarm chili! Turnoffs; insecurity and guys who come on too strong!!!!"

The two Polish Annas surely had clear notions of what they loved and hated, but like the rest of us, they were limited in terms of vocabulary, and this made them appear less than sophisticated. The teacher forged on, and we learned that Carlos, the Argentine bandonion player, loved wine, music, and, in his words, "making sex with the womens of the world." Next came a beautiful young Yugoslav who identified herself as an optimist, saying that she loved everything that life had to offer.

The teacher licked her lips, revealing a hint of the saucebox we would later come to know. She crouched low for her attack, placed her hands on the young woman's desk, and leaned close, saying, "Oh yeah? And do you love your little war?"

While the optimist struggled to defend herself, I scrambled to think of an answer to what had obviously become a trick question. How often is one asked what he loves in this world? More to the point, how often is one asked and then publicly ridiculed for his answer? I recalled my mother, flushed with wine, pounding the tabletop late one night, saying, "Love? I love a good steak cooked rare. I love my cat, and I love . . ." My sisters and I leaned forward, waiting to hear our names. "Tums," our mother said. "I love Tums."

The teacher killed some time accusing the Yugoslavian girl of masterminding a program of genocide, and I jotted frantic notes in the margins of my pad. While I can honestly say that I love leafing through medical textbooks devoted to severe dermatological conditions, the hobby is beyond the reach of my French vocabulary, and acting it out would only have invited controversy.

When called upon, I delivered an effortless list of things that I detest: blood sausage, intestinal pâtés, brain pudding. I'd learned these words the hard way. Having given it some thought, I then declared my love for IBM typewriters, the French word for *bruise*, and my electric floor waxer. It was a short list, but still I managed to mispronounce *IBM* and assign the wrong gender to both the floor waxer and the typewriter. The teacher's reaction led me to believe that these mistakes were capital crimes in the country of France.

"Were you always this *palicmkrexis?*" she asked. "Even a *fiuscrzsa ticiwelmun* knows that a typewriter is feminine."

I absorbed as much of her abuse as I could understand, thinking—but not saying—that I find it ridiculous to assign a gender to an inanimate object incapable of disrobing and making an occasional fool of itself. Why refer to Lady Crack Pipe or Good Sir Dishrag when these things could never live up to all that their sex implied?

The teacher proceeded to belittle everyone from German Eva, who hated laziness, to Japanese Yukari, who loved paintbrushes and soap. Italian, Thai, Dutch, Korean, and Chinese—we all left class foolishly believing that the worst was over. She'd shaken us up a little, but surely that was just an act designed to weed out the deadweight. We didn't know it then, but the coming months would teach us what it was like to spend time in the presence of a wild animal, something completely unpredictable. Her temperament was not based on a series of good and bad days but, rather, good and bad moments. We soon learned to dodge chalk and protect our heads and stomachs whenever she approached us with a question. She hadn't yet punched anyone, but it seemed wise to protect ourselves against the inevitable.

Though we were forbidden to speak anything but French, the teacher would occasionally use us to practice any of her five fluent languages.

"I hate you," she said to me one afternoon. Her English was flawless. "I really, really hate you." Call me sensitive, but I couldn't help but take it personally.

After being singled out as a lazy *kfdtinvfm*, I took to spending four hours a night on my homework, putting in even more time whenever we were assigned an essay. I suppose I could have gotten by with less, but I was determined to create some sort of identity for myself: David the hard worker, David the cut-up. We'd have one of those "complete this sentence" exercises, and I'd fool with the thing for hours, invariably settling on something like "A quick run around the lake? I'd love to! Just give me a moment while I strap on my wooden leg." The teacher, through word and action, conveyed the message that if this was my idea of an identity, she wanted nothing to do with it.

My fear and discomfort crept beyond the borders of the classroom and accompanied me out onto the wide boulevards. Stopping for a coffee, asking directions, depositing money in my bank account: these things were out of the question, as they involved having to speak. Before beginning school, there'd been no shutting me up, but now I was convinced that everything I said was wrong. When the phone rang, I ignored it. If someone asked me a question, I pretended to be deaf. I knew my fear was getting the best of me when I started wondering why they don't sell cuts of meat in vending machines.

My only comfort was the knowledge that I was not alone. Huddled in the hallways and making the most of our pathetic French, my fellow students and I engaged in the sort of conversation commonly overheard in refugee camps.

"Sometime me cry alone at night."

"That be common for I, also, but be more strong, you. Much work and someday you talk pretty. People start love you soon. Maybe tomorrow, okay."

Unlike the French class I had taken in New York, here there was no sense of competition. When the teacher poked a shy Korean in the eyelid with a freshly sharpened pencil, we took no comfort in the fact that, unlike Hyeyoon Cho, we all knew the irregular past tense of the verb *to defeat*. In all fairness, the teacher hadn't meant to stab the girl, but neither did she spend much time apologizing, saying only, "Well, you should have been *vkkdyo* more *kdeynfulh*."

Over time it became impossible to believe that any of us would ever improve. Fall arrived and it rained every day, meaning we would now be scolded for the water dripping from our coats and umbrellas. It was mid-October when the teacher singled me out, saying, "Every day spent with you is like having a cesarean section." And it struck me that, for the first time since arriving in France, I could understand every word that someone was saying.

Understanding doesn't mean that you can suddenly speak the language. Far from it. It's a small step, nothing more, yet its rewards are intoxicating and deceptive. The teacher continued her diatribe and I settled back, bathing in the subtle beauty of each new curse and insult.

"You exhaust me with your foolishness and reward my efforts with nothing but pain, do you understand me?"

The world opened up, and it was with great joy that I responded, "I know the thing that you speak exact now. Talk me more, you, plus, please, plus."

POSSIBILITIES FOR WRITING

1. To what extent do you think Sedaris captures the experience of trying to learn a foreign language? To what extent do you think he exaggerates what happens in a foreign language classroom?

2. To what extent did you find the essay funny? Explain how Sedaris achieves his humorous effects. What is the purpose of the many nonsense words Sedaris includes?

3. Write an essay about your own experience learning or attempting to learn a foreign language. You may wish to compare or contrast your experience with Sedaris's. Or you may wish to compare learning a foreign language with learning another subject or learning another skill, such as playing a musical instrument, or learning computer skills.

DAVID SEDARIS

Cyclops

In "Cyclops," David Sedaris provides a quasi-autobiographical essay about his family, with a focus on his father. In the essay, Sedaris conveys something of his father's paranoia, particularly his father's fear that catastrophes are ever ready and waiting to happen to his family. Sedaris creates a humorous portrait of his father by using hyperbole, or exaggeration, as a rhetorical strategy.

The essay is organized around a series of anecdotes, or little stories that reveal aspects of his family's behavior. The stories are linked by their humor and their common theme of imminent danger. One of the intriguing aspects of the essay is trying to decide how much is factual and just where Sedaris stretches the truth to achieve his comic purpose.

When he was young my father shot out his best friend's eye with a BB gun. That is what he told us. "One foolish moment and, Jesus, if I could take it back, I would." He winced, shaking his fist as if it held a rattle. "It eats me alive," he said. "I mean to tell you that it absolutely tears me apart."

On one of our summer visits to his hometown, my father took us to meet this guy, a shoe salesman whose milky pupil hugged the corner of his mangled socket. I watched the two men shake hands and turned away, sickened and ashamed by what my father had done.

Our next-door neighbor received a BB gun for his twelfth birthday and accepted it as a personal challenge to stalk and maim any living creature: sunbathing cats, sparrows, slugs, and squirrels—if it moved, he shot it. I thought this was an excellent idea, but every time I raised the gun to my shoulder, I saw my father's half-blind friend stumbling forth with an armload of Capezios. What would it be like to live with that sort of guilt? How could my father look himself in the mirror without throwing up?

While watching television one afternoon my sister Tiffany stabbed me in the eye with a freshly sharpened pencil. The blood was copious, and I rode to the hospital knowing that if I was blinded, my sister would be my slave for the rest of her life. Never for one moment would I let her forget what she'd done to me. There would be no swinging cocktail parties in her future, no poolside barbeques or episodes of carefree laughter, not one moment of joy—I would make sure of that. I'd planned my vengeance so thoroughly that I was almost disappointed when the doctor announced that this was nothing but a minor puncture wound, located not on but beneath the eye.

"Take a look at your brother's face," my father said, pointing to my Band-Aid. "You could have blinded him for life! Your own brother, a Cyclops, is that what you want?" Tiffany's suffering eased my pain for an hour or two, but then I began to feel sorry for her. "Every time you reach for a pencil, I want you to think about what you've done to your brother," my father said. "I want you to get on your knees and beg him to forgive you."

There are only so many times a person can apologize before it becomes annoying. I lost interest long before the bandage was removed, but not my father. By the time he was finished, Tiffany couldn't lift a dull crayon without breaking into tears. Her pretty, suntanned face assumed the characteristics of a wrinkled, grease-stained bag. Six years old and the girl was broken.

Danger was everywhere and it was our father's lifelong duty to warn us; attending the country club's Fourth of July celebration, we were told how one of his Navy buddies had been disfigured for life when a cherry bomb exploded in his lap. "Blew his balls right off the map," he said. "Take a second and imagine what that must have felt like!" Racing to the farthest edge of the golf course, I watched the remainder of the display with my hands between my legs.

Fireworks were hazardous, but thunderstorms were even worse. "I had a friend, used to be a very bright, good-looking guy. He was on top of the world until the day he got struck by lightning. It caught him right between the eyes while he was trout fishing and cooked his brain just like you'd roast a chicken. Now he's got a metal plate in his forehead and can't even chew his own food; everything has to be put in a blender and taken through a straw."

If the lightning was going to get me, it would have to penetrate walls. At the first hint of a storm I ran to the basement, crouching beneath a table and covering my head with a blanket. Those who watched from their front porches were fools. "The lightning can be attracted by a wedding ring, even the fillings in your teeth," my father said. "The moment you let down your guard is guaranteed to be the day it strikes."

In junior high I signed up for shop class, and our first assignment was to build a napkin holder. "You're not going to be using a table saw, are you?" my father asked. "I knew a guy, a kid about your size, who was using a table saw when the blade came loose, flew out of the machine, and sliced his face right in half." Using his index finger, my father drew an imaginary line from his forehead to his chin. "The guy survived, but nobody wanted anything to do with him. He turned into an alcoholic and wound up marrying a Chinese woman he'd ordered through a catalog. Think about it." I did.

My napkin holder was made from found boards and, once finished, weighed in at close to seven pounds. My bookshelves were even worse. "The problem with a hammer," I was told, "is that the head can fly off at any moment and, boy, let me tell you, you've never imagined pain like that."

After a while we began to wonder if my father had any friends who could still tie their own shoes or breathe without the aid of a respirator. With the exception of the shoe salesman, we'd never seen any of these people, only heard about them whenever one of us attempted to deep-fry chicken or operate the garbage disposal. "I've got a friend who buys a set of gloves and throws one of them away. He lost his right hand doing the exact same thing you're doing. He had his arm down the drain when the cat rubbed against the switch to the garbage disposal. Now he's wearing clip-on ties and having the restaurant waiters cut up his steak. Is that the kind of life you want for yourself?"

He allowed me to mow the lawn only because he was too cheap to pay a landscaper and didn't want to do it himself. "What happened," he said, "is that the guy slipped, probably on a pile of crap, and his leg got caught up in the blade. He found his foot, carried it to the hospital, but it was too late to sew it back on. Can you imagine that? The guy drove fifteen, twenty miles with his foot in his lap."

Regardless of the heat, I mowed the lawn wearing long pants, knee-high boots, a football helmet, and a pair of goggles. Before starting, I scouted the lawn for rocks and dog feces, slowly combing the area as if it were mined. Even then I pushed the mower haltingly, aways fearing that this next step might be my last.

Nothing bad ever happened, and within a few years I was mowing in shorts and sneakers, thinking of the supposed friend my father had used to illustrate his warning. I imagined this man jumping into his car and pressing on the accelerator with his bloody stump, a warm foot settled in his lap like a sleeping puppy. Why hadn't he just called an ambulance to come pick him up? How, in his shock, had he thought to search the weeds for his missing foot? It didn't add up.

I waited until my junior year of high school to sign up for driver's education. Before taking to the road, we sat in the darkened classroom, watching films that might have been written and directed by my father. *Don't do it*, I thought, watching the prom couple attempt to pass a lumbering dump truck. Every excursion ended with the young driver wrapped around a telephone pole or burned beyond recognition, the camera focusing in on a bloody corsage littering the side of the highway.

I drove a car no faster than I pushed the lawn mower, and the instructor soon lost patience.

"That license is going to be your death warrant," my father said on the day I received my learner's permit. "You're going to get out there and kill someone, and the guilt is going to tear your heart out."

The thought of killing myself had slowed me down to five miles per hour. The thought of killing someone else stopped me completely.

My mother had picked me up from a play rehearsal one rainy night when, cresting a hill, the car ran over something it shouldn't have. This was not a brick or a misplaced boot but some living creature that cried out when caught beneath the tire. "Shit," my mother whispered, tapping her forehead against the steering wheel. "Shit, shit shit." We covered our heads against the rain and searched the darkened street until we found an orange cat coughing up blood into the gutter.

"You killed me," the cat said, pointing at my mother with its flattened paw. "Here I had so much to live for, but now it's over, my whole life wiped out just like that." The cat wheezed rhythmically before closing its eyes and dying.

"Shit," my mother repeated. We walked door to door until finding the cat's owner, a kind and understanding woman whose young daughter shared none of her qualities. "You killed my cat," she screamed, sobbing into her mother's skirt. "You're mean and you're ugly and you killed my cat."

"She's at that age," the woman said, stroking the child's hair.

My mother felt bad enough without the lecture that awaited her at home. "That could have been a child!" my father shouted. "Think about that the next time you're tearing down the street searching for kicks." He made it sound as if my mother ran down cats for sport. "You think this is funny," he said, "but we'll see who's laughing when you're behind bars awaiting trial for manslaughter." I received a variation on the same speech after sideswiping a mailbox. Despite my mother's encouragement, I surrendered my permit and never drove again. My nerves just couldn't take it. It seemed much safer to hitchhike.

My father objected when I moved to Chicago, and waged a full-fledged campaign of terror when I announced I would be moving to New York. "New York! Are you out of your mind? You might as well take a razor to your throat because, let me tell you something, those New Yorkers are going to eat you alive." He spoke of friends who had been robbed and bludgeoned by packs of roving gangs and sent me newspaper clippings detailing the tragic slayings of joggers and vacationing tourists. "This could be you!" he wrote in the margins.

I'd lived in New York for several years when, traveling upstate to attend a wedding, I stopped in my father's hometown. We hadn't visited since our grandmother moved in with us, and I felt my way around with a creepy familiarity until I found my father's old apartment, but his friend's shoe store had been converted into a pool hall. When I called to tell him about it, my father said, "What shoe store? What are you talking about?"

"The place where your friend worked," I said. "You remember, the guy whose eye you shot out."

"Frank?" he said. "I didn't shoot his eye out; the guy was born that way."

My father visits me now in New York. We'll walk through Washington Square, where he'll yell, "Get a look at the ugly mug on that one!" referring to a three-hundred-pound biker with grinning skulls tattooed like a choker around his neck. A young man in Central Park is photographing his girl-friend, and my father races to throw himself into the picture. "All right, sweetheart," he says, placing his arm around the startled victim, "it's time to get comfortable." I cower as he marches into posh grocery stores, demanding to speak to the manager. "Back home I can get this exact same cantaloupe for less than half this price," he says. The managers invariably suggest that he do just that. He screams at waiters and cuts in line at tony restaurants. "I have a friend," I tell him, "who lost his right arm snapping his fingers at a waiter."

"Oh, you kids," he says. "Not a one of you has got so much as a teaspoon of gumption. I don't know where you got it from, but in the end, it's going to kill you."

POSSIBILITIES FOR WRITING

1. Explain how Sedaris begins his essay "Cyclops." What impression of his father does he create in this opening? How does the author react to his father's accidental shooting of a friend?

2. Why do you think Sedaris includes the story of his sister stabbing him in the eye with a pencil? What comic effects does he draw from this family story? Explain the extent to which you find "Cyclops" funny. How do you think Sedaris wants us to respond to his father's stories—and to the essay as a whole?

3. Write an essay in which you tell three or four brief connected stories about a member of your family. The little stories—or anecdotes— should, collectively, paint a portrait in words of this family member.

Leonard Shlain (1937–2009) was an associate professor of surgery and Chairman of Laparoscopic Surgery at the California Pacific Medical Center in San Francisco. He is the author of Art & Physics: Parallel Visions in Space, Time & Light (1991), The Alphabet Versus the Goddess: The Conflict Between Word and Image (1998), and Sex, Time and Power: How Women's Sexuality Changed the Course of Human Evolution (2003). In addition to winning several literary awards for his books, Dr. Shlain holds a number of patents on surgical devices. His final book, Leonardo's Brain is published posthumously.

LEONARD SHLAIN

Nonverbal/Verbal

In "Nonverbal/Verbal," a chapter from *The Alphabet Versus the Goddess*, Shlain argues that the development of literacy, particularly alphabetic literacy, has had devastating consequences for women. Most importantly, Shlain contends, alphabetic literacy, with a right brain dominance typically associated with men, has effectively short-circuited left brain values, traditionally associated with women. One consequence has been male dominance and power in literate cultures.

As in other chapters from *The Alphabet Versus the Goddess*, Shlain sets up a series of interrelated dichotomies—between verbal and nonverbal forms of communication, between left and right brain functions, between speech and gesture, and between words and images. Shlain uses these and numerous other conflicting or alternative categories to clarify his ideas and advance his argument.

In oral communication the eye, ear, brain, senses and faculties acted together in busy co-operation and rivalry, each eliciting, stimulating, and supplementing the other.

—HAROLD INNIS

The evidence indicates that learning to read and write a language in youth influences the way the hemispheres work.

—ROBERT ORNSTEIN

To speak, we need the cooperation of *both* hemispheres of the brain, and we use *both* areas of the retina and we employ *both* hands. Although speech is generated primarily from the dominant left brain, articulation requires the activation of muscles controlled equally by both hemispheres. Retinal cones and rods both engage when we speak and listen; in many instances, the listener's eye gathers more about the meaning of the speaker's message than does his ear. Gesture is also a bicameral activity with both hands participating. Their role varies, depending on the emotional content of the conversation and the ethnic background of the speakers, but gestures are always present.

When written words began to supersede spoken words, the left brain's dominance markedly increased. To write and read, an individual uses *primarily* the left hemisphere, *only* the hunting cones and *only* the killing hand. With the strokes of a thousand chisels, styli, brushes, and pens, literacy diminished the right brain's complementary role in creating and deciphering language, dismissing with it the importance of both the rods of the retina and the left hand.

While no one knows exactly when speech began, enough scientific data has accumulated to engage in cautious speculation. Gestures probably preceded vocalizations. A few milliseconds before the vocal cords begin to vibrate, the muscles of the hands and face begin to twitch. Of the 408 muscles in our bodies, a disproportionately high number are located in the face, and many exist primarily for expressing emotions.

Another human feature that developed in conjunction with gesture is the peculiar color of our hands. Among the varied species of primates, only humans—including highly melanotic native Africans—lack pigment on their palms. One explanation of this unique feature is that it once served the hands' function in communication. Before the full development of spoken language, our ancestors sat around the fire speaking and gesturing to each other. It would have been a distinct advantage for the palms to be pale and thus more visible in dim light.

Gesture is such a vital component of speech that it is nearly impossible to have a conversation without it. In some cases it is the more expressive mode. Anyone asked to describe a spiral staircase will inevitably accompany the spoken answer with a corkscrew motion of the hand. This pantomime is far more descriptive than words could be.

Hearing is the most important sense for understanding speech, but while listening one also continually monitors the speaker's facial expressions and body language visually. The retina's rods allow an appreciation of gestalts and slight movements in the periphery; more than cones, they are expert at gathering subtle visual clues. The speaker's fingers nervously drumming on a desktop may not be heard by the listener's ear, but peripheral vision does not "lose sight" of this revealing information. Nor does it miss him shaking his head from side to side (indicating his rejection) while he is saying that he agrees wholeheartedly with your position. (Of these two contradictory messages, the listener intuitively knows that the nonverbal one is more accurate.)

Vision is also important to the speaker. While talking, he constantly watches the listener for nonverbal feedback. If he believes that his message is producing a desired (or undesired) effect, he can switch his mode of speech in mid-sentence. He can also reduce what he says to a kind of oral shorthand if he is confident that the listener's nods of assent mean his unfinished sentences and incomplete thoughts are being anticipated and understood.

Millions tune in to watch presidential debates. Asked why they feel it necessary to observe the candidates on television when they have already read their positions in the newspaper, many reply that they want to *see* how each candidate comports himself. Ignoring speech's content, the viewer's right brain evaluates the candidate's sincerity, cleverness, honesty, cunning, and forthrightness. The conduct of a conversation is, in many cases, more illuminating than its content, reinforcing the wisdom of the Chinese aphorism, "Let us draw closer to the fire so that we may better see what we are saying."

Some time in our distant past, speech supplanted gesture as the principal means of human communication. However, the left brain's speech centers never completely eliminated the influence that the older right brain has on both the creation and comprehension of oral language. If the spoken word was the result of delicately balanced assignments of the feminine and the masculine sides of the brain, then the invention of writing completely upset this balance.

A letter writer has no instant visual feedback to assess the impact of his words on the recipient, and a letter deprives the reader of the body language, facial expression, and other clues she would normally garner from the letter writer. "Reading between the lines" is a far more difficult exercise than evaluating the nonverbal clues of speech. Ferdinande de Sassure, an early researcher in the field, noted, "Writing veils the appearance of language; it is not a guise for language but a disguise."

Speech and writing differ significantly in a purely mechanical aspect. All spoken languages fall within a narrow range of meter: too rapid, and the listener will have difficulty comprehending; too slow, and the listener will be bored; too monotonic, and the listener will tune out; too histrionic, and the listener will become overburdened. The speaker sets the pace and the listener must follow. In reading, the opposite is the case: the reader's left brain is in complete control.

Music appreciation resides principally in the right hemisphere. Inflection and rhythm are musical qualities that are crucial components of speech. A change in the enunciation and emphasis of certain phrases and words can subtly redirect the entire meaning of the speaker's message. A speaker can imply or exaggerate double entendres, puns, and humorous interpretations simply by varying his inflection. The written word, in contrast, is silent. Writers use punctuation marks in an attempt to overcome this serious disadvantage, but while these symbols enliven prose, a question mark is a pallid substitute for an arched eyebrow above a mocking smirk.

With speech, both speaker and listener must occupy proximate physical spaces at the same moment for any interaction to take place.* Speech generation and listener comprehension are *simultaneous* events. The written word's message is deciphered sometime in the future and usually in another location. It is *linear*. Speech is framed in the *here* and *now*. Writing's context is *there* and *then*.

Speech is the consummate act of improvisation and everyone, at one time or another, has been surprised by her or his own eloquence. Every day, we speak complex sentences that we did not plan in advance. Somehow, in the interstices of Broca's left-brain speech center, grammatically correct phrases are hurriedly stitched together and emerge as relatively seamless diction. In most conversations, there is little editorial interference. This helps the listener evaluate the speaker's message. Slips of the tongue cannot be retrieved. In contrast, a writer has far more control than the speaker, more time to "collect his thoughts" and calculate their effect, allowing him to edit and revise what the reader sees.

Also missing from the written word is the aesthetic quality of the speaker's voice. Different people's voices—dull, sexy, forced, slippery, seductive, earnest, convincing, or stentorian—evoke different emotional responses. While consciously attending to the content of spoken language, the listener is also evaluating speech's emotional tenor subliminally.[†]

While the right brain can sometimes evaluate the nonverbal content of handwriting, this paltry amount of nuance pales when compared to the nonverbal clues available from the full panoply of facial expression. And in modern times, the printing press and then the typewriter further diminished the right brain's participation by replacing the individuality of handwriting with standardized and impersonal type.

*For the vast majority of humankind's history, this condition held true. Recent technological developments, such as the telegraph, radio, telephone, etc., have added new caveats.
[†]Listening to radio supplies us with only auditory clues. We imagine how the radio personality looks based solely on voice quality. When we actually see photographs of someone we have known only through his or her voice, the image jars as it is usually quite different from the face we had imagined.

While speakers and listeners fully engage both their rods and cones during conversation, reading requires *only* a small circle of tunnel vision to follow the linear progression of words on a page. Information contained in the paragraph further down the page is of no interest until the reader gets there.

The writer's eye uses only cone vision to follow the trail of ink emerging from the pen tip as it advances across a page. Handwriting, like reading, proceeds in a linear, sequential fashion, and like all cone vision tasks, requires a high level of concentration. If we are writing (or reading) in a room where there are distracting peripheral stimuli, we generally will rise to turn off a television or move to a quieter place. In contrast, our conversational skills allow us to banter at crowded cocktail parties, oblivious to the welter of incoming visual and competing auditory information.

The font of the print on this page contains serifs. They are the horizontal "finishes" at the top and bottom of most letters. Serifs form what amounts to a set of rails, marking out tracks that the cones of the eye can easily follow. They serve to keep the reader's visual train of thought rolling smoothly over the print. They accentuate the sequential nature of the written word. There are no serifs in a frown or a smile.

Speech requires the active participation of both halves of the paired somatic muscles of vocalization. The formation of the word *tree* involves an equal effort of right and left sides of the diaphragm, both vocal cords, cooperation between the tongue's opposite sides, and the pursing of both halves of the lips. Anyone who has ever returned from the dentist's office after having one side of the tongue and lips paralyzed with anesthetic is acutely aware that the articulation of words depends on the musculature of both sides of the mouth.

Writing involves the muscles of *only* one side of the body. Pure writing, using stylus, quill, pencil, or pen, engages the dominant hand, which the dominant hemisphere controls. Right-brain participation is markedly reduced. The left hand has no role during this activity. Evolution selected the dominant hand to be the aggressor, the hand that wields the club, swings the sword, and pulls the trigger. Placing the pen in the fighting hand etches aggression into the written word differentiating it from speech, which depends more on a bicameral cooperative effort.

Nonverbal clues, concrete gestalts, music, inflection, spontaneity, simultaneity, aesthetics, emotion, slips of the tongue, gesticulation, and *peripheral vision* are all features best processed by the right brain. Speech—and its reciprocal, listening—are hemispheric activities requiring a large amount of traffic in both directions across the corpus callosum.

The written word issues from *linearity, sequence, reductionism, abstraction, control, central vision,* and the *dominant hand*—all hunter/killer attributes. Writing represented a shift of tectonic proportions that fissured the integrated nature of gatherer/hunter communication and brain cooperation. Writing made the left brain, flanked by the incisive cones of the eye and the aggressive right hand, dominant over the right. The triumphant march of literacy that began five thousand years ago conquered right-brain values, and, with them, the Goddess. Patriarchy and misogyny have been the inevitable result.

POSSIBILITIES FOR WRITING

1. Summarize Shlain's argument in this piece. Include examples of the different kinds of evidence he accumulates to develop and support his argument.
2. What is the purpose of Shlain's use of epigraphs and his inclusion of asterisked footnotes? How effectively does he use each of these? What do they contribute to his argument?
3. Write your own essay about the differences between verbal and nonverbal communication. You can use examples from your own experience, including personal narrative, as well as examples based on your reading and your observation of others. You may wish to illustrate with some examples from film, advertising, or television.

Lee Siegel (b. 1957) *was born and raised in the Bronx, New York, and received his B.A., M.A. and M Phil. from Columbia University. He worked as an editor at* The New Leader *and* ARTnews *before turning to writing full-time in 1998. In 2002, Siegel received the National Magazine Award for Reviews and Criticism. Siegel has written several essays for art catalogues, and several introductions to reprinted classics, and has authored several books, including:* Falling Upwards: Essays in Defense of the Imagination *(2006),* Not Remotely Controlled: Notes on Television *(2007), and* Against the Machine: How the Web Is Reshaping Culture and Commerce—and Why It Matters, *a polemic that offers a perspective on the Internet that explores a range of its consequences, good and bad.*

LEE SIEGEL

The World Is All That Is the Case

In "The World Is All That Is the Case," Siegel identifies a number of ways the Internet shapes the way people live today. In a spirit of critical inquiry, he asks some basic questions about the consequences of the Internet's reshaping of culture, particularly how people behave and interact socially. Among his concerns is the way the Internet universe is driven by and saturated in economic matters, "assimilating human existence to an economic model," and thereby "embed[ding] human life in an economic model."

Siegel admits that the Internet is a marvelous invention, an amazing life changer, and a powerful tool that aids the production of work, including Siegel's own work as a writer. But he worries that too few people are thinking about the ways the Internet has already changed our lives, and he has decided to be one of the few to challenge the view that the Web is anything other than a mixed blessing.

I go to starbucks, sit down, open my laptop, and turn it on. In the old days—ten years ago—I would be sitting with a pen and notebook, partly concentrating on my writing and partly aware of the people in the room around me. Back in that prehistoric time, my attention faced outward. I might see someone I know, or someone I'd like to know. I might passively enjoy trying to figure out why that couple in the middle of the room are speaking so intensely—are they moving closer together to relish their intimacy or because there is a crisis in their intimacy? And who is that guy with the fedora—and why the red sneakers? Is he an original, or the copy of an original? I might be watching everyone, but some people might be watching me, too. My situation is just as permeable as theirs. A stranger could come over to my table at any minute, his sudden physical presence before me unexpected, incalculable, absolutely enigmatic in the seconds before he becomes one kind of situation or another.

But here I am, sitting in live future—I mean the present—in front of my laptop. Just about everyone around me has a laptop open also. The small mass of barely variegated gray panels looks like a scene out of Fritz Lang's *Metropolis,* but with modems and Danishes. I can hardly see anyone else's face behind the screens, and no one seems to be doing anything socially or psychologically that might be fun to try to figure out. They are bent into their screens and toward their self-interest. My attention, too, is turned toward my ego. But I am paying attention in a different way from what I do when I read a book or a newspaper. I am opening e-mail sent to me, writing e-mail expressing one or another desire that belongs to me, clicking on Google looking for information to be used by me. Ten years ago, the space in a coffee-house abounded in experience. Now that social space has been con-tracted into isolated points of wanting, all locked into separate phases of inwardness.

The new situation doesn't represent the "lack of community" sud-denly produced by the Internet. That is the hackneyed complaint made, again and again, by people who don't seem to have thought through the unlovely aspects of "community"—its smug provincialism and punitive conventionalism, its stasis and xenophobia—which was in any case jeopardized and transformed by the advent of modernity two hundred years ago. The simple fact is that sometimes you don't want the quiet conformities induced by "community"; sometimes you simply want to be alone, yet together with other people at the same time. The old-fashioned café provided a way to both share and aban-don solitude, a fluid, intermediary experience that humans are always trying to create and perfect. The Internet could have been its fulfill-ment. But sitting absorbed in your screenworld is a whole other story. You are socially and psychologically cut off from your fellow caffeine addicts, but mentally beset by e-mails, commercial "pop-ups," and a million temptations that may enchant in the moment—aimed as they are at your specific and immediate interests and desires—but in retro-spect are time-wasting ephemera. It's not community that the laptopiza-tion of the coffeehouse has dispelled. It's the concrete, undeniable, immutable fact of our being in the world.

Before our screens, experience is collapsed into gratifying our desires on the one hand, and on the other either satisfying or refusing to satisfy the soliciting desires of other people—or entities. As the Viennese philosopher Ludwig Wittgenstein famously said, "The world is all that is the case." We have been flung into the world whether we like it or not. But the Internet creates a vast illusion that the physical, social world of interacting minds and hearts does not exist. In this new situation, the screen is all that is the case, along with the illusion that the screen projects of a world tamed, digested, abbreviated, rationalized, and ordered into a trillion connected units, called sites. This new world turns the most consequential fact of human life—other people—into seemingly manipulable half presences wholly available to our fantasies. It's a world controlled by our wrist and finger.

Yet the untamed, undigested, unrationalized, uncontrolled world is still there. People as thinking, feeling beings still exist. What form, then, do we take, in a world where there is—how else can I put it?—no world at all? To put it another way: What kind of idea do we have of the world when, day after day, we sit in front of our screens and enter further and further into the illusion that we ourselves are actually creating our own external reality out of our own internal desires? We become impatient with realities that don't gratify our impulses or satisfy our picture of reality. We find it harder to accept the immutable limitations imposed by identity, talent, personality. We start to behave in public as if we were acting in private, and we begin to fill our private world with gargantuan public appetites. In other words, we find it hard to bear simply being human.

This situation is not a crisis of technology. Rather, it is a social development that has been embodied in the new technology of the Internet, bur not created by the Internet. The sudden onset of Web culture is really a dramatic turn in the timeless question of what it means to be a human being. What a shame that transformative new technologies usually either inspire uncritical celebration or incite bouts of nostalgia for a prelapsarian age that existed before said technology—anything for an uprising against cellphones and a return to the glorious phone booths of yore! The advent of new technologies pretty quickly becomes a pitched battle between the apostles of edge and Luddites wielding alarmist sentiments like pitchforks. Because each side is a caricature of itself, no one takes what is at stake very seriously at all.

And they are caricatures, for anyone who thinks technological innovation is bad in and of itself is an unimaginative crank. (I would rather go live on Pluto than return to the days of the phone booth and the desperate search for change.) But anyone who denies that technology has the potential to damage us if it is not put to good use is either cunning or naive. In the case of the Internet, the question is whether we let this remarkably promising opportunity—which, as we'll see, has until now largely been developed in service to commerce and capital—shape us to its needs or put it in the service of our own. Do we keep acquiescing in the myopic glibness and carelessness that characterize how so many of us are using the Internet? Do we keep surrendering to the highly purposeful way vested interests are foisting it upon us?

Comfortable Upheaval

The future, we were once told, shocked. Well, the future is here. But no one is shocked.

The sensational evidence of upheaval is everywhere. You can read about it in the newspaper or see it on the news by the hour. A lonely middle-aged carpenter in Arizona meets a Brazilian woman online, visits her in Rio de Janeiro twice, and then, on his third encounter with her, is murdered by his new girlfriend, her real boyfriend, and a hired assassin. A sting operation sweeps up hundreds of pedophiles luring their prey in Internet chat rooms. Computer hackers use the Internet to nearly bring down the government of Estonia. An anonymous Web site reveals the identities of federally protected witnesses in capital cases. Social-networking sites like MySpace and the video-blog site called YouTube turn the most graphic inhumanity—a Texas policeman puts up photos of a dismembered woman; anonymous users post footage of American soldiers in Iraq being gunned down—into numbing new forms of entertainment.

The Internet's most consequential changes in our lives, however, are the ones woven into our everyday routines. Maybe your teenage son—or daughter—spends hours every day and night corresponding with dozens of new "friends" on MySpace or Facebook; perhaps he's uploading a forty-minute-long video of himself dancing naked, alone in his room, onto YouTube, one of the world's most highly trafficked sites. Maybe your officemate is addicted to political blogs like Little Green Footballs, or Instapundit, or Firedoglake, in which dozens, sometimes hundreds, of people, argue with each other passionately, sometimes abusively, on interminable threads of commenters. Or your other officemate spends all of his time buying merchandise on eBay, or your boss, a high-powered attorney, closes her door on her lunch hour and logs on to JDate, a Jewish dating service, where she fields inquiries from dozens of men.

Perhaps your husband is, at this very moment, shut away in his office somewhere in your home, carrying on several torrid online affairs at the same time under his various aliases: "Caliente," "Curious," "ActionMan." When he emerges from his sequestered lair, red-faced and agitated, is it because he has been arguing for moderation with "KillBush46" on the political blog Daily Kos, has failed in his bid to purchase genuine military-issue infrared night goggles on eBay, or has been masturbating while instant-messaging "Prehistorical2"?

Then again, maybe your husband died four years ago from a rare disease, and thanks to information you discovered on the Web, you were able to find a drug that kept him alive for twice as long as he would have lived without it. An Internet grief support group helped get you through the pain of your loss and introduced you to people who are now trusted friends. They led you, in turn, to an online dating service where you met your second husband, and began a new life.

Like all significant technologies, the Internet is a blessing and a curse. Or, rather, it is obviously a blessing and obscurely a curse. It would be tedious to recite the Internet's wonders as a tool for research and a medium for connectivity in detail here—in any case, those wonders have been touted far and wide for the last decade by an all-too-willing media. But the transformations are real. For the first time in human history, a person can have romance, friendship, and sex (sort of); be fed, clothed, and entertained; receive medical, legal, and just about every other type of advice; collect all sorts of information, from historical facts to secrets about other people—all without leaving home. For the first time in human history, a technology exists that allows a person to lead as many secret lives, under a pseudonym, as he is able to manage. For the first time in human history, a person can broadcast his opinions, beliefs, and most intimate thoughts—not to mention his face, or any other part of his body—to tens of millions of other people.

The simple fact is that more and more people are able to live in a more comfortable and complete self-enclosure than ever before.

The Big Lie

Since the rise of the Internet just ten years ago, the often irrational boosterism behind it has been for the most part met by criticism that is timid, defensive, and unfocused. The Internet is possibly the most radical transformation of private and public life in the history of humankind, but from the way it is publicly discussed, you would think that this gigantic jolt to the status quo had all the consequences of buying a new car. "The Internet," the *New York Times* casually reports, represents "a revolution in politics and human consciousness." Online sex is "changing the lives of billions" in Asia, writes *Time* magazine with a shrug, and follows that astounding headline with what amounts to a lifestyle article ("A continent of 3 billion human beings is getting sexy and kicking the guilt . . . say a sincere hosanna to the Internet, which not only allows wired Asians to hook up but also to find out about whatever may titillate or tantalize them"). Everyone agrees the Internet has the same "epochal" significance that the printing press once did. But after the printing press made its appearance in Europe, three hundred years had to go by before the "revolutionary" new invention began to seep down from the scholar's cloister into everyday life. Even the telephone and television, the most transformative technologies of modern times, took decades to reshape "human consciousness," to borrow the *Times*'s grandiose tone. The Internet has radically changed almost every level of human experience, throughout most of the world, in just a few years. So why can't people be honest about the downside as well as the upside of what's happening to us?

Of course no one wants to stand athwart the future shaking a finger, mocking and scowling and scolding. No one wants to be a wet blanket at the party. Americans don't like naysayers, and we don't like backward lookers/Ours has got to be the only culture in the world where saying that someone belongs to "history" is a fatal insult. So what you usually get by way of criticism are sunny, facile gestures toward criticism. A typical example is the Pew Internet & American Life Project. Its September 2006 report on the current state and future of Internet culture has been widely used by anxious or self-interested journalists to forecast, among other things, the death of newspapers and print magazines. According to the Pew Project, "Internet users have become more likely to note big improvements in their ability to shop and the way they pursue their hobbies and interests. A majority of internet users also consistently report that the internet helps them to do their job and improves the way they get information about health care." Pew also notes "addiction problems" for many Web visitors, but quickly concludes that for many respondents to the survey, " 'addiction' is an inappropriate notion to attach to people's interest in virtual environments." The report then adds this creepy glance into the future: "Tech 'refuseniks' will emerge as a cultural group characterized by their choice to live off the network. Some will do this as a benign way to limit information overload, while others will commit acts of violence and terror against technology-inspired change."

To my mind, it could well be that one reason why the Pew report is so upbeat about its subject is that eight of the twelve people on the advisory board of the Pew Internet & American Life Project, at the time the report was written, had a financial or professional stake in Internet companies. Pew asserts that its staff is independent of the advisory board. Be that as it may, the authors of the Pew report view any opposition to the Internet's darker effects as resistance to "technology-inspired change" rather than skepticism that embraces technology but recoils at some of its effects. Naturally, in their eyes, much of the opposition could not possibly be rational. It would have to come in the form of "violence and terror."

Along with Web boosters like the authors of the Pew study is another type of potent promoter: the utopian technophile. We will meet several different varieties of these along our way. One of the most energetic and persuasive is Kevin Kelly, Internet guru, co-founder of *Wired* magazine, and the author of two hugely influential books on Internet culture—*Out of Control: The New Biology of Machines, Social Systems, and the Economic World* and *New Rules for the New Economy: 10 Radical Strategies for a Connected World.* While the Pew report covered general patterns of usage, Kelly has a vision of social and cultural transformation:

> *What will entertainment technology look like in 20 years? Let's listen to what technology says. First, technology has no preference between real and simulations—(so) neither will our stories. The current distinction between biological actors and virtual actors will cease, just as the distinction between real locations and virtual locations has almost gone. The choice will simply come down to what is less expensive. The blur between real and simulated will continue to blur the line between documentary and fiction. As straight documentaries continue to surge in popularity in the next 20 years, so will hybrids between fiction and non-fiction. We'll see more reality shows that are scripted, scripted shows that run out of control, documentaries that use actors, actors that are robotic creations, news that is staged, stories that become news and the total collision and marriage between fantasy and the found.*

Now, Kelly may well be right. Yet in his feverish devotion to "technology," he sees nothing wrong with fake documentaries, deceitful "reality" shows, and "news that is staged." If technology decides that truth and falsehood shall be blurred, then for Kelly their "total collision and marriage"—whatever that means, exactly—is as historically determined, inevitable, and necessary as the Marxist belief in the dictatorship of the proletariat.

Despite the fact that Kelly cheerily predicts the imminent extinction of "old" media, nearly the entire journalistic establishment has embraced, in various degrees, his exuberant view of a dystopic future. For it is dystopic. What sane person wants a culture in which the border between truthfulness and lying is constantly being eroded? Nothing affects our values and perceptions, our thoughts and feelings, like the shows we watch, the movies we see, the books we read—and we watch far more than we read; Americans spend a large amount, if not a majority, of their leisure time being entertained. Kelly sees the engine of the Internet driving these cataclysmic changes in the culture. But journalists and other commentators are so afraid of appearing behind the times, or of being left behind, that the role the Internet plays in the disappearing borders of truth rarely gets talked about in public.

We know where we stand on a politician's lies; we know how to respond when we feel, for example, that the government's deceptions and lies led us into the Iraq war. But no one is making a cogent connection between the rise of the Internet and the accelerating blur of truth and falsity in culture—even though culture's subtle effects on our minds are a lot more profound in the long run than a politician's lies, which usually get discovered and exposed sooner or later. Instead of crying out against the manipulation of truth by "entertainment technology," as Kelly chillingly calls what used to be described as "having fun," we watch the general mendacity get turned into a joke—the comedian Stephen Colbert's celebrated quip about "truthiness"—and turn back to our various screens with a laugh.

People like the Pew group and Kevin Kelly are in a mad rush to keep the Web entrepreneurially viable or to push a fervent idealism. But in their blinkered eagerness to sell their outlooks—to focus our attention on what they are selling as an inevitable future—they rush right past the most obvious questions: How will the Internet affect the boundaries between people? As "information" consists more and more of reports from people's psyches, how will we be able to express intimate thoughts and feelings without sounding hackneyed and banal? As increasing numbers of people become dependent on the Internet, and the Internet is driven more and more by commerce—the sensational stock prices and sales of Google, MySpace, and YouTube, for example—how do we keep an obsession with the bottom line from overwhelming our lives? How do we carve out a space for a life apart from the Internet, and apart from economics?

Upgrade and be Happy

Anyway, who wants to glower at the Internet when it brings such a cornucopia of wonders? Bill Gates describes what he considers the full potential of the Internet's developments:

> They will enable equal access to information and instantaneous communication with anyone in the world. They will open up vast markets and opportunities to businesses of any size. They will transcend national borders, making possible a frictionless global economy. They will allow workers to be even more efficient and productive, and will have the potential to make jobs more stimulating and fulfilling. They will give developing nations the ability to leapfrog the industrial era and move straight into the information age. They will help people and businesses in countries with large, dispersed populations to stay in touch, and help the smallest nations participate as equals in the global economy.

Gates says he is not blind to the Internet's pitfalls, either:

> As more and more people store personal information on the Internet, how will we ensure that information is kept secure? As our economy becomes more dependent on bits than on atoms, how will we protect these resources from being damaged or devalued by hackers? As the barriers to information come down, how will we protect our children from negative and predatory influences? And as the Internet dissolves national borders, how will we help indigenous cultures coexist with an increasingly homogenous global culture?

Gates's radiant view of the future and his predictions of the problems that might obstruct the Internet's promise are reiterated throughout the media. They are the standard description of the Internet's bright side and its dark side. But there is something dark about Gates's sunniness; there is something rosy about his premonition of difficulties along the way. Consider the bad news first. Are the problems Gates foresees really problems at all? They have a red-herringish quality about them; they are by no means insoluble. Indeed, Gates frames these dilemmas produced by new technology in such a way that their resolution lies exclusively in the invention of newer technology.

For the way to keep information secure is to develop software that will do so. We can protect against hackers by constructing systems that thwart them. Advanced computer programs will shield our children from the dangers unleashed as "the barriers to information come down." (Notice how Gates makes even sexual predators seem like the necessary consequence of an unmitigated good: How could more information ever be anything but a marvelous beneficence? And who would use "negative and predatory influences" on children as an argument against opening the floodgates of information?)

As for the disruptions that the Internet might bring to impoverished, illiterate populations, Gates formulates this conflict as a cultural, not a social, clash. The answer, he implies, is simply to introduce the "indigenous" cultures to the techniques that are making the world "increasingly homogenous." Rather than honestly face the strange new perils the Internet has created, Gates's "realism" strengthens the impression of the Internet's power, permanence, and necessity. For Gates, the only answer to the Internet's dark side is the Internet, itself.

One of the striking characteristics of conversation about the Internet is this circular, hermetic quality. The "key words and phrases," as the search engines like to say, in Gates's rosy picture of the future give you a sense of how he would answer the dilemmas posed by new technology: "access," "markets," "businesses," "economy," "efficient," "productive," "leapfrog the industrial era." Gates doesn't worry that the Internet will upset deep, irrational human needs and desires. For him, deep, irrational human needs and desires don't exist outside the super-rationally ordered universe of the Internet. And since economics is the simplest means of rationalizing human life, Gates believes that being human can be defined strictly in economic terms.

Microsoft, however, had a long arrival. Over thirty years ago, in *The Coming of Post-Industrial Society*, the sociologist Daniel Bell predicted Bill Gates. Decades before Gates made the computer the means of assimilating human existence to an economic model, Bell saw how the computer would eventually embed everyday life in an economic framework.

POSSIBILITIES FOR WRITING

1. What is the main point Siegel makes in the essay? Where is it most clearly stated? Summarize Siegel's argument in one paragraph.

2. To what extent do you think Siegel is fair and balanced in his discussion of the values and dangers of the Internet? Identify one passage in which he demonstrates a balanced approach and explain how successfully he offers a balanced view. What evidence can you find that suggests he may favor one side or the other—the positive or negative impact the Internet has had on our lives?

3. Write an essay in which you explore what you see as the virtues and vices—the values and dangers of the Internet. You may use some of Siegel's examples, if you wish. However, if you do, be sure to include them among others that he does not mention.

Leslie Marmon Silko (b. 1948), who is of native Laguna, Mexican, and Anglo-American ancestry, was born in Albuquerque, New Mexico, and raised on the nearby Laguna Pueblo Reservation. After earning a degree from the University of New Mexico, she taught at a community college, then began her career as a writer with the poetry collection Laguna Woman *(1974). Her first novel,* Ceremony, *appeared in 1977, followed by* Almanac of the Dead *(1991) and, most recently,* Gardens in the Dunes *(1999). Her short stories are collected in* Storyteller *(1981);* Yellow Woman and a Beauty of the Spirit *(1996) is a collection of essays. Silko is a recipient of the prestigious MacArthur Foundation prize.*

LESLIE MARMON SILKO

Landscape, History, and the Pueblo Imagination

The focus of Silko's "Landscape, History, and the Pueblo Imagination" is landscape less as aesthetic object or private property than as something alive and to be appreciated, even revered. Silko describes the cycle of life and death in nature, stressing how the remains of things that have died nourish those still alive. For Silko and for the Native American tradition she reflects, all things should be celebrated, whether living or dead, because they possess spirit or being. For Silko there is a mystery at the center of life. "We do not know," she reminds us, exactly "how all beings share in the spirit of the Creator."

Landscape, for Silko, includes not just what we can see. Landscape also includes the very viewers who survey it. And since people are part of the landscape that they see and inhabit, they should respect and honor it. From her perspective, all the inhabitants of the landscape are part of the grand unified design of creation that Silko and her tradition postulate.

You see that after a thing is dead, it dries up. It might take weeks or years, but eventually if you touch the thing, it crumbles under your fingers. It goes back to dust. The soul of the thing has long since departed. With the plants and wild game the soul may have already been borne back into bones and blood or thick green stalk and leaves. Nothing is wasted. What cannot be eaten by people or in some way used must then be left where other living creatures may benefit. What domestic animals or wild scavengers can't eat will be fed to the plants. The plants feed on the dust of these few remains.

The ancient Pueblo people buried the dead in vacant rooms or partially collapsed rooms adjacent to the main living quarters. Sand and clay used to construct the roof make layers many inches deep once the roof has collapsed. The layers of sand and clay make for easy gravedigging.

The vacant room fills with cast-off objects and debris. When a vacant room has filled deep enough, a shallow but adequate grave can be scooped in a far corner. Archaeologists have remarked over formal burials complete with elaborate funerary objects excavated in trash middens of abandoned rooms. But the rocks and adobe mortar of collapsed walls were valued by the ancient people. Because each rock had been carefully selected for size and shape, then chiseled to an even face. Even the pink clay adobe melting with each rainstorm had to be prayed over, then dug and carried some distance. Corn cobs and husks, the rinds and stalks and animal bones were not regarded by the ancient people as filth or garbage. The remains were merely resting at a midpoint in their journey back to dust. Human remains are not so different. They should rest with the bones and rinds where they all may benefit living creatures—small rodents and insects—until their return is completed. The remains of things—animals and plants, the clay and the stones—were treated with respect. Because for the ancient people all these things had spirit and being.

The antelope merely consents to return home with the hunter. All phases of the hunt are conducted with love. The love the hunter and the people have for the Antelope People. And the love of the antelope who agree to give up their meat and blood so that human beings will not starve. Waste of meat or even the thoughtless handling of bones cooked bare will offend the antelope spirits. Next year the hunters will vainly search the dry plains for antelope. Thus it is necessary to return carefully the bones and hair, and the stalks and leaves to the earth who first created them. The spirits remain close by. They do not leave us.

The dead become dust, and in this becoming they are once more joined with the Mother. The ancient Pueblo people called the earth the Mother Creator of all things in this world. Her sister, the Corn Mother, occasionally merges with her because all succulent green life rises out of the depths of the earth.

Rocks and clay are part of the Mother. They emerge in various forms, but at some time before, they were smaller particles or great boulders. At a later time they may again become what they once were. Dust.

A rock shares this fate with us and with animals and plants as well. A rock has being or spirit, although we may not understand it. The spirit may differ from the spirit we know in animals or plants or in ourselves. In the end we all originate from the depths of the earth. Perhaps this is how all beings share in the spirit of the Creator. We do not know.

From the Emergence Place

Pueblo potters, the creators of petroglyphs and oral narratives, never conceived of removing themselves from the earth and sky. So long as the human consciousness remains *within* the hills, canyons, cliffs, and the plants, clouds, and sky, the term *landscape*, as it has entered the English language, is misleading. "A portion of territory the eye can comprehend in a single view" does not correctly describe the relationship between the human being and his or her surroundings. This assumes the viewer is somehow *outside* or *separate from* the territory he or she surveys. Viewers are as much a part of the landscape as the boulders they stand on. There is no high mesa edge or mountain peak where one can stand and not immediately be part of all that surrounds. Human identity is linked with all the elements of Creation through the clan: you might belong to the Sun Clan or the Lizard Clan or the Corn Clan or the Clay Clan. Standing deep within the natural world, the ancient Pueblo understood the thing as it was—the squash blossom, grasshopper, or rabbit itself could never be created by the human hand. Ancient Pueblos took the modest view that the thing itself (the landscape) could not be improved upon. The ancients did not presume to tamper with what had already been created. Thus *realism,* as we now recognize it in painting and sculpture, did not catch the imaginations of Pueblo people until recently.

The squash blossom itself is *one thing:* itself. So the ancient Pueblo potter abstracted what she saw to be the key elements of the squash blossom—the four symmetrical petals, with four symmetrical stamens in the center. These key elements, while suggesting the squash flower, also link it with the four cardinal directions. By representing only its intrinsic form, the squash flower is released from a limited meaning or restricted identity. Even in the most sophisticated abstract form, a squash flower or a cloud or a lightning bolt became intricately connected with a complex system of relationships which the ancient Pueblo people maintained with each other, and with the populous natural world they lived within. A bolt of lightning is itself, but at the same time it may mean much more. It may be a messenger of good fortune when summer rains are needed. It may deliver death, perhaps the result of manipulations by the Gunnadeyahs, destructive necromancers. Lightning may strike down an evil-doer. Or lightning may strike a person of good will. If the person survives, lightning endows him or her with heightened power.

Pictographs and petroglyphs of constellations or elk or antelope draw their magic in part from the process wherein the focus of all prayer and concentration is upon the thing itself, which, in its turn, guides the hunter's hand. Connection with the spirit dimensions requires a figure or form which is all-inclusive. A "lifelike" rendering of an elk is too restrictive. Only the elk *is* itself. A *realistic* rendering of an elk would be only one particular elk anyway. The purpose of the hunt rituals and magic is to make contact with *all* the spirits of the Elk.

The land, the sky, and all that is within them—the landscape—includes human beings. Interrelationships in the Pueblo landscape are complex and fragile. The unpredictability of the weather, the aridity and harshness of much of the terrain in the high plateau country explain in large part the relentless attention the ancient Pueblo people gave the sky and the earth around them. Survival depended upon harmony and cooperation not only among human beings, but among all things—the animate and the less animate, since rocks and mountains were known to move, to travel occasionally.

The ancient Pueblos believed the Earth and the Sky were sisters (or sister and brother in the post-Christian version). As long as good family relations are maintained, then the Sky will continue to bless her sister, the Earth, with rain, and the Earth's children will continue to survive. But the old stories recall incidents in which troublesome spirits or beings threaten the earth. In one story, a malicious ka'tsina, called the Gambler, seizes the Shiwana, or Rainclouds, the Sun's beloved children. The Shiwana are snared in magical power late one afternoon on a high mountain top. The Gambler takes the Rainclouds to his mountain stronghold where he locks them in the north room of his house. What was his idea? The Shiwana were beyond value. They brought life to all things on earth. The Gambler wanted a big stake to wager in his games of chance. But such greed, even on the part of only one being, had the effect of threatening the survival of all life on earth. Sun Youth, aided by old Grandmother Spider, outsmarts the Gambler and the rigged game, and the Rainclouds are set free. The drought ends, and once more life thrives on earth.

Through the Stories We Hear Who We Are

All summer the people watch the west horizon, scanning the sky from south to north for rain clouds. Corn must have moisture at the time the tassels form. Otherwise pollination will be incomplete, and the ears will be stunted and shriveled. An inadequate harvest may bring disaster. Stories told at Hopi, Zuni, and at Acoma and Laguna describe drought and starvation as recently as 1900. Precipitation in west-central New Mexico averages fourteen inches annually. The western pueblos are located at altitudes over 5,600 feet above sea level, where winter temperatures at night fall below freezing. Yet evidence of their presence in the high desert plateau country goes back ten thousand years. The ancient Pueblo people not only survived in this environment, but many years they thrived. In A.D. 1100 the people at Chaco Canyon had built cities with apartment buildings of stone five stories high. Their sophistication as sky-watchers was surpassed only by Mayan and Inca astronomers. Yet this vast complex of knowledge and belief, amassed for thousands of years; was never recorded in writing.

Instead, the ancient Pueblo people depended upon collective memory through successive generations to maintain and transmit an entire culture, a world view complete with proven strategies for survival. The oral narrative, or "story," became the medium in which the complex of Pueblo knowledge and belief was maintained. Whatever the event or the subject, the ancient people perceived the world and themselves within that world as part of an ancient continuous story composed of innumerable bundles of other stories.

The ancient Pueblo vision of the world was inclusive. The impulse was to leave nothing out. Pueblo oral tradition necessarily embraced all levels of human experience. Otherwise, the collective knowledge and beliefs comprising ancient Pueblo culture would have been incomplete. Thus stories about the Creation and Emergence of human beings and animals into this World continue to be retold each year for four days and four nights during the winter solstice. The "humma-hah" stories related events from the time long ago when human beings were still able to communicate with animals and other living things. But, beyond these two preceding categories, the Pueblo oral tradition knew no boundaries. Accounts of the appearance of the first Europeans in Pueblo country or of the tragic encounters between Pueblo people and Apache raiders were no more and no less important than stories about the biggest mule deer ever taken or adulterous couples surprised in cornfields and chicken coops. Whatever happened, the ancient people instinctively sorted events and details into a loose narrative structure. Everything became a story.

Traditionally everyone, from the youngest child to the oldest person, was expected to listen and to be able to recall or tell a portion, if only a small detail, from a narrative account or story. Thus the remembering and retelling were a communal process. Even if a key figure, an elder who knew much more than others, were to die unexpectedly, the system would remain intact. Through the efforts of a great many people, the community was able to piece together valuable accounts and crucial information that might otherwise have died with an individual.

Communal storytelling was a self-correcting process in which listeners were encouraged to speak up if they noted an important fact or detail omitted. The people were happy to listen to two or three different versions of the same event or the same humma-hah story. Even conflicting versions of an incident were welcomed for the entertainment they provided. Defenders of each version might joke and tease one another, but seldom were there any direct confrontations. Implicit in the Pueblo oral tradition was the awareness that loyalties, grudges, and kinship must always influence the narrator's choices as she emphasizes to listeners this is the way *she* has always heard the story told. The ancient Pueblo people sought a communal truth, not an absolute. For them this truth lived somewhere within the web of differing versions, disputes over minor points, outright contradictions tangling with old feuds and village rivalries.

A dinner-table conversation, recalling a deer hunt forty years ago when the largest mule deer ever was taken, inevitably stimulates similar memories in listeners. But hunting stories were not merely after-dinner entertainment. These accounts contained information of critical importance about behavior and migration patterns of mule deer. Hunting stories carefully described key landmarks and locations of fresh water. Thus a deer-hunt story might also serve as a "map." Lost travelers, and lost piñon-nut gatherers, have been saved by sighting a rock formation they recognize only because they once heard a hunting story describing this rock formation.

The importance of cliff formations and water holes does not end with hunting stories. As offspring of the Mother Earth, the ancient Pueblo people could not conceive of themselves within a specific landscape. Location, or "place," nearly always plays a central role in the Pueblo oral narratives. Indeed, stories are most frequently recalled as people are passing by a specific geographical feature or the exact place where a story takes place. The precise date of the incident often is less important than the place or location of the happening. "Long, long ago," "a long time ago," "not too long ago," and "recently" are usually how stories are classified in terms of time. But the places where the stories occur are precisely located, and prominent geographical details recalled, even if the landscape is well-known to listeners. Often because the turning point in the narrative involved a peculiarity or special quality of a rock or tree or plant found only at that place. Thus, in the case of many of the Pueblo narratives, it is impossible to determine which came first: the incident or the geographical feature which begs to be brought alive in a story that features some unusual aspect of this location.

There is a giant sandstone boulder about a mile north of Old Laguna, on the road to Paguate. It is ten feet tall and twenty feet in circumference. When I was a child, and we would pass this boulder driving to Paguate village, someone usually made reference to the story about Kochininako, Yellow Woman, and the Estrucuyo, a monstrous giant who nearly ate her. The Twin Hero Brothers saved Kochininako, who had been out hunting rabbits to take home to feed her mother and sisters. The Hero Brothers had heard her cries just in time. The Estrucuyo had cornered her in a cave too small to fit its monstrous head. Kochininako had already thrown to the Estrucuyo all her rabbits, as well as her moccasins and most of her clothing. Still the creature had not been satisfied. After killing the Estrucuyo with their bows and arrows, the Twin Hero Brothers slit open the Estrucuyo and cut out its heart. They threw the heart as far as they could. The monster's heart landed there, beside the old trail to Paguate village, where the sandstone boulder rests now.

It may be argued that the existence of the boulder precipitated the creation of a story to explain it. But sandstone boulders and sandstone formations of strange shapes abound in the Laguna Pueblo area. Yet most of them do not have stories. Often the crucial element in a narrative is the terrain—some specific detail of the setting.

A high dark mesa rises dramatically from a grassy plain fifteen miles southeast of Laguna, in an area known as Swanee. On the grassy plain one hundred and forty years ago, my great-grandmother's uncle and his brother-in-law were grazing their herd of sheep. Because visibility on the plain extends for over twenty miles, it wasn't until the two sheepherders came near the high dark mesa that the Apaches were able to stalk them. Using the mesa to obscure their approach, the raiders swept around from both ends of the mesa. My great-grandmother's relatives were killed, and the herd lost. The high dark mesa played a critical role: the mesa had compromised the safety which the openness of the plains had seemed to assure. Pueblo and Apache alike relied upon the terrain, the very earth herself, to give them protection and aid. Human activities or needs were maneuvered to fit the existing surroundings and conditions. I imagine the last afternoon of my distant ancestors as warm and sunny for late September. They might have been traveling slowly, bringing the sheep closer to Laguna in preparation for the approach of colder weather. The grass was tall and only beginning to change from green to a yellow which matched the late-afternoon sun shining off it. There might have been comfort in the warmth and the sight of the sheep fattening on good pasture which lulled my ancestors into their fatal inattention. They might have had a rifle whereas the Apaches had only bows and arrows. But there would have been four or five Apache raiders, and the surprise attack would have canceled any advantage the rifles gave them.

Survival in any landscape comes down to making the best use of all available resources. On that particular September afternoon, the raiders made better use of the Swanee terrain than my poor ancestors did. Thus the high dark mesa and the story of the two lost Laguna herders became inextricably linked. The memory of them and their story resides in part with the high black mesa. For as long as the mesa stands, people within the family and clan will be reminded of the story of that afternoon long ago. Thus the continuity and accuracy of the oral narratives are reinforced by the landscape—and the Pueblo interpretation of that landscape is *maintained*.

POSSIBILITIES FOR WRITING

1. Consider Silko's final story about the slaughter of her own ancestors. In what ways does this story explain, elaborate on, and summarize the central points she makes throughout the essay?
2. Compare Silko's observations with those of N. Scott Momaday in "The Way to Rainy Mountain" (pages 419–425). Based on these two essays, what are some similarities and differences between the two writers' native cultures?
3. Write an essay about a landscape that has significant meaning for you. How similar and different is it for you to attempt to view landscape as Silko describes here?

Susan Sontag (1933–2004) *was one of America's most prominent intellectuals, having been involved with the world of ideas all her life. After studying at the University of California at Berkeley, she earned a B.A. in philosophy from the University of Chicago at the age of eighteen, after which she studied religion at the Union Theological Seminary in New York, then philosophy and literature at Harvard, receiving master's degrees in both fields. Sontag also studied at Oxford and the Sorbonne. From the other side of the desk, she taught and lectured extensively at universities around the world, but for many years she made her academic home at Columbia and Rutgers universities. Sontag's books range widely, and include a collection of stories, I, etcetera (1978); a play, Alice in Bed (1993); and six volumes of essays, including* Against Interpretation (1966), Illness as Metaphor (1978), *and* On Photography (1977). *Among her four novels are* The Volcano Lover (1992), *which was a best-seller, and* In America (2000), *which won the National Book Critics Circle Award. In addition, Sontag wrote and directed four feature-length films and was a human rights activist for more than two decades. She was also a MacArthur Fellow.*

SUSAN SONTAG

A Woman's Beauty: Put-Down or Power Source?

In "A Woman's Beauty: Put-Down or Power Source?" Sontag displays her historical interest as well as her interest in current attitudes toward gender roles. In arguing against the dangerous and limiting ideals to which women have subjected themselves (and been subjected by men), Sontag brings to bear a brisk analysis of Greek and Christian perspectives, implicating both in their consequences for contemporary women's obsessive and compulsive efforts to make themselves beautiful.

Unlike many contemporary essays, Sontag's essays lack a strong autobiographical impulse. One might expect such a personal strain in an essay on women's beauty—it certainly would not be out of place—but Sontag assiduously avoids the personal note. But Sontag is less concerned either with her own experience of beauty or with past perspectives on beauty in and of themselves. She is far more interested in how the past can help us understand the present, and how past perspectives affect modern women's fascination with and desire for personal beauty.

For the Greeks, beauty was a virtue: a kind of excellence. Persons then were assumed to be what we now have to call—lamely, enviously—*whole* persons. If it did occur to the Greeks to distinguish between a person's "inside" and "outside," they still expected that inner beauty would be matched by beauty of the other kind. The well-born young Athenians who gathered around Socrates found it quite paradoxical that their hero was so intelligent, so brave, so honorable, so seductive—and so ugly. One of Socrates' main pedagogical acts was to be ugly—and teach those innocent, no doubt splendid-looking disciples of his how full of paradoxes life really was.

They may have resisted Socrates' lesson. We do not. Several thousand years later, we are more wary of the enchantments of beauty. We not only split off—with the greatest facility—the "inside" (character, intellect) from the "outside" (looks); but we are actually surprised when someone who is beautiful is also intelligent, talented, good.

It was principally the influence of Christianity that deprived beauty of the central place it had in classical ideals of human excellence. By limiting excellence (*virtus* in Latin) to *moral* virtue only, Christianity set beauty adrift—as an alienated, arbitrary, superficial enchantment. And beauty has continued to lose prestige. For close to two centuries it has become a convention to attribute beauty to only one of the two sexes: the sex which, however Fair, is always Second. Associating beauty with women has put beauty even further on the defensive, morally.

A beautiful woman, we say in English. But a handsome man. "Handsome" is the masculine equivalent of—and refusal of—a compliment which has accumulated certain demeaning overtones, by being reserved for women only. That one can call a man "beautiful" in French and in Italian suggests that Catholic countries—unlike those countries shaped by the Protestant version of Christianity—still retain some vestiges of the pagan admiration for beauty. But the difference, if one exists, is of degree only. In every modern country that is Christian or post-Christian, women *are* the beautiful sex—to the detriment of the notion of beauty as well as of women.

To be called beautiful is thought to name something essential to women's character and concerns. (In contrast to men—whose essence is to be strong, or effective, or competent.) It does not take someone in the throes of advanced feminist awareness to perceive that the way women are taught to be involved with beauty encourages narcissism, reinforces dependence and immaturity. Everybody (women and men) knows that. For it is "everybody," a whole society, that has identified being feminine with caring about how one *looks*. (In contrast to being masculine—which is identified with caring about what one *is* and *does* and only secondarily, if at all, about how one looks.) Given these stereotypes, it is no wonder that beauty enjoys, at best, a rather mixed reputation.

It is not, of course, the desire to be beautiful that is wrong but the obligation to be—or to try. What is accepted by most women as a flattering idealization of their sex is a way of making women feel inferior to what they actually are—or normally grow to be. For the ideal of beauty is administered as a form of self-oppression. Women are taught to see their bodies in *parts,* and to evaluate each part separately. Breasts, feet, hips, waistline, neck, eyes, nose, complexion, hair, and so on—each in turn is submitted to an anxious, fretful, often despairing scrutiny. Even if some pass muster, some will always be found wanting. Nothing less than perfection will do.

In men, good looks is a whole, something taken in at a glance. It does not need to be confirmed by giving measurements of different regions of the body; nobody encourages a man to dissect his appearance, feature by feature. As for perfection, that is considered trivial—almost unmanly. Indeed, in the ideally good-looking man a small imperfection or blemish is considered positively desirable. According to one movie critic (a woman) who is a declared Robert Redford fan, it is having that cluster of skin-colored moles on one cheek that saves Redford from being merely a "pretty face." Think of the depreciation of women—as well as of beauty—that is implied in that judgment.

"The privileges of beauty are immense," said Cocteau. To be sure, beauty is a form of power. And deservedly so. What is lamentable is that it is the only form of power that most women are encouraged to seek. This power is always conceived in relation to men; it is not the power to do but the power to attract. It is a power that negates itself. For this power is not one that can be chosen freely—at least, not by women—or renounced without social censure.

To preen, for a woman, can never be just a pleasure. It is also a duty. It is her work. If a woman does real work—and even if she has clambered up to a leading position in politics, law, medicine, business, or whatever—she is always under pressure to confess that she still works at being attractive. But in so far as she is keeping up as one of the Fair Sex, she brings under suspicion her very capacity to be objective, professional, authoritative, thoughtful. Damned if they do—women are. And damned if they don't.

One could hardly ask for more important evidence of the dangers of considering persons as split between what is "inside" and what is "outside" than that interminable half-comic half-tragic tale, the oppression of women. How easy it is to start off by defining women as caretakers of their surfaces, and then to disparage them (or find them adorable) for being "superficial." It is a crude trap, and it has worked for too long. But to get out of the trap requires that women get some critical distance from that excellence and privilege which is beauty, enough distance to see how much beauty itself has been abridged in order to prop up the mythology of the "feminine." There should be a way of saving beauty *from* women—and *for* them.

POSSIBILITIES FOR WRITING

1. Consider the extent to which you agree (or disagree) with Sontag regarding what she says about the plight of contemporary women with respect to beauty. To what extent are men responsible for women's obsession with beauty? To what extent are women themselves responsible? Explain.

2. Sontag makes a brief historical excursion to consider the place of beauty in classical Greek culture and in early Christian times. How effective is this excursion into history? How important is it for Sontag's argument? And how persuasive is Sontag's use of these references?

3. Do your own little study of women's attitudes to beauty by surveying women you know in varying age groups. Consider both what they say and what they do with regard to the use of beauty products. Write up your findings and your analysis of the significance of beauty for women today.

Elizabeth Cady Stanton (1815–1902), an important leader of the early women's movement, was born in Johnstown, New York, and received a rigorous education for a woman of her day at the Troy Female Seminary. After attending a congress of abolitionists during which women were barred from participating, she was inspired to promote greater equality for women. She helped organize the first women's rights convention in Seneca Falls, New York, in 1848, and she continued to be a strong leader in the movement to gain women the right to vote, to liberalize divorce laws, and to help women achieve parity with men in terms of education, employment, and legal status. The mother of seven children, she was nevertheless a tireless organizer, lecturer, and writer for the cause, as president of major women's suffrage associations from 1869 until her death.

ELIZABETH CADY STANTON

Declaration of Sentiments and Resolutions

Elizabeth Cady Stanton's "Declaration of Sentiments and Resolutions" was created at the Seneca Falls Convention, at which women gathered in Seneca Falls, New York, to assert their rights and demand equal respect as full United States citizens. In the "Declaration," Stanton makes clear and purposeful reference to the United States Declaration of Independence. At certain points, Stanton uses the exact wording of the American Declaration. But she adds "women" to the equation.

Stanton also follows the logical structure of the Declaration of Independence, arguing that men have mistreated women, denied women their "inalienable" rights, and generally established "an absolute tyranny" over them, a tyranny analogous to that which England had established over the American colonies. In addition, Stanton also creates a list of examples she cites as evidence of men's tyrannical treatment of women. From this evidence she draws the conclusion that women be given "immediate admission to all the rights and privileges which belong to them as citizens of the United States."

When, in the course of human events, it becomes necessary for one portion of the family of man to assume among the people of the earth a position different from that which they have hitherto occupied, but one to which the laws of nature and of nature's God entitle them, a decent respect to the opinions of mankind requires that they should declare the causes that impel them to such a course.

We hold these truths to be self-evident: that all men and women are created equal; that they are endowed by their Creator with certain inalienable rights; that among these are life, liberty, and the pursuit of happiness; that to secure these rights governments are instituted, deriving their just powers from the consent of the governed. Whenever any form of government becomes destructive of these ends, it is the right of those who suffer from it to refuse allegiance to it, and to insist upon the institution of a new government, laying its foundation on such principles, and organizing its powers in such form, as to them shall seem most likely to effect their safety and happiness. Prudence indeed, will dictate that governments long established should not be changed for light and transient causes; and accordingly all experience hath shown that mankind are more disposed to suffer, while evils are sufferable, than to right themselves by abolishing the forms to which they were accustomed. But when a long train of abuses and usurpations, pursuing invariably the same object evinces a design to reduce them under absolute despotism, it is their duty to throw off such government, and to provide new guards for their future security. Such has been the patient sufferance of the women under this government, and such is now the necessity which constrains them to demand the equal station to which they are entitled.

The history of mankind is a history of repeated injuries and usurpations on the part of man toward woman, having in direct object the establishment of an absolute tyranny over her. To prove this, let facts be submitted to a candid world.

He has never permitted her to exercise her inalienable right to the elective franchise.

He has compelled her to submit to laws, in the formation of which she had no voice.

He has withheld from her rights which are given to the most ignorant and degraded men—both natives and foreigners.

Having deprived her of this first right of a citizen, the elective franchise, thereby leaving her without representation in the halls of legislation, he has oppressed her on all sides.

He has made her, if married, in the eye of the law, civilly dead.

He has taken from her all right in property, even to the wages she earns.

He has made her, morally, an irresponsible being, as she can commit many crimes with impunity, provided they be done in the presence of her husband. In the covenant of marriage, she is compelled to promise obedience to her husband, he becoming, to all intents and purposes, her master—the law giving him power to deprive her of her liberty, and to administer chastisement.

He has so framed the laws of divorce, as to what shall be the proper causes, and in case of separation, to whom the guardianship of the children shall be given, as to be wholly regardless of the happiness of women—the law, in all cases, going upon a false supposition of the supremacy of man, and giving all power into his hands.

After depriving her of all rights as a married woman, if single, and the owner of property, he has taxed her to support a government which recognizes her only when her property can be made profitable to it.

He has monopolized nearly all the profitable employments, and from those she is permitted to follow, she receives but a scanty remuneration. He closes against her all the avenues to wealth and distinction which he considers most honorable to himself. As a teacher of theology, medicine, or law, she is not known.

He has denied her the facilities for obtaining a thorough education, all colleges being closed against her.

He allows her in Church, as well as State, but a subordinate position, claiming Apostolic authority for her exclusion from the ministry, and, with some exceptions, from any public participation in the affairs of the Church.

He has created a false public sentiment by giving to the world a different code of morals for men and women, by which moral delinquencies which exclude women from society, are not only tolerated, but deemed of little account in man.

He has usurped the prerogative of Jehovah himself, claiming it as his right to assign for her a sphere of action, when that belongs to her conscience and to her God.

He has endeavored, in every way that he could, to destroy her confidence in her own powers, to lessen her self-respect, and to make her willing to lead a dependent and abject life.

Now, in view of this entire disfranchisement of one-half the people of this country, their social and religious degradation—in view of the unjust laws above mentioned, and because women do feel themselves aggrieved, oppressed, and fraudulently deprived of their most sacred rights, we insist that they have immediate admission to all the rights and privileges which belong to them as citizens of the United States.

In entering upon the great work before us, we anticipate no small amount of misconception, misrepresentation, and ridicule; but we shall use every instrumentality within our power to effect our object. We shall employ agents, circulate tracts, petition the State and National legislatures, and endeavor to enlist the pulpit and the press in our behalf.

We hope this Convention will be followed by a series of Conventions embracing every part of the country.

POSSIBILITIES FOR WRITING

1. Analyze the list of grievances Stanton enumerates. In particular, consider the extent to which these follow a logical sequence, building one upon another. Do you find that they lead successfully to her larger conclusion? Why or why not?
2. Based on your reading of Stanton's Declaration, how were women viewed in 1848, when the document was drafted and delivered—that is, what arguments *against* Stanton's position seem to have prevailed at the time? For example, how might denying women any right to vote, the most controversial grievance listed in the document, have been justified? You might do some research in responding to this question.
3. Draft your own Declaration based on Jefferson's pages 306–314 and Stanton's. Cast yourself as a member of an aggrieved party, explain your grievances, and end with a call to action. Your effort may be serious, or you may focus on more light-hearted grievances (those of first-year college students, for example).

Brent Staples (b. 1951) *grew up in the poor neighborhood of Chester, Pennsylvania, and attended Widener University on scholarship, later receiving a doctorate in psychology from the University of Chicago. After a short stint as a teacher, he found a job as a reporter with the* Chicago Sun-Times *and was later hired by the* New York Times, *where he is now a member of the editorial board and contributes opinion pieces under his own by-line. His 1994 memoir* Parallel Time: Growing Up in Black and White *explores his experiences as a black youth trying to escape the poverty and violence that surrounded his family and the tragic inability of his younger brother to do so.*

BRENT STAPLES

Just Walk on By: Black Men and Public Space

The title, "Just Walk on By: Black Men and Public Space," conveys the casual manner of Brent Staples's essay about a black male's power to intimidate white people. Staples tells a series of stories and then reflects on their significance. The first story, which is a paradigm for the others, reveals the fear that he as a large black man induces in others, particularly in white women. He describes people's responses to seeing him—locking their cars, walking on the opposite of the street, holding tightly to their pocketbooks. And he describes the actions he takes to alleviate their unfounded fear of him—whistling melodies from classical music, for example.

Acknowledging that women and men, black and white are victimized disproportionately by young black males through violent crime, Staples offers some reasons why this is so. But he also explains his own very real fear that, as a black male, he may be victimized by other people's mistaken fear of him, since he is basically a timid and unthreatening soul. The precautions he takes are his attempt to minimize that fear and to protect himself from its potentially dangerous consequences.

My first victim was a woman—white, well dressed, probably in her early twenties. I came upon her late one evening on a deserted street in Hyde Park, a relatively affluent neighborhood in an otherwise mean, impoverished section of Chicago. As I swung onto the avenue behind her, there seemed to be a discreet, uninflammatory distance between us. Not so. She cast back a worried glance. To her, the youngish black man—a broad six feet two inches with a beard and billowing hair, both hands shoved into the pockets of a bulky military jacket—seemed menacingly close. After a few more quick glimpses, she picked up her pace and was soon running in earnest. Within seconds she disappeared into a cross street.

That was more than a decade ago, I was twenty-two years old, a graduate student newly arrived at the University of Chicago. It was in the echo of that terrified woman's footfalls that I first began to know the unwieldy inheritance I'd come into—the ability to alter public space in ugly ways. It was clear that she thought herself the quarry of a mugger, a rapist, or worse. Suffering a bout of insomnia, however, I was stalking sleep, not defenseless wayfarers. As a softy who is scarcely able to take a knife to a raw chicken—let alone hold one to a person's throat—I was surprised, embarrassed, and dismayed all at once. Her flight made me feel like an accomplice in tyranny. It also made it clear that I was indistinguishable from the muggers who occasionally seeped into the area from the surrounding ghetto. That first encounter, and those that followed, signified that a vast, unnerving gulf lay between nighttime pedestrians—particularly women—and me. And I soon gathered that being perceived as dangerous is a hazard in itself. I only needed to turn a corner into a dicey situation, or crowd some frightened, armed person in a foyer somewhere, or make an errant move after being pulled over by a policeman. Where fear and weapons meet—and they often do in urban America—there is always the possibility of death.

In that first year, my first away from my hometown, I was to become thoroughly familiar with the language of fear. At dark, shadowy intersections, I could cross in front of a car stopped at a traffic light and elicit the *thunk, thunk, thunk, thunk* of the driver—black, white, male, or female—hammering down the door locks. On less traveled streets after dark, I grew accustomed to but never comfortable with people crossing to the other side of the street rather than pass me. Then there were the standard unpleasantries with policemen, doormen, bouncers, cabdrivers, and others whose business it is to screen out troublesome individuals *before* there is any nastiness.

I moved to New York nearly two years ago and I have remained an avid night walker. In central Manhattan, the near-constant crowd cover minimizes tense one-on-one street encounters. Elsewhere—in SoHo, for example, where sidewalks are narrow and tightly spaced buildings shut out the sky—things can get very taut indeed.

After dark, on the warrenlike streets of Brooklyn where I live, I often see women who fear the worst from me. They seem to have set their faces on neutral, and with their purse straps strung across their chests bandolier-style, they forge ahead as though bracing themselves against being tackled. I understand, of course, that the danger they perceive is not a hallucination. Women are particularly vulnerable to street violence, and young black males are drastically overrepresented among the perpetrators of that violence. Yet these truths are no solace against the kind of alienation that comes of being ever the suspect, a fearsome entity with whom pedestrians avoid making eye contact.

It is not altogether clear to me how I reached the ripe old age of twenty-two without being conscious of the lethality nighttime pedestrians attributed to me. Perhaps it was because in Chester, Pennsylvania, the small, angry industrial town where I came of age in the 1960s, I was scarcely noticeable against a backdrop of gang warfare, street knifings, and murders. I grew up one of the good boys, had perhaps a half-dozen fistfights. In retrospect, my shyness of combat has clear sources.

As a boy, I saw countless tough guys locked away; I have since buried several, too. They were babies, really—a teenage cousin, a brother of twenty-two, a childhood friend in his mid-twenties—all gone down in episodes of bravado played out in the streets. I came to doubt the virtues of intimidation early on. I chose, perhaps unconsciously, to remain a shadow—timid, but a survivor.

The fearsomeness mistakenly attributed to me in public places often has a perilous flavor. The most frightening of these confusions occurred in the late 1970s and early 1980s, when I worked as a journalist in Chicago. One day, rushing into the office of a magazine I was writing for with a deadline story in hand, I was mistaken for a burglar. The office manager called security and, with an ad hoc posse, pursued me through the labyrinthine halls, nearly to my editor's door. I had no way of proving who I was. I could only move briskly toward the company of someone who knew me.

Another time I was on assignment for a local paper and killing time before an interview. I entered a jewelry store on the city's affluent Near North Side. The proprietor excused herself and returned with an enormous red Doberman pinscher straining at the end of a leash. She stood, the dog extended toward me, silent to my questions, her eyes bulging nearly out of her head. I took a cursory look around, nodded, and bade her good night.

Relatively speaking, however, I never fared as badly as another black male journalist. He went to nearby Waukegan, Illinois, a couple of summers ago to work on a story about a murderer who was born there. Mistaking the reporter for the killer, police officers hauled him from his car at gunpoint and but for his press credentials would probably have tried to book him. Such episodes are not uncommon. Black men trade tales like this all the time.

Over the years, I learned to smother the rage I felt at so often being taken for a criminal. Not to do so would surely have led to madness. I now take precautions to make myself less threatening. I move about with care, particularly late in the evening. I give a wide berth to nervous people on subway platforms during the wee hours, particularly when I have exchanged business clothes for jeans. If I happen to be entering a building behind some people who appear skittish, I may walk by, letting them clear the lobby before I return, so as not to seem to be following them. I have been calm and extremely congenial on those rare occasions when I've been pulled over by the police.

And on late-evening constitutionals I employ what has proved to be an excellent tension-reducing measure: I whistle melodies from Beethoven and Vivaldi and the more popular classical composers. Even steely New Yorkers hunching toward nighttime destinations seem to relax, and occasionally they even join in the tune. Virtually everybody seems to sense that a mugger wouldn't be warbling bright, sunny selections from Vivaldi's *Four Seasons*. It is my equivalent of the cowbell that hikers wear when they know they are in bear country.

POSSIBILITIES FOR WRITING

1. Staples's essay was published in the mid-1980s and has since been widely anthologized. How do you account for its popularity? In responding, consider both the way it is written, the points Staples has to make, and the essay's relevance today. Do you think this popularity is justified? Why or why not?

2. Rather than confront the fears and prejudice of the strangers he encounters, Staples explains that he goes out of his way to accommodate them. How does he do so? *Why* does he do so? How do you respond to his actions and motives?

3. Write about any times you have made strangers uncomfortable because of the way you "alter public space." How did you respond? Alternatively, write about any times you have judged others as threatening solely because of their appearance. Were your responses justified? Do you think people tend to mistrust one another based too much on appearances?

Shelby Steele (b. 1946) *grew up in Chicago, the son of biracial parents who were active in the civil rights movement. He attended Coe College, Southern Illinois University, and the University of Utah, and he is currently a professor of English at San Jose State University. His* The Content of Our Character: A New Vision of Race in America *(1990), a collection of essays, received wide attention because of its reasoned stand against affirmative action; it also won the National Book Critics Circle Award. Among Steele's books are* The Dream Deferred: A Second Betrayal of Black Freedom in America *(1999), and* White Guilt *(2006).*

SHELBY STEELE

On Being Black and Middle Class

In "On Being Black and Middle Class," Shelby Steele provides a forthright account of his identity as a middle-class black American. As a black man, Steele feels an allegiance to and identifies with black Americans of the working classes. As a member of the American middle class, Steele identifies with the values and culture of middle Americans, who happen to be mostly white. Steele's essay explores this dual identity.

One of the more complicated and controversial aspects of Steele's essay is his contention that poorer, less-educated African Americans are typically considered to be more authentically "black" than middle-class African Americans. Steele contests this idea, arguing that simplistic stereotypes of blacks perpetuated by the media and popular culture oversimplify the complex issues associated with being a middle-class black American.

Not long ago, a friend of mine, black like myself, said to me that the term "black middle class" was actually a contradiction in terms. Race, he insisted, blurred class distinctions among blacks. If you were black, you were just black and that was that. When I argued, he let his eyes roll at my naiveté. Then he went on. For us, as black professionals, it was an exercise in self-flattery, a pathetic pretension, to give meaning to such a distinction. Worse, the very idea of class threatened the unity that was vital to the black community as a whole. After all, since when had white America taken note of anything but color when it came to blacks? He then reminded me of an old Malcolm X line that had been popular in the sixties. Question: What is a black man with a Ph.D.? Answer: A nigger.

For many years I had been on my friend's side of this argument. Much of my conscious thinking on the old conundrum of race and class was shaped during my high school and college years in the race-charged sixties, when the fact of my race took on an almost religious significance. Progressively, from the mid-sixties on, more and more aspects of my life found their explanation, their justification, and their motivation in race. My youthful concerns about career, romance, money, values, and even styles of dress became a subject to consultation with various oracular sources of racial wisdom. And these ranged from a figure as ennobling as Martin Luther King, Jr., to the underworld elegance of dress I found in jazz clubs on the South Side of Chicago. Everywhere there were signals, and in those days I considered myself so blessed with clarity and direction that I pitied my white classmates who found more embarrassment than guidance in the fact of *their* race. In 1968, inflated by my new power, I took a mischievous delight in calling them culturally disadvantaged.

But now, hearing my friend's comment was like hearing a priest from a church I'd grown disenchanted with. I understood him, but my faith was weak. What had sustained me in the sixties sounded monotonous and off the mark in the eighties. For me, race had lost much of its juju, its singular capacity to conjure meaning. And today, when I honestly look at my life and the lives of many other middle-class blacks I know, I can see that race never fully explained our situation in American society. Black though I may be, it is impossible for me to sit in my single-family house with two cars in the driveway and a swing set in the back yard and *not* see the role class has played in my life. And how can my friend, similarly raised and similiarly situated, not see it?

Yet despite my certainty I felt a sharp tug of guilt as I tried to explain myself over my friend's skepticism. He is a man of many comedic facial expressions and, as I spoke, his brow lifted in extreme moral alarm as if I were uttering the unspeakable. His clear implication was that I was being elitist and possibly (dare he suggest?) anti-black—crimes for which there might well be no redemption. He pretended to fear for me. I chuckled along with him, but inwardly I did wonder at myself. Though I never doubted the validity of what I was saying, I felt guilty saying it. Why?

After he left (to retrieve his daughter from a dance lesson) I realized that the trap I felt myself in had a tiresome familiarity and, in a sort of slow-motion epiphany, I began to see its outline. It was like the suddenly sharp vision one has at the end of a burdensome marriage when all the long-repressed incompatibilities come undeniably to light.

What became clear to me is that people like myself, my friend, and middle-class blacks generally are caught in a very specific double bind that keeps two equally powerful elements of our identity at odds with each other. The middle-class values by which we were raised—the work ethic, the importance of education, the value of property ownership, of respectability, of "getting ahead," of stable family life, of initiative, of self-reliance, etc.—are, in themselves, raceless and even assimilationist. They urge us toward participation in the American mainstream, toward integration, toward a strong identification with the society—and toward the entire constellation of qualities that are implied in the word "individualism." These values are almost rules for how to prosper in a democratic, free-enterprise society that admires and rewards individual effort. They tell us to work hard for ourselves and our families and to seek our opportunities whenever they appear, inside or outside the confines of whatever ethnic group we may belong to.

But the particular pattern of racial identification that emerged in the sixties and that still prevails today urges middle-class blacks (and all blacks) in the opposite direction. This pattern asks us to see ourselves as an embattled minority, and it urges an adversarial stance toward the mainstream, an emphasis on ethnic consciousness over individualism. It is organized around an implied separatism.

The opposing thrust of these two parts of our identity results in the double bind of middle-class blacks. There is no forward movement on either plane that does not constitute backward movement on the other. This was the familiar trap I felt myself in while talking with my friend. As I spoke about class, his eyes reminded me that I was betraying race. Clearly, the two indispensable parts of my identity were a threat to each other.

Of course when you think about it, class and race are both similar in some ways and also naturally opposed. They are two forms of collective identity with boundaries that intersect. But whether they clash or peacefully coexist has much to do with how they are defined. Being both black and middle class becomes a double bind when class and race are defined in sharply antagonistic terms, so that one must be repressed to appease the other.

But what is the "substance" of these two identities, and how does each establish itself in an individual's overall identity? It seems to me that when we identify with any collective we are basically identifying with images that tell us what it means to be a member of that collective. Identity is not the same thing as the fact of membership in a collective; it is, rather, a form of self-definition, facilitated by images of what we wish our membership in the collective to mean. In this sense, the images we identify with may reflect the aspirations of the collective more than they reflect reality, and their content can vary with shifts in those aspirations.

But the process of identification is usually dialectical. It is just as necessary to say what we are *not* as it is to say what we are—so that finally identification comes about by embracing a polarity of positive and negative images. To identify as middle class, for example, I must have both positive and negative images of what being middle class entails; then I will know what I should and should not be doing in order to be middle class. The same goes for racial identity.

In the racially turbulent sixties the polarity of images that came to define racial identification was very antagonistic to the polarity that defined middle-class identification. One might say that the positive images of one lined up with the negative images of the other, so that to identify with both required either a contortionist's flexibility or a dangerous splitting of the self. The double bind of the black middle class was in place. . . .

The black middle class has always defined its class identity by means of positive images gleaned from middle- and upper-class white society, and by means of negative images of lower-class blacks. This habit goes back to the institution of slavery itself, when "house" slaves both mimicked the whites they served and held themselves above the "field" slaves. But in the sixties the old bourgeois impulse to dissociate from the lower classes (the "we-they" distinction) backfired when racial identity suddenly called for the celebration of this same black lower class. One of the qualities of a double bind is that one feels it more than sees it, and I distinctly remember the tension and strange sense of dishonesty I felt in those days as I moved back and forth like a bigamist between the demands of class and race.

Though my father was born poor, he achieved middle-class standing through much hard work and sacrifice (one of his favorite words) and by identifying fully with solid middle-class values—mainly hard work, family life, property ownership, and education for his children (all four of whom have advanced degrees). In his mind these were not so much values as laws of nature. People who embodied them made up the positive images in his class polarity. The negative images came largely from the blacks he had left behind because they were "going nowhere."

No one in my family remembers how it happened, but as time went on, the negative images congealed into an imaginary character named Sam, who, from the extensive service we put him to, quickly grew to mythic proportions. In our family lore he was sometimes a trickster, sometimes a boob, but always possessed of a catalogue of sly faults that gave up graphic images of everything we should not be. On sacrifice: "Sam never thinks about tomorrow. He wants it now or he doesn't care about it." On work: "Sam doesn't favor it too much."

On children: "Sam likes to have them but not to raise them." On money: "Sam drinks it up and pisses it out." On fidelity: "Sam has to have two or three women." On clothes: "Sam features loud clothes. He likes to see and be seen." And so on. Sam's persona amounted to a negative instruction manual in class identity.

I don't think that any of us believed Sam's faults were accurate representations of lower-class black life. He was an instrument of self-definition, not of sociological accuracy. It never occurred to us that he looked very much like the white racist stereotype of blacks, or that he might have been a manifestation of our own racial self-hatred. He simply gave us a counterpoint against which to express our aspirations. If self-hatred was a factor, it was not, for us, a matter of hating lower-class blacks but of hating what we did not want to be.

Still, hate or love aside, it is fundamentally true that my middle-class identity involved a dissociation from images of lower-class black life and a corresponding identification with values and patterns of responsibility that are common to the middle class everywhere. These values sent me a clear message: be both an individual and a responsible citizen; understand that the quality of your life will approximately reflect the quality of effort you put into it; know that individual responsibility is the basis of freedom and that the limitations imposed by fate (whether fair or unfair) are no excuse for passivity.

Whether I live up to these values or not, I know that my acceptance of them is the result of lifelong conditioning. I know also that I share this conditioning with middle-class people of all races and that I can no more easily be free of it than I can be free of my race. Whether all this got started because the black middle class modeled itself on the white middle class is no longer relevant. For the middle-class black, conditioned by these values from birth, the sense of meaning they provide is as immutable as the color of his skin.

I started the sixties in high school feeling that my class-conditioning was the surest way to overcome racial barriers. My racial identity was pretty much taken for granted. After all, it was obvious to the world that I was black. Yet I ended the sixties in graduate school a little embarrassed by my class background and with an almost desperate need to be "black." The tables had turned. I knew very clearly (though I struggled to repress it) that my aspirations and my sense of how to operate in the world came from my class background, yet "being black" required certain attitudes and stances that made me feel secretly a little duplicitous. The inner compatibility of class and race I had known in 1960 was gone.

For blacks, the decade between 1960 and 1969 saw racial identification undergo the same sort of transformation that national identity undergoes in times of war. It became more self-conscious, more narrowly focused, more prescribed, less tolerant of opposition. It spawned an implicit party line, which tended to disallow competing forms of identity. Race-as-identity was lifted from the relative slumber it knew in the fifties and pressed into service in a social and political war against oppression. It was redefined along sharp adversarial lines and directed toward the goal of mobilizing the great mass of black Americans in this warlike effort. It was imbued with a strong moral authority, useful for denouncing those who opposed it and for celebrating those who honored it as a positive achievement rather than as a mere birthright.

The form of racial identification that quickly evolved to meet this challenge presented blacks as a racial monolith, a singular people with a common experience of oppression. Differences within the race, no matter how ineradicable, had to be minimized. Class distinctions were one of the first such differences to be sacrificed, since they not only threatened racial unity but also seemed to stand in contradiction to the principle of equality which was the announced goal of the movement for racial progress. The discomfort I felt in 1969, the vague but relentless sense of duplicity, was the result of a historical necessity that put my race and class at odds, that was asking me to cast aside the distinction of my class and identify with a monolithic view of my race.

If the form of this racial identity was the monolith, its substance was victimization. The civil rights movement and the more radical splinter groups of the late sixties were all dedicated to ending racial victimization, and the form of black identity that emerged to facilitate this goal made blackness and victimization virtually synonymous. Since it was our victimization more than any other variable that identified and unified us, moreover, it followed logically that the purest black was the poor black. It was images of him that clustered around the positive pole of the race polarity; all other blacks were, in effect, required to identify with him in order to confirm their own blackness.

Certainly there were more dimensions to the black experience than victimization, but no other had the same capacity to fire the indignation needed for war. So, again out of historical necessity, victimization became the overriding focus of racial identity. But this only deepened the double bind for middle-class blacks like me. When it came to class we were accustomed to defining ourselves against lower-class blacks and identifying with at least the values of middle-class whites; when it came to race we were now being asked to identify with images of lower-class blacks and to see whites, middle class or otherwise, as victimizers. Negative lining up with positive, we were called upon to reject what we had previously embraced and to embrace what we had previously rejected. To put it still more personally, the Sam figure I had been raised to define myself against had now become the "real" black I was expected to identify with.

The fact that the poor black's new status was only passively earned by the condition of his victimization, not by assertive, positive action, made little difference. Status was status apart from the means by which it was achieved, and along with it came a certain power—the power to define the terms of access to that status, to say who was black and who was not. If a lower-class black said you were not really "black"—a sell-out, an Uncle Tom—the judgment was all the more devastating because it carried the authority of his status. And this judgment soon enough came to be accepted by many whites as well.

In graduate school I was once told by a white professor, "Well, but . . . you're not really black. I mean, you're not disadvantaged." In his mind my lack of victim status disqualified me from the race itself. More recently I was complimented by a black student for speaking reasonably correct English, "proper" English as he put it. "But I don't know if I really want to talk like that," he went on. "Why not?" I asked. "Because then I wouldn't be black no more," he replied without a pause.

To overcome his marginal status, the middle-class black had to identify with a degree of victimization that was beyond his actual experience. In college (and well beyond) we used to play a game called "nap matching." It was a game of one-upmanship, in which we sat around outdoing each other with stories of racial victimization, symbolically measured by the naps of our hair. Most of us were middle class and so had few personal stories to relate, but if we could not match naps with our own biographies, we would move on to those legendary tales of victimization that came to us from the public domain.

The single story that sat atop the pinnacle of racial victimization for us was that of Emmett Till, the Northern black teenager who, on a visit to the South in 1955, was killed and grotesquely mutilated for supposedly looking at or whistling at (we were never sure which, though we argued the point endlessly) a white woman. Oh, how we probed his story, finding in his youth and Northern upbringing the quintessential embodiment of black innocence, brought down by a white evil so portentous and apocalyptic, so gnarled and hideous, that it left us with a feeling not far from awe. By telling his story and others like it, we came to *feel* the immutability of our victimization, its utter indigenousness, as a thing on this earth like dirt or sand or water.

Of course, these sessions were a ritual of group identification, a means by which we, as middle-class blacks, could be at one with our race. But why were we, who had only a moderate experience of victimization (and that offset by opportunities our parents never had), so intent on assimilating or appropriating an identity that in so many ways contradicted our own? Because, I think, the sense of innocence that is always entailed in feeling victimized filled us with a corresponding feeling of entitlement, or even license, that helped us endure our vulnerability on a largely white college campus.

In my junior year in college I rode to a debate tournament with three white students and our faculty coach, an elderly English professor. The experience of being the lone black in a group of whites was so familiar to me that I thought nothing of it as our trip began. But then halfway through the trip the professor casually turned to me and, in an isn't-the-world-funny sort of tone, said that he had just refused to rent an apartment in a house he owned to a "very nice" black couple because their color would "offend" the white couple who lived downstairs. His eyebrows lifted helplessly over his hawkish nose, suggesting that he too, like me, was a victim of America's racial farce. His look assumed a kind of comradeship: he and I were above this grimy business of race, though for expediency we had occasionally to concede the world its madness.

My vulnerability in this situation came not so much from the professor's blindness to his own racism as from his assumption that I would participate in it, that I would conspire with him against my own race so that he might remain comfortably blind. Why did he think I would be amenable to this? I can only guess that he assumed my middle-class identity was so complete and all-encompassing that I would see his action as nothing more than a trifling concession to the folkways of our land, that I would in fact applaud his decision not to disturb propriety. Blind to both his own racism and to me—one blindness serving the other—he could not recognize that he was asking me to betray my race in the name of my class.

His blindness made me feel vulnerable because it threatened to expose my own repressed ambivalence. His comment pressured me to choose between my class identification, which had contributed to my being a college student and a member of the debating team, and my desperate desire to be "black." I could have one but not both; I was double-bound.

Because double binds are repressed there is always an element of terror in them: the terror of bringing to the conscious mind the buried duplicity, self-deception, and pretense involved in serving two masters. This terror is the stuff of vulnerability, and since vulnerability is one of the least tolerable of all human feelings, we usually transform it into an emotion that seems to restore the control of which it has robbed us; most often, that emotion is anger. And so, before the professor had even finished his little story, I had become a furnace of rage. The year was 1967, and I had been primed by endless hours of nap-matching to feel, at least consciously, completely at one with the victim-focused black identity. This identity gave me the license, and the impunity, to unleash upon this professor one of those volcanic eruptions of racial indignation familiar to us from the novels of Richard Wright. Like Cross Damon in *Outsider*, who kills in perfectly righteous anger, I tried to annihilate the man. I punished him not according to the measure of his crime but according to the measure of my vulnerability, a measure set by the cumulative tension of years of repressed terror. Soon I saw that terror in *his* face, as he stared hollow-eyed at the road ahead. My white friends in the back seat, knowing no conflict between their own class and race, were astonished that someone they had taken to be so much like themselves could harbor a rage that for all the world looked murderous.

Though my rage was triggered by the professor's comment, it was deepened and sustained by a complex of need, conflict, and repression in myself of which I had been wholly unaware. Out of my racial vulnerability I had developed the strong need of an identity with which to defend myself. The only such identity available was that of me as victim, him as victimizer. Once in the grip of this paradigm, I began to do far more damage to myself than he had done.

Seeing myself as a victim meant that I clung all the harder to my racial identity, which, in turn, meant that I suppressed my class identity. This cut me off from all the resources my class values might have offered me. In those values, for instance, I might have found the means to a more dispassionate response, the response less of a victim attacked by a victimizer than of an individual offended by a foolish old man. As an individual I might have reported this professor to the college dean. Or I might have calmly tried to reveal his blindness to him, and possibly won a convert. (The flagrancy of his remark suggested a hidden guilt and even self-recognition on which I might have capitalized. Doesn't confession usually signal a willingness to face oneself?) Or I might have simply chuckled and then let my silence serve as an answer to his provocation. Would not my composure, in any form it might take, deflect into his own heart the arrow he'd shot at me?

Instead, my anger, itself the hair-trigger expression of a long-repressed double bind, not only cut me off from the best of my own resources, it also distorted the nature of my true racial problem. The righteousness of this anger and the easy catharsis it brought buoyed the delusion of my victimization and left me as blind as the professor himself.

As a middle-class black I have often felt myself *contriving* to be "black." And I have noticed this same contrivance in others—a certain stretching away from the natural flow of one's life to align oneself with a victim-focused black identity. Our particular needs are out of sync with the form of identity available to meet those needs. Middle-class blacks need to identify racially; it is better to think of ourselves as black and victimized than not black at all; so we contrive (more unconsciously than consciously) to fit ourselves into an identity that denies our class and fails to address the true source of our vulnerability.

For me this once meant spending inordinate amounts of time at black faculty meetings, though these meetings had little to do with my real racial anxieties or my professional life. I was new to the university, one of two blacks in an English department of over seventy, and I felt a little isolated and vulnerable, though I did not admit it to myself. But at these meetings we discussed the problems of black faculty and students within a framework of victimization. The real vulnerability we felt was covered over by all the adversarial drama the victim/victimized polarity inspired, and hence went unseen and unassuaged. And this, I think, explains our rather chronic ineffectiveness as a group. Since victimization was not our primary problem—the university had long ago opened its doors to us—we had to contrive to make it so, and there is not much energy in contrivance. What I got at these meetings was ultimately an object lesson in how fruitless struggle can be when it is not grounded in actual need.

At our black faculty meetings, the old equation of blackness with victimization was ever present—to be black was to be a victim; therefore, not to be a victim was not to be black. As we contrived to meet the terms of this formula there was an inevitable distortion of both ourselves and the larger university. Through the prism of victimization the university seemed more impenetrable than it actually was, and we more limited in our powers. We fell prey to the victim's myopia, making the university an institution from which we could seek redress but which we could never fully join. And this mind-set often led us to look more for compensations for our supposed victimization than for opportunities we could pursue as individuals.

The discomfort and vulnerability felt by middle-class blacks in the sixties, it could be argued, was a worthwhile price to pay considering the progress achieved during that time of racial confrontation. But what may have been tolerable then is intolerable now. Though changes in American society have made it an anachronism, the monolithic form of racial identification that came out of the sixties is still very much with us. It may be more loosely held, and its power to punish heretics has probably diminished, but it continues to catch middle-class blacks in a double bind, thus impeding not only their own advancement but even, I would contend, that of blacks as a group.

The victim-focused black identity encourages the individual to feel that his advancement depends almost entirely on that of the group. Thus he loses sight not only of his own possibilities but of the inextricable connection between individual effort and individual advancement. This is a profound encumbrance today, when there is more opportunity for blacks than ever before, for it reimposes limitations that can have the same oppressive effect as those the society has only recently begun to remove.

It was the emphasis on mass action in the sixties that made the victim-focused black identity a necessity. But in the eighties and beyond, when racial advancement will come only through a multitude of individual advancements, this form of identity inadvertently adds itself to the forces that hold us back. Hard work, education, individual initiative, stable family life, property ownership—these have always been the means by which ethnic groups have moved ahead in America. Regardless of past or present victimization, these "laws" of advancement apply absolutely to black Americans also. There is no getting around this. What we need is a form of racial identity that energizes the individual by putting him in touch with both his possibilities and his responsibilities.

It has always annoyed me to hear from the mouths of certain arbiters of blackness that middle-class blacks should "reach back" and pull up those blacks less fortunate than they—as though middle-class status were an unearned and essentially passive condition in which one needed a large measure of noblesse oblige to occupy one's time. My own image is of reaching back from a moving train to lift on board those who have no tickets. A noble enough sentiment—but might it not be wiser to show them the entire structure of principles, efforts, and sacrifice that puts one in a position to buy a ticket any time one likes? This, I think, is something members of the black middle class can realistically offer to other blacks. Their example is not only a testament to possibility but also a lesson in method. But they cannot lead by example until they are released from a black identity that regards that example as suspect, that sees them as "marginally" black, indeed that holds *them* back by catching them in a double bind.

To move beyond the victim-focused black identity we must learn to make a difficult but crucial distinction: between actual victimization, which we must resist with every resource, and identification with the victim's status. Until we do this we will continue to wrestle more with ourselves than with the new opportunities which so many paid so dearly to win.

POSSIBILITIES FOR WRITING

1. Central to Steele's argument here is the idea of "victimization." What does this term mean for Steele, both explicitly and implicitly? How does his use of the term affect his argument? Can you think of other terms to substitute that might be used to counter his argument?

2. Steele assumes certain markers of class distinctions among blacks, particularly in his discussion of the fictional "Sam" and of standard English speech. Do these seem accurate to you? Are these markers also true of class distinctions among whites and other ethnic groups? How do you make class distinctions?

3. Consider current images of African Americans in television series, advertising, and movies. To what extent do these images seem to suggest a spectrum of experience, or do certain social classes or stereotypes predominate?

Jonathan Swift (1667–1745) was born to English parents in Dublin, Ireland, and received a degree from Trinity College there. Unable to obtain a living in Ireland, he worked for some years as a secretary to a nobleman in Surrey, England, during which time he became acquainted with some of the most important literary figures of his day. He eventually returned to Ireland to assume a clerical post but still spent much of his time among the literary set in London. Swift published several volumes of romantic poetry and a wide variety of literary lampoons and political broadsides, but he is best known today for Gulliver's Travels *(1726), a sharp satire of human foibles. Appointed Dean of Dublin's St. Patrick's Cathedral in 1713, Swift was a tireless defender of the Irish in their struggle against England's harsh, sometimes unbearable rule.*

JONATHAN SWIFT

A Modest Proposal

Jonathan Swift's "A Modest Proposal" is among the most famous satires in English. In it Swift—or rather the persona or speaker he creates to make the modest proposal—recommends killing Irish babies at one year of age. The speaker makes this proposal as a way to solve a severe economic problem that occasions great human suffering: the overpopulation of the Irish people, particularly among Irish Catholics.

The essay's power resides partly in Swift's never lifting the mask he wears, portraying his speaker as a man with a serious public service proposal. It resides, too, in the tone of consummate seriousness and scientific objectivity with which it is offered. And it also derives from Swift's use of irony and digression, from his leaving unspoken the proposal's violation of morality. The consummate reasonableness of the speaker and the wonderful summary of benefits his enacted proposal would provide show Swift wearing his mask to the very end of the essay.

It is a melancholy object to those who walk through this great town or travel in the country, when they see the streets, the roads, and cabin doors, crowded with beggars of the female-sex, followed by three, four, or six children, all in rags and importuning every passenger for an alms. These mothers, instead of being able to work for their honest livelihood, are forced to employ all their time in strolling to beg sustenance for their helpless infants, who, as they grow up, either turn thieves for want of work, or leave their dear native country to fight for the Pretender in Spain, or sell themselves to the Barbadoes.

I think it is agreed by all parties that this prodigious number of children in the arms, or on the backs, or at the heels of their mothers, and frequently of their fathers, is in the present deplorable state of the kingdom a very great additional grievance; and therefore whoever could find out a fair, cheap, and easy method of making these children sound, useful members of the commonwealth would deserve so well of the public as to have his statue set up for a preserver of the nation.

But my intention is very far from being confined to provide only for the children of professed beggars; it is of a much greater extent, and shall take in the whole number of infants at a certain age who are born of parents in effect as little able to support them as those who demand our charity in the streets.

As to my own part, having turned my thoughts for many years upon this important subject, and maturely weighed the several schemes of other projectors, I have always found them grossly mistaken in their computation. It is true, a child just dropped from its dam may be supported by her milk for a solar year, with little other nourishment; at most not above the value of two shillings, which the mother may certainly get, or the value in scraps, by her lawful occupation of begging; and it is exactly at one year old that I propose to provide for them in such a manner as instead of being a charge upon their parents or the parish, or wanting food and raiment for the rest of their lives, they shall on the contrary contribute to the feeding, and partly to the clothing, of many thousands.

There is likewise another great advantage in my scheme, that it will prevent those voluntary abortions, and that horrid practice of women murdering their bastard children, alas, too frequent among us, sacrificing the poor innocent babes, I doubt, more to avoid the expense than the shame, which would move tears and pity in the most savage and inhuman breast.

The number of souls in this kingdom being usually reckoned one million and a half, of these I calculate there may be about two hundred thousand couples whose wives are breeders; from which number I subtract thirty thousand couples who are able to maintain their own children, although I apprehend there cannot be so many under the present distresses of the kingdom; but this being granted, there will remain an hundred and seventy thousand breeders. I again subtract fifty thousand for those women who miscarry, or whose children die by accident or disease within the year. There only remain an hundred and twenty thousand children of poor parents annually born. The question therefore is, how this number shall be reared and provided for, which, as I have already said, under the present situation of affairs, is utterly impossible by all the methods hitherto proposed. For we can neither employ them in handicraft or agriculture; we neither build houses (I mean in the country) nor cultivate land. They can very seldom pick up a livelihood by stealing till they arrive at six years old, except where they are of towardly parts; although I confess they learn the rudiments much earlier, during which time they can however be looked upon only as probationers, as I have been informed by a principal gentleman in the county of Cavan, who protested to me that he never knew above one or two instances under the age of six, even in a part of the kingdom so renowned for the quickest proficiency in that art.

I am assured by our merchants that a boy or a girl before twelve years old is no salable commodity; and even when they come to this age they will not yield above three pounds, or three pounds and half a crown at most on the Exchange; which cannot turn to account either to the parents or the kingdom, the charge of nutriment and rags having been at least four times that value.

I shall now therefore humbly propose my own thoughts, which I hope will not be liable to the least objection.

I have been assured by a very knowing American of my acquaintance in London, that a young healthy child well nursed is at a year old a most delicious, nourishing, and wholesome food, whether stewed, roasted, baked, or boiled; and I make no doubt that it will equally serve in a fricassee or a ragout.

I do therefore humbly offer it to public consideration that of the hundred and twenty thousand children, already computed, twenty thousand may be reserved for breed, whereof only one fourth part to be males, which is more than we allow to sheep, black cattle, or swine; and my reason is that these children are seldom the fruits of marriage, a circumstance not much regarded by our savages, therefore one male will be sufficient to serve four females. That the remaining hundred thousand may at a year old be offered in sale to the persons of quality and fortune through the kingdom, always advising the mother to let them suck plentifully in the last month, so as to render them plump and fat for a good table. A child will make two dishes at an entertainment for friends; and when the family dines alone, the fore or hind quarter will make a reasonable dish, and seasoned with a little pepper or salt will be very good boiled on the fourth day, especially in winter.

I have reckoned upon a medium that a child just born will weigh twelve pounds, and in a solar year if tolerably nursed increaseth to twenty-eight pounds.

I grant this food will be somewhat dear, and therefore very proper for landlords, who, as they have already devoured most of the parents, seem to have the best title to the children.

Infant's flesh will be in season throughout the year, but more plentiful in March, and a little before and after. For we are told by a grave author, an eminent French physician, that fish being a prolific diet, there are more children born in Roman Catholic countries about nine months after Lent than at any other season; therefore, reckoning a year after Lent, the markets will be more glutted than usual, because the number of popish infants is at least three to one in this kingdom; and therefore it will have one other collateral advantage, by lessening the number of Papists among us.

I have already computed the charge of nursing a beggar's child (in which list I reckon all cottagers, laborers, and four fifths of the farmers) to be about two shillings per annum, rags included; and I believe no gentleman would repine to give ten shillings for the carcass of a good fat child, which, as I have said, will make four dishes of excellent nutritive meat, when he hath only some particular friend or his own family to dine with him. Thus the squire will learn to be a good landlord, and grow popular among the tenants; the mother will have eight shillings net profit, and be fit for work till she produces another child.

Those who are more thrifty (as I must confess the times require) may flay the carcass; the skin of which artificially dressed will make admirable gloves for ladies, and summer boots for fine gentlemen.

As to our city of Dublin, shambles may be appointed for this purpose in the most convenient parts of it, and butchers we may be assured will not be wanting; although I rather recommend buying the children alive, and dressing them hot from the knife as we do roasting pigs.

A very worthy person, a true lover of his country, and whose virtues I highly esteem, was lately pleased in discoursing on this matter to offer a refinement upon my scheme. He said that many gentlemen of this kingdom, having of late destroyed their deer, he conceived that the want of venison might be well supplied by the bodies of young lads and maidens, not exceeding fourteen years of age nor under twelve, so great a number of both sexes in every county being now ready to starve for want of work and service; and these to be disposed of by their parents, if alive, or otherwise by their nearest relations. But with due deference to so excellent a friend and so deserving a patriot, I cannot be altogether in his sentiments; for as to the males, my American acquaintance assured me from frequent experience that their flesh was generally tough and lean, like that of our schoolboys, by continual exercise, and their taste disagreeable; and to fatten them would not answer the charge. Then as to the females, it would, I think with humble submission, be a loss to the public, because they soon would become breeders themselves: and besides, it is not improbable that some scrupulous people might be apt to censure such a practice (although indeed very unjustly) as a little bordering upon cruelty; which, I confess, hath always been with me the strongest objection against any project, how well soever intended.

But in order to justify my friend, he confessed that this expedient was put into his head by the famous Psalmanazar, a native of the island Formosa, who came from thence to London above twenty years ago, and in conversation told my friend that in his country when any young person happened to be put to death, the executioner sold the carcass to persons of quality as a prime dainty; and that in his time the body of a plump girl of fifteen, who was crucified for an attempt to poison the emperor, was sold to his Imperial Majesty's prime minister of state, and other great mandarins of the court, in joints from the gibbet, at four hundred crowns. Neither indeed can I deny that if the same use were made of several plump young girls in this town, who without one single groat to their fortunes cannot stir abroad without a chair, and appear at the playhouse and assemblies in foreign fineries which they never will pay for, the kingdom would not be the worse.

Some persons of a desponding spirit are in great concern about that vast number of poor people who are aged, diseased, or maimed, and I have been desired to employ my thoughts what course may be taken to ease the nation of so grievous an encumbrance. But I am not in the least pain upon that matter, because it is very well known that they are every day dying and rotting by cold and famine, and filth and vermin, as fast as can be reasonably expected. And as to the younger laborers, they are now in almost as hopeful a condition. They cannot get work, and consequently pine away for want of nourishment to a degree that if at any time they are accidentally hired to common labor, they have not strength to perform it; and thus the country and themselves are happily delivered from the evils to come.

I have too long digressed, and therefore shall return to my subject. I think the advantages by the proposal which I have made are obvious and many, as well as of the highest importance.

For first, as I have already observed, it would greatly lessen the number of Papists, with whom we are yearly overrun, being the principal breeders of the nation as well as our most dangerous enemies; and who stay at home on purpose to deliver the kingdom to the Pretender, hoping to take their advantage by the absence of so many good Protestants, who have chosen rather to leave their country than to stay at home and pay tithes against their conscience to an Episcopal curate.

Secondly, the poorer tenants will have something valuable of their own, which by law may be made liable to distress, and help to pay their landlord's rent, their corn and cattle being already seized and money a thing unknown.

Thirdly, whereas the maintenance of an hundred thousand children, from two years old and upwards, cannot be computed at less than ten shillings a piece per annum, the nation's stock will be thereby increased fifty thousand pounds per annum, besides the profit of a new dish introduced to the tables of all gentlemen of fortune in the kingdom who have any refinement in taste. And the money will circulate among ourselves, the goods being entirely of our own growth and manufacture.

Fourthly, the constant breeders, besides the gain of eight shillings sterling per annum by the sale of their children, will be rid of the charge of maintaining them after the first year.

Fifthly, this food would likewise bring great custom to taverns, where the vintners will certainly be so prudent as to procure the best receipts for dressing it to perfection, and consequently have their houses frequented by all the fine gentlemen, who justly value themselves upon their knowledge in good eating; and a skillful cook, who understands how to oblige his guests, will contrive to make it as expensive as they please.

Sixthly, this would be a great inducement to marriage, which all wise nations have either encouraged by rewards or enforced by laws and penalties. It would increase the care and tenderness of mothers toward their children, when they were sure of a settlement for life to the poor babes, provided in some sort by the public, to their annual profit instead of expense. We should see an honest emulation among the married women, which of them could bring the fattest child to the market. Men would become as fond of their wives during the time of their pregnancy as they are now of their mares in foal, their cows in calf, or sows when they are ready to farrow; nor offer to beat or kick them (as is too frequent a practice) for fear of a miscarriage.

Many other advantages might be enumerated. For instance, the addition of some thousand carcasses in our exportation of barreled beef, the propagation of swine's flesh, and improvement in the art of making good bacon, so much wanted among us by the great destruction of pigs, too frequent at our tables, which are no way comparable in taste or magnificence to a well-grown, fat, yearling child, which roasted whole will make a considerable figure at a lord mayor's feast or any other public entertainment. But this and many others I omit, being studious of brevity.

Supposing that one thousand families in this city would be constant customers for infants' flesh, besides others who might have it at merry meetings, particularly weddings and christenings, I compute that Dublin would take off annually about twenty thousand carcasses, and the rest of the kingdom (where probably they will be sold somewhat cheaper) the remaining eighty thousand.

I can think of no one objection that will possibly be raised against this proposal, unless it should be urged that the number of people will be thereby much lessened in the kingdom. This I freely own, and it was indeed one principal design in offering it to the world. I desire the reader will observe, that I calculate my remedy for this one individual kingdom of Ireland and for no other that ever was, is, or I think ever can be upon earth. Therefore let no man talk to me of other expedients: of taxing our absentees at five shillings a pound: of using neither clothes nor household furniture except what is of our own growth and manufacture: of utterly rejecting the materials and instruments that promote foreign luxury: of curing the expensiveness of pride, vanity, idleness, and gaming in our women: of introducing a vein of parsimony, prudence, and temperance: of learning to love our country, in the want of which we differ even from Laplanders and the inhabitants of Topinamboo: of quitting our animosities and factions, nor acting any longer like the Jews, who were murdering one another at the very moment their city was taken: of being a little cautious not to sell our country and conscience for nothing: of teaching landlords to have at least one degree of mercy toward their tenants: lastly, of putting a spirit of honesty, industry, and skill into our shopkeepers; who, if a resolution could now be taken to buy only our native goods, would immediately unite to cheat and exact upon us in the price, the measure, and the goodness, nor could ever yet be brought to make one fair proposal of just dealing, though often and earnestly invited to it.

Therefore I repeat, let no man talk to me of these and the like expedients, till he hath at least some glimpse of hope that there will ever be some hearty and sincere attempt to put them in practice.

But as to myself, having been wearied out for many years with offering vain, idle, visionary thoughts, and at length utterly despairing of success, I fortunately fell upon this proposal, which, as it is wholly new, so it hath something solid and real, of no expense and little trouble, full in our own power, and whereby we can incur no danger in disobliging England. For this kind of commodity will not bear exportation, the flesh being of too tender a consistence to admit a long continuance in salt, although perhaps I could name a country which would be glad to eat up our whole nation without it.

After all, I am not so violently bent upon my own opinion as to reject any offer proposed by wise men, which shall be found equally innocent, cheap, easy, and effectual. But before something of that kind shall be advanced in contradiction to my scheme, and offering a better, I desire the author or authors will be pleased maturely to consider two points. First, as things now stand, how they will be able to find food and raiment for an hundred thousand useless mouths and backs. And secondly, there being a round million of creatures in human figure throughout this kingdom, whose sole subsistence put into a common stock would leave them in debt two millions of pounds sterling, adding those who are beggars by profession to the bulk of farmers, cottagers, and laborers, with their wives and children who are beggars in effect; I desire those politicians who dislike my overture, and may perhaps be so bold to attempt an answer, that they will first ask the parents of these mortals whether they would not at this day think it a great happiness to have been sold for food at a year old in the manner I prescribe, and thereby have avoided such a perpetual scene of misfortunes as they have since gone through by the oppression of landlords, the impossibility of paying rent without money or trade, the want of common sustenance, with neither house nor clothes to cover them from the inclemencies of the weather, and the most inevitable prospect of entailing the like or greater miseries upon their breed forever.

I profess, in the sincerity of my heart, that I have not the least personal interest in endeavoring to promote this necessary work, having no other motive than the public good of my country, by advancing our trade, providing for infants, relieving the poor, and giving some pleasure to the rich. I have no children by which I can propose to get a single penny; the youngest being nine years old, and my wife past childbearing.

POSSIBILITIES FOR WRITING

1. Throughout "A Modest Proposal," Swift uses language that dehumanizes the Irish people. Point out examples of such language, and explain their effect both in terms of Swift's satire and his underlying purpose.

2. Though Swift never fully drops his mask, he does make a number of veiled appeals toward sympathy for the Irish and legitimate suggestions for alleviating their predicament. Citing the text, examine when and where he does so. How can you recognize his seriousness?
3. Write a "modest proposal" of your own in which you offer an outrageous solution to alleviate some social problem. Make sure that readers understand that your proposal is satirical and that they recognize your real purpose in writing.

Margaret Talbot (b. 1946) writes for the New York Times *magazine, where she has published several major stories. Formerly an editor at* Lingua Franca *and the* New Republic, *she has written for the* Washington Post, Slate, Vogue, the New Yorker, *and the* Atlantic Monthly. *Her essays have been featured in* The Anchor Essay Annual *(1997, 1998) and* The Art of the Essay: 1999.

MARGARET TALBOT

Les Très Riches Heures de Martha Stewart

In "Les Très Riches Heures de Martha Stewart," Margaret Talbot analyzes the phenomenon of Martha Stewart as cultural icon and successful businesswoman. First published in the *New Republic,* Talbot's essay considers Martha Stewart not only in relation to the enterprises she created but also in relation to the lifestyle she came to represent and embody.

Talbot's essay was published in 1996. Since then, after a continuing spiral of successful new spinoffs, including a budget line of Martha Stewart products sold at K-Mart stores, Stewart was tried and convicted and served five months in prison. Released in March 2005, she launched a highly publicized comeback.

Every age gets the household goddess it deserves. The '60s had Julia Child, the sophisticated French chef who proved as permissive as Dr. Spock. She may have proselytized for a refined foreign cuisine from her perch at a Boston PBS station, but she was always an anti-snob, vowing to "take a lot of the la dee dah out of French cooking." With her madras shirts and her penumbra of curls, her 6'2" frame and her whinny of a voice, she exuded an air of Cambridge eccentricity—faintly bohemian and a little tatty, like a yellowing travel poster. She was messy and forgiving. When Julia dropped an egg or collapsed a soufflé, she shrugged and laughed. "You are alone in the kitchen, nobody can see you, and cooking is meant to be fun," she reminded her viewers. She wielded lethal-looking kitchen knives with campy abandon, dipped her fingers into crème anglaise and wiped her chocolate-smeared hands on an apron tied carelessly at her waist. For Child was also something of a sensualist, a celebrant of appetite as much as a pedant of cooking.

In the '90s, and probably well into the next century, we have Martha Stewart, corporate overachiever turned domestic superachiever, Mildred Pierce in earth-toned Armani. Martha is the anti-Julia. Consider the extent of their respective powers. At the height of her success, Child could boast a clutch of bestselling cookbooks and a *gemütlich* TV show shot on a single set. At what may or may not be the height of her success, here's what Stewart can claim: a 5-year-old magazine, *Martha Stewart Living*, with a circulation that has leapt to 1.5 million; a popular cable TV show, also called "Martha Stewart Living" and filmed at her luscious Connecticut and East Hampton estates; a dozen wildly successful gardening, cooking and lifestyle books; a mail-order business, Martha-by-Mail; a nationally syndicated newspaper column, "Ask Martha"; a regular Wednesday slot on the "Today" show; a line of $110-a-gallon paints in colors inspired by the eggs her Araucana hens lay; plans to invade cyberspace—in short, an empire.

Julia limited herself to cooking lessons, with the quiet implication that cooking was a kind of synecdoche for the rest of bourgeois existence; but Martha's parish is vaster, her field is all of life. Her expertise, as she recently explained to *Mediaweek* magazine, covers, quite simply, "Beautiful soups and how to make them, beautiful houses and how to build them, beautiful children and how to raise them." (From soups to little nuts.) She presides, in fact, over a phenomenon that, in other realms, is quite familiar in American society and culture: a cult, devoted to her name and image.

In the distance between these two cynosures of domestic life lies a question: What does the cult of Martha mean? Or, to put it another way, what have we done, exactly, to deserve her?

If you have read the paper or turned on the television in the last year or so, you have probably caught a glimpse of the WASPy good looks, the affectless demeanor, the nacreous perfection of her world. You may even know the outlines of her story. Middle-class girl from a Polish-American family in Nutley, New Jersey, works her way through Barnard in the early '60s, modeling on the side. She becomes a stockbroker, a self-described workaholic and insomniac who by the '70s is making six figures on Wall Street, and who then boldly trades it all in . . . for life as a workaholic, insomniac evangelist for domesticity whose business now generates some $200 million in profits a year. (She herself, according to the *Wall Street Journal*, makes a salary of $400,000 a year from Time, Inc., which generously supplements this figure with a $40,000 a year clothing allowance and other candies.) You may even have admired her magazine, with its art-book production values and spare design, every kitchen utensil photographed like an Imogen Cunningham nude, every plum or pepper rendered with the loving detail of an eighteenth-century botanical drawing, every page a gentle exhalation of High Class.

What you may not quite realize, if you have not delved deeper into Stewart's oeuvre, is the ambition of her design for living—the absurd, self-parodic dream of it. To read Martha Stewart is to know that there is no corner of your domestic life that cannot be beautified or improved under careful tutelage, none that should not be colonized by the rhetoric and the discipline of quality control. Work full time though you may, care for your family though you must, convenience should never be your watchword in what Stewart likes to call, in her own twee coinage, "homekeeping." Convenience is the enemy of excellence. "We do not pretend that these are 'convenience' foods," she writes loftily of the bread and preserves recipes in a 1991 issue of the magazine. "Some take days to make. But they are recipes that will produce the very best results, and we know that is what you want." Martha is a kitchen-sink idealist. She scorns utility in the name of beauty. But her idealism, of course, extends no further than surface appearances, which makes it a very particular form of idealism indeed.

To spend any length of time in Martha-land is to realize that it is not enough to serve your guests homemade pumpkin soup as a first course. You must present it in hollowed-out, hand-gilded pumpkins as well. It will not do to serve an Easter ham unless you have baked it in a roasting pan lined with, of all things, "tender, young, organically-grown grass that has not yet been cut." And, when serving a "casual" lobster and corn dinner al fresco, you really ought to fashion dozens of cunning little bamboo brushes tied with raffia and adorned with a chive so that each of your guests may butter their corn with something pretty.

To be a Martha fan (or more precisely, a Martha adept) is to understand that a terracotta pot is just a terracotta pot until you have "aged" it, painstakingly rubbing yogurt into its dampened sides, then smearing it with plant food or "something you found in the woods" and patiently standing by while the mold sprouts. It is to think that maybe you could do this *kind* of thing, anyway—start a garden, say, in your scruffy backyard—and then to be brought up short by Martha's enumeration, in *Martha Stewart's Gardening*, of forty-nine "essential" gardening tools. These range from a "polesaw" to a "corn fiber broom" to three different kinds of pruning shears, one of which—the "loppers"—Martha says she has in three different sizes. You have, perhaps, a trowel. But then Martha's garden is a daunting thing to contemplate, what with its topiary mazes and state-of-the-art chicken coop; its "antique" flowers and geometric herb garden. It's half USDA station, half Sigginghurst. And you cannot imagine making anything remotely like it at your own house, not without legions of artisans and laborers and graduate students in landscape design, and a pot of money that perhaps you'll unearth when you dig up the yard.

In *The Culture of Narcissism*, Christopher Lasch describes the ways in which pleasure, in our age, has taken on "the qualities of work," allowing our leisure-time activities to be measured by the same standards of accomplishment that rule the workplace. It is a phenomenon that he memorably characterizes as "the invasion of play by the rhetoric of achievement." For Lasch, writing in the early '70s, the proliferation of sex-advice manuals offered a particularly poignant example. Today, though, you might just as easily point to the hundreds of products and texts, from unctuous home-furnishings catalogs to upscale "shelter" magazines to self-help books like *Meditations for Women Who Do Too Much*, that tell us exactly how to "nest" and "cocoon" and "nurture," how to "center" and "retreat," and how to measure our success at these eminently private pursuits. Just as late-nineteenth-century marketers and experts promised to bring Americans back in touch with the nature from which modern industrial life had alienated them, so today's "shelter" experts—the word is revealingly primal—promise to reconnect us with a similarly mystified home. The bourgeois home as lost paradise, retrievable through careful instruction.

Martha Stewart is the apotheosis of this particular cult of expertise, and its most resourceful entrepreneur. She imagines projects of which we would never have thought—gathering dewy grass for our Easter ham, say—and makes us feel the pressing need for training in them. And she exploits, brilliantly, a certain estrangement from home that many working women feel these days. For women who are working longer and longer hours at more and more demanding jobs, it's easy to think of home as the place where chaos reigns and their own competence is called into doubt: easy to regard the office, by comparison, as the bulwark of order. It is a reversal, of course, of the hoary concept of home as a refuge from the tempests of the marketplace. But these days, as the female executives in a recent study attested, the priority they most often let slide is housekeeping: they'll abide disorder at home that they wouldn't or couldn't abide at the office. No working couple's home is the oasis of tranquility and Italian marble countertops that Marthaism seems to promise. But could it be? Should it be? Stewart plucks expertly at that chord of doubt.

In an era when it is not at all uncommon to be cut off from the traditional sources of motherwit and household lore—when many of us live far from the families into which we were born and have started our own families too late to benefit from the guidance of living parents or grandparents—domestic pedants like Martha Stewart rightly sense a big vacuum to fill. Stewart's books are saturated with nostalgia for lost tradition and old moldings, for her childhood in Nutley and for her mother's homemade preserves. In the magazine, her "Remembering" column pines moralistically for a simpler era, when beach vacations meant no television or video games, just digging for clams and napping in hammocks. Yet Stewart's message is that such simplicity can only be achieved now through strenuous effort and a flood of advice. We might be able to put on a picnic or a dinner party without her help, she seems to tell us, but we wouldn't do it properly, beautifully, in the spirit of excellence that we expect of ourselves at work.

It may be that Stewart's special appeal is to women who wouldn't want to take their mother's word anyway, to babyboomer daughters who figure that their sensibilities are just too different from their stay-at-home moms', who can't throw themselves into housekeeping without thinking of their kitchen as a catering business and their backyards as a garden show. In fact, relatively few of Martha's fans are housewives—72 percent of the subscribers to *Martha Stewart Living* are employed outside the home as managers or professionals—and many of them profess to admire her precisely because she isn't one, either. As one such Martha acolyte, an account executive at a Christian radio station, effused on the Internet: "[Stewart] is my favorite independent woman and what an entrepreneur! She's got her own television show, magazine, books and even her own brand of latex paint. . . . Martha is a feisty woman who settles for nothing less than perfection."

For women such as these, the didactic faux-maternalism of Martha Stewart seems the perfect answer. She may dispense the kind of home-keeping advice that a mother would, but she does so in tones too chill and exacting to sound "maternal," singling out, for example, those "who will always be too lazy" to do her projects. She makes housekeeping safe for the professional woman by professionalizing housekeeping. And you never forget that Stewart is herself a mogul, even when she's baking rhubarb crisp and telling you, in her Shakeresque mantra, that "it's a Good Thing."

It is tempting to see the Martha cult purely as a symptom of anti-feminist backlash. Though she may not directly admonish women to abandon careers for hearth and home, Stewart certainly exalts a way of life that puts hearth and home at its center, one that would be virtually impossible to achieve without *somebody's* full-time devotion. (Camille Paglia has praised her as "someone who has done a tremendous service for ordinary women—women who identify with the roles of wife, mother, and homemaker.") Besides, in those alarming moments when Stewart slips into the social critic's mode, she can sound a wee bit like Phyllis Schlafly—less punitive and more patrician, maybe, but just as smug about the moral uplift of a well-ordered home. Her philosophy of cultivating your own walled garden while the world outside is condemned to squalor bears the hallmarks of Reagan's America—it would not be overreading to call it a variety of conservatism. "Amid the horrors of genocidal war in Bosnia and Rwanda, the AIDS epidemic and increasing crime in many cities," Stewart writes in a recent column, "there are those of us who desire positive reinforcement of some very basic tenets of good living." And those would be? "Good food, gardening, crafts, entertaining and home improvement." (Hollow out the pumpkins, they're starving in Rwanda.)

Yet it would, in the end, be too simplistic to regard her as a tool of the feminine mystique, or as some sort of spokesmodel for full-time mommies. For one thing, there is nothing especially June Cleaverish, or even motherly, about Stewart. She has taken a drubbing, in fact, for looking more convincing as a business-woman than a dispenser of milk and cookies. (Remember the apocryphal tale that had Martha flattening a crate of baby chicks while backing out of a driveway in her Mercedes?) Her habitual prickliness and Scotchguard perfectionism are more like the badges of the striving good girl, still cut to the quick by her classmates' razzing when she asked for extra homework.

Despite the ritual obeisance that Martha pays to Family, moreover, she is not remotely interested in the messy contingencies of family life. In the enchanted world of Turkey Hill, there are no husbands (Stewart was divorced from hers in 1990), only loyal craftsmen, who clip hedges and force dogwood with self-effacing dedication. Children she makes use of as accessories, much like Parisian women deploy little dogs. The books and especially the magazine are often graced with photographic spreads of parties and teas where children pale as waxen angels somberly disport themselves, their fair hair shaped into tasteful blunt cuts, their slight figures clad in storybook velvet or lace. "If I had to choose one essential element for the success of an Easter brunch," she writes rather menacingly in her 1994 *Menus for Entertaining*, "it would be children." The homemade Halloween costumes modeled by wee lads and lasses in an October 1991 issue of *Martha Stewart Living* do look gorgeous—the Caravaggio colors, the themes drawn from nature. But it's kind of hard to imagine a 5-year-old boy happily agreeing to go as an acorn this year, instead of say, Batman. And why should he? In Marthaland, his boyhood would almost certainly be overridden in the name of taste.

If Stewart is a throwback, it's not so much to the 1950s as to the 1850s, when the doctrine of separate spheres did allow married or widowed women of the upper classes a kind of power—unchallenged dominion over the day-to-day functioning of the home and its servants, in exchange for ceding the public realm to men. At Turkey Hill, Stewart is the undisputed chatelaine, micromanaging her estate in splendid isolation. (This hermetic pastoral is slightly marred, of course, by the presence of cameras.) Here the domestic arts have become ends in themselves, unmoored from family values and indeed from family.

Stewart's peculiar brand of didacticism has another nineteenth-century precedent—in the domestic science or home economics movement. The domestic scientists' favorite recipes—"wholesome" concoctions of condensed milk and canned fruit, rivers of white sauce—would never have passed Martha's muster; but their commitment to painstakingly elegant presentation, their concern with the look of food even more than its taste, sound a lot like Stewart's. And, more importantly, so does their underlying philosophy. They emerged out of a tradition: the American preference for food writing of the prescriptive, not the descriptive, kind, for food books that told you, in M. F. K. Fisher's formulation, not about eating but about what to eat. But they took this spirit much further. Like Stewart, these brisk professional women of the 1880s and '90s believed that true culinary literacy could not be handed down or casually absorbed; it had to be carefully taught. (One of the movement's accomplishments, if it can be called that, was the home ec curriculum.)

Like Stewart, the domestic scientists were not bent on liberating intelligent women from housework. Their objective was to raise housework to a level worthy of intelligent women. They wished to apply rational method to the chaos and the drudgery of housework and, in so doing, to earn it the respect accorded men's stuff like science and business. Neither instinct, nor intuition, nor mother's rough-hewn words of advice would have a place in the scientifically managed home of the future. As Laura Shapiro observes in *Perfection Salad*, her lively and perceptive history of domestic science, the ideal new housewife was supposed to project, above all, "self-sufficiency, self-control, and a perfectly bland façade." Sound familiar?

It is in their understanding of gender roles, however, that the doyennes of home ec most closely prefigure Marthaism. Like Stewart, they cannot be classified either as feminists or traditionalists. Their model housewife was a pseudo-professional with little time for sublimating her ego to her husband's or tenderly ministering to his needs. She was more like a factory supervisor than either the Victorian angel of the home or what Shapiro calls the courtesan type, the postwar housewife who was supposed to zip through her chores so she could gussy herself up for her husband. In Martha's world, too, the managerial and aesthetic challenges of "homekeeping" always take priority, and their intricacy and ambition command a respect that mere wifely duties never could. Her husbandless hauteur is rich with the self-satisfaction of financial and emotional independence.

* * *

In the end, Stewart's fantasies have as much to do with class as with gender. The professional women who read her books might find themselves longing for a breadwinner, but a lifestyle this beautiful is easier to come by if you've never needed a breadwinner in the first place. Stewart's books are a dreamy advertisement for independent wealth— or, more accurately, for its facsimile. You may not have a posh pedigree, but with a little effort (okay, a lot) you can adopt its trappings. After all, Martha wasn't born to wealth either, but now she attends the weddings of people with names like Charles Booth-Cliborn (she went to his in London, the magazine tells us) and caters them for couples named Sissy and Kelsey (see her *Wedding Planner*, in which their yacht is decorated with a "Just Married" sign).

She is not an American aristocrat, but she plays one on TV. And you can play one, too, at least in your own home. Insist on cultivating only those particular yellow plums you tasted in the Dordogne, buy your copper cleaner only at Delherin in Paris, host lawn parties where guests come "attired in the garden dress of the Victorian era," and you begin to simulate the luster of lineage. Some of Stewart's status-augmenting suggestions must strike even her most faithful fans as ridiculous. For showers held after the baby is born, Martha "likes presenting the infant with engraved calling cards that the child can then slip into thank you notes and such for years to come." What a great idea. Maybe your baby can gum them for a while first, thoughtfully imprinting them with his signature drool.

The book that best exemplifies her class-consciousness is *Martha Stewart's New Old House*, a step-by-step account of refurbishing a Federal-style farmhouse in Westport, Connecticut. Like all her books, it contains many, many pictures of Martha; here she's frequently shown supervising the work of plasterers, carpenters and other "seemingly taciturn men." *New Old House* establishes Stewart's ideal audience: a demographic niche occupied by the kind of people who, like her, can afford to do their kitchen countertops in "mottled, gray-green, hand-honed slate from New York state, especially cut" for them. The cost of all this (and believe me, countertops are only the beginning) goes unmentioned. If you have to ask, maybe you're not a Martha kind of person after all.

In fact, Stewart never seems all that concerned with reassuring her readers of their ability to afford such luxuries or their right to enjoy them. She's more concerned with establishing her own claims. Her reasoning seems to go something like this: the houses that she buys and renovates belong to wealthy families who passed them down through generations. But these families did not properly care for their patrimony. The widowed Bulkeley sisters, erstwhile owners of Turkey Hill, had let the estate fall "into great disrepair. All the farms and out-buildings were gone. . . . The fields around had been sold off by the sisters in 2-acre building lots; suburbia encroached." The owner of the eponymous New Old House was a retired librarian named Miss Adams who "had little interest in the house other than as a roof over her head. Clearly a frugal spirit, she had no plans to restore the house, and she lived there until she could no longer cope with the maintenance and upkeep of the place. The house was in dire need of attention, and since no other family member wanted to assume responsibility, Miss Adams reluctantly decided to sell her family home. I wanted very much to save the Adams house, to put it to rights, to return its history to it, to make it livable once again."

It's a saga with overtones of Jamesian comedy; a family with bloodlines but no money is simultaneously rescued and eclipsed by an energetic upstart with money but no bloodlines. The important difference—besides the fact that Martha is marrying the house, not the son—is that she also has taste. And it's taste, far more than money, she implies, that gives her the right to these splendid, neglected piles of brick. Unlike the "frugal" Misses Bulkeley, she will keep suburbia at bay; unlike the careless Miss Adams, she would never resort to "hideous rugs" in (yuck) shades of brown. They don't understand their own houses; she does, and so she *deserves* to own their houses. But leave it to Martha to get all snippy about these people's aesthetic oversights while quietly celebrating their reversion to type. They're useful to her, and not only because their indifference to decor bolsters her claim to their property. Like the pumpkin pine floors and original fixtures, these quaintly cheeseparing New Englanders denote the property's authenticity.

The fantasy of vaulting into the upper crust that Martha Stewart fulfilled, and now piques in her readers, is about more than just money, of course. Among other things, it's about time, and the luxurious plenitude of it. Living the Martha way would mean enjoying a surfeit of that scarce commodity, cooking and crafting at the artisanal pace her projects require. Trouble is, none of us overworked Americans has time to spare these days—and least of all the upscale professional women whom Stewart targets. Martha herself seemed to acknowledge this when she told *Inside Media* that she attracts at least two classes of true believers: the "Be-Marthas," who have enough money and manic devotion to follow many of her lifestyle techniques, and the "Do-Marthas," who "are a little bit envious" and "don't have as much money as the Be-Marthas."

To those fulsome categories, you could surely add the "watch Marthas" or the "read Marthas," people who might consider, say, making their own rabbit-shaped wire topiary forms, but only consider it, who mostly just indulge in the fantasy of doing so, if only they had the time. There is something undeniably soothing about watching Martha at her absurdly time-consuming labors. A female "media executive" explained the appeal to Barbara Lippert in *New York* magazine: "I never liked Martha Stewart until I started watching her on Sunday mornings. I turn on the TV, and I'm in my pajamas, still in this place between sleep and reality. And she's showing you how to roll your tablecloths in parchment paper. She's like a character when she does her crafts. It reminds me of watching Mr. Green Jeans on Captain Kangaroo. I remember he had a shoebox he took out that was filled with craft things. There would be a close-up on his hands with his buffed nails. And then he would show you how to cut an oaktag with a scissor, or when he folded paper, he'd say: 'There you go, boys and girls,' and it was very quiet. It's like she brings out this great meditative focus and calm."

The show does seem strikingly unfrenetic. Unlike just about everything else on TV, including the "Our Home" show, which follows it on

Lifetime, it eschews Kathy Lee-type banter, perky music, swooping studio shots and jittery handheld cameras. Instead there's just Martha, alone in her garden or kitchen, her teacherly tones blending with birdsong, her recipes cued to the seasons. Whimsical recorder music pipes along over the credits. Martha's crisply ironed denim shirts, pearl earrings, and honey-toned highlights bespeak the fabulousness of Connecticut. Her hands move slowly, deliberately over her yellow roses or her Depression glasses. Martha is a Puritan who prepares "sinful" foods—few of her recipes are low-fat or especially health-conscious—that are redeemed by the prodigious labors, the molasses afternoons, involved in serving them. (She preys upon our guilt about overindulgence, then hints at how to assuage it.) Here at Turkey Hill, time is as logy as a honey-sated bumblebee. Here on Lifetime, the cable channel aimed at baby-boom women, Martha's stately show floats along in a sea of stalker movies, Thighmaster commercials and "Weddings of a Lifetime" segments, and by comparison, I have to say, she looks rather dignified. Would that we all had these *très riches heures*.

But if we had the hours, if we had the circumstances, wouldn't we want to fill them with something of our own, with a domestic grace of our own devising? Well, maybe not anymore. For taste is no longer an expression of individuality. It is, more often, an instrument of conformism, a way to assure ourselves that we're living by the right codes, dictated or sanctioned by experts. Martha Stewart's "expertise" is really nothing but another name for the perplexity of her cowed consumers. A lifestyle cult as all-encompassing as hers could thrive only at a time when large numbers of Americans have lost confidence in their own judgment about the most ordinary things. For this reason, *Martha Stewart Living* isn't really living at all.

POSSIBILITIES FOR WRITING

1. Summarize the reasons Talbot presents for Martha Stewart's success. Consider both Stewart's personal qualities and talents and the social conditions and circumstances that enabled her to succeed.
2. Look through one of Martha Stewart's magazines and evaluate the extent to which Talbot's analysis of what Stewart represents is reflected in that issue. Provide your own perspective on the Martha Stewart characteristics you find embodied there.
3. Choose a popular cultural icon from the world of sports, music, fashion, or other area of interest. Write an essay analyzing the reasons for this person's success. Consider both personal qualities and talents and social and cultural conditions that support his or her rise to success.

Amy Tan (b. 1952) grew up in Oakland, California, her parents having immigrated from China only shortly before her birth. She graduated from San Francisco State University with degrees in English and linguistics and began her writing career in the business world, drafting presentations, marketing materials, and producing various corporate publications. Tan began pursuing fiction writing as a break from the stress of her job, and in 1987, after years of literary workshops, she produced The Joy Luck Club, a group of interrelated stories about four Chinese immigrant mothers and their assimilated, second-generation daughters. It was an immediate success both with critics and readers and was followed by The Kitchen's God's Wife (1991), The Hundred Secret Senses (1995), The Bonesetter's Daughter (2001), and Saving Fish from Drowning (2005) all dealing with similar themes of family and culture.

AMY TAN

Mother Tongue

In "Mother Tongue," Amy Tan describes the various kinds of English she uses—from the "broken" English she uses in speaking with her mother, to the formal and sophisticated English she employs in public settings. Tan plays upon the meaning of the term "mother tongue," referring both to English as one's native language and to the English her own mother uses, that is, her mother's English, which is not her mother's "mother tongue."

For Amy Tan herself, English is a variety of tongues. English is more than a single and monolithic way of using the language. Tan finds in her mother's "broken" English, for example, a powerful self-presence, even though the mother's use of English is riddled with grammatical errors and idiomatic incongruities. Part of the pleasure of Tan's essay is the way the writer plays off various kinds of English against one another. Part of the essay's power lies in its invitation to see how English provides multiple possibilities for conveying ideas and expressing oneself. An additional but related aspect of Tan's essay is its revelation of culturally conflicting perspectives—and how language, in this case English, both reflects and exacerbates them.

I am not a scholar of English or literature. I cannot give you much more than personal opinions on the English language and its variations in this country or others.

I am a writer. And by that definition, I am someone who has always loved language. I am fascinated by language in daily life. I spend a great deal of my time thinking about the power of language — the way it can evoke an emotion, a visual image, a complex idea, or a simple truth. Language is the tool of my trade. And I use them all—all the Englishes I grew up with.

Recently, I was made keenly aware of the different Englishes I do use. I was giving a talk to a large group of people, the same talk I had already given to half a dozen other groups. The nature of the talk was about my writing, my life, and my book, *The Joy Luck Club*. The talk was going along well enough, until I remembered one major difference that made the whole talk sound wrong. My mother was in the room. And it was perhaps the first time she had heard me give a lengthy speech, using the kind of English I have never used with her. I was saying things like "The intersection of memory upon imagination" and "There is an aspect of my fiction that relates to thus-and-thus"—a speech filled with carefully wrought grammatical phrases, burdened, it suddenly seemed to me, with nominalized forms, past perfect tenses, conditional phrases, all the forms of standard English that I had learned in school and through books, the forms of English I did not use at home with my mother.

Just last week, I was walking down the street with my mother, and I again found myself conscious of the English I was using, the English I do use with her. We were talking about the price of new and used furniture and I heard myself saying this: "Not waste money that way." My husband was with us as well, and he didn't notice any switch in my English. And then I realized why. It's because over the twenty years we've been together I've often used that same kind of English with him, and sometimes he even uses it with me. It has become our language of intimacy, a different sort of English that relates to family talk, the language I grew up with.

So you'll have some idea of what this family talk I heard sounds like, I'll quote what my mother said during a recent conversation which I videotaped and then transcribed. During this conversation, my mother was talking about a political gangster in Shanghai who had the same last name as her family's, Du, and how the gangster in his early years wanted to be adopted by her family, which was rich by comparison. Later, the gangster became more powerful, far richer than my mother's family, and one day showed up at my mother's wedding to pay his respects. Here's what she said in part:

"Du Yusong having business like fruit stand. Like off the street kind. He is Du like Du Zong—but not Tsung-ming Island people. The local people call putong, the river east side, he belong to that side local people. That man want to ask Du Zong father take him in like become own family. Du Zong father wasn't look down on him, but didn't take seriously, until that man big like become a mafia. Now important person, very hard to inviting him. Chinese way, came only to show respect, don't stay for dinner. Respect for making big celebration, he shows up. Mean gives lots of respect. Chinese custom. Chinese social life that way. If too important won't have to stay too long. He come to my wedding. I didn't see, I heard it. I gone to boy's side, they have YMCA dinner. Chinese age I was nineteen."

You should know that my mother's expressive command of English belies how much she actually understands. She reads the *Forbes* report, listens to *Wall Street Week*, converses daily with her stockbroker, reads all of Shirley MacLaine's books with ease—all kinds of things I can't begin to understand. Yet some of my friends tell me they understand 50 percent of what my mother says. Some say they understand 80 to 90 percent. Some say they understand none of it, as if she were speaking pure Chinese. But to me, my mother's English is perfectly clear, perfectly natural. It's my mother tongue. Her language, as I hear it, is vivid, direct, full of observation and imagery. That was the language that helped shape the way I saw things, expressed things, made sense of the world.

Lately, I've been giving more thought to the kind of English my mother speaks. Like others, I have described it to people as "broken" or "fractured" English. But I wince when I say that. It has always bothered me that I can think of no other way to describe it other than "broken," as if it were damaged and needed to be fixed, as if it lacked a certain wholeness and soundness. I've heard other terms used, "limited English," for example. But they seem just as bad, as if everything is limited, including people's perceptions of the limited English speaker.

I know this for a fact, because when I was growing up, my mother's "limited" English limited *my* perception of her. I was ashamed of her English. I believed that her English reflected the quality of what she had to say. That is, because she expressed them imperfectly her thoughts were imperfect. And I had plenty of empirical evidence to support me: the fact that people in department stores, at banks, and at restaurants did not take her seriously, did not give her good service, pretended not to understand her, or even acted as if they did not hear her.

My mother has long realized the limitations of her English as well. When I was fifteen, she used to have me call people on the phone to pretend I was she. In this guise, I was forced to ask for information or even to complain and yell at people who had been rude to her. One time it was a call to her stockbroker in New York. She had cashed out her small portfolio and it just so happened we were going to go to New York the next week, our very first trip outside California. I had to get on the phone and say in an adolescent voice that was not very convincing, "This is Mrs. Tan."

And my mother was standing in the back whispering loudly, "Why he don't send me check, already two weeks late. So mad he lie to me, losing me money."

And then I said in perfect English, "Yes, I'm getting rather concerned. You had agreed to send the check two weeks ago, but it hasn't arrived."

Then she began to talk more loudly. "What he want, I come to New York tell him front of his boss, you cheating me?" And I was trying to calm her down, make her be quiet, while telling the stockbroker, "I can't tolerate any more excuses. If I don't receive the check immediately, I am going to have to speak to your manager when I'm in New York next week." And sure enough, the following week there we were in front of this astonished stockbroker, and I was sitting there red-faced and quiet, and my mother, the real Mrs. Tan, was shouting at his boss in her impeccable broken English.

We used a similar routine just five days ago, for a situation that was far less humorous. My mother had gone to the hospital for an appointment, to find out about a benign brain tumor a CAT scan had revealed a month ago. She said she had spoken very good English, her best English, no mistakes. Still, she said, the hospital did not apologize when they said they had lost the CAT scan and she had come for nothing. She said they did not seem to have any sympathy when she told them she was anxious to know the exact diagnosis, since her husband and son had both died of brain tumors. She said they would not give her any more information until the next time and she would have to make another appointment for that. So she said she would not leave until the doctor called her daughter. She wouldn't budge. And when the doctor finally called her daughter, me, who spoke in perfect English—lo and behold—we had assurances the CAT scan would be found, promises that a conference call on Monday would be held, and apologies for any suffering my mother had gone through for a most regrettable mistake.

I think my mother's English almost had an effect on limiting my possibilities in life as well. Sociologists and linguists probably will tell you that a person's developing language skills are more influenced by peers. But I do think that the language spoken in the family, especially in immigrant families which are more insular, plays a large role in shaping the language of the child. And I believe that it affected my results on achievement tests, IQ tests, and the SAT. While my English skills were never judged as poor, compared to math, English could not be considered my strong suit. In grade school I did moderately well, getting perhaps B's, sometimes B-pluses, in English and scoring perhaps in the sixtieth or seventieth percentile on achievement tests. But those scores were not good enough to override the opinion that my true abilities lay in math and science, because in those areas I achieved A's and scored in the ninetieth percentile or higher.

This was understandable. Math is precise; there is only one correct answer. Whereas, for me at least, the answers on English tests were always a judgment call, a matter of opinion and personal experience. Those tests were constructed around items like fill-in-the-blank sentence completion, such as "Even though Tom was _____, Mary thought he was _____." And the correct answer always seemed to be the most bland combinations of thoughts, for example, "Even though Tom was shy, Mary thought he was charming," with the grammatical structure "even though" limiting the correct answer to some sort of semantic opposites, so you wouldn't get answers like, "Even though Tom was foolish, Mary thought he was ridiculous." Well, according to my mother, there were very few limitations as to what Tom could have been and what Mary might have thought of him. So I never did well on tests like that.

The same was true with word analogies, pairs of words in which you were supposed to find some sort of logical, semantic relationship—for example, "*Sunset* is to *nightfall* as _____ is to _____." And here you would be presented with a list of four possible pairs, one of which showed the same kind of relationship: *red* is to *stoplight, bus* is to *arrival, chills* is to *fever, yawn* is to *boring.* Well, I could never think that way. I knew what the tests were asking, but I could not block out of my mind the images already created by the first pair, "*sunset* is to *nightfall*"—and I would see a burst of colors against a darkening sky, the moon rising, the lowering of a curtain of stars. And all the other pairs of words—red, bus, stoplight, boring—just threw up a mass of confusing images, making it impossible for me to sort out something as logical as saying: "A sunset precedes nightfall" is the same as "a chill precedes a fever." The only way I would have gotten that answer right would have been to imagine an associative situation, for example, my being disobedient and staying out past sunset, catching a chill at night, which turns into feverish pneumonia as punishment, which indeed did happen to me.

I have been thinking about all this lately, about my mother's English, about achievement tests. Because lately I've been asked, as a writer, why there are not more Asian Americans represented in American literature. Why are there few Asian Americans enrolled in creative writing programs? Why do so many Chinese students go into engineering? Well, these are broad sociological questions I can't begin to answer. But I have noticed in surveys—in fact, just last week—that Asian students, as a whole, always do significantly better on math achievement tests than in English. And this makes me think that there are other Asian-American students whose English spoken in the home might also be described as "broken" or "limited." And perhaps they also have teachers who are steering them away from writing and into math and science, which is what happened to me.

Fortunately, I happen to be rebellious in nature and enjoy the challenge of disproving assumptions made about me. I became an English major my first year in college, after being enrolled as pre-med. I started writing nonfiction as a freelancer the week after I was told by my former boss that writing was my worst skill and I should hone my talents toward account management.

But it wasn't until 1985 that I finally began to write fiction. And at first I wrote using what I thought to be wittily crafted sentences, sentences that would finally prove I had mastery over the English language. Here's an example from the first draft of a story that later made its way into *The Joy Luck Club*, but without this line: "That was my mental quandary in its nascent state." A terrible line, which I can barely pronounce.

Fortunately, for reasons I won't get into today, I later decided I should envision a reader for the stories I would write. And the reader I decided upon was my mother, because these were stories about mothers. So with this reader in mind—and in fact she did read my early drafts—I began to write stories using all the Englishes I grew up with: the English I spoke to my mother, which for lack of a better term might be described as "simple"; the English she used with me, which for lack of a better term might be described as "broken"; my translation of her Chinese, which could certainly be described as "watered down"; and what I imagined to be her translation of her Chinese if she could speak in perfect English, her internal language, and for that I sought to preserve the essence, but neither an English nor a Chinese structure. I wanted to capture what language ability tests can never reveal: her intent, her passion, her imagery, the rhythms of her speech, and the nature of her thoughts.

Apart from what any critic had to say about my writing, I knew I had succeeded where it counted when my mother finished reading my book and gave me her verdict: "So easy to read."

POSSIBILITIES FOR WRITING

1. Tan's focus here is on the "different Englishes" she uses. What are these, and what occasions her shift from one to another? Consider, as well, her feelings about these various "Englishes" and about her mother's "fractured" English. In what ways are these both limiting and liberating for communication?

2. Tan is pleased when her mother's verdict on her first novel was that it was "So easy to read." Do you find Tan's style in this essay "easy to read"? In an essay, evaluate her style, quoting from the text to support your viewpoint.

3. How does your language and that of your peers differ from that of a different generation of speakers—your parents, say, or your children? How does the language you use in formal situations differ from that you use in less formal ones? In an essay, describe the different sorts of "Englishes" you encounter in your life.

He also became a physician, graduating from Princeton University and

Lewis Thomas (1913–1993) *was born in Flushing, New York, the son of a family doctor. He also became a physician, graduating from Princeton University and Harvard Medical School, and he spent most of his career on the faculty at Yale University's medical school. He also served as president of the Sloan-Kettering Memorial Cancer Center. In the early 1970s, he began contributing a monthly essay to the* New England Journal of Medicine. *Personal and informal in nature, these short pieces achieved immediate popularity that spread well beyond the medical community. Thomas published his first collection,* The Lives of a Cell, *in 1974; it won the National Book Award. Four other collections followed, including* Late Night Thoughts on Listening to Mahler's Ninth Symphony *(1984) and* The Fragile Species *(1992), all praised for their insight and grace.*

LEWIS THOMAS

The Corner of the Eye

In "The Corner of the Eye," Lewis Thomas emphasizes the importance of seeing, noticing, observing. Seeing, in fact, provides the foundation for the thoughtful speculation Thomas offers in this essay. For Thomas, the corner of the eye suggests something glimpsed or hinted at, a suggestion that teases thought. In the corner of the mind ideas lie hidden, waiting to be discovered.

Thomas begins the essay with an example of something that can be seen only out of the corner of one's eye—small, faint stars, which when looked at directly, vanish from our field of vision. He provides another kind of example—a metaphorical one—when he describes listening to music and hearing its meaning in the "corner of the mind." And he provides a third example with his comments about computers and artificial intelligence. This kind of movement of mind is characteristic of Thomas's thinking, and of the kinds of essays he writes. They suggest the virtues of indirectness, Thomas's usual method of essaying.

There are some things that human beings can see only out of the corner of the eye. The niftiest examples of this gift, familiar to all children, are small, faint stars. When you look straight at one such star, it vanishes; when you move your eyes to stare into the space nearby, it reappears. If you pick two faint stars, side by side, and focus on one of the pair, it disappears and now you can see the other in the corner of your eye, and you can move your eyes back and forth, turning off the star in the center of your retina and switching the other one on. There is a physiological explanation for the phenomenon: we have more rods, the cells we use for light perception, at the periphery of our retinas, more cones, for perceiving color, at the center.

Something like this happens in music. You cannot really hear certain sequences of notes in a Bach fugue unless at the same time there are other notes being sounded, dominating the field. The real meaning in music comes from tones only audible in the corner of the mind.

I used to worry that computers would become so powerful and sophisticated as to take the place of human minds. The notion of Artificial Intelligence used to scare me half to death. Already, a large enough machine can do all sorts of intelligent things beyond our capacities: calculate in a split second the answers to mathematical problems requiring years for a human brain, draw accurate pictures from memory, even manufacture successions of sounds with a disarming resemblance to real music. Computers can translate textbooks, write dissertations of their own for doctorates, even speak in machine-tooled, inhuman phonemes any words read off from a printed page. They can communicate with one another, holding consultations and committee meetings of their own in networks around the earth.

Computers can make errors, of course, and do so all the time in small, irritating ways, but the mistakes can be fixed and nearly always are. In this respect they are fundamentally inhuman, and here is the relaxing thought: computers will not take over the world, they cannot replace us, because they are not designed, as we are, for ambiguity.

Imagine the predicament faced by a computer programmed to make language, not the interesting communication in sounds made by vervets or in symbols by brilliant chimpanzee prodigies, but real human talk. The grammar would not be too difficult, and there would be no problem in constructing a vocabulary of etymons, the original, pure, unambiguous words used to name real things. The impossibility would come in making the necessary mistakes we humans make with words instinctively, intuitively, as we build our kinds of language, changing the meanings to imply quite different things, constructing and elaborating the varieties of ambiguity without which speech can never become human speech.

Look at the record of language if you want to glimpse the special qualities of the human mind that lie beyond the reach of any machine. Take, for example, the metaphors we use in everyday speech to tell ourselves who we are, where we live, and where we come from.

The earth is a good place to begin. The word "earth" is used to name the ground we walk on, the soil in which we grow plants or dig clams, and the planet itself; we also use it to describe all of humanity ("the whole earth responds to the beauty of a child," we say to each other).

The earliest word for earth in our language was the Indo-European root *dhghem*, and look what we did with it. We turned it, by adding suffixes, into *humus* in Latin; today we call the complex polymers that hold fertile soil together "humic" acids, and somehow or other the same root became "humility." With another suffix the word became "human." Did the earth become human, or did the human emerge from the earth? One answer may lie in that nice cognate word "humble." "Humane" was built on, extending the meaning of both the earth and ourselves. In ancient Hebrew, *adamha* was the word for earth, *adam* for man. What computer could run itself through such manipulations as those?

We came at the same system of defining ourselves from the other direction. The word *wiros* was the first root for man; it took us in our vanity on to "virile" and "virtue," but also turned itself into the Germanic word *weraldh*, meaning the life of man, and thence in English to our word "world."

There is a deep hunch in this kind of etymology. The world of man derives from this planet, shares origin with the life of the soil, lives in humility with all the rest of life. I cannot imagine programming a computer to think up an idea like that, not a twentieth-century computer, anyway.

The world began with what it is now the fashion to call the "Big Bang." Characteristically, we have assigned the wrong words for the very beginning of the earth and ourselves, in order to evade another term that would cause this century embarrassment. It could not, of course, have been a bang of any sort, with no atmosphere to conduct the waves of sound, and no ears. It was something else, occurring in the most absolute silence we can imagine. It was the Great Light.

We say it had been chaos before, but it was not the kind of place we use the word "chaos" for today, things tumbling over each other and bumping around. Chaos did not have that meaning in Greek; it simply meant empty.

We took it, in our words, from chaos to cosmos, a word that simply meant order, cosmetic. We perceived the order in surprise, and our cosmologists and physicists continue to find new and astonishing aspects of the order. We made up the word "universe" from the whole affair, meaning literally turning everything into one thing. We used to say it was a miracle, and we still permit ourselves to refer to the whole universe as a marvel, holding in our unconscious minds the original root meaning of these two words, miracle and marvel—from the ancient root word *smei*, signifying a smile. It immensely pleases a human being to see something never seen before, even more to learn something never known before, most of all to think something never thought before. The rings of Saturn are the latest surprise. All my physicist friends are enchanted by this phenomenon, marveling at the small violations of the laws of planetary mechanics, shocked by the unaccountable braids and spokes stuck there among the rings like graffiti. It is nice for physicists to see something new and inexplicable; it means that the laws of nature are once again about to be amended by a new footnote.

The greatest surprise of all lies within our own local, suburban solar system. It is not Mars; Mars was surprising in its way but not flabbergasting; it was a disappointment not to find evidences of life, and there was some sadness in the pictures sent back to earth from the Mars Lander, that lonely long-legged apparatus poking about with its jointed arm, picking up sample after sample of the barren Mars soil, looking for any flicker of life and finding none; the only sign of life on Mars was the Lander itself, an extension of the human mind all the way from earth to Mars, totally alone.

Nor is Saturn the great surprise, nor Jupiter, nor Venus, nor Mercury, nor any of the glimpses of the others.

The overwhelming astonishment, the queerest structure we know about so far in the whole universe, the greatest of all cosmological scientific puzzles, confounding all our efforts to comprehend it, is the earth. We are only now beginning to appreciate how strange and splendid it is, how it catches the breath, the loveliest object afloat around the sun, enclosed in its own blue bubble of atmosphere, manufacturing and breathing its own oxygen, fixing its own nitrogen from the air into its own soil, generating its own weather at the surface of its rain forests, constructing its own carapace from living parts: chalk cliffs, coral reefs, old fossils from earlier forms of life now covered by layers of new life meshed together around the globe, Troy upon Troy.

Seen from the right distance, from the corner of the eye of an extraterrestrial visitor, it must surely seem a single creature, clinging to the round warm stone, turning in the sun.

POSSIBILITIES FOR WRITING

1. Thomas ranges widely in subject matter here. Analyze the essay to discover the connections (some of which are implicit) among Thomas's subjects. How would you summarize his central point?

2. Thomas refers to "special qualities of the human mind that lie beyond the reach of any machine." What are the differences for Thomas between the human mind and computers? How do you respond? As computers have become increasingly sophisticated, have these "special qualities" been more nearly approached?

3. Thomas ends by noting our capacity for surprise (and its pleasures). In an essay explore the nature and kinds of surprises that we as humans can encounter.

Henry David Thoreau (1817–1862) was born in Concord, Massachusetts, where he spent most of his life. A graduate of Harvard, he was an early protégé of Ralph Waldo Emerson, whom he served for several years as an assistant and under whose tutelage he began to write for publication. Thoreau was philosophically a strict individualist and antimaterialist, and in 1845 he retired for two years to an isolated cabin on Walden Pond, near Concord, where he lived in comparative solitude, studying the natural world, reading, and keeping a journal that would become the basis for Walden (1854), a lyrical but deeply reasoned account of his experiences there and what they meant to him, as well as four later volumes. His work has influenced generations of writers, thinkers, and even political movements in terms of determining what constitutes true human and natural value.

HENRY DAVID THOREAU

Why I Went to the Woods

In this excerpt from the second chapter of *Walden*, Thoreau explains why he "went to the woods," that is, why he took a sabbatical from civilization to get away from it all for a while. (Thoreau spent two years and two months at Walden pond, where he built himself a cabin, grew his own food, and subsisted simply, as an experiment to see how little he would really need to live.) Essentially, Thoreau wanted time to read, write, and think. He wanted to make time for nature. And he wanted to test himself, to see just how much he could simplify his life, to determine how much time he could save to do what he really wanted to do with every minute of every day.

The appeal of Thoreau's central idea and fundamental ideal is especially acute for twenty-first century America, where people strive to accomplish as much as they can as fast as they can so as to accumulate everything they think they need. Thoreau postulates an opposite ideal: to see how little we really require to live our lives, with an appreciation for what is truly essential and a respect for the rhythms of the natural world.

I went to the woods because I wished to live deliberately, to front only the essential facts of life, and see if I could not learn what it had to teach, and not, when I came to die, discover that I had not lived. I did not wish to live what was not life, living is so dear; nor did I wish to practice resignation, unless it was quite necessary. I wanted to live deep and suck out all the marrow of life, to live so sturdily and Spartan-like as to put to rout all that was not life, to cut a broad swath and shave close, to drive life into a corner, and reduce it to its lowest terms, and, if it proved to be mean, why then to get the whole and genuine mean-ness of it, and publish its meanness to the world; or if it were sublime, to know it by experience, and be able to give a true account of it in my next excursion. For most men, it appears to me, are in a strange uncertainty about it, whether it is of the devil or of God, and have *somewhat hastily* concluded that it is the chief end of man here to "glorify God and enjoy him forever."

Still we live meanly, like ants; though the fable tells us that we were long ago changed into men; like pygmies we fight with cranes; it is error upon error, and clout upon clout, and our best virtue has for its occasion a superfluous and evitable wretchedness. Our life is frittered away by detail. An honest man has hardly need to count more than his ten fingers, or in extreme cases he may add his ten toes, and lump the rest. Simplicity, simplicity, simplicity! I say, let your affairs be as two or three, and not a hundred or a thousand; instead of a million count half a dozen, and keep your accounts on your thumb-nail. In the midst of this chopping sea of civilized life, such are the clouds and storms and quicksands and thousand-and-one items to be allowed for, that a man has to live, if he would not founder and go to the bottom and not make his port at all, by dead reckoning, and he must be a great calculator indeed who succeeds. Simplify, simplify. Instead of three meals a day, if it be necessary eat but one; instead of a hundred dishes, five; and reduce other things in proportion. Our life is like a German Confederacy, made of up petty states, with its boundary forever fluctuating, so that even a German cannot tell you how it is bounded at any moment. The nation itself, with all its so-called internal improvements, which, by the way are all external and superficial, is just such an unwieldy and overgrown establishment, cluttered with furniture and tripped up by its own traps, ruined by luxury and heedless expense, by want of calculation and a worthy aim, as the million households in the lands; and the only cure for it, as for them, is in a rigid economy, a stern and more than Spartan simplicity of life and elevation of purpose. It lives too fast. Men think that it is essential that the *Nation* have commerce, and export ice, and talk through a telegraph, and ride thirty miles an hour, without a doubt, whether *they* do or not; but whether we should live like baboons or like men, is a little uncertain. If we do not get our sleepers, and forge rails, and devote days and nights to the work, but go to tinkering upon our *lives* to improve *them*, who will build railroads? And if railroads are not built, how shall we get to heaven in season? But if we stay at home and mind our business, who will want railroads? We do not ride on the railroad; it rides upon us. Did you ever think what those sleepers are that underlie the railroad? Each one is a man, an Irishman, or a Yankee man. The rails are laid on them, and they are covered with sand, and the cars run smoothly over them.

They are sound sleepers, I assure you. And every few years a new lot is laid down and run over; so that, if some have the pleasure of riding on a rail, others have the misfortune to be ridden upon. And when they run over a man that is walking in his sleep, a supernumerary sleeper in the wrong position, and wake him up, they suddenly stop the cars, and make a hue and cry about it, as if this were an exception. I am glad to know that it takes a gang of men for every five miles to keep the sleepers down and level in their beds as it is, for this is a sign that they may sometimes get up again.

Why should we live with such hurry and waste of life? We are determined to be starved before we are hungry. Men say that a stitch in time saves nine, and so they take a thousand stitches to-day to save nine tomorrow. As for *work*, we haven't any of any consequence. We have the Saint Vitus' dance, and cannot possibly keep our heads still. If I should only give a few pulls at the parish bell-rope, as for a fire, that is, without setting the bell, there is hardly a man on his farm in the outskirts of Concord, notwithstanding that press of engagements which was his excuse so many times this morning, nor a boy, nor a woman, I might almost say, but would foresake all and follow that sound, not mainly to save property from the flames, but, if we will confess the truth, much more to see it burn, since burn it must, and we, be it known, did not set it on fire—or to see it put out, and have a hand in it, if that is done as handsomely; yes, even if it were the parish church itself. Hardly a man takes a half-hour's nap after dinner, but when he wakes he holds up his head and asks, "What's the news?" as if the rest of mankind had stood his sentinels. Some give directions to be waked every half-hour, doubtless for no other purpose; and then, to pay for it, they tell what they have dreamed. After a night's sleep the news is as indispensable as the breakfast. "Pray tell me anything new that has happened to a man anywhere on this globe"—and he reads it over his coffee and rolls, that a man has had his eyes gouged out this morning on the Wachito River; never dreaming the while that he lives in the dark unfathomed mammoth cave of this world, and has but the rudiment of an eye himself.

For my part, I could easily do without the post-office. I think that there are very few important communications made through it. To speak critically, I never received more than one or two letters in my life—I wrote this some years ago—that were worth the postage. The penny-post is, commonly, an institution through which you seriously offer a man that penny for his thoughts which is so often safely offered in jest. And I am sure that I never read any memorable news in a newspaper. If we read of one man robbed, or murdered, or killed by accident, or one house burned, or one vessel wrecked, or one steamboat blown up, or one cow run over on the Western Railroad, or one mad dog killed, or one lot of grasshoppers in the winter—we never need read of another. One is enough. If you are acquainted with the principle, what do you care for a myriad instances and applications? To a philosopher all *news*, as it is called, is gossip, and they who edit and read it are old women over their tea. Yet not a few are greedy after this gossip. There was such a rush, as I hear, the other day at one of the offices to learn the foreign news by the last arrival, that several large squares of plate glass belonging to the establishment were broken by the pressure—news which I seriously think a ready wit might write a twelvemonth, or twelve years, beforehand with sufficient accuracy. As for Spain, for instance, if you know how to throw in Don Carlos and the Infanta, and Don Pedro and Seville and Granada, from time to time in the right proportions—they may have changed the names a little since I saw the papers—and serve up a bullfight when other entertainments fail, it will be true to the letter, and give us as good an idea of the exact state or ruin of things in Spain as the most succinct and lucid reports under this head in the newspapers; and as for England, almost the last significant scrap of news from that quarter was the revolution of 1649; and if you have learned the history of her crops for an average year, you never need attend to that thing again, unless your speculations are of a merely pecuniary character. If one may judge who rarely looks into the newspapers, nothing new does ever happen in foreign parts, a French revolution not excepted.

What news! how much more important to know what that is which was never old! "Kieou-he-yu (great dignitary of the state of Wei) sent a man to Khoung-tseu to know his news. Khoung-tseu caused the messenger to be seated near him, and questioned him in these terms: What is your master doing? The messenger answered with respect: My master desires to diminish the number of his faults, but he cannot come to the end of them. The messenger being gone, the philosopher remarked: What a worthy messenger! What a worthy messenger!" The preacher, instead of vexing the ears of drowsy farmers on their day of rest at the end of the week—for Sunday is the fit conclusion of an ill-spent week, and not the fresh and brave beginning of a new one—with this one other draggle-tail of a sermon, should shout with thundering voice, "Pause! Avast! Why so seeming fast, but deadly slow?"

Shams and delusions are esteemed for soundless truths, while reality is fabulous. If men would steadily observe realities only, and not allow themselves to be deluded, life, to compare it with such things as we know, would be like a fairy tale and the Arabian Nights' Entertainments. If we respected only what is inevitable and has a right to be, music and poetry would resound along the streets. When we are unhurried and wise, we perceive that only great and worthy things have any permanent and absolute existence, that petty fears and petty pleasures are but the shadow of the reality. This is always exhilarating and sublime. By closing the eyes and slumbering, and consenting to be deceived by shows, men establish and confirm their daily life of routine and habit everywhere, which still is built on purely illusory foundations. Children, who play life, discern its true law and relations more clearly than men, who fail to live it worthily, but who think that they are wiser by experience, that is, by failure. I have read in a Hindoo book, that "there was a king's son, who, being expelled in infancy from his native city, was brought up by a forester, and, growing up to maturity in that state, imagined himself to belong to the barbarous race with which he lived. One of his father's ministers having discovered him, revealed to him what he was, and the misconception of his character was removed, and he knew himself to be a prince. So soul," continues the Hindoo philosopher, "from the circumstances in which it is placed, mistakes its own character, until the truth is revealed to it by some holy teacher and then it knows itself to be *Brahme*." I perceive that we inhabitants of New England live this mean life that we do because our vision does not penetrate the surface of things. We think that that *is* which *appears* to be. If a man should walk through this town and see only the reality, where, think you, would the "Milldam" go to? If he should give us an account of the realities he beheld there, we should not recognize the place in his description. Look at the meetinghouse, or a courthouse, or a jail, or a shop, or a dwelling-house, and say what that thing really is before a true gaze, and they would all go to pieces in your account of them. Men esteem truth remote, in the outskirts of the system, behind the farthest star, before Adam and after the last man. In eternity there is indeed something true and sublime. But all these times and places and occasions are now and here. God himself culminates in the present moment, and will never be more divine in the lapse of all the ages. And we are enabled to apprehend at all what is sublime and noble only by the perpetual instilling and drenching of the reality that surrounds us. The universe constantly and obediently answers to our conceptions; whether we travel fast or slow, the track is laid for us. Let us spend our lives in conceiving then. The poet or the artist never yet had so fair and noble a design but some of his posterity at least could accomplish it.

Let us spend one day as deliberately as Nature, and not be thrown off the track by every nutshell and mosquito's wing that falls on the rails. Let us rise early and fast, or breakfast, gently and without perturbation; let company come and let company go, let the bells ring and the children cry—determined to make a day of it. Why should we knock under and go with the stream? Let us not be upset and overwhelmed in that terrible rapid and whirlpool called a dinner, situated in the meridian shallows. Weather this danger and you are safe, for the rest of the way is downhill. With unrelaxed nerves, with morning vigor, sail by it, looking another way, tied to the mast like Ulysses. If the engine whistles, let it whistle till it is hoarse for its pains. If the bell rings, why should we run? We will consider what kind of music they are like. Let us settle ourselves and work and wedge our feet downward through the mud and slush of opinion, and prejudice, and tradition, and delusion, and appearance, that alluvion which covers the globe, through Paris and London, through New York and Boston and Concord, through Church and State, through poetry and philosophy and religion, till we come to a hard bottom and rocks in place, which we can call *reality*, and say, This is, and no mistake; and then begin, having a *point d'appui*, below freshet and frost and fire, a place where you might found a wall or a state, or set a lamppost safely, or perhaps a gauge, not a Nilometer, but a Realometer, that future ages might know how deep a freshet of shams and appearances had gathered from time to time. If you stand right fronting and face to face to a fact, you will see the sun glimmer on both its surfaces, as if it were a cimeter, and feel its sweet edge dividing you through the heart and marrow, and so you will happily conclude your mortal career. Be it life or death, we crave only reality. If we are really dying, let us hear the rattle in our throats and feel cold in the extremities; if we are alive, let us go about our business.

Time is but the stream I go afishing in. I drink at it; but while I drink I see the sandy bottom and detect how shallow it is. Its thin current slides away but eternity remains. I would drink deeper; fish in the sky, whose bottom is pebbly with stars. I cannot count one. I know not the first letter of the alphabet. I have always been regretting that I was not as wise as the day I was born. The intellect is a cleaver; it discerns and rifts its way into the secret of things. I do not wish to be any more busy with my hands than is necessary. My head is hands and feet. I feel all my best faculties concentrated in it. My instinct tells me that my head is an organ for burrowing, as some creatures use their snout and fore paws, and with it I would mine and burrow my way through these hills. I think that the richest vein is somewhere hereabouts; so by the divining-rod and thin rising vapors, I judge; and here I will begin to mine.

POSSIBILITIES FOR WRITING

1. Analyze the recommendations that Thoreau is making here. What are his general recommendations? What are his specific recommendations? How might these recommendations be applied to life as it is lived in the twenty-first century?
2. Thoreau's writing is characterized by extensive use of metaphor. Choose several of these to analyze in detail. How well does metaphor contribute to clarifying Thoreau's ideas?
3. Throughout the essay, Thoreau includes what are for him statements of observed truth—for example, "Our life is frittered away by detail" and "I perceive that we . . . live this mean life that we do because our vision does not penetrate the surface of things." Choose one of these ideas that you find interesting as the basis for an essay of your own.

Sojourner Truth (c. 1797–1883) was born a slave in Ulster County, New York, with the given name Isabella. When slavery was abolished in the state, she worked for a time with a Quaker family and was caught up in the religious fervor then sweeping American Protestantism. In 1843, announcing that she had received messages from heaven, she took on the name Sojourner Truth and began a career as an itinerant preacher, advocating the abolishment of slavery and the advancement of women's rights. While basically illiterate, she was nevertheless a highly effective speaker and a powerful physical presence, and she had an intense following. After the Civil War, she counseled newly freed slaves and petitioned for a "Negro state" on public lands in the West. Her memoirs, dictated to Olive Gilbert, were published as Narratives of Sojourner Truth *(1878).*

SOJOURNER TRUTH

And Ain't I a Woman?

The following speech was made by Sojourner Truth, a black female slave, when she attended a women's rights convention held in Akron, Ohio in May of 1851. Sojourner Truth was the only black woman in attendance. On the second day of the convention she approached the podium, and addressed the audience in a deep and powerful voice. The speech was recorded by Frances D. Gage, who presided at the convention, and was later transcribed.

Part of the power of Sojourner Truth's short speech is its spontaneous refutation of those who spoke before her. Part of the pleasure for readers of the speech is listening to her rebuttal of implied arguments made by the speakers who preceded her. Readers can infer the type of arguments they made about why women were inferior to men from how Sojourner Truth addresses those implied arguments.

Well children, where there is so much racket there must be somethin' out o'kilter. I think that 'twixt the Negroes of the North and the South and the women at the North, all talkin' 'bout rights, the white men will be in a fix pretty soon. But what's all this here talkin' 'bout?

That man over there say that women needs to be helped into carriages, and lifted over ditches, and to have the best place everywhere. Nobody ever helps me into carriages, or over mud-puddles, or give me any best place! And ain't I a woman? Look at me! Look at my arm! I have ploughed, and planted, and gathered into barns, and no man could head me! And ain't l a woman? I could work as much and eat as much as a man—when I could get it—and bear the lash as well! And ain't I a woman? I have borne thirteen children, and seen 'em mos' all sold off to slavery, and when I cried out with my mother's grief, none but Jesus heard me! And ain't I a woman?

Then they talk about this thing in the head; what's this they call it? ["Intellect," whispered some one near.] That's it honey. What's that got to do with women's rights or Negro's rights? If my cup won't hold but a pint and yours holds a quart, wouldn't you be mean not to let me have my little measure full?

Then that little man in black there, he says women can't have as much rights as men, 'cause Christ wasn't a woman! Where did your Christ come from? Where did your Christ come from? From God and a woman! Man had nothin' to do with Him.

If the first woman God ever made was strong enough to turn the world upside down all alone, these women together ought to be able to turn it back and get it right side up again; and now they is asking to do it, they better let 'em. 'Bliged to you for hearin' me, and now ole Sojourner hasn't got nothin' more to say.

POSSIBILITIES FOR WRITING

1. There are a number of striking points packed into this very brief argument—about both slavery and women's rights. Analyze each of the assertions Sojourner Truth makes, whether explicit or implied, and how she supports each assertion.

2. Read "And Ain't I a Woman?" along with Elizabeth Cady Stanton's "Declaration of Sentiments and Resolutions" (pages 592–595). Although the two speeches are very different, consider in particular what they have in common. Then think about how the two women go about achieving their point.

3. "Translate" Sojourner Truth's speech into standard, more formal English. Then analyze the differences between the two texts, taking into account differences when the two are read aloud.

Mark Twain (1835–1910) was born Samuel L. Clemens in Florida, Missouri, and spent most of his childhood in the river town of Hannibal. As a young man, he worked as a printer and as a journalist, and for five years he piloted steamboats on the Misssssippi River. He began his writing career in earnest when he journeyed west in the 1860s, reporting for newspapers in Virginia City, Nevada, and later in San Francisco. Initially known for his humorous "tall tales," Twain soon became a popular lecturer. After marrying and settling in Hartford, Connecticut, he produced a string of popular works, including the classic novels of adolescence The Adventures of Tom Sawyer *(1876) and* The Adventures of Huckleberry Finn *(1884). In* Life on the Mississippi *(1883), he recounted his experiences as a river boat pilot. He remains one of the best loved and most widely read of American writers.*

MARK TWAIN

Reading the River

Mark Twain is best known for his classic novel, *The Adventures of Huckleberry Finn*. One of the central characters of that book is the Mississippi River, where much of the book's action occurs. Twain also wrote another book about the river, *Life on the Mississippi*, from which the following excerpt has been taken. In this selection, Twain describes his experience as an apprentice steamboat pilot, who had to learn to "read" the river to ensure the safe passage of his boat, his passengers, and his crew.

Twain suggests that in studying the river analytically, the pilot loses his sense of its aura and beauty. For the steamboat pilot, the romance of the river is displaced by technical understanding of and professional respect for its shifting currents and eddies, its changing contours and depths. Something is gained with the pilot's accumulating knowledge, but something is also surely lost.

653

It turned out to be true. The face of the water in time became a wonderful book—a book that was a dead language to the uneducated passenger but which told its mind to me without reserve, delivering its most cherished secrets as clearly as if it uttered them with a voice. And it was not a book to be read once and thrown aside, for it had a new story to tell every day. Throughout the long twelve hundred miles there was never a page that was void of interest, never one that you could leave unread without loss, never one that you would want to skip, thinking you could find higher enjoyment in some other thing. There never was so wonderful a book written by man, never one whose interest was so absorbing, so unflagging, so sparklingly renewed with every reperusal. The passenger who could not read it was charmed with a peculiar sort of faint dimple on its surface (on the rare occasions when he did not overlook it altogether) but to the pilot, that was an italicized passage; indeed it was more than that, it was a legend of the largest capitals with a string of shouting exclamation-points at the end of it, for it meant that a wreck or a rock was buried there that could tear the life out of the strongest vessel that ever floated. It is the faintest and simplest expression the water ever makes, and the most hideous to a pilot's eye. In truth, the passenger who could not read this book saw nothing but all manner of pretty pictures in it, painted by the sun and shaded by the clouds, whereas to the trained eye these were not pictures at all, but the grimmest and most dead-earnest of reading matter.

Now when I had mastered the language of this water and had come to know every trifling feature that bordered the great river as familiarly as I knew the letters of the alphabet, I had made a valuable acquisition. But I had lost something, too. I had lost something which could never be restored to me while I lived. All the grace, the beauty, the poetry, had gone out of the majestic river! I still kept in mind a certain wonderful sunset which I witnessed when steamboating was new to me. A broad expanse of the river was turned to blood; in the middle distance the red hue brightened into gold, through which a solitary log came floating, black and conspicuous; in one place a long, slanting mark was broken by boiling, tumbling rings, that were as many-tinted as an opal; where the ruddy flush was faintest, was a smooth spot that was covered with graceful circles and radiating lines, ever so delicately traced; the shore on our left was densely wooded and the somber shadow that fell from this forest was broken in one place by a long, ruffled trail that shone like silver; and high above the forest wall a clean-stemmed dead tree waved a single leafy bough that glowed like a flame in the unobstructed splendor that was flowing from the sun. There were graceful curves, reflected images, woody heights, soft distances, and over the whole scene, far and near, the dissolving lights drifted steadily, enriching it every passing moment with new marvels of coloring.

I stood like one bewitched. I drank it in, in a speechless rapture. The world was new to me and I had never seen anything like this at home. But as I have said, a day came when I began to cease from noting the glories and the charms which the moon and the sun and the twilight wrought upon the river's face; another day came when I ceased altogether to note them. Then, if that sunset scene had been repeated, I should have looked upon it without rapture, and should have commented upon it inwardly after this fashion: "This sun means that we are going to have wind to-morrow; that floating log means that the river is rising, small thanks to it; that slanting mark on the water refers to a bluff reef which is going to kill somebody's steamboat one of these nights, if it keeps on stretching out like that; those tumbling 'boils' show a dissolving bar and a changing channel there; the lines and circles in the slick water over yonder are a warning that that troublesome place is shoaling up dangerously; that silver streak in the shadow of the forest is the 'break' from a new snag and he has located himself in the very place he could have found to fish for steamboats; that tall dead tree, with a single living branch, is not going to last long, and then how is a body ever going to get through this blind place at night without the friendly old landmark?

No, the romance and beauty were all gone from the river. All the value any feature of it had for me now was the amount of usefulness it could furnish toward compassing the safe piloting of a steamboat. Since those days, I have pitied doctors from my heart. What does the lovely flush in a beauty's cheek mean to a doctor but a "break" that ripples above some deadly disease? Are not all her visible charms sown thick with what are to him the signs and symbols of hidden decay? Does he ever see her beauty at all, or doesn't he simply view her professionally and comment upon her unwholesome condition all to himself? And doesn't he sometimes wonder whether he has gained most or lost most by learning his trade?

POSSIBILITIES FOR WRITING

1. This passage is built around three different examples of comparison and contrast in paragraphs 1, 2–3, and 4. How do each of these work to elaborate on Twain's point? How does the analogy of reading apply in each case?

2. Describe a subject of your own, choosing as Twain does, from the vantage point first of a novice and then of someone more experienced with the subject. Don't ignore possibilities for humor here.

3. Try to observe a familiar setting with fresh eyes. Describe what you see there, paying special note to things you hadn't noticed before and things you had begun to take so for granted that you no longer noticed them consciously. What does such close observation suggest to you about everyday perception?

Alice Walker (b. 1944) *grew up in Eatonton, Georgia, the only daughter of a sharecropping family. A gifted student, she won scholarships to attend historically black Spelman College and, later, Sarah Lawrence. Walker published her first volume of poetry when she was twenty-four, and this was soon followed by a novel and a collection of short stories. Her fame increased with* The Color Purple (1982), *a novel which won the Pulitzer Prize. During the 1970s and 1980s Walker was an ongoing contributor to Ms.* magazine, *where many of the essays collected in* In Search of Our Mothers' Gardens: Womanist Prose (1983) *and* Living by the Word (1988) *originally appeared. One of the most striking African American voices of her generation, Walker most recently published the short story collection* The Way Forward Is with a Broken Heart (2000).

A L I C E   W A L K E R

Beauty: When the Other Dancer Is the Self

Alice Walker's essay about beauty grows out of a childhood experience during which she suffered an eye injury that left a psychological scar as well as a physical one. Walker shows how she learned to live with her wound, how she learned to accept her physical imperfection, and how she overcame her damaged self-regard, transforming it into a serene self-acceptance, scar and all.

By organizing her essay chronologically in a series of scenes narrated in the present tense, Walker increases its dramatic immediacy. She unifies her essay by describing the movement from being "cute" to being scarred and then to becoming psychologically and emotionally healed. As she traces this progression of her experience, Walker moves beyond her initial self-regard and self-pity to a larger vision of appreciation for all that is beautiful in life.

It is a bright summer day in 1947. My father, a fat, funny man with beautiful eyes and a subversive wit, is trying to decide which of his eight children he will take with him to the county fair. My mother, of course, will not go. She is knocked out from getting most of us ready: I hold my neck stiff against the pressure of her knuckles as she hastily completes the braiding and then her ribboning of my hair.

My father is the driver for the rich old white lady up the road. Her name is Miss Mey. She owns all the land for miles around, as well as the house in which we live. All I remember about her is that she once offered in pay my mother thirty-five cents for cleaning her house, raking up piles of her magnolia leaves, and washing her family's clothes, and that my mother—she of no money, eight children, and a chronic earache—refused it. But I do not think of this in 1947. I am two and a half years old. I want to go everywhere my daddy goes. I am excited at the prospect of riding in a car. Someone has told me fairs are fun. That there is room in the car for only three of us doesn't faze me at all. Whirling happily in my starchy frock, showing off my biscuit-polished patent-leather shoes and lavender socks, tossing my head in a way that makes my ribbons bounce, I stand, hands on hips, before my father. "Take me, Daddy," I say with assurance; "I'm the prettiest!"

Later, it does not surprise me to find myself in Miss Mey's shiny black car, sharing the back seat with the other lucky ones. Does not surprise me that I thoroughly enjoy the fair. At home that night I tell the unlucky ones all I can remember about the merry-go-round, the man who eats live chickens, and the teddy bears, until they say: that's enough, baby Alice. Shut up now, and go to sleep.

It is Easter Sunday, 1950. I am dressed in a green, flocked, scalloped hem dress (handmade by my adoring sister, Ruth) that has its own smooth satin petticoat and tiny hot-pink roses tucked into each scallop. My shoes, new T-strap patent leather, again highly biscuit-polished. I am six years old and have learned one of the longest Easter speeches to be heard that day, totally unlike the speech I said when I was two: "Easter lilies/pure and white/blossom in/the morning light." When I rise to give my speech I do so on a great wave of love and pride and expectation. People in the church stop rustling their new crinolines. They seem to hold their breath. I can tell they admire my dress, but it is my spirit, bordering on sassiness (womanishness), they secretly applaud.

"That girl's a little *mess*," they whisper to each other, pleased.

Naturally I say my speech without stammer or pause, unlike those who stutter, stammer, or, worst of all, forget. This is before the word "beautiful" exists in people's vocabulary, but "Oh, isn't she the *cutest* thing!" frequently floats my way. "And got so much sense!" they gratefully add . . . for which thoughtful addition I thank them to this day.

It was great fun being cute. But then, one day, it ended.

I am eight years old and a tomboy. I have a cowboy hat, cowboy boots, checkered shirt and pants, all red. My playmates are my brothers, two and four years older than I. Their colors are black and green, the only difference in the way we are dressed. On Saturday nights we all go to the picture show, even my mother; Westerns are her favorite kind of movie.

Back home, "on the ranch," we pretend we are Tom Mix, Hopalong Cassidy, Lash LaRue (we've even named one of our dogs Lash LaRue); we chase each other for hours rustling cattle, being outlaws, delivering damsels from distress. Then my parents decide to buy my brothers guns. These are not "real" guns. They shoot "BBs," copper pellets my brothers say will kill birds. Because I am a girl, I do not get a gun. Instantly I am relegated to the position of Indian. Now there appears a great distance between us. They shoot and shoot at everything with their new guns. I try to keep up with my bow and arrows.

One day while I am standing on top of our makeshift "garage"— pieces of tin nailed across some poles—holding my bow and arrow and looking out toward the fields, I feel an incredible blow in my right eye. I look down just in time to see my brother lower his gun.

Both brothers rush to my side. My eye stings, and I cover it with my hand. "If you tell," they say, "we will get a whipping. You don't want that to happen, do you?" I do not. "Here is a piece of wire," says the older brother, picking it up from the roof; "say you stepped on one end of it and the other flew up and hit you." The pain is beginning to start. "Yes," I say. "Yes, I will say that is what happened." If I do not say this is what happened, I know my brothers will find ways to make me wish I had. But now I will say anything that gets me to my mother.

Confronted by our parents we stick to the lie agreed upon. They place me on a bench on the porch and I close my left eye while they examine the right. There is a tree growing from underneath the porch that climbs past the railing to the roof. It is the last thing my right eye sees. I watch as its trunk, its branches, and then its leaves are blotted out by the rising blood.

I am in shock. First there is intense fever, which my father tries to break using lily leaves bound around my head. Then there are chills: my mother tries to get me to eat soup. Eventually, I do not know how, my parents learn what has happened. A week after the "accident" they take me to see a doctor. "Why did you wait so long to come?" he asks, looking into my eye and shaking his head. "Eyes are sympathetic," he says. "If one is blind, the other will likely become blind too."

This comment of the doctor's terrifies me. But it is really how I look that bothers me most. Where the BB pellet struck there is a glob of whitish scar tissue, a hideous cataract, on my eye. Now when I stare at people—a favorite pastime, up to now—they will stare back. Not at the "cute" little girl, but at her scar. For six years I do not stare at anyone, because I do not raise my head.

Years later, in the throes of a mid-life crisis, I ask my mother and sister whether I changed after the "accident." "No," they say, puzzled. "What do you mean?"

What do I mean?

I am eight, and, for the first time, doing poorly in school, where I have been something of a whiz since I was four. We have just moved to the place where the "accident" occurred. We do not know any of the people around us because this is a different county. The only time I see the friends I knew is when we go back to our old church. The new school is the former state penitentiary. It is a large stone building, cold and drafty, crammed to overflowing with boisterous, ill-disciplined children. On the third floor there is a huge circular imprint of some partition that has been torn out.

"What used to be here?" I ask a sullen girl next to me on our way past it to lunch.

"The electric chair," says she.

At night I have nightmares about the electric chair, and about all the people reputedly "fried" in it. I am afraid of the school, where all the students seem to be building criminals.

"What's the matter with your eye?" they ask, critically.

When I don't answer (I cannot decide whether it was an "accident" or not), they shove me, insist on a fight.

My brother, the one who created the story about the wire, comes to my rescue. But then brags so much about "protecting" me. I become sick.

After months of torture at the school, my parents decide to send me back to our old community, to my old school. I live with my grandparents and the teacher they board. But there is no room for Phoebe, my cat. By the time my grandparents decide there *is* room, and I ask for my cat, she cannot be found. Miss Yarborough, the boarding teacher takes me under her wing, and begins to teach me to play the piano. But soon she marries an African—a "prince," she says—and is whisked away to his continent.

At my old school there is at least one teacher who loves me. She is the teacher who "knew me before I was born" and bought my first baby clothes. It is she who makes life bearable. It is her presence that finally helps me turn on the one child to the school who continually calls me "one-eyed bitch." One day I simply grab him by his coat and beat him until I am satisfied. It is my teacher who tells me my mother is ill.

My mother is lying in bed in the middle of the day, something I have never seen. She is in too much pain to speak. She has an abscess in her ear. I stand looking down on her, knowing that if she dies, I cannot live. She is being treated with warm oils and hot bricks held against her cheek. Finally a doctor comes. But I must go back to my grandparents' house. The weeks pass but I am hardly aware of it. All I know is that my mother might die, my father is not so jolly, my brothers still have their guns, and I am the one sent away from home.

"You did not change," they say.

Did I imagine the anguish of never looking up?

I am twelve. When relatives come to visit I hide in my room. My cousin Brenda, just my age, whose father works in the post office and whose mother is a nurse, comes to find me. "Hello." she says. And then she asks, looking at my recent school picture, which I did not want taken, and on which the "glob," as I think of it, is clearly visible, "You still can't see out of that eye?"

"No," I say and flop back on the bed over my book.

That night, as I do almost every night, I abuse my eye. I rant and rave at it, in front of the mirror. I plead with it to clear up before morning. I tell it I hate and despise it. I do not pray for sight. I pray for beauty.

"You did not change." they say.

I am fourteen and baby-sitting for my brother Bill, who lives in Boston. He is my favorite brother and there is a strong bond between us. Understanding my feelings of shame and ugliness he and his wife take me to a local hospital, where the "glob" is removed by a doctor named O. Henry. There is still a small bluish crater where the scar tissue was, but the ugly white stuff is gone. Almost immediately I become a different person from the girl who does not raise her head. Or so I think. Now that I've raised my head I win the boyfriend of my dreams. Now that I've raised my head I have plenty of friends. Now that I've raised my head classwork comes from my lips as faultlessly as Easter speeches did, and I leave high school as valedictorian, most popular student, and *queen*, hardly believing my luck. Ironically, the girl who was voted most beautiful in our class (and was) was later shot twice through the chest by a male companion, using a "real" gun, while she was pregnant. But that's another story in itself. Or is it?

"You did not change," they say.

It is now thirty years since the "accident." A beautiful journalist comes to visit and to interview me. She is going to write a cover story for her magazine that focuses on my latest book. "Decide how you want to look on the cover," she says. "Glamorous, or whatever."

Never mind "glamorous," it is the "whatever" that I hear. Suddenly all I can think of is whether I will get enough sleep the night before the photography session: if I don't, my eye will be tired and wander, as blind eyes will.

At night in bed with my lover I think up reasons why I should not appear on the cover of a magazine. "My meanest critics will say I've sold out," I say. "My family will now realize I write scandalous books."

"But what's the real reason you don't want to do this?" he asks.

"Because in all probability," I say in a rush, "my eye won't be straight."

"It will be straight enough," he says. Then, "Besides, I thought you'd made your peace with that."

And I suddenly remember that I have.

I remember:

I am talking to my brother Jimmy, asking if he remembers anything unusual about the day I was shot. He does not know I consider that day the last time my father, with his sweet home remedy of cool lily leaves, chose me, and that I suffered and raged inside because of this. "Well," he says, "all I remember is standing by the side of the highway with Daddy, trying to flag down a car. A white man stopped, but when Daddy said he needed somebody to take his little girl to the doctor, he drove off."

I remember:

I am in the desert for the first time. I fall totally in love with it. I am so overwhelmed by its beauty. I confront for the first time consciously, the meaning of the doctor's words years ago: "Eyes are sympathetic. If one is blind, the other will likely become blind too." I realize I have dashed about the world madly, looking at this, looking at that, storing up images against the fading of the light. *But I might have missed seeing the desert!* The shock of that possibility—and gratitude for over twenty-five years of sight—sends me literally to my knees. Poem after poem comes—which is perhaps how poets pray.

On Sight

I am so thankful I have seen
The Desert
And the creatures in the desert
And the desert Itself.

The desert has its own moon
Which I have seen
With my own eye.

There is no flag on it.
Trees of the desert have arms
All of which are always up
That is because the moon is up
The sun is up
Also the sky
The stars
Clouds
None with flags

If there *were* flags, I doubt
the trees would point.
Would you?

But mostly, I remember this:

I am twenty-seven and my baby daughter is almost three. Since her birth I have worried about her discovery that her mother's eyes are different from other people's. Will she be embarrassed? I think. What will she say? Every day she watches a television program called "Big Blue Marble." It begins with a picture of the earth as it appears from the moon. It is bluish, a little battered-looking, but full of light, with whitish clouds swirling around it. Every time I see it I weep with love, as if it is a picture of Grandma's house. One day when I am putting Rebecca down for her nap, she suddenly focuses on my eye. Something inside me cringes, gets ready to try to protect myself. All children are cruel about physical differences, I know from experience, and that they don't always mean to be in another matter. I assume Rebecca will be the same.

But no-o-o-o. She studies my face intently as we stand, her inside and me outside her crib. She even holds my face maternally between her dimpled little hands. Then, looking every bit as serious and lawyerlike as her father, she says, as if it may just possibly have slipped my attention: "Mommy, there's a *world* in your eye," (As in, "Don't be alarmed, or do anything crazy.") And then, gently, but with great interest: "Mommy, where did you *get* that world in your eye?"

For the most part, the pain left then. (So what, if my brothers grew up to buy even more powerful pellet guns for their sons and to carry real guns themselves. So what, if a young "Morehouse man" once nearly fell off the steps of Trevor Arnett Library because he thought my eyes were blue.) Crying and laughing I ran to the bathroom, while Rebecca mumbled and sang herself off to sleep. Yes indeed, I realized, looking into the mirror. There *was* a world in my eye. And I saw that it was possible to love it: that in fact, for all it had taught me of shame and anger and inner vision, I *did* love it. Even to see it drifting out of orbit in boredom, or rolling up out of fatigue, not to mention floating back at attention in excitement (bearing witness, a friend has called it), deeply suitable to my personality, and even characteristic of me.

That night I dream I am dancing to Stevie Wonder's song "Always" (the name of the song is really "As," but I hear it as "Always"). As I dance, whirling and joyous, happier than I've ever been in my life, another bright-faced dancer joins me. We dance and kiss each other and hold each other through the night. The other dancer has obviously come through all right, as I have done. She is beautiful, whole and free. And she is also me.

POSSIBILITIES FOR WRITING

1. Trace Walker's image of herself from childhood onward as it is related to the disfiguring of her eye. Note particularly that paragraphs 34—40 take place prior to the following paragraphs that end the essay. The final image of the two dancers resolves the essay, but does it seem to you a true resolution for Walker? Why or why not?
2. Walker's picture of herself here is of someone who is highly self-absorbed, in some cases, perhaps, even vain. Do you find her generally sympathetic or not? Point to specific passages in the text that contribute to your response.
3. Like Walker as child, people can be highly self-conscious about some aspect of their appearance. In your experience—both in terms of your thoughts about your own appearance and thoughts about their appearance friends may have shared with you—is such self-consciousness generally justified or not?

DAVID FOSTER WALLACE

Consider the Lobster

"Consider the Lobster," originally published in *Gourmet* magazine in 2004, was selected for *Best American Essays 2005*, and serves as the title essay of a 2008 collection of his nonfiction prose. The essay grew out of Wallace's visit to the Maine Lobster Festival and serves as a kind of "review" of that sprawling and popular annual event.

Wallace's distinctive signature style is in evidence throughout the essay, characterized by a rich panoply of details, sprawling sentences with surprising words and images, and a profusion of lengthy footnotes. About midway through the essay, Wallace shifts from describing the Maine Lobster Festival and the variety of ways lobster is prepared, cooked, and eaten, to an investigation of the ethics of killing and eating lobsters for human enjoyment and nourishment. In the process, Wallace raises a number of disturbing questions, which have yet to be satisfactorily answered.

THE ENORMOUS, pungent, and extremely well-marketed Maine Lobster Festival is held every late July in the state's midcoast region, meaning the western side of Penobscot Bay, the nerve stem of Maine's lobster industry. What's called the midcoast runs from Owl's Head and Thomaston in the south to Belfast in the north. (Actually, it might extend all the way up to Bucksport, but we were never able to get farther north than Belfast on Route 1, whose summer traffic is, as you can imagine, unimaginable.) The region's two main communities are Camden, with its very old money and yachty harbor and five-star restaurants and phenomenal B&Bs, and Rockland, a serious old fishing town that hosts the festival every summer in historic Harbor Park, right along the water.[1]

[1] There's a comprehensive native apothegm: "Camden by the sea, Rockland by the smell."

Tourism and lobster are the midcoast region's two main industries, and they're both warm-weather enterprises, and the Maine Lobster Festival represents less an intersection of the industries than a deliberate collision, joyful and lucrative and loud. The assigned subject of this *Gourmet* article is the 56th Annual MLF, 30 July–3 August 2003, whose official theme this year was "Light-houses, Laughter, and Lobster." Total paid attendance was over 100,000, due partly to a national CNN spot in June during which a senior editor of *Food & Wine* magazine hailed the MLF as one of the best food-themed galas in the world. 2003 festival highlights: concerts by Lee Ann Womack and Orleans, annual Maine Sea Goddess beauty pageant, Saturday's big parade, Sunday's William G. Atwood Memorial Crate Race, annual Amateur Cooking Competition, carnival rides and midway attractions and food booths, and the MLF's Main Eating Tent, where something over 25,000 pounds of fresh-caught Maine lobster is consumed after preparation in the World's Largest Lobster Cooker near the grounds' north entrance. Also available are lobster rolls, lobster turnovers, lobster sauté, Down East lobster salad, lobster bisque, lobster ravioli, and deep-fried lobster dumplings. Lobster thermidor is obtainable at a sit-down restaurant called the Black Pearl on Harbor Park's northwest wharf. A large all-pine booth sponsored by the Maine Lobster Promotion Council has free pamphlets with recipes, eating tips, and Lobster Fun Facts. The winner of Friday's Amateur Cooking Competition prepares Saffron Lobster Ramekins, the recipe for which is now available for public downloading at www.mainelobsterfestival.com. There are lobster T-shirts and lobster bobblehead dolls and inflatable lobster pool toys and clamp-on lobster hats with big scarlet claws that wobble on springs. Your assigned correspondent saw it all, accompanied by one girlfriend and both his own parents—one of which parents was actually born and raised in Maine, albeit in the extreme northern inland part, which is potato country and a world away from the touristic midcoast.[2]

For practical purposes, everyone knows what a lobster is. As usual, though, there's much more to know than most of us care about—it's all a matter of what your interests are. Taxonomically speaking, a lobster is a marine crustacean of the family Homaridae, characterized by live pairs of jointed legs, the first pair terminating in large pincerish claws

[2]N.B. All personally connected parties have made it clear from the start that they do not want to be talked about in this article.

used for subduing prey. Like many other species of benthic carnivore, lobsters are both hunters and scavengers. They have stalked eyes, gills on their legs, and antennae. There are a dozen or so different kinds worldwide, of which the relevant species here is the Maine lobster, *Homarus americanus.* The name "lobster" comes from the Old English *loppestre,* which is thought to be a corrupt form of the Latin word for locust combined with the Old English *loppe,* which meant spider.

Moreover, a crustacean is an aquatic arthropod of the class Crustacea, which comprises crabs, shrimp, barnacles, lobsters, and freshwater crayfish. All this is right there in the encyclopedia. And arthropods are members of the phylum Arthropoda, which phylum covers insects, spiders, crustaceans, and centipedes/millipedes, all of whose main commonality, besides the absence of a centralized brain-spine assembly, is a chitinous exoskeleton composed of segments, to which appendages are articulated in pairs.

The point is that lobsters are basically giant sea insects.[3] Like most arthropods, they date from the Jurassic period, biologically so much older than mammalia that they might as well be from another planet. And they are—particularly in their natural brown-green state, brandishing their claws like weapons and with thick antennae awhip—not nice to look at. And it's true that they are garbagemen of the sea, eaters of dead stuff,[4] although they'll also eat some live shellfish, certain kinds of injured fish, and sometimes one another.

But they are themselves good eating. Or so we think now. Up until sometime in the 1800s, though, lobster was literally low-class food, eaten only by the poor and institutionalized. Even in the harsh penal environment of early America, some colonies had laws against feeding lobsters to inmates more than once a week because it was thought to be cruel and unusual, like making people eat rats. One reason for their low status was how plentiful lobsters were in old New England, "Unbelievable abundance" is how one source describes the situation, including accounts or Plymouth Pilgrims wading out and capturing all they wanted by hand, and of early Boston's seashore being littered with lobsters after hard storms—these latter were treated as a smelly nuisance and ground up for fertilizer. There is also the fact that premodern lobster was cooked dead and then preserved, usually packed in salt or

---

[3]Midcoasters' native term for a lobster is, in fact, "bug," as in "Come around on Sunday and we'll took up some bugs."
[4]Factoid: Lobster traps are usually baited with dead herring.

crude hermetic containers. Maine's earliest lobster industry was based around a dozen such seaside canneries in the 1840s, from which lobster was shipped as far away as California, in demand only because it was cheap and high in protein, basically chewable fuel.

Now, of course, lobster is posh, a delicacy, only a step or two down from caviar. The meat is richer and more substantial than most fish, its taste subtle compared to the marine-gaminess of mussels and clams. In the US pop-food imagination, lobster is now the seafood analog to steak, with which it's so often twinned as Surf 'n' Turf on the really expensive part of the chain steakhouse menu.

In fact, one obvious project of the MLK, and of its omni-presently sponsorial Maine Lobster Promotion Council, is to counter the idea that lobster is unusually luxe or unhealthy or expensive, suitable only for effete palates or the occasional blow-the-diet treat. It is emphasized over and over in presentations and pamphlets at the festival that lobster meat has fewer calories, less cholesterol, and less saturated fat than chicken.[5] And in the Main Eating Tent, you can get a "quarter" (industry shorthand for a 1¼-pound lobster), a four-ounce cup of melted butter, a bag of chips, and a soft roll w/ butter-pat for around $12.00, which is only slightly more expensive than supper at McDonald's.

Be apprised, though, that the Maine Lobster Festival's democratization of lobster comes with all the massed inconvenience and aesthetic compromise of real democracy. See, for example, the aforementioned Main Eating Tent, for which there is a constant Disneyland-grade queue, and which turns out to be a square quarter mile of awning-shaded cafeteria lines and rows of long institutional tables at which friend and stranger alike sit cheek by jowl, cracking and chewing and dribbling. It's hot, and the sagged roof traps the steam and the smells, which latter are strong and only partly food-related. It is also loud, and a good percentage of the total noise is masticatory. The suppers come in styrofoam trays, and the soft drinks arc iceless and flat, and the coffee is convenience-store coffee in more styrofoam, and the utensils are plastic (there are none of the special long skinny forks for pushing out the tail meat, though a few savvy diners bring their own). Nor do they give you near enough napkins considering how messy lobster is to eat, especially when you're squeezed onto benches alongside children of

---

[5]Of course, the common practice of dipping the lobster meat in melted butter torpedoes all these happy fat-specs, which none of the council's promotional stuff ever mentions, any more than potato industry PR talks about sour cream and bacon bits.

various ages and vastly different levels of fine-motor development—not to mention the people who've somehow smuggled in their own beer in enormous aisle-blocking coolers, or who all of a sudden produce their own plastic tablecloths and spread them over large portions of tables to try to reserve them (the tables) for their own little groups. And so on. Any one example is no more than a petty inconvenience, of course, but the MLF turns out to be full of irksome little downers like this—see for instance the Main Stage's headliner shows, where it turns out that you have to pay $20 extra for a folding chair if you want to sit down; or the North Tent's mad scramble for the Nyquil-cup-sized samples of finalists' entries handed out after the Cooking Competition; or the much-touted Maine Sea Goddess pageant finals, which turn out to be excruciatingly long and to consist mainly of endless thanks and tribute to local sponsors. Let's not even talk about the grossly inadequate Port-A-San facilities or the fuel that there's nowhere to wash your hands before or after eating. What the Maine Lobster Festival really is is a midlevel county fair with a culinary hook, and in this respect it's not unlike Tidewater crab festivals, Midwest corn festivals. Texas chili festivals, etc., and shares with these venues the core paradox of all teeming commercial demotic events: It's not for everyone.[6] Nothing against the

[6]In truth, there's a great deal to be said about the differences between working-class Rockland and the heavily populist flavor of its festival versus comfortable and elltist Camden with its expensive view and shops given entirely over to $200 sweaters and great rows of Victorian homes converted to upscale B&Bs. And about these differences as two sides of the great coin that is US tourism. Very little of which will be a scald here, except to amplify the above-mentioned paradox and to reveal your assigned correspondent's own preferences. I confess that I have never understood why so many people's idea of a fun vacation is to don flip-flops and sunglasses and crawl through maddening traffic to loud, hot, crowded tourist venues in order to sample a "local flavor" that is by definition ruined by the presence of tourists. This may (as my festival companions keep pointing out) all be a matter of personality and hardwired taste: the fast that I do not like tourist venues means that I'll never understand their appeal and so am probably not the one to talk about it (the supposed appeal). But, since this FN will almost surely not survive magazine-editing anyway, here goes:

As I see it. It probably really is good for the soul to be a tourist, even if it's only once in a while. Not good for the soul in a refreshing or enlivening way, though, but rather in a grim, steely-eyed, let's-look-honestly-at-the-facts-and-find-some-way-to-deal-with-them way. My personal experience has not been that traveling around the country is broadening or relaxing, or that radical changes is place and context have a salutary effect, but rather that international tourism is radically constricting, and humbling in the hardest way—hostile to my fantasy of being a true individual, of living somehow outside and above it all. (Coming up is the part that my companions find especially unhappy and repellent, a sure way to spoil the fun of vacation travel:) To be a mass tourist, for me, is to become a pure late-date American: alien, ignorant, greedy for something you cannot ever have, disappointed in a way you can never admit. It is to spoil, by way of sheer ontology, the very unspoiledness you are there to experience. It is to impose yourself on places that in all non-economic ways would be better, realer, without you. It is, in lines and gridlock and transaction after transaction, to confront a dimension of yourself that is as inescapable as it is painful: As a tourist, you become economically significant but existentially loathsome, and insect on a dead thing.

euphoric senior editor of *Food & Wine,* but I'd be surprised if she'd ever actually been here in Harbor Park, amid crowds of people slapping canal-zone mosquitoes as they eat deep-fried Twinkies and watch Professor Paddywhack, on six-foot stilts in a raincoat with plastic lobsters protruding from all directions on springs, terrify their children.

Lobster is essentially a summer food. This is because we now prefer our lobsters fresh, which means they have to be recently caught, which for both tactical and economic reasons takes place at depths less than 25 fathoms. Lobsters tend to be hungriest and most active (i.e., most trappable) at summer water temperatures of 45–50 degrees. In the autumn, most Maine lobsters migrate out into deeper water, either for warmth or to avoid the heavy waves that pound New England's coast all winter. Some burrow into the bottom. They might hibernate; nobody's sure. Summer is also lobsters' molting season—specifically early- to mid-July. Chitinous arthropods grow by molting, rather the way people have to buy bigger clothes as they age and gain weight. Since lobsters can live to be over 100, they can also get to be quite large, as in 30 pounds or more—though truly senior lobsters are rare now because New England's waters are so heavily trapped.[7] Anyway, hence the Culinary distinction between hard- and soft-shell lobsters, the latter sometimes a.k.a. shedders. A soft-shell lobster is one that has recently molted. In midcoast restaurants, the summer menu often offers both kinds, with shedders being slightly cheaper even though they're easier to dismantle and the meat is allegedly sweeter. The reason for the discount is that a molting lobster uses a layer of seawater for insulation while its new shell is hardening, so there's slightly less actual meat when you crack open a shedder, plus a redolent gout of water that gets all over everything and can sometimes jet out lemon-like and catch a tablemate tight in the eye. If it's winter or you're buying lobster someplace far from New England; on the other hand, you can almost bet that the lobster is a hard-shell, which for obvious reasons travel better.

As an a la carte entrée, lobster can be baked, broiled, steamed, grilled, sautéed, stir-fried, or microwaved. The most common method, though, is boiling. If you're someone who enjoys having lobster at home, this is probably the way you do it, since boiling is so easy. You

---

[7]Datum: In a good year, the US industry produces around 80,000,000 pounds of lobster, and Maine accounts for more than half that total.

need a large kettle w/ cover, which you fill about half full with water (the standard advice is that you want 2.5 quarts of water per lobster). Seawater is optimal, or you can add two tbsp salt per quart from the tap. It also helps to know how much your lobsters weigh. You get the water boiling, put in the lobsters one at a time, cover the kettle, and bring it back up to a boil. Then you bank the heat and let the kettle simmer—ten minutes for the first pound of lobster, then three minutes for each pound after that. (This is assuming you've got hard-shell lobsters, which, again, if you don't live between Boston and Halifax is probably what you've got. Fox shedders, you're supposed to subtract three minutes from the total.) The reason the kettle's lobsters turn scarlet is that boiling somehow suppresses every pigment in their chitin but one. If you want an easy test of whether the lobsters are done, you try pulling on one of their antennae—if it comes out of the head with minimal effort, you're ready to eat.

A detail so obvious that most recipes don't even bother to mention it is that each lobster is supposed to be alive when you put it in the kettle. This is part of lobster's modern appeal—it's the freshest food there is. There's no decomposition between harvesting and eating. And not only do lobsters require no cleaning or dressing or plucking, they're relatively easy for vendors to keep alive. They come up alive in the traps, are placed in containers of seawater, and can—so long as the water's aerated and the animals' claws are pegged or banded to keep them from tearing one another up under the stresses of captivity[8]— survive right up until they're boiled. Most of us have been in supermarkets or restaurants that Feature tanks of live lobsters, from which you can pick out your supper while it watches you point. And part of the overall spectacle of the Maine Lobster Festival is that you can see actual lobstermen's vessels docking at the wharves along the northeast grounds and unloading fresh-caught product, which is transferred by

---

[8]N.B. Similar reasoning underlies the practice of what's termed "debeaking" broiler chickens and brood hens in modern factory farms. Maximum commercial efficiency requires that enormous poultry populations be confined in unnaturally close quarters, under which conditions many birds go crazy and peck one another to death. As a purely observational side note, be apprised that debeaking is usually an automated process and that the chickens receive no anesthetic. It's not clear to me whether most *Gourmet* readers know about debeaking, or about related practices like dehorning cattle in commercial feed lots, cropping swine's tails in factory hog farms to keep psychotically bored neighbors from chewing them off, and so forth. It so happens that your assigned correspondent knew almost nothing about standard meat-industry operations before starting work on this article.

hand or cart 150 yards to the great clear tanks stacked up around the festival's cooker—which is as mentioned, billed as the World's Largest Lobster Cooker and can process over 100 lobsters at a time for the Main Eating Tent.

So then here is a question that's all but unavoidable at the World's Largest Lobster Cooker, and may arise in kitchens across the US: Is it all right to boil a sentient creature alive just for our gustatory pleasure? A related set of concerns: Is the previous question irksomely PC or sentimental? What does "all right" even mean in this context? Is the whole thing just a matter of personal choice?

As you may or may not know, a certain well-known group called People for the Ethical Treatment of Animals thinks that the morality of lobster-boiling is not just a matter of individual conscience. In fact, one of the very first things we hear about the MLF . . . well, to set the scene: We're coming in by cab from the almost indescribably odd and rustic Knox County Airport[9] very late on the night before the festival opens, sharing the cab with a wealthy political consultant who lives on Vinalhaven Island in the bay half the year (he's headed for the island ferry in Rockland). The consultant and cabdriver are responding to informal journalistic probes about how people who live in the midcoast region actually view the MLF, as in is the festival just a big-dollar tourist thing or is it something local residents look forward to attending, take genuine civic pride in, etc. The cabdriver (who's in his seventies, one of apparently a whole platoon of retirees the cab company puts on to help with the summer rush, and wears a US-flag lapel pin, and drives in what can only be called a very *deliberate* way) assures us that locals do endorse and enjoy the MLF, although he himself hasn't gone in years, and now come to think of it no one he and his wife know has, either. However, the demilocal consultant's been to recent festivals a couple times (one gets the impression it was at his wife's behest), of which his most vivid impression was that "you have to line up for an ungodly long time to get your lobsters, and meanwhile there are all these ex-flower children coming up and down along the line handing out pamphlets that say the lobsters die in terrible pain and you shouldn't eat them."

And it turns out that the post-hippies of the consultant's recollection were activists from PETA. There were no PETA people in obvious

---

[9]The terminal used to be somebody's house, for example, and the lost-luggage-reporting room was clearly once a pantry.

view at the 2003 MLF,[10] but they've been conspicuous at many of the recent festivals. Since at least the mid-1990s, articles in everything from the *Camden Herald* to the *New York Times* have described PETA urging boycotts of the Maine Lobster Festival, often deploying celebrity spokesmen like Mary Tyler Moore for open letters and ads saying stuff like "Lobsters are extraordinarily sensitive" and "To me, eating a lobster is out of the question." More concrete is the oral testimony of Dick, our florid and extremely gregarious rental-car liaison,[11] to the effect that PETA's been around so much during recent years that a kind of brittlely tolerant homeostasis now obtains between the activists and the festival's locals, e.g.: "We had some incidents a couple years ago. One lady took most of her clothes off and painted herself like a lobster, almost got herself arrested. But for the most part they're let alone. (Rapid series of small ambiguous laughs, which with Dick happens a lot.) They do their thing and we do our thing."

This whole interchange takes place on Route 1, 30 July, during a four-mile, 50-minute ride from the airport[12] to the dealership to sign car-rental papers. Several irreproducible segues down the road from the PETA anecdotes. Dick—whose son-in-law happens to be a professional lobsterman and one of the Main Eating Tent's regular suppliers—explains what he and his family feel is the crucial mitigating factor in the whole morality-of-boiling-lobsters-alive issue: "There's a part of the brain in people and animals that lets us feel pain, and lobsters' brains don't have this part."

---

[10]It turned out that one Mr. William R. Rivas-Rivas, a high-ranking PETA official out of the group's Virginia headquarters, was indeed there this year, albeit solo, working the festival's main and side entrances on Saturday, 2 August, handing out pamphlets and adhesive stickers emblazoned with "Being Boiled Hurts," which is the tagline in most of PETA's published material about lobsters. I learned that he'd been there only later, when speaking with Mr. Rivas-Rivas on the phone. I'm not sure how we missed seeing him *in situ* at the festival, and I can't see much to do except apologize for the oversight—although it's also true that Saturday was the day of the big MLF parade through Rockland, which basic journalistic responsibility seemed to require going to (and which, with all the due respect, meant that Saturday was maybe not the best day for PETA to work the Harbor Park grounds, especially if it was going to be just one person for one day, since a lot of diehard MLF partisans were off-site watching the parade (which, again with no offense intended, was in truth kind of cheesy and boring, consisting mostly of slow homemade floats and various midcoast people waving at one another, and with an extremely annoying man dressed as Blackbeard ranging up and down the length of the crowd saying "Arrr" over and over and brandishing a plastic sword at people, etc.; plus it rained)).
[11]By profession, Dick is actually a car salesman; the midcoast region's National Car Rental franchise operates out of a Chevy dealership in Thomaston.
[12]The short version regarding why we were back at the airport after already arriving the previous night involves lost luggage and a miscommunication about where and what the midcoast's National franchise was—Dick came out personally to the airport and got us, out of no evident motive but kindness. (He also talked nonstop the entire way, with a very distinctive speaking style that can be described only as manically laconic; the truth is that I now know more about this man than I do about some members of my own family.)

Besides the fact that it's incorrect in about nine different ways, the main reason Dick's statement is interesting is that its thesis is more or less echoed by the festival's own pronouncement on lobsters and pain, which is part of a Test Your Lobster IQ quiz that appears in the 2003 MLF program courtesy of the Maine Lobster Promotion Council:

> *The nervous system of a lobster is very simple, and is in fact most similar to the nervous system of the grasshopper. It is decentralized with no brain. There is no cerebral cortex, which in humans is the area of the brain that gives the experience of pain.*

Though it sounds more sophisticated, a lot of the neurology in this latter claim is still either false or fuzzy. The human cerebral cortex is the brain-part that deals with higher faculties like reason, metaphysical self-awareness, language, etc. Pain reception is known to be part of a much older and more primitive system of nociceptors and prostaglandins that are managed by the brain stem and thalamus.[13]

On the other hand, it is true that the cerebral cortex is involved in what's variously called suffering, distress, or the emotional experience of pain—i.e., experiencing painful stimuli as unpleasant, very unpleasant, unbearable, and so on.

Before we go any further, let's acknowledge that the questions of whether mid how different kinds of animals feel pain, and of whether and why it might be justifiable to inflict pain on them in order to eat them, turn out to be extremely complex and difficult. And comparative neuroanatomy is only part of the problem. Since pain is a totally subjective mental experience, we do not have direct access to anyone or anything's pain but our own; and even just the principles by which we can infer that other human beings experience pain and have a legitimate interest in not feeling pain involve hard-core philosophy—metaphysics, epistemology, value theory, ethics. The fact that even the most highly evolved nonhuman mammal can't use language to communicate with us about their subjective mental experience is only the first layer of additional complication in trying to extend our reasoning about pain and morality to animals. And everything gets progressively more abstract and convoluted as we move farther and farther out from

[13]To elaborate by way of example: The common experience of accidentally touching a hot stove and yanking your hand back before you're even aware that anything's going on is explained by the fact that many of the processes by which we detect and avoid painful stimuli do not involve the cortex. In the case of the hand and stove, the brain is bypassed altogether; all the important neurochemical action takes place in the spine.

the higher-type mammals into cattle and swine and dogs and cats and rodents, and then birds and fish, and finally invertebrates like lobsters.

The more important point here, though, is that the whole animal-cruelty-and-eating issue is not just complex, it's also uncomfortable. It is, at any rate, uncomfortable for me, and for just about everyone I know who enjoys a variety of foods and yet does not want to see herself as cruel or unfeeling. As far as I can tell, my own main way of dealing with this conflict has been to avoid thinking about the whole unpleasant thing. I should add that it appears to me unlikely that many readers of *Gourmet* wish to think about it, either, or to be queried about the morality of their eating habits in the pages of a culinary monthly. Since, however, the assigned subject of this article is what it was like to attend the 2003 MLF, and thus to spend several days in the midst of a great mass of Americans all eating lobster, and thus to be more or less impelled to think hard about lobster and the experience of buying and eating lobster, it turns out that there is no honest way to avoid certain moral questions.

There are several reasons for this. For one thing, it's not just that lobsters get boiled alive, it's that you do it yourself—or at least it's done specifically for you, on-site.[14] As mentioned, the World's Largest Lobster Cooker, which is highlighted as an attraction in the festival's program, is right out there on the MLF's north grounds for everyone to see. Try to imagine a Nebraska Beef Festival[15] at which part of the festivities is watching trucks pull up and the live cattle get driven down the ramp and slaughtered right there on the World's Largest Killing Floor or something—there's no way.

The intimacy of the whole thing is maximized at home, which of course is where most lobster gets prepared and eaten (although note

[14]Morality-wise, let's concede that this cuts both ways. Lobster-eating is at least not abetted by the system of corporate factory farms that produces most beef, pork, and chicken. Because, if nothing else, of the way they're marketed and packaged for sale, we eat these latter meats without having to consider that they were once conscious, sentient creatures to whom horrible things were done. (N.B. "Horrible" here meaning really, really horrible. Write off to PETA or peta.org for their free "Meet Your Meat" video, narrated by Mr. Alec Baldwin, if you want to see just about everything meat-related you don't want to see or think about. (N. B., Not that PETA's any sort of font of unspun truth. Like many partisans in complex moral disputes, the PETA people are fanatics, and a lot of their rhetoric seems simplistic and self-righteous. But this particular video, replete with actual factory-farm and corporate-slaughterhouse footage, is both credible and traumatizing.))
[15]Is it significant that "lobster," "fish," and "chicken" are our culture's words for both the animal and the meat, whereas most mammals seem to require euphemisms like "beef" and "pork" that help us separate the meat we eat from the living creature the meat once was? Is this evidence that some kind of deep uncase about eating higher animals is endemic enough to show up in English usage, but that the unease diminishes as we move out of the mammalian order? (And is "lamb"/"lamb" the counterexample that sinks the whole theory, or are there special, biblico-historical reasons for that equivalence?)

already the semiconscious euphemism "prepared," which in the case of lobsters really means killing them right there in our kitchens). The basic scenario is that we come in from the store and make our little preparations like getting the kettle filled and boiling, and then we lift the lobsters out of the bag or whatever retail container they came home in . . . whereupon some uncomfortable things start to happen. However stuporous a lobster is from the trip home, for instance, it tends to come alarmingly to life when placed in boiling water. If you're tilting it from a container into the steaming kettle, the lobster will sometimes try to cling to the container's sides or even to hook its claws over the kettle's rim like a person trying to keep from going over the edge of a roof. And worse is when the lobster's fully immersed. Even if you cover the kettle and turn away, you can usually hear the cover rattling and clanking as the lobster tries to push it off. Or the creature's claws scraping the sides of the kettle as it thrashes around. The lobster, in other words, behaves very much as you or I would behave if we were plunged into boiling water (with the obvious exception of screaming[16]). A blunter way to say this is that the lobster acts as if it's in terrible pain, causing some cooks to leave the kitchen altogether and to take one of those little lightweight plastic oven-timers with them into another room and wait until the whole process is over.

There happen to be two main criteria that most ethicists agree on for determining whether a living creature has the capacity to suffer and so has genuine interests that it may or may not be our moral duty to consider.[17] One is how much of the neurological hardware required for pain-experience the animal comes equipped with—nociceptors, prostaglandins, neuronal opioid receptors, etc. The other criterion is whether the animal demonstrates behavior associated with pain.

[16]There's relevant populist myth about the high-pitched whistling sound that sometimes issues from a pot of boiling lobster. The sound is really vented steam from the layer of seawater between the lobster's flesh and its carapace (this is why shedders whistle more than hard-shells), but the pop version has it that the sound is the lobster's rabbit like death-scream. Lobsters communicate via pheromones in their urine and don't have anything close to the vocal equipment for screaming, but the myth's very persistent—which might, once again, point to a low-level cultural unease about the boiling thing.

[17]"Interests" basically means strong and legitimate preferences, which obviously require some degree of consciousness, responsiveness to stimuli, etc. See, for instance, the utilitarian philosopher Peter Singer, whose 1974 *Animal Liberation* is more of less the bible of the modern animal-rights movement:

> It would be nonsense to say that it was not in the interests of a stone to be kicked along the road by a schoolboy. A stone does not have interests because it cannot suffer. Nothing that we can do it could possibly make any difference to its welfare. A mouse, on the other hand, does have an interest in not being kicked along the road, because it will suffer if it is.

And it takes a lot of intellectual gymnastics and behaviorist hairsplitting not to see struggling, thrashing, and lid-clattering as just such pain-behavior. According to marine zoologists, it usually takes lobsters between 35 and 45 seconds to die in boiling water. (No source I could find talks about how long it takes them to die in superheated steam; one rather hopes it's faster.)

There are, of course, other ways to kill your lobster on-site and so achieve maximum freshness. Some cooks' practice is to drive a sharp heavy knife point-first into a spot just above the midpoint between the lobster's eyestalks (more or less where the Third Eye is in human foreheads). This is alleged either to kill the lobster instantly or to render it insensate, and is said at least to eliminate some of the cowardice involved in throwing a creature into boiling water and then fleeing the room. As far as I can tell from talking to proponents of the knife-in-head method, the idea is that it's more violent but ultimately more merciful, plus that a willingness to exert personal agency and accept responsibility for stabbing the lobster's head honors the lobster somehow and entitles one to eat it (there's often a vague sort of Native American spirituality-of-the-hunt flavor to pro-knife arguments). But the problem with the knife method is basic biology: Lobsters' nervous systems operate off not one but several ganglia, a.k.a. nerve bundles, which are sort of wired in series and distributed all along the lobster's underside, from stem to stern. And disabling only the frontal ganglion does not normally result in quick death or unconsciousness.

Another alternative is to put the lobster in cold saltwater and then very slowly bring it up to a full boil. Cooks who advocate this method are going on the analogy to a frog, which can supposedly be kept from jumping out of a boiling pot by heating the water incrementally. In order to save a lot of research-summarizing, I'll simply assure you that the analogy between frogs and lobsters turns out not to hold—plus, if the kettle's water isn't aerated seawater, the immersed lobster suffers from slow suffocation, although usually not decisive enough suffocation to keep it from still thrashing and clattering when the water gets hot enough to kill it. In fact, lobsters boiled incrementally often display a whole bonus set of gruesome, convulsion like reactions that you don't see in regular boiling.

Ultimately, the only certain virtues of the home-lobotomy and slow-heating methods are comparative, because there are even worse/crueler ways people prepare lobster. Time-thrifty cooks sometimes microwave them alive (usually after poking several vent-holes in the carapace, which is a precaution most shellfish-microwavers learn about the hard way). Live dismemberment, on the other hand, is big in Europe—some chefs cut the lobster in half before cooking; others like to tear off the claws and tail and toss only these parts into the pot.

And there's more unhappy news respecting suffering-criterion number one. Lobsters don't have much in the way of eyesight or hearing, but they do have an exquisite tactile sense one facilitated by hundreds of thousands of tiny hairs that protrude through their carapace. "Thus it is," in the words of T. M. Prudden's industry classic *About Lobster*, "that although encased in what seems a solid, impenetrable armor, the lobster can receive stimuli and impressions from without as readily as if it possessed a soft and delicate skin." And lobsters do have nociceptors,[18] as well as invertebrate versions of the prostaglandins and major neurotransmitters via which our own brains register pain.

Lobsters do not, on the other hand, appear to have the equipment for making or absorbing natural opioids like endorphins and enkephalins, which are what more advanced nervous systems use to try to handle intense pain. From this fact, though, one could conclude either that lobsters are maybe even *more* vulnerable to pain, since they lack mammalian nervous systems' built-in analgesia, or, instead, that the absence of natural opioids implies an absence of the really intense pain-sensations that natural opioids are designed to mitigate. I for one can detect a marked upswing in mood as I contemplate this latter possibility. It could be that their lack of endorphin/enkephalin hardware means that lobsters' raw subjective experience of pain is so radically different from mammals' that it may not even deserve the term "pain." Perhaps lobsters are more like those frontal-lobotomy patients one reads about who report experiencing pain in a totally different way than you and I. These patients evidently do feel physical pain, neurologically speaking, but don't dislike it—though neither do they like it; it's more that they feel it but don't feel anything *about* it—the point being that the pain is not distressing to them or something they want to get away from. Maybe lobsters, who are also without frontal lobes, are detached from the neurological-registration-of-injury-or-hazard we call pain in just the same way. There is, after all, a difference between (1) pain as a purely neurological event, and (2) actual suffering,

CONSIDER THE LOBSTER

677

---

[18]This is the neurological term for special pain-receptors that are "sensitive to potentially damaging extremes of temperature, to mechanical forces, and to chemical substances which are released when body tissues are damaged."

which seems crucially to involve an emotional component, an awareness of pain as unpleasant, as something to fear/dislike/want to avoid.

Still, after all the abstract intellection, there remain the facts of the frantically clanking lid, the pathetic clinging to the edge of the pot. Standing at the stove, it is hard to deny in any meaningful way that this is a living creature experiencing pain and wishing to avoid/escape the painful experience. To my lay mind, the lobster's behavior in the kettle appears to be the expression of a *preference;* and it may well be that an ability to form preferences is the decisive criterion for real suffering.[19] The logic of this (preference → suffering) relation may be easiest to see in the negative case. If you cut certain kinds of worms in half, the halves will often keep crawling around and going about their vermiform business as if nothing had happened. When we assert, based on their post-op behavior, that these worms appear not to be suffering, what we're really saying is that there's no sign the worms know anything bad has happened or would *prefer* not to have gotten cut in half.

Lobsters, though, are known to exhibit preferences, Experiments have shown that they can detect changes of only a degree or two in water temperature; one reason for their complex migratory cycles (which can often cover 100-plus miles a year) is to pursue the temperatures they like best.[20] And, as mentioned, they're bottom-dwellers and do not like bright light—if a lank of food-lobsters is out in the sunlight or a store's fluorescence, the lobsters will always congregate in whatever part is darkest. Fairly solitary in the ocean, they also clearly dislike the crowding that's part of their captivity in tanks, since (as also mentioned)

---

[19]"Preference" is maybe roughly synonymous with "interests" but it is a better term for our purposes because it's less abstractly philosophical—"*preference*" seems more personal, and it's the whole idea of a living creature's personal experience that's at issue.

[20]Of course, the most common sort of counterargument here would begin by objecting that "like best" is really just a metaphor, and a misleadingly anthropomorphic one at that. The counterarguer would posit that the lobster seeks to maintain a certain optimal ambient temperature out of nothing but unconscious instinct (with a similar explanation for the low-light affinities upcoming in the main text). The thrust of such a counterargument will be that the lobster's thrashings and clankings in the kettle express not unpreferred pain but involuntary reflexes, like your leg shooting out when the doctor hits your knee. Be advised that there are professional scientists, including many researchers who use animals in experiments, who hold to the view that nonhuman creatures have no real feelings at all, merely "behaviors." Be further advised that this view has a long history that goes all the way back to Descartes, although its modern support comes mostly from behaviorist psychology.

To these what-looks-like-pain-is-really-just-reflexes counterarguments, however, there happen to be all sorts of scientific and pro-animal rights counter-counterarguments. And then further attempted rebuttals and redirects, and so on. Suffice it to say that both the scientific and the philosophical arguments on either side of the animal-suffering issue are involved, abstruse, technical, often informed by self-interest or ideology, and in the end so totally inconclusive that as a practical matter. In the kitchen or restaurant, it all still seems to come down to individual conscience, going with (no pun) your gut.

one reason why lobsters' claws are banded on capture is to keep them from attacking one another under the stress of close-quarter storage.

In any event, at the MLF, standing by the bubbling tanks outside the World's Largest Lobster Cooker, watching the fresh-caught lobsters pile over one another, wave their hobbled claws impotently, huddle in the rear corners, or scrabble frantically back from the glass as you approach, it is difficult not to sense that they're unhappy, or frightened, even if it's some rudimentary version of these feelings . . . and, again, why does rudimentariness even enter into it? Why is a primitive, inarticulate form of suffering less urgent or uncomfortable for the person who's helping to inflict it by paying for the food it results in? I'm not trying to give you a PETA-like screed here—at least I don't think so. I'm trying, rather, to work out and articulate some of the troubling questions that arise amid all the laughter and saltation and community pride of the Maine Lobster Festival. The truth is that if you, the festival attendee, permit yourself to think that lobsters can suffer and would rather not, the MLF begins to take on the aspect of something like a Roman circus or medieval torture-fest.

Does that comparison seem a bit much? If so, exactly why? Or what about this one: Is it possible that future generations will regard our present agribusiness and eating practices in much the same way we now view Nero's entertainments or Mengele's experiments? My own initial reaction is that such a comparison is hysterical, extreme—and yet the reason it seems extreme to me appears to be that I believe animals are less morally important than human beings;[21] and when it comes to defending such a belief, even to myself, I have to acknowledge that (a) I have an obvious selfish interest in this belief, since I like to eat certain kinds of animals and want to be able to keep doing it, and (b) I haven't succeeded in working out any sort of personal ethical system in which the belief is truly defensible instead of just selfishly convenient.

Given this article's venue and my own lack of culinary sophistication, I'm curious about whether the reader can identify with any of these reactions and acknowledgments and discomforts. I'm also concerned not to come off as shrill or preachy when what I really am is more like confused. For those *Gourmet* readers who enjoy well-prepared and -presented meals involving beef, veal, lamb, pork, chicken, lobster,

[21]Meaning *a lot* less important, apparently, since the moral comparison here is not the value of one human's life vs. the value of one animal's life, but rather the value of one animal's life vs. the value of one human's taste for a particular kind of protein. Even the most diehard carniphile will acknowledge that it's possible to live and eat well without consuming animals.

etc.: Do you think much about the (possible) moral status and (probable) suffering of the animals involved? If you do, what ethical convictions have you worked out that permit you not just to eat but to savor and enjoy flesh-based viands (since of course refined *enjoyment,* rather than mere ingestion, is the whole point of gastronomy)? If, on the other hand, you'll have no truck with confusions or convictions and regard stuff like the previous paragraph as just so much fatuous navel-gazing, what makes it feel truly okay, inside, to just dismiss the whole thing out of hand? That is, is your refusal to think about any of this the product of actual thought, or is it just that you don't want to think about it? And if the latter, then why not? Do you ever think, even idly, about the possible reasons for your reluctance to think about it? I am not trying to bait anyone here—I'm genuinely curious. After all, isn't being extra aware and attentive and thoughtful about one's food and its overall context part of what distinguishes a real gourmet? Or is all the gourmet's extra attention and sensibility just supposed to be sensuous? Is it really all just a matter of taste and presentation?

These last few queries, though, while sincere, obviously involve much larger and more abstract questions about the connections (if any) between aesthetics and morality—about what the adjective in a phrase like "The Magazine of Good Living" is really supposed to mean—and these questions lead straightaway into such deep and treacherous waters that it's probably best to stop the public discussion right here. There are limits to what even interested persons can ask of each other.

POSSIBILITIES FOR WRITING

1. Describe your experience of reading "Consider the Lobster." To what extent did you find yourself, at various points, experiencing different feelings and thoughts? Was there any point in reading the essay in which you became uncomfortable? Explain.

2. Using some of the details Wallace provides, write a much briefer review of the 2003 Maine Lobster Festival—five hundred words or so. Try to give an overview of the event, and decide whether to make your review strictly a factual report or to include a judgement about its quality and/or its value.

3. Taking off from the second half of Wallace's essay about the ethics of killing lobsters for food, write an essay in which you explore this issue. Explain whether you think it is or is not justified, with your reasons. You may quote from Wallace, if you wish.

Eudora Welty (1909–2001) was born in Jackson, Mississippi, and attended the Mississippi State College for Women and the University of Wisconsin. She is best known for her portraits of people and life in the deep South, especially her home state of Mississippi. During World War II she was on the staff of the New York Times Book Review, testimony to the insatiable appetite for reading she developed as a child. She began publishing collections of stories in 1941 with Curtain of Green and Other Stories. *She won a Pulitzer Prize in 1980 for* The Collected Stories, *which contains work spanning forty years. Welty has also written novels, including* The Optimist's Daughter, *which won the Pulitzer Prize in 1982, and criticism, collected in* The Eye of the Story. *Her 1984 memoir,* One Writer's Beginnings, *describes her early experience with language, learning, and literature. Her writing, whether factual or fictional, entertains as it informs, and provides a vivid evocation of place.*

EUDORA WELTY

From Listening

In this excerpt from her memoir, *One Writer's Beginnings,* Eudora Welty shares her evocative childhood memories of school and learning. She brings her early world of books and reading, of school and teachers, vividly to life in a series of brief sketches and anecdotes.

Welty characterizes her first-grade teacher, Miss Duling, as the quintessential schoolmarm—dedicated as much to the moral rectitude and social improvement of her students as to their intellectual development. Without sentimentalizing her, Welty memorializes Miss Duling, describing with grace and verve her no-nonsense approach to educating her young charges by means of a set of high and inflexible standards and with an imperious manner. Although other teachers are mentioned, some appreciably, it is Miss Duling who captures Welty's imagination and, through her vivid prose, ours as well.

From the first I was clamorous to learn—I wanted to know and begged to be told not so much what, or how, or why, or where, as when. How soon?

> Pear tree by the garden gate,
> How much longer must I wait?

This rhyme from one of my nursery books was the one that spoke for me. But I lived not at all unhappily in this craving, for my wild curiosity was in large part suspense, which carries its own secret pleasure. And so one of the godmothers of fiction was already bending over me.

From *One Writer's Beginnings* (1984).

When I was five years old, I knew the alphabet, I'd been vaccinated (for smallpox), and I could read. So my mother walked across the street to Jefferson Davis Grammar School and asked the principal if she would allow me to enter the first grade after Christmas.

"Oh, all right," said Miss Duling. "Probably the best thing you could do with her."

Miss Duling, a lifelong subscriber to perfection, was a figure of authority, the most whole-souled I have ever come to know. She was a dedicated schoolteacher who denied herself all she might have done or whatever other way she might have lived (this possibility was the last that could have occurred to us, her subjects in school). I believe she came of well-off people, well-educated, in Kentucky, and certainly old photographs show she was a beautiful, high-spirited-looking young lady—and came down to Jackson to its new grammar school that was going begging for a principal. She must have earned next to nothing; Mississippi then as now was the nation's lowest-ranking state economically, and our legislature has always shown a painfully loud reluctance go give money to public education. That challenge *brought* her.

In the long run she came into touch, as teacher or principal, with three generations of Jacksonians. My parents had not, but everybody else's parents had gone to school to her. She'd taught most of our leaders somewhere along the line. When she wanted something done—some civic oversight corrected, some injustice made right overnight, or even a tree spared that the fool telephone people were about to cut down—she telephoned the mayor, or the chief of police, or the president of the power company, or the head doctor at the hospital, or the judge in charge of a case, or whoever, and calling them by their first names, *told* them. It is impossible to imagine her meeting with anything less than compliance. The ringing of her brass bell from their days at Davis School would still be in their ears. She also proposed a spelling match between the fourth grade at Davis School and the Mississippi Legislature, who went through with it; and that told the Legislature.

Her standards were very high and of course inflexible, her authority was total; why *wouldn't* this carry with it a brass bell that could be heard ringing for a block in all directions? That bell belonged to the figure of Miss Duling as though it grew directly out of her right arm, as wings grew out of an angel or a tail out of the devil. When we entered, marching, into her school, by strictest teaching, surveillance, and order we learned grammar, arithmetic, spelling, reading, writing, and geography; and he, not the teachers, I believe, wrote out the examinations: need I tell you, they were "hard."

She's not the only teacher who has influenced me, but Miss Duling, in some fictional shape or form, has stridden into a larger part of my work than I'd realized until now. She emerges in my perhaps inordinate number of schoolteacher characters. I loved those characters in the writing. But I did not, in life, love Miss Duling. I was afraid of her high-arched bony nose, her eyebrows lifted in half-circles above her hooded, brilliant eyes, and of the Kentucky R's in her speech, and the long steps she took in her hightop shoes. I did nothing but bear her bearing-down authority, and did not connect this (as of course we were meant to) with our own need or desire to learn, perhaps because I already had this wish, and did not need to be driven.

She was impervious to lies or foolish excuses or the insufferable plea of not knowing any better. She wasn't going to have any frills, either, at Davis School. When a new governor moved into the mansion, he sent his daughter to Davis School; her name was Lady Rachel Conner. Miss Duling at once called the governor to the telephone and told him, "She'll be plain Rachel here."

Miss Duling dressed as plainly as a Pilgrim on a Thanksgiving poster we made in the schoolroom, in a longish black-and-white checked gingham dress, a bright thick wool sweater the red of a railroad lantern— she'd knitted it herself—black stocking and her narrow elegant feet in black hightop shoes with heels you could hear coming, rhythmical as a parade drum down the hall. Her silky black curly hair was drawn back out of curl, fastened by high combs, and knotted behind. She carried her spectacles on a gold chain hung around her neck. Her gaze was in general sweeping, then suddenly at the point of concentration upon you. With a swing of her bell that took her whole right arm and shoulder, she rang it, militant and impartial, from the head of the front steps of Davis School when it was time for us all to line up, girls on one side, boys on the other. We were to march past her and the school building, while the fourth-grader she nabbed played time on the piano, mostly to a tune we could have skipped to, but we didn't skip into Davis School.

Little recess (open-air exercises) and big recess (lunch-boxes from home opened and eaten on the grass, on the girls' side and the boys' side of the yard) and dismissal were also regulated by Miss Duling's bell. The bell was also used to catch us off guard with fire drill.

It was examinations that drove my wits away, as all emergencies do. Being expected to measure up was paralyzing. I failed to make 100 on my spelling exam because I missed one word and that word was "uncle." Mother, as I knew she would, took it personally. "You couldn't spell *uncle?* When you've got those five perfectly splendid uncles in West Virginia? What would *they* say to that?"

It was never that Mother wanted me to beat my classmates in grades; what she wanted was for me to have my answers right. It was unclouded perfection I was up against.

My father was much more tolerant of possible error. He only said, as he steeply and impeccably sharpened my pencils on examination morning, "Now just keep remembering: the examinations were made out for the *average* student to pass. That's the majority. And if the majority can pass, think how much better *you* can do."

I looked to my mother, who had her own opinions about the majority. My father wished to treat it with respect, she didn't. I'd been born left-handed, but the habit was broken when I entered the first grade in Davis School. My father had insisted. He pointed out that everything in life had been made for the convenience of right-handed people, because they were the majority, and he often used "what the majority wants" as a criterion for what was for the best. My mother said she could not promise him, could not promise him at all, that I wouldn't stutter as a consequence. Mother had been born left-handed too; her family consisted of five left-handed brothers, a left-handed mother, and a father who could write with both hands at the same time, also backwards and forwards and upside down, different words with each hand. She had been broken of it when she was young, and she said she used to stutter.

"But you still stutter," I'd remind her, only to hear her say loftily, "You should have heard me when I was your age."

In my childhood days, a great deal of stock was put, in general, in the value of doing well in school. Both daily newspapers in Jackson saw the honor roll as news and published the lists, and the grades, of all the honor students. The city fathers gave the children who made the honor roll free season tickets to the baseball games down at the grandstand. We all attended and all worshiped some player on the Jackson Senators: I offered up my 100's in arithmetic and spelling, reading and writing, attendance and, yes, deportment—I must have been a prig!—to Red McDermott, the third baseman. And our happiness matched that of knowing Miss Duling was on her summer vacation, far, far away in Kentucky.

Every school week, visiting teachers came on their days for special lessons. On Mondays, the singing teacher blew into the room fresh from the early outdoors, singing in her high soprano "How do you do?" to do-mi-sol-do, and we responded in chorus from our desks, "I'm ve-ry well" to do-sol-mi-do. Miss Johnson taught us rounds—"Row row row your boat gently down the stream"—and "Little Sir Echo," with half the room singing the words and the other half being the echo, a competition. She was from the North, and she was the one who wanted us all to stop the Christmas carols and see snow. The snow falling that morning outside the window was the first most of us had ever seen, and Miss Johnson threw up the window and held out wide her own black cape and caught flakes on it and ran, as fast as she could go, up and down the aisles to show us the real thing before it melted.

Thursday was Miss Eyrich and Miss Eyrich was Thursday. She came to give us physical training. She wasted no time on nonsense. Without greeting, we were marched straight outside and summarily divided into teams (no choosing sides), put on the mark, and ordered to get set for a relay race. Miss Eyrich cracked out "Go!" Dread rose in my throat. My head swam. Here was my turn, nearly upon me. (Wait, have I been touched—was that slap the touch? Go on! Do I go on without our passing a word? What word? Now am I racing too fast to turn around? Now I'm nearly home, but where is the hand waiting for mine to touch? Am I too late? Have I lost the whole race for our side?) I lost the relay race for our side before I started, through living ahead of myself, dreading to make my start, feeling too late prematurely, and standing transfixed by emergency, trying to think of a password. Thursdays will make me hear Miss Eyrich's voice, "On your mark—get set—GO!"

Very composedly and very slowly, the art teacher, who visited each room on Fridays, paced the aisle and looked down over your shoulder at what you were drawing for her. This was Miss Ascher. Coming from behind you, her deep, resonant voice reached you without being a word at all, but a sort of purr. It was much the sound given out by our family doctor when he read the thermometer and found you were running a slight fever: "Um-hm. Um-hm." Both alike, they let you go right ahead with it.

The school toilets were in the boys' and girls' respective basements. After Miss Duling had rung to dismiss school, a friend and I were making our plans for Saturday from adjoining cubicles. "Can you come spend the day with me?" I called out, and she called back, "I might could."

"Who—said—MIGHT—COULD?" It sounded like "Fe Fi Fo Fum!"

We both were petrified, for we knew whose deep measured words these were that came from just outside our doors. That was the voice of Mrs. McWillie, who taught the other fourth grade across the hall from ours. She was not even our teacher, but a very heavy, stern lady who dressed entirely in widow's weeds with a pleated black shirtwaist with a high net collar and velvet ribbon, and a black skirt to her ankles, with black circles under her eyes and a mournful, Presbyterian expression. We children took her to be a hundred years old. We held still.

"You might as well tell me," continued Ms. McWillie. "I'm going to plant myself right here and wait till you come out. Then I'll see who it was I heard saying 'MIGHT-COULD.'"

If Elizabeth wouldn't go out, of course I wouldn't either. We knew her to be a teacher who would not flinch from standing there in the basement all afternoon, perhaps even all day Saturday. So we surrendered and came out. I priggishly hoped Elizabeth would clear it up which child it was—it wasn't me.

"So it's you." She regarded us as a brace, made no distinction: whoever didn't say it was guilty by association. "If I ever catch you down here one more time saying 'MIGHT-COULD,' I'm going to carry it to Miss Duling. You'll be kept in every day for a week! I hope you're both sufficiently ashamed of yourselves?" Saying "might-could" was bad, but saying it in the basement made bad grammar a sin. I knew Presbyterians believed that you could go to Hell.

Mrs. McWillie never scared us into grammar, of course. It was my first-year Latin teacher in high school who made me discover I'd fallen in love with it. It took Latin to thrust me into bona fide alliance with words in their true meaning. Learning Latin (once I was free of Caesar) fed my love for words upon words, words in continuation and modification, and the beautiful, sober, accretion of a sentence. I could see the achieved sentence finally standing there, as real, intact, and built to stay as the Mississippi State Capitol at the top of my street, where I could walk through it on my way to school and hear underfoot the echo of its marble floor, and over me the bell of its rotunda.

On winter's rainy days, the schoolrooms would grow so dark that sometimes you couldn't see the figures on the blackboard. At that point, Mrs. McWillie, that stern fourth-grade teacher, would let her children close their books, and she would move, broad in widow's weeds like darkness itself, to the window and by what light there was she would stand and read aloud "the King of the Golden River." But I was excluded—in the other fourth grade, across the hall. Miss Louella Varnado, my teacher, didn't copy Mrs. McWillie; we had a spelling match: you could spell in the dark. I did not then suspect that there was any other way I could learn the story of "The King of the Golden River" than to have been assigned in the beginning to Mrs. McWillie's cowering fourth grade, then wait for her to treat you to it on the rainy day of her choice. I only now realize how much the treat depended, too, on there not having been money enough to put electric lights in Davis School. John Ruskin had to come in through courtesy of darkness. When in time I found the story in a book and read it to myself, it didn't seem to live up to my longings for a story with that name; as indeed, how could it?

POSSIBILITIES FOR WRITING

1. What specific details does Welty use to characterize her first-grade teacher, Miss Duling? What qualities of character does Welty emphasize about Miss Duling? And what effect did Miss Duling have on Welty in both the short and the long term?

2. Identify three other teachers that Welty mentions. What does she emphasize about each? What do her memories of all her teachers share? What significance do these teachers have for Welty and for the reader?

3. Write an essay about one or more of your own teachers. You may wish to describe a teacher or teachers from long ago, or you may focus on a more recent teacher. Consider setting up your essay as a contrast between two teachers.

E. B. WHITE

Once More to the Lake

E. B. White's "Once More to the Lake" describes a visit to a Maine lake that White makes with his family, which evokes memories of the annual trip he made there when he was a young boy. Reflecting on his recent trip in the context of the time he spent at the lake as a youth, White creates a lyrical remembrance of the place and a speculative essay about the passage of time, about change and changlessness, and about mortality.

One of the most striking features of the essay is the way White describes himself, his father, and his son. White explains, for example, how, as he watched his son doing the things he did when he was a boy at the lake—preparing the fishing tackle box, running the boat's outboard motor, casting his fishing line—White felt that he was "living a dual existence." Inhabiting the essay's present as the adult father of his son, White sees himself in his son as the boy he had been when his father occupied the paternal role that White himself later occupies. "It gave me," he writes "a creepy sensation." Just how creepy we only understand with White's culminating realization at the end of the essay.

One summer, along about 1904, my father rented a camp on a lake in Maine and took us all there for the month of August. We all got ring-worm from some kittens and had to rub Pond's Extract on our arms and legs night and morning, and my father rolled over in a canoe with all his clothes on; but outside of that the vacation was a success and from then on none of us ever thought there was any place in the world like that lake in Maine. We returned summer after summer—always on August 1 for one month. I have since become a salt-water man, but sometimes in summer there are days when the restlessness of the tides and the fearful cold of the sea water and the incessant wind that blows across the afternoon and into the evening make me wish for the placidity of a lake in the woods. A few weeks ago this feeling got so strong I bought myself a couple of bass hooks and a spinner and returned to the lake where we used to go, for a week's fishing and to revisit old haunts.

I took along my son, who had never had any fresh water up his nose and who had seen lily pads only from train windows. On the journey over to the lake I began to wonder what it would be like. I wondered how time would have marred this unique, this holy spot—the coves and streams, the hills that the sun set behind, the camps and the paths behind the camps. I was sure that the tarred road would have found it out, and I wondered in what other ways it would be desolated. It is strange how much you can remember about places like that once you allow your mind to return into the grooves that lead back. You remember one thing, and that suddenly reminds you of another thing. I guess I remembered clearest of all the early mornings, when the lake was cool and motionless, remembered how the bedroom smelled of the lumber it was made of and of the wet woods whose scent entered through the screen. The partitions in the camp were thin and did not extend clear to the top of the rooms, and as I was always the first up I would dress softly so as not to wake the others, and sneak out into the sweet outdoors and start out in the canoe, keeping close along the shore in the long shadows of the pines. I remembered being very careful never to rub my paddle against the gunwale for fear of disturbing the stillness of the cathedral.

The lake had never been what you would call a wild lake. There were cottages sprinkled around the shores, and it was in farming country although the shores of the lake were quite heavily wooded. Some of the cottages were owned by nearby farmers, and you would live at the shore and eat your meals at the farmhouse. That's what our family did. But although it wasn't wild, it was a fairly large and undisturbed lake and there were places in it that, to a child at least, seemed infinitely remote and primeval.

I was right about the tar: it led to within half a mile of the shore. But when I got back there, with my boy, and we settled into a camp near a farmhouse and into the kind of summertime I had known, I could tell that it was going to be pretty much the same as it had been before—I knew it, lying in bed the first morning, smelling the bedroom and hearing the boy sneak quietly out and go off along the shore in a boat. I began to sustain the illusion that he was I, and therefore, by simple transposition, that I was my father. This sensation persisted, kept cropping up all the time we were there. It was not an entirely new feeling, but in this setting it grew much stronger. I seemed to be living a dual existence. I would be in the middle of some simple act, I would be picking up a bait box or laying down a table fork, or I would be saying something, and suddenly it would be not I but my father who was saying the words or making the gesture. It gave me a creepy sensation.

We went fishing the next morning. I felt the same damp moss covering the worms in the bait can, and saw the dragonfly alight on the tip of my rod as it hovered a few inches from the surface of the water. It was the arrival of this fly that convinced me beyond any doubt that everything was as it always had been, that the years were a mirage and that there had been no years. The small waves were the same, chucking the rowboat under the chin as we fished at anchor, and the boat was the same boat, the same color green and the ribs broken in the same places, and under the floorboards the same fresh-water leavings and débris—the dead helgramite, the wisps of moss, the rusty discarded fishhook, the dried blood from yesterday's catch. We stared silently at the tips of our rods, at the dragonflies that came and went. I lowered the tip of mine into the water, tentatively, pensively dislodging the fly, which darted two feet away, poised, darted two feet back, and came to rest again a little farther up the rod. There had been no years between the ducking of this dragonfly and the other one—the one that was part of memory. I looked at the boy, who was silently watching his fly, and it was my hands that held his rod, my eyes watching. I felt dizzy and didn't know which rod I was at the end of.

We caught two bass, hauling them in briskly as though they were mackerel, pulling them over the side of the boat in a businesslike manner without any landing net, and stunning them with a blow on the back of the head. When we got back for a swim before lunch, the lake was exactly where we had left it, the same number of inches from the dock, and there was only the merest suggestion of a breeze. This seemed an utterly enchanted sea, this lake you could leave to its own devices for a few hours and come back to, and find that it had not stirred, this constant and trustworthy body of water. In the shallows, the dark, water-soaked sticks and twigs, smooth and old, were undulating in clusters on the bottom against the clean ribbed sand, and the track of the mussel was plain. A school of minnows swam by, each minnow with its small individual shadow, doubling the attendance, so clear and sharp in the sunlight. Some of the other campers were in swimming, along the shore, one of them with a cake of soap, and the water felt thin and clear and unsubstantial. Over the years there had been this person with the cake of soap, this cultist, and here he was. There had been no years.

Up to the farmhouse to dinner through the teeming, dusty field, the road under our sneakers was only a two-track road. The middle track was missing, the one with the marks of the hooves and the splotches of dried, flaky manure. There had always been three tracks to choose from in choosing which track to walk in; now the choice was narrowed down to two. For a moment I missed terribly the middle alternative. But the way led past the tennis court, and something about the way it lay there in the sun reassured me; the tape had loosened along the backline, the alleys were green with plantains and other weeds, and the net (installed in June and removed in September) sagged in the dry noon, and the whole place steamed with midday heat and hunger and emptiness. There was a choice of pie for dessert, and one was blueberry and one was apple, and the waitresses were the same country girls, there having been no passage of time, only the illusion of it as in a dropped curtain—the waitresses were still fifteen; their hair had been washed, that was the only difference—they had been to the movies and seen the pretty girls with the clean hair.

Summertime, oh, summertime, pattern of life indelible, the fadeproof lake, the woods unshatterable, the pasture with the sweetfern and the juniper forever and ever, summer without end; this was the background, and the life along the shore was the design, the cottagers with their innocent and tranquil design, their tiny docks with the flagpole and the American flag floating against the white clouds in the blue sky, the little paths over the roots of the trees leading from camp to camp and the paths leading back to the outhouses and the can of lime for sprinkling, and at the souvenir counters at the store the miniature birchbark canoes and the postcards that showed things looking a little better than they looked. This was the American family at play, escaping the city heat, wondering whether the newcomers in the camp at the head of the cove were "common" or "nice," wondering whether it was true that the people who drove up for Sunday dinner at the farmhouse were turned away because there wasn't enough chicken.

It seemed to me, as I kept remembering all this, that those times and those summers had been infinitely precious and worth saving. There had been jollity and peace and goodness. The arriving (at the beginning of August) had been so big a business in itself, at the railway station the farm wagon drawn up, the first smell of the pine-laden air, the first glimpse of the smiling farmer, and the great importance of the trunks and your father's enormous authority in such matters, and the feel of the wagon under you for the long ten-mile haul, and at the top of the last long hill catching the first view of the lake after eleven months of not seeing this cherished body of water. The shouts and cries of the other campers when they saw you, and the trunks to be unpacked, to give up their rich burden. (Arriving was less exciting nowadays, when you sneaked up in your car and parked it under a tree near the camp and took out the bags and in five minutes it was all over, no fuss, no loud wonderful fuss about trunks.)

Peace and goodness and jollity. The only thing that was wrong now, really, was the sound of the place, an unfamiliar nervous sound of the outboard motors. This was the note that jarred, the one thing that would sometimes break the illusion and set the years moving. In those other summertimes all motors were inboard; and when they were at a little distance, the noise they made was a sedative, an ingredient of summer sleep. They were one-cylinder and two-cylinder engines, and some were make-and-break and some were jump-spark, but they all made a sleepy sound across the lake. The one-lungers throbbed and fluttered, and the twin-cylinder ones purred and purred, and that was a quiet sound, too. But now the campers all had outboards. In the daytime, in the hot mornings, these motors made a petulant, irritable sound; at night, in the still evening when the afterglow lit the water, they whined about one's ears like mosquitoes. My boy loved our rented outboard, and his great desire was to achieve single-handed mastery over it, and authority, and he soon learned the trick of choking it a little (but not too much), and the adjustment of the needle valve. Watching him I would remember the things you could do with the old one-cylinder engine with the heavy flywheel, how you could have it eating out of your hand if you got really close to it spiritually. Motorboats in those days didn't have clutches, and you would make a landing by shutting off the motor at the proper time and coasting in with a dead rudder. But there was a way of reversing them, if you learned the trick, by cutting the switch and putting it on again exactly on the final dying revolution of the flywheel, so that it would kick back against compression and begin reversing. Approaching a dock in a strong following breeze, it was difficult to slow up sufficiently by the ordinary coasting method, and if a boy felt he had complete mastery over his motor, he was tempted to keep it running beyond its time and then reverse it a few feet from the dock. It took a cool nerve, because if you threw the switch a twentieth of a second too soon you would catch the flywheel when it still had speed enough to go up past center, and the boat would leap ahead, charging bull-fashion at the dock.

We had a good week at the camp. The bass were biting well and the sun shone endlessly, day after day. We would be tired at night and lie down in the accumulated heat of the little bedrooms after the long hot day and the breeze would stir almost imperceptibly outside and the smell of the swamp drift in through the rusty screens. Sleep would come easily and in the morning the red squirrel would be on the roof, tapping out his gay routine. I kept remembering everything, lying in bed in the mornings—the small steamboat that had a long rounded stern like the lip of a Ubangi, and how quietly she ran on the moonlight sails, when the older boys played their mandolins and the girls sang and we ate doughnuts dipped in sugar, and how sweet the music was on the water in the shining night, and what it had felt like to think about girls then. After breakfast we would go up to the store and the things were in the same place—the minnows in a bottle, the plugs and spinners disarranged and pawed over by the youngsters from the boys' camp, the Fig Newtons and the Beeman's gum. Outside, the road was tarred and cars stood in front of the store. Inside, all was just as it had always been, except there was more Coca-Cola and not so much Moxie and root beer and birch beer and sarsaparilla. We would walk out with the bottle of pop apiece and sometimes the pop would backfire up our noses and hurt. We explored the streams, quietly, where the turtles slid off the sunny logs and dug their way into the soft bottom; and we lay on the town wharf and fed worms to the tame bass. Everywhere we went I had trouble making out which was I, the one walking at my side, the one walking in my pants.

One afternoon while we were there at that lake a thunderstorm came up. It was like the revival of an old melodrama that I had seen long ago with childish awe. The second-act climax of the drama of the electrical disturbance over a lake in America had not changed in any important respect. This was the big scene, still the big scene. The whole thing was so familiar, the first feeling of oppression and heat and a general air around camp of not wanting to go very far away. In midafternoon (it was all the same) a curious darkening of the sky, and a lull in everything that had made life tick; and then the way the boats suddenly swung the other way at their moorings with the coming of a breeze out of the new quarter, and the premonitory rumble. Then the kettle drum, then the snare, then the bass drum and cymbals, then crackling light against the dark, and the gods grinning and licking their chops in the hills. Afterward the calm, the rain steadily rustling in the calm lake, the return of light and hope and spirits, and the campers running out in joy and relief to go swimming in the rain, their bright cries perpetuating the deathless joke about how they were getting simply drenched, and the children screaming with delight at the new sensation of bathing in the rain, and the joke about getting drenched linking the generations in a strong indestructible chain. And the comedian who waded in carrying an umbrella.

When the others went swimming, my son said he was going in, too. He pulled his dripping trunks from the line where they had hung all through the shower and wrung them out. Languidly, and with no thought of going in, I watched him, his hard little body, skinny and bare, saw him wince slightly as he pulled up around his vitals the small, soggy, icy garment. As he buckled the swollen belt, suddenly my groin felt the chill of death.

POSSIBILITIES FOR WRITING

1. Analyze White's essay to focus on its themes of change and changelessness. To what extent, might White say, is change itself changeless?

2. White is justly noted for his writing style, particularly his attention to concrete yet evocative descriptive detail. Choose several passages that appeal to you, and examine White's use of language in them. How would you characterize White's style?

3. Describe a place that holds a personal sense of history for you. It may be a place you have returned to after a long absence, as the lake is for White, or a place that simply holds many memories. Focus on your responses to and feelings about the place both in the past and from your present perspective.

GEOFFREY WOLFF

The Duke of Deception

In this excerpt, the opening chapter from his biographical *The Duke of Deception*, Geoffrey Wolff describes his father, whose behavior and style provide Wolff with the title for his book. Wolff's father is shown to be a liar, a cheat, and a fraud, yet the author characterizes him as witty and charming as well. Unsatisfied with his life as it was, Wolff's father invented a reality more in tune with his hopes and expectations, something that would provide him with more status and prestige than he actually possessed, and that would allow him to live in the style to which he wished to become accustomed.

Wolff is unsparingly honest in this portrait of his father. He describes how his father conned others, including for a while, his son, and how his son was his ultimate confidence victim. In describing first what his father pretended to be, Wolff highlights his father's values—the values of a gentleman, which he wished to and actually did pass on to his son. The trouble, however, was that Wolff's father, the duke of "deception," was himself no gentleman at all. He was a conniving and manipulative fraud, scheming and clever, and ultimately a felon, who died lonely and alone. Wolff's book, including this excerpt from it, is his attempt to come to grips with his patrimony.

Wolff's writing here is brisk and taut. This opening chapter is brief and pointed. In it Wolff lays out the themes he explores more expansively as the book develops. This part is an "essay" in the original meaning of the French verb from which the English word "essay" derives—"essayer" to try or attempt. Wolff's piece is an attempt to capture the esseuce of his father's life and self. In the process Wolff aims to come to some kind of peace about his father and to better understand himself.

I listen for my father and I hear a stammer. This was explosive and unashamed, not a choking on words but a spray of words. His speech was headlong, edgy, breathless: there was neither room in his mouth nor time in the day to contain what he burned to utter. I have a remnant of that stammer, and I wish I did not; I stammer and blush, my father would stammer and grin. He depended on a listener's good will. My father depended excessively upon people's good will.

As he spoke straight at you, so did he look at you. He could stare down anyone, though this was a gift he rarely practiced. To me, everything about him seemed outsized. Doing a school report on the Easter Islanders I found in an encyclopedia pictures of their huge sculptures, and there he was, massive head and nose, nothing subtle or delicate. He was in fact (and how diminishing those words, *in fact*, look to me now) an inch or two above six feet, full bodied, a man who lumbered from here to there with deliberation. When I was a child I noticed that people were respectful of the cubic feet my father occupied; later I understood that I had confused respect with resentment.

I recollect things, a gentleman's accessories, deceptively simple fabrications of silver and burnished nickle, of brushed Swedish stainless, of silk and soft wool and brown leather. I remember his shoes, so meticulously selected and cared for and used, thin-soled, with cracked uppers, older than I was or could ever be, shining dully and from the depths. Just a pair of shoes? No: I knew before I knew any other complicated thing that for my father there was nothing he possessed that was "just" something. His pocket watch was not "just" a timepiece, it was a miraculous instrument with a hinged front and a representation on its back of porcelain ducks rising from a birch-girt porcelain pond. It struck the hour unassertively, musically, like a silver tine touched to a crystal glass, no hurry, you might like to know it's noon.

He despised black leather, said black shoes reminded him of black attaché cases, of bankers, lawyers, look-before-you-leapers anxious not to offend their clients. He owned nothing black except his dinner jacket and his umbrella. His umbrella doubled as a shooting-stick, and one afternoon at a polo match at Brandywine he was sitting on it when a man asked him what he would do if it rained, sit wet or stand dry? I laughed. My father laughed also, but tightly, and he did not reply: nor did he ever again use this quixotic contraption. He took things, *things*, seriously.

My father, called Duke, taught me skills and manners; he taught me to shoot and to drive fast and to read respectfully and to box and to handle a boat and to distinguish between good jazz music and bad jazz music. He was patient with me, led me to understand for myself why Billie Holiday's understatements were more interesting than Ella Fitzgerald's complications. His codes were not novel, but they were rigid, the rules of decorum that Hemingway prescribed. A gentleman kept his word, and favored simplicity of sentiment; a gentleman chose his words with care, as he chose his friends. A gentleman accepted responsibility for his acts, and welcomed the liberty to act unambiguously. A gentleman was a stickler for precision and punctilio; life was no more than an inventory of small choices that together formed a man's character, entire. A gentleman was this, and not that; a *man* did, did not, said, would not say.

My father could, however, be coaxed to reveal his bona fides. He had been schooled at Groton and passed along to Yale. He was just barely prepared to intimate that he had been tapped for "Bones," and I remember his pleasure when Levi Jackson, the black captain of Yale's 1948 football team, was similarly honored by that secret society. He was proud of Skull and Bones for its hospitality toward the exotic. He did sometimes wince, however, when he pronounced Jackson's Semitic Christian name, and I sensed that his tolerance for Jews was not inclusive; but I never heard him indulge express bigotry, and the first of half a dozen times he hit me was for having called a neighbor's kid a guinea.

There was much luxury in my father's affections, and he hated what was narrow, pinched, or mean. He understood exclusion, mind you, and lived his life believing the world to be divided between a few *us's* and many *thems*, but I was to understand that aristocracy was a function of taste, courage, and generosity. About two other virtues—candor and reticence—I was confused, for my father would sometimes proselytize the one, sometimes the other.

If Duke's preoccupation with bloodlines was finite, this did not cause him to be unmindful of his ancestors. He knew whence he had come, and whither he meant me to go. I saw visible evidence of this, a gold signet ring which I wear today, a heavy bit of business inscribed arsy-turvy with lions and flora and a motto, *nulla vestigium retrorsit.* "Don't look back" I was told it meant.

After Yale—class of late nineteen-twenty something, or early nineteen-thirty something—my father batted around the country, living a high life in New York among school and college chums, flying as a test pilot, marrying my mother, the daughter of a rear admiral. I was born a year after the marriage, in 1937, and three years after that my father went to England as a fighter pilot with Eagle Squadron, a group of American volunteers in the Royal Air Force. Later he transferred to the OSS, and was in Yugoslavia with the partisans; just before the Invasion he was parachuted into Normandy, where he served as a sapper with the Resistance, which my father pronounced *ray-zee-staunce.*

His career following the war was for me mysterious in its particulars; in the service of his nation, it was understood, candor was not always possible. This much was clear: my father mattered in the world, and was satisfied that he mattered, whether or not the world understood precisely why he mattered.

A pretty history for an American clubman. Its fault is that it was not true. My father was a bullshit artist. True, there were many boarding schools, each less pleased with the little Duke than the last, but none of them was Groton. There was not Yale, and by the time he walked from a room at a mention of Skull and Bones I knew this, and he knew that I knew it. No military service would have him: his teeth were bad. So he had his teeth pulled and replaced, but the Air Corps and Navy and Army and Coast Guard still thought he was a bad idea. The ring I wear was made according to his instructions by a jeweler two blocks from Schwab's drugstore in Hollywood, and was never paid for. The motto, engraved backwards so that it would come right on a red wax seal, is dog Latin and means in fact "leave no trace behind," but my father did not believe me when I told him this.

My father was a Jew. This did not seem to him a good idea, and so it was his notion to disassemble his history, begin at zero, and re-create himself. His sustaining line of work till shortly before he died was as a confidence man. If I now find his authentic history more surprising, more interesting, than his counterfeit history, he did not. He would not make peace with his actualities, and so he was the author of his own circumstances, and indifferent to the consequences of this nervy program.

There were some awful consequences, for other people as well as for him. He was lavish with money, with others' money. He preferred to stiff institutions: jewelers, car dealers, banks, fancy hotels. He was, that is, a thoughtful buccaneer, when thoughtfulness was convenient. But people were hurt by him. Much of his mischief was casual enough. I lost a tooth when I was six, and the Tooth Fairy, "financially inconvenienced" or "temporarily out of pocket," whichever was then his locution, left under my pillow an IOU, a sight draft for two bits, or two million.

I wish he hadn't selected from among the world's possible disguises the costume and credentials of a yacht club commodore. Beginning at scratch he might have reached further, tried something a bit more bold and odd, a bit less inexorably conventional, a bit less calculated to please. But it is true, of course, that a confidence man who cannot inspire confidence in his marks is nothing at all, so perhaps his tuneup of his bloodline, educational *vita*, and war record was merely the price of doing business in a culture preoccupied with appearances.

I'm not even now certain what I wish he had made of himself: I once believed that he was most naturally a fictioneer. But for all his preoccupation with make-believe, he never tried seriously to write it. A confidence man learns early in his career that to commit himself to paper is to court trouble. The successful bunco artist does his game, and disappears himself: Who was that masked man? No one, no one at all, *nulla vestigium [sic] retrorsit [sic]*, not a trace left behind.

Well, I'm left behind. One day, writing about my father with no want of astonishment and love, it came to me that I am his creature as well as his get. I cannot now shake this conviction, that I was trained as his instrument of perpetuation, put here to put him into the record. And that my father knew this, calculated it to a degree. How else explain his eruption of rage when I once gave up what he and I called "writing" for journalism? I had taken a job as the book critic of *The Washington Post*, was proud of myself: it seemed then like a wonderful job, honorable and enriching. My father saw it otherwise: "You have failed me," he wrote, "you have sold yourself at discount" he wrote to me, his prison number stamped below his name.

He was wrong then, but he was usually right about me. He would listen to anything I wished to tell him, but would not tell me only what I wished to hear. He retained such solicitude for his clients. With me he was strict and straight, except about himself. And so I want to be strict and straight with him, and with myself. Writing to a friend about this book, I said that I would not now for anything have had my father be other than what he was, except happier, and that most of the time he was happy enough, cheered on by imaginary successes. He gave me a great deal, and not merely life, and I didn't want to bellyache; I wanted, I told my friend, to thumb my nose on his behalf at everyone who had limited him. My friend was shrewd, though, and said that he didn't believe me, that I couldn't mean such a thing, that if I followed out its implications I would be led to a kind of ripe sentimentality, and to mere piety. Perhaps, he wrote me, you would not have wished him to lie to himself, to lie about being a Jew. Perhaps you would have him fool others but not so deeply trick himself. "In writing about a father," my friend wrote me about our fathers, "one clambers up a slippery mountain, carrying the balls of another in a bloody sack, and whether to eat them or worship them or bury them decently is never cleanly decided."

So I will try here to be exact. I wish my father had done more headlong, more elegant inventing. I believe he would respect my wish, be willing to speak with me seriously about it, find some nobility in it. But now he is dead, and he had been dead two weeks when they found him. And in his tiny flat at the edge of the Pacific they found no address book, no batch of letters held with a rubber band, no photograph. Not a thing to suggest that he had ever known another human being.

POSSIBILITIES FOR WRITING

1. What is your response to Wolff's description of his father? Do the pieces seem to add up? What about Wolff's writing evokes your response?
2. Compare Wolff's essay with Scott Russell Sanders's "Under the Influence" (pages 529–542). What sorts of legacies do both adult sons carry from their fathers? How do they cope with their memories? What importance does the act of writing about his father have for each?
3. Wolff quotes a letter from a friend which suggests the complexity of the feelings of adult children for their parents. Try writing about a parent without platitudes and sentimentality but honestly, describing both strengths and failings.

Mary Wollstonecraft (1759–1797), *a radical feminist centuries before the term had been coined, was born in London to a well-off family whose fortune was squandered by her dissolute father. Forced to earn a living, she took on the only jobs open to an educated woman of the time: schoolmistress, companion, and governess. In her mid-twenties, Wollstonecraft became part of a circle of radical English thinkers and artists, and in 1790 she published* A Vindication of the Rights of Man, *an impassioned defense of the French Revolution which earned her great attention both positive and negative. Even more controversial was her* A Vindication of the Rights of Woman *(1792), a revolutionary examination of the status of women in eighteenth-century society that earned her the epithet "hyena in petticoats." She died of complications related to the birth of her second child, Mary Shelley.*

MARY WOLLSTONECRAFT

A Vindication of the Rights of Woman

Mary Wollstonecraft wrote her eighteenth-century *A Vindication of the Rights of Woman* as a defense of women's rights and as an encouragement for women to believe in their strength of mind and spirit. In this excerpt, she provides a bracing antidote to the conventional image of women as frail and fragile, delicate and demure. Wollstonecraft will have none of that, as she urges women to abandon the "soft phrases," "delicacy of sentiment," and "refinement of taste," with which they are presumably comfortable and to which they are presumed to have been accustomed. Wollstonecraft dismisses that characterization of her sex as a dangerous way to subordinate women to the control of men. She presents an image of woman, not as a weaker vessel but as an equal vessel, one who should develop her character as a human being on an equal footing with a man.

Wollstonecraft's language throughout is strong and unapologetic, and her arguments direct and forceful. Wollstonecraft's rhetoric is unrelenting, as she argues that if women possess inferior intelligence and wisdom to men, why do men give them the responsibility of raising children and governing a family? Why, indeed?

My own sex, I hope, will excuse me, if I treat them like rational creatures, instead of flattering their *fascinating* graces, and viewing them as if they were in a state of perpetual childhood, unable to stand alone. I earnestly wish to point out in what true dignity and human happiness consists—I wish to persuade women to endeavor to acquire strength, both of mind and body, and to convince them that the soft phrases, susceptibility of heart, delicacy of sentiment, and refinement of taste, are almost synonymous with epithets of weakness, and that those beings who are only the objects of pity and that kind of love, which has been termed its sister, will soon become objects of contempt.

Dismissing, then, those pretty feminine phrases, which the men condescendingly use to soften our slavish dependence, and despising that weak elegancy of mind, exquisite sensibility, and sweet docility of manners, supposed to be the sexual characteristics of the weaker vessel, I wish to show that elegance is inferior to virtue, that the first object of laudable ambition is to obtain a character as a human being, regardless of the distinction of sex; and that secondary views should be brought to this simple touchstone.

This is a rough sketch of my plan; and should I express my conviction with the energetic emotions that I fed whenever I think of the subject, the dictates of experience and reflection will be felt by some of my readers. Animated by this important object, I shall disdain to cull my phrases or polish my style; I aim at being useful, and sincerity will render me unaffected; for, wishing rather to persuade by the force of my arguments, than dazzle by the elegance of my language, I shall not waste my time in rounding periods, or in fabricating the turgid bombast of artificial feelings, which, coming from the head, never reach the heart. I shall be employed about things, not words! and, anxious to render my sex more respectable members of society, I shall try to avoid that flowery diction which has slided from essays into novels, and from novels into familiar letters and conversation.

These pretty superlatives, dropping glibly from the tongue, vitiate the taste, and create a kind of sickly delicacy that runs away from simple unadorned truth; and a deluge of false sentiments and overstretched feelings, stifling the natural emotions of the heart, render the domestic pleasures insipid, that ought to sweeten the exercise of those severe duties, which educate a rational and immortal being for a nobler field of action.

The education of women has, of late, been more attended to than formerly; yet they are still reckoned a frivolous sex, and ridiculed or pitied by the writers who endeavor by satire or instruction to improve them. It is acknowledged that they spend many of the first years of their lives in acquiring a smattering of accomplishments; meanwhile strength of body and mind are sacrificed to libertine notions of beauty, to the desire of establishing themselves—the only way women can rise in the world—by marriage. And this desire making mere animals of them, when they marry they act as such children may be expected to act—they dress; they paint, and nickname God's creatures. Surely these weak beings are only fit for a seraglio!—Can they be expected to govern a family with judgment, or take care of the poor babes whom they bring into the world?

If then it can be fairly deduced from the present conduct of the sex, from the prevalent fondness for pleasure which takes place of ambition, and those nobler passions that open and enlarge the soul; that the instruction which women have hitherto received has only tended, with the constitution of civil society, to render them insignificant objects of desire—mere propagators of fools!—if it can be proved that in aiming to accomplish them, without cultivating their understandings, they are taken out of their sphere of duties, and made ridiculous and useless when the short-lived bloom of beauty is over,* I presume that *rational* men will excuse me for endeavoring to persuade them to become more masculine and respectable.

Indeed the word masculine is only a bugbear: there is little reason to fear that women will acquire too much courage or fortitude; for their apparent inferiority with respect to bodily strength, must render them, in some degree, dependent on men in the various relations of life; but why should it be increased by prejudices that give a sex to virtue, and confound simple truths with sensual reveries?

Women are, in fact, so much degraded by mistaken notions of female excellence, that I do not mean to add a paradox when I assert, that this artificial weakness produces a propensity to tyrannize, and gives birth to cunning, the natural opponent of strength, which leads them to play off those contemptible infantine airs that undermine esteem even whilst they excite desire. Let men become more chaste and modest, and if women do not grow wiser in the same ratio, it will be clear that they have weaker understandings. It seems scarcely necessary to say, that I now speak of the sex in general. Many individuals have more sense than their male relatives; and, as nothing preponderates where there is a constant struggle for an equilibrium, without it has naturally more gravity, some women govern their husbands without degrading themselves, because intellect will always govern.

*A lively writer, I cannot recollect his name, asks what business women turned of forty have to do in the world?

POSSIBILITIES FOR WRITING

1. Wollstonecraft argues here that what in her day was regarded as proper conduct for women allowed men to define them as weak and frivolous. What conduct does she refer to, and what would she substitute in its place? What advice does she have for men?

2. In paragraph 7, Wollstonecraft writes that, although she is encouraging women to become more masculine, "their apparent inferiority with respect to bodily strength must render them, in some degree, dependent on men in the various relations of life." In the context of her whole argument, what point is she making here? To what extent do you think this attitude still exists today? Why?

3. Would you say that women at the beginning of the twenty-first century have achieved equality with men? You may base your essay on personal observations as well as research if you wish.

Virginia Woolf (1882–1941) *was born Virginia Stephen into one of London's most prominent literary families. Essentially self-educated in her father's vast library, by her early twenties Woolf was publishing reviews and critical essays in literary journals. Her first novel appeared in 1915, but it was the publication of* Mrs. Dalloway *in 1925 and* To the Lighthouse *in 1927 that established her reputation as an important artistic innovator. Four more novels followed, and her criticism and essays were collected in* The Common Reader *(1925, 1932),* Three Guineas *(1938), and* The Death of the Moth and Other Essays *(1942), edited posthumously by her husband after her tragic suicide. Her* Collected Essays *(1967) numbers four volumes. Woolf is also remembered for* A Room of One's Own *(1929), an early feminist consideration of the difficulties facing women writers.*

VIRGINIA WOOLF

The Death of the Moth

In her classic essay "The Death of the Moth," Virginia Woolf writes memorably about a moth she chances to see while gazing out her window on a sunny September morning. Watching the moth fly within a small square of window pane, Woolf speculates about the life force that animates the moth and about the myriad forms of life she notices in the fields. With his seemingly unflagging energy, the moth represents for Woolf, the pure energy of "life itself."

Woolf begins with seeing, with careful description of the moth based on attentive observation. The essay moves quickly, however, to speculation, as Woolf reflects on the moth's significance. At first Woolf pities the pathetic little moth with its severely circumscribed and limited life. But as she watches it longer, she begins to analogize the life of the moth with human life. Her attitude shifts toward respect for the moth's attempts to live its brief life as exuberantly as it can.

Moths that fly by day are not properly to be called moths; they do not excite that pleasant sense of dark autumn nights and ivy-blossom which the commonest yellow-underwing asleep in the shadow of the curtain never fails to rouse in us. They are hybrid creatures, neither gay like butterflies nor sombre like their own species. Nevertheless the present specimen, with his narrow hay-coloured wings, fringed with a tassel of the same colour, seemed to be content with life. It was a pleasant morning, mid-September, mild, benignant, yet with a keener breath than that of the summer months. The plough was already scoring the field opposite the window, and where the share had been, the earth was pressed flat and gleamed with moisture. Such vigour came rolling in from the fields and the down beyond that it was difficult to keep the eyes strictly turned upon the book. The rooks too were keeping one of their annual festivities; soaring round the tree tops until it looked as if a vast net with thousands of black knots in it had been cast up into the air; which, after a few moments sank slowly down upon the trees until every twig seemed to have a knot at the end of it. Then, suddenly, the net would be thrown into the air again in a wider circle this time, with the utmost clamour and vociferation, as though to be thrown into the air and settle slowly down upon the tree tops were a tremendously exciting experience.

The same energy which inspired the rooks, the ploughmen, the horses, and even, it seemed, the lean bare-backed downs, sent the moth fluttering from side to side of his square of the window-pane. One could not help watching him. One was, indeed, conscious of a queer feeling of pity for him. The possibilities of pleasure seemed that morning so enormous and so various that to have only a moth's part in life, and a day moth's at that, appeared a hard fate, and his zest in enjoying his meagre opportunities to the full, pathetic. He flew vigorously to one corner of his compartment, and, after waiting there a second, flew across to the other. What remained for him but to fly to a third corner and then to a fourth? That was all he could do, in spite of the size of the downs, the width of the sky, the far-off smoke of houses, and the romantic voice, now and then, of a steamer out at sea. What he could do he did. Watching him, it seemed as if a fibre, very thin but pure, of the enormous energy of the world had been thrust into his frail and diminutive body. As often as he crossed the pane, I could fancy that a thread of vital light became visible. He was little or nothing but life.

Yet, because he was so small, and so simple a form of the energy that was rolling in at the open window and driving its way through so many narrow and intricate corridors in my own brain and in those of other human beings, there was something marvellous as well as pathetic about him. It was as if someone had taken a tiny bead of pure life and decking it as lightly as possible with down and feathers, had set it dancing and zig-zagging to show us the true nature of life. Thus displayed one could not get over the strangeness of it. One is apt to forget all about life, seeing it humped and bossed and garnished and cumbered so that it has to move with the greatest circumspection and dignity. Again, the thought of all that life might have been had he been born in any other shape caused one to view his simple activities with a kind of pity.

After a time, tired by his dancing apparently, he settled on the window ledge in the sun, and, the queer spectacle being at an end, I forgot about him. Then, looking up, my eye was caught by him. He was trying to resume his dancing, but seemed either so stiff or so awkward that he could only flutter to the bottom of the window-pane; and when he tried to fly across it he failed. Being intent on other matters I watched these futile attempts for a time without thinking, unconsciously waiting for him to resume his flight, as one waits for a machine, that has stopped momentarily, to start again without considering the reason of its failure. After perhaps a seventh attempt he slipped from the wooden ledge and fell, fluttering his wings, on to his back on the window sill. The helplessness of his attitude roused me. It flashed upon me that he was in difficulties; he could no longer raise himself; his legs struggled vainly. But, as I stretched out a pencil, meaning to help him to right himself, it came over me that the failure and awkwardness were the approach of death. I laid the pencil down again.

The legs agitated themselves once more. I looked as if for the enemy against which he struggled. I looked out of doors. What had happened there? Presumably it was midday, and work in the fields had stopped. Stillness and quiet had replaced the previous animation. The birds had taken themselves off to feed in the brooks. The horses stood still. Yet the power was there all the same, massed outside indifferent, impersonal, not attending to anything in particular. Somehow it was opposed to the little hay-coloured moth. It was useless to try to do anything. One could only watch the extraordinary efforts made by those tiny legs against an oncoming doom which could, had it chosen, have submerged an entire city, not merely a city, but masses of human beings; nothing, I knew, had any chance against death. Nevertheless after a pause of exhaustion the legs fluttered again. It was superb this last protest, and so frantic that he succeeded at last in righting himself. One's sympathies, of course, were all on the side of life. Also, when there was nobody to care or to know, this gigantic effort on the part of an insignificant little moth, against a power of such magnitude, to retain what no one else valued or desired to keep, moved one strangely. Again, somehow, one saw life, a pure bead. I lifted the pencil again, useless though I knew it to be. But even as I did so, the unmistakable tokens of death showed themselves. The body relaxed, and instantly grew stiff. The struggle was over. The insignificant little creature now knew death. As I looked at the dead moth, this minute wayside triumph of so great a force over so mean an antagonist filled me with wonder. Just as life had been strange a few minutes before, so death was now as strange. The moth having righted himself now lay most decently and uncomplainingly composed. O yes, he seemed to say, death is stronger than I am.

POSSIBILITIES FOR WRITING

1. The moth in Woolf's essay becomes a potent symbol for life and then also for death more generally. How does Woolf manage to do this? Point to specific passages in the essay that directly or by implication tie the moth to the world beyond itself.
2. For all its concreteness, this essay is quite philosophical. How would you characterize Woolf's conception of the universe, based on the ideas that this essay provokes?
3. In order to explore your feelings about an abstract concept—love, courage, greed, humility, loss, or another of your choice—construct an essay, as Woolf does, around a central symbol. Describe your symbol in primarily concrete terms so that the concept itself becomes concrete.

Professions for Women

In the following essay, which first saw the light of day as a talk delivered in 1931 to the Women's Service League in England, Virginia Woolf addresses the issue of what it means to be a woman writer. Her larger theme involves a consideration of those professions that are open to women, professions deemed appropriate for or suitable to women's talents, inclinations, abilities, and dispositions.

Woolf tells a story, about how, as a writer and critic, she had to overthrow conventional notions of what it meant to think and write like a woman. In reviewing books by men, Woolf was haunted by a presence she names "The Angel in the House." This "angel" was a stereotypical woman of the Victorian era, a woman who was more comfortable flattering than condemning, more at ease using "all the arts of wiles of [her] sex" rather than honestly evaluating, even criticizing the books she read, especially if they had been written by men. Woolf says that she had to kill this haunting presence, to liberate herself from its influence, if she was to have a mind of her own and express what she really thought.

When your secretary invited me to come here, she told me that your Society is concerned with the employment of women and she suggested that I might tell you something about my own professional experiences. It is true I am a woman; it is true I am employed, but what professional experiences have I had? It is difficult to say. My profession is literature; and in that profession there are fewer experiences for women than in any other, with the exception of the stage—fewer, I mean, that are peculiar to women. For the road was cut many years ago—by Fanny Burney, by Aphra Behn, by Harriet Martineau, by Jane Austen, by George Eliot—many famous women, and many more unknown and forgotten, have been before me, making the path smooth, and regulating my steps. Thus, when I came to write, there were very few material obstacles in my way. Writing was a reputable and harmless occupation. The family peace was not broken by the scratching of a pen. No demand was made upon the family purse. For ten and sixpence one can buy paper enough to write all the plays of Shakespeare—if one has a mind that way. Pianos and models, Paris, Vienna and Berlin, masters and mistresses, are not needed by a writer. The cheapness of writing paper is, of course, the reason why women have succeeded as writers before they have succeeded in the other professions.

But to tell you my story—it is a simple one. You have only got to figure to yourselves a girl in a bedroom with a pen in her hand.

She had only to move that pen from left to right—from ten o'clock to one. Then it occurred to her to do what is simple and cheap enough after all—to slip a few of those pages into an envelope, fix a penny stamp in the corner, and drop the envelope in the red box at the corner. It was thus that I became a journalist; and my effort was rewarded on the first day of the following month—a very glorious day it was for me—by a letter from an editor containing a check for one pound ten shillings and sixpence. But to show you how little I deserve to be called a professional woman, how little I know of the struggles and difficulties of such lives, I have to admit that instead of spending that sum upon bread and butter, rent, shoes and stockings, or butcher's bills, I went out and bought a cat—a beautiful cat, a Persian cat, which very soon involved me in bitter disputes with my neighbors.

What could be easier than to write articles and to buy Persian cats with the profits? But wait a moment. Articles have to be about something. Mine, I seem to remember, was about a novel by a famous man. And while I was writing this review, I discovered that if I were going to review books I should need to do battle with a certain phantom. And the phantom was a woman, and when I came to know her better I called her after the heroine of a famous poem, The Angel in the House. It was she who used to come between me and my paper when I was writing reviews. It was she who bothered me and wasted my time and so tormented me that at last I killed her. You who come of a younger and happier generation may not have heard of her—you may not know what I mean by the Angel in the House. I will describe her as shortly as I can. She was intensely sympathetic. She was immensely charming. She was utterly unselfish. She excelled in the difficult arts of family life. She sacrificed herself daily. If there was chicken, she took the leg; if there was a draught she sat in it—in short she was so constituted that she never had a mind or a wish of her own but preferred to sympathize always with the minds and wishes of others. Above all—I need not say it—she was pure. Her purity was supposed to be her chief beauty—her blushes, her great grace. In those days—the last of Queen Victoria—every house had its Angel. And when I came to write I encountered her with the very first words. The shadow of her wings fell on my page; I heard the rustling of her skirts in the room. Directly, that is to say, I took my pen in hand to review that novel by a famous man, she slipped behind me and whispered: "My dear, you are a young woman. You are writing about a book that has been written by a man. Be sympathetic; be tender; flatter; deceive; use all the arts and wiles of our sex.

Never let anybody guess that you have a mind of your own. Above all, be pure." And she made as if to guide my pen. I now record the one act for which I take some credit to myself, though the credit rightly belongs to some excellent ancestors of mine who left me a certain sum of money—shall we say five hundred pounds a year?—so that it was not necessary for me to depend solely on charm for my living. I turned upon her and caught her by the throat. I did my best to kill her. My excuse, if I were to be had up in a court of law, would be that I acted in self-defense. Had I not killed her she would have killed me. She would have plucked the heart out of my writing. For, as I found, directly I put pen to paper, you cannot review even a novel without having a mind of your own, without expressing what you think to be the truth about human relations, morality, sex. And all these questions, according to the Angel in the House, cannot be dealt with freely and openly by women; they must charm, they must conciliate, they must—to put it bluntly—tell lies if they are to succeed. Thus, whenever I felt the shadow of her wing or the radiance of her halo upon my page, I took up the inkpot and flung it at her. She died hard. Her fictitious nature was of great assistance to her. It is far harder to kill a phantom than a reality. She was always creeping back when I thought I had despatched her. Though I flatter myself that I killed her in the end, the struggle was severe; it took much time that had better have been spent upon learning Greek grammar; or in roaming the world in search of adventures. But it was a real experience; it was an experience that was bound to befall all women writers at that time. Killing the Angel in the House was part of the occupation of a woman writer.

But to continue my story. The Angel was dead; what then remained? You may say that what remained was a simple and common object—a young woman in a bedroom with an inkpot. In other words, now that she had rid herself of falsehood, that young woman had only to be herself. Ah, but what is "herself"? I mean, what is a woman? I assure you, I do not know. I do not believe that you know. I do not believe that anybody can know until she has expressed herself in all the arts and professions open to human skill. That indeed is one of the reasons why I have come here—out of respect for you, who are in process of showing us by your experiments what a woman is, who are in process of providing us, by your failures and successes, with that extremely important piece of information.

But to continue the story of my professional experiences. I made one pound ten and six by my first review; and I bought a Persian cat with the proceeds. Then I grew ambitious. A Persian cat is all very well, I said; but a Persian cat is not enough. I must have a motor car. And it was thus that I became a novelist—for it is a very strange thing that people will give you a motor car if you will tell them a story. It is a still stranger thing that there is nothing so delightful in the world as telling stories. It is far pleasanter than writing reviews of famous novels. And yet, if I am to obey your secretary and tell you my professional experiences as a novelist, I must tell you about a very strange experience that befell me as a novelist. And to understand it you must try first to imagine a novelist's state of mind. I hope I am not giving away professional secrets if I say that a novelist's chief desire is to be as unconscious as possible. He has to induce in himself a state of perpetual lethargy. He wants life to proceed with the utmost quiet and regularity. He wants to see the same faces, to read the same books, to do the same things day after day, month after month, while he is writing, so that nothing may break the illusion in which he is living—so that nothing may disturb or disquiet the mysterious nosings about, feelings round, darts, dashes and sudden discoveries of that very shy and illusive spirit, the imagination. I suspect that this state is the same both for men and women. Be that as it may, I want you to imagine me writing a novel in a state of trance. I want you to figure to yourselves a girl sitting with a pen in her hand, which for minutes, and indeed for hours, she never dips into the inkpot. The image that comes to my mind when I think of this girl is the image of a fisherman lying sunk in dreams on the verge of a deep lake with a rod held out over the water. She was letting her imagination sweep unchecked round every rock and cranny of the world that lies submerged in the depths of our unconscious being. Now came the experience, the experience that I believe to be far commoner with women writers than with men. The line raced through the girl's fingers. Her imagination had rushed away. It had sought the pools, the depths, the dark places where the largest fish slumber. And then there was a smash. There was an explosion. There was foam and confusion. The imagination had dashed itself against something hard. The girl was roused from her dream. She was indeed in a state of the most acute and difficult distress. To speak without figure she had thought of something, something about the body, about the passions which it was unfitting for her as a woman to say. Men, her reason told her, would be shocked. The consciousness of what men will say of a woman who speaks the truth about her passions had roused her from her artist's state of unconsciousness. She could write no more. The trance was over. Her imagination could work no longer. This I believe to be a very common experience with women writers—they are impeded by the extreme conventionality of the other sex. For though men sensibly allow themselves great freedom in these respects, I doubt that they realize or can control the extreme severity with which they condemn such freedom in women.

These then were two very genuine experiences of my own. These were two of the adventures of my professional life. The first—killing the Angel in the House—I think I solved. She died. But the second, telling the truth about my own experiences as a body, I do not think I solved. I doubt that any woman has solved it yet. The obstacles against her are still immensely powerful—and yet they are very difficult to define. Outwardly, what is simpler than to write books? Outwardly, what obstacles are there for a woman rather than for a man? Inwardly, I think the case is very different; she has still many ghosts to fight, many prejudices to overcome. Indeed it will be a long time still, I think, before a woman can sit down to write a book without finding a phantom to be slain, a rock to be dashed against. And if this is so in literature, the freest of all professions for women, how is it in the new professions which you are now for the first time entering?

Those are the questions that I should like, had I time, to ask you. And indeed, if I have laid stress upon these professional experiences of mine, it is because I believe that they are, though in different forms, yours also. Even when the path is nominally open—when there is nothing to prevent a woman from being a doctor, a lawyer, a civil servant—there are many phantoms and obstacles, as I believe, looming in her way. To discuss and define them is I think of great value and importance; for thus only can the labor be shared, the difficulties be solved. But besides this, it is necessary also to discuss the ends and the aims for which we are fighting, for which we are doing battle with these formidable obstacles. Those aims cannot be taken for granted; they must be perpetually questioned and examined. The whole position, as I see it—here in this hall surrounded by women practising for the first time in history I know not how many different professions—is one of extraordinary interest and importance. You have won rooms of your own in the house hitherto exclusively owned by men. You are able, though not without great labor and effort, to pay the rent. You are earning your five hundred pounds a year. But this freedom is only a beginning; the room is your own, but it is still bare. It has to be furnished; it has to be decorated; it has to be shared. How are you going to furnish it, how are you going to decorate it? With whom are you going to share it, and upon what terms? These, I think, are questions of the utmost importance and interest. For the first time in history you are able to ask them; for the first time you are able to decide for yourselves what the answers should be. Willingly would I stay and discuss those questions and answers—but not tonight. My time is up; and I must cease.

POSSIBILITIES FOR WRITING

1. What is Woolf's advice to the women to whom she delivered this speech? What might the "Angel of the House," the metaphorical rock, and "rooms of your own" represent for professional women of her day?
2. Describe Woolf's style here, focusing in particular on her use of concrete and metaphoric language, as well as the persona she presents. What do you find especially noteworthy about her voice?
3. Only in a few fields have professional women today achieved high rank in the same numbers as men. What might Woolf's observations of seventy years ago contribute to explaining this disparity? Do men continue to view women (and women, indeed, to view themselves) as Woolf describes? To what extent or do you think other factors have come into play?

credits

first published in "World Tomorrow," May 1928.

Pico Iyer, "Nowhere Man" by Pico Iyer from *Utne Reader*, May/June 1997 issue. Copyright by Pico Iyer. Reprinted by permission of the author.

Yoshida Kenko "Essay in Idleness" by Yoshida Kenko, Essay, #189.

Jamaica Kincaid, "On Seeing England for the First Time" originally published by *Transition* by Jamaica Kincaid. Copyright © 1991 by Jamaica Kincaid. Reprinted with the permission of The Wylie Agency, LLC.

Martin Luther King, Jr., "Letter from Birmingham Jail" by Martin Luther King Jr. Reprinted by arrangement with the Estate of Martin Luther King jr., c/o Writers House as the agent for the proprietor New York, NY. Copyright 1963 Martin Luther King Jr., copyright renewed 1991 Coretta Scott King.

Stephen King, "Why We Crave Horror Movies" by Stephen King. Reprinted with permission. © Stephen King. All rights reserved. Originally appeared in *Playboy* (1982).

Maxine Hong Kingston, "On Discovery", from *China Men* by Maxine Hong Kingston, copyright © 1977, 1978, 1979, 1980 by Maxine Hong Kingston. Used by permission of Alfred A. Knopf, a division of Random House, Inc.

August Kleinzahler "The Dog, The Family: A Household Tale" from *Cutty, One Rock* by August Kleinzahler. Copyright © 2004, 2005 by August Kleinzahler. Reprinted by permission of Farrar, Straus and Giroux, LLC.

Robin Tolmach Lakoff, "You Are What You Say" by Robin Tolmach Lakoff. Ms., July 1974. Reprinted by permission of the author.

D. H. Lawrence, "Benjamin Franklin" from *Studies in Classic American Literature* by D. H. Lawrence. Copyright 1923 by Thomas Seltzer, Inc., renewed 1950 by Frieda Lawrence. Copyright © 1961 by The Estate of the late Mrs. Frieda Lawrence. Used by permission of Viking Penguin, a division of Penguin Group (USA) Inc.

Niccolò Machiavelli, "The Morals of the Prince" from *The Prince: A Norton Critical Edition, Second Edition* by Niccolo Machiavelli, translated by Robert M. Adams. Copyright © 1992, 1977 by W. W. Norton & Company, Inc. Used by permission of W. W. Norton & Company, Inc.

Nancy Mairs, " On Being a Cripple" from *Plaintext* by Nancy Mairs. Copyright © 1986 by The Arizonna Board of Regents. Reprinted by permission of the University of Arizonna Press.

Karl Marx, excerpts from *The Communist Manifesto* by Karl Marx, Frederic L. Bender, editor. © 1988 by W. W. Norton & Company, Inc. Used by permission of W. W. Norton & Company, Inc.

H. L. Mencken, "Portrait of an Ideal World" from *A Mencken Chrestomathy* by H. L. Mencken. © 1926 by Alfred A. Knopf, and renewed 1954 by H. L. Mencken. Used by permission of Alfred A. Knopf, a division of Random House, Inc.

Laura Miller, "Cat People vs. Dog People" by Laura Miller. This article first appeared in Salon.com at http:www.Salon.com. An online version remains in the Salon archives. Reprinted with permission.

N. Scott Momaday, "The Way to Rainy Mountain" from *The Way to Rainy Mountain* by N. Scott Momaday, 1969. Reprinted by permission of The University of New Mexico Press.

Michel de Montaigne, "Of Smells" by Michel del Montaigne. From *The Complete Essays of Montaigne* by Michel de Montaigne translated by Donald M. Frame. Copyright © 1958 by the Board of Trustees of the Leland Stanford Junior University. All rights reserved. Used with the permission of Stanford University Press, www.sup.org.

Bharati Mukherjee, "Imagining Homelands" by Bharati Mukherjee. Copyright © 1999 by Bharati Mukherjee. Originally published in *Letters of Transit: Reflections on Exile, Identity, Language and Loss.* Reprinted by permission of the author.

Nuala O'Faolain, "Introduction" by Nuala O'Faolain from *Are You Somebody?* by

Nuala O'Faolain, © 1996 by Nuala O'Faolain. Reprinted by arrangement with Henry Holt and Company, LLC.

George Orwell, "Politics and the English Language" from Shooting an Elephant and Other Essays by George Orwell. Copyright 1950 by Harcourt, Inc., and renewed 1979 by Sonia Brownell Orwell. Reprinted by permission of Harcourt, Inc.

George Orwell, "Shooting an Elephant" from Shooting an Elephant and Other Essays by George Orwell. Copyright 1950 by Sonia Brownell Orwell, and renewed 1978 by Sonia Pitt-Rivers, reprinted by permission of Harcourt, Inc. Reproduced by permission of A. M. Heath & Co. Ltd. on behalf of Bill Hamilton as the Literary Executor of the Estate of the late Sonia Brownell Orwell and Martin Secker & Warburg Ltd.

Cynthia Ozick, "The Seam of the Snail" from Metaphor and Memory by Cynthia Ozick. Copyright © 1989 by Cynthia Ozick. Used by permission of Alfred A. Knopf, a division of Random House, Inc.

Katherine Anne Porter, "The Necessary Enemy" from The Days Before (New York: Harcourt, Brace and Company, 1952). Originally published in Mademoiselle (October 1948) as "Love and Hate". Reprinted with the permission of The Permissions Company on behalf of Barbara Thompson Davis, Literary trustee for the Estate of Katherine Anne Porter.

Anna Quindlen, "Between the Sexes, A Divide" by Anna Quindlen. © 1988, The New York Times. Reprinted by permission.

Clotaire Rapaille, "Working for a Living: The Codes for Work and Money" from The Culture Code an Ingenious Way to Understand Why People Around the World Live and Buy as They Do by Clotaire Rapaille, copyright © 2006 by Clotaire Rapaille. Used by permission of Broadway Books, a division of Random House, Inc.

Richard Rodriguez, "Aria: Memoir of a Bilingual Childhood" by Richard Rodriguez. Copyright © 1980 by Richard Rodriguez. Originally appeared in The American Scholar. Reprinted by permission of Georges Borchardt Inc., for the author.

Judy Ruiz, "Oranges and Sweet Sister Boy" by Judy Ruiz, originally appeared in Iowa Woman, 1988.

Scott Russell Sanders, "Under the Influence" copyright © 1989 by Scott Russell Sanders; first published in Harper's, from the author's Secrets of the Universe (Beacon, 1991); reprinted by permission of the author.

Luc Sante, "What Secrets Tell" by Luc Sante, The New York Times, Syndicate. Copyright 2000 by Luc Sante. Reprinted by permission.

David Sedaris "Me Talk Pretty One Day" from Me Talk Pretty One Day by David Sedaris. Copyright © 2000 by David Sedaris. Reprinted by permission of Little, Brown and Co.

David Sedaris, "Cyclops" from Naked by David Sedaris. Copyright © 1997 by David Sedaris. By permission of Little, Brown & Company.

Leonard Shlain, "Nonverbal/Verbal" from The Alphabet Versus the Goddess by Leonard Shlain. Copyright © 1998 by Leonard Shlain. Used by permission of Viking Penguin, a division of Penguin Group (USA) Inc.

Lee Siegel "The World That is the Case" by Lee Siegel from Against the Machine: How the Web is Reshaping Culture and Commerce-and Why It Matters, 2008, pg 15–30.

Leslie Marmon Silko, "Landscape, History and the Pueblo Imagination" by Leslie Marmon Silko. Copyright © 1986 by Leslie Marmon Silko. Reprinted with the permission of The Wylie Agency, Inc.

Susan Sontag, From "A Woman's Beauty: Put-Down or Power Source?" by Susan Sontag, Vogue, 1975. Reprinted by permission of the author.

Brent Staples, "Black Men and Public Space" by Brent Staples. Reprinted by permission of the author.

Shelby Steele, "On Being Black and Middle Class" adapted from The Content of Our Character by Shelby Steele. © 1990

additional titles of interest

For Instructors: Pearson Penguin Packages

The Pearson composition team is proud to offer a variety of Penguin paperbacks at a significant discount when packaged with any of our textbooks. For a complete list of titles available, as well as information about how to package these titles with your text, please visit www.pearsonhighered.com/penguin.

MyCompLab

Your students can save time and improve results with MyCompLab, a state-of-the-art resource for use in first year writing courses, either as a media supplement or as a course management system. MyCompLab offers students a composing space, where writing assignments can be created and graded, and a wealth of resources for improving writing.